The Role of the Synagogue
in the Aims of Jesus

The Role of the Synagogue in the Aims of Jesus

Jordan J. Ryan

Fortress Press
Minneapolis

THE ROLE OF THE SYNAGOGUE IN THE AIMS OF JESUS

Cover image: Anders Runesson
Cover design: Tory Herman

Print ISBN: 978-1-5064-2811-6
eBook ISBN: 978-1-5064-3844-3

The paper used in this publication meets the minimum requirements of American National Standard for Information Sciences — Permanence of Paper for Printed Library Materials, ANSI Z329.48-1984.

Manufactured in the U.S.A.

For my parents, and for the street youth of Toronto
whose lives they touched
(Isa 58:6–12; Luke 6:20)

Contents

Part II. The Historical Jesus and the Synagogue

Acknowledgments

This project could not have been completed without the help and support of the family members, friends, and colleagues who have journeyed alongside me throughout my doctoral studies and through the preparation of this work. There are too many to name here, and so, my expressions of gratitude here will have to be limited to those who have made the most direct impact.

Anders Runesson, my *doktorvater*, has been an excellent mentor, teacher, and friend. Much of my thought and identity as a scholar has been shaped by interactions and conversations with him. My doctoral committee members, Stephen Westerholm and Eileen Schuller, are invaluable resources, and have also contributed much to my academic development. I consider myself fortunate to have learned from them. Dan Machiela was also very helpful and willing to impart wisdom throughout my time at McMaster, and for that, I am grateful. Thanks is also due to Philippa Carter, who was a superb work supervisor and from whom I have learned much about teaching. I am also grateful to the Religious Studies administrative staff, particularly Doreen Drew, for their tireless work.

To my colleagues and friends at McMaster and the University of Toronto: thank you for your friendships and for the many long conversations that have made my graduate studies so much more enjoyable. There are far too many of you to name, so I will only list a few who have been especially influential and supportive: John Bolton, Ryan Watson, Jonathan Bernier, Miriam Decock, Anthony Meyer, Michael Johnson, Wally Cirafesi, Greg Fewster, and Bruce Worthington.

I would also like to extend my gratitude to the members of the Magdala Center Archaeological Project. Marcela Zapata-Meza deserves very special thanks for her friendship, her willingness to aid with my research, and for teaching me so much about archaeological methods and fieldwork. Rosaura Sanz, Andrea Garza, and Meztli Hernández also deserve particular mention here for their help. Arfan Najjar of the Israel Antiquities Authority has also contributed much to my research, and it was a pleasure to have worked with and learned from him at Magdala. My thanks also goes out to Fr. Eamon Kelly, whose help and support during my research trips to Israel in both 2012 and 2014 were much appreciated. I am also grateful to the Canadian Friends of the École Biblique, who made a stay at the École Biblique in Jerusalem possible. A good portion of the archaeological research for this project was carried out during my time at the École, and I am thankful for that opportunity.

Some of my colleagues also deserve some thanks for the comments and thoughts that they have offered on this research. Steven Fine and Craig Evans have been especially helpful. I thank them for the kindness and encouragement that they have given to a young scholar like me. I would also like to thank Chris Keith for his thoughts on some of the methodological issues covered in this work.

A special word of thanks is due to my parents, Bill and Lillian, who have been constant sources of inspiration and encouragement. My sister, Caitlin, also deserves my gratitude for her constant willingness to discuss the finer points of the study of the ancient Mediterranean world, and for sharing the formative experience of archaeological excavation and research with me in 2012. She also deserves thanks for assisting with some of the photography in this volume. Angeline, my mother-in-law, has been kind, understanding, and caring throughout my studies. My wife, Joy, has been a constant source of support and love, and has exhibited the utmost patience throughout the writing of my thesis as well as the research process that led up to it. Thank you for being with me for every step of this journey.

Figures and Tables

Abbreviations

AJEC	Ancient Judaism and Early Christianity.
ASSB	Runesson, Binder, and Olsson, 2008.
AYB	Anchor Yale Bible.
BASOR	Bulletin of the American Schools of Oriental Research.
BAR	Biblical Archaeology Review.
BECNT	Baker Exegetical Commentary on the New Testament.
BTB	Biblical Theology Bulletin.
CBNTS	Coniectanea Biblica New Testament Series.
CBQ	Catholic Biblical Quarterly.
CIJ	Frey, 1936–1952.
HdO	Handbuch der Orientalistik.
ICC	International Critical Commentary.
IEJ	Israel Exploration Journal.
JBL	Journal of Biblical Literature.
JETS	Journal of the Evangelical Theological Society.
JJMJS	Journal of the Jesus Movement in its Jewish Setting.
JJS	Journal of Jewish Studies.
JSHJ	Journal for the Study of the Historical Jesus.
JSNT	Journal for the Study of the New Testament.
JSJSupp	Journal for the Study of Judaism Supplement Series.
JSNTSupp	Journal for the Study of the New Testament Supplement Series.

JSOTSupp Journal for the Study of the Old Testament Supplement Series.

JQR *Jewish Quarterly Review.*

LNTS Library of New Testament Studies.

LXX Septuagint.

MT Masoretic Text.

NAC New American Commentary.

NCBC New Cambridge Bible Commentary.

NIGTC New International Greek Testament Commentary.

NICNT New International Commentary on the New Testament.

NTS *New Testament Studies.*

OTS Old Testament Studies.

PTMS Princeton Theological Monograph Series.

RBL *Review of Biblical Literature.*

RBS Resources for Biblical Studies.

SBT Studies in Biblical Theology.

SNTU Studien zum Neuen Testament und seiner Umwelt.

TOTC Tyndale Old Testament Commentary.

TSAJ Texts and Studies in Ancient Judaism.

WBC Word Biblical Commentary.

WUNT Wissenschaftliche Untersuchungen zum Neuen Testament.

ZAW Zeitschrift für die alttestamentliche Wissenschaft.

1

Introduction and *Status Quaestionis*

Jesus and Early Synagogues

The synagogue was a vital aspect of Jewish societal, political, and religious life in Galilee and Judea during the late Second Temple period. According to the evangelists, it also played an essential role in the life and career of Jesus. As the Gospels report, it was Jesus's custom to attend synagogue gatherings on the Sabbath (Luke 4:16), and it was also the primary venue for his teaching and preaching activities outside of Jerusalem (Mark 1:38; Matt 4:23; Luke 4:14–15, 43–44; John 18:20). Given this, the fact that research on the synagogue has thus far had a minor impact on historical Jesus studies is surprising. This is all the more striking in light of the turn toward the recovery of Jesus's Jewish background in historical Jesus scholarship since the latter half of the twentieth century. The goal of this project is to draw the threads of historical Jesus research and synagogue scholarship together, in order to apply the findings of recent synagogue scholarship to the study of Jesus's historical actions, aims, and words.

There can be no doubt that Jesus cannot be understood apart from his historical context. Much effort has rightly been put into understanding Jesus within the context of the Jewish society, culture, and religion of his day. In the words of Geza Vermes, "the historical Jesus can be retrieved only within the context of first-century Galilean

Judaism. The Gospel image must therefore be inserted into the historical canvas of Palestine in the first century CE."[1] The synagogue, as I shall demonstrate, was an important facet of Jewish life, society, religion, culture, and identity within Judea and Galilee during the time of Jesus. Thus, in consonance with the testimony of the evangelists, the synagogue was also a major facet of Jesus's life, society, religion, culture, and identity. It thereby stands to reason that if we desire to understand Jesus as a first-century Galilean Jew, that understanding must be conditioned by current research on the early synagogue, the institution in which Jesus's thought was shaped and in which his message was delivered.

A common and deceptively intuitive misconception is that the synagogues of the time of Jesus were generally similar in form and function to modern synagogues. As such, it is easy to see the synagogues in the Gospels primarily as "religious" institutions. Current synagogue research, however, has highlighted the political role played by synagogues on the local-official level. As Anders Runesson has put it, the synagogue was "a religio-political town hall of sorts."[2] One of the emphases of this project will be on the synagogue's identity as a simultaneously "religious" and "political" institution. By understanding Jesus's interactions, teachings, and actions within the synagogue as occurring within a religio-political setting, we may be able to shed new light on the political dimension of Jesus's aims and proclamation. Numerous attempts have been made in recent years to recover the political aspects of Jesus's thought, intentions, and deeds, often resulting in an anti-imperial reading of Jesus and the Gospels.[3] However, these works have tended to focus on the national and imperial political levels, giving little consideration to the local level. As a result, despite being a major political institution with which Jesus interacted and which he utilized as a platform for his teaching and proclamation, the synagogue has played a negligible role thus far in political examinations of Jesus. Studying the synagogue can offer a corrective for

---

1. Geza Vermes, *The Real Jesus: Then and Now* (Minneapolis: Fortress Press, 2010), 52.
2. Anders Runesson, "Saving the Lost Sheep of the House of Israel: Purity, Forgiveness, and Synagogues in the Gospel of Matthew," *Melilah* 11 (2014): 8–24 (9).
3. E.g., Douglas E. Oakman, *The Political Aims of Jesus* (Minneapolis: Fortress Press, 2012); Richard A. Horsley, *Jesus and Empire* (Minneapolis: Fortress Press, 2003); Richard A. Horsley and Tom Thatcher, *John, Jesus, and the Renewal of Israel* (Grand Rapids: Eerdmans, 2013); John Dominic Crossan, *God and Empire: Jesus Against Rome, Then and Now* (New York: HarperCollins, 2007); Warren Carter, *Matthew and Empire: Initial Explorations* (Harrisburg: Trinity, 2001); Warren Carter, *John and Empire: Initial Explorations* (New York: T&T Clark, 2008); Seán Freyne, *Jesus, A Jewish Galilean* (London and New York: T&T Clark, 2004).

this oversight, putting us in touch with politics "on the ground" in the towns and villages where Jesus taught, healed, exorcised, and proclaimed his message of the Kingdom.

Mark 1:38–39	Matthew 4:23–25	Luke 4:14–15; 43–44	John 18:20
He answered, 'Let us go on to the neighbouring towns, so that I may proclaim the message there also; for that is what I came out to do.' And he went throughout **Galilee**, proclaiming the message in their *synagogues* and casting out demons.	Jesus went throughout **Galilee**, teaching in their *synagogues* and proclaiming the good news of the kingdom and curing every disease and every sickness among the people. So his fame spread throughout all Syria, and they brought to him all the sick, those who were afflicted with various diseases and pains, demoniacs, epileptics, and paralytics, and he cured them.	Then Jesus, filled with the power of the Spirit, returned to **Galilee**, and a report about him spread through all the surrounding country. He began to teach in their *synagogues* and was praised by everyone (vv. 14–15). But he said to them, 'I must proclaim the good news of the kingdom of God to the other cities also; for I was sent for this purpose.' So he continued proclaiming the message in the *synagogues* of **Judea** (vv. 43–44).	Jesus answered, 'I have spoken openly to the world; I have always taught in *synagogues* and in the *temple*, where all the Jews come together. I have said nothing in secret.'

Table 1. Comparison of the synagogue summary passages in the four canonical Gospels.

Every historical investigation needs a starting point—a problem or datum which raises questions that need to be answered. For this investigation, that starting point is the data in the Gospels which indicate that the synagogue functioned as the locus for Jesus's program in Galilee and Judea (Mark 1:38–39; Matt 4:23–25; Luke 4:14–15, 43–44; John 18:20; see the table below for comparison). These passages all reflect a common memory of the synagogue as the primary context for Jesus's activities of proclamation, teaching, exorcism, and healing, especially while he was in Galilee. This is an indication that, regardless of the literal "authenticity" or "verifiability" of the incidents in any passage, Jesus was remembered at a very early stage in the tradition as having used the synagogue as a platform for carrying out his program.[4]

4. Indeed, as James Dunn has argued, Jesus remembered may be the only realistic objective of any quest for the historical Jesus. See James D. G. Dunn, *Jesus Remembered* (Christianity in the Making 1; Grand Rapids: Eerdmans, 2003), 882.

Similarly, Jesus indicates in Mark 1:38 that his intention is to "proclaim the message" (Gk. κηρύξω) in the towns near Capernaum. This statement of intent is followed up in v. 39, in which we are told that he "went throughout the Galilee proclaiming the message in their synagogues." Thus, we may infer that proclamation in the synagogues is equated with proclamation to the towns of Galilee.

What does all of this mean for the historical understanding of Jesus? First, it means that any historical reconstruction of Jesus, his acts of healing and exorcism, and the message that he proclaimed should be properly contextualized by being firmly situated within the early Galilean synagogues, and should thus be informed by current research on early synagogues. This much is immediately apparent, and contextualization is certainly a task worth pursuing in its own right.[5] Nevertheless, even if this first task is accomplished, we are still faced with the crucial interpretive task of understanding what the data itself means. In other words, we must ask *why* Jesus used synagogues as the locus of his actions. Thus, our second task is to determine what role the synagogue played in Jesus's aims. This goal is of particular historical value since it gets at the "inside of the event" of Jesus's actions.[6] As a result, it is this task of determining the role played by synagogues in Jesus's aims that will be the primary occupation of the present study. That having been said, the two tasks are interrelated, and we cannot hope to determine the role played by synagogues in Jesus's aims unless Jesus and his actions are firmly contextualized in the first-century synagogue and rooted in current synagogue research.

Now that the basic tasks of this study have been defined, the remainder of this chapter will be devoted to charting the course for the discussion to follow, locating it within the context of past and present scholarship.

---

5. Cf. R. G. Collingwood, who argues that one of the characteristics of history is that the historian's picture "must be localized in time and space." See R. G. Collingwood, *The Idea of History* (ed. Jan van der Dussen; rev. and enl. ed.; Oxford: Clarendon, 1993 [1946]), 246. Contextualization is both essential for this reason, as well as for providing crucial evidence for the interpretation of the matter that is being contextualized.

6. On the importance of intention and the "inside of the event," see Ben F. Meyer, *Aims of Jesus* (PTMS 48; Eugene: Pickwick, 2002 [1979]), 76ff., cf. 111–13; Ben F. Meyer, *Critical Realism & the New Testament* (PTMS 17; Eugene: Pickwick, 1989), 157–70; Collingwood, *Idea of History*, 213ff. The distinction between the "inside" and "outside" of the event originates with Collingwood, and its importance and relevance for the study of Jesus was apprehended by Meyer.

Jesus According to Historians:
Methods and Portraits, Past and Present

A brief review of the history of the academic study of the historical Jesus with particular attention paid to method will help to situate the present project, both in light of recent methodological developments and of the history of the discipline in general. The academic historical examination of Jesus is typically recognized to have been inaugurated by Hermann Samuel Reimarus (d. 1768), whose seminal work was first published both posthumously and anonymously between 1774 and 1778 by G.E. Lessing.[7] Not only is Reimarus's work usually considered to be the first critical historical work on Jesus, but it is also notable for being the first political reading of Jesus, depicting him as a failed revolutionary concerned with the liberation of Israel from Roman oppression. Reimarus astutely noticed that neither Jesus nor John the Baptist directly explained the term "kingdom of God" to their audiences, which led him to the conclusion that the kingdom proclaimed by Jesus should be understood in the same terms that would have been familiar to his early Jewish audience. Thus, according to Reimarus, Jesus proclaimed a temporal Jewish kingdom with himself at its head as a messianic king. As he writes, "the prevailing idea of the Messiah and his kingdom was that he would be a great temporal king and would establish a powerful kingdom in Jerusalem, whereby he would free them of all servitude and make them masters over other people."[8]

It is notable that Reimarus's portrait of Jesus, despite its many shortcomings, was based on an interpretation of Jesus's *intention* as distinguished from that of the post-Easter apostles,[9] which he determined by historically contextualizing Jesus's message within the Judaism of his day. This procedure produced a Jesus with political ambition and a concern for the liberation of Israel.

Reimarus's provocative writings may well have been the initial spark that kindled the "First Quest" for the historical Jesus.[10] However, the

---

7. Reference here is made to the modern English translation, Hermann Samuel Reimarus, *Reimarus: Fragments* (ed. Charles H. Talbert; trans. Ralph S. Fraser; Eugene: Wipf & Stock, 2009 [1774–1778]). See also the original English translation, G. E. Lessing, ed., *Fragments from Reimarus: Consisting of Brief Critical Remarks on the Object of Jesus and His Disciples as Seen in the New Testament*, trans. Charles Voysey (London: Williams and Norgate, 1879). Reimarus's original title for the work was *Apologie oder Schutzschrift für die vernünftigen Verehrer Gottes*.

8. Reimarus, *Fragments*, "The Intention of Jesus and His Disciples," 1.30.

9. Ibid., 1.31.

10. A complete review of this period is beyond the purview of this work. However, an excellent

scholarship that followed customarily understood Jesus as an apolitical or pre-political figure, and interpreted his proclamation of the kingdom of God accordingly.[11] For example, in his 1863 *Vie de Jésus*, Ernest Renan understood Jesus's conception of the kingdom of God in terms of "the spiritual kingdom, and the deliverance of the soul," whereas the notion of a temporal revolution "does not appear to have impressed him [Jesus] greatly."[12] Albrecht Ritschl conceived of Jesus's notion of the kingdom of God in moral terms.[13] Johannes Weiss (writing in 1892) and Albert Schweitzer (circa 1901) both forcefully argued that Jesus's proclamation of the kingdom should be understood in thoroughly eschatological terms.[14] Indeed, it was not until the 1960s that an interest in the political aspects of the life of Jesus arose once more, in the form of the hypothesis that Jesus was a zealot or zealot sympathizer, a social revolutionary against Israel's Roman overlords.[15]

Although his particular interpretation of Jesus and his message was not followed by subsequent scholarship, the distinction that Reimarus made between the thought and message of the historical Jesus on the one hand, and that of his followers on the other, was significant for the development of the quest for the historical Jesus. The notion that, in some sense, to use the words of Rudolf Bultmann, "the proclaimer became the proclaimed"[16] became a fixture of historical Jesus research. Thus, distinguishing between the historical Jesus and the

overview and introduction to the "First Quest" and the major works of that period can be found in Gregory W. Dawes, ed., *The Historical Jesus Quest: Landmarks in the Search for the Jesus of History* (Louisville: Westminster John Knox, 2000), which collects and introduces excerpts of major works from Reimarus to Käsemann. It is also worth recognizing that the traditional division of the history of historical Jesus scholarship into three quests is not without its problems, as will become apparent in the discussion below. The standard periodization is retained here for the sake of convenience and continuity with standard reviews of the history of scholarship.

11. Dawes notes that the interpretation of the kingdom of God is a *leitmotif* in the work of the early questers. Cf. Dawes, *Historical Jesus Quest*, x.

12. Ernest Renan, *Life of Jesus* (trans. William G. Hutchinson; London: Walter Scott Ltd., 1893 [1863]), 171–72.

13. See part I of Albrecht Ritschl, "Instruction in the Christian Religion," in *Three Essays* (trans. Philip Hefner; Eugene: Wipf & Stock, 2005), 222ff.

14. See esp. Johannes Weiss, *Jesus' Proclamation of the Kingdom of God* (trans. Richard Hyde Hiers and David Larrimore Holland; Philadelphia: Fortress Press, 1971 [1892]); and Albert Schweitzer, *The Mystery of the Kingdom of God: The Secret of Jesus' Messiahship and Passion* (trans. Walter Lowrie; New York: Dodd, Mead and Company, 1914), originally published as the second part of Albert Schweitzer, *Das Abendmahl: im Zusammenhang mit dem Leben Jesu und der Geschichte des Urchristentums* (Tübingen and Leipzig: Mohr Siebeck, 1901).

15. Most notably, S. G. F. Brandon, *Jesus and the Zealots* (New York: Charles Scribner's Sons, 1967), and Oscar Cullmann, *Jesus and the Revolutionaries* (New York: Harper Collins, 1970). Robert Eisler, *Iēsous Basileus ou Basileusas* (2 vols.; Heidelberg: Carl Winters Universitäitsbuchhandlung, 1929–1930) might be considered a forerunner to this approach.

16. Rudolf Bultmann, *The Theology of the New Testament (1948-1953)*, trans. Kendrick Grobel with an introduction by Robert Morgan (Waco: Baylor University Press, 2007).

exalted Jesus proclaimed by the evangelists and the apostles was the primary methodological preoccupation of the "First Quest."

The early quest for the historical Jesus was, methodologically speaking, an interpretive endeavour, as scholars attempted to make sense of Jesus's actions and teachings. However, the efforts of the First Questers were vulnerable to some important critiques. As Martin Kähler argued, the "Lives of Jesus" produced by the Quest present an image of Jesus that is "refracted" through the spirits of their authors, who play the role of "stage manager behind the scenes, manipulating, according to his own dogmatic script, the fascinating spectacle of a colorful biography."[17] Likewise, Schweitzer came to the eventual conclusion that the Jesus produced by much of the First Quest never existed. Rather, "he is the figure designed by rationalism, endowed with life by liberalism, and clothed by modern theology in historical garb."[18] A further objection arose that the Jesus of history could not be distilled from the Gospels.[19] Moreover, the sentiment that the historical Jesus was of little use for theology—a position maintained in various forms by such influential thinkers as Kähler, Bultmann, and Karl Barth—put a damper on the enthusiasm for the Quest.[20]

A major development came with the advent of form criticism and its focus on isolating individual pericopes of early tradition from the narrative context, provided by the evangelists, in which they are embedded.[21] The preoccupation of the form critics with the *Sitz im Leben* of these pericopes within the life of the early church left less room again for the historical reconstruction of Jesus, especially since it was accepted that the individual pericopes had been shaped by their use in

17. Martin Kähler, *The So-Called Historical Jesus and the Historic Biblical Christ* (trans. Carl E. Braaten; Philadelphia: Fortress Press, 1964 [1892]), reprinted in Dawes, *Historical Jesus Quest*, 225–26.
18. Albert Schweitzer, *The Quest of the Historical Jesus: A Critical Study of its Progress from Reimarus to Wrede* (trans. W. Montgomery; New York: Macmillan, 1968), 398; trans. of *Von Reimarus zu Wrede: eine Geschichte der Leben-Jesu-Forschung* (Tübingen: Mohr Siebeck, 1906).
19. Relatively early examples of this position include, for instance, Martin Kähler, *So-Called Historical Jesus*; and William Wrede, *The Messianic Secret* (trans. J. C. G. Greig; London: James Clarke & Co., 1971 [1901]). Wrede argued that even the earliest Gospel, Mark, is written from the perspective of faith and should not be regarded as a reliable source for the reconstruction of the Jesus of history.
20. See Kähler, *So-Called Historical Jesus*; Rudolf Bultmann, "Liberal Theology and the Latest Theological Movement," in Gregory W. Dawes, *The Historical Jesus Quest: Landmarks in the Search for the Jesus of History* (Louisville: Westminster John Knox, 2000), 242–68; repr. from Rudolf Bultmann, *Faith and Understanding* (New York: Harper & Row, 1969); trans. of *Glauben und verstehen* (Tübingen: Mohr Siebeck, 1933); and Karl Barth, *Church Dogmatics*, vol. 1:2: *The Doctrine of the Word of God* (London: T&T Clark, 1956), section 19.4.
21. Some of the most important works in Gospel form criticism include Martin Dibelius, *Die Formgeschitchte des Evangeliums* (3rd ed. Günther Bornkamm; Tübingen: Mohr Siebeck, 1971 [1919]); and Rudolf Bultmann, *History of the Synoptic Tradition* (trans. John Marsh; Peabody: Hendrickson, 1963); trans. of *Geschichte der Synoptischen Tradition* (Göttingen: Vandenhoeck & Ruprecht, 1931).

the life of early Christian communities even prior to their inclusion in a Gospel. This shaping of the tradition units by community concerns, illuminated by the retrieval of the *Sitz im Leben*, led to skepticism about the historian's ability to recover the sense of these tradition units within the setting of Jesus's teaching. The Gospels could thus be understood by the form critics to be the product of faith, rather than historical sources for the life and teaching of Jesus.[22] Although the period in which these developments came about—from Schweitzer up until the early 1950s (1906–1953)—is often termed the "No Quest" period, it is important to recognize that research on Jesus did, in fact, continue through this period.[23] To name just two important examples, C. H. Dodd's *Parables of the Kingdom* (1935) was published in this period, as was T. W. Manson's *The Teaching of Jesus* (1931).[24]

One of the most influential developments in historical Jesus research came about at a lecture given in 1953 by Ernst Käsemann.[25] This lecture is typically regarded as the beginning of a revitalization of scholarly interest in the historical Jesus, referred to as the "New Quest." Käsemann recognized as a problem that scholars only had access to the historical Jesus through the *kerygma* of the early Christian community.[26] Indeed, Käsemann acknowledges a general skepticism about the historical value of the Gospel sources, saying that "the historical credibility of the Synoptic tradition has become doubtful all along the line."[27] However, Käsemann had a method for determining the historical authenticity of a given tradition, by means of determining the distinctive elements of Jesus's teaching: "In only one case do we have more or less safe ground under our feet; when there are no grounds

---

22. For example, consider Bultmann's statement to the effect that "the Christ who is preached [in the Gospels] is not the historic Jesus, but the Christ of the faith and the cult," in Bultmann, *History of the Synoptic Tradition*, 370–71. Nevertheless, we must be careful not to push Bultmann's skepticism too far. To the contrary, in the introduction to *Jesus and the Word*, although Bultmann expresses pessimism about reconstructing the life and personality of Jesus, he nevertheless sets out to examine Jesus's message. See the introduction to Rudolf Bultmann, *Jesus and the Word* (trans. Louise Pettibone Smith and Erminie Huntress Lantero; London: Collins, 1958 [1926]), esp. 14–15.

23. Cf. the opinion of Stanley E. Porter, *Criteria for Authenticity in Historical Jesus Research* (Sheffield: Sheffield Academic Press, 2000), 36ff., esp. 40–45.

24. C. H. Dodd, *The Parables of the Kingdom* (London: James Nisbet & Co., 1935); T. W. Manson, *The Teaching of Jesus: Studies of its Form and Content* (Cambridge: Cambridge University Press, 1931). Further examples and discussion of research on Jesus published during this period can be found in Porter, *Criteria for Authenticity*, 36–45. Note also that Bultmann himself also published *Jesus and His Word*, a work concerned with the message of Jesus, during this period (circa 1926).

25. Published in English as Ernst Käsemann, "The Problem of the Historical Jesus," in *Essays on New Testament Themes* (trans. J.W. Montague; London: SCM, 1964 [1954]), 15–47; repr. Gregory Dawes, ed. *The Historical Jesus Quest* (Louisville: Westminster John Knox, 2000), 279–313. Pagination here follows this reprint.

26. Käsemann, "Problem of the Historical Jesus," 289.

27. Ibid., 302.

either for deriving a tradition from Judaism or for ascribing it to primitive Christianity."[28] This methodological principle came to be known as the "criterion of dissimilarity," and it provided some assurance of historical results in spite of a general lack of confidence in the Gospel sources.

The criterion of dissimilarity became a major methodological component of historical Jesus research in the years to follow, both throughout the New Quest and beyond. The criterion of dissimilarity was joined by other criteria for authenticity, which were developed in the years following Käsemann's lecture—primarily, the criteria of coherence, multiple attestation, embarrassment, and Aramaic language.[29] Bolstered by the use of redaction criticism, which sought to identify, isolate, and examine the editorial impact of the evangelists on the Gospels,[30] the criteria of authenticity became the default methodological fixture of historical Jesus research.

The so-termed "Third Quest" has no definitive beginning. Rather, it emerged slowly over a period of decades.[31] As a result, it is also hard to define precisely what constitutes the "Third Quest."[32] Russell Morton sums up the usual thought on the matter well in saying, "The so-called Third Quest of the Historical Jesus represents not so much a single quest as the common interest of a number of researchers: to understand Jesus within the context of Second-Temple Judaism."[33]

The concern for Jesus's context within Judaism was already present in Geza Vermes's *Jesus the Jew* (1973),[34] but the "Third Quest" came into

---

28. Ibid. See also Bultmann's earlier formulation of this same principle in Bultmann, *History of the Synoptic Tradition*, 205.

29. Lists and descriptions of the criteria from the "New Quest" period can be found in Norman Perrin, *Rediscovering the Teaching of Jesus* (London: SCM, 1967), 37–45; and Reginald H. Fuller, *A Critical Introduction to the New Testament* (Naperville: Allenson, 1966), 95–98. For more recent lists and discussions, see John P. Meier, *A Marginal Jew: Rethinking the Historical Jesus* (5 vols.; New York: Doubleday, 1991–2016), 1:168ff.; Gerd Theissen and Annette Merz, *The Historical Jesus: A Comprehensive Guide* (trans. John Bowden; Minneapolis: Fortress Press, 1998), 114–18; Porter, *Criteria for Authenticity*, 69–99; Tom Holmén, "Authenticity Criteria," in *Encyclopedia of the Historical Jesus* (ed. Craig A. Evans; New York and London: Routledge, 2007), 43–54.

30. On the use of redaction criticism in historical Jesus research, see Norman Perrin, *What Is Redaction Criticism?* (Minneapolis: Fortress Press, 1969), 68–73; C. Clifton Black, "Redaction Criticism," in *Encyclopedia of the Historical Jesus* (ed. Craig A. Evans; New York and London: Routledge, 2007), 491–94.

31. On the coining of the term "Third Quest," see N. T. Wright, "Doing Justice to Jesus: A Response to J.D. Crossan," *Scottish Journal of Theology* 50, no. 3 (1997): 359–79. Notably, Wright did not conceive of the "Third Quest" solely in terms of interest in Jesus's Jewish context.

32. This may itself be an indication that the "three quest" terminology and standard periodization is flawed.

33. Russell Morton, "Quest of the Historical Jesus," in *Encyclopedia of the Historical Jesus* (ed. Craig A. Evans; (New York and London: Routledge, 2007), 472–79 (476).

34. Geza Vermes, *Jesus the Jew: A Historian's Reading of the Gospels* (Philadelphia: Fortress Press, 1973).

its heyday in the 1980s and 1990s, with the work of figures such as E. P. Sanders, N. T. Wright, and John P. Meier.[35] Other influential scholars, such as Robert Funk, John Dominic Crossan, Burton Mack, and the Jesus Seminar,[36] who were not necessarily interested in Jesus's Jewish context, so much as in a Jesus stripped of the interpretive elements layered on top of him by his early followers, were also active during this period. The work of these scholars is usually associated with the "Third Quest" as well, presumably due to temporal proximity. However, Wright (who is credited with coining the term "Third Quest") distinguished between the "Third Quest," which he considered to be in the tradition of the work of Schweitzer, and these scholars, whom he considered to belong to a "Renewed New Quest,"[37] in the tradition of Wrede's more thorough skepticism and Bultmann's "deJudaized Jesus."[38]

Regardless of the inherent messiness of the standard periodization, the criteria of authenticity remained a methodological staple throughout the 1980s and 1990s. This state of affairs has continued into the new millennium. However, despite the long reign that the criteria have enjoyed as the default methodological tool in historical Jesus research, they have now begun to fall out of favour. One of the most important methodological developments in recent years has been signalled by the publication of *Jesus, Criteria, and the Demise of Authenticity*,[39] in which a united front of contributors have called the criteria-based approach to the study of the historical Jesus into serious question.[40] Although criticism of the criteria approach is certainly not a new development,[41] the publication of this volume is an indication that the criteria approach has been unseated from its place as the default methodology in the

---

35. E. P. Sanders, *Jesus and Judaism* (Philadelphia: Fortress Press, 1985); N. T. Wright, *Jesus and the Victory of God* (Minneapolis: Fortress Press, 1996); Meier, *A Marginal Jew* (vol. 1).

36. Robert W. Funk, *Honest to Jesus: Jesus for a New Millennium* (San Francisco: HarperSanFrancisco, 1993); John Dominic Crossan, *The Historical Jesus: The Life of a Mediterranean Jewish Peasant* (San Francisco: HarperCollins, 1991); Burton Mack, *A Myth of Innocence: Mark and Christian Origins* (Philadelphia: Fortress Press, 1988); Robert W. Funk, Roy W. Hoover, and the Jesus Seminar, *The Five Gospels: What Did Jesus Really Say?* (New York: HarperCollins, 1997).

37. Wright, *Victory of God*, 28–82.

38. Ibid., 79, 81. See also p. 28.

39. Chris Keith and Anthony Le Donne, eds., *Jesus, Criteria, and the Demise of Authenticity* (London and New York: T&T Clark, 2012).

40. Contributors include Morna D. Hooker, Anthony Le Donne, Chris Keith, Jens Schröter, Loren T. Stuckenbruck, Dagmar Winter, Rafael Rodríguez, Mark Goodacre, Scot McKnight, and Dale C. Alison.

41. See, for example, the work of Morna Hooker, whose thought on the matter is exemplified in "On Using the Wrong Tool," *Theology* 75 (1972): 570–81. Similarly, see D. G. A. Calvert, "An Examination of the Criteria for Distinguishing the Authentic Words of Jesus," *New Testament Studies* 18 (1972): 209–19.

minds of many scholars. This has left a methodological vacuum in the discipline, needing to be filled.

Around the turn of the millennium, interest began to grow in memory studies and the application of social memory theory to the Gospels. Particularly important in this regard was the publication of the volume, *Memory, Tradition, and Text*, edited by Alan Kirk and Tom Thatcher.[42] Since then, a deluge of works on Jesus and the Gospels employing social memory have been published.[43] Chris Keith has proposed what he calls the "memory approach," which he offers as a procedural alternative, based upon the insights of social memory theory, to the criteria approach.[44]

While the impetus for the present work stems directly from current developments in synagogue studies and historical Jesus research, the above reflection upon the history of the quest for the historical Jesus and the methods employed in its service also points us back to its origin. Despite all of the problems and shortcomings of Reimarus's work, the present study holds several features in common with his thought and procedure. First, the issue of Jesus's *intention*, which was at the heart of Reimarus's portrait of Jesus, will be examined and explored, particularly in relation to the synagogues of Galilee. The intention of historical actors, the "inside" of historical events, plays an important role within both Collingwoodian and critical realist historiography,[45] and in this respect, Reimarus was far ahead of his time. Second, this examination of Jesus's intention will be informed by historical contextualization within the Judaism of his day. In this case, special emphasis will be placed upon the context of Jesus's activities within early synagogues in the Land of Israel. Third, the present study will be attentive to the political dimension of Jesus's message, actions, and intentions,

---

42. Alan Kirk and Tom Thatcher, eds., *Memory, Tradition, and Text: Uses of the Past in Early Christianity* (Semeia 52; Atlanta: Society of Biblical Literature, 2005).

43. Important recent examples include Chris Keith, *Jesus' Literacy: Scribal Culture and the Teacher from Galilee* (LNTS 413; London: T&T Clark, 2011); Chris Keith, *Jesus Against the Scribal Elite: The Origins of the Conflict* (Grand Rapids: Baker Academic, 2014); Anthony Le Donne, *The Historiographical Jesus: Memory, Typology, and the Son of David*, (Waco: Baylor University Press, 2005); Rafael Rodríguez, *Structuring Early Christian Memory: Jesus in Tradition, Performance, and Text* (LNTS 407; London and New York: T&T Clark, 2010); and Dale C. Allison, Jr., *Constructing Jesus: Memory, Imagination, and History* (Grand Rapids: Baker Academic, 2010). Of a different tenor, though still employing memory theory to some extent, see also Richard Bauckham, *Jesus and the Eyewitnesses: The Gospels as Eyewitness Testimony* (Grand Rapids: Eerdmans, 2006); Robert K. McIver, *Memory, Jesus, and the Synoptic Gospels* (Leiden: Brill, 2011).

44. See especially Chris Keith, *Jesus' Literacy: Scribal Culture and the Teacher from Galilee* (LNTS 413; London and New York: T&T Clark, 2011), 61–70; and Chris Keith, *Jesus Against the Scribal Elite* (Grand Rapids: Baker Academic, 2014), 69–84.

45. This will be covered in our discussion of historical method in this chapter. Further, see appendices A and B.

especially as they concern the synagogues of the Land of Israel.[46] This will be done with caution and in relation to the evidence.

Historiography, Hermeneutics, and the Historical Jesus

Although I recognize the contributions that both the memory- and the criteria-based approaches offer to the study of Jesus, I have proposed in an article that was recently published in the *Journal for the Study of the Historical Jesus* that a different path be forged, one that is solidly grounded in the philosophy of history and historiography.[47] Our discipline has much to learn from theorists of history outside of the biblical studies fold. As such, the historical method employed in this project was developed in conversation with major works of historiographical thought of the twentieth and twenty-first centuries. In particular, the posthumously published work of R. G. Collingwood (d. 1943) in philosophy of history, *The Idea of History*,[48] contains insights that are relevant and applicable to current discussions. These insights have the potential to form a foundation for methodological procedures in future research. The method utilized in this book is based upon Collingwood's thought, supplemented by an epistemological hermeneutic drawn from the critical realist cognitional theory of Bernard Lonergan. As a result, the method, philosophy, and approach of this project owes more to works of philosophy of history and historiography of the twentieth and twenty-first centuries than to mainstream historical Jesus scholarship of the past century.

Five of Collingwood's insights about the nature of history are worth introducing in order to provide some basic orientation, before we delve into our investigation. First, according to Collingwood, history is *inferential*. History is not like the empirical sciences. Since the objects of a historian's study are in the past, and the past cannot be observed directly by the senses, the past is comprehended by arguing to it from

---

46. I use the *Land* and *Land of Israel* (Heb. *'eretz Israel*) to refer to the former traditional territory of the kingdoms of Israel and Judah in the Iron Age and the region associated with the Jewish homeland in the first century CE, as distinct from the Diaspora. In the second century, this region was incorporated into the Roman province of Palestine after 135 CE. It is referred to variously as "Palestine," "Israel," and "the Land." To be clear, I use the term here not for any political reasons whatsoever, but for the sake of historical reference alone; that is, my subjects, Jesus of Nazareth and his fellow first-century Jews, would have thought of this region in terms of its significance as "the Land" of Israel rather than as the territory that would be incorporated into the Roman province of Syria-Palestine in the second century.

47. See Jordan J. Ryan, "Jesus at the Crossroads of Inference and Imagination: The Relevance of R. G. Collingwood's Philosophy of History for Current Methodological Discussions in Historical Jesus Research," *JSHJ* 13, no. 1 (2015): 66–89.

48. Collingwood, *The Idea of History*.

evidence. This leads to the second point—that history must be rooted in *evidence*, or it is not history at all. The strength of a historian's reconstruction of the past is based on its appeal to evidence. Third, history is *imaginative*. It is both critical and constructive. The historian's imagination is required in order to fill gaps between points of data provided by the evidence and to interpret it. Evidence tempers the historical imagination, allowing the historian to discern between more or less plausible conclusions and interpretations. Fourth, history is concerned with the *inside of the event*, the thoughts, aims, and intentions of historical actors, as well as the *outside of the event*, the physical actions involved in a past event. Fifth, history is not *only* concerned with determining the truth of the statements of witnesses and sources. Collingwood critiqued this form of history harshly, calling it "scissors-and-paste." Rather, the historian's aim is to *understand* what a given relevant piece of evidence or datum means in relation to their investigation, regardless of whether it is true or false. This does not mean that a historian is never interested in determining the truth of a statement. It simply means that the determination of statement's truth or falsehood is not, in itself, the aim of historical inquiry.

A fuller account of the historiographical method and hermeneutics employed here, and the rationale underlying them, is outlined in two essays found in the appendices of this book. Appendix A outlines the Collingwoodian principles of history and their relevance for the study of the historical Jesus, while appendix B addresses the hermeneutical and epistemological dimensions of history writing in light of the critical realist thought of Bernard Lonergan and Ben F. Meyer, in conversation with postmodern historiography. Neither essay is required for the reader to appreciate or grasp the interpretations or arguments presented in this book. Nevertheless, readers interested in historiography, hermeneutics, and method in historical Jesus studies are highly encouraged to read them in order to fully grasp the finer points of the procedure of this study.

Recent Developments in Synagogue Research

A brief overview of recent scholarship on ancient synagogues will help to set the stage for the discussion in later chapters. Synagogue research has advanced by leaps and bounds since the close of the last millennium. Recent developments have produced what might be described as an emerging "new perspective" on early synagogues. This "new perspective" is characterized by a recognition of the coexistence and intertwining of the multiple aspects of the synagogue discussed above, particularly the "liturgical" (religious) and "non-liturgical" (especially communal and political) aspects.[49] Although there are exceptions, this recognition of the different aspects of the synagogue frequently accompanies an acknowledgment of a typological distinction between two types of synagogues. In the late 1990s, discussion of the origin of synagogues resulted in competing definitions of the synagogue as either a Greco-Roman association, similar to a club or guild, or a public municipal institution, similar to a town hall. Strong evidence exists, however, for *both* of these definitions, which led to the conclusion first proposed by Anders Runesson in his dissertation, published in 2001,[50] that *there were, in fact, two types of institutions designated by synagogue terms*: semi-public association synagogues and public synagogues. These advances in scholarship have also been bolstered by new archaeological evidence. Since the mid-1990s, remains of Second-Temple-period synagogue buildings have been positively identified at Qiryat Sefer (1995),[51] Jericho (1998),[52] Modi'in (2000),[53] and Magdala (2009).[54] A

---

49. Examples include Donald D. Binder, *Into the Temple Courts: The Place of the Synagogues in the Second Temple Period* (SBL Dissertation Series 169; Atlanta: Society of Biblical Literature, 1999); Lee I. Levine, *The Ancient Synagogue: The First Thousand Years* (2nd ed.; New Haven and London: 2005); Anders Runesson, *The Origins of the Synagogue: A Socio-Historical Study* (Coniectanea Biblica, New Testament Series 37; Stockholm: Almqvist & Wiksell, 2001); Birger Olsson, "The Origins of the Synagogue: An Evaluation," in *The Ancient Synagogue From Its Origins Until 200 C.E.: Papers Presented at an International Conference at Lund University, October 14-17, 2001* (ed. Birger Olsson, and Magnus Zetterholm; CBNTS 39; Stockholm: Almqvist & Wiksell, 2003), 132–38; James F. Strange, "Archaeology and Ancient Synagogues up to about 200 C.E." in *The Ancient Synagogue From Its Origins Until 200 C.E.: Papers Presented at an International Conference at Lund University, October 14-17, 2001* (ed. Birger Olsson, and Magnus Zetterholm; CBNTS 39; Stockholm: Almqvist & Wiksell, 2003), 37–62; Ralph J. Korner, "Before Church: Political, Ethno-Religious, and Theological Implications of the Collective Designation of Pauline Christ-Followers as *Ekklēsiai*" (PhD diss., McMaster University, 2014); Rachel Hachlili, *Ancient Synagogues - Archaeology and Art: New Discoveries and Current Research* (HdO 105; Leiden and Boston: Brill, 2013); Mordechai Aviam and William Scott Green, "The Ancient Synagogue: Public Space in Ancient Judaism," in *Judaism From Moses to Muhammad: An Interpretation* (ed. Jacob Neusner, William Scott Green, and Alan J. Avery-Peck; Leiden and Boston: Brill, 2005), 183–200; Jonathan Bernier, *Aposynagōgos and the Historical Jesus in John: Rethinking the Historicity of the Johannine Expulsion Passages* (Biblical Interpretation 122; Leiden and Boston: Brill, 2013; Graham H. Twelftree, "Jesus and the Synagogue," in *Handbook for the Study of the Historical Jesus* (ed. Tom Holmén and Stanley E. Porter; 4 vols.; Leiden: Brill, 2011), 4:3105–3134; Eric C. Stewart, *Gathered Around Jesus: An Alternative Spatial Practice in the Gospel of Mark* (Matrix: The Bible in Mediterranean Context 6; Eugene: Wipf & Stock, 2009).

50. Runesson, *Origins*.

51. Anders Runesson, Donald D. Binder, and Birger Olsson, *The Ancient Synagogue from its Origins to 200 C.E.: A Source Book* (Ancient Judaism and Early Christianity 72; Leiden and Boston: Brill, 2008), no. 35. Abbreviated as *ASSB*. See fig. 14.

52. *ASSB*, no. 15. See fig. 18.

53. *ASSB*, no. 29. See fig. 15.

54. Jürgen K. Zangenberg, Archaeological News From the Galilee: Tiberias, Magdala and Rural Galilee," *Early Christianity* 1 (2010): 471–84 (476–78). Cf. Dina Avshalom-Gorni and Arfan Najar,

late-first-century synagogue has also been identified at Khirbet Qana.[55] New discoveries continue to be made. In the summer of 2016, the discovery of a possible Second-Temple-period synagogue building at Tel Rechesh was announced.[56] Other potential early synagogue buildings have recently been identified at Diab,[57] Et-Tawani,[58] and Khirbet Majdouliya.[59]

These developments in scholarship and recent archaeological discoveries provide a new interpretive framework within which scholarship on early Judaism, Galilean studies, and research on Jesus and the Gospels might operate. As discussed above, one of the aims of the present study is to consider the Gospel data on the historical Jesus in light of the interpretive paradigm provided by these advances.

Scholarship on Jesus and the Synagogue

The present work is the first book-length treatment of the issue of the relationship of Jesus to the synagogues of his day. However, this work is preceded and anticipated by a handful of much shorter works, and by a brief but storied history of the impact of reconstructions of "the synagogue" upon historical Jesus research. This will be discussed and evaluated in much greater depth in chapter 6, but some introduction here will help to set the stage.

The history of the impact of reconstructions of "the synagogue" on historical Jesus research can be divided into three phases. In the earliest phase, "the synagogue" was reconstructed in scholarship in terms of its relationship to "the church," usually either as a foil or counterpart. Perhaps the most important example of this can be found in the work of J. Louis Martyn. Martyn's influential 1968 study, *History and Theology in the Fourth Gospel*, which received a new edition as recently as 2003,[60] proposed a two-level reading of the Gospel of John, in which the

"Migdal: Preliminary Report," *Hadashot* 125 (2013), http://www.hadashot-esi.org.il/report_detail_eng.aspx?id=2304&mag_id=120. See figs. 3–13.
55. *ASSB*, no. 3.
56. The report appeared across various news media, though a formal academic publication is pending. See, e.g., Nir Hasson, "Archaeologists in Israel Find Ancient Synagogue Predating Second Temple Ruin," *Haaretz* (August 16, 2016), http://www.haaretz.com/israel-news/1.736752.
57. Binyamin Har-Even, "A Second Temple Synagogue at Horvat Diab in Western Benjamin," *Qadmoniot* 151 (2016): 49–53.
58. Binyamin Har-Even, "Khirbet Tawani: A Settlement From the Second Temple, Roman-Byzantine and Early Muslim Periods," *The Frontier and Desert in the Land of Israel* 7 (2012): 15–29.
59. A formal report is not yet available. See the announcement in Robin Ngo, "Roman-Era Structure Believed to be Synagogue Exposed in Israel." December 29, 2014, http://www.biblicalarchaeology.org/daily/ancient-cultures/daily-life-and-practice/roman-era-structure-believed-to-be-synagogue-exposed-in-israel/.

aposynagōgos passages (9:22, 12:42, and 16:2) are understood to reflect the exclusion of the Johannine community from the synagogues of their own day. Here, the synagogue is depicted in an adversarial relationship to Jesus's later followers, "the church." This notion that John can be read on two levels, one of which tells the story of the community, has had a remarkable impact on the role of the Fourth Gospel in historical Jesus research.

During the second phase, serious questions were raised about the existence of synagogue buildings during the Second Temple period, and thus, during the life of Jesus. These questions effectively leveled a charge of anachronism against Luke, the only one of the four canonical evangelists to clearly reference a synagogue building. This doubt over the existence of synagogue buildings began with the publication of an article by Howard Clark Kee on the topic in 1990,[61] which spawned a debate lasting more than a decade between those who accepted Kee's hypothesis[62] and their detractors,[63] who pointed out that Kee's proposal is not supported by the evidence from the Second Temple period. This debate had the effect of delaying the application of synagogue

---

60. J. Louis Martyn, *History and Theology in the Fourth Gospel* (NTL; Louisville and London: Westminster John Knox, 2003[1968]).

61. Howard Clark Kee, "The Transformation of the Synagogue After 70 C.E.: Its Import for Early Christianity," *NTS* 36 (1990): 1–24.

62. Heather A. McKay, "Ancient Synagogues: The Continuing Dialectic between Two Major Views," *Currents in Research: Biblical Studies* 6: (1998): 103–42; Heather A. McKay, *Sabbath and Synagogue: The Question of Sabbath Worship in Ancient Judaism* (Religions in the Greco Roman World 122; Leiden, New York, and Köln: Brill, 1994); L. Michael White, "Reading the Ostia Synagogue: A Reply to A. Runesson," *Harvard Theological Review* 92 (1992): 222–37; L. Michael White, *The Social Origins of Christian Architecture* (2 vols.; Valley Forge: Trinity Press International, 1996–1997); L. Michael White, "Synagogue and Society in Imperial Ostia: Archaeology and Epigraphic Evidence," *Harvard Theological Review* 92 (1999): 409–33; Carsten Claussen, *Versammlung, Gemeinde, Synagoge: die hellenistisch-jüdische Umfeld der frühchristlichen Gemeinden* (Studien zur Umwelt des Neuen Testaments 27; Göttingen: Vandenhoeck & Ruprecht, 2002); Carsten Claussen, "Meeting, Community, Synagogue – Different Frameworks of Ancient Jewish Congregations in the Diaspora," in *The Ancient Synagogue From its Origins until 200 C.E.* (ed. Birger Olsson, and Magnus Zetterholm; Stockholm: Almqvist & Wiksell, 2003), 144–67; Richard A. Horsley, *Galilee: History, Politics, People* (Valley Forge: Trinity Press International, 1995), 222–37, cf. Richard A. Horsley, *Archaeology, History, and Society in Galilee: The Social Context of Jesus and the Rabbis* (Valley Forge: Trinity Press International, 1996), 131–53.

63. For example, Richard E. Oster, "Supposed Anachronism in Luke-Acts' Use of ΣΥΝΑΓΩΓΗ," *NTS* 39 (1993): 178–208; Kenneth Atkinson, "On Further Defining the First-Century Synagogue: Fact or Fiction? A Rejoinder to H. C. Kee," *NTS* 43 (1997): 491–502; John S. Kloppenborg Verbin, "Dating Theodotos (*CIJ* II 1404)," *JJS* 51, no. 2 (2000): 243–80; Binder, *Into the Temple Courts*, 92–111; Lee I. Levine, "The First-Century Synagogue: Critical Reassessments and Assessments of the Critical," in *Religion and Society in Roman Palestine: Old Questions, New Approaches* (ed. Douglas R. Edwards; New York: Routledge, 2004), 70–102; E. P. Sanders, *Jewish Law From Jesus to the Mishnah: Five Studies* (London: SCM, 1990), 341–43; Rainer Riesner, "Synagogues in Jerusalem," in *The Book of Acts in its Palestinian Setting* (ed. Richard Bauckham; Grand Rapids: Eerdmans, 1995), 179–210; P.W. van der Horst, "Was the Synagogue a Place of Sabbath Worship Before 70 C.E.?" in *Jews, Christians, and Polytheists: Cultural Interaction during the Greco-Roman Period*, (ed. Steven Fine; London: Routledge, 1999), 18–43; Runesson, *Origins*, 149–52.

data to the quest for the historical Jesus due to the controversy and confusion that it created around Second-Temple-period synagogues.

The third and final phase is directly related to the significant advances in synagogue studies that occurred around the turn of the millennium and beyond. In this present phase, scholars have begun to recognize the potential for the recent advances in synagogue studies to contribute to research on the historical Jesus. However, only a handful of works effectively utilizing these insights have been published. Jonathan Bernier has produced a monograph which challenges Martyn's two-level reading of the *aposynagōgos* passages, partly on the basis of current synagogue research.[64] Graham Twelftree has published an article on "Jesus and the Synagogue" in the *Handbook for the Study of the Historical Jesus,* which details some recent developments in synagogue research and employs a redaction-critical approach to the issue of the authenticity of the synagogue passages in the Gospels.[65] Runesson has also briefly considered the issue of the relationship of the historical Jesus to the synagogue in an article titled "The Gospels, the Historical Jesus, and Jewish Society: The Importance of the Synagogue for Understanding the New Testament."[66] Although his treatment of the historical Jesus is very short (comprising less than ten pages), he raises some interesting preliminary questions and issues that are worth pursuing.

Conclusion: Charting a Path

The present study is located at the intersection of synagogue studies and historical Jesus research, and as such, our path is partially laid out for us by the current state of affairs and recent developments in both of these fields. The study is divided into two parts. Part I will examine the Second Temple synagogue in light of recent scholarship and archaeological discoveries, and will produce a basic portrait of its roles and functions within Jewish society in the Land. This will lead into part II, which will be concerned directly with the historical Jesus. It is in part II that I will examine and address the primary research questions of this project, and present a historical reconstruction of the role of the synagogue in the aims of Jesus.

Part I, comprising chapters 2 to 4, presents a portrait of the Second

---

4. Bernier, *Aposynagōgos*, passim.

5. Twelftree, "Jesus and the Synagogue," 4:3105–3134.

6. Anders Runesson, "The Historical Jesus, the Gospels, and First-Century Jewish Society: The Importance of the Synagogue for Understanding the New Testament," in *A City Set on a Hill: Festschrift in Honour of James F. Strange,* ed. Daniel Warner (Fayetteville: Borderstone, 2014), 265–97 (287–92).

Temple public synagogue in light of the findings and advancements of contemporary synagogue studies. Chapter 2 will discuss and examine evidence concerning the definition of the "synagogue" in recent scholarship. This will entail a discussion of current research on the origins of the synagogue. This will dovetail into chapter 3, in which I will examine the evidence pertaining to the synagogue as Jesus knew it, in order to produce an overview and reconstruction of public synagogues in the Land of Israel during the late Second Temple period. Specifically, I will discuss early public synagogues' functions, officials, and attendees, as well as architecture within the sociopolitical setting of Jewish towns and villages. Chapter 4 will then review the impact of scholarly reconstructions of "the synagogue" on the study of Jesus and the Gospels, with particular emphasis on work written since the 1990s. Here, the findings of the previous chapters in part I will be brought to bear in order to review and critique past scholarship, both on a historiographical basis and on the basis of current advances in synagogue research.

Once this has been accomplished, we will turn to the Gospel data and the historical Jesus in part II, made up of chapters 5 through 9. Chapter 5 will examine the synagogue summary statements (Mark 1:38; Matt 4:23; Luke 4:14–15, 43–44; John 18:20). In so doing, I will set out to determine the role of the synagogue in the aims of Jesus and to contextualize the activities of Jesus's program in light of the reconstruction of the public synagogue presented in chapters 2 and 3. I will argue that the synagogue was intrinsic rather than incidental to the aims of Jesus, and that it was both the vehicle and the means by which he intended to bring the Kingdom of God, as he conceived of it, into existence. The work in this chapter will present the basic hypothesis of the project, which will be evaluated in light of the evidence discussed in the chapters to follow.

Chapters 6 through 9 will investigate specific narratives in the Gospels involving synagogues. Chapter 6 will examine Jesus's reading from the scroll of Isaiah in the synagogue at Nazareth (Luke 4:16–30 and parallels). Chapter 7 will discuss the role played by healings and exorcisms in Jesus's synagogue program and will specifically examine three miracle narratives set in synagogue contexts: Mark 1:21–28/Luke 4:31–37, Luke 13:10–17, and Mark 3:1–6/Matt 12:9–14/Luke 6:6–11. Chapter 8 will investigate and interpret Jesus's teaching in the synagogue at Capernaum in John 6:25–71. Chapter 9 will briefly explore Jesus's aims regarding Jerusalem and its temple in light of recent research on the relationship between the synagogue and temple. Consideration will be given to John 18:20 and to the Johannine *aposynagōgos* passages there. The investigation will be brought to a close in chapter 10, which will present the conclusions of the study.

PART I

Early Synagogues

2

Defining "Synagogue": Synagogue Origins and Development in Recent Research

Introduction

We cannot understand Jesus's use of, conditioning by, relation to, or interaction with the Galilean synagogues without some idea of what synagogues actually were—how they came about, and what function they held in early Jewish society. Our current understanding of the definition of the "synagogue" has advanced considerably since the turn of the millennium, thanks to the combined work of a number of scholars on the origins of the synagogue. In this chapter, I will review the current state of scholarship on the origins of the "synagogue" in order to determine the sort of institution that we are discussing. Recognizing the origins of the "synagogue" helps to clarify its role within early Jewish society. The understanding of the "synagogue" produced by this review of recent scholarship will inform and ground the historical examination and synthesis of synagogue functions, people, and architecture in the chapter to follow.

Synagogue Terminology

Before we begin our discussion of the synagogue in the Second Temple period, it is necessary to clarify what, precisely, is being referred to by the term "synagogue." Runesson has suggested that a suitable understanding of "synagogue" requires the consideration of four aspects: the spatial, the liturgical, the nonliturgical, and the institutional.[1] The spatial aspect pertains to the building itself, including architecture and archaeology, as well as artwork, decoration, and furniture. The liturgical aspect includes the "religious" activities that took place within the synagogue. The nonliturgical aspect refers to the social, communal dimensions of the synagogue. Finally, the institutional aspect pertains to organization, structure, operation, offices, and leadership within the synagogue.

The institutions designated by synagogue terms in antiquity incorporate all of these aspects. A focus on one of the four to the neglect of the others will have a distorting effect upon a given reconstruction.[2] As such, the reconstruction of the early synagogue undertaken in this study will consider all four of these aspects over the course of the investigation.

It must also be recognized that the Jewish institution referred to in English by the term "synagogue" had a variety of designations in antiquity.[3] The two most commonly used terms were *synagōgē*, which is the most typical term found in the New Testament, and *proseuchē*.[4] However, there are a great many more Greek, Latin, and Hebrew terms that are all used to refer to a Jewish establishment with spatial, liturgical, nonliturgical, and institutional aspects, including *ekklēsia*, *oikos*, *topos*, *hagios topos*, *hieros peribolos*, *hieron*, *synagōgion*, *sabbateion*, *semneion*, *didaskaleion*, *amphitheatron*, *eucheion*, *proseuktērion*, *thiasos*, *templum*, *proseucha*, *bet mo'ed*, *bet ha-Torah*, and *bet ha-knesset*.[5] The object of all of these terms is what in English is termed "synagogue." There are a number of reasons why we might encounter different terms with

---

1. Runesson, *Origins*, 29–37. Cf. Runesson, Binder, and Olsson, *ASSB*, 7–9; Birger Olsson, "Origins of the Synagogue," 133. See also Bernier, *Aposynagōgos*, 57.

2. Cf. Runesson, *Origins*, 30–31. Examples of such a focus on the liturgical aspect include Louis Finkelstein, "The Origin of the Synagogue," in *The Synagogue: Studies in Origins, Archaeology, and Architecture* (ed. Joseph Gutman; New York: Ktav, 1975), 3–13, and Emil Schürer, *A History of the Jewish People in the Time of Jesus* (ed. Geza Vermes, Fergus Millar, and Matthew Black; 2 vols.; rev. ed.; Edinburgh: T&T Clark, 1973–1986; repr. Edinburgh: T&T Clark, 1885) 2: 245.

3. For an in-depth examination of the various synagogue terms and their usages in antiquity, see Binder, *Into the Temple Courts*, 91–154.

4. See the table of synagogue terms in ibid, 152, cf. Runesson, *Origins*, 171–74.

5. Cf. Runesson, Binder, and Olsson, *ASSB*, 10–11.

similar referents. For instance, there may be different regional usages, along with diversity in language (Greek, Latin, and Hebrew). Some scholars have also argued that different terms may have been used to describe various aspects of synagogue functions or activities.[6]

It is also important to note that synagogue terms can potentially refer both to buildings and to congregations.[7] The term synagōgē, for example, simply means "a gathering," and was used interchangeably to refer to both assemblies and to buildings for assembly. In the LXX, the term typically refers to the assembled congregation of Israel. With the lone exception of Sus 28 (LXX), none of the over two hundred instances of synagōgē in the LXX refer to a building.[8] Similarly, *Psalms of Solomon* 10:7 uses synagōgai to refer to the "congregations of Israel," and an inscription from Panticapaeum in the Bosporan Kingdom uses synagōgē to refer to the Jewish community of the city, as distinguished from proseuchē, which is used in the same inscription to refer to the synagogue building belonging to the Jewish community.[9]

The above discussion has highlighted the need for some variance and flexibility in our approach to the "synagogue." Allowance needs to be made for variegation among the data.[10] Nevertheless, in the most basic sense, the term "synagogue" refers to Jewish gatherings, both the assemblies themselves and the edifices in which they met.

The Origins of the Synagogue in Current Scholarship

The question of the definition of the "synagogue" in early Jewish society is closely tied to the issue of its origins. In the late 1990s, discussion of the origin of synagogues resulted in competing definitions of the

---

6. For example, *sabbateion* recalls the synagogue's function as the place where the Torah was read on the Sabbath. Some scholars also suggest that *proseuchē*, one of the most common synagogue terms in the diaspora, refers to the act of prayer performed in synagogues. See, e.g., Martin Hengel, "Proseuche und Synagoge: Jüdische Gemeinde, Gotteshaus und Gottesdienst in der Diaspora und in Palästina," in *The Synagogue: Studies in Origins, Archaeology and Architecture* (The Library of Biblical Studies, ed. J. Gutmann; New York: Ktav, 1975), 27–54; Levine, *The Ancient Synagogue*, 23; Stephen K. Catto, *Reconstructing the First-Century Synagogue: A Critical Analysis of Current Research* (LNTS 363; London and New York: T&T Clark, 2007), 125–26, 150. Note, however, that some scholars have doubted that communal prayer was performed in synagogues. See, for example, McKay, *Sabbath and Synagogue*.

7. Cf. Runesson, *Origins*, 232. For an extensive overview of synagogue terms and usages with distinction made between references to buildings and to congregations, see Binder, *Into the Temple Courts*, 91–154.

8. Cf. Binder, *Into the Temple Courts*, 92–93. For examples of synagōgē as a term for the congregation of Israel in the LXX, consider Lev 8:3 and Deut 5:22.

9. *ASSB* 124, cf. *ASSB* 125; See also *CIRB* 70 = *AGRW* 86.

10. In general agreement with the conclusions of Catto, *First-Century Synagogue*, 199–201. See also Levine, *Ancient Synagogue*, 172.

synagogue as either a Greco-Roman association, similar to a club or guild, or a public municipal institution, similar to a town hall. Strong evidence exists, however, for *both* of these definitions, which led to the conclusion originally proposed by Runesson (mentioned in chapter 1 above) that there were actually two types of institutions that were designated by synagogue terms: semi-public association synagogues and public synagogues.[11] A brief examination of the arguments and evidence pertaining to each of these two definitions will serve to demonstrate the merits of them both and to clarify the respective roles and features of semi-public and public synagogues.

The City Gate Hypothesis

In 1996, Lee I. Levine published an article arguing that the synagogue developed from the earlier city gate complex.[12] Shortly afterward, this hypothesis was followed in modified forms by both Donald Binder and Runesson,[13] and has since been refined and restated in both editions of Levine's comprehensive monograph on the subject of the ancient synagogue.[14] Up to this point in time, hypotheses pertaining to the origin of the synagogue had proposed diverse periods as the genesis of the synagogue.[15] The diversity of hypotheses and proposed periods is

---

11. Runesson, *Origins.*
12. Lee I. Levine, "Nature and Origin."
13. Binder, *Into the Temple Courts;* Runesson, *Origins.*
14. Lee I. Levine, *The Ancient Synagogue: The First Thousand Years* (1st ed.; New Haven and London: Yale University Press, 2000); cf. Levine, *The Ancient Synagogue* (2005). Unless otherwise stated, references to follow are to the 2005 edition.
15. For example, among the periods proposed are the reign of Manasseh, in Louis Finkelstein, "The Origin of the Synagogue," *Proceedings of the American Academy for Jewish Research 1928-1930* (vol. 1: 1928–1930), 49–59; H. E. von Waldow, "The Origin of the Synagogue Reconsidered," in *From Faith to Faith: Essays in Honour of Donald G. Miller on his Seventieth Birthday* (ed. D.Y. Hadidian; Pittsburgh: Pickwick, 1979), 269–86; the reign of Josiah, in J. Morgenstern, "The Origin of the Synagogue," *Studi Orientalistici* 2 (1956): 192–201; Jacob Weingreen, "Origin of the Synagogue," *Hermathena* 98 (1964): 68–84; Moshe Weinfeld, *Deuteronomy and the Deuteronomic School* (Oxford: Oxford University Press, 1972), cf. Moshe Weinfeld, *Deuteronomy 1-11: A New Translation with Introduction and Commentary* (AB 5; New York: Doubleday, 1991); during the Babylonian period, in (for example) Carolus Sigonius, *De republica Hebraeorum libri VII* (Coloniae: 1583); A. Menes, "Tempel und Synagoge," *ZAW* 9 (1932): 268–76; Eleazar Lipa Sukenik, *Ancient Synagogues in Palestine and Greece* (London: Oxford University Press, 1934); H. H. Rowley, *Worship in Ancient Israel: Its Forms and Meaning* (London: SPCK, 1967), 224–27; E. W. Nicholson, *Preaching to the Exiles; A Study of the Prose Tradition in the Book of Jeremiah* (Oxford: Basil Blackwell, 1970), 134–35; Azriel Eisenberg, *The Synagogue Through the Ages* (New York: Bloch, 1974), esp. 30–31; Hershel Shanks, *Judaism in Stone: The Archaeology of Ancient Synagogues* (New York: Harper & Row, 1979), 21ff.; Schürer, *History of the Jewish People,* 2: 424–26; during the Hellenistic period in the diaspora, in M. Friedländer, *Synagoge und Kirche in ihren Anfängen* (Berlin: Georg Reimer, 1908); L. Michael White, *Building God's House in the Roman World: Architectural Adaptation Among Pagans, Jews, and Christians* (Harvard Theological Studies 42; vol. 1 of *The Social Origins of Christian Architecture;* Valley Forge: Trinity Press International, 1996); Peter Richardson, "Early Synagogues as Collegia in the Diaspora and in Palestine," in *Voluntary Associations in the Graeco-Roman World* (ed. John S. Kloppenborg and Stephen G. Wilson; London: Routledge, 1996),

demonstrative of the mystery that shrouds the historical origin and development of the synagogue. As Levine has eloquently put it, the mysterious nature of the origin of the synagogue is due to the fact that new phenomena, such as the synagogue once was, "often germinate unobtrusively only later to emerge in our sources in a relatively developed form."[16]

Levine notes a tendency among these theories to assume that the synagogue came about as a result of dramatic new religious circumstances.[17] Similarly, Runesson detects a common element within most theories of synagogue origins, which he calls the "deprivation argument."[18] Variations of this argument share a view of the origin of the synagogue as a response to the "deprivation of religious activities caused by some form of absence of the Jerusalem temple."[19] The essential logic behind the variants of this theory is that, in the period following the destruction of the first temple, the Jews needed an alternative religious institution in order to maintain their religious identity, and the synagogue developed in order to fill the void left by the destruction of the temple.[20]

Despite the diversity of these theories pertaining to synagogue origins, Levine has noted that most of them share in common an assumption of the priority of the religious component of the ancient synagogue.[21] Rather than understanding the synagogue in terms of its

---

90–109; J. G. Griffiths, "Egypt and the Rise of the Synagogue," in *Ancient Synagogues: Historical Analysis and Archaeological Discovery* (Studia Post-Biblica 1, ed. D. Urman et al., Leiden: Brill, 1995), 3–16; Hengel, "Proseuche und Synagoge," 27–54; during the Hellenistic period in the Land, e.g., G. L. Bauer, *Beschreibung der gottesdienstlichen Verfassung der alten Hebräer* (2 vols.; Leipzig: 1806); Isaak. M. Jost, *Geschichte der Israeliten seit der Zeit der Maccabäer bis auf unsre Tage* (Berlin: Schlesingerschen Buch und Musikhandlung, 1822), 136–37; L. Zunz, *Die gottesdienstlichen Vorträge der Juden* (Berlin: A. Asher, 1832), 1–3; Joseph Gutmann, "Synagogue Origins: Theories and Facts, in *Ancient Synagogues: The State of Research* (ed. Joseph Gutmann; Brown Judaic Studies; Chico: Scholars Press, 1981); Steven Fine, *This Holy Place: On the Sanctity of the Synagogue During the Greco-Roman Period* (Christianity and Judaism in Antiquity 11; Notre Dame: University of Notre Dame Press, 1997); during the Roman period following 70 CE, Howard Clark Kee, "The Transformation of the Synagogue after 70 C.E.: Its Import for Early Christianity," *NTS* 36 (1990): 1–24, further refined in Howard Clark Kee, "Defining the First-Century Synagogue: Problems and Progress," *NTS* 41 (1995): 481–500; Horsley, *Galilee*, 222–37; Horsley, *Archaeology, History, and Society in Galilee*, 131–53; Rachel Hachlili, "The Origin of the Synagogue: A Re-Assessment," *JSJ* 28 (1997): 34–47. Note that those scholars who place the emergence of the synagogue after 70 CE generally consider there to have been an institutional forerunner in earlier periods, though the synagogue emerged as a more formal institution after the destruction of the Jerusalem temple. For an in-depth review and discussion of theories on the origin of the synagogue, see Runesson, *Origins*, 67–168. For a brief review, see Levine, *Ancient Synagogue*, 21–28, cf. Binder, *Into the Temple Courts*, 204–26.

16. Levine, "Nature and Origin," 426.
17. Ibid., 427.
18. Runesson, *Origins*, 163.
19. Ibid.
20. Ibid., 120.
21. Levine, "Nature and Origin," 427.

religious dimension, Levine notes that the evidence appears to indicate that the primary characteristic of the synagogue is its nature as a *communal institution*.[22] Likewise, Runesson has observed that the deprivation argument is rooted in a "liturgical definition" of the synagogue, to the neglect of its nonliturgical elements.[23] Consideration of the nonliturgical elements, such as the public and communal dimensions of the synagogue, renders the deprivation approach problematic.[24]

Levine's solution to the problem of the mystery of synagogue origins is to propose that the ancient city gate was the forerunner of the synagogue, and that the synagogue emerged gradually in the Hellenistic period, when gate architecture changed.[25] In so doing, Levine has revitalized, built upon, and modernized a theory which had earlier been held by Löw,[26] Silber,[27] and Hoenig.[28] The point of departure for this is the identification of the public communal function of the ancient synagogue in early Jewish society.[29] Levine notes that first-century sources depict the synagogue being used "as a courtroom, school, hostel, a place for political meetings, social gatherings, housing charity funds, a setting for manumissions, meals (sacred or otherwise), and, of course, a number of religious-liturgical functions."[30] In earlier sources, the city gate was the locus of these functions.[31]

Levine's proposal represents a significant advance in the scholarly understanding of the function and origin of the synagogue. The city gate hypothesis is preferable to the deprivation argument precisely because it is firmly rooted in the evidence, both literary and archaeological.[32] We have evidence concerning the communal functions of the

---

22. Levine, *Ancient Synagogue*, 430ff.
23. Runesson, *Origins*, 164.
24. Ibid.
25. Levine, *Ancient Synagogue*, 34ff., cf. Levine, "Nature and Origin," 436ff.
26. Leopold Löw, "Der synagogale Rituus," *Monatschrift für Geschichte und Wissenshaft des Judenthums* 33 (1884): 97–114, 161–71, 215–44, 305–26.
27. Mendel Silber, *The Origin of the Synagogue* (New Orleans: Steeg, 1915).
28. Sidney B. Hoenig, "The Ancient City-Square: The Forerunner of the Synagogue," in *Judentum:Allemeines, palestinisches Judentu* (ed. W. Haase; ANRW 2:19:1; Berlin: de Gruyter, 1979), 448–76.
29. The public, communal function of the Second-Temple-period synagogue is widely recognized, even outside of the corpus of the work of Levine, Binder, Runesson, and Runesson's students. See, e.g., Fine, *This Holy Place*, 3; Steven Fine, "From Meeting House to Sacred Realm," in *Sacred Realm: The Emergence of the Synagogue in the Ancient World* (ed. Steven Fine; New York and Oxford: Oxford University Press, 1996), 21–24; Rachel Hachlili "Synagogues: Before and After the Roman Destruction of the Temple," *BAR* 41, no. 3 (2015), n.p.; Chad Spigel, "First Century Synagogues," Bible Odyssey, http://www.bibleodyssey.org/places/related-articles/first-century-synagogues, n.p.; Horsley, *Galilee*, 223–33; Horsley, *Archaeology, History, and Society*, 145–53; Eric M. Meyers and Mark A. Chancey, *Alexander to Constantine* (Archaeology of the Land of the Bible 3; New Haven: Yale University Press, 2012), 216–17.
30. Levine, *Ancient Synagogue*, 29, cf. Levine, "Nature and Origin," 430–31.
31. Levine, *Ancient Synagogue*, 30ff.

synagogue in the late Second Temple period, on the one hand, and evidence locating those same functions in the city gates in earlier evidence from the Hebrew Bible, on the other. It is thus a robust thread of historical imagination that connects these two points, establishing a firm developmental relationship between the two.

Synagogues as Associations

There are certain institutions designated by synagogue terms from the Second Temple period which are difficult to understand as public communal institutions. Some synagogues belonged to particular groups. The "synagogue of the freedmen" (Acts 6:9) in Jerusalem, for example, appears to be one such institution. Philo also describes the Torah reading ritual of the Essenes as taking place in "sacred places, which they call synagogues" (Gk. οἳ καλοῦντι συναγωγαί).[33] The Essenes should be understood as a "sect" or a voluntary association. As a result, their synagogues should be understood to belong to their group and not to the Jewish community as a whole. Furthermore, a synagogue located in Jerusalem, such as the one mentioned in the Theodotos inscription,[34] could hardly have been the seat of local community functions, such as courtroom judgment, since this would have been performed in the Jerusalem temple.[35] This issue is acute in diaspora settings, where it is difficult to imagine a Jewish synagogue performing the same communal administrative functions associated with the city gate as in locales in the Jewish homeland, since administrative control of diaspora cities and towns was in Gentile hands.

Roughly contemporaneous with Levine's first publication detailing the city gate hypothesis in 1996, Peter Richardson published an article making a case for the identification of early synagogues as a type of Greco-Roman voluntary association.[36] This identification has since

---

32. Cf. Collingwood, *IH*, 246; Lonergan, *Method*, 186ff.

33. *Prob.* 81–82. On this, see Runesson, *Origins*, 223ff.

34. *CIJ* 2.1404; *ASSB* no. 26.

35. Runesson, *Origins*, 227. On the date of this inscription, see John S. Kloppenborg Verbin, "Dating Theodotos (*CIJ* 1404)," *JJS* 51, no. 2 (2000): 243–80; cf. John S. Kloppenborg, "The Theodotos Synagogue Inscription and the Problem of First-Century Synagogue Buildings," in *Jesus and Archaeology*, (ed. James H. Charlesworth; Grand Rapids: Eerdmans, 2006), 236–82.

36. Peter Richardson, "Early Synagogues as *Collegia*," 90–109. This article was later republished as a chapter of Peter Richardson, *Building Jewish in the Roman East* (Waco: Baylor University Press, 2004), 111–33. Further page references will be to the 2004 edition. On what Richardson means by *collegia* (or "association"), see John S. Kloppenborg, "*Collegia* and *Thiasoi*: Issues in function, taxonomy and membership," in *Voluntary Associations in the Ancient World* (ed. John S. Kloppenborg and Stephen G. Wilson; London: Routledge, 1996), 16–30.

been followed and further explored by Philip Harland.[37] Voluntary associations in the Greco-Roman world were semi-public groups, and are roughly analogous to clubs.[38] This hypothesis is able to make better sense of evidence from the diaspora by understanding diaspora synagogues as associations belonging to the Jewish community of their locales. Identifying synagogues as associations also provides a typological tool for understanding synagogues that appear to belong to particular groups rather than to the population of a locale as a whole.

It is important to note that the bulk of the positive evidence presented by both Richardson and Harland comes from the diaspora.[39] This is particularly evident in Richardson's attempt to make an architectural case for synagogues as associations.[40] Although Richardson is able to make a compelling case for the architectural similarity between the archaeological remains of voluntary association buildings and synagogues from the diaspora, he notes only two cases in the Land—at Jericho and Qumran—in which the architectural remains fit the pattern that he establishes for association buildings and diaspora synagogues.[41] The public communal nature of the other synagogue buildings in the Land on the basis of architecture, such as those at Gamla, Modi'in, and Qiryat Sefer, is likely.[42] Indeed, Richardson himself agrees that "the majority of Palestinian synagogues were simple communal meeting halls."[43] The public nature of some synagogues in the Land is also supported by literary evidence. Josephus's description of a public political gathering in a synagogue in Tiberias implies that the edifice, which was large enough to hold the Tiberian assembly, was a municipal institution used by the public for communal gatherings.[44]

---

37. See Philip A. Harland, *Associations, Synagogues and Congregations: Claiming a Place in Ancient Mediterranean Society* (Minneapolis: Fortress Press, 2003). The understanding of synagogues as associations is also implicit in Richard S. Ascough, Philip A. Harland, and John S. Kloppenborg, *Associations in the Greco-Roman World: A Sourcebook* (Waco: Baylor University Press, 2012).

38. For an in-depth discussion of voluntary associations, see Kloppenborg, "*Collegia* and *Thiasoi*."

39. Harland's lack of distinction between the land of Israel and the Diaspora despite his heavy reliance on Diaspora evidence has also been noted by Bernier, *Aposynagōgos*, 58.

40. Richardson, "Synagogues as Associations."

41. Ibid., 113. The buildings referred to are *ASSB* nos. 15 and 41. It is also not entirely clear whether or not the room at Qumran referred to by Richardson should be identified as a synagogue. On this, see the comments to *ASSB* no. 41, in Runesson, Binder, and Olsson, *ASSB*, 72ff.

42. *ASSB* nos. 10, 29, and 35. Note the comments about the Gamla building's function as a "Jewish community centre serving both religious and secular needs" by Zvi Yavor, "The Architecture and Stratigraphy of the Eastern and Western Quarters," in *Gamla II: The Architecture* (ed. Danny Syon and Zvi Yavor; Jerusalem: Israel Antiquities Authority, 2010), 13–112 (61).

43. Peter Richardson, "An Architectural Case for Synagogues as Associations," in *The Ancient Synagogue From Its Origins Until 200 C.E.: Papers Presented at an International Conference at Lund University, October 14-17, 2001* (ed. Birger Olsson, and Magnus Zetterholm; CBNTS 39; Stockholm: Almqvist & Wiksell, 2003), 90–117 (113).

44. *Vita* 276–81, 294–95.

Distinguishing Between Public and Association Synagogues

A synagogue in a Gentile city such as Thessalonica (see Acts 17:1–4) could accurately be described as an association of the Jews of Thessalonica, for which membership was determined on the basis of ethnicity. The situation could potentially be quite different for a synagogue in a town in the Jewish homeland. While the synagogue of the Jews of Thessalonica could be called a semi-public association, the synagogue of the Jews of Capernaum would simply be the public assembly (or assembly place) of the people of that town. This is because the Jews of Capernaum, by and large, constituted the people of the town. Even if we were to take a small minority gentile population into consideration, it must be granted that the majority Jewish population controlled the town.[45] *Control of the town is the primary determining factor in this respect.* A specific party or group in a Jewish locale could form a semi-public association synagogue if they wished,[46] but the local assembly of the town can hardly be called a voluntary association.

Thus, there appears to be two sets of evidence that are at odds. Some evidence is best explained by understanding the synagogue as a public institution that developed from the ancient city gate, while other evidence is best explained by understanding synagogues as voluntary associations. This has led Runesson to the proposal that there were, in fact, two types of institutions designated by synagogue terms: public synagogues and association synagogues.[47] Runesson's hypothesis is to be preferred because it best explains the evidence.[48] As a result of the recognizable explanatory power of the "two types" synagogue typology, it has enjoyed positive reception and acceptance in recent publications by New Testament scholars.[49]

---

45. Ann Killebrew makes a distinction between Greco-Roman cities with mixed populations of pagans and Jews and Jewish villages, whose populations "tended to be more homogenous in their social, economic, and religious make-up, usually comprising large extended families with strong kinship ties." Ann E. Killebrew, "Village and Countryside," in *The Oxford Handbook of Jewish Daily Life in Roman Palestine* (ed. Catherine Hezser; Oxford and New York: Oxford University Press, 2010), 189–209 (194–95). Cf. also the study of Jewish settlements in Ze'ev Safrai, *The Economy of Roman Palestine* (London: Routledge, 1994), 9–60.

46. Such as the case might be with the Jericho synagogue (*ASSB* no. 15). See Anders Runesson, "The Nature and Origins of the First-Century Synagogue," *Bible and Interpretation*, July 2004, http://www.bibleinterp.com/articles/Runesson-1st-Century_Synagogue_1.shtml. See also Ehud Netzer, "A Synagogue from the Hasmonean Period Recently Exposed in the Western Plain of Jericho," *Israel Exploration Journal* 49 (1999): 219–21.

47. Runesson, *Origins*, 213–35. See esp. 233.

48. This is an example of the application of the historiographical principle of inference to the best explanation. On this, see McCullagh, *The Logic of History*, 49ff.

49. E.g., Twelftree, "Jesus and the Synagogue," 3109–110; Bernier, *Aposynagōgos*, 57–60; Keith, *Scribal Elite*, 33ff., esp. 33 no. 59; Birger Olsson, "Origins of the Synagogue," 133; Donald D. Binder, "The

The determination of a distinction between the two types of synagogues clarifies the function and role played by each type. As a result, the nature of the synagogues depicted in the gospels can also be substantially clarified, thereby allowing for a deeper and more accurate understanding of the role that they play in the gospel narratives. The synagogues in the gospel narratives are *public synagogues*.[50] Jesus is able to enter freely from synagogue to synagogue across Galilee,[51] which precludes any notion of these synagogues having been closed to outsiders. This presumes that the synagogues visited by Jesus were public places, open to the general populace. They are depicted as gathering places belonging to the local populations and open for outsiders—such as Jesus—to enter, participate in services, and interact with the people gathered within.[52] Moreover, there is no clear indication that the synagogues that Jesus visits in the Gospels belong to a particular group. As an example to the contrary, Luke 7:5 describes the synagogue in Capernaum as though it were owned by the town, rather than by a specific association.[53] Though there are Pharisees present in Mark 3:1–6 (and parallels), they do not seem to be in control of the assembly. In fact, the Pharisaic interpretation of the Sabbath Law is actually openly and successfully challenged by Jesus in this pericope, which points toward a public rather than a Pharisaic association setting. Furthermore, the sayings in the Jesus tradition concerning synagogues describe functions that assume public institutional settings rather than semi-private association settings.[54] John 18:20 especially exemplifies

Origins of the Synagogue: An Evaluation," in *The Ancient Synagogue From Its Origins Until 200 C.E.: Papers Presented at an International Conference at Lund University, October 14-17, 2001* (ed. Birger Olsson, and Magnus Zetterholm; CBNTS 39; Stockholm: Almqvist & Wiksell, 2003), 122–23; Stewart, *Gathered Around Jesus*, esp. 139; Meyers and Chancey, *Alexander to Constantine*, 203–4; Richard S. Ascough, "Paul, Synagogues, and Associations: Reframing the Question of Models for Pauline Christ Groups," *JJMJS* 2 (2015): 27–52, esp. 39–40; Ralph J. Korner, "*Ekklēsia* as a Jewish Synagogue Term: Some Implications for Paul's Socio-Religious Location," *JJMJS* 2 (2015): 53–78, esp. 60–61.

50. Cf. Runesson, *Origins*, 355ff.; Runesson, "Importance of the Synagogue," 12ff.; Twelftree, "Jesus and the Synagogue," esp. 3133.

51. Statements that Jesus taught in the various synagogues of Galilee can be found at Matt 4:23, 9:35, Mark 1:39, and Luke 4:15, cf. John 18:20. Paul can also freely enter into a number of *association* synagogues in the diaspora. He does so on the basis of his Jewish ethnicity, which grants him "membership" in the Jewish synagogue associations. In other association synagogues, such as those found in the Land, ethnicity might not be the determining factor for admission. This is likely the case with the synagogue of the Freedmen from Acts 6:9.

52. Mark 1:21, 23, 39, 3:1, 6:2; Matt 4:23, 9:35, 12:9, 13:54; Luke 4:15, 16, 31–33, 44, 6:6, 7:5 (note that the synagogue here appears to be owned by the people of Capernaum rather than a specific association), 13:10; John 6:59, 18:20.

53. Cf. *m. Ned.* 5:5.

54. Mark 12:39 (cf. Matt 23:6; Luke 20:46), 13:9; Matt 6:2, 5, 23:34; Luke 11:43, 12:11, 21:12; John 16:2, 18:20. It is worth noting that a case has been made for understanding the *aposynagōgos* passages in John (9:22, 12:42, 16:2) in light of disaffiliation from associations by John S. Kloppenborg, "Disaffiliation in Associations and the ἀποσυναγωγός of John," *HTS Teologeise Studies* 61, no 1, article

this, as the point being made by that saying is only intelligible if it can be assumed that synagogues are open, public gathering places such as the Jerusalem temple rather than semi-private association settings.

Recognition of the public/association typology helps to determine what data is useful for understanding the particular synagogue institutions that appear in the gospel narratives. Because the synagogues that Jesus interacted with were public synagogues, the dataset that will be most pertinent to our investigation will necessarily be that which pertains to the Land of Israel, since public synagogues could not exist in the diaspora. Furthermore, it is important to distinguish between data that clearly pertains to semi-public synagogues belonging to a particular association in the Land, on the one hand, and public synagogues, on the other.

Public Assembly in Jerusalem During the Second Temple Period

Since Jerusalem was the location of the temple, the situation there was different from the rest of the Land. The temple most likely served as the civic centre and primary place of public assembly for Jerusalem. Binder has pointed out that the temple's architecture, with its colonnades and stoas, reflects that of a Hellenistic civic centre insofar as it resembles an *agora*, which was originally a cultic and civic centre, and only secondarily attracted business and commerce.[55] The public assembly in Jerusalem appears to have shifted from the Water Gate to the temple complex by the time that 1 Esdras 9:38 was written (second century BCE). Here, the Torah reading in Nehemiah 8:1–12 is retold, but rather than taking place at the Water Gate, it is located "in the open square before the east gate of the temple." Indeed, the architecture of the Jerusalem temple, with its open and publically accessible space in the form of porticoes, plazas, and courts, reflects its nature and function as communal space.[56] Thus, much like public synagogue buildings, there was also a public spatial aspect to the Jerusalem temple complex.[57]

---

962 (2011). However, this interpretation has been critiqued as a "fallacy of perfect analogy" by Bernier, *Aposynagōgos*, 63–64.

55. Binder, *Into the Temple Courts*, 218.

56. For a description and analysis of the architecture of the Jerusalem, see Leen Ritmeyer, "Imagining the Temple Known to Jesus and to Early Jews," in *Jesus and Temple: Textual and Archaeological Explorations* (ed. James H. Charlesworth; Minneapolis: Fortress Press, 2014), 19–57; and Dan Bahat, "The Second Temple in Jerusalem," in *Jesus and Temple: Textual and Archaeological Explorations* (ed. James H. Charlesworth; Minneapolis: Fortress Press, 2014), 59–74.

57. A more direct relationship between the architecture of the temple and the synagogue has been advanced by both Binder and Strange. See Binder, *Into the Temple Courts*, 222–26 and James F.

Josephus has followed 1 Esdras's relocation of the movement of the assembly described in Nehemiah 8:1–12 from the Water Gate to the temple complex, from which we may infer that the septennial Torah-reading ceremony likely took place in the temple courts during the first century CE.[58] There are also a number of places elsewhere in the works of Josephus in which the temple courts function as a place of public assembly.[59] Trials also took place in the temple courts.[60] We may infer from this evidence that, in Jerusalem, synagogue functions (that is, Torah reading, public assembly, and judgement) took place in the temple precincts.[61] This sheds some light on the equivalence that is presumed between the temple and synagogue as public assembly places in Jesus's saying in John 18:20.

Conclusion

Our review of recent scholarship on the origins of the "synagogue" has determined two competing definitions of "the synagogue." While some scholars support a definition of the "synagogue" as a type of Greco-Roman association, others define it as a Jewish public institution derived from earlier city gate assemblies. There are merits to both definitions, which are each supported by distinct sets of evidence. This has led to the conclusion that the best explanation of the evidence as a whole is that there were two types of institutions designated by synagogue terms: association synagogues and public synagogues.

The synagogues visited by Jesus in the Gospel narratives are best classified as public synagogues. This means that they developed from gate assemblies, and were public religio-political institutions with a

---

Strange, "First Century Galilee from Archaeology and from the Texts," in *Archaeology and the Galilee; Texts and Contexts in Graeco-Roman and Byzantine Periods* (ed. Douglas R. Edwards and C. Thomas McCollough; Atlanta: Scholars Press, 1997), 39–48 (43–44); Strange, "Archaeology and Ancient Synagogues," 45–46. See also Anders Runesson, *Origins*, 29–37; Olsson, "Origins of the Synagogue," 133.

58. *Ant.* 11.154–58. Cf. the observations of Binder, *Into the Temple Courts*, 219–20.

59. *War* 1.122, 2.1–5, 2.294–95, 2.320–24; *Ant.* 17.200–201. Cf. Binder, *Into the Temple Courts*, 220.

60. See *War* 4.336. According to the Mishnah, three courts were located in the Temple complex at the gate of the Temple Mount, at the gate of the Temple court, and in the Chamber of Hewn Stone (*Sanh.* 11.2). Given that the Sanhedrin probably met in the Temple precincts, it is most likely that the trials in Acts 4:5ff. and Acts 22:30ff. both took place in the Temple. See Ritmeyer, "Imagining the Temple," 42–43.

61. Cf. Runesson, *Origin*, 352–53. For consideration of the Temple as "synagogue" in relation to the *aposynagōgos* passages in John, see Bernier, *Aposynagōgos*, 66ff. There is a public assembly (*ekklēsia*) of the people of Jerusalem mentioned in 1 Macc 5:16 and 14:19, and it is a reasonable guess that these assemblies would have taken place in the primary public space of the city, the temple courts. A public assembly (*ekklēsia*) is also mentioned with some frequency in Ben Sira (15:5, 21:17, 23:24, 31:11, 33:19, 38:33, 39:10, 44:15). We shall deal with this institution in more depth in chapter 3.

variety of legal-liturgical, judicial, and conciliar functions. In Jerusalem, these functions were located in the temple courts. Armed with this definition of the synagogues visited by Jesus as public institutions, we may now turn to the task of examining the evidence pertaining to Second Temple public synagogues. In so doing, I will bring the evidence together, connected by robust threads of historical imagination, into a portrait of public synagogues as Jesus and his Galilean contemporaries knew them.

3

The Public Synagogue as Jesus Knew It: Functions, People, and Architecture

Introduction

In this chapter, I will investigate the functions of public synagogues, the people who met in them, and the architecture of synagogue buildings. The distinction between public and association synagogues outlined in the previous chapter provides a helpful categorization that will allow us to place limits and controls on the data that will serve as evidence for the present investigation.

While recent scholarly reconstructions of early synagogues have been occupied with avoiding anachronism,[1] less care has been taken to avoid anatopism and anatypism. For example, Binder mixes evidence from the Land and the diaspora,[2] while Levine tends to generalize between the two, minimizing distinctions between them.[3] Stephen

---

1. See Kee, "Transformation of the Synagogue"; Richard E. Oster, "Supposed Anachronism"; Atkinson, "Further Defining." The scholarly discourse surrounding the issue of anachronism, the existence of synagogues during the Second Temple period, and the development of the synagogue after the destruction of the temple in 70 CE will be treated in detail in chapter 4. It is worth noting that the question of the existence of synagogues prior to 70 CE occasionally still continues to be posed, e.g., Evans, *Jesus and His World*, 38–62; Hachlili, "Synagogues: Before and After the Roman Destruction of the Temple."
2. Although he examines them separately in earlier chapters, throughout the description of func-

Catto is careful to note the provenance of the data that he treats in his reconstruction,[4] but makes no distinction between data pertaining to association and public synagogues.[5] As a result, he tends toward anatypism, focussing on the liturgical aspects of early synagogues and leaving his treatment of the nonliturgical (political and communal) aspect relatively underdeveloped.

The emphasis in this chapter will be placed on evidence pertaining to public synagogues in the Land of Israel. The picture of public synagogues that will emerge from the evidence is that of a religio-political institution operating at the local-official level. The aim is not to present a totally revolutionary portrait of early synagogues, but to produce a historical synthesis from the relevant evidence of the public synagogues in the Land prior to 70 CE *as Jesus and his Galilean contemporaries would have known them.* In so doing, I aim to draw out and highlight the aspects of the data that will serve as the most important evidence for the task of contextualizing and understanding Jesus.

A few words are necessary concerning references made to New Testament sources in this chapter. One potential difficulty involved with applying synagogue scholarship and data to the study of Jesus is that the New Testament provides some crucial information on Second-Temple-period synagogues. As a result, data from the Gospels and Acts are regularly utilized in current synagogue scholarship as evidence for reconstructing the Second Temple synagogue. The matter is summed up well by Levine, who writes that "New Testament sources reveal facets of synagogue life virtually unknown elsewhere."[6] Excising New Testament material from the present study altogether would be problematic, since it would most likely produce a portrait of Second Temple synagogues that would differ in certain respects from current mainstream scholarship.

It is important to be conscious of the fact that the historical value of the Gospels as sources on the synagogue is recognized in mainstream synagogue scholarship.[7] This study shares that perspective. As a result,

---

tionaries in Binder, *Into the Temple Courts*, 343–87, and synagogues functions in pp. 389–50, the evidence from the Land and the diaspora are mixed freely together without sufficient distinction.

3. See, e.g., Levine, *Ancient Synagogue*, 136.

4. In Catto, *Reconstructing*, passim.

5. Cf. Birger Olsson, review of Stephen K. Catto, *Reconstructing the First-Century Synagogue: A Critical Analysis of Current Research, RBL* 11.

6. Lee I. Levine, "The Synagogues of Galilee," in *Galilee in the Late Second Temple and Mishnaic Periods: Life, Culture, and Society* (ed. David A. Fiensy and James Riley Strange; vol. 1 *Galilee in the Late Second Temple and Mishnaic Periods*; Minneapolis: Fortress Press, 2014), 140.

7. For a recent summary of the reasons for this, see Levine, "Synagogues of Galilee," 141. Although a charge of anachronism was raised against Luke's depiction of the synagogue in the 1990s, this

references to these texts can be found throughout this chapter. To be clear, what I am *not* doing is using the Gospels to interpret themselves or one another. What I am doing is treating them as potential evidence for understanding both Jesus and early synagogues, and then, utilizing one of those constructions to inform the other. This in itself is not fallacious.[8] Nevertheless, I recognize the need for caution. Thus, I want to emphasize that these texts do not stand alone. Rather, I am casting them alongside plentiful evidence drawn from other sources, both literary and material, in the web of inference and imagination.[9] So doing demonstrates in itself how well the Gospels and Acts fit into the portrait of the synagogue that emerges from the archaeology and literature of the Second Temple period.

Scripture Reading: Torah and Nevi'im

The communal reading of Jewish scripture was a characteristic feature of synagogue institutions during the Second Temple period.[10] This was true for both public and association synagogues in the Second Temple period, in the Land as well as in the diaspora. Literary sources evidencing the reading of Torah in synagogues include Acts 15:21; Josephus (*Ap.* 2.175, *Ant.* 16.43, *War* 2.292); The Theodotos Inscription (*CIJ* 2.1404); and Philo (*Prob.* 80–83, *Embassy* 156).

The sources are diverse. We may infer that *CIJ* 2.1404 (the Theodotos Inscription from Jerusalem), *Prob.* 80–83 (which concerns Essene *synagōgai*), and *War* 2.292 (on Caesarea Maritima, a mixed-population, Gentile-dominated city) refer to association synagogues. As a result, their relevance for our purposes is limited. The references in Acts

charge has been roundly rejected in current mainstream scholarship. This issue is treated in detail in chapter 4. See also Catto, *Reconstructing*, passim.
8. There is, after all, nothing fallacious about using one reasonable historical inference drawn from a source to inform another inference drawn from the same source. Historians do this all the time. The logical fallacy of circularity in history concerns the assumption of what is to be proven, and is not relevant here. See David Hackett Fischer, *Historians' Fallacies: Toward a Logic of History* (New York: Harper & Row, 1970), 49–51.
9. Cf. Collingwood's notion of the historian's interpretive web as the "touchstone" for historical criticism. See Collingwood, *Idea of History*, 244, discussed in appendix A.
10. Rachel Hachlili has also noted general agreement among scholars that "reading and teaching the Torah was the key liturgical function" of synagogues, in Hachlili, *Ancient Synagogues*, 47, cf. also Olsson, "An Evaluation," 134, and Runesson, *Origins*, passim; Lester L. Grabbe, "Synagogue and Sanhedrin in the Frist Century," in *Handbook for the Study of the Historical Jesus*, ed. Tom Holmén and Stanley E. Porter; 4 vols. (Leiden: Brill, 2011), 1723–44 (1728–29). On the relationship of synagogue architecture to public reading, see James F. Strange, "Archaeology and Ancient Synagogues," 43–44. See also Steven Fine, "From Meeting House to Sacred Realm," in *Sacred Realm: The Emergence of the Synagogue in the Ancient World*, ed. Steven Fine (New York and Oxford: Oxford University Press, 1996), 21–47 (22); cf. Steven Fine, *This Holy Place*, 25.

15:21, *Ap.* 2.175, *Ant.* 16.43, and *Embassy* 156, however, are all general blanket statements that seem to describe public gatherings for the reading of Torah, and probably refer indiscriminately to the Land and the diaspora. According to Acts 15:21, "in every city, for generations past, Moses has had those who proclaim him, for he has been read aloud every Sabbath in the synagogues." In the narrative of Acts, this statement is uttered at a meeting in a Judean context in Jerusalem by James the Just. The reference to "every city" is nonspecific, though given the location of the utterance in Jerusalem, κατὰ πόλιν ("every city") should at least be understood to include the Land,[11] if not every city in the Roman world.

Some corroboration, though it comes from a later source, can also be found in the early Rabbinic writings. For example, *m. Meg.* 3:1 presumes that Torah scrolls are typically located within synagogues. Moreover, the discussion of Torah readings in *m. Meg.* 3:4–4:9 directly follows teachings concerning synagogues in 3:1–3, as though the two are intimately connected. The most important evidence from the early Rabbinic corpus concerning the reading of scripture within synagogues comes from *t. Meg.* 2:18, which specifically lists the reading of scripture as a typical activity performed in a synagogue.[12]

Archaeology contributes important evidence to this matter. As James Strange has noted, the architecture of early synagogue buildings in the Land indicates a design emphasizing hearing rather than seeing, which makes sense if the buildings in question were designed with the communal reading of scripture in mind.[13] This is because columns are typically situated in places where they obscure the vision of people seated on benches.

The synagogue at Magdala contains two rectangular carved stone blocks, each with two half-cylindrical grooves that run down the top surface on both the right- and left-hand sides (fig. 6). One was discovered in secondary use in the main meeting room, and the other *in situ* in a central location in a smaller "study room" (fig. 5). It has been suggested that these stones may have been used as surfaces for reading texts, and that each of the grooves would be suited to hold a scroll roller.[14] This is currently the best interpretation of the artifacts,

---

11. Cf. Runesson, *Origins*, 220.
12. See also *m. Meg.* 3:12, 21.
13. Strange, "Archaeology and Ancient Synagogues," 43–44. See figs. 2–3, 14–18.
14. E.g., Anders Runesson, "Synagogues Without Rabbis or Christians? Ancient Institutions Beyond Normative Discourses," (paper presented at the "Erasure History: Approaching the Missing Sources of Antiquity" conference, Toronto, Ontario, November 11, 2011).

though it is possible that future studies may present some alternative hypotheses.

An important piece of evidence comes from the excavations at Masada, where fragments of Deuteronomy and Ezekiel were found inside a small room in the synagogue building.[15] Given the association of the Torah with synagogues in the literature, the discovery of Deuteronomy in the Masada synagogue corroborates the literary evidence. Even more intriguing is the discovery of the Ezekiel fragments, since Ezekiel belongs to the Nevi'im. This discovery may speak to the growing use of the Nevi'im alongside the Torah in synagogue liturgical settings in the Second Temple Period.

In 2 Maccabees 15:9, Judas Maccabee encourages his troops with readings from "the Law and the Prophets" (ἐκ τοῦ νόμου καὶ τῶν προφητῶν). This reflects a trend in the Second Temple period to associate the Nevi'im with the Torah, which can also be seen in the prologue of Sirach. In the New Testament, frequent reference is made to the Jewish scriptures as "the Law and the Prophets."[16] Acts 13:15 is of special note, since it recounts the reading of "the Law and the Prophets" in an association synagogue setting in Pisidian Antioch.

All of this is indicative of the emergence of *haftarah* readings (readings from the Nevi'im) as an extension of Torah readings in the late Second Temple period.[17] The narrative of Jesus's reading from Isaiah in the synagogue at Nazareth in Luke 4:16ff. is best understood in light of *haftarah* readings during this era, and is itself evidence for this practice.[18]

The practice of reading Torah in the synagogue continued into the second century and beyond, as evidenced by the Mishnah and Tosefta.[19] Although the difficulties associated with their use in reconstructions of the early first century are well known,[20] early rabbinic lit-

---

15. *ASSB*, no. 28. On this discovery and other texts found at Masada, see Shemaryahu Talmon, "Hebrew Fragments From Masada," in *Masada VI* (Jerusalem: Israel Exploration Society, 1999).

16. Matt 5:17, 7:12, 22:40; Luke 16:16; Acts 13:15; Rom 3:21. See also 4 Macc 18:10.

17. In agreement with Levine, *Ancient Synagogue*, 153–55; Binder, *Into the Temple Courts*, 400–402.

18. For an interpretation of this passage in light of the Jewish background on *haftarah* readings, see R. Steven Notley, "Jesus' Jewish Hermeneutical Method in the Nazareth Synagogue," in *Early Christian Literature and Intertextuality*, vol. 2, Exegetical Studies, ed. Craig A. Evans and H.D. Zacharias (London: T&T Clark, 2009), 46–59.

19. E.g. *t. Meg.* 2:18, 3:21, 4:4. In the Mishnah, the Torah scrolls appear to be located within an ark in the local synagogue (*m. Meg.* 3:1–2). The location of the ark and scrolls is assumed when Torah reading practices and passing in front of the ark are discussed in *m. Meg.* 4.

20. The problem is essentially twofold. First, there are concerns regarding the date of rabbinic traditions, and second, serious issues have been raised concerning the genre and authority of rabbinic texts. As regards the problem of chronology, despite the chronological distance between the compilation of these texts and the earlier tradents, the nature of oral tradition and transmission in

erature provides a point of reference in the second century to which to attach a thread of historical imagination from the first-century evidence, thereby establishing continuity and shared tradition throughout the intervening period. Instructions for readings from the Nevi'im (*haftarah*) are discussed alongside Torah readings in *m. Meg.* 4:4.[21] While the synagogue (*bet knesset*) is not actually mentioned directly, I concur with the evaluation of Runesson, Binder, and Olsson that these traditions "apply to the reading rituals of communal assemblies," and thus, to a synagogue context.[22]

The Politics of Interpretation

All of the evidence that we have examined indicates that the synagogue was the location for public readings from the Torah and the Nevi'im and that it was closely associated with this purpose. It is important to recognize that during the time of Jesus, the Torah was not only a sacred text, but also functioning normative law in Jewish-controlled areas.[23] Although the legal-official status of the Torah in the early Sec-

---

rabbinic Judaism allows for the possibility that early traditions were preserved with some accuracy. Concerning the nature of Oral Torah and the oral transmission of the sayings of the sages in rabbinic literature, see Shmuel Safrai, "Oral Tora," in *The Literature of the Sages Part One: Oral Tora, Halakha, Tosefta, Talmud, Externa Tractates* (ed. Shmuel Safrai and Peter J. Tomson; vol. 1 of *Literature of the Sages*; Philadelphia: Fortress Press, 1987), 35–119, and the now classic study by Birger Gerhardsson, *Memory and Manuscript: Oral Tradition and Written Transmission in Rabbinic Judaism and Early Christianity* (Acta Seminarii Neotestamentici Upsaliensis 22; Lund: C.W.K. Gleerup, 1961). A good discussion of how Rabbinic material might be used in Jesus research can be found in Geza Vermes, "Reflections on Improving Methodology in Jesus Research," in *Jesus Research: New Methodologies and Perceptions, The Second Princeton-Prague Symposium on Jesus Research* (ed. James H. Charlesworth with Brian Rhea and Petr Pokorný; Grand Rapids: Eerdmans, 2014), 17–27 (18–21).

21. It is worth noting that, according to *m. Meg.* 4:4, while it is not permitted to skip from place to place in the Torah readings, it is permissible in the readings from the Nevi'im. This is an interesting tradition in light of Jesus's reading from the scroll of Isaiah in Luke 4:18–20, in which Jesus skips from his reading of Isa 61:1–2 to 58:6 and back again. This issue will be explored in chapter 6.

22. Runesson, Binder, and Olsson, *Ancient Synagogue Source Book*, 113. This evaluation is even more likely once it is considered alongside *t. Meg.* 2:18 and 3:21, in which the reading of scripture is considered to be normative within a synagogue context.

23. Cf., e.g., Philip S. Alexander, "Jewish Law in the Time of Jesus: Towards a Clarification of the Problem," in *Law and Religion: Essays on the Place of the Law in Israel and Early Christianity*, ed. Barnabas Lindars (Cambridge: J. Clarke, 1988), 44–58; James W. Watts, "The Political and Legal Uses of Scripture," in *From the Beginnings to 600* (ed. James Carleton Paget and Joachim Schaper; vol. 1 of *The New Cambridge History of the Bible*; Cambridge: Cambridge University Press, 2013), 345–64, esp. 356–58; Thomas Kazen, *Scripture, Interpretation, or Authority?: Motives and Arguments in Jesus' Halakic Conflicts* (WUNT 320; Tübingen: Mohr Siebeck, 2013), 296–98; Anders Runesson, "Entering a Synagogue With Paul: First-Century Torah Observance," in *Torah Ethics and Early Christian Identity*, ed. Susan J. Wendel and David M. Miller (Grand Rapids: Eerdmans, 2016), 11–26, esp. 15–20; Michael LeFebvre, *Collections, Codes, and Torah: The Re-Characterization of Israel's Written Law* (OTS 451; London and New York: T&T Clark, 2006), passim, esp. 182, 239–40, 258–60.

ond Temple period is unclear,[24] there is evidence for the legal status of the Torah from the Hellenistic period to the late Second Temple period.

By the Hellenistic period, we see the Torah being applied to situations that are beyond the boundaries of what we might categorize as strictly religious. It is applied to the performance of marriage contracts (Tob 1:8; 7:12–13), battle plans (1 Macc 3:48), Sabbath observance (1 Macc 2:34–41), and criminal justice (Sus 62).[25] The Torah did not only govern "religious" life, or the temple cult. It governed everyday life.[26] Thus, we see that Josephus makes no distinction between "religious" law and secular or "political" (statutory) law in *Ap.* 2.170–2.171. He places the Torah on the same level as Roman governmental law (*Ap.* 2.176–178).[27] According to Josephus, Moses ordained the Jewish government to be a "theocracy" (*Ap.* 2.165, Gk. *theokratia*).[28] The Torah is the foundation of that theocracy, divine instruction for divine rule.[29] Transgression of the proper practice of Torah could have serious and very real consequences.[30] I would suggest that it is in light of this understanding of the Torah that we should view elements in the Jesus tradition, such as Matthew 5:21–22, which deals with legal liability to both human and divine courts (see chapter 5 below), or the dispute over healing on the Sabbath between Jesus and the *archisynagōgos* in Luke 13:10–17.[31]

As a result of the Torah being functional civil law in the Land, the

---

24. See the articles contained in James W. Watts, ed., *Persia and Torah: The Theory of Imperial Authorization of the Pentateuch* (Atlanta: Society of Biblical Literature, 2001); cf. also LeFebvre, *Re-Characterization*, passim.

25. As argued by Watts, "Political and Legal," 357.

26. This apparently extended beyond the destruction of the Temple in 70 CE. On local Jewish law and its co-existence with Hellenistic law in regard to the second-century legal papyri from the Judean desert, see Joseph Mélèze Modrzejewski, "What is Hellenistic Law? The Documents of the Judaean Desert in the Light of the Papyri from Egypt," *in Law in the Documents of the Judaean Desert* (ed. R. Katzoff and D. Schaps; JSJSup 96; Leiden and Boston: Brill, 2005), 7–21, esp. 9–14. Consider, for example, P.Yad. 18, a marriage contract containing the phrase "you will be my wife according to the law of Moses and the Judeans." On marriage contracts specifically, see David Instone-Brewer, "1 Corinthians 7 in the Light of the Jewish Greek and Aramaic Marriage and Divorce Papyri," *Tyndale Bulletin* 52, no. 2 (2001): 225–43.

27. Similarly, he contrasts the "illegal" severe judicial laws imposed by Herod with the Mosaic law in *Ant.* 16.1–4, which indicates that Josephus thought of the Torah as normative legislation on par (or even more legitimate than) laws enacted by a ruler such as Herod.

28. As argued by John Barclay, this term here has to do with God's sovereignty rather than priestly governance. See John M.G. Barclay, *Against Apion: Translation and Commentary* (Flavius Josephus: Translation and Commentary 10; Leiden and Boston: Brill, 2007), 262. However, on priests as human government, see *Ap.* 2.185, cf. Barclay, *Apion*, 273–74.

29. Cf. *Ant.* 4.196–98.

30. Cf., e.g., Josephus, *Ap.* 2.215–19, 276–77, *Ant.* 4.210; *m. Mak.* 3:1–15; John 10:31–33, cf. Lev 24:10–23. See Barclay, *Apion*, 294–95.

31. Cf. Jordan J. Ryan, "Jesus and Synagogue Disputes: The Institutional Context of Luke 13:10-17," *CBQ* 79, no. 1 (2017): 41–59. This passage will be discussed in chapter 7.

reading and interpretation of the Torah which occurred in public synagogues were, simultaneously and inextricably, both political and religious acts. The reading and interpretation of the Nevi'im could also have religio-political implications. The local-official character of the public synagogue meant that it was uncontrolled by a central, supralocal authority. As such, the interpretation of the law was open for discussion and debate within the local public synagogues. As Runesson has pointedly observed,

> A certain village or town could thus be dominated by an influential group striving to control the local-official level ideologically. Such a struggle for domination is likely to have been the case in many of the villages and towns of Galilee (and elsewhere in Palestine) and it is in this context that we are to understand the mission of Jesus and other groups such as Judas the Galilean and his followers, the Herodians, the Sadducees, and the Pharisees.[32]

Sources from both the Land and the diaspora indicate that discussion was a part of the practice of public scripture reading, and interpretive discourse following readings and teaching was apparently common in both public and association synagogues.[33]

Scripture reading in first-century synagogues was not tied to a specific lectionary, nor should we imagine formal sermons taking place as in modern synagogues or churches.[34] Rather, the main activity at synagogue gatherings after the reading of the Torah and the Nevi'im was open discussion in which, as Carl Mosser writes, "anyone could offer insights or dispute the interpretive claims of others."[35] The political and socio-legal aspects of the reading and interpretation of the Torah have frequently been overlooked in recent scholarship. Levine, for example, distinguishes between the functions of the synagogue as a religious institution, including the reading and interpretation of scripture, and its communal (political, legal, official) functions.[36] This dis-

---

32. Runesson, *Origins*, 221–22.
33. E.g., Philo, *Hypoth.* 7.13; *Somn.* 2.127; Neh 8:1–8; Luke 4:22–30; Mark 6:2. Interactive discussion of a teaching closely related to passages from the Torah also occurs in the Johannine account of Jesus's teaching in the Capernaum synagogue (John 6:25–59, cf. Catto, *First Century Synagogue*, 124). Cf., e.g., Carl Mosser, "Torah Instruction, Discussion, and Prophecy in First-Century Synagogues," in *Christian Origins and Hellenistic Judaism: Social and Literary Contexts for the New Testament* (Texts and Editions for New Testament Study 10; ed. Stanley E. Porter and Andrew W. Pitts; Leiden and Boston: Brill, 2013), 523–51, passim; Binder, *Into the Temple Courts*, 403; Runesson, "Entering a Synagogue," 16–19. Later tradition also mentions interpretation (targum) following a reading (*t. Meg.* 3:20).
34. Mosser, "Torah Instruction," passim.
35. Ibid., 550.

tinction is somewhat misleading, since the reading and interpretation of scripture was as much political and communal as it was religious. Similarly, Catto's discussion of scripture reading is limited to its nature as a worship practice.[37] Rather than separating the "religious" from the "communal" or the "political,"[38] it is preferable to consider them to be two sides of the same coin.

The Public Synagogue as a Local-Official Institution

The public synagogue was a public assembly and, if we imagine a building or location, a public assembly place for the town.[39] This is indicated by the very term *synagōgē*, the common term used for the public synagogue in the New Testament, which is derived from the verb *synagō*, meaning "to bring together, gather together, collect, convene."[40] One of the clearest statements of the synagogue's function as a primary assembly place comes from John 18:20, where Jesus says: "I have spoken openly to the world; I have always taught in synagogues and in the temple, *where all the Jews come together*. I have said nothing in secret."[41] The point being made in this passage—that Jesus teaches publically rather than in secret—is only coherent if synagogues are understood by Jesus's hearers and John's readers as being a place for communal gathering and open to the general public.

Important evidence concerning the local-official character of the synagogue from the late Second Temple period comes from Josephus. In *Life* 276–303, Josephus describes several gatherings that took place in the synagogue (*proseuchē*) in Tiberias. Of these, one (initially *Life* 277–79, though the meeting reconvenes in 280–82) is a local-official political assembly, while another (290–303) was a public fast and prayer service.[42] Another political gathering of the town is also recounted at 284–89.

The attendees of the assemblies appear to have been the town council (*boulē*), and the "body of the people" (*dēmotikon ochlon*) of Tiberias.

---

36. See the discussion in Levine, *Ancient Synagogue*, 135–73.

37. Catto, *First-Century Synagogue*, 116–25.

38. In light of this, though I recognize that "Torah" is probably better translated as "instruction" rather than "law," I am not sure that this distinction is actually of much help to the historian in this situation. It is easy to make too much of this distinction. Regardless of how the Hebrew term is translated into English, the evidence and scholarship discussed above indicates that it was treated or regarded as functional law in Jewish locales during the late Second-Temple period.

39. Cf. Levine, *Ancient Synagogue*, 139; Runesson, *Origins*, 216ff.; Olsson, "An Evaluation," 133.

40. H. G. Liddell and Robert Scott, *IGEL*, 7th ed. (Oak Harbor: Logos Research Systems, Inc.), 766.

41. Emphasis my own.

42. Cf. Runesson, Binder, and Olsson, *Ancient Synagogue Source Book*, 78.

Accordingly, the building in question was very large (cf. *Vita* 277),[43] and designed with public assembly in mind. Leaders of at least two of the three Tiberian political factions—Jesus, son of Sapphias, and Justus, son of Pistus—are mentioned as being in attendance, both of whom belong to pro-war factions.[44] The two political gatherings are both concerned with the then-ongoing revolt against Rome, although the first of them (277–82) is most directly concerned with a change in leadership over the town.[45] The goal of the major players appears to be to persuade the townspeople and to win them over through public speech and rhetoric. It is important to note that the people present at this meeting in the synagogue do not represent a single dominant faction or group, but rather, the town as a whole.[46] This does not necessarily mean that every single person in the town literally attended the meeting, but that the gathering represented the public assembly, rather than a particular interest group. As such, we see the partisan faction members here attempting to persuade the general populace to accept their points of view.

In Judith, which was written in the Second Temple period though recounting fictional events from an earlier era (eighth century BCE),[47] we encounter references to the *ekklēsia* of Bethulia in Judea.[48] I concur with Ralph Korner's opinion that the depiction of this public assembly is anachronistic, and that it is modelled on a Hasmonean-era Judean public synagogue assembly.[49] Within the narrative of Judith, the Bethulian *ekklēsia* is a local-official public assembly. According to 6:16, the key congregants in the assembly appear to be the elders of the city (τοὺς πρεσβυτέρους τῆς πόλεως). Nevertheless, it is clear that the gathering was open and involved the town as a whole, as we are also told that all of the young men and the women of the town "ran together" into the *ekklēsia*.[50] The function of the assembly is generally political, having to do with the impending military threat of Holofernes's army,

---

43. Josephus tells us elsewhere that the *boulē* of Tiberias alone had 600 members (*War*, 2.641).
44. On the factions, see *Life* 32–36. These two are mentioned by name in 277 and 278.
45. Josephus tells us that Jonathan said that "their city had need of a better leader" (Gk. "ἔφη δὲ στρατηγοῦ κρείττονος χρείαν τὴν πόλιν αὐτῶν ἔχειν").
46. Cf. Jordan Ryan, "Tiberias," in *Lexham Bible Dictionary*, ed. John D. Barry and Lazarus Wentz (Bellingham: Lexham, 2012), n.p.
47. Cf. George W.E. Nickelsburg, *Jewish Literature between the Bible and the Mishnah*, 2nd ed. (Minneapolis: Fortress Press, 2005), 97–102. Nickelsburg dates the extant composition of Judith to the Hasmonean period, though allows that the tale may have originated in the Persian period. See also Benedikt Otzen, *Tobit and Judith* (Sheffield: Sheffield Academic, 2002), 132.
48. Judith 6:16, 21; 7:29; 14:6.
49. Ralph J. Korner, "Before Church," 107. On *ekklēsia* as a synagogue term, see Korner, "*Ekklēsia* as a Jewish Synagogue Term."
50. Gk. καὶ συνέδραμον πᾶς νεανίσκος αὐτῶν καὶ αἱ γυναῖκες εἰς τὴν ἐκκλησίαν.

although this is not divorced from the religious dimension of the meeting. The reaction of the people of Bethulia, described in 6:18–19, to the discussion of the oncoming threat is to fall down and worship God (πεσόντες ὁ λαὸς προσεκύνησαν τῷ θεῷ) (v. 18), offering up a prayer for deliverance (v. 19). Here, we see a striking example of the intertwining of the religious and the political, in the form of communal acts of worship and prayer during a meeting convened for the discussion of a political matter.

A public institution referred to as a *synagōgē* appears several times in Ben Sira (LXX).[51] The *synagōgē* in Ben Sira appears to be a public assembly in which an individual could seek honor or be shamed (1:30, 4:7).[52] Honor was an essential aspect of public life. According to Bruce Malina and Richard Rohrbaugh, "honour is public reputation. It is name or place. It is one's status or standing in the community *together with the public recognition of it*."[53] Moreover, in 41:18, the reader is instructed to be ashamed "of a crime, before a judge or magistrate, and of a breach of the law, before the congregation (*synagōgē*) and the people." This passage indicates the judicial function of the *synagōgē* as well as its status as an official institution.

Ben Sira also makes a significant number of references to an institution designated by the term *ekklēsia*.[54] Like the *synagōgē*, the *ekklēsia* was also a public assembly, a place of judgement (23:24, 38:33),[55] as well as a place in which one could attain honor (15:5, 21:17, 31:11, 39:10, 44:15) or experience shame (23:24, 38:33).[56] Given the cognate meanings of *ekklēsia* and *synagōgē*, the potential of both to function as synagogue terms,[57] and the identical functions of the institutions signified

---

51. Sir 1:30, 4:7, 41:18.
52. On the public assembly in Ben Sira, see Eckhard J. Schnabel, *Law and Wisdom from Ben Sira to Paul* (WUNT 16; Tübingen: Mohr Siebeck, 1985), 57–59.
53. Malina and Rohrbaugh, *Social-Science Commentary on the Synoptic Gospels*, 369–70.
54. Sir 15:5, 21:17, 23:24, 24:2, 31:11, 33:19, 38:33, 39:10, 44:15.
55. On the juridical responsibilities of the *ekklēsia* in Ben Sira, see Patrick Tiller, "The Sociological Settings of the Components of 1 Enoch," in *The Early Enoch Literature* (ed. Gabriele Boccaccini and John J. Collins; JSJSupp 121; Leiden and Boston: Brill 2007), 237–55 (247). Tiller sees 23:24 as indicative of the juridical responsibilities of the assembly where imperial law was not involved, but nevertheless, says that "we do not know what assembly he [Ben Sira] is referring to." I suggest here that the most likely candidate is the public synagogue, which is known to have had judicial functions.
56. On honor and shame in the public sphere in Ben Sira, see David deSilva, "The Wisdom of Ben Sira: Honour, Shame, and the Maintenance of the Values of a Minority Culture," *CBQ* 58 (1996): 433–55; Daniel J. Harrington, *Jesus Ben Sira of Jerusalem: A Biblical Guide to Living Wisely*, Interfaces (Collegeville: Liturgical Press, 2005), 86–88. In the wisdom literature of the Hebrew Bible, the concepts of honor and shame are typically expressed in terms of wisdom (חָכְמָה) and folly (אִוֶּלֶת). See W. R. Domeris, "Shame and Honor in Proverbs: Wise Women and Foolish Men," *Old Testament Essays* 8, no. 1 (1995): 86–102.
57. Cf. Runesson, *Origins*, 172; Runesson, Binder, and Olsson, *Ancient Synagogue Source Book*, 10–11; Korner, "Before Church," 88–101.

by these words, I suggest that they both refer to an assembly, which we may understand as a public synagogue.[58]

Ben Sira's depiction of the synagogue highlights its role as the place wherein public eminence and personal advancement could be achieved.[59] Honor, understood in terms of the acknowledgement of one's wisdom and deeds within the public assembly is presented as an ideal to be sought after. The ability to successfully speak persuasively in such a setting depended heavily upon the recognition of one's honor and the wisdom of one's speech. Speaking wisely in the synagogue (15:5, 21:17) is highly regarded in Ben Sira, and indicates the importance of public discussion within synagogue settings. The mention of the proclamation of one's acts of charity within the synagogue in 31:11 is particularly noteworthy, given the reference in Matt 6:2 to hypocrites who "sound a trumpet" before them when giving alms in the synagogues. The practice of almsgiving is also mentioned in the rabbinic material,[60] and appears to have been a normative function of the public synagogue.

According to an anonymous tradition preserved in *m. Ned.* 5:5, the public synagogue (*bet ha-kneset*) belonged to the local municipality, along with the town square, the bathhouse, and the Law scrolls. As such, it did not belong to any one faction or group, but to the people of the town as a whole. This passage appears to be descriptive in nature, and probably reflects general Jewish society in the Land at the time when the Mishnah was compiled.[61] Given the coherence with earlier data, it is plausible that this passage reflects an early tradition, or a social situation that existed in the Second Temple period as well as in the later Roman era. The location of the synagogue at the municipal level means that synagogue officials were accountable to the local community rather than a supra-local authority.[62]

The picture that emerges from the data is one of the synagogue as

---

58. A similar suggestion has been made by Bernier, *Aposynagōgos*, 66-67. See also the discussion of the *ekklēsia* passages in Runesson, *Origins*, 311-13, cf. Korner, "Before Church," 126-27.

59. Cf. Antonino Minissale, "The metaphor of 'falling': hermeneutic key to the Book of Sirach," in *The Wisdom of Ben Sira: Studies on Tradition, Redaction, and Theology* (ed. Angelo Passaro and Giuseppe Bellia; Deuterocanonical and Cognate Literature Studies 1; Berlin and New York: Walter de Gruyter, 2008), 253-75, (260). On honor and shame in synagogue settings, see Jordan J. Ryan, "Jesus and Synagogue Disputes: Recovering the Institutional Context of Luke 13:10-17," *CBQ* 71, no. 1 (2017): 41-59.

60. The earliest perhaps being *t. Shab.* 16:22. Almsgiving in a synagogue setting is also firmly attested by an inscription found in the synagogue at Hammat Tiberias (cf. Levine, *Ancient Synagogue*, 385).

61. Runesson, Binder, and Olsson, *Ancient Synagogue Sourcebook*, 114 (no. 84).

62. Cf. Levine, *Ancient Synagogue*, 381; Runesson, Binder, and Olsson, *Ancient Synagogue Sourcebook*, 114 (no. 84).

a local-official institution and meeting place for political and community gatherings. The synagogue appears to have been open to the town as a whole, and the evidence from Judith and Josephus indicates that the representatives of the town—in these sources called the *presbyteroi* and *boulē*, respectively—convened in synagogue space for official meetings along with any townspeople who wished to attend. This coheres quite well with what has been discussed above concerning the local-official functions and assemblies that took place at the city gates in earlier sources. It is important to recognize the political dimension of the synagogue as the town assembly place and locus of political ambition and activity. Any impulse to separate or distinguish this from the "religious" or "liturgical" aspects of the synagogue should be resisted. Public synagogue activities were not necessarily *either* "religious" or "political," but could, in fact, be simultaneously and inseparably religio-political.

The Legal-Judicial Function

The legal-judicial capacity of the public synagogue is closely related to its identity as a religio-political institution, and should be understood to be a subordinate function of this identity.[63] This function appears to have been common to public synagogues in the Land as well as to certain synagogue communities in the diaspora, which had been granted the right of adjudication.[64]

The judicial function of synagogues in the Land is strongly attested in the Gospels and Acts. References to punitive judgment in synagogues of the Land can be found in Mark 13:9, (cf. Luke 21:12, Matt 10:17–18), Matthew 23:34, and Acts 22:19. Mention of a trial set in a synagogue can also be found in Luke 12:11–12. Punishments could

---

63. In fact, both Levine, *Ancient Synagogue*, 143 and Binder, *Into the Temple Courts*, 445–49, treat the legal-judicial function as part of the communal, religio-political dimension. It is also worth noting that the connection between the synagogue as the place where the Torah was read and the place where justice was carried out should further caution us against a nonlegal understanding of the function of Torah in synagogue settings.

64. E.g., Susanna 28 (LXX); Josephus, *Ant.* 14.235, 259–61 (Sardis). Related to this is the matter of locales in which the Jewish community was constituted as a *politeuma*, or where it was granted limited self-governance. The most important example of this is probably the Alexandrian Jewish community, cf. *Ant.* 14.117, cf. *Ap.* 237, 61. See John M.G. Barclay, *Jews in the Mediterranean Diaspora: From Alexander to Trajan (323 BCE - 117 CE)* (Berkeley: University of California Press, 1996), 49–71, and Victor Tcherikover, *Hellenistic Civilization and the Jews* (Grand Rapids: Baker Academic, 1999), 320–27. These synagogues are still best understood as semi-public associations rather than fully public synagogues. This is because they only serve a specific demographic sector of the population of a given locale, and because the Jewish community was not in political control of the city as a whole.

include floggings (Matt 10:17, 23:34; Mark 13:9; Acts 22:19) and imprisonment (Luke 21:12, Acts 22:19). This evidence from the New Testament coheres well with the judicial function of the city gate complexes attested in the Hebrew Bible.[65] An additional datum from Sirach 23:24 may serve to draw this evidence together. In this passage, an adulterous woman is brought for punitive judgement into the *ekklēsia*,[66] which, we have argued above, is to be understood as a term referring to the public synagogue. According to Deuteronomy 22:24, the city gates were the location of judgment for adultery in earlier times. It is reasonable to consider this passage in Sirach as evidence that the synagogue came to replace the city gate as the place of judgment. That the synagogue continued to have a judicial function beyond the first century is attested by rabbinic literature.[67]

Synagogue People: Who Attended the Public Synagogue?

Like any institution, public synagogues required functionaries in order to operate. One of the best known synagogue functionaries is the *archisynagōgos* (lit. "assembly leader"), referred to in Hebrew as the *rosh knesset* (lit. "head of assembly"). The Theodotus inscription (*CIJ* 2.1404), which was discovered in Jerusalem, describes the eponymous Theodotos as a priest (*hiereus*) and *archisynagōgos*, son of an *archisynagōgos*, and grandson of an *archisynagōgos*, who built the synagogue to which the inscription was attached. The *archisynagōgos* is described as a benefactor in this inscription, having "built" (Gk. *oikodomeō*) the synagogue.[68] However, this evidence must be tempered by the fact that the institution described in the Theodotos inscription is best identified as an association synagogue.[69] It is appropriate to presume some correspondence between the *archisynagōgoi* of public and association synagogues, although it is important to recall that association synagogues lacked the local-official capacity of public synagogues.

The Mishnah and Tosefta contain some valuable information about the *rosh ha-knesset* (= Gk. *archisynagōgos*). Both *m. Yoma* 7:1 and *m. Sotah*

---

65. Ruth 4:1–12; Deut 17:5; 21:19; 22:15, 24; 25:7; 2 Sam 15:2; see also Amos 5:15 and Zech 8:16.

66. Although the connection to the public synagogue has only been made relatively recently, scholars have tended to recognize the public institutional setting of the punishment described here. See, e.g., Patrick W. Skeehan and Alexander A. Di Lella, *The Wisdom of Ben Sira: A New Translation and Commentary* (AYB 39; New Haven: Yale, 2007), 325; Schnabel, *Law and Wisdom*, 58.

67. E.g., *m. Makkot* 3.12. On judgment in the synagogue in the Rabbinic literature, see Levine, *Ancient Synagogue*, 395–96.

68. Compare Luke 7:5, according to which a centurion "built" (Gk. *oikodomeō*) a synagogue at Capernaum.

69. Cf. Runesson, *Origins*, 227; Bernier, *Aposynagōgos*, 62.

7:7–8 describe a Torah-reading ceremony that took place in the Jerusalem temple. According to these passages, the *rosh ha-knesset* was one of the officials, along with the *hazzan*, involved in handing the Torah scroll to the high priest (the king, in *m. Sotah* 7:8) before he reads from it. Given the temple's "public synagogue" functions and its historical relationship to public Torah-reading ceremonies, the ceremony described here—involving synagogue functionaries in a temple setting—is historically plausible.[70] According to *t. Meg.* 3:21, the *rosh ha-knesset* is not supposed to read from the Torah scroll at a public reading unless he is instructed to do so by others, because "a person does not lower himself on his own initiative." This can be understood as an implication that the *rosh ha-knesset* is expected to be supervising the reading, and thus, it would be an act of lowering to perform the reading himself.[71] The depiction of the *rosh ha-knesset* in the rabbinic literature fits well with the Jesus tradition, in which the *archisynagōgos* is presumed to be a person of respect and authority within the synagogue community whose opinion on legal matters could be influential.[72]

Earlier scholarship had a tendency to view the *archisynagōgos*'s role as primarily religious.[73] The identification of the *archisynagōgos* as a benefactor responsible for the construction and upkeep of the synagogue building has been proposed by Ismar Elbogen, and has been followed by others.[74] Tessa Rajak and David Noy have taken this position a step further, arguing that the *archisynagōgos* was an honorary title for a benefactor.[75] Levine and Binder both see the *archisynagōgos* as a multifunctional role encompassing religious, financial, political, and administrative responsibilities.[76] This multifunctional understand-

---

70. Cf. Levine, *Ancient Synagogue*, 420–21; Runesson, Binder, and Olsson, *ASSB*, 51.
71. Cf. Jacob Neusner, *The Tosefta: Translated from the Hebrew with a New Introduction* (2 vols.; Peabody: Hendrickson, 2002), 1:649. See the interpretation in square brackets for *t. Meg.* 3:21.
72. Cf. Luke 13:10–17; Mark 5:22 and parallels.
73. E.g., Samuel Krauss, *Synagogale Altertümer* (Berlin: Hildesheim, 1922), 114–21; Emil Schürer, *Die Gemeindeverfassung der Juden in Rom in der Kaiserzeit nach den Inschriften dargestellt* (Leipzig: J. C. Hinrichs, 1879), 27–28; Jean Juster, *Les Juifs dans l'Empire Romain: leur condition juridique, économique et sociale*, vol. 1 (Paris: Paul Geuthner, 1914), 450–53. More recently, Paul R. Trebilco, *Jewish Communities in Asia Minor*, (SNTS 69; Cambridge and New York: Cambridge University Press, 1991), 104ff.
74. Ismar Elbogen, *Jewish Liturgy: A Comprehensive History* (1913; trans. Raymond P. Scheindlin; Philadelphia: The Jewish Publication Society, 1993); Harry J. Leon and Carolyn Osiek, *The Jews of Ancient Rome*, updated ed. (Peabody: Hendrickson, 1995), 171–72; Wolfgang Schrage, "Συναγωγή" in *Theological Dictionary of the New Testament*, vol. 3, ed. Gerhard Kittel, Geoffrey William Bromiley, and Gerhard Friedrich (Grand Rapids: Eerdmans, 1964–1976), 798–852; Louis H. Feldman, "Diaspora Synagogues: New Light from Inscriptions and Papyri," in *Sacred Realm: The Emergence of the Synagogue in the Ancient Worl*, ed. Steven Fine (New York and Oxford: Oxford University Press, 1996), 48–66 (58–59).
75. Tessa Rajak and David Noy, "Archisynagogoi: Office, Title, and Social Status in the Greco-Jewish Synagogue," *The Journal of Roman Studies* 83 (1993): 75–93.
76. Levine, *Ancient Synagogue*, 415–27; Binder, *Into the Temple Courts*, 352.

ing has the most explanatory power. The picture that emerges from the evidence is one of a prestigious title held by a respected community member—probably a benefactor—for a synagogue functionary charged with the oversight of the ceremonial reading and interpretation of the law. The level at which they functioned was that of the institutional level of the synagogue itself, not the local-official, municipal level. The *archisynagōgoi* were nevertheless involved with the political dimension of the synagogue insofar as they were charged with the oversight of the ceremonial reading and interpretation of the Law.

The attendant, referred to in Hebrew as *hazzan* and in Greek as *hypēretēs*,[77] was a minor functionary, who was also associated with the Torah-reading ceremony. An attendant (*hypēretēs*) appears in the Lukan account of Jesus reading from Isaiah in the synagogue at Nazareth. In Luke 4:17, the scroll is "given to him" (ἐπεδόθη αὐτῷ), and in v. 20, Jesus rolls the scroll and returns it to the attendant (πτύξας τὸ βιβλίον ἀποδοὺς τῷ ὑπηρέτῃ). Luke's depiction of the role of the attendant during the Second Temple period coheres quite well with the description of the role of this functionary in the aforementioned Mishnaic account of scripture readings in the temple in *m. Yoma* 7:1 and *m. Sotah* 7:7–8. The attendant also had duties relating to the civic function of the synagogue.[78] According to *m. Mak.* 3:12, the flogging of forty lashes (cf. Deut 25:2–3) is administered by a *hazzan ha-knesset*. That such a punishment would be carried out by a synagogue official is to be expected in light of the synagogue's judicial function and the mentions of beatings in synagogues in the New Testament.[79]

The Greek word *archōn* denotes a ruler or chief in its most literal sense, and it is typically used in the Hellenistic world to refer to someone occupying a public office, such as a magistrate.[80] Officials denoted by this term appear in a number of inscriptions involving synagogues from the diaspora,[81] but our concern is for the situation in the Land.

---

77. On the correspondence between these two terms, see Levine, *Ancient Synagogue*, 437.

78. Cf. Horsley, *Galilee*, 230.

79. Matt 10:17, 23:34; Mark 13:9; Acts 22:19.

80. See the range of applications of this term in its entry in Henry George Liddell, Robert Scott, Henry Stuart Jones, and Roderick McKenzie, *A Greek-English Lexicon*, rev. and augmented (Oxford and New York: Clarendon, 1996). See also Juster, *Les Juifs*, 443–47. In the LXX translation of the Hexateuch, the term *archōn* is sometimes used to designate the rulers of the congregation (*synagōgē*) of Israel, cf. Binder, *Into the Temple Courts*, 345. See LXX Exod 16:22, 34:31; Num 1:16; 31:13, 26, 32:2; Josh 9:15, 19, 22:30. It is clear in these texts that the term is operating on a national-official level. The primary present concern, however, is for the local-official level, the level on which the synagogue operated.

81. E.g., *CJCZ* 70-72; *DF* 33. Levine has noted inscriptional evidence that, at least in Rome, the title of *archōn* was associated with officials attached to synagogues, in Levine, *Ancient Synagogue*, 427. However, similar evidence is lacking from the rest of the diaspora as well as from the Land.

The evidence from the Land indicates that the *archontes* functioned on the local-official level as municipal magistrates. According to Josephus, Moses appointed seven men to rule (ἄρχω) over each city (Gk. Ἀρχέτωσαν δὲ καθ' ἑκάστην πόλιν ἄνδρες ἑπτὰ οἵ).[82] In my opinion, the number of *archontes* in this passage reflects Josephus's own ideal practice, to which he ascribes Mosaic authority. Elsewhere, Josephus mentions that he appointed seven "judges" (Gk. δικαστάς) for each city.[83] Given the coherence of this with his presentation of the Mosaic appointment of seven *archontes* over each city, it seems likely that these "judges" were *archontes*.[84]

The judicial capacity of the *archōn* is similarly reflected in Luke 12:58, in which Jesus recommends that one should settle with an accuser on the way when being brought before the *archōn*.[85] Luke also mentions followers of Jesus being brought before "synagogues, *archontes* (NRSV 'magistrates'), and authorities" (Gk. τὰς συναγωγὰς καὶ τὰς ἀρχὰς καὶ τὰς ἐξουσίας), which seems to suggest that the *archontes* and "authorities" met in synagogue, although other interpretations are also possible. Nevertheless, on the level of the Lukan narrative or that of the historical Jesus, we are compelled to envision the judicial system of the Land, and thus, a synagogue setting with Jewish officials.[86]

The most important data from the Land for our purposes comes from Josephus's account of the meetings to discuss his leadership, which took place in the synagogue at Tiberias, recounted in *Vita* 277–303. These meetings, which have been discussed above, were convened and presided over by Jesus ben Sapphias, who was "the *archōn*" (*Vita* 134, 278, 294; Gk. ὁ ἄρχων) of Tiberias. At the time of the First Jewish Revolt, Tiberias appears to have been ruled on a local-official level by one *archōn*,[87] and a council (*boulē*) with ten "leading men" (*prōtoi*).[88] The

---

82. Josephus, *Ant.* 4.214.
83. Josephus, *War* 2.571.
84. Cf. Binder, *Into the Temple Courts*, 346.
85. Similarly, see Sir 41:18.
86. It is worth mentioning that Luke 8:41 calls Jairus one of the *archōn tēs synagōgēs*, while Matt 9:18 (cf. v. 23) refers to him simply as an *archōn*. It is probable that Luke's designation is a periphrastic way to say "*archisynagōgos*" (cf. v. 49). It is also possible that at an earlier stage in the tradition, Jairus was an *archōn* (as in Matthew) and Luke here is attempting to clarify Jairus's office. At any rate, though it is tempting to do so, it is difficult to make a solid connection between the office of *archōn* and the synagogue in this tradition.
87. Josephus refers to Jesus ben Sapphias as "the *archōn*" (ὁ ἄρχων) in *Vita* 278 and 294, with a definite article. No other Tiberian *archōn* or *archontes* are mentioned. This is somewhat contrary to the aforementioned evidence from *Ant.* 4.214, which seems to point to seven *archontes* being appointed to each city. *Ant.* 4.214 likely presents Josephus's prescriptive ideal for his own time, rather than a description of actual practice.
88. This may be inferred from the evidence in *Vita* 169, 278, and 300, in combination with mention of

Tiberian *archōn* seems to have been the head of the town assembly, acting as a primary speaker, as seen in the meetings in the synagogue (e.g., *Vita* 278ff.). He has the power to dismiss the townspeople from a gathering in the synagogue (*Vita* 300), and to compel the council to remain. This particular meeting was a religious gathering (cf. *Vita* 290, 295), though the conversation is explicitly political, and once the townspeople are dismissed, it is transformed into an overtly political meeting of the town council. This demonstrates the blurred line between "religion" and "politics" in synagogue gatherings, and is indicative of the political clout wielded by the *archōn*.

The picture of the *archōn* that emerges from the evidence is one of a municipal magistrate, a political and judicial authority operating on the local-official level. The *archontes* do not appear to have been a part of the institutional structure of the synagogue, as were the *archisynagōgoi* or the *hazzanim*, since they belonged to the institutional structure of the municipality. Nevertheless, the synagogue appears to have functioned as the customary venue for the local-official and legal-judicial functions that they oversaw.[89]

This brings us to local councils. As we have seen above, the public synagogue was the habitual meeting place for the Tiberian *boulē*. The *boulē* was a typical feature of the local government system of a Hellenistic *polis*,[90] and was essentially a local governing body composed of the municipality's representatives, performing both deliberative and judicial functions. Korner has noted that in Hellenistic cities, the *boulē* met with and presented their recommended courses of action to the populace (the *dēmos*) for ratification or revision at public assemblies (*ekklēsiai*).[91] It is worth considering in connection with this that the architecture of public synagogue buildings, with their quadrilateral design and stepped benches, resembles that of a *bouleuterion*, the customary meeting place of the *boulē* in Gentile cities.[92] Members of *boulai*

the "leading men" of the *boulē* in *Vita* 64, 69, 296, and 381. Cf. Runesson, Binder, and Olsson, *ASSB*, 78; Binder, *Into the Temple Courts*, 346. See also Lee Levine, "Synagogues of Galilee," 34.

89. Whether a municipality had a purpose-built structure for such gatherings, made use of a multipurpose building, or met in open public space is inconsequential. "The synagogue" was a local-official, religio-political institution, and the presence of municipal or regional officials within it is natural, even if those officials were not necessarily connected to the institutional structure of the synagogue itself.

90. See Tcherikover, *Hellenistic Civilization and the Jews* (repr. ed.; Baker Academic, 2011 [1959]), 107–8. On the role of *boulai* in general, see Alan K. Bowman, *The Town Councils of Roman Egypt* (Toronto: A. M. Hakkert, 1971), 7–11. On the *boulē* in relationship to the *dēmos* and *ekklēsia*, see Korner, "Before Church," 30–34.

91. Korner, "Before Church," 30–33.

92. Cf. Yigael Yadin's comments on the architecture of the synagogue at Masada. See Yigael Yadin, "The Synagogue at Masada," in *Ancient Synagogues Revealed*, edited by Lee I. Levine (Jerusalem:

were drawn from the local aristocracy, and thus, from a high social level.[93]

Local councils were by no means unique to cities with a Hellenistic constitution, such as Tiberias (a Jewish locale with a Hellenistic constitution).[94] Traditional Jewish towns and villages also appear to have been typically governed by local councils, referred to variously as the elders (Gk. presbyteroi, gerōn), dynatoi ("powerful men"), or the synedrion ("council").[95] In the assembly described in Judith 6:16, the elders of Bethulia seem to have been the key decision-making congregants of the city's public synagogue (ekklēsia),[96] which likely reflects the earlier traditions relating to the gathering of the elders in the gates. The elders also appear within a local-official synagogue context in the narrative of Susanna (see Sus 28 LXX). The elders (presbyteroi) of Capernaum are also associated with the local public synagogue building in Luke 7:3-5. We may also note that the judicial function of the local synedrion is mentioned in connection with corporal punishment in synagogues in Mark 13:9.

Since synagogues were public assemblies and assembly places, a connection between local councils and synagogues is natural. As we shall see when we discuss architecture below, public synagogue buildings were designed for communal assembly, and so, the customary use of the Tiberian synagogue by the boulē as a venue in Vita 277–303 makes a good deal of sense. Even in locales where there was no synagogue building, local councils probably met with the public in the open-air

---

Israel Exploration Society, 1981), 19–23. I will return to this issue when we discuss synagogue architecture later in this chapter.

93. Cf. Junghwa Choi, *Jewish Leadership in Palestine from 70 CE to 1135 CE* (AJEC 83; Leiden and Boston: Brill, 2013), 121–23; Joyce Reynolds, "Cities," in *The Administration of the Roman Empire*, ed. David Braund (Exeter: University of Exeter, 1988), 15–52, esp. 25ff.

94. On Tiberias's Hellenistic constitution, see Schürer, *History of the Jewish People*, 2:179–80.

95. Cf. Schürer, *History of the Jewish People*, 2:184–85; Binder, *Into the Temple Courts*, 360–61. On village councils from a Roman perspective, see Choi, *Jewish Leadership*, 125ff. Compare Samuel Rocca, *Herod's Judea: A Mediterranean State in the Classic World* (Eugene: Wipf & Stock, 2008), 263–71. On the Greek term synedrion and its transliterated Hebrew form as a term for local councils in the Land, see Mark 13:9 (cf. Matt 10:17); *m. Mak.* 1:10; *m. Sanh.* 1:6; *t. Sanh.* 7:1. The use of the term to refer to councils is ubiquitous in Greco-Roman sources (see the entry in LSJ), e.g., Aelius Aristides, *Orations*, 13; Xenophon, *Hellenica*, 1.31; Xenophon, *Memorabilia*, 4.2; Sophocles, *Ajax*, 749; Diodorus Siculus, *Hist. Lib.* 14.82.2, 15.28.4, 17.4.2. Josephus also refers to a local council made up of his friends that he called in Tiberias as a synedrion in *Life* 368. See also Judith 6:1, 11:9. On synedrion as a designation for councils, see the classic study of Solomon Zeitlin, "The Political Synedrion and the Religious Sanhedrin" *Jewish Quarterly Review* 36, no. 2 (1945): 109–40, though the distinction that he makes between "councils" and "courts" is problematic. The best explanation of the greatest amount of evidence is that councils could perform judicial functions.

96. Note also the role of the presbyteroi in the founding of the Theodotos synagogue, in *CIJ* 2.1404. This, however, is best identified as an association synagogue.

places of communal assembly, just as they did in the earlier town assemblies depicted in the Hebrew Bible.[97]

Scribes (Gk. *grammateus*; Heb. *sôphēr*) appear in synagogue settings in the synoptic Gospel narratives.[98] The narrative in Mark 1:21–22 indicates that the scribes were the customary teachers in synagogue settings. This inference is supported by the mention of the convention of scribal teaching in Matthew 7:29, and by the references elsewhere in the Gospels to specific scribal teachings.[99] Jesus's statement in Mark 12:38–39 that the scribes desire the "first seats" (πρωτοκαθεδρίας) in the synagogues points to the prominent status of scribes in synagogue settings.[100] Moreover, this implies that there was prestige attached to seating placement in the synagogues.

Although one might get the impression from the Gospel portrayals that the scribes were a distinct unified group or faction, this was not the case.[101] As Saldarini has argued, the title of "scribe" is roughly equivalent to the English term "secretary," and covers a broad range of roles and activities across a spectrum of social and political levels,[102] all of which require a high level of reading and writing. On the low end of this spectrum would be village scribes,[103] who provided legal, bureaucratic, and secretarial services requiring literacy skills for village communities.[104] On the higher end would be scribes working in the upper echelons of government, such as Diophantus, who was Herod's royal scribe.[105] The picture of the scribes encountered by Jesus in the synagogues of Galilee that emerges from the data is that of literate, educated bureaucrats and low-level officials. Their higher levels of lit-

---

97. As envisioned by Horsley, *Archaeology, History, and Society*, 145ff. However, his reconstruction problematically rejects the existence of synagogue buildings during the late Second Temple period.

98. Mark 1:21–22, 12:38–39 (cf. Matt 23:6; Luke 20:46); Luke 6:6–7.

99. Mark 9:11, 12:35. This is supported by evidence in the Mishnah, e.g., *m. Yad.* 3:2; *m. Tehar.* 4:7; *m. Parah* 11:5; *m. Sanh.* 11:3.

100. Although it is not possible to be certain, the "first seats" were probably those located on the first row of benches from the floor across from the building entrance, cf. Binder, *Into the Temple Courts*, 367.

101. As convincingly and forcefully argued by Anthony J. Saldarini, *Pharisees, Scribes and Sadducees in Palestinian Society: A Sociological Approach* (Biblical Resource Series; Grand Rapids: Eerdmans, 2001), 241ff. See also the perspectives on the role of scribes presented in Sanders, *Judaism: Practice and Belief*, 170–81; Christine Schams, *Jewish Scribes in the Second-Temple Period* (JSOTSup 291; Sheffield: Sheffield Academic Press, 1998).

102. Cf. Saldarini, *Pharisees, Scribes and Sadducees*, 241–42.

103. E.g., Josephus, *War*, 1.479.

104. As indicated by data pertaining to the function of the *kōmogrammateus* in Egyptian papyri, e.g., P. Cair. Zen 59275; P. Teb. 44–51; *CPJ* III 478. Cf. Schams, *Jewish Scribes*, 135–36. Data indicating similar functions of scribes in the Land can be found in the Mishnah: *m. Git* 3:1; *m. B. Bat.* 10:3; *m. B. Metzi'a* 5:11.

105. Josephus, *War*, 1.529.

eracy, education, and legal expertise granted them authority as teachers within synagogue settings.[106]

Public synagogue gatherings were also attended by the townspeople, who would have typically constituted the majority of the congregants. The presence of the townspeople is usually a given in public synagogue settings, since it was they who constituted the "gathering." It is important to recall at this point that the public synagogue belonged to the town as a whole, and that it was not controlled by a supra-local power, nor by any specific partisan group.[107]

A public presence is typically implied or understood in Gospel passages depicting synagogue gatherings.[108] Sometimes, the public presence is mentioned directly. The "crowd" (*ochlos*) plays an explicit and prominent role in the dispute between Jesus and an *archisynagōgos* in Luke 13:1–17. Likewise, the gatherings at the synagogue in Tiberias in *Vita* 277ff. include both the townspeople and their representatives. In Susanna 28 (LXX),[109] we are told that all of the "Sons of Israel" who were present in the city gathered (*synedreuō*) in the synagogue. One of the more interesting attestations of a public presence at a synagogue gathering can be seen in the depiction of the Bethulian assembly (*ekklēsia*) in Judith 6:16. While the principal congregants are the elders, the young men and women of the town also come to the assembly, which is indicative of the scope in terms of both age and gender of synagogue assembly attendees. It is worth noting at this point that women could certainly be present at synagogue gatherings, as indicated by this passage and by the presence of a crippled woman in a synagogue in Luke 13:10–17.[110]

In sizable towns, it would not have been possible for the entirety of the populace to fit inside a synagogue building,[111] although small rural

---

06. On this, see also Keith, *Scribal Elite*, 33–36.

07. Cf. Runesson, *Origins*, 221–23. Of course, the possibility that the perspective of a single influential group or party could come to dominate the local assembly is not excluded.

08. E.g., Mark 6:1–6 (cf. Matt 13:54–58; Luke 4:16–30), 1:21–27 (cf. Luke 4:3–37), 1:39 (cf. Matt 4:23, 9:35; Luke 4:44); John 18:20.

09. Although the setting of the narrative is in Babylon, Susanna probably had a Semitic *Vorlage* stemming from the Land, cf. Levine, *Ancient Synagogue*, 41; and Carey A. Moore, *Daniel, Esther, and Jeremiah: The Additions* (AB 44; New York: Doubleday, 1977), 91–92. Given the evident legal-judicial authority wielded by the apparently public synagogue assembly in this text, it would be reasonable to see the text as coming from the Land, and thus, reflecting synagogue customs of the Land.

10. On the role and presence of women in synagogues, see Bernadette J. Brooten, *Women Leaders in the Ancient Synagogue* (Brown Judaic Studies 36; Chico: Scholar's Press, 1982), cf. Bernadette J. Brooten, "Female Leadership in the Ancient Synagogue," in *From Dura to Sepphoris: Studies in Jewish Art and Society in Late Antiquity*, ed. Lee I. Levine and Zeev Weiss (Portsmouth: Journal of Roman Archaeology, 2000), 215–23; Levine, *Ancient Synagogue*, 499–518.

11. Cf. the findings of Spigel, *Seating Capacities*.

villages, such as Qiryat Sefer or Nazareth, may have been able to house the majority of the populace in a single edifice.[112] However, this does not mean that there was no public presence at all in synagogue buildings in larger towns, or that we should conclude that synagogues buildings that could not house the majority of the population of a given locale must belong to an association or "sect."[113]

Not all of the population would have to be present for there to be a public presence at a synagogue gathering. No matter how large the synagogue (*proseuchē*) in Tiberias might have been, it is difficult to imagine a building that could have housed the entirety of the population of such a major city. Nevertheless, the gatherings depicted in the Tiberian synagogue by Josephus in *Vita* 277ff. are clearly gatherings of members of the public along with the city council and the *archōn*. This is most clearly indicated in *Vita* 300, in which the *archōn* dismisses the townspeople (*dēmos*), but asks the council (*boulē*) to remain. This passage witnesses the concurrent presence of the public along with the council and *archōn* in a synagogue building, while also simultaneously demonstrating that the local-official leadership could also meet in a synagogue setting apart from the public.

Townspeople played an active role in synagogue gatherings. They were engaged in the proceedings, and were able to voice their opinions about what was being said or discussed.[114] Indeed, the ability to speak well in the public assembly (*ekklēsia*) is counted among the desirable traits of a wise person by Ben Sira (15:5, 21:17). Thus, it seems as if anyone with something worthwhile to say was encouraged to say it (cf. Sir 21:17). This may help to explain how Jesus could enter synagogues in places where he was a visitor and teach.

Persuasion of the majority of the assembled townspeople was necessary for a particular public decision to go forward or for a particular interpretation of the Torah or Nevi'im to be accepted in a given locale. Thus, the townspeople could have a major impact on the deliberative function of their local public synagogue. This is illustrated quite well by the assemblies in the Tiberian synagogue,[115] wherein the key players of the assembly attempt to persuade the assembled majority to adopt

---

112. Cf. the discussion of Qiryat Sefer in Spigel, *Seating Capacities*, 293-96.
113. This is discussed by Richard Bauckham regarding the Magdala synagogue in Richard Bauckham, "Further Thoughts on the Migdal Synagogue Stone," *Novum Testamentum* 57 (2015): 113-35 (131), but is ultimately rejected by Bauckham in light of the fact that the artwork of the "Magdala stone" reflects common Judaism rather than the beliefs or practices of a specific group.
114. E.g., Mark 6:2-3 (cf. Matt 13:54-56; Luke 4:22); John 6:28, 30-31, 34, 41-42, 52; Josephus, *Vita* 279, 299-301.
115. Josephus, *Vita* 277ff.

their perspective.[116] Similarly, the resolution of Jesus's dispute with an *archisynagōgos* over the legality of Sabbath healings at a synagogue gathering in Luke 13:10–17 is achieved by means of the rhetorical persuasion of the crowd (v. 17) of the validity of Jesus's position. If Susanna reflects public synagogue traditions of the Land, then Susanna 41 may also indicate that the assembled townspeople also had a significant role to play in judgment and sentencing. To be clear, the local-official politics of the Land did not approximate an egalitarian democracy. As the data indicates, those members of the public with more recognized honor and wisdom had a better chance of being successful. This is most likely why the evidence indicates that elites such as council members, benefactors, scribes, or officials do most of the talking in public synagogue settings. Furthermore, honor could be gained or conferred through engaging in successful, persuasive speech in a synagogue. For example, the narrative of Susanna concludes by stating that Daniel "had a great reputation among the people" (v. 64) as a result of his actions in the synagogue.

Honor in Ben Sira, expressed in terms of wisdom,[117] is construed as *public* communal recognition of standing or reputation.[118] Honor must be recognized by the synagogue assembly for it to have meaning. For example, Sir 31:11 speaks of the assembly proclaiming the charity of a wise rich person. Likewise, 38:33 mentions the attainment of eminence in the assembly, and 44:15 says that the assembly will declare the wisdom of the descendants of godly men. The assembly also confers shame, as seen in 42:11, which warns that a headstrong daughter can put you to shame in public gatherings. Similarly, Sir 23:24 says that an adulterous woman "will be brought before the assembly and her punishment will extend to her children." This implies not only that she will be shamed by being brought before the assembly, but also that the public assembly will be responsible for her punishment.

In Susanna, the elders direct their address not to a judge or magistrate. Rather, it would appear as though they address the assembly. In v. 41, we are told that "all the synagogue" (ἡ συναγωγὴ πᾶσα) believed the testimony of the elders because they were "elders and judges of

---

6. See esp. Josephus, *Vita* 279, 299–303.

7. Concerning the expressions of honor and shame and wisdom and folly (respectively), see W. R. Domeris, "Shame and Honor in Proverbs: Wise Women and Foolish Men," *Old Testament Essays* 8, no. 1 (1995): 86–102. On honor in Ben Sira more generally, see David deSilva, "The Wisdom of Ben Sira: Honour, Shame, and the Maintenance of the Values of a Minority Culture," *CBQ* 58 (1996): 433–55.

8. Cf. the definition of honor in Malina and Rohrbaugh, *Social-Science Commentary on the Synoptic Gospels*, 369–70.

the people." Thus, it is they who deliver the final verdict. The Theodotian recension adds that the synagogue "condemned her (Susanna) to be killed." Likewise, when Daniel appears in the narrative, he too addresses the assembly (ἡ συναγωγὴ) directly (v. 52), and presumes that the people (ὁ λαὸς) of the assembly will carry out justice (v. 59). The synagogue assembly carries out the sentence of the Law for the false witness in vv. 60–62, throwing them into a gully where an angel casts fire into their midst. Both Daniel and the elders address them because they are the ones who will need to be persuaded, since *they decide the outcome of the trial.*

The townspeople also participated in religious acts of worship in synagogue settings. Examples of this include the public fast mentioned by Josephus in *Vita* 290, and the worship and prayer depicted in the Bethulian *ekklēsia* in Judith 6:18–19.

Members of particular Jewish associations, factions, or "sects," should generally be counted among the townspeople unless otherwise indicated. This includes Pharisees, Sadducees, members of the Jesus movement, and any other such groups. While it is possible for the perspective of a partisan group to have dominated a particular public synagogue, this would have been achieved by persuading the populace to adopt their point of view, not because any particular partisan group, such as the Pharisees, ran public synagogues.[119] They were not *ipso facto* a part of the institutional structure of public synagogues, although it was possible for someone belonging to a partisan group to hold a public or institutional office, or for a scribe to be affiliated with a particular group.[120]

The understanding of the various attendees and functionaries of public synagogues that has emerged from the evidence highlights the religio-political nature of the public synagogue. It is important to recognize the distinction between synagogue functionaries, such as the attendant and the *archisynagōgos*, and local-official functionaries. The presence of both within synagogue gatherings wonderfully illustrates the intertwining and inseparability of the religious and the political in the public synagogue. Moreover, the use of synagogue settings as a venue for the meetings of local-official functionaries indicates that the public synagogue was embedded in the administrative structure of the town.

119. Cf. Runesson, *Origins*, 221–23. Contra Ellis Rivkin, *A Hidden Revolution* (Nashville: Abingdon, 1978), 103.
120. E.g., Luke 6:7.

Perhaps one of the most important aspects of this discussion has been the role played by the townspeople in synagogue gatherings. The evidence indicates that the congregants wielded a significant amount of deliberative power. Persuasion of the majority within the public synagogue was an important and determinative aspect of Jewish religious and political life during the Second Temple period.

Public Synagogue Buildings

The architectural form of public synagogue buildings reveals much about their function, and can help stimulate the historical imagination,[121] allowing the historian to better contextualize, understand, and envision the setting of the Gospel synagogue narratives. This section will present a basic overview of synagogue buildings for the specific purpose of reconstructing and imagining public synagogue building forms and functions at the time of Jesus.

The remains of eight buildings dating to the Second Temple period that are typically identified as synagogues are extant in the Land of Israel, at Capernaum, Gamla, Herodium, Jericho, Magdala, Masada, Modi'in (Umm el-Umdan), and Qiryat Sefer.[122] An additional synagogue building dating to the late first century after the destruction of the Jerusalem Temple has been discovered at Khirbet Qana.[123] Although it dates to the first century, its post-70 CE date technically precludes us from including it in the list of Second-Temple-period synagogues. Of the pre-70 buildings, only the structure at Jericho (fig. 18) may be identified with some measure of confidence as an association synagogue.[124]

---

121. On the concept of the historical imagination in the historian's craft, see appendix A.

122. Two other recent discoveries are also worth mentioning here. A Second-Temple-period building that can probably be identified as a synagogue has been found at et-Tuwani. The building was rectangular in shape, and featured stone hewn benches. No columns have been found on site, and only the Western side survives. See Hachlili, *Ancient Synagogues*, 26. News media outlets have also broken news of the discovery of a synagogue dated to "the Roman period" (i.e., prior to the late-third or early-fourth centuries CE) by Michael Osband at Khirbet Majdouliya. See Nir Hasson, "Roman-era Structure Thought to Be Synagogue Found in Golan Heights," *Haaretz*, December 26, 2014, http://www.haaretz.com/life/archaeology/.premium-1.633939. Details of this excavation, including a more precise date, have yet to be published. The photographs that appeared in *Haaretz* depict a quadrilateral building with what appear to be benches of well-dressed stone, as well as elements of columns. These may both yet prove to be significant discoveries for the study of early synagogues, but the major details are not readily available for study as of now.

123. C. Thomas McCollough, "Final Report on the Archaeological Excavations at Khirbet Qana: Field II, the Synagogue," (2013), http://asorblog.org/2013/11/19/final-report-on-the-archaeological-excavations-at-khirbet-qana-field-ii-the-synagogue; cf. C. Thomas McCollough, "Khirbet Qana," in *The Archaeological Record from Cities, Towns, and Villages*. Vol. 2 of *Galilee in the Late Second Temple and Mishnaic Periods*, ed. David A. Fiensy and James Riley Strange (Minneapolis: Fortress Press, 2015), 127–45 (141).

124. Despite holding general architectural features in common with other synagogues of the Land,

Very little of the architecture of the building identified as a Second Temple synagogue remains at Capernaum, making analysis difficult. The rest of these buildings share architectural and design characteristics that are indicative of Jewish public assembly.

In addition to the eight buildings (nine if we include Khirbet Qana) that can be identified with some measure of confidence, there are also a handful of recently discovered structures that may also be identified as synagogue buildings. However, the identification of these buildings as synagogues are either uncertain at this time, or require further analysis pending the publication of excavation results. This group includes remains discovered at Diab,[125] Et-Tawani,[126] Khirbet Majdouliya,[127] Kefar Shikhin,[128] and Tel Rechesh.[129] We will discuss these discoveries and will assess the plausibility of the identification of them as synagogue buildings below. Of course, any conclusions drawn about recent discoveries will have to be provisional for the time being, at least until further publications provide the information necessary for a more confident analysis.

The synagogue at Gamla (figs. 1–2; *ASSB* no. 10) in the Golan Heights is the largest of the extant public synagogue remains. Its main hall measures 20 x 16 square meters, and features several additional rooms. Gamla was a fairly large town with a population of between 3,000

---

the structure at Jericho's (*ASSB* no. 15) identity as a synagogue has sometimes been called into question because its location meant that it could only serve a small portion of the community. See, for example, David Stacy, "Was there a synagogue in Hasmonean Jericho?" *Bible and Interpretation*, (2004), http://www.bibleinterp.com/articles/Hasmonean_Jericho.shtml. However, such an argument depends on a definition of synagogues only as public institutions, and as Runesson has pointed out, the structure at Jericho is probably best identified as an association synagogue. See Runesson, "Nature and Origins of the 1st-Century Synagogue," n.p. In connection with this, it is important to note that the Jericho synagogue features a *triclinium* for dining. On this, see Ehud Netzer, "A Synagogue from the Hasmonean Period Recently Exposed in the Western Plain of Jericho," *Israel Exploration Journal* 49 (1999): 205. As Richardson has observed, *triclinia* are a feature of association buildings. See Richardson, "Architectural Case," passim. However, *triclinia* are not found in any of the other, more clearly public synagogue buildings extant in the Land. This is further evidence that the Jericho structure (*ASSB* no. 15) should probably be identified as an association synagogue.

125. Binyamin Har-Even, "A Second Temple Synagogue at Horvat Diab in Western Benjamin," *Qadmoniot* 151 (2016): 49–53.

126. Binyamin Har-Even, "Khirbet Tawani: A Settlement from the Second Temple, Roman-Byzantine and Early Muslim Periods," *The Frontier and Desert in the Land of Israel* 7 (2012): 15–29.

127. See Robin Ngo, "Roman-Era Structure Believed to be Synagogue Exposed in Israel." December 29, 2014. Online: http://www.biblicalarchaeology.org/daily/ancient-cultures/daily-life-and-practice/roman-era-structure-believed-to-be-synagogue-exposed-in-israel/.

128. See James Riley Strange, "Kefar Shikhin," in *The Archaeological Record From Cities, Towns, and Villages*. Vol. 2 of *Galilee in the Late Second Temple and Mishnaic Periods*, ed. David A. Fiensy and James Riley Strange (Minneapolis: Fortress Press, 2015), 88–108 (103–5).

129. A formal academic publication is pending. See, e.g., Nir Hasson, "Archaeologists in Israel Find Ancient Synagogue Predating Second Temple Ruin," *Haaretz* (August 16, 2016), http://www.haaretz.com/israel-news/1.736752.

and 4,000 people.[130] A *miqveh* was located near its entrance. Spigel estimates that the synagogue could have realistically accommodated 407–454 people, with a maximum capacity of 509–536.[131] The building is located near the town entrance, and is constructed of well-dressed basalt ashlars with a pressed-earth floor for its central area. It was built in the late first century BCE, and went out of use when the town was destroyed and abandoned in 67 CE during the First Jewish Revolt.

At Capernaum in Galilee, the black basalt foundations of a fairly large public building dating to the first century CE (*ASSB* no. 8) were discovered underneath a monumental late antique limestone synagogue, which is dated variously between the fourth to sixth centuries.[132] It is located in a central area of the locale. Although the remains of this building are very scant, based on its size and location under a later synagogue, they are best interpreted as belonging to a first-century synagogue.[133] This is probably the same synagogue at Capernaum mentioned in the Gospels.[134]

The synagogue building discovered at Magdala (Migdal) in Galilee (figs. 3–8) was constructed in the mid first century BCE, but was not clearly used as a synagogue until the early first century CE.[135] It fea-

---

30. Cf. Danny Syon and Zvi Yavor, "Gamla – Old and New," *Qadmoniot* 121 (2001): 2–33 (20).

31. Spigel, *Ancient Synagogue Seating Capacities*, 82.

32. Heinrich Kohl and Carl Watzinger, *Antike Synagogen in Galiläa* (Leipzig: Henrichs, 1916), 4–40; Virgilio Corbo, "Resti della sinagoga del primo secolo a Cafarnao," in *Studia Hierosolymitana* (3 vols.; 3rd ed.; ed. G.C. Biottini; Jerusalem: Franciscan Printing, 1982), 3:313–57; Stanislao Loffreda, "Ceramica Ellenistico-Romana nel Sottosuolo della Sinagoga di Cafarnao," in *Studia Hierosolymitana* (3 vols.; 3rd ed.; ed. G.C. Biottini; Jerusalem: Franciscan Printing, 1982), 3:273–313; Stanislao Loffreda, "The Late Chronology of the Synagogue of Capernaum," in *Ancient Synagogues Revealed*, ed. Lee I. Levine (Jerusalem: Israel Exploration Society, 1981), 52–56; Stanislao Loffreda, *Recovering Capharnaum* (Jerusalem: Franscican Printing, 1993), 32–49; Gideon Foerster, "Notes on Recent Excavations at Capernaum," in *Ancient Synagogues Revealed*, ed. Lee I. Levine (Jerusalem: Israel Exploration Society, 1981), 57–59; Michael Avi-Yonah, "Some Comments on the Capernaum Excavations," in *Ancient Synagogues Revealed*, ed. Lee I. Levine (Jerusalem: Israel Exploration Society, 1981), 60–62; Binder, *Into the Temple Courts*, 186–93; Zvi Uri Ma'oz, "When Were the Galilean Synagogues First Constructed?" *Eretz Israel* 25 (1996): 416–26; Leslie J. Hoppe, *The Synagogues and Churches of Ancient Palestine* (Collegeville: Liturgical, 1994), 33–40; James F. Strange, "Ancient Texts, Archaeology as Text, and the Problem of the First Century Synagogue," in *Evolution of the Synagogue*, ed. Howard C. Kee and Lynn H. Cohick (Harrisburg: Trinity Press International, 1999), 27–45; Levine, *Ancient Synagogue*, 71. See also the discussion by Jodi Magness, Eric M. Meyers, and James F. Strange in Alan J. Avery-Peck and Jacob Neusner, eds., *Judaism in Late Antiquity, Part 3: Where We Stand: Issues and Debates in Ancient Judaism*, vol. 4: *The Special Problem of the Ancient Synagogue* (Leiden: Brill, 2001).

33. The identification of the basalt pavement as a Second-Temple-period synagogue has sometimes been the subject of debate. At present, the issue seems to have mostly been resolved in favor of the identification of these remains as belonging to a first-century-CE synagogue. For a summary of the issues and a convincing interpretation of the history of the site, see Anders Runesson, "Architecture, Conflict and Identity Formation," in *Religion, Ethnicity and Identity in Ancient Galilee*, ed. Jürgen K. Zangenberg, Harold W. Attridge and Dale B. Martin (Tübingen; Mohr Siebeck, 2007), 231–57.

34. Mark 1:21–29; Luke 4:31–37, Luke 7:5–9; John 6:25–59. See also Mark 3:1–6.

35. Avshalom-Gorni and Najar, "Migdal."

tures more extravagant ornamentation than other early synagogues, but unlike the Gamla synagogue, its benches are constructed from reused architectural elements of other buildings, rather than well-dressed ashlars. Its main hall covers about 120 square meters. Benches line all four walls. A walkway separates the benches along the wall from a lower set of benches surrounding the quadrilateral centre space. The synagogue could probably hold between 120 and 200 people in the assembly hall.[136] It was apparently abandoned after the siege of the town during the First Jewish Revolt. At present, excluding the meager remains at Capernaum, it is the only first-century synagogue building that has been discovered in Galilee, within the range of Jesus's activities. This fact, along with some of its unique features (discussed below), means that the Magdala synagogue is particularly relevant to this study.

Modi'in in Judea boasts a synagogue building (fig. 15; *ASSB* no. 29) dating to the second half of the first century BCE. It measured 11 x 6.5 meters, and featured benches lining all four walls. The centre of the north bench is pronounced, and may have been a special seat.[137] It had a plastered floor, and an attached courtyard with a *miqveh*.

A synagogue (fig. 14; *ASSB* no. 35) dated to the first century CE. was discovered in the centre of the settlement at Qiryat Sefer in Judea. It measures 9.6 x 9.6 meters, is constructed of well-cut ashlars, and features decorated stone lintels. It features benches along three of its walls. The Qiryat Sefer synagogue is a one-room, rural village synagogue, and consists only of a small entrance hall and an assembly hall.[138] Two small rooms adjoin the synagogue, one probably containing a pool and the other being a small storage space, but they were inaccessible from inside the main building.[139] Qiryat Sefer, which covers an area of 10.7 dunams,[140] had an estimated population of only about 107–160.[141] By Spigel's estimate, the synagogue could seat 82–101 peo-

---

136. See Richard Bauckham and Stefano De Luca, "Magdala As We Now Know It," *Early Christianity* 6 (2015): 91–118 (109), who state that the excavators estimate that the synagogue could hold 120. However, in light of the comparative findings of Spigel, *Ancient Synagogue Seating Capacities*, I might estimate a higher upper range closer to 200. For example, the reasonably conservative estimate Spigel gives for Phase II of the synagogue at Nabratein, which has a floor space of 122 square meters, is 174–188 people. In personal correspondence, Anders Runesson has also offered an estimate of around 200 people.

137. Hachlili, *Ancient Synagogues*, 34.

138. See Yitzhak Magen, Yoav Tzionit, and Orna Sirkis, "Khirbet Badd 'Isa – Qiryat Sefer," in *The Land of Benjamin* (ed. Noga Haimovich-Carmin; JSP 3; Jerusalem: Israel Antiquities Authority, 2004), 179–241 (204–5).

139. Magen, Tzionit, and Sirkis, "Khirbet Badd 'Isa," 205. The small storage space is comparable, in modern terms, to a shed.

140. Magen, Tzionit, and Sirkis, "Khirbet Badd 'Isa," 179, 217.

ple, which constitutes a majority of the population.[142] This is the smallest Second Temple synagogue building discovered to date. The existence of a synagogue building in a community of this size indicates that even the smallest of Jewish settlements could have a synagogue building. It is thus plausible that the various small rural villages of Galilee could have boasted public synagogue buildings.

The synagogue at Masada (fig. 16; *ASSB* no. 28) and its sibling at Herodium (fig. 17; *ASSB* no. 11) constitute special cases. Both were converted for use as synagogues from other structures by the rebels during the First Jewish Revolt. Thus, neither was in use as a synagogue during the time of Jesus. They served as public synagogues for the inhabitants of these fortresses during the war. The synagogue at Herodium was converted from a triclinium. It measures 15.15 x 10.6 meters, and features benches along all four of its walls. A *miqveh* was located at its entrance. The synagogue at Masada was converted from a stable.[143] It features plastered, tiered benches along its walls, and had a main hall measuring 15 x 12 meters.

A Second-Temple-period building that could potentially be identified as a synagogue has been found at Et-Tawani.[144] The building is rectangular, and features a hall measuring 8 meters in width lined with stone hewn benches. Only portions of the western side of the building have survived, making further determinations about the size and function of the structure difficult. No columns have been found on site. The existence of benches along the wall is similar to the synagogue buildings described above, and may indicate that the building was used for public assembly. As a result, I am willing to accept the identification of this building as a synagogue provisionally. However, due to the present condition of the building, it is difficult to clearly determine the structure's function.

A building dated to the Second Temple period discovered at Diab has also been identified as a synagogue by the excavator.[145] Much like the other structures identified as synagogues listed above, the building is quadrilateral with benches lining all four of the walls. No columns were discovered. However, the hall is quite small (3.5 x 7.5 meters), so there may have been no need for columns. Nevertheless, the very small size

41. Spigel, *Seating Capacities*, 293.
42. Ibid., 295.
43. Ehud Netzer, *Masada III: The Buildings* (Jerusalem: Israel Exploration Society, 1991), 412–13.
44. Har-Even, "Khirbet Tawani ," 15–29; Hachlili, *Ancient Synagogues*, 26.
45. Binyamin Har-Even, "A Second Temple Synagogue at Horvat Diab in Western Benjamin," *Qadmoniot* 151 (2016): 49–53.

of the building and the lack of columns, which are a typical feature of other synagogue buildings from the Roman period, may be cause for uncertainty about the structure's function and identification.

Limestone architectural fragments that have been identified as belonging to a synagogue have been discovered at Kefar Shikhin.[146] The remains are difficult to date, but James R. Strange has suggested that they belong to a synagogue that was probably built no earlier than the second century using elements of an earlier public building (such as a synagogue) or private villa. The remains include columns, a threshold (in two pieces), and a section of a wall composed of bossed stones. The bossed stones, in particular, appear to have been cut from larger bossed stones and are clearly in secondary use, coming from the earlier building. The fragmentary nature of the remains of the earlier structure that have been reused in the later synagogue makes it difficult to make any clear decisions about the building's identity or function.

A monumental public building has been uncovered at Khirbet Majdouliya (alt. "Majduliyya").[147] This edifice is a quadrilateral building with benches built along the walls. Remains of columns have also been found on site. Michael Osband, the excavator, has rightly noted that the fact that the structure is a monumental public building located in a Jewish area points strongly toward its identification as a synagogue.[148] Moreover, the general architectural pattern of the building fits the typical pattern of other synagogue buildings. An official publication is lacking at this time. In my opinion, it is quite likely that this structure is indeed a synagogue. The building dates broadly to the Roman period, but it is difficult to determine whether the building should be dated more precisely to the late Second Temple period (the early Roman period), or to a time when the Temple was no longer standing (the middle and late Roman periods) without an official publication or site report.

The discovery of a building at Tel Rechesh that has been identified as a synagogue was announced in 2016.[149] The building is part of a large farm complex. At present, only the Western half of the structure has been excavated. It features a hall measuring 8 x 9 meters with a sin-

---

146. James Riley Strange, "Kefar Shikhin," 103–5.
147. An official publication or report is currently lacking. See, however, the announcement in Ngo, "Roman-Era Structure." Additional information can be found at the excavation's website, https://archgolan.wordpress.com/majduliyya/.
148. Quoted in Ngo, "Roman-Era Structure."
149. See Hasson, "Ancient Synagogue," n.p. More concrete information can be found on the "Bornblum Eretz Israel Synagogue Website," which is maintained by Kinneret College, one of the institutions involved in the excavation. See http://synagogues.kinneret.ac.il/synagogues/tel-rekhesh/.

gle row of limestone benches lining at least three of its walls. A single column or pilaster base has thus far been uncovered. The structure is dated to the first century CE on the basis of ceramic evidence. The architectural elements uncovered thus far are indeed consistent with the typical architecture of early synagogue buildings. Tel Rechesh was a Jewish village during the early Roman period,[150] and the architecture of the structure indicates that it could have been used for local gathering. These facts are in favour of the identification of this building as a synagogue. However, as of the time of writing, the structure is not yet fully excavated, and no formal publication is yet available. As a result, we will need to wait for more information to be made available before this edifice can be fully incorporated into our data pool.

The number of synagogue buildings discovered in the Land might seem surprisingly low. However, it is important to recognize that it is very difficult and expensive to excavate large portions of sites. Often, only a portion of a site's land coverage can be excavated. Moreover, buildings are often destroyed and built over, as with the synagogue building at Capernaum. Four of the extant synagogue buildings (at Gamla, Herodium, Magdala, and Masada) were discovered in areas that had been abandoned after the First Jewish Revolt. This is not coincidence, since the abandonment of these areas meant that these buildings were not torn down and built over. As the discovery of the synagogue at Magdala in 2009 indicates, it is quite possible that more data will become available as further excavations are carried out.

Basic Architectural Pattern and Artwork

The typical architectural form shared by these buildings consists of a quadrilateral main assembly area with stepped benches lining three or four of the walls and supporting columns (fig. 1).[151] This left an

---

50. Shuichi Hasegawa and Yitzhak Paz, "Tel Rekhesh – 2013," *Hadashot Arkheologiyot* 127 (2015): n.p., http://www.hadashot-esi.org.il/report_detail_eng.aspx?id=24892&mag_id=122. Note that this report predates the discovery of the synagogue.
51. Note that the proposed synagogue buildings at Diab and Et-Tawani lack the typical columns. This may have to do with the smaller size of the buildings. I am not of the opinion that these outliers should force us to reconsider the standard architectural typology, as they both generally reflect most of the basic pattern in all other respects. However, it is worth noting that the size of the synagogue at Diab might speak against its ability to be used as a gathering place. There is also a building from the late first or early second century CE discovered at Horvat Ethri that has been identified as a synagogue but does not fit the typical architectural pattern, as it lacks benches and its three columns are located in a row in the middle of the hall (*ASSB*, no. 12). For the detailed archaeological report on the potential synagogue at Horvat Ethri, see Boaz Zissu and Amir Ganor, "Horvat 'Ethri – A Jewish Village From the Second Temple Period and the Bar Kokhba Revolt in the Judean Foothills," *JJS* 60, no. 1 (2009): 90–136 (101–10). This public building complex included a

open area in the centre on the ground level. The columns supported clerestory walls, and light would have entered the assembly hall through the clerestory windows.[152]

This architectural form is public in nature. Some scholars who deny the existence of Second-Temple-period synagogue buildings have suggested that the building at Gamla should be identified as a private dwelling,[153] but this is an extremely problematic suggestion. Such an identification has difficulty making sense of the stepped benches and their arrangement. The size and general seating capacity of the Gamla synagogue, estimated by Spigel to be around 454–536,[154] is also better explained as indicative of public rather than domestic architectural space.

The basic architectural template resembles other civic buildings of the ancient Mediterranean. Several scholars have remarked on the similarities between the synagogue buildings of the Land and Hellenistic *ekklēsiastēria* or *bouleutēria*,[155] which were Greek civic assembly

---

main hall (measuring 13 x 7 meters), a vestibule (3.5 x 13 meters), an outer court, an inner courtyard, and a ritual bath. I agree that this structure was some sort of public building (cf. Runesson, Binder, and Olsson, *Ancient Synagogue*, 38), but it worth stating that it may be that not all public buildings discovered in Jewish locales should necessarily be identified as synagogues simply on the basis of being public buildings alone. The benches, after all, are instrinsic to the assembly and deliberative functions of synagogues. Nevertheless, it is at least possible that the building at Horvat Ethri may have had wooden or removable benches that have not survived in context. It is also conceivable that the assembled public could have sat on the floor. At any rate, we should view the lack of benches at the Horvat Ethri synagogue as a potential outlier (though not one without explanation) rather than as a direct challenge to the standard architectural pattern. It is also worth noting that, according to Zissu and Ganor, the building was restored during the Late Roman period, and "its internal space was reorganised, while the external walls remained unchanged. This activity altered the original plan and makes it difficult to analyse and understand the remains of the initial phase" (Zissu and Ganor, "Horvat 'Ethri," 103). As a result of this remodelling process (in the third century CE, cf. Zissu and Ganor, "Horvat 'Ethri," 108), it is difficult to make any judgments about the internal architecture of the building as it would have existed in the first or second centuries CE Zissu and Ganor suggest that the earlier phase of the building had benches that were either wooden or were dismantled ("Horvat 'Ethri," 108).

152. See Strange, "Archaeology and Ancient Synagogues," 43.

153. E.g., Horsley, *Galilee*, 224; Kee, "Transformation," 8. It is worth mentioning that both also suggest that a building discovered at Magdala that was identified as a synagogue is also a domestic dwelling. However, the building that Kee and Horsley are referring to is not the synagogue discovered in the 2009 salvage excavations by the Israel Antiquities Authority. They are referring to a smaller building discovered on the Franciscan side of the excavations and identified as a synagogue (*ASSB* no. 27) by Virgilio Corbo, "Scavi Archaelogici a Magdala," *Liber Annuus* 24 (1974): 5–37; cf. Virgilio Corbo, "La Citta romana di Magdala," in *Studia Hierosolymitana in onore del P. Bellarmino Bagatti*, ed. I. Mancini and M. Piccirillo (Jerusalem: Franciscan Printing Press, 1976), 365–68. However, Ehud Netzer has convincingly demonstrated that this building served from the time it was built as a springhouse rather than a synagogue, in Ehud Netzer, "Did the Magdala Springhouse Serve as a Synagogue?" in *Synagogues in Antiquity*, ed. A. Kasher, A. Oppenheimer, and U. Rappaport (Jerusalem: Yad Izhak Ben Zvi, 1987), 165–72. Unless specifically stated otherwise, references in this study to the synagogue at Magdala are to the more solidly identified structure discovered in 2009 by the Israel Antiquities Authority salvage excavation.

154. Spigel, *Seating Capacities*, 207.

155. E.g., Yigael Yadin, "The Excavation of Masada 1963/1964: Preliminary Report," *Israel Exploration*

buildings. The *ekklēsiastērion* was a very large structure, and housed the popular assembly of citizens. As its name indicates, the *bouleutērion* was the meeting place for the local *boulē*. The *bouleutērion*, which seated several hundred people, provides a close point of comparison in terms of building size and capacity.[156] These Hellenistic civic buildings also featured stepped benches and open space in the centre, much like synagogues.

Unlike many later synagogues and churches with forward-facing seating placing the focal point at the front of the congregation, the seating arrangement of early synagogues places the focus at the centre of the room. This architectural layout is designed for discussion. In particular, the quadrilateral seating arrangement facilitates discussion, especially between people seated on opposite sides of the assembly hall as well as with anyone in the open central area. This would have allowed congregants to easily engage anyone speaking in the centre or sitting opposite from them in debate or discussion.[157]

Most early synagogue buildings were sparsely decorated. This stands in stark contrast to later synagogues in the Land, which can sometimes feature ornate mosaic pavements.[158] Aniconism was generally observed in this period, in keeping with the biblical prohibition against graven images (Exod 20:4; Deut 4:16, 27:15).[159] The decoration surviving at Gamla is limited to architectonic elements—Doric columns, and a lintel that features a rosette and date palms.[160] Similarly, at Qiryat Sefer, two decorated lintels belonging to the synagogue have been found.[161] One has a *tabula ansata*, and the other has a geometric motif. Some remnants of thick red plaster on one of the column bases suggests that the

Journal 15 (1965): 1–120 (78); cf. Yadin, "Masada," 20n1; Levine, *Ancient Synagogue*, 55, 75; Binder, *Into the Temple Courts*, 222; Strange, "Archaeology and Ancient Synagogues," 42; Zvi Ma'oz, "The Synagogue of Gamla and the Typology of Second-Temple Synagogues," in *Ancient Synagogues Revealed*, ed. Lee I. Levine (Jerusalem: Israel Exploration Society, 1981), 35–41.

56. The Athenian *bouleutērion* famously housed a *boulē* of 500 (see, e.g., Aristotle, *Ath. Pol.* 24.3). This is roughly comparative to Spigel's estimation of the Gamla synagogue's seating capacity of 454–536 people, in Spigel, *Seating Capacities*, 207.

57. Cf. Mosser, "Torah Instruction," 550.

58. See, for example, the well-known mosaic pavements in the synagogues at Bet Aleph, En Gedi, Sepphoris, Huqoq, or Hamat Tiberias. For studies that cover both late antique synagogue art as well as early synagogue art, see Lee I. Levine, *Visual Judaism in Late Antiquity: Historical Contexts of Jewish Art* (New Haven: Yale University Press, 2012), see esp. 226; Hachlili, *Ancient Synagogues*. On the artwork of late antique synagogues, see also Steven Fine, *Art and Judaism in the Greco-Roman World: Toward New Jewish Archaeology* (Cambridge: Cambridge University Press, 2005), esp. 165–209.

59. On this, see Rachel Hachlili, *Ancient Jewish Art and Archaeology in the Land of Israel* (HdO; Leiden and New York: Brill, 1988), 65–83. A poignant example of Jewish aniconic attitudes during the late Second Temple period is found in Josephus's description of the destruction of Antipas' palace in Tiberias, in *Vita* 65–67.

60. See Zvi Ma'oz, "The Synagogue of Gamla," 39.

61. Cf. Magen, Tzionit, and Sirkis, "Khirbet Badd 'Isa," 200, 203 (fig. 38), 204 (fig. 40).

interior would have been painted red.[162] Fragments of red, white, and yellow painted plaster were also found in the synagogue at Modi'in.[163] Red painted plaster has been discovered on the columns of the Magdala synagogue (fig. 8). Remnants of a fresco, primarily red with yellow and blue panels, have been found on the walls.[164] This should prevent us from imagining the inside of synagogues to have been drab, colored only by stones, dirt, and mud.

The Magdala synagogue is a notable exception to the generally austere decoration of Second Temple synagogues. A portion of a tricolored mosaic floor has been discovered on the floor, featuring a rosette and a meander pattern.[165] However, the mosaic appears to have been left unfinished, as the meander pattern breaks off evenly at both ends. It is important to observe the existence of a mosaic pavement in a synagogue before 70 CE, since this is evidence of continuity between Second Temple synagogues and synagogues that postdate the destruction of the temple.

Perhaps the most important discovery pertaining to Second-Temple-synagogue artwork is an ornately carved limestone piece known as the "Magdala stone." The "Magdala stone" is a decorated four-footed rectangular block, measuring about 0.6 meters in length, 0.5 meters in width, and 0.4 meters in height,[166] which was found in the central floor area of the Magdala synagogue.[167] It was not discovered in the exact centre of the room, but just slightly south and east of the center. However, the stone is portable enough to have been moved. The Magdala stone is decorated with carved reliefs imagery on five of its sides (figs. 9–12). The façade features two pillars on either side supporting an archway. A seven-branched menorah flanked by two amphorae is pictured between the pillars. The menorah has three legs and stands atop a square object with a diamond shape on its interior. The combination of the iconic seven-branched menorah with elements of monumental architecture immediately bring the Jerusalem temple to mind.

---

162. Magen, Tzionit, and Sirkis, "Khirbet Badd 'Isa," 205.
163. See *ASSB* no. 29.
164. Avshalom Gorni and Najar, "Magdala."
165. Ibid.
166. According to the measurements in Mordechai Aviam, "The Decorated Stone at Migdal: A Holistic Interpretation and a Glimpse into the Life of Galilean Jews at the Time of Jesus," *Novum Testamentum* 55 (2013): 205–20 (208).
167. The Magdala stone was discovered underneath a column that had apparently been purposefully placed on top of the stone, perhaps to protect it. This detail is not mentioned in the preliminary reports that are currently available so far as I am aware, but was learned through personal communication with Arfan Najar during the time I spent onsite participating in the 2012 excavation season. This pillar can be seen in Avshalom-Gorni and Najar, "Migdal," fig. 9.

Although the function of the stone is currently unknown, there is general agreement in current publications that this face of the stone depicts temple imagery.[168]

The presence of an object representing the temple in a Galilean synagogue is striking, and indicative of a strong connection and relationship between Galilee and Jerusalem. It also indicates a symbolic connection between synagogue assemblies and the Jerusalem temple. We can say with confidence that Galilee and the synagogues on the one hand, and Jerusalem and the temple on the other, were certainly not opposed. Both the synagogue and the temple were important institutions and symbols for early Jewish identity formation and community organization, as well as Jewish religion and politics.

The function of the Magdala stone is unclear. Aviam has suggested that it may have been used as the base for a table used for reading the Torah,[169] a sort of lectern. However, as Binder has pointed out, the table would have needed to be anchored to the base to avoid it slipping off, and there is no evidence of anchor points on the stone.[170] Binder has made three alternative suggestions—that the stone may have served as the base for a lampstand, as a chair for a functionary, or a base for an offering vessel—but none of these suggestions are particularly convincing or certain. At present, the lack of data has led me to suspend judgment on the matter. In fact, its practical function is so unclear that I question whether it even had one at all. The possibility that the stone may have simply been decorative or symbolic cannot be excluded.[171] However, even if the practical function of the stone remains unknown, it served the symbolic functions, whether intentional or otherwise, of reinforcing Judean identity and encouraging a connection between the synagogue assembly and the Jerusalem temple, along with the deity that resided within its holiest place.

Purity and Synagogues: *Miqva'ot* and Handwashing

Ritual baths, or *miqva'ot*, are frequently discovered nearby or in con-

---

68. Various proposals have been made, including a base for a lectern (Aviam, "Decorated Stone," 211–12), the base for a lampstand, as a chair for a functionary, or a base for an offering vessel (Donald D. Binder, "The Mystery of the Magdala Stone," in *A City Set on a Hill: Essays in Honor of James F. Strange*, ed. Daniel A. Warner and Donald D. Binder [Fayetteville: Borderstone, 2014], 26), or a purely symbolic function (Bauckham, "Migdal Synagogue Stone," 114).

69. Aviam, "Decorated Stone," 216.

70. Binder, "Mystery of the Magdala Stone," 42.

71. A similar argument has been made by Richard Bauckham and Stefano de Luca, "Magdala As We Now Know It," *EC* 6 (2015): 91–118, esp. 111.

nection with synagogue buildings. The public synagogues at Gamla, Herodium, Masada, Modi'in, and Qiryat Sefer all have *miqva'ot* situated adjacent or very close by.[172] A *miqveh* has also been found adjacent to the association synagogue at Jericho, and the Theodotos inscription from Jerusalem mentions "water installations."[173]

A plastered basin, fed by a plastered channel leading from a cistern, is also located on the top level of the assembly hall of the Gamla synagogue near the Eastern wall.[174] This same channel continues from the basin into the *miqveh* near the building's main entrance. A similar basin with a channel leading into a *miqveh* has also been found in the Jericho synagogue. According to Yavor, this basin was probably used for hand-washing, and may have been a predecessor of the *gorna*, a stone basin referred to in Talmudic sources for hand and foot washing.[175]

What is the connection between these installations and synagogues? Was there a special need for purity in synagogue contexts? The answers are not readily apparent. Binder has argued that the synagogue was an extension of the temple, and that the purity laws of the temple extended, at least in some degree, to the synagogue.[176] However, as Susan Haber has pointed out, while the law concerning ritual purity in the temple is alluded to in Second Temple sources, no mention is made of purity laws connected to the synagogue in this period.[177] Moreover, she notes the logistical difficulties of cleansing the entire congregation prior to entering the building. In agreement with Haber, I concur that the best explanation of the data is that the connection was mostly practical.[178] Public *miqva'ot* were located near public synagogues

---

172. See *ASSB* nos. 10 (Gamla), 11 (Herodium), 28 (Masada), 29 (Modi'in), and 35 (Qiryat Sefer). Note that at Masada and Qiryat Sefer, the *miqva'ot* are located slightly further away. At Masada, the *miqveh* is located about 15 meters away from the synagogue. Levine, *Ancient Synagogue*, 75 n. 112 says that no *miqveh* has been discovered near the synagogue at Qiryat Sefer, but the recently published excavation report describes a *miqveh* located near the center of the settlement, about 13 meters away from the synagogue. See Magen, Tzionit, and Sirkis, "Khirbet Badd 'Isa," 185. Although no *miqveh* has been discovered in direct connection with the Magdala synagogue, four *miqva'ot* have been found in two nearby (but not adjacent) structures, see Ronny Reich and Marcela Zapata Meza, "A Preliminary Report on the *Miqwa'ot* of Migdal," *IEJ* 64, no. 1 (2014): 63–71. Only three *miqva'ot* are mentioned in this report, but another *miqveh* has since been found during the 2015 summer season. However, the distance to the synagogue is too far to make a direct connection. Moreover, the spatial setting of these miqva'ot is probably that of a private dwelling, with no clear relation to the synagogue.
173. See *ASSB* nos. 15 (Jericho) and 26 (Jerusalem).
174. See Yavor, "Architecture and Stratigraphy," 52–54.
175. Yavor, "Architecture and Stratigraphy," 54. On the *gorna*, see, e.g., *Y. Meg.* 3:3.
176. Binder, *Into the Temple Courts*, 391–99.
177. Susan Haber, "Common Judaism, Common Synagogue? Purity, Holiness, and Sacred Space at the Turn of the Common Era," in *"They Shall Purify Themselves": Essays on Purity in Early Judaism*, ed. Adele Reinhartz (Atlanta: Society of Biblical Literature, 2008), 161–79 (169).
178. Cf. Haber, "Common Synagogue," 170. Alternatively, it is worth mentioning that Ronny Reich

because they were public gathering places and the communal center of the locale.

The basins found at Gamla and Jericho may have been used to wash one's hands after handling scrolls containing sacred scripture. According to *m. Yad.* 3:5, "all holy writings make the hands unclean."[179] Thus, it is reasonable to infer that handwashing, or perhaps even immersion of the hands or body in a *miqveh* after handling sacred texts, may have been practiced in locations where this tradition was known and upheld. If this interpretation of the data is correct, then the existence of such basins may be good evidence of the presence of scrolls containing scripture at these synagogues.

Secondary Rooms

Some synagogues had additional rooms aside from the main hall. These rooms provide some further insight into synagogue functions and roles. The Gamla synagogue (figs. 1–2), for example, features a number of small additional rooms both near the building's entrance and at the back of the hall.[180] The largest and most significant of these rooms is what the excavators refer to as a "study room," a rectangular room seating about 25 people at the back of the synagogue, with benches lining at least three of the four walls.[181] This "study room" was not entered directly through the main hall, but through another room off of the main assembly area, though it did have a window opening onto the main hall. Zvi Yavor has quite reasonably noted that the small size and arrangement of the room suggests that the room was used for study in smaller groups, though he notes that other communal functions could have taken place there.[182]

My opinion—and without further evidence, it can be nothing more than opinion—is that while the room was probably used for study, it may have also been used to hold meetings of smaller subgroups or

has suggested that synagogues may have required the use of *miqva'ot* in connection with sacred meals and with the handling of scripture, in Ronny Reich, "The Synagogue and the *Miqweh* in Eretz-Israel in the Second Temple, Mishnaic and Talmudic Periods," in *Ancient Synagogues: Historical Analysis and Archaeological Discovery*, ed. Dan Urman and Paul Virgil McCracken Flesher (Leiden and Boston: Brill, 1998), 289–97, esp. 296.

79. On this phenomenon, see John Barton, *Holy Writings, Sacred Texts: The Canon in Early Christianity* (Louisville: Westminster John Knox, 1997), 108–21; cf. Martin Goodman, "Sacred Scriptures and 'Defiling the Hands,'" *JTS* 41 (1990): 99–107 (103–4).

80. See Yavor, "Architecture and Stratigraphy," 55–58.

81. Ibid., 56. The bench on the Western side may have been too narrow to serve as seating.

82. Yavor, "Architecture and Stratigraphy," 55–56. Previously, it was also suggested that the room might have been a place for impure people or others not allowed into the main assembly hall, in Danny Syon and Zvi Yavor, "Gamla - Old and New," *Qadmoniot* 121 (2000): 10.

councils, such as the *prōtoi* or *presbytēroi*, apart from the main congregation. The window on to the main hall could have been used for communication between the assembly and the council.

The synagogue at Magdala (figs. 4 and 5) has two rooms in addition to the main assembly hall. The smaller of these two rooms is located in a short hallway off of the main room. It features a mosaic floor, and may have been used for storage, perhaps for Torah scrolls.[183] The larger of the auxiliary rooms at Magdala is referred to by the excavators as "the vestibule," so-called because the synagogue's entrance has been reconstructed on the western side of the room.[184] Like the main hall, this room also features benched seating (fig. 5). A limestone block with two semi-cylindrical grooves along either end of its upward face, mentioned earlier in this chapter, stands in the center of the room (fig. 6), in the middle of a small basalt frame on the floor. The excavators have suggested that this block may have been the base for a chair or table,[185] but I think it is more likely that this served as a small table for reading scrolls. Scroll rollers could be placed in the two grooves, allowing the reader to easily scroll back and forth between various sections of the text.

I find the identification of this room as a vestibule to be somewhat problematic. First, the architectural elements of the synagogue's entryway were discovered out of context, and were not reconstructed in their current location until 2013–2014 (fig. 7).[186] Second, the reconstructed entrance is made awkward by the location of the limestone block and its frame by the proposed entrance (cf. fig. 3). The stone frame and the block's location at the room's central focal point strongly indicates that it was a key element of the room's design, so it is curious to have the entrance located in a place which would appear to disrupt this. I suggest that the entrance may have been located on the south side. There is a small hallway that abuts the road on the south side of the building, which seems to be the most natural place for an entrance. As indicated by the plan in fig. 3, the remains of what may be a step are be located on the road right outside the south hallway.

---

183. Cf. Bauckham and De Luca, "Magdala As We Now Know It," 106–7.
184. See Avshalom-Gorni and Najar, "Migdal."
185. Ibid.
186. I first came to this site as a participant in the 2012 excavation season, and at that time, the elements of the doorway were not yet incorporated into the reconstruction of this room. Note, however, that according to the publication of Avshalom-Gorni and Najar, "Magdala," the remains of the entrance were not discovered. It is possible that they mean that the remains of the entrance were not discovered *in situ*, since in personal conversation, Arfan Najar indicated that he believed that the architectural elements of the entryway depicted in fig. 7 belonged to the synagogue.

As it stands, the best clues to the function of this secondary room are the limestone block and the seating arrangement. I infer from this evidence that, much like the secondary "study room" in the synagogue at Gamla, this secondary room was probably used for teaching and studying involving texts in smaller groups,[187] and perhaps also for meetings of smaller councils and subgroups. It is worth mentioning that a secondary room with benches lining at least three of its walls was also discovered at the late-first-century synagogue at Khirbet Qana.[188] This room is quite comparable in form to the "study room" at Gamla, and so we should imagine that it had similar functions to the Gamla synagogue's "study room."

The synagogue at Masada features a small additional room. It was under the floor of this room that the portions of scrolls of Deuteronomy and Ezekiel, mentioned above, were found buried.[189] This led Yadin to suggest that this was a sort of *genizah*, though it is unclear as to whether the texts were buried while the rebels were living at Masada or whether the texts were buried before they took their own lives.[190] It is, however, somewhat natural to imagine that the texts may have been kept in this room while they were in use. At any rate, this is indicative of the presence or storage of sacred texts in the synagogue buildings of the Land and sacred texts, not only the Torah, but also the Nevi'im, just as in Luke's depiction of Jesus's reading from Isaiah in Luke 4:16–21.

Synagogue Buildings: Summary and Conclusions

As the evidence presented above has shown, public synagogue buildings generally reflect the nature of their functions, evidenced in the literature that we have discussed earlier in this chapter. Above all, the architecture of these edifices expresses the communal nature and functions of public synagogues. Assembly halls were designed for common gathering, deliberation, and discussion. The ancillary "study rooms" also reflect these functions, though on a smaller scale.[191] The

---

87. As suggested also by Mordechai Aviam, "Zwischen Meer und See – Geschichte und Kultur Galiläas von Simon Makkabäus bis zu Flavius Josephus," in *Bauern, Fischer und Propheten - Galiläa zur Zeit Jesu* (ed. Jürgen K. Zangenberg and Jens Schröter; Darmstadt: Verlag Philipp von Zabern), 35; Bauckham and De Luca, "Magdala As We Now Know It," 106. Note also that according to Avshalom Gorni and Najar, "Magdala," "the vestibule might also have been a kind of small seminary used for studying."

88. See Richardson, *Building Jewish*, 66; *ASSB* no. 3.

89. See Yadin, "Masada," 21–22 for an account of this discovery. See also Netzer, *Masada III*, 410.

90. Yadin, "Masada," 21.

91. For further discussion of these secondary rooms, see appendix C below.

active, conversive, and sometimes disputative nature of synagogue meetings is manifest in the very form of public synagogue buildings.

It is sometimes claimed that while the literary data points to the liturgical or religious functions of synagogues, the archaeological data mostly indicates nonliturgical, communal functions.[192] I am not convinced that the two can be separated altogether, nor that archaeological data pointing to liturgical functions is entirely lacking. As I have argued above, it is difficult to separate the "liturgical" function of scripture reading and interpretation from the "nonliturgical" local-official dimension of the public synagogue. Moreover, when the archaeological data is connected to the literary data using the historical imagination, the relationship between the liturgical and communal functions becomes clearer. The archaeological evidence thus deepens and illuminates the understanding of public synagogues that emerges from the literary evidence. Taken together, the archaeological evidence and the literary evidence highlight and reveal the jointly "religious" or "liturgical" and communal, local-official nature of public synagogues in the late Second Temple period.

Summary and Synthesis

The purpose of this chapter has been to consider the data in order to produce a sketch of the public synagogue as Jesus knew it. I have been careful to place emphasis on the most relevant evidence for this task, and the result of this study has been the emergence of a coherent picture of public synagogues and synagogue life in the Land during the time of Jesus. Our discussion so far allows us to draw several key conclusions about the nature of the public synagogue as Jesus knew it. I will summarize them here:

1. Scripture reading and study were central facets of public synagogue functions. Both the Torah and Nevi'im were read at synagogue gatherings. Interpretation of scripture, especially the Torah, accompanied the readings. Interpretation was not done individually, but in community. The assembly participated in active discussion of the teaching and interpretation of scripture that was presented to them. Because the Torah functioned as law in Jewish locales, the reading, teaching, and interpretation of the

---

192. See, e.g., Hachlili, *Ancient Synagogues*, 49; Levine, *Ancient Synagogue*, 169.

Torah, though ostensibly a "religious" act, also had clear socio-legal and political valences.

2. Public synagogues were communal local-official institutions. They belonged to the town rather than to a particular group. Decisions pertaining to the locale as a whole on issues such as justice, local legal practice, and military action, were made in synagogue settings. The evidence strongly indicates that the presence and participation of members of the public was an expected element of public synagogue gatherings.

3. Because of the key role played by the public in decisions made at public synagogue gatherings, rhetoric and persuasion was a fundamental component of the proceedings. The evidence indicates that these tasks were most often undertaken by elite members of the assembly, such as council members (elders, etc.), local magistrates, *archisynagōgoi*, or scribes. The success or failure of such speech acts can be broadly conceived in terms of honor and shame.

4. The functionaries that are encountered in narratives set in public synagogues can be divided into two categories. The first category includes functionaries who belonged to the institutional structure of the synagogue itself, such as *archisynagōgoi*, or synagogue attendants (*hyperetai*). The second category includes functionaries who belong to the institutional structure of the town, village, or city, such as the *archōn*, or local council members. Although functionaries belonging to the first category had no direct political or local-official authority, they were nevertheless influential members of the synagogue community by virtue of their positions or their benefaction.

5. The assembly halls of public synagogue buildings share a common architectural pattern. The remains of the six extant undisputable instances of Second Temple public synagogues (at Gamla, Herodion, Masada, Magdala, Modi'in, and Qiryat Sefer) all feature a quadrilateral meeting hall with benches lining at least three of the walls, an open area in the center of the room, and columns. This design reflects the synagogue's communal, local-official functions.

6. The "liturgical" dimension of the public synagogue is also reflected in the archaeological data. This includes the concern for hearing rather than seeing in assembly halls, the text fragments discovered in the synagogue at Masada, the washbasins dis-

covered at several synagogue sites, and the "reading stones" found at Magdala.

7. The artwork of the Magdala temple stone hints at a strong connection between Galilean synagogues and the Jerusalem temple. This provides an example of clearly "religious" artwork discovered in synagogue space in the Land.

By drawing the threads of the evidence, arguments, and inferences presented in this chapter and the chapter that precedes it together, we are able to produce an imaginative hypothetical synthesis of a public synagogue that could have existed in Galilean towns such as Capernaum, Cana, or Nazareth. The imagination of such a hypothetical institution is required by the Gospel data, which speaks generically of Jesus's teaching and proclamation in unspecified Galilean synagogues,[193] and which does not always identify the location of episodes that take place within synagogue contexts.[194]

Now that we have produced a sketch of the public synagogue as Jesus knew it, we are prepared to address the primary burdens of this project. The data, arguments, and conclusions presented here will be applied as evidence for the joint historical tasks of contextualizing and interpreting Jesus's activities within the synagogues of Galilee, and determining the role played by synagogues within his aims. Armed now as we are with a robust historical praxis and with a sketch of Second-Temple-period synagogues firmly rooted in the evidence, we can also examine and critique the ways in which reconstructions of the synagogue have impacted the study of Jesus and the Gospels.

193. Mark 1:39; Matt 4:23, 9:35; Luke 4:15; John 18:20.
194. E.g., Luke 13:10–17.

Gallery: Synagogue Archaeology
and Architecture

Fig. 1. The synagogue at Gamla. Photograph courtesy of Anders Runesson.

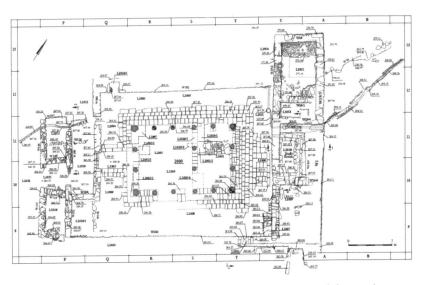

Fig. 2. Floorplan of the Gamla synagogue. Courtesy of Danny Syon and the Israel Antiquities Authority.

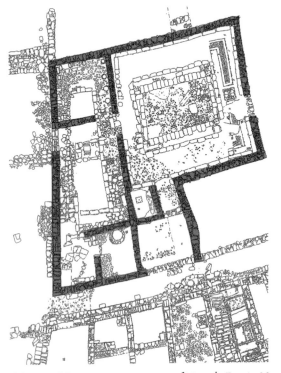

Fig. 3. Floorplan of the Magdala synagogue. Courtesy of Marcela Zapata-Meza.

Fig. 4. The main assembly hall of the Magdala synagogue.

Fig. 5. The "study room" of the Magdala synagogue.

Fig. 6. Carved limestone block possibly used as a reading table. Photograph courtesy of Anders Runesson.

Fig. 7. Architectural elements of the Magdala synagogue assembled out of context in June of 2012.

Fig. 8. Architectural elements of the Magdala synagogue assembled out of context in June of 2012.

Fig. 9. Façade of the Magdala stone. Photograph courtesy of Anders Runesson.

Fig. 10. Rear face of the Magdala stone. Photograph courtesy of Anders Runesson.

Fig. 11. Side panel of the Magdala stone. Photograph courtesy of Anders Runesson.

Fig. 12. Top surface of the Magdala stone. Photograph courtesy of Anders Runesson.

Fig. 13. The street outside the Magdala synagogue. The synagogue is pictured to the left.

Fig. 14. The synagogue at Qiryat Sefer. Photograph courtesy of Wally V. Cirafesi.

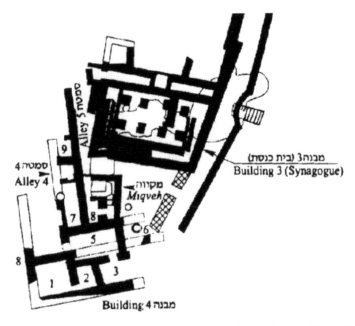

Fig. 15. Floorplan of the Modi'in synagogue. Courtesy of the Israel Antiquities Authority.

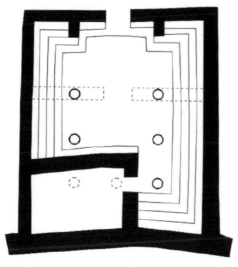

Fig. 16. Floorplan of the Masada synagogue. Courtesy of Dieter Mitternacht.

Fig. 17. The synagogue at Herodium.

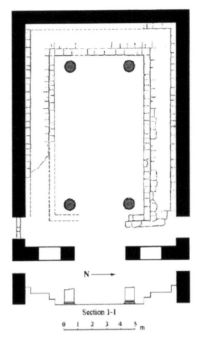

Fig. 17. Floorplan of the Herodium synagogue. Ehud Netzer. Courtesy of the Israel Exploration Society.

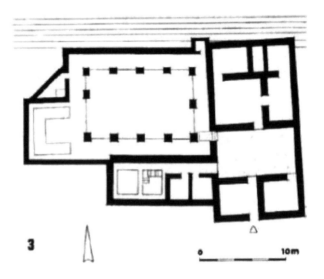

Fig. 18. Floorplan of the association synagogue at Jericho. Courtesy of the Israel Exploration Society.

Excursus:
Early Post-Second-Temple-Period
Synagogues

It is sometimes suggested that the depictions of synagogues in the Gospels are anachronistic, and therefore, historically unreliable.[1] The logic behind this notion is that synagogues underwent significant changes after the destruction of the Jerusalem temple in 70 CE,[2] and that the evangelists, writing after 70 CE, projected aspects of the synagogue as it was known to them at that time back into the 30s CE.

This suggestion is closely related to the denial of the existence of synagogue buildings during the Second Temple period,[3] but can also stand on its own apart from this notion. Even if we affirm the existence of Second-Temple-period synagogue buildings, it is still possible that the evangelists' portrayal of synagogues of the time of Jesus has been anachronistically impacted by their experiences of synagogues in the post-Second Temple period. Compounding the matter is the notion that the evangelists were writing in the diaspora, and so, elements of the diaspora synagogue may have also impacted their portrayal of the synagogues of the Land. The problem is laid out by Twelftree, who writes:

---

1. See, e.g., Twelftree, "Jesus and the Synagogue," 3106; Paul V. M. Flesher, "Palestinian Synagogues Before 70 C.E.: A Review of the Evidence," in *Ancient Synagogues*; 2 vols.; ed. Dan Urman and Paul V. M. Flesher (Leiden: Brill, 1995), 1:27–39 (32); Levine, *Ancient Synagogue*, 438; Hans Conzelmann, *Acts of the Apostles* (Hermeneia; Philadelphia: Fortress Press, 1987), xliii–xlv, 187; Étienne Nodet, *The Historical Jesus?: Necessity and Limits of an Inquiry* (Jewish and Christian Texts in Contexts and Related Studies; trans. J. Edward Crowley; London and New York: T&T Clark, 2008 [2003]), 63–64.
2. On this idea, see Hachlili, "Synagogues: Before and After the Roman Destruction of the Temple."
3. See the discussion in chapter 4.

In setting out what we know about the synagogue in the time and place of Jesus we are able to take into account an inscription, archaeological evidence and literary sources. We need to exercise considerable care and restraint in using data from the New Testament for it is likely that early Christian experiences of the synagogues in the Diaspora have been projected chronologically back and cross-culturally into the period and experience of Jesus and his followers in Palestine.[4]

Are the evangelists' depictions of the synagogue anachronistic? Are they anatopistic? Against the suggestion of anatopism, Runesson rightly points out that the Gospel accounts depict Jesus interacting with public synagogues, which did not exist in the diaspora.[5] The public nature of the synagogues in the Gospels will become clearer as we examine the Gospel data in the chapters to follow. For now, it is sufficient to note along with Runesson that the portrayal of synagogues in the Gospels fits better within a Palestinian milieu than a Diasporic one.

What of the possibility that the evangelists' portrayal of synagogues of the time of Jesus has been coloured by their experience of synagogues of their own time? Even though we can dismiss the issue of anatopism, it is still possible that the evangelists modeled their depictions of synagogue settings on post-70 CE Palestinian public synagogues. It is, after all, readily apparent that the monumental Palestinian synagogues of Late Antiquity, with their ornate architecture, Torah shrines, and complex iconic mosaics developed in considerable ways from the much simpler Second Temple synagogue buildings. Runesson's response to this suggestion is not entirely satisfactory, as he dismisses the issue, writing that "synagogues in the 80s or 90s would have looked much the same as synagogues in the 30s"[6] without further discussion of the evidence. This issue warrants further examination, if for no other reason than to help put the matter to rest and to thereby allay further confusion.

The archaeological evidence does not indicate that public synagogues changed drastically in the years immediately following the destruction of the temple. For example, a building that has been identified as a synagogue has been discovered at Khirbet Qana in Galilee. This structure has been dated to the late-first to early-second centuries on the basis of ceramic evidence and carbon-14 testing.[7] The architecture

4. Twelftree, "Jesus and the Synagogue," 3106.
5. Runesson, "Importance of the Synagogue," 288–89.
6. Ibid., 288.
7. C. Thomas McCollough, "Khirbet Qana," in *The Archaeological Record From Cities, Towns, and Villages.*

of the building matches that of other public synagogues of the Land of Israel quite well. Consider the description contained in the final excavation report on the synagogue:

> Excavations in the interior of the building exposed two layers of plaster floors and remnants of plaster benches along three walls of the structure. We also recovered large amounts of painted interior wall plaster. The excavation of the soil covering the plaster floor in the interior of the building revealed footers for 8 columns, each 2.5 m from the respective eastern and western walls and 5 m apart. Reused drums and column bases were exposed in the southeast corner, and in the northeast corner a reused capital was also recovered. Analysis of the form and decoration of the capital concluded that it was similar to ones used in the Gamla synagogue and should be dated to the Early Roman period.[8]

The structure described here lines up exactly with the architectural pattern that we have seen in Second-Temple-period synagogues, as discussed in chapters 2 and 3. The Qana synagogue is a quadrilateral edifice featuring a gathering hall sporting supporting columns and benches lining at least three of the walls. Direct architectural parallels have been drawn to the Gamla synagogue, including the form and decoration of the capital mentioned above, and the plastering of the aisle floors but not the central nave.[9]

The remains of the synagogue discovered at Khirbet Qana,[10] which roughly date to the period when the Gospels are typically thought to have been written, do not indicate any major shifts or developments from earlier public synagogue remains. In fact, the identification of this building as a synagogue is tied to its *similarities* to other synagogue buildings, such as that at Gamla.[11]

The synagogue discovered at Nabratein[12] has three phases, the earliest of which dates to the mid-second century CE.[13] This building is

---

Vol. 2 of *Galilee in the Late Second Temple and Mishnaic Periods*, ed. David A. Fiensy and James Riley Strange (Minneapolis: Fortress Press, 2015), 127–45 (141).

8. McCollough, "Final Report."

9. McCollough, "Khirbet Qana," 141.

10. *ASSB* no. 2.

11. Cf. McCollough, "Khirbet Qana," 141; McCollough, "Final Report," n.p.

12. *ASSB* no. 30.

13. Cf. Eric M. Meyers and Carol L. Meyers, "Nabratein: Synagogue and Environs," in *The Archaeological Record From Cities, Towns, and Villages*, vol. 2 of *Galilee in the Late Second Temple and Mishnaic Periods*, ed. David A. Fiensy and James Riley Strange (Minneapolis: Fortress Press, 2015), 405. For full treatment, see Eric M. Meyers and Carol L. Meyers, *Excavations at Ancient Nabratein: Synagogue and Environs* (Meiron Excavation Project 6; Winona Lake: Eisenbrauns, 2009). The specific dates of the first phase of this synagogue are 135–250 CE. The second phase dates from 250–363 CE, and the final phase dates from 564–700 CE.

quite small, measuring 11.2 by 9.35 meters, and boasts a meeting hall with four columns and benches lining three of its walls.[14] There are no benches along the south wall, which instead has two platforms that have been identified as *bemas*. The excavators suggest that a Torah shrine may have stood on one of these platforms, but no direct evidence of this has been discovered.[15]

The *bemas* at Nabratein are a feature lacking from earlier synagogues, and may represent a development in synagogue form. Otherwise, the Nabratein synagogue is reminiscent of the Qiryat Sefer synagogue, especially in terms of size and seating capacity. Spigel estimates that the Nabratein synagogue could have sat 83 to 87 people.[16] This is quite close to Spigel's low estimate of 82 people for the Qiryat Sefer synagogue.[17]

The fact that the first notable development in synagogue form, the addition of *bemas*, is not attested until the mid-second century CE, long after the Gospels were written, speaks against major developments emerging immediately after the fall of the temple. Moreover, we must also note that, in most ways, the first phase of the Nabratein synagogue follows the architectural pattern and form of earlier synagogues, and does not indicate any specific major changes in function.

What of the literary evidence? The Mishnah and Tosefta bear clear witness to the continuing public nature of the synagogue in the second and third centuries CE. Synagogue ownership is civic, as indicated by the following passage from *m. Ned.* 5:5, which I have mentioned already in chapter 3: "What are the things that belong to the town? For example, the town square, the bathhouse, the synagogue, the ark, and the scrolls." Civic ownership is further witnessed by *m. Meg.* 3:1 and *t. Meg.* 2:12. Moreover, *m. Ned.* 9:2 presumes that synagogues are public buildings that one would be expected to enter under normal circumstances.

Early rabbinic literature also indicates that the synagogue functions known from the Second-Temple-period sources continued on after 70 CE. The judicial function of synagogues and the meting out of corporal punishment in synagogue settings is indicated in *m. Mak.* 3:12, which interestingly also depicts the involvement of synagogue functionaries in corporal punishment. Similarly, *m. Shebu.* 4:10 describes the syna-

---

14. Cf. Meyers and Meyers, "Nabratein," 405–6.
15. *ASSB* no. 30. This is a reasonable suggestion despite the lack of direct evidence, since *bemas* with Torah shrines were common by the fourth century CE and could have emerged in the mid–second century.
16. Spigel, *Synagogue Seating Capacities*, 91, 95.
17. Ibid., 295.

gogue as a place where one could seek witnesses to give evidence on one's behalf. The practice of performing acts of charity in synagogue settings is also indicated by *t. Shab.* 16:22, though it should be noted that the Shammaites here are against charitable acts being done in synagogue settings. As discussed in chapter 3, the characteristic function of the synagogue, public reading from Jewish scriptures, is attested and discussed in the Mishnah and Tosefta.[18]

When we compare the literary and material evidence from the early post-Second-Temple period discussed in this excursus with the Second-Temple-period evidence discussed in chapters 2 and 3, we find that the basic form and functions of public synagogues did not change drastically after the destruction of the temple. We may confidently join the points of evidence from the Second Temple period to those discussed from the second and early third centuries with a robust thread of imagination. Thus, we may definitively conclude that public synagogues at the time when the Gospels were written were not significantly different from public synagogues at the time of Jesus. Simply put, the evidence does not support the notion that the depiction of synagogues in the Gospels is anachronistic.

18. See *m. Meg.* 4:5, 4:6; *t. Meg.* 2:18, 3:12, 3:21. Based on the mentions that readings take place in the synagogue in these passages, it is probable that the readings described throughout *Megillah* in both the Tosefta and Mishnah take place in synagogue settings. Note that readings from the Torah and Nevi'im are both discussed.

4

———

How "the Synagogue" Has Impacted the Study of Jesus in Previous Research: An Evaluation

Introduction

Although the present study is, to my knowledge, the first book-length study of the historical Jesus and the synagogue, research on the synagogue has sometimes impacted the study of Jesus and the Gospels. In recent years, there have also been a few article-length works that deal with or focus on the early synagogue in relation to Jesus research, as well as a couple of studies on Jesus that incorporate some elements of recent research on the synagogue. As the following survey will demonstrate, the question of the role of the synagogue in Jesus's aims has not yet been adequately addressed. Moreover, although there has been some awareness of the importance of the synagogue as a context for Jesus and the movement that formed around him in Galilee, no major attempts have yet been made in contemporary scholarship to interpret Jesus and his movement within a synagogue context in light of recent synagogue research.

Three Phases in Previous Scholarship

This chapter will concentrate specifically on how reconstructions of "the synagogue" have impacted the scholarly reconstruction of the historical Jesus. Particular attention will be paid to relatively recent scholarship, especially from 1990 onward. Older scholarship on the first-century synagogue tends to be complicated by the overuse of rabbinic sources in order to speak to common first-century practice.[1] Moreover, the greatest growth in the history of synagogue studies has come since the turn of the millennium in the form of several significant archaeological discoveries,[2] and the publication of a number of substantial studies.[3]

The history of the impact of reconstructions of the synagogue on the study of Jesus and the Gospels in previous scholarship can be roughly divided into three phases. In the first phase, "the synagogue" was conceived in relationship to "the church." During the second phase, scholars questioned the existence of synagogue buildings during the time of Jesus. This led to a charge of anachronism against Luke's portrayal of the synagogue, since Luke is the only one of the four evangelists to explicitly identify a building as a "synagogue." Throughout the third and most recent phase, scholars have attempted to recover the synagogue as a context for Jesus. However, this has typically been expressed

1. E.g., Schürer, *History of the Jewish People*, 2:52–83; Israel Abrahams, "The Freedom of the Synagogue," in *Studies in Pharisaism and the Gospels*, 2 vols. (Cambridge: Cambridge University Press, 1917), 1:1–17. This was part of a larger problematic trend in scholarship on Second Temple Judaism. On this, see Sanders, *Practice and Belief*, 10–12.
2. Remains of buildings identified as Second Temple synagogues discovered within the Land of Israel since 2000 include the structures at Qiryat Sefer (*ASSB* no. 35), Modi'in (*ASSB* no. 29), and Magdala. Additionally, remains of a synagogue dated to the late first century or early second century have also been discovered at Khirbet Qana (*ASSB* no. 3). See chapter 3 above.
3. Examples of book-length monograph studies with an emphasis on the ancient synagogue since 1999 include Binder, *Into the Temple Courts*; Runesson, *Origins*; Levine, *Ancient Synagogue*; Carsten Claussen, *Versammlung, Gemeinde, Synagoge*; Harland, *Associations, Synagogues, and Congregations*; Richardson, *Building Jewish*; Catto, *First-Century Synagogue*; Steven Fine, *Art and Judaism in the Greco-Roman World: Toward a New Jewish Archaeology*, 2nd ed. (Cambridge: Cambridge University Press, 2010); Hachlili, *Ancient Synagogues*. Examples of published essay collections on the synagogue include Steven Fine, ed., *Jews, Christians, and Polytheists in the Ancient Synagogue: Cultural Interaction during the Greco-Roman Period* (Baltimore Studies in the History of Judaism; London: Routledge, 1999); Howard Clark Kee and Lynn H. Cohick, eds., *Evolution of the Synagogue: Problems and Progress* (Harrisburg: Trinity Press International); Alan J. Avery-Peck and Jacob Neusner, eds., *Judaism in Late Antiquity*, Part 3, *Where We Stand: Issues and Debates in Ancient Judaism*, vol. 4, *The Special Problem of the Ancient Synagogue* (Leiden: Brill, 2001); Birger Olsson, and Magnus Zetterholm, eds., *The Ancient Synagogue From its Origins until 200 C.E.* (CBNTS 39; Stockholm: Almqvist & Wiksell, 2003). Three dissertation projects involving synagogue research have also recently been written at McMaster University, including Jonathan Bernier, *Aposynagōgos*; Korner, "Before Church"; and Andrew R. Krause, "Rhetoric, Spatiality, and the First-Century Synagogue: The Description and Narrative Use of Jewish Institutions in the Works of Flavius Josephus," (PhD diss., McMaster University, 2015). Bernier's dissertation research has since been published as Bernier, *Aposynagōgos*.

in terms of the authenticity or historical plausibility of the synagogue passages in the Gospels. A critical examination of these three phases will help to determine the direction of my own project by highlighting some problems, lacunae, and unanswered questions in previous scholarship on Jesus and the synagogue.

Phase One: Relating "The Synagogue" to "The Church"

Prior to the 1990s, the synagogue did not frequently enter as a major factor into discussions of the historical Jesus. When it did appear in studies of Jesus or the Gospels, it was often considered in terms of its relationship to the Christian "church," frequently as its foil or counterpart. It is worth noting that in some instances, the connection between the synagogue and Jesus or his followers, the early "church," is described in comparatively positive terms, wherein the synagogue is seen as the birthplace or prototype of the "church."[4] Some early scholarship, though conceiving of the Second Temple synagogue in light of later rabbinic material, even considers the synagogue to have been a positive and normative setting for Jesus's life and ministry.[5]

Despite this, anticipation of the eventual separation between "church" and "synagogue" is often found lurking behind even the more positive conceptions of the relationship between the two institutions. Thus, in what is probably the earliest example in modern academic scholarship of a study devoted specifically to the relationship between Jesus and the synagogue (circa 1900), Edwin Knox Mitchell follows a statement describing "the synagogue" as the precursor of "the church," with the unfortunate assertion that "the disciples of Jesus and the early converts to the Christian faith did not leave the synagogue until they were forced to do so by the hostility of those who refused to accept the gospel."[6]

It has sometimes been argued or assumed that the synagogue was dominated by the Pharisees, or that it was a Pharisaic institution.[7]

---

4. Examples from relatively early scholarship include Edwin Knox Mitchell, "The Jewish Synagogue and the Relation of Jesus to It," *The Biblical World* 16, no.1 (1900): 10–17, esp. 17; and Adolf Schlatter, *Der Glaube im Neuen Testament*, 2nd ed. (Stuttgart: Calwer Verlag, 1896), 7–8.

5. E.g., Mitchell, "Jewish Synagogue," 17; Donald Wayne Riddle, "Jesus in Modern Research," *The Journal of Religion* 17, no. 2 (1937): 170–82 (174).

6. Mitchell, "Jewish Synagogue," 17. Note also the somewhat anti-Jewish shift in tone in Schlatter's later work, wherein he pits "the church" against "the synagogue" and speaks of "the hollow pride of the synagogue," in Adolf Schlatter, *Die Theologie des Neuen Testaments. Zweiter Teil: Die Lehre der Apostel* (Calw & Stuttgart: Verlag der Vereinsbuchhandlung, 1910), 239, 242.

7. E.g., Kee, "Transformation of the Synagogue," 14ff., Gutmann, "Synagogue Origins," 4; R. Travers Herford, *The Pharisees* (London: G. Allen, 1924), 88–109; Robert M. Grant, *Historical Introduction to*

Since the Pharisees are depicted as major antagonists of Jesus in the Gospels, such an understanding results in a portrayal of the synagogue as hostile to Jesus and his later followers. This type of reconstruction is exemplified by the work of Ellis Rivkin. Rivkin considers the synagogue to be *"exclusively a Pharisaic institution,"*[8] and thus, reads the Gospel passages pertaining to the synagogue in light of perceived conflict with the Pharisaic-dominated synagogue. His key piece of evidence for this is the mention of fear of being "cast out of the synagogue" (ἀποσυνάγωγοι γένωνται) "because of the Pharisees" (διὰ τοὺς Φαρισαίους) in John 12:42.[9] Passages such as this one and Matthew 23:34 are treated as evidence of conflict between the synagogue and the Christian community.[10] The conflict, however, began with Jesus himself, who engaged the Pharisees within their own synagogues.[11]

There are two consequences for the study of the historical Jesus that come as a result of such a proposal. First, in seeing passages such as John 12:42 and Matthew 23:34 as having historical referents in the time of the evangelists, Rivkin presents a challenge to the reliability of these passages as evidence for events that took place during the life of Jesus. Second, the interpretation of the synagogue as adverse to Jesus and his followers transforms the synagogue from being Jesus's social context into the seat of the opposition against him and an institution to be confronted.

This is a problematic perspective. In the first place, it is built upon the tenuous foundations of the hypothesis of virtual Pharisaic primacy and control in the Land during the late Second Temple period.[12] Second, the evidence connecting the Pharisees with synagogue governance is very thin.[13] The Pharisees are neither consistently nor frequently connected to the synagogues in the Gospels.[14] Matthew 23:34

the New Testament (New York: Harper & Row, 1963), 274–75; Martin Hengel, *The Pre-Christian Paul,* (London: SCM, 1991), 57; Martin Hengel and Roland Deines, "E. P. Sanders' 'Common Judaism,'" *JTS* 46, no. 1 (1995): 1–70 (32–33). Against this position, see Sanders, *Practice and Belief,* 399–412, esp. 401, cf. 450; Richard A. Horsley, "Synagogues in Galilee and the Gospels," in *Evolution of the Synagogue: Problems and Progress,* ed. Howard Clark Kee and Lynn H. Cohick (Harrisburg: Trinity Press International, 1999), 46–69 (64–69).

8. Rivkin, *A Hidden Revolution,* 103, emphasis original. This understanding of the synagogue is also featured in his earlier work, Ellis Rivkin, "Ben Sira and the Non-Existence of the Synagogue: A Study in Historical Method," in *In the Time of the Harvest: Essays in honor of Abba Hillel Silver on the Occasion of his 70th Birthday* (ed. D.J. Silver; New York: Macmillan, 1963), 320–54.

9. Rivkin, *Hidden Revolution,* 103.

10. Ibid., 103–4; 269–71.

11. Ibid., 275.

12. This has been severely critiqued by Sanders, *Practice and Belief,* 448–51; 458–90.

13. See also Horsley, "Synagogues in Galilee," 64–69; Levine, *Ancient Synagogue,* 41.

14. In agreement, see Shaye J. D. Cohen, "Were Pharisees and Rabbis the Leaders of Communal Prayer

and John 12:42 need not be interpreted as evidence for the Pharisaic control of the synagogue. It is much more likely that they simply indicate the threat of conflict between the Jesus movement and Pharisees within a public synagogue context, as in Mark 3:1–6 (cf. Matt 12:9–14, Luke 6:6–11).

The fear of being cast out of the synagogue in John 9:22, 12:42, and 16:2 is rendered all but unintelligible if the synagogue is understood to be an exclusively Pharisaic institution. Why would followers of Jesus, presumably non-Pharisees, be so gravely concerned about being excluded from Pharisaic gatherings? Outside of the Gospels, one finds even less of a connection. There is no clear evidence from the Second Temple period linking synagogue rule or offices directly with the Pharisees.

The basic notion of the existence of evidence of conflict between "the synagogue" and "the church" within the Gospels has had a significant effect upon the study of the historical Jesus. The work of J. Louis Martyn on the *aposynagōgos* passages in the Gospel of John has been especially influential in this.[15] His seminal work, *History and Theology in the Fourth Gospel* has had three editions, originally appearing in 1968, with a revised and enlarged edition released in 1979, and a third edition as recently as 2003.[16] The third edition, released thirty-five years after the original publication, is a testament to the lasting influence that this study has enjoyed.[17]

Martyn argues that the passages in John that refer to the threat of expulsion from the synagogue (the state of *aposynagōgos*) reflect the history of the late-first-century Johannine community, whose members have been excluded from participation in synagogues due to the institution of the *birkat ha-minim* ("Benediction against Heretics") by the post-70 CE rabbinic leadership at Yavneh. This position is outlined in a chapter revealingly titled "He is Excluded from the Synagogue and Enters the Church,"[18] which is itself contained within a section named "A Synagogue-Church Drama: Erecting the Wall of Separation."[19] These

and Torah Study in Antiquity?" in *Evolution of the Synagogue: Problems and Progress* (ed. Howard Clark Kee and Lynn H. Cohick; Harrisburg: Trinity Press International, 1999), 89–105.

15. John 9:22, 12:42, and 16:2.

16. J. Louis Martyn, *History and Theology in the Fourth Gospel* (New York: Harper & Row, 1968); J. Louis Martyn, *History and Theology in the Fourth Gospel*, rev. and enl. ed. (Nashville: Abingdon, 1979); J. Louis Martyn, *History and Theology in the Fourth Gospel*, 3rd ed. (Classics of the New Testament Library; Louisville: Westminster John Knox, 2003). Unless otherwise stated, references will be to the third edition. The original publication date in 1968 is, however, important to note.

17. On this, see D. Moody Smith, "The Contribution of J. Louis Martyn for Understanding the Gospel of John," in *History and Theology in the Fourth Gospel*, 3rd ed.; (Classics of the New Testament Library; Louisville: Westminster John Knox, 2003), 1–19.

titles are indicative of Martyn's understanding of "the synagogue" primarily in terms of an adversative relationship to "the church" within the context of his historical analysis.

Martyn's hypothesis has not only influenced the way in which the *aposynagōgos* passages are read in mainstream historical scholarship, but also how the Fourth Gospel has been read. It advances a two-level reading of John's narrative, wherein the first level refers to the events of the life of Jesus, while the second level refers to the events of the history of the Johannine community in the period after 70 CE.[20] This two-level reading of the Johannine narrative has been remarkably impactful, and the interpretation of the *aposynagōgos* passages as references to events pertaining to an expulsion of Johannine Christians from synagogues has been followed by a number of scholars, even into the present time.[21] Although the direct identification of the *aposynagōgos* passages with the *birkat ha-minim* has not been affirmed by all of these scholars, the core notion that the *aposynagōgos* passages are evidence that the Fourth Gospel can be read on two levels is commonly presumed.

The hermeneutical mode of reading John on two different levels has complicated the use of John as a historical source for the events of the life of Jesus. It becomes difficult to determine what elements of the data can or should be attributed to the time of Jesus, since it is unclear precisely how and to what extent the events that have occurred on the

18. Martyn, *History and Theology*, 46–66. The "He" here refers to the man born blind introduced in John 9:1.

19. Martyn, *History and Theology*, 33–66.

20. Cf. Martyn, *History and Theology*, 38–40.

21. Anderson, *The Fourth Gospel and the Quest for Jesus*; John Ashton, *Understanding the Fourth Gospel*, 2nd ed. (Oxford: Oxford University Press, 2007); Raymond Brown, *Community of the Beloved Disciple: The Life, Loves, and Hates of an Individual Church in New Testament Times* (New York: Paulist, 1979); Raymond Brown, *An Introduction to the Gospel of John*, ed. Francis J. Maloney (New York: Doubleday, 2003); Marius Heemstra, *The Fiscus Judaicus and the Parting of the Ways* (Tübingen: Mohr Siebeck, 2010); Joel Marcus, "*Birkat ha-Minim* Revisited,' *NTS* 55 (2009): 523–51; Kloppenborg, "Disaffiliation in Associations,"; David Rensberger, *Johannine Faith and Liberating Community* (Philadelphia: Westminster, 1988); Lance Byron Richey, *Roman Imperial Ideology and the Gospel of John* (Washington, DC: Catholic Biblical Association of America, 2007). In addition to these instances of scholars who have followed Martyn in a more direct fashion, Bernier has identified a number of scholars who he considers to be "Neo-Martynian," insofar as they follow Martyn's two-level approach, but do not consider there to have been mechanisms in place for formal expulsion from the synagogue either during the time of Jesus, nor in the period immediately following 70 CE. Examples include Carter, *John and Empire*; Raimo Hakola, *Identity Matters: John, the Jews, and Jewishness* (Leiden: Brill, 2005); Raimo Hakola and Adele Reinhartz, "John's Pharisees," in *In Quest of the Historical Pharisees*, ed. Jacob Neusner and Bruce D. Chilton (Waco: Baylor University Press, 2007), 131–47; Adele Reinhartz, "Reading History in the Fourth Gospel," in *What We Have Heard from the Beginning: The Past, Present, and Future of Johannine Studies*, ed. Tom Thatcher (Waco: Baylor University Press, 2007), 190–94; Tom Thatcher, *Greater Than Caesar: Christology and Empire in the Fourth Gospel* (Minneapolis: Fortress Press, 2009); Thatcher, *Why John Wrote a* Gospel. See Bernier, *Aposynagōgos*, 12–13.

second level have impacted the narrative of the first level.[22] As Klink has aptly stated the matter, there appears to be a tendency for the second level of history, that of the community, to "eclipse" the first level, that of the life of Jesus.[23]

The Martynian hypothesis has had the side-effect of cutting the Johannine Jesus off from his context within the synagogue of his day. The two-level reading of the *aposynagōgos* passages abstracts the Johannine Jesus and those who followed him during his lifetime from the conflict that occurred within the synagogue, and which appears in different narrative forms in the synoptic Gospels. The lack of references within *History and Theology in the Fourth Gospel* to the passages in John's narrative which situate Jesus and his teaching within the synagogue is noteworthy in light of this fact.[24] Taken within the Johannine narrative context, the *aposynagōgos* passages describe a fear of serious religio-political consequences resulting from a conflict between the Jesus group and the influential Pharisees within a synagogue context. The abstraction of this data to a second historical level removes it from our potential evidence concerning Jesus and the movement that surrounded him before his death.

This same tendency to consider the presentation of the synagogue in the Gospels primarily in light of the relationship between "the synagogue" and "the church" can also be detected in an article by Charles Perrot, titled "La synagogue dans le Nouveau Testament," which appeared in a special synagogue-oriented issue of *Le Monde de la Bible* in 1989.[25] Perrot's concern is with ruptures and continuity, the latter of which is conceived mostly in terms of the reading of scripture in both institutions, between "the Church" ("l'Église") and "the Synagogue ("la Synagogue"). In the Gospels, his focus is primarily on a particular Lukan motif that he calls "de la Synagogue aux nations,"[26] the movement of the Christian community out of the synagogue to the gentiles.

Perrot reads the Lukan narrative of Jesus in the synagogue at Nazareth as an early announcement of this theme.[27] In his estimation, the Lukan narrative of Jesus teaching in the synagogues of Galilee and

---

22. Cf. Blomberg, *Historical Reliability of John's Gospel*, 62.

23. Edward W. Klink III, "The Overrealized Expulsion in the Gospel of John," in *Aspects of Historicity in the Fourth Gospel* (Early Christianity and Its Literature 2; ed. Paul N. Anderson, Felix Just, and Tom Thatcher; vol. 2 of *John Jesus and History*; Atlanta: Society of Biblical Literature, 2009), 175–84 (175).

24. John 6:59, 18:20.

25. Charles Perrot, "La synagogue dans le Nouveau Testament," *Le Monde De la Bible* 57 (1989): 36–39.

26. Ibid., 36.

27. Ibid.

being *expelled* from the synagogue at Nazareth exemplifies a pattern, which is systematized in Acts through the accounts of Paul encountering violent resistance when teaching in the synagogues of the diaspora. Thus, Jesus's expulsion from the synagogue is indicative of the beginning of the rupture between "church" and "synagogue." Although Perrot is not explicitly making a historical claim about Jesus here, it is notable that this interpretation approximates a Martynian two-level reading, though with reference to Luke and early Pauline Christianity rather than the Johannine community. As with Martyn, interpreting the data in this way tends toward the abstraction of Jesus and his earliest followers from their historical context within the synagogues of the Land.

Phase Two: The Existence of Synagogue Buildings and the Charge of Anachronism

Throughout much of the 1990s, scholarship on Jesus and the synagogue was primarily concerned with whether or not there were synagogue buildings before 70 CE, and if the references to *synagōgai* in the gospels should be understood to refer to open-air assemblies rather than structures. The scholar most associated with this perspective is Howard Clark Kee, who first published on this topic in *NTS* in 1990,[28] and would later restate his position in another *NTS* article in 1995.[29] Responses to Kee's work also appeared in *NTS*, first by Richard Oster in 1993,[30] to whom Kee offered a response in 1994,[31] and later by Kenneth Atkinson in 1997.[32]

The primary significance of this position for the study of Jesus and the Gospels is that if Kee is correct, then the descriptions of synagogue buildings and practices as seen in Luke-Acts do not belong in a pre-70 CE context within the land, but have been imported from a post-70 diaspora milieu.[33] Luke alone, among the evangelists, uses *synagōgē* to refer unequivocally to buildings, once in a setting within the Land (Luke 7:5) and once within the diaspora (Acts 18:7). If Luke's presenta-

---

28. Kee, "Transformation of the Synagogue," 1–24.
29. Howard Clark Kee, "Defining the First-Century CE Synagogue: Problems and Progress," *NTS* 41 (1995): 481–500.
30. Richard E. Oster, "Supposed Anachronism," 178–208.
31. Howard Clark Kee, "The Changing Meaning of Synagogue: A Response to Richard Oster," *NTS* 40 (1994): 281–83.
32. Kenneth Atkinson, "On Further Defining the First-Century Synagogue: Fact or Fiction? A Rejoinder to H.C. Kee," *NTS* 43 (1997): 491–502.
33. Kee, "Transformation of the Synagogue," 18–19.

tion of the synagogue is anachronistic and anatopic, then the reliability of Luke-Acts as a source for the early synagogue and for Jesus's interaction with the synagogue (e.g., Luke 4:16–30) would be called into question.

Kee's hypothesis hinges on a late dating of *CIJ* 2.1404, also known as the Theodotos Inscription.[34] This inscription, discovered in Jerusalem by the Weill excavations in 1913, clearly uses the word *synagōgē* to refer to an edifice, since it mentions that a donor, Theodotos, *built* the *synagōgē* (ᾠκοδόμησε τὴν συναγωγὴν) to which the inscription was attached. It is also typically dated to the first century CE.[35] Kee dates the inscription to the late second to early third centuries CE on the authority of unnamed "responsible archaeologists and epigraphers who saw it prior to publication."[36]

The hypothesis of the nonexistence of synagogue buildings in the Second Temple period has largely been rejected in current scholarship. The early negative evaluations of Kee's work in *NTS* by Oster and Atkinson are indicative of this.[37] Oster's identification of the use of *synagōgē* to refer to a structure rather than an assembly in an inscription from Berenike (*CJZC* 72), which mentions repairs (ἐπισκευὴν) made to a *synagōgē* during the reign of Nero, constitutes significant evidence against Kee's position.[38] The basic problem identified by most scholars is that the evidence speaks against the hypothesis,[39] as there are numerous data that witness to the existence of synagogue buildings prior to 70 CE and to the use of *synagōgē* to refer to structures.[40]

Another serious objection came with the publication of Kloppenborg's study on the date of the Theodotos Inscription.[41] Kloppenborg is able to conclude that "Consideration of the stratigraphy of the site of the discovery virtually rules out a date later than 70 CE."[42] Moreover,

34. See also *ASSB*, no. 26.
35. Refer to the original publication by Gustav Adolf Deissmann, *Light from the Ancient East: the New Testament Illustrated by Recently Discovered Texts of the Graeco-Roman World*, 4th ed. (New York: George H. Doran, 1927), 439–41.
36. Kee, "Transformation of the Synagogue," 7. Cf. his similar statements in Kee, "Defining," 8.
37. Oster, "Supposed Anachronism," and Atkinson, "Further Defining."
38. Oster, "Supposed Anachronism," 187–88. According to Kloppenborg Verbin, "Dating Theodotos," 248, this inscription is "at the least an exception to the rule that Kee proposes, and at worst it is fatal to his thesis."
39. E.g., E. P. Sanders, *Jewish Law*, 341–43; Riesner, "Synagogues in Jerusalem," 179–210; Binder, *Into the Temple Courts*, 92–111; P. W. van der Horst, "Was the Synagogue a Place of Sabbath Worship Before 70 C.E.?" in *Jews, Christians, and Polytheists: Cultural Interaction during the Greco-Roman Period*, (ed. Steven Fine; London: Routledge, 1999), 18–43; Runesson, *Origins*, 149–52; Lee I. Levine, "The First-Century Synagogue," 70–102; Catto, *First-Century Synagogue*, 152–98; Bernier, *Aposynagōgos*, 56–57.
40. Luke 7:5; Acts 18:7; *CJZC* 72; Philo, *Quod omnis* 81; Josephus, *War*, 2.285, 2.289.
41. Kloppenborg, "Dating Theodotos."

the paleography of the inscription indicates a date within the Herodian or early Roman periods.[43] This confirmation of the pre-70 CE date of the Theodotos Inscription and its use of *synagōgē* to refer unequivocally to a building militates against Kee's position and the charge of anachronism and geographical displacement in Luke-Acts' depiction of synagogues.

Despite the objections raised against it and its eventual rejection in mainstream scholarship, the hypothesis that *synagōgē* referred to informal meetings and that synagogue buildings did not exist during the time of Jesus had supporters in the 1990s, most notably Heather McKay,[44] L. Michael White,[45] and Carsten Claussen.[46] Richard Horsley likewise rejects the existence of synagogue *buildings* in the Second Temple period, but nevertheless recognizes that there were formal, religio-political synagogue gatherings in this period.[47]

Although Kee's proposal has not been well received by most scholars of ancient synagogues, it is important to recognize the significant impact that it has had upon the study of Jesus and the synagogue. The debate over the existence of synagogue buildings in the Land prior to 70 CE, and the charge of inaccuracy against Luke-Acts' portrayal of the synagogue took place over a decade. This has had the effect of delaying progress on the application of synagogue studies to historical Jesus research and of muddying the waters with respect to the interpretation of the material evidence for early synagogues.

In 2007, Stephen K. Catto published a monograph titled *Reconstructing the First-Century Synagogue: A Critical Analysis of Current Research.*[48] As the title indicates, this work is an analysis of previous scholarship on the basis of the extant evidence. It is, however, questionable as to whether or not the analysis presented here is of research that would

---

42. Ibid., 276.
43. Ibid., 276–77.
44. McKay, "Ancient Synagogues," passim; McKay, *Sabbath and Synagogue*, passim.
45. L. Michael White, "Reading the Ostia Synagogue: A Reply to A. Runesson," *Harvard Theological Review* 92 (1992): 222–37; L. Michael White, *The Social Origins of Christian Architecture*, 2 vols. (Valley Forge: Trinity Press International, 1996–1997); L. Michael White, "Synagogue and Society in Imperial Ostia: Archaeology and Epigraphic Evidence," *Harvard Theological Review* 92 (1999): 409–33.
46. Carsten Claussen, *Versammlung, Gemeinde, Synagoge*; Claussen, "Meeting, Community," 144–67.
47. Horsley, *Galilee*, 222–37, cf. Horsley, *Archaeology, History, and Society*, 131–53. This general rejection of the identification of synagogue buildings has continued to persist in his more recent work, despite the recent advances in synagogue scholarship and the discovery of buildings identified as synagogues since the turn of the millennium, e.g., Horsley, *Jesus: Power, People, and Performance* (Minneapolis: Fortress Press, 2008), 92; Horsley and Thatcher, *John, Jesus, and the Renewal of Israel*, 29n19. In the latter, note that the more recent discoveries at Qiryat Sefer, Modi'in, and Magdala (II) are not mentioned.
48. Catto, *First-Century Synagogue*.

have been current at the time of its publication.[49] Catto's primary concern throughout is with the evaluation of the minimalist perspective on the existence of pre-70 CE synagogue buildings espoused by Kee, White, Horsley, Claussen, and McKay.[50] This is because the focus of his project is the application of synagogue research to New Testament studies,[51] which is carried out in the form of an evaluation of the charge of anachronism brought against Luke-Acts' depiction of the synagogue.[52]

On the basis of his review of the evidence, Catto concludes that synagogue buildings existed in the Land in the first century, and that Luke-Acts is neither anachronistic nor anatopistic in its portrayal of the pre-70 CE synagogue in the Land.[53] However, he also soberly cautions against the immediate assumption that whenever Jesus or Paul is said to enter a synagogue in Luke-Acts, a building is to be imagined.[54]

Although Catto's conclusion is convincing and agreeable, he has covered little new ground.[55] Moreover, it is difficult to escape the sense that despite its title, Catto's monograph is not so much engaged with scholarship current in 2007 as it is with the minimalist position that was more current in the 1990s.[56] As we have seen, this had already been the focus of substantial critiques and it is reasonable to consider it to have been a minority position at best by 2007. More problematic is its insufficient discussion of terminological issues and definitions.[57] This

---

49. The view that this work is lacking in certain respects as a review of *current* (circa 2007) research is reflected in the reviews that appeared in *RBL*: Jonathan Bernier, review of Stephen K. Catto, *Reconstructing the First-Century Synagogue: A Critical Analysis of Current Research, RBL*, November 16, 2008; Birger Olsson, review of Stephen K. Catto, *Reconstructing the First-Century Synagogue: A Critical Analysis of Current Research, RBL*, November 16, 2008. Bernier's comment on the matter in his review is pointed: "for a monograph on the current state of 'synagogue' research, one would like to see more in the way of current 'synagogue' research."

50. Cf. Catto, *First-Century Synagogue*, 2–5.

51. Ibid., 13.

52. Ibid., 152–98.

53. Ibid., 194–98.

54. Catto, *First-Century Synagogue*, 195.

55. Cf. Olsson, review of *Reconstructing the First-Century Synagogue* (by Catto).

56. Thus, note the lack of references made by Catto to then-recent publications on synagogue archaeology. E.g., on Delos, Monika Trümper, "The Oldest Synagogue Building in the Diaspora: The Delos Synagogue Reconsidered," *Hesperia* 74, no. 4 (2004): 513–98. On Capernaum, Jodi Magness, "The Question of the Synagogue: The Problem of Typology," in *The Special Problem of the Ancient Synagogue* (vol. 4 of *Judaism in Late Antiquity*, Part 3: *Where We Stand: Issues and Debates in Ancient Judaism*; ed. Alan J. Avery-Peck and Jacob Neusner; Leiden: Brill, 2001), 1–48; Jodi Magness, "A Response to Eric M. Meyers and James F. Strange," in *The Special Problem of the Ancient Synagogue* (vol. 4 of *Judaism in Late Antiquity*, Part 3: *Where We Stand: Issues and Debates in Ancient Judaism* (ed. Alan J. Avery-Peck and Jacob Neusner; Leiden: Brill, 2001), 79–91; Anders Runesson, "Architecture, Conflict, and Identity Formation: Jews and Christians in Capernaum From the 1st to the 6th Century," in *The Ancient Galilee in Interaction: Religion, Ethnicity, and Identity*, ed. Harold W. Attridge, Dale Martin, and Jürgen Zangenberg (Tübingen: Mohr Siebeck, 2007), 231–57.

57. Cf. Olsson, review of *Reconstructing the First-Century Synagogue* (by Catto).

is apparent in Catto's failure to address the then-emerging question of the competing definitions of the synagogue as either a voluntary association or public institution.[58]

Despite its shortcomings, Catto's study should nevertheless be seen as the final closing word on the debate over the existence of synagogue buildings before 70 CE and the charge of anachronism or anatopism against Luke-Acts' depiction of the synagogue. The plausible relevance of Luke-Acts' synagogue passages for studies concerning the Second Temple period has been sufficiently and confidently demonstrated at this juncture. Catto's monograph thus stands as evidence of the length and breadth of the delaying effect that Kee's minimalistic proposal, first published in 1990, has had on the application of current research on the synagogue to the study of Jesus. If progress is to be made toward this end, it is imperative that scholarship move past the debate over the existence of synagogue buildings before 70 CE.

Phase Three: Authenticity, Plausibility, and the Recovery of the Synagogue as a Context for Jesus's Galilean Ministry

The significant advances in synagogue studies around and since the turn of the millennium have brought about new opportunities to apply current research on early synagogues to the study of the historical Jesus. Along with the advancements of knowledge has finally come a trickle of works that deal with the topic of the historical Jesus and the Second-Temple-period synagogue. However, as the following survey will show, New Testament scholars have been surprisingly slow to incorporate the majority of the new material into the study of Jesus and the Gospels. There have nevertheless been some noteworthy exceptions. The typical concern of the majority of scholarly works that deal with the historical Jesus and the synagogue since the turn of the millennium has been the *authenticity* of passages in the Gospels which involve the synagogue.

The influential volume titled *Jesus and Archaeology*, published in 2006,[59] contains an article by James Dunn that directly addresses the

---

58. The currency of this issue in the early and mid-2000s is exemplified by (e.g.) Peter Richardson, "An Architectural Case for Synagogues as Associations," in *The Ancient Synagogue From Its Origins Until 200 C.E.: Papers Presented at an International Conference at Lund University, October 14–17, 2001* (ed. Birger Olsson, and Magnus Zetterholm; Coniectanea Biblica New Testament Series 39; Stockholm: Almqvist & Wiksell, 2003), 90–117; Levine, *Ancient Synagogue* (2005); in which a case for synagogues as public institutions is made; and Runesson, *Origins* (2001).

59. James H. Charlesworth, ed., *Jesus and Archaeology* (Grand Rapids: Eerdmans, 2006).

relationship between the historical Jesus and the synagogue.[60] The article's purpose, as communicated by the article's title, is to answer one particular question: "Did Jesus attend the synagogue?" Dunn's investigation produces a positive answer to this question. He undertakes the task of answering this question by posing two subordinate questions: 1) "Can we speak of 'Galilean Judaism'?" and 2) "Were there synagogues in first-century Galilee?"[61] It must be noted that the concerns addressed by asking the question in this way are *authenticity* and *definition*. At stake is the historical accuracy of the Gospels' depiction of Jesus as regularly attending, preaching, and teaching in the synagogue, and the validity of the translation of the Greek term *synagōgē* by the English term "synagogue," which Dunn equates with buildings that were used for worship, reading Torah, and prayer.[62]

Although his conclusions are generally persuasive, there are two major issues that limit the usefulness of Dunn's study as an examination of the historical Jesus's relationship to the synagogue. In the first place, the endeavour is an instantiation of the scissors-and-paste approach to history.[63] By aiming only to prevent testimony from being jettisoned, this approach makes its contribution entirely on the level of the data without going beyond it toward historical reconstruction and interpretation of the data.[64] While this sort of study is not problematic in itself, it leaves much to be determined and understood. Thus, the reader is left without a sense of where or how the data fits into the life, aims, and mission of the historical Jesus, nor why it matters at all. Second, by phrasing his answer to the primary question in terms of the two particular subordinate questions that he poses, Dunn ends up reviewing ground that had already been extensively covered by other scholars. As a result, there is virtually no new territory explored by his study.

Contained within the pages of the four-volume *Handbook for the Study of the Historical Jesus*, published in 2011, is a chapter contributed by Graham Twelftree, aptly titled "Jesus and the Synagogue."[65] This chapter's promising purpose, as described by the author, "is to set out what we can know about the synagogue in the time and place of the ministry of

---

60. James D. G. Dunn, "Did Jesus Attend the Synagogue?" in *Jesus and Archaeology* (Grand Rapids: Eerdmans, 2006), 206–22.
61. Ibid., 206.
62. Ibid., 216–17.
63. See Collingwood, *Idea of History*, 257–61. Cf. also Lonergan, *Method in Theology*, 205–6.
64. On this, see appendix A. The issue was also covered briefly in chapter 1.
65. Graham H. Twelftree, "Jesus and the Synagogue," in *Handbook for the Study of the Historical Jesus* (ed. Tom Holmén, and Stanley E. Porter; Leiden and Boston: Brill, 2011), 4:3105–34.

the historical Jesus so that, in conjunction with an examination of the gospel data, this information can be used to help shed light on Jesus through understanding his relationship with the synagogue."[66]

Before turning to the Gospel data, Twelftree first undertakes an analysis of archaeological and literary data external to the Gospels pertaining to the Second Temple synagogue. There is much to be commended in this endeavour. Most importantly, Twelftree refers to and makes use of current works and advances in synagogue scholarship, especially Runesson's distinction between public and semi-public synagogues.[67]

Although Twelftree's treatment of the external synagogue evidence is informative, his examination of the Gospel data is methodologically problematic. On the passages in the Gospels concerning Jesus and the synagogue, he writes, "a critical examination of this material shows that many references cannot be traced back to the earliest traditions about Jesus."[68] As this statement indicates, Twelftree's primary concern in his treatment of the Gospel data is *authenticity*. In support of this statement, he cites Jürgen Becker's assertion that "most of the statements that put Jesus in the synagogue are redactional."[69] This citation is indicative of the methodological procedure that Twelftree applies to the Gospel material. Redaction criticism is the primary tool that he employs for his historical investigation.[70] The end result of his analysis is shockingly minimalistic, as the only Gospel data that he admits as authentic are Luke 11:43, Mark 12:38–39, and Mark 1:23–27.[71] Of these passages, only Mark 1:23–27 actually locates Jesus within a synagogue, since Luke 11:43 and Mark 12:38–39 are both sayings expressing criticism of people who seek honor within synagogue settings.

The extreme minimalistic findings of Twelftree's study require a response, since I will be examining much of the data that he regards as inauthentic in this project. Even if we set aside the problems associated with a scissors-and-paste approach to history, redaction criticism is at best an imperfect method for the craft of history, and its use as a his-

---

66. Ibid., 4:3105.
67. Ibid., 4:3110, no. 33. The distinction between public and semi-public synagogues is employed throughout the chapter.
68. Ibid., 4:3125.
69. Ibid., 3125, no. 154; Jürgen Becker, *Jesus of Nazareth*, trans. James E. Crouch (New York and Berlin: Walter de Gruyter, 1998), 29.
70. On the perceived relevance of redaction criticism for historical Jesus studies, see the now dated discussion in Perrin, *What Is Redaction Criticism?*, 68–74.
71. Twelftree, "Jesus and the Synagogue," 4:3132.

torical tool has been critiqued.[72] It is important to recognize that much like form and source criticism, its genetic relatives, redaction criticism is properly a literary tool in design.[73] It was not originally intended for historiographical purposes.[74] Moreover, redaction criticism's basis in form criticism[75] opens its use as a historical tool up to the problems which have been raised concerning form criticism's use within historical Jesus research,[76] and the general problems that have been raised concerning the form-critical paradigm.[77]

One of the difficulties with the use of redaction criticism as a historical method is that it typically requires the criterion of dissimilarity in order to operate.[78] Redaction criticism can be useful for determining the interests or emphases of the individual evangelists or the tendencies of the transmission and remembering process of the early followers of Jesus. However, this alone does not actually tell us anything directly about the historical character of the data. At the very least, a tacit application of the principle of dissimilarity is required in order for this information to have a bearing on the question of authenticity.[79] Once dissimilarity is thrown into the mix, any traditions or elements that reflect the interests or beliefs of the evangelists or the early Jesus movement are excluded, which by logical extension includes any cases in which redactional activity can be detected.

Dissimilarity alone, however, is a shaky foundation, and its *negative* application has been subject to severe criticism.[80] Some scholars have

---

72. E.g., Hooker, 570–81, esp. 579; Birger Gerhardsson, *The Reliability of the Gospel Tradition* (Grand Rapids: Baker Academic, 2001), 82–86; D. A. Carson, "Redaction Criticism: On the Legitimacy and Illegitimacy of a Literary Tool," in *Scripture and Truth*, ed. D. A. Carson and John D. Woodbridge (Grand Rapids: Baker, 1992), 119–42; Stephen Smith, "The Changing Face of Redaction Criticism," *Churchman* 107 (1993): 130–45; Craig L. Blomberg, *The Historical Reliability of the Gospels*, 2nd ed. (Downers Grove: IVP Academic, 2007), 68–75.

73. Cf. Chris Keith, "Indebtedness," 33; Hooker, "Wrong Tool."

74. This can be grasped upon review of the history of the development of redaction criticism, esp. in relation to form criticism, in Perrin, *Redaction Criticism*, 1–39.

75. Ibid., 1–24, cf. 71.

76. See esp. Hooker, "Wrong Tool," Keith, "Indebtedness," and Calvert, "Examination of the Criteria," 209–19.

77. Much of the problematization of the form-critical paradigm has come about as a result of developments in research on social memory theory and orality. E.g., Christopher Tuckett, "Form Criticism," in *Jesus and Memory: Traditions in Oral and Scribal Perspectives*, ed. Werner Kelber and Samuel Byrskog (Waco: Baylor University Press, 2009), 21–38; Alan Kirk, "Memory," in *Handbook for the Study of the Historical Jesus*, 4 vols., ed. Tom Holmén and Stanley E. Porter (Leiden and Boston: Brill, 2011), 1:809–42, esp. 813; Werner H. Kelber, *The Oral and the Written Gospel: The Hermeneutics of Speaking and Writing in the Synoptic Tradition, Mark, Paul, and Q* (Bloomington: Indiana University Press, 1983).

78. Cf. Hooker, "Wrong Tool," 579; Black, "Redaction Criticism," 491–94.

79. Cf. Black, "Redaction Criticism," 494.

80. E.g., Hooker, "Wrong Tool"; Calvert, "Examination"; Craig A. Evans, "Authenticity Criteria in Life of Jesus Research," *Christian Scholar's Review* 19, no. 1 (1989): 6–31; Theissen and Merz, *Historical*

even proposed that, on the contrary, traditions that bear *similarity* to Second Temple Judaism or that evince continuity between Jesus and his early followers are plausibly authentic.[81]

Twelftree's historical investigation assumes that evidence of redactional activity is evidence of inauthenticity.[82] In my opinion, redaction criticism has a place in Jesus research insofar as it can show us how the evangelists, or early Christian communities, remembered and shaped the material that went into the Gospels. However, evidence of redactional shaping is not evidence of total inauthenticity. The insights of social memory theory have shown that the Gospel material, as with any memory, has been shaped and interpreted through the process of remembering, but this does not mean that there is no original event being remembered. Moreover, we cannot exclude the very real possibility that redactional activity might be corrective or undertaken with additional historical knowledge.[83] Thus, as Gerhardsson writes, "as far as redactional operations are concerned, they need not have been totally unhistorical. Such changes could also be made with knowledge of historical realities."[84]

An example of this can be seen in Twelftree's interpretation of Matthew 9:35. He determines that Matthew 9:35 relies upon Mark 6:6b, and thus, concludes that in this case, "we are taken no further back towards the historical Jesus than Matthew's creativity."[85] This is a problematic claim. The fact that Matthew 9:35 is generically related to Mark 6:6 does not mean that it cannot be evidence of Jesus's activities in the synagogues of Galilee. Noting that a witness' statement differs

---

Jesus, 115ff.; Wright, *Jesus and the Victory of God*, 131–33; E.P. Sanders, *Jesus and Judaism* (Minneapolis: Fortress Press, 1985), 16, 145; Stanley E. Porter, "A Dead End or a New Beginning? Examining the Criteria for Authenticity in Light of Albert Schweitzer," in *Jesus Research: An International Perspective*, vol. 1, ed. James H. Charlesworth and Petr Pokorný (Grand Rapids: Eerdmans, 2009), 16–35 (25–28); Winter, "Saving the Quest for Authenticity," *passim*; cf. the critique of the criterion of embarrassment by Rafael Rodríguez, "The Embarrassing Truth About Jesus: The Criterion of Embarrassment and the Failure of Historical Authenticity," in *Jesus, Criteria, and the Demise of Authenticity*, ed. Chris Keith and Anthony Le Donne (London and New York: T&T Clark, 2012), 132–51. This criterion is so commonly critiqued that an exhaustive list is neither possible nor necessary for the present purposes. Note, however, that the positive use of the criterion (i.e., to indicate the historical plausibility of a passage) has not been subjected to the same level of criticism.

81. Gerd Theissen and Dagmar Winter, *The Quest for the Plausible Jesus: The Question of Criteria*, trans. M. Eugene Boring (Louisville: Westminster John Knox, 2002), 172–225; Theissen and Merz, *Historical Jesus*, 117ff.; Wright, *Jesus and the Victory of God*, 131–33.

82. Cf. his treatment of the Lucan material on pp. 4:3126–28. Typically, where Twelftree considers a statement to have been modified from or modelled on an earlier statement made in Mark or Q, he renders a judgment of inauthenticity. The same can be said for instances in which something has been added to a statement drawn from an earlier source.

83. Cf. Blomberg, *Reliability of the Gospels*, 72–74; Gerhardsson, *Gospel Tradition*, 83–84.

84. Gerhardsson, *Gospel Tradition*, 84.

85. Twelftree, "Jesus and the Synagogue," 4:3129.

from that of another witness, especially in a situation where the truth of one statement does not exclude the possibility of the truth of the other, is not sufficient reason to discard that statement. Even if the first statement relies on the second, the first witness could have additional information, or may have made a correct inference on the basis of the information at their disposal. In this instance, it is entirely plausible that Matthew was aware that Jesus taught in the synagogues during his peripatetic teaching journeys around Galilee, and added this information as a point of expansion and clarity.

Another problem involves the identification of preferred terms as indications of redactional activity—and thus, inauthenticity. For instance, concerning the opening of Mark 3:1 ("Again he entered the synagogue"), he writes, "There is sufficient evidence to suggest that Mark is responsible for this opening statement which includes the mention of the synagogue."[86] Although this evidence is not actually discussed in the main text, Twelftree identifies Mark's use of πάλιν in this passage as evidence of redaction in a footnote, since it "is often used in Mark's introductions to link a story back to a previous one."[87] Once the introduction has been removed, the setting of the incident of the healing of the man with the withered hand becomes indistinct.

The presence of πάλιν in the introduction of Mark 3:1 does not preclude the historical plausibility of the statement that Jesus "entered the synagogue." Twelftree is correct in identifying a characteristic of Mark's writing style, but this has no certain bearing on the historical reference or plausibility of the statement in question. Mark presumably retold or put into writing traditions that he had received, and so, he is naturally responsible for the wording of his Gospel. This does not obviate his ability to speak historically or to preserve historical traditions. Are we to assume that Mark is not able to speak truthfully in his own words about a tradition that he had inherited? Mark is indeed responsible for the introduction in Mark 3:1, but only in the same way that he is responsible for his Gospel as a whole. Unless we conceive of a situation in which Mark wrote down every pre-Markan tradition exactly as he had received it and that anything bearing his authorial mark is an original Markan creation, there is no reason to extrapolate from Mark's use of πάλιν that the setting of the incident within a synagogue is secondary.

---

86. Ibid., 4:3131.
87. Ibid., 4:3131. In this case, the previous story is that of the incident in the synagogue at Capernaum in 1:21ff.

Twelftree's study represents significant progress. He takes recent synagogue scholarship into account, and presents a viable reconstruction of the Second Temple synagogue that is based on the extant evidence. However, it also has serious shortcomings, since he does not actually apply his reconstruction or recent synagogue scholarship to the majority of the Gospel data, as he discards almost all of it as inauthentic on redaction-critical bases. The result of Twelftree's redaction-critical approach is a portrait of Jesus who is detached from the historical context of the synagogues of Galilee, on the one hand, and from the strong, unanimous memory of his frequent presence in the synagogue that has been preserved by evangelists, on the other.

At the end of Twelftree's study, the reader is left with nothing more than two sayings critiquing synagogue practice, and one instance of an exorcism set in a synagogue. However, Twelftree states in his conclusion that "in seeking an audience, perhaps on almost any day, the synagogue would have been the most obvious venue, but not simply as a place to preach but also to debate and to perform healings,"[88] despite having discarded the data in the Gospels that directly evince this very claim (e.g., Mark 1:39; Matt 4:23, 9:35; Luke 4:15; John 18:20). The conclusion that he reaches cannot be derived from the results produced by his redaction-critical study, but is clearly consistent with the data that he has discarded. One wonders if he would have arrived at the same conclusion if he had not been aware of this discarded data in the first place.

A different approach to the Gospel data is taken by Runesson, whose contribution on the topic of the relevance of synagogue research for the study of Jesus and the Gospels to a *Festschrift* in honor of James F. Strange includes a consideration of the relationship between the historical Jesus and the Second Temple synagogue.[89] Runesson's approach to this issue operates within a decidedly post-criteria framework,[90] favoring especially contextual plausibility, as well as memory, orality, genre analysis and intention. He writes,

> Rather than operating with simple stratification of Jesus tradition based on selected criteria, a historically more reliable foundation seems to emerge through the application of a methodological frame *prioritizing contextual plausibility*, paying due attention to the role of memory in oral cul-

88. Ibid., 4:3133.
89. Runesson, "Importance of the Synagogue," 21–26.
90. Ibid., 21.

tures as well as to genre analysis of the Gospels in order to discern aims intertwined with the process of textualization.[91]

The overarching concern of these considerations (plausibility, memory, orality, genre analysis, and intention) is the determination of the relevance of the data for historical Jesus research. Such a concern marks a progression away from the scissors-and-paste burdens of authenticity and criteria, but its level of operation is still at that of the data itself rather than historical inference, interpretation, and imagination. In other words, these methodological operations can only help the historian to determine the relevance and character of the data. The application of that data as evidence within a framework of imagination from which to infer historical knowledge and to perform historical reconstruction is still up to the historian once the data's character has been established.[92] Nevertheless, the establishment of the relevance of the data is a precondition for historical reconstruction, and investigation into the nature of the data is helpful for understanding it.

Runesson's primary burden is to briefly survey important aspects of the early synagogue "in order to describe the setting in which the historical Jesus carried out his public activities and in which the Gospels were written."[93] This allows for a comparison of the data concerning synagogues in the Gospels with what can be known about synagogues from outside sources in order to determine the historical and sociocultural plausibility of the Gospel data.[94] It is only once the Gospel data has been cast alongside Runesson's survey of synagogue material and scholarship that he turns to a direct application to the historical Jesus.

Runesson's short study of the relation between the historical Jesus and the synagogue asks and answers three questions.

First: do the descriptions and assumptions of the nature and settings of synagogues in the Gospels match the text-external, archaeological, literary, and inscriptional evidence of first-century synagogues in the region? Second, in order to eliminate or affirm the possibility of anachronisms in the Gospels, is it possible to prove developments in synagogues immediately after 70 CE, so that texts written after this time may have been affected by a different perception of synagogues? Third, is there evidence of differences between the synagogues in the land of Israel and those of the Diaspora, so that Gospel writers located outside the land could be

91. Ibid. Emphasis my own.
92. On the scope of the historian's task, see appendix A.
93. Runesson, "Importance of the Synagogue," 3.
94. Ibid.

assumed to have conveyed, intentionally or unintentionally, information colored by their own Diaspora experience?[95]

All three of these are directed toward the establishment of the plausibility of the data. By applying data and scholarship pertaining to the Second Temple synagogue to these questions, Runesson is able to conclude in favor of the general plausibility of the Gospel synagogue passages and against the charges of anatopism and anachronism.

The greatest contribution of Runesson's article to the question of the relation between the historical Jesus and the synagogue is in its determination of the relevance of the Gospel data by establishing its historical plausibility. This is not history in itself, but the evaluation of the potential relevance of a data pool is a precondition for historical investigation. However, the interpretation and application of that data as evidence is not achieved by the establishment of relevance, but by further investigation by the historian through the processes of question and answer, inference, and the historical imagination. Moreover, although the determination of plausibility might be preferable to redaction-critical or criteria-based approaches, it nevertheless deals with the same basic concern—that of the potential relevance or non-relevance of the data. If we are primarily concerned with the determination of what is plausible, we are still largely operating at the level of the data and not at the level of inference.

Runesson himself recognizes the limitations of his study in saying that "much remains to be done, but such efforts require monograph-length studies."[96] Nevertheless, Runesson's article is a step in the right direction. Not only does it directly apply the results of synagogue research to the study of Jesus and the Gospels, but more importantly, it does so outside of the restrictive framework of "authenticity" and the traditional methods that have complicated earlier scholarship.

In *Jesus and His World: The Archaeological Evidence*, Craig A. Evans posits the synagogue as the context in which Jesus's thought and development should be understood.[97] In order to demonstrate this, he poses two questions: "What archaeological evidence is there for synagogues in the time of Jesus? And if they existed, what did they look like and what was their function?"[98] The first of these questions is explicitly asked in relation to Kee's argument for the nonexistence of synagogue

---

95. Ibid., 21–22.
96. Ibid., 26.
97. Evans, *Jesus and His World*, 36.
98. Ibid., 37.

buildings before 70 CE.[99] Although Evans does review the literary and inscriptional evidence,[100] his primary focus in this particular work is on archaeological (in this case, architectural) evidence. Evans rightly considers the discovery of buildings identified as synagogues, combined with the literary material, to be evidence of the existence of synagogue buildings prior to 70 CE.[101] Consequently, the bulk of Evans's discussion of the synagogue in relation to the historical Jesus is concerned with a survey of the eight pre-70 CE synagogue buildings that had been identified when the work was published with some confidence within the Land of Israel.[102]

It is important to be aware that Evans's work is designed to introduce archaeological evidence pertaining to the Gospels to nonexperts.[103] Indeed, it functions admirably in the capacity for which it was intended, as it presents much of the basic information pertaining to the extant synagogue remains in a succinct and efficient manner. However, this means that the evidence is not considered in detail nor should one expect much in the way of in-depth analysis. This is, however, probably a function of the genre and intention of the work.

While *Jesus and His World* provides a good introduction to the archaeological evidence pertaining to Second Temple synagogues in the Land, its conclusions and analysis regarding the synagogue are not novel. Evans's interaction with Kee in an introductory work published in 2012 is further testament to the ongoing effect that Kee's hypothesis has had upon the incorporation of synagogue data into historical Jesus studies. So far as the function of synagogues is concerned, Evans mostly focuses on the synagogue as a place for education and for the study of the Torah, which he then links to the issue of literacy in the first century. One cannot help but feel as though Evans has missed an opportunity to introduce readers to the public and local-official roles played by the synagogue.

In his dissertation, published in 2013 as *Aposynagōgos and the Historical Jesus in John*,[104] Jonathan Bernier argues for the historical plausibility of the *aposynagōgos* passages in the Gospel of John. In so doing, he pro-

---

99. Ibid., 38–44.

100. Ibid., 39–44.

101. Ibid., 44.

102. Ibid., 44–58. Along with these, the claim made by the excavators that an additional synagogue was discovered at Shuafat (see *ASSB* no. 42) is also discussed. Evans, however, upholds the same skepticism as Runesson et al. See Alexander Onn and Y. Rafyunu, "Jerusalem: Khirbeth a-ras," *Hadashot Arkheologiyot*, 100 (1993): 60.

103. Evans, *Jesus and His World*, xi.

104. Bernier, *Aposynagōgos*.

vides a viable "post-Martynian" alternative to the Martynian two-level reading of these passages,[105] which undermines much of the impetus for reading the Fourth Gospel as a history of the Johannine community. Bernier's alternative is the suggestion that "the historian should focus attention first and foremost on that level which is often called the literal,"[106] which is to say, the level of the Johannine story of Jesus.

One of the strengths of Bernier's study is his methodological approach, which eschews the traditional criteria-based approach, and is instead firmly grounded in Ben Meyer's critical realist epistemology.[107] This allows him to avoid a scissors-and-paste approach in favor of an inferential approach to history. In particular, Bernier adopts Meyer's historiographical concept of oblique and direct patterns of inference,[108] both of which play a role in his investigation.

A major component of Bernier's argument involves the interpretation of the *aposynagōgos* passages in light of recent advances in synagogue studies.[109] Bernier rightly considers the interpretation of the *aposynagōgos* passages within the context of synagogue research to be useful for the determination of the historical plausibility of their interpretation as references to events within the lifetime of Jesus. He espouses the public/association typological distinction developed by Runesson,[110] and appeals especially to the work of Levine, Binder, Olsson, and Runesson concerning the public dimension of the early synagogue.[111] This leads Bernier to the conclusion that "in the *aposynagōgos* passages John seems to have in mind Jerusalem's public assembly that moved from the city gates to the temple mount."[112]

Bernier's use of current synagogue research in his study exemplifies the significant potential for synagogue studies to contribute to the historical understanding of Jesus and the Gospels. Moreover, the alternative that he provides to the two-level Martynian reading of the *aposynagōgos* passages goes a long way toward the recovery of the Fourth Gospel as a historical source for the life of Jesus. Also important for the particular purposes of the present project is the establishment of the

---

105. Ibid., 18–26.
106. Ibid., 22.
107. Ibid., 23–25.
108. As detailed in Meyer, *Aims of Jesus*, 85–86.
109. Bernier, *Aposynagōgos*, 54–68.
110. Ibid., 59–61. Cf. the position advanced by Runesson, *Origins*.
111. Bernier, *Aposynagōgos*, 65–68. Reference is made in particular to Levine, *Ancient Synagogue*; Binder, *Into the Temple Courts*; Runesson, Binder, and Olsson, *ASSB*; and Runesson, *Origins*.
112. Bernier, *Aposynagōgos*, 75. Cf. Runesson, *Origins*, 352–53 on Jerusalem's public synagogue activities taking place in temple space.

plausible reference of the *aposynagōgos* passages to events during the life of Jesus, which is an indication of their potential relevance as data for the study of the role played by the synagogue in Jesus's aims and ministry. Like Runesson's work on Jesus and the synagogue, Bernier's study is primarily concerned with the level of the data and the determination of its relevance for the study of the historical Jesus. More work has yet to be done toward the interpretation of that data and its place as evidence within the historical reconstruction of the aims of Jesus.

In his *Jesus against the Scribal Elite*, published in 2014, Chris Keith situates the origin of the conflict between Jesus and the scribal elite within the context of the Galilean synagogues.[113] According to Keith, the beginning of the dispute is closely tied to the matter of Jesus's role as a synagogue teacher and interpreter of the scriptures. In occupying the position of a scribal-literate authority despite his status as a scribal-illiterate tradesman, Jesus trespassed well-kept boundaries of social position, and as a result, the literate scribal elite "attempted to demonstrate publicly that Jesus was not a scribal-literate authority."[114] Keith aptly regards the synagogue as the appropriate primary setting for the opening stages of this conflict.[115]

Keith's identification of the synagogue as the contextual setting for the debate is insightful and appropriate, especially given the public nature of the synagogue institution and the very public nature of the interaction between Jesus and the scribal-literate authorities. Nevertheless, *Jesus against the Scribal Elite* is lacking in engagement with or application of synagogue data and synagogue research. Indeed, the actual presentation of information concerning the synagogue is surprisingly sparse and limited primarily to a brief discussion of synagogue roles.[116]

The discussion of synagogue roles is limited only to two classes: scribal-literate teachers, and manual laborers.[117] This division of roles within the synagogue is unknown in synagogue studies, and the lack of reference to the in-depth studies of synagogue functionaries in the work of Binder and Levine is conspicuous,[118] especially in light of the

---

13. Keith, *Scribal Elite*.
14. Ibid., 151.
15. Cf. the conclusion in ibid., 156: "the conflict that ended up on a Roman cross in Jerusalem began in synagogues in Galilee."
16. Ibid., 33–36.
17. Ibid.
18. Levine, *Ancient Synagogue*, 414–529; Binder, *Into the Temple Courts*, 343–87.

omission of any mention of roles typically discussed in synagogue scholarship, such as the *archisynagōgos, archōn, presbyteros,* or *prostatēs,* none of which is typically tied in any clear or direct way to scribal-literacy. Some roles, especially the role of scribe (*grammateus*), would necessitate scribal-literacy, but the limitation of discussion of synagogue roles to two questionable categories creates a problematic dichotomy upon which too much of the argument is founded. This might have been avoided by closer interaction with the work of synagogue scholars on synagogue roles and functionaries.

Despite Keith's appropriate recognition of the synagogue as context, *Jesus against the Scribal Elite* is much more focussed upon and intentional in the use of scholarship and background information pertaining to scribal-literacy than it is with synagogue data and scholarship. There are a couple of indications that the author may not be well-versed in current scholarship and advances in synagogue research. For example, the limestone synagogue at Capernaum is dated curiously early to the third-fourth centuries CE.[119] A third-century CE date for the synagogue is unlikely,[120] due to the ceramic and numismatic evidence discovered in sealed strata, which indicate a much later construction date, probably in the early fifth or late fourth century.[121] Similarly, he states that "archaeologists have not yet unearthed a first-century synagogue in Galilee,"[122] despite the discovery of the first-century synagogue at Magdala five years prior to the publication of *Jesus against the Scribal Elite.*[123] Keith's omission of this discovery is conspicuous, given his citation of Evans's *Jesus and His World,* which contains discussion and photographs of the Magdala synagogue.[124]

When one casts these relatively minor issues alongside the lack of references to major studies on the synagogue,[125] one cannot help but come to the conclusion that *Jesus and the Scribal Elite* does not make much of an effort to contextualize Jesus and his conflict with the

---

119. Keith, *Scribal Elite,* 34.
120. Contra Foerster, "Notes on Recent Excavations at Capernaum," 57–59. Foerster dates the limestone synagogue to the third century on art historical grounds.
121. The excavator, Stanislao Loffreda, prefers a date within the fourth or fifth century. See Loffreda, "Late Chronology," passim. Jodi Magness has suggested an even later date in the sixth century, in Jodi Magness, "Question of the Synagogue."
122. Keith, *Against the Scribal Elite,* 33.
123. Information concerning this discovery was available as early as 2010, in Zangenberg, "Archaeological News," 475–78.
124. Evans, *Jesus and His World,* 53–55.
125. Binder, *Into the Temple Courts* and Runesson, *Origins* do not appear in Keith's bibliography at all. Levine, *Ancient Synagogue* is referenced once (p. 35), while Catto, *First-Century Synagogue* is cited twice (both on p. 35).

scribal elite within a synagogue setting, insofar as it does not effectively utilize synagogue data or research. However, so far as Keith's argument and hypothesis is concerned, this is more a matter of missed opportunity rather than glaring omission. While the recognition of the synagogue as Jesus's context and of Jesus's role as a synagogue teacher is appropriate, this recognition has little impact on the results of Keith's study.

Conclusion

Given the prominence of the synagogue as a social and historical setting within the narratives of all four of the canonical Gospels, it is surprising that synagogue data and research has not played a substantive role in historical Jesus scholarship. It is even more striking that when reconstructions of "the synagogue" have played more important roles, such as in the work of Martyn and Kee, those reconstructions have tended to abstract the synagogue out of the literal level of the narrative in the Second Temple period into the sociogeographical context of the evangelists and the temporal context of the composition of the Gospels after the destruction of the temple in 70 CE.[126]

Several factors have delayed or complicated the application of synagogue data and synagogue research to the modern study of the historical Jesus. Chief among these over the past quarter century has been the hypothesis originally advanced by Kee, which called into question the existence of synagogue buildings prior to 70 CE.[127] Despite its problematic relationship to the extant evidence and its rejection by synagogue scholars, this theory has continued to cause confusion in scholarship on Jesus and the Gospels up to the present day.

The challenge and interpretive ramifications of the minimalist position were considerable enough to require a response, but that response can be found in its negative reception and evaluation in synagogue scholarship of the 1990s and early 2000s. Further response is no longer required. The present investigation will consider the matter of the existence of synagogue buildings prior to 70 CE to have been settled. The evidence is overwhelmingly in favor of the existence of synagogue buildings in the Land during the time of Jesus.

The application of the insights of synagogue studies to Jesus research has also been delayed by the methodological concern for the

26. This is done with John by Martyn and with Luke by Kee.
27. Kee, "Transformation of the Synagogue."

historical authenticity of the Gospel synagogue data. For instance, the authenticity of certain passages, such as the *aposynagōgos* passages, has been called into doubt, which has complicated their use in historical reconstructions.[128] However, as vexing as this issue is in itself, it is symptomatic of a greater methodological difficulty. The very procedure of historical investigation which prioritizes and privileges the determination of historical authenticity is itself a problem. Such a procedure is vulnerable both to Collingwood's critique of scissors-and-paste,[129] as well as to the criticisms presented by the insights of social memory theory.[130]

Studies whose aim is to determine the reliability of the data by establishing historical plausibility may produce valuable insights into the data, but history does not stop at the establishment of relevance. It is, if anything, more of a starting point than an end in itself. Furthermore, it is questionable as to whether or not one can make a definitive judgment about the plausibility of a given datum apart from a larger picture of the past woven of inference and imagination produced through historical investigation.[131] The problem is tied to an insufficient grasp of the scope of the historian's task in previous scholarship on Jesus and synagogues. It is not enough to merely pass judgment on the plausibility or authenticity of data. The historian's task also involves the interpretation and application of the data. In other words, given that we have a wealth of information in the Gospels about Jesus and synagogues, we need to determine not only the truth or falsity of that information, but also what it means for our understanding of Jesus and his aims.

Although the studies of Dunn, Runesson, and Evans all come to reasonable conclusions, there is still much work to be done in terms of analysis, application, interpretation, imagination, and reconstruction. While the present project will ask questions concerning the relevance or plausibility of certain data, the determination of relevance or plausibility will not be considered to be an end in itself, but an element of inferential historical reconstruction and investigation.

The problematic tendency to conceive of the synagogue in terms of its conflict with "the church" or as an institution in conflict with Jesus himself is now mostly a thing of the past, though the effects of

---

128. Esp. in Martyn, *History and Theology*.
129. Collingwood, *Idea of History*, 257–82 (passim), esp. 274–82.
130. E.g., Keith, *Jesus' Literacy*, 41–68.
131. On the nature of the historian's task, see appendix A.

this conception of the synagogue can still be detected in contemporary scholarship through its legacy in the Martynian tradition. Bernier's post-Martynian hypothesis provides a more plausible alternative reading of the data.

The history of scholarship concerning Jesus's relationship to the synagogue tells the story of the recovery of the synagogue as the context for Jesus's thought, actions, and movement. Progress has been made on this front over the past decade. Indeed, one of the most common characteristics of work that we have surveyed from the Third Phase is the recognition of the relevance of the synagogue as a sociohistorical context for the historical Jesus. While this represents a significant advancement in itself, several issues remain to be addressed:

1. What effect does the contextualization of Jesus's miracles, teaching, and proclamation of the Kingdom of God within a synagogue setting have upon the interpretation and understanding of these activities?
2. Given the prominence of the synagogue within the accounts of Jesus's activity in Galilee, what role did the synagogue play in Jesus's aims?
3. Some previous scholarship (e.g., Horsley, Runesson, Levine) has noted the political dimension of the public synagogue. This insight has yet to be applied in historical Jesus research. How might this this be incorporated into current research on Jesus and politics?
4. If Bernier's post-Martynian hypothesis is followed, how might the inclusion of Johannine synagogue passages impact our reconstruction of the role played by the synagogue in Jesus's aims?

PART II

The Historical Jesus
and the Synagogue

5

Kingdom and Synagogue: The Synagogue and Jesus's Program

The Synagogue Summary Statements

Each of the four evangelists describes Jesus's activity within synagogues as a hallmark of his ministry. In other words, the Gospels do not portray the synagogue as *incidental* to Jesus's program, but as *intrinsic* to it. It is this data that opened our investigation in chapter 1. Now that we are equipped with our reconstruction of "the synagogue" as Jesus knew it, we return to this data and the questions that it raised.

As mentioned in chapter 1, the synoptic Gospels all contain summary statements of Jesus's Galilean program, which situate it in synagogues:

> "Let us go on to the neighboring towns, so that I may proclaim the message there also; for that is what I came out to do." And he went throughout Galilee, proclaiming the message in their synagogues and casting out demons. (Mark 1:38–39)

> Jesus went throughout Galilee, teaching in their synagogues and proclaiming the good news of the kingdom and curing every disease and every sickness among the people. (Matt 4:23)[1]

> Then Jesus, filled with the power of the Spirit, returned to Galilee, and a report about him spread through all the surrounding country. He began to teach in their synagogues and was praised by everyone. (Luke 4:15–16)

Two other related passages can be grouped with these summary statements, though neither situates the synagogue activity specifically in Galilee:

> But he said to them, "I must proclaim the good news of the kingdom of God to the other cities also; for I was sent for this purpose." So he continued proclaiming the message (κηρύσσω) in the synagogues of Judea. (Luke 4:43–44)

> Jesus answered, "I have spoken openly to the world; I have always taught in synagogues and in the temple, where all the Jews come together. I have said nothing in secret." (John 18:20)

These last two require some further comments. Luke 4:43–44 presents both textual and historical problems. Unlike the other synoptic synagogue summary statements, v. 44 specifically indicates that Jesus was proclaiming the message in the synagogues of Judea (εἰς τὰς συναγωγὰς τῆς Ἰουδαίας) rather than Galilee. Some notable manuscripts (including A, D, Γ, Δ, Θ, Ψ) replace "Judea" with "Galilee." Nevertheless, the NA28 has printed "Judea." This is because the best manuscripts (P[75], א, and B) evince this reading, and moreover, it is the *lectio difficilior*.[2] The "Galilee" reading can be explained as an attempt to assimilate to Mark 1:39 and Matthew 4:23 (see above),[3] and to its context within the Lukan narrative,[4] which places Jesus in Capernaum prior to this pericope and by the Sea of Galilee in the episode following it. The "Judea" reading is more difficult to explain. This leads to the conclusion that "Judea" is likely the correct reading.

The fact that this pericope comes between an episode taking place in Capernaum and another taking place by the Sea of Galilee may also be indicative of a historical problem. Interestingly, Luke is the only evangelist to specifically describe Jesus travelling to Judean synagogues, and his Gospel is the only one that depicts an episode taking place in a Judean synagogue (Luke 13:10–17). Given that Luke's source, Mark, has

---

1. See also Matt 9:35.
2. Cf., e.g., Joseph A. Fitzmyer, *The Gospel According to Luke* (3 vols.; AYB 28; New York: Doubleday, 1981), 1:557–58; Darrell L. Bock, *Luke* (2 vols.; BECNT; Grand Rapids: Baker, 1994); 1:445.
3. Thus, Bock, *Luke*, 1:445.
4. So Fitzmyer, *Luke*, 1:558.

Jesus travelling only to synagogues in Galilee, it seems as though there is some specific intent behind Luke's testimony that Jesus was active in Judean synagogues. It is tempting to dismiss Luke's testimony here, but it is nevertheless hard to explain his decision to locate Jesus's synagogue activity within "Judea" rather than "Galilee," especially given that he mentions Jesus's Galilean synagogue program in 4:14–15. The best solution is to take Luke's usage of "Judea" here to be inclusive, in the sense of "the entirety of the Jewish homeland," since he uses it in this way elsewhere (1:5, 6:17, 7:17, 23:5; Acts 10:37).[5] This would mean that, according to Luke, Jesus's synagogue program took place in both Galilee *and* Judea.

From a historical perspective, Luke's testimony here is important. It breaks up the neat, convenient synoptic narrative of a Galilean ministry that was followed by a final, fateful trip through Judea to Jerusalem at the very end of Jesus's life by introducing forays into Judea early on in Jesus's career. When cast alongside the narrative of the Fourth Gospel, which has Jesus making multiple trips back and forth from Galilee to Judea, Luke's indication that Jesus was active in both Judean and Galilean synagogues makes a good deal of sense.[6] These two facts of Johannine coherence and reading against the synoptic grain lead me to the conclusion that Luke's testimony should be taken seriously. However, given that the three other Gospels do not contain any episodes set in Judean synagogues, and that Luke does not feature an episode taking place in a Judean synagogue until 13:10–17, it is clear that Jesus's activity in Galilean synagogues was remembered much more strongly. I suggest that the best inference to make from the evidence is that Jesus's synagogue program took place primarily in Galilee, since this is where he was based (cf. Mark 2:1; Matt 4:13). Nevertheless, Jesus probably did not limit his area of activity to Galilee alone, and likely made forays into Judea, where he entered synagogues to teach and proclaim his message.

The saying in John 18:20 is a reply given by Jesus to the high priest

---

5. This is a popular explanation among commentators. See, e.g., Fitzmyer, *Luke*, 1:558; Bock, *Luke*, 1:441; Robert C. Tannehill, *Luke* (ANTC; Nashville: Abingdon, 1996), 98; John T. Carroll, *Luke: A Commentary* (NTL: Louisville: Westminster John Knox, 2012), 122; François Bovon, *A Commentary on the Gospel of Luke*, 3 vols. (Hermeneia; Minneapolis: Fortress Press, 2002), 1:165.

6. E.g., Paul N. Anderson, "Aspects of Historicity in the Fourth Gospel: Consensus and Convergences," in *Aspects of Historicity in the Fourth Gospel*, vol. 2 of *John Jesus and History*, ed. Paul N. Anderson, Felix Just, and Tom Thatcher (Atlanta: Society of Biblical Literature, 2009), 379–86 (382); Horsley and Thatcher, *John, Jesus & the Renewal of Israel*, 2. Further evidence that coheres with this can be found in Matt 10:5–6, wherein Jesus sends the Twelve out to the whole Land of Israel, not just Galilee, and in the "how often have I desired to gather your children together" saying in Matt 23:37/Luke 13:34, speaking of Jerusalem.

when he is questioned about his teaching. The reference to habitual teaching in the synagogue is curious within the context of John's narrative, since only one block of teaching is located within a synagogue setting in the Fourth Gospel (see John 6:59). This saying thus likely reflects the strength of the memory of Jesus having regularly taught in synagogues.

This saying is set in Jerusalem. However, the statement is general, and Jesus is not depicted teaching in a Jerusalem synagogue in John, nor in any of the other Gospels. Jesus's undisputed venue of choice while in Jerusalem was the temple.[7] The inference that can be made from this is that the teaching in synagogues mentioned here most likely refers to Jesus's teaching outside of Jerusalem, and thus, primarily to his activities in Galilee and perhaps also in Judea. This is all the more likely when considered alongside the fact that the only episode set within a synagogue in John takes place in Capernaum.[8]

We thus have a collection of summary statements that locate Jesus's program of teaching and proclamation in Galilee and beyond within synagogues. This evidence will anchor our investigation. It is a logical starting point, the first visible node from which the imaginative web of historical reconstruction will be spun. It is difficult to dispute the inference from this evidence that the historical Jesus taught and proclaimed his message in synagogues.[9] It is a manifestly plausible scenario. As our reconstruction of early synagogues in chapters 2 and 3 has shown, synagogues were a major part of Jewish civic and religious life during the late Second Temple period. Moreover, the synagogues that Jesus interacted with were local public institutions where townspeople would gather. As such, an itinerant Jewish teacher such as Jesus would have naturally made use of local synagogues as go-to venues for teaching and proclamation, since he could expect to find an audience in the assembled public.[10] Furthermore, the unanimity of the evange-

---

7. Mark 11:27, 12:35, 13:1, 14:49; Matt 21:14, 23, 24:1; Luke 19:47, 20:1, 21:37–38, 22:53; John 5:14, 7:14, 28, [8:2], 8:20, 10:23.

8. John 6:59.

9. Hence, even a group as skeptical as the Jesus Seminar considers it to be unequivocal that Jesus was active in the synagogues of Galilee, having assigned it a "red" rating. See Robert W. Funk and the Jesus Seminar, *The Acts of Jesus: The Search for the Authentic Deeds of Jesus* (New York: Polebridge, 1998), 61. Surprisingly, Twelftree, who rejects the authenticity of the summary statements out of hand on redaction critical grounds, nevertheless affirms that the synagogue would have been the most obvious venue for Jesus to preach, perform healings, and debate. See Twelftree, "Jesus and the Synagogue," 3133. According to Runesson, "Importance of the Synagogue," 290, "it is almost certain that Jesus proclaimed the kingdom in Galilean public institutions without restriction."

10. Cf. Twelftree, "Jesus and the Synagogue," 3133.

lists indicates a very strong memory in the tradition of Jesus teaching and proclaiming in synagogue settings.[11]

What does this mean? What can be inferred about the historical Jesus from the summary statements? More specifically, what can we learn from this data about Jesus's aims? In the summary statements, the evangelists unambiguously report Jesus carrying out two types of actions in the synagogues: teaching (Matt 4:23; Luke 4:15–16; John 18:20) and proclaiming (Mark 1:39; Luke 4:43–44).[12] Before turning to specific episodes in the Gospels that take place in synagogues, these two actions require further investigation. Given that the acts of teaching and proclaiming in synagogues were habitual and intrinsic to Jesus's program, it is not enough to say simply *that* Jesus did these things. If we are to have any hope of coming to some understanding of Jesus's aims, then we must know what this data means. In other words, what did it mean for Jesus to teach in synagogues? What was he teaching? Why was he teaching it? Similarly, what was he proclaiming, and why?

It is worth noting that with the exception of John 18:20, all of these statements explicitly refer to events taking place at relatively early stages of Jesus's career. It will be important to keep this in mind as we proceed, since it may indicate that whatever historical knowledge can be gleaned from this data specifically pertains to the early phases of Jesus's career.

By highlighting these two actions and examining them individually, I am not trying to draw a hard distinction between them. They are very

---

11. We might say that the multiple attestation of the evangelists across both the synoptic and Johannine traditions itself serves as evidence of the accuracy of the witnesses' statements. It is mutual corroboration, and while it does not definitively establish "authenticity" (if indeed there is such a thing), it is nevertheless an index of the statement's veracity. This is not irrelevant information, since it helps us understand how to interpret the data. We should resist the impulse to allow our discipline's growing distaste for the criteria approach to turn us away entirely from some of the good and useful historiographical elements that may undergird some of the criteria themselves. I am by no means advocating that the criteria can or should be rehabilitated. I am only saying that corroboration of evidence is in itself a good historiographical principle. On indices in historical Jesus research, see Meyer, *Aims of Jesus*, 85–87; Denton, *Historiography and Hermeneutics*, 120–21. On multiple attestation and historical method, see Mark Goodacre, "Criticizing the Criterion of Multiple Attestation: The Historical Jesus and the Question of Source," in *Jesus, Criteria, and the Demise of Authenticity* (ed. Chris Keith and Anthony Le Donne; London and New York: T&T Clark, 2012), 152–69 (152–53).

12. The ambiguity of the grammatical construction in Matt 4:23 makes it difficult to determine whether the actions of "proclaiming the good news of the Kingdom" (Gk. κηρύσσων τὸ εὐαγγέλιον τῆς βασιλείας), and "healing every disease and every sickness among the people" (Gk. θεραπεύων πᾶσαν νόσον καὶ πᾶσαν μαλακίαν ἐν τῷ λαῷ) are understood to have taken place "in their synagogues" (ἐν ταῖς συναγωγαῖς αὐτῶν) along with teaching. The same goes for "casting out demons" in Mark 1:39. The matter is moot, however, since as we shall see, there is ample evidence elsewhere that Jesus performed these acts in synagogues.

much two sides of the same coin. As will become clear in the discussion to follow, the teaching clarifies and illuminates the proclamation. What we will first examine below is the *object* of the proclamation, which is at the heart of Jesus's aims. We will then turn to a discussion of the *content* of the teaching, and how it relates to that object.

As the investigation proceeds, it is important to be aware of what I am actually doing when I consider and interpret the words of Jesus as reported by the evangelists. It is essential to recognize that, as always, we are seeking the *vox* rather than the *verba* of the historical Jesus. Although I am examining the words of Jesus as reported by the evangelists, I am not claiming that we can know that the words attributed to Jesus by them are the exact words of Jesus. The act of translation alone, not to mention the processes of remembering and writing the past, makes this difficult to determine.[13] Nevertheless, we should not despair and give up the historical endeavour. What I will be doing is using the *words* reported by the evangelists to have been said by Jesus as *evidence* for reconstructing the *voice* of Jesus. This is an important epistemological distinction. If we seek to get at the inside of the event, the best way to do that is to treat the remembrances of Jesus's words and actions as reported by the evangelists as artifacts, evidence of what the historical Jesus thought, said, and did.

Proclaiming the Kingdom in Their Synagogues

What was Jesus proclaiming in the synagogues? Mark 1:39 does not specify this, though a summary of Jesus's proclamation can be found in 1:14–15: "Jesus came to Galilee, proclaiming the good news of God, and saying, 'The time is fulfilled, and the kingdom of God has come near; repent, and believe in the good news.'"[14] Likewise, the Lukan Jesus

---

13. On translation and the transmission of traditions, see Gerhardsson, *Reliability of the Gospel Tradition*, 51.

14. Whether or not this represents an actual direct saying is irrelevant for our purposes, since Mark 1:15 represents the voice of Jesus, cf., e.g., Marius Reiser, *Jesus and Judgment: The Eschatological Proclamation in Its Jewish Context* (Minneapolis: Fortress Press, 1997), 255. See also G. R. Beasley-Murray, *Jesus and the Kingdom of God* (Grand Rapids: Eerdmans, 1986), 71–75; cf. G.R. Beasley-Murray, "Jesus and the Kingdom of God," *Baptist Quarterly* 32 (1987): 141–47 (142). It is sometimes asserted that this saying is problematic because Jesus rarely speaks of repentance (e.g., Funk, Hoover, and the Jesus Seminar, *Five Gospels*, 41). However, repentance is directly spoken of in Mark 6:12; Matt 11:21–24/Luke 10:13–16; Matt 12:38–42/Luke 11:29–32; Luke 5:32, 13:1–5, 15:7, 10, 16:30, 17:3–4. Indirectly, we might read themes of repentance into Luke 15:11–32 and 18:9–14. Thus, it seems as though this claim can only be made within a scissors-and-paste approach to history, by excising all of this corresponding data. There are, then, no reasonable grounds for disregarding Mark 1:15 or treating with suspicion so long as we are willing to regard it as representing the *vox* of Jesus.

summarizes the basic content of his proclamation in the synagogues in Luke 4:43, saying, "I must proclaim the good news of the Kingdom of God to the other cities also; for I was sent for this purpose."

Thus, the "the Kingdom of God" was the core element of Jesus's proclamation in the synagogues. This much is clear according to the synoptic tradition. However, what Jesus meant by "the Kingdom of God" is less clear. We can infer a few further details from Mark's summary of the proclamation in 1:14–15. The Kingdom's advent is imminent,[15] its imminence is "good news" (Gk. εὐαγγέλιον),[16] and its coming requires a response of repentance.[17] Nevertheless, the precise meaning and character of the Kingdom that Jesus proclaimed is enigmatic. Although Jesus speaks of it in parables, nowhere in any of the four Gospels is it directly explicated. We cannot hope to understand Jesus's synagogue proclamation nor his aims apart from his conception of the Kingdom of God. What, then, can we know about the kingdom that Jesus proclaimed?

Kingdom and Eschatology

The notion of the "Kingdom" or "reign" (Gk. *basileia*) of God in early Jewish thought is often steeped in eschatological hope. Glimpses of this can already be seen in some texts of the Hebrew Bible. In Isaiah 52:7, God's reign is presented as an image of the expectation of redemption and salvation. In a striking parallel to the Gospel traditions, the Greek translation of this passage in the LXX describes the coming reign of Israel's God (Gk. βασιλεύσει σου ὁ θεός)[18] as "good news" (Gk. εὐαγγελιζόμενος ἀγαθά). Images of God's salvific, redemptive rule can also be seen in Obadiah 21 and Zephaniah 3:15. These texts present hopeful images of restoration following catastrophe. Likewise, as Brant Pitre has recently pointed out, Micah 4:1–8 speaks of a coming, future kingdom with God as its ruler, providing a parallel to Jesus's prayer for the coming of the Kingdom in Matthew 6:10/Luke 11:12.[19] Given

---

5. Further support for this inference is found in Matt 3:2, 4:17, 6:10, 10:7, 16:28; Mark 9:1; Luke 9:27, 10:9, 10:11, 11:2, 19:11 (the fact that the disciples thought that the Kingdom would appear immediately indicates that they had been given reason to believe that it was imminent).

6. Cf. the association of "Kingdom" with "good news" by either Jesus or the evangelists in Matt 4:23, 9:35, 10:7, 24:14; Luke 4:43, 8:1, 16:16. The instances in which the association of "Kingdom" with "good news" in the Gospels come from the narrator rather than from Jesus are also significant. This is because they evince a strong memory of a connection between "Kingdom" and "gospel" in Jesus's proclamation amongst his early followers.

7. Cf. Meyer, *Aims of Jesus*, 132.

8. Note the future tense of "βασιλεύσει."

9. Brant Pitre, *Jesus and the Last Supper* (Grand Rapids: Eerdmans, 2015), 169.

the reference in Micah 4:10 to the Babylonian exile and the subsequent return from exile, it is clear that in this text too we are presented with an image of God's reign as a coming restorative event in the wake of catastrophe.

The association of God's kingship with restoration is strongly present in Ezekiel 20:33–37. The clear connection between God's kingly reign and restoration is both striking and highly instructive, so it is fitting to cite this passage here:

> As I live, says the Lord GOD, surely with a mighty hand and an outstretched arm, and with wrath poured out, *I will be king over you*. I will *bring you out from the peoples and gather you out of the countries where you are scattered*, with a mighty hand and an outstretched arm, and with wrath poured out; and I will bring you into the wilderness of the peoples, and there I will enter into judgment with you face to face. As I entered into judgment with your ancestors in the wilderness of the land of Egypt, so I will enter into judgment with you, says the Lord GOD. I will make you pass under the staff, and *will bring you within the bond of the covenant*.

The historical backdrop of this passage is the Babylonian exile. What we see here is the notion that there will come a time when God will reign as king over his people. When this happens, the exiles and scattered people of Israel will be gathered. In a reenactment of the exodus from Egypt, they will be gathered into the wilderness and judged, and will be brought into "the bond of the covenant." In short, when God reigns as king, Israel will be restored, its people judged, the covenant renewed, and the exodus story, Israel's foundational narrative, will be repeated.

Elsewhere in the Hebrew Bible, the God of Israel's reign is established over and against the opposition of Gentile powers.[20] This notion of an eschatological conflict appears to have developed over time. During the late Second Temple period, the establishment of the reign of God was sometimes depicted in terms of a dualistic struggle or battle between God and the demonic forces.[21] What is common to all of these conceptions is the idea that a time is coming but is not yet when God will establish his salvific, redemptive universal rule over Israel and the earth. This is not to say that prior to that time, God is dethroned or powerless. To the contrary, some streams of tradition emphasize God's *present* reign.[22] We need not necessarily consider these ideas to be in

---

20. Isa 24:21–23, 33:17–22; Zech 14:1–9; Dan 7. Cf. Theissen and Merz, *Historical Jesus*, 248.
21. See *T. Dan* 5:10–13; 1QM, esp. 6:6; *Assumption of Moses* 10, esp. v. 1; *Sib. Or.* 3.767.

tension with each other. Rather, as Jürgen Becker has put it, "The view is that God rules already as king, but not until the near future will he do so in any complete sense."[23]

Interestingly, the Gospels appear to assume that the early Jewish understanding of the kingdom of God was futurist and eschatological in nature. Thus, the Pharisees ask Jesus when the kingdom of God is to come (Luke 17:20), and Joseph of Arimathea is said to have been "waiting expectantly for the kingdom" (Mark 15:43, cf. Luke 23:51).

As we shall see, there is an eschatological dimension to Jesus's proclamation of the Kingdom of God.[24] By this, I do not mean that it envisions the end of the space-time continuum, but that it envisions the end of the current order and the beginning of a new one. Some scholars have presented a noneschatological portrait of Jesus and his Kingdom proclamation,[25] but the evangelists clearly present the Kingdom in eschatological terms. It has a future element. Thus, Jesus proclaims in Mark 1:15 and its parallels that the Kingdom of God has "come near" (ἐγγίζω). It is imminent, but not yet.[26] This is further supported by the statement in Mark 9:1 that "There are some standing here who will not taste death until they see that the Kingdom of God has come with power." The kingdom *will* host an eschatological banquet, to which people from the east and west, north and south (referring either to Gentiles, dispersed Jews, or both), *will* come (Luke 13:29, cf. Matt 8:11). It *will be* like (Gk. ὁμοιωθήσεται) ten bridesmaids (Matt 25:1). Moreover, according to Matthew's version of the Olivet Discourse, the proclamation of the good news of the kingdom throughout the world will bring about the *eschaton* (Matt 24:14). Perhaps most tellingly, the "your kingdom come" petition in the Lord's Prayer (Luke 11:2, Matt 6:10) encapsulates the desire for the establishment of the kingdom in a near-but-not-yet time.

One of the distinctive characteristics of Jesus's kingdom proclama-

22. E.g., in 4Q403 1, I, 25 and 30–36; *Pss. Sol.* 17. In the Hebrew Bible, see Pss. 47, 145:13; Dan 4:3.

23. Jürgen Becker, *Jesus of Nazareth* (trans. James E. Crouch; New York and Berlin: Walter de Gruyter, 1998), 90.

24. This is now probably the dominant perspective in mainstream scholarship. See, e.g., Meyer, *Aims of Jesus*, esp. 134; Sanders, *Jesus and Judaism*, esp. 232; Becker, *Jesus of Nazareth*, esp. 107; Theissen and Merz, *The Historical Jesus*, esp. 275; Schröter, *Jesus of Nazareth*, 126ff.; Wright, *Jesus and the Victory of God*, 202–9; Beasley-Murray, *Jesus and the Kingdom of God*, 341–44; Allison, *Constructing Jesus*; Pitre, *Jesus and the Last Supper*, 168–71. This is merely a small sampling of relatively recent scholarship stretching from 1979 (Meyer) to 2015 (Pitre) and is by no means an exhaustive list. As mentioned in chapter 1, the eschatological interpretation of Jesus's Kingdom proclamation in early modern scholarship goes back to Weiss, *Jesus' Proclamation*, passim; and Schweitzer, *Quest of the Historical Jesus* (cf. Schweitzer, *Mystery of the Kingdom of God*).

25. E.g., Burton Mack, *Myth of Innocence*. More recently, see Oakman, *Political Aims of Jesus*, esp. 119–23.

26. Compare, however, Dodd, *Parables of the Kingdom*, 36–37.

tion in the synoptic Gospels is that it has a present element as well as a future element. It is both now and not yet. It is imminent, *moreover* it is already breaking out. As C. H. Dodd demonstrated in *The Parables of the Kingdom*, there are sayings in the Jesus tradition that indicate that Jesus proclaimed the kingdom "as a present fact, which men must recognize, whether by their actions they accept or reject it."[27] The eschatology of the kingdom is, in part, a realized eschatology.

This need not be at odds with the future dimension of the kingdom. Jesus believed that the reign of God was at hand, and saw it already coming into being in his own work.[28] Thus, in the double-tradition version of the Beelzebul controversy, Jesus says "if it is by the finger of God that I cast out the demons, then the kingdom of God has come upon you (Gk. ἔφθασεν ἐφ' ὑμᾶς)" (Luke 11:20, cf. Matt 12:28). The aorist tense here is indicative of the already present nature of the reign of God. A similar understanding of the realized presence of the kingdom can also be seen in Jesus's response to the Pharisees when they ask when the kingdom of God was coming: "The kingdom of God is not coming with things that can be observed; nor will they say, 'Look, here it is!' or 'There it is!' For, in fact, *the kingdom of God is among you*" (Luke 17:21).

A noneschatological reading of Jesus's kingdom proclamation reads against the grain of the coming salvific, redemptive reign of God in the Hebrew Bible and early Palestinian Jewish texts. Admittedly, there are examples from diaspora Hellenistic Jewish texts of a more "sapiential" kingdom,[29] but the Palestinian tradition, which is the most likely milieu of Jesus the Galilean Jew, mostly envisions the reign of God as: a) something that is yet to come, and b) redemptive. More importantly, a noneschatological reading of Jesus's kingdom proclamation is a quintessentially scissors-and-paste hypothesis that can only be arrived at by excising the Gospel data that speaks of the kingdom as future or imminent.[30] Even if we were to excise all of that material, it would still be difficult to account for the fact that Jesus's kingdom proclamation was strongly and evidently remembered in eschatological terms by the evangelists. In this, I am reminded of Dale Alison's

---

27. Ibid., 36.
28. Kümmel suggested a "double eschatology" as a mediation between the thorough-going, futurist eschatology of Weiss and Schweitzer on the one hand and the realized eschatology of Dodd on the other. Werner Georg Kümmel, *Promise and Fulfilment: The Eschatological Message of Jesus* (trans. Dorothea M. Barton; Naperville: A. R. Allenson, 1957), passim, see esp. 155.
29. Crossan, *Historical Jesus*, 287–91. Crossan points specifically to examples drawn from the writings of Philo and the Wisdom of Solomon, both of which hail from Alexandria.
30. See, for example, the treatment of the eschatological elements of the double-tradition material as later interpretation by Oakman, *Political Aims of Jesus*, 119–23.

much-celebrated statement that "our choice is not between an apocalyptic Jesus and some other Jesus; it is between an apocalyptic Jesus and no Jesus at all. . . . The pertinent material is sufficiently abundant that removing it all should leave one thoroughly skeptical about the mnemonic competence of the tradition."[31]

We must, then, conclude that Jesus's proclamation in the synagogues was an eschatological proclamation with both present and future dimensions. This fits plausibly within the traditional milieu of early Palestinian Judaism, which indicates that Jesus's Galilean Jewish audience would have been able to perceive the eschatological character of the proclamation.

What Did Jesus Mean by "The Kingdom of God"?

So far, we have determined that the kingdom of God as Jesus proclaimed it in the synagogues is imminent, that it is "good news," that it requires a response of repentance, and that it has both present and future eschatological dimensions. All of this provides some good initial orientation. Nevertheless, it is still necessary to provide a precise account of what "the kingdom of God" meant for Jesus.

In light of the images of the restorative reign of God in the Nevi'im presented above, a number of scholars have suggested that Jesus's proclamation of the kingdom of God is tied to the restoration of Israel. Consider the following examples of accounts of Jesus's conception of the kingdom of God:

> It is my contention that an examination of Jesus' words and actions suggest that the non-negotiable in Jesus' proclamation was, in fact, the presence of the kingdom and that Jesus, like his contemporaries, did conceive of this kingdom as a new social order in a way that was broadly consistent with the widespread expectation that the outcome of God's eschatological action would be a restoration of Israel's national life.[32]

> The coming of God's kingdom for which Jesus instructs his disciples to pray means nothing less than the ingathering of Israel and the Gentiles to the promised land in a new exodus.[33]

---

31. Alison, *Constructing Jesus*, 43.
32. Steven M. Bryan, "Jesus and Israel's Eschatological Constitution," in *Handbook for the Study of the Historical Jesus* (ed. Tom Holmén and Stanley E. Porter; Leiden and Boston: Brill, 2011), 3:2835–53 (2838).
33. Pitre, *Jesus and the Last Supper*, 171.

Thus the kingdom expected by Jesus is not quite that expected by Paul – in the air, and not of flesh and blood –, but not that of an actual insurrectionist either. It is like the present world – it has a king, leaders, a temple, and twelve tribes – but it is not just a rearrangement of the present world. God must step in and provide a new temple, the restored people of Israel, and presumably a renewed social order, one in which 'sinners' will have a place.[34]

While the rulers stand under God's condemnation, the kingdom of God is emerging as the renewal of the people of Israel in its ideal twelve tribes.[35]

The favourite and most important subject of Jesus' teaching is clearly the Kingdom of God. Like many Jews of his day, he saw this as the promised era of God's universal rule and the restoration of the chosen people to wholeness and relationship with God, an era where his will comes to be done on earth just as in heaven.[36]

The views cited above are only a small sampling of a much larger trend.[37] What we see here is an emerging dominant hypothesis that Jesus's kingdom proclamation, and by extension, his aims, were tied to the eschatological hope for the restoration of Israel.

The connection between Jesus's aims and the restoration of Israel has been frequently discussed, so there is no need to elaborate upon it in depth. It will serve my present purposes to simply present what I consider to be the most convincing evidence indicating a connection between Jesus's aims and restoration. This evidence and the initial inferences that it produces will then serve as a spring board for an investigation into whether and how the primary setting of Jesus's proclamation of the kingdom of God within synagogues might impact, elaborate, support, or speak against the restoration hypothesis. The strongest evidence in favor of connecting Jesus's aims with the restoration of Israel is listed below:

1. The reign of God is linked to images of the restoration of Israel in the prophetic writings of the Hebrew Bible discussed above. This

---

34. Sanders, *Jesus and Judaism*, 232.
35. Horsley and Thatcher, *John, Jesus & the Renewal of Israel*, 73.
36. Markus Bockmuehl, *This Jesus: Martyr, Lord, Messiah* (Downers Grove: InterVarsity, 1994), 81.
37. Other well-known examples of relatively recent scholarship espousing some variety of the restoration hypothesis include Meyer, *Aims of Jesus*, esp. 132–33; Allison, *Constructing Jesus*; Freyne, *Jewish Galilean*; Meier, *A Marginal Jew*, esp. 3:148–53; Wright, *Jesus and the Victory of God*, passim; Gerhard Lohfink, *Jesus of Nazareth: What He Wanted, Who He Was*, trans. Linda M. Maloney (Collegeville: Liturgical, 2012 [2011]), esp. 58–71; Paula Fredriksen, *Jesus of Nazareth, King of the Jews: A Jewish Life and the Emergence of Christianity* (London: Macmillan, 1999), esp. 95–98.

is exemplified especially by texts such as Micah 4:1–10, Ezekiel 20:33–37, and Isaiah 52, in which God's reign is depicted as a coming time of restoration following the disaster of the Babylonian exile.[38] As discussed in chapter 5, the Nevi'im were read in synagogues during this period. If Jesus and his synagogue audiences were familiar with any textual traditions whatsoever concerning the reign of God, it is most likely that they would have been familiar with the images of the reign of God found in the Nevi'im. In Jesus's case, the fact that he was proclaiming the kingdom of God is strong evidence for the inference that he was aware of the traditional conceptions of it. Although other possibilities cannot be excluded, the most probable place for Jesus to have encountered these concepts was in synagogues.

2. Luke-Acts contains two passages indicating that Jesus's followers thought that he aimed to restore Israel. Both instances occur in post-resurrection settings. In Luke 24:21, Jesus's followers on the road to Emmaus say of Jesus that "we had hoped that he was the one to redeem Israel." Similarly, just prior to Jesus's ascension in Acts 1, his disciples ask "Lord, is this the time when you will restore the kingdom to Israel?" (Acts 1:6). The importance of this data has been underappreciated in historical Jesus research. Presumably, this is due to concerns regarding the historicity of post-resurrection narratives. However, the value of these passages as evidence for the matter at hand is independent of the issue of the literal historicity of the events that they narrate and of the historicity of Jesus's resurrection. Even if we bracket off the matter of the resurrection, the intention of both passages is to redirect and address concerns that Jesus did not meet the expectation that he would bring about the restoration of Israel during his lifetime by redefining that hope.[39] This expectation itself requires explanation, and when combined with the other evidence listed here, these passages support the notion that Jesus said and did things that would create it.

3. Jesus called twelve "apostles" into his inner circle,[40] and according

---

38. See also, perhaps, Zeph 3:14–20.

39. Good discussion of this issue in relation to the eschatology of Luke-Acts can be found in David L. Tiede, "The Exaltation of Jesus and the Restoration of Israel in Acts 1," *Harvard Theological Review* 79:1–3 (1986): 278–86; and Craig S. Keener, *Acts: An Exegetical Commentary*, 4 vols. (Grand Rapids: Baker Academic, 2012), 1:682–84.

40. Mark 3:14–16, cf. 4:10, 6:7, 9:35, 10:32, 11:11, 14:10, 17, 20, 43; Matt 10:1–4, 5a, 11:1, 26:14, 20, 47; Luke 6:13–16, 8:1, 9:1, 9:12, 18:31, 22:3, 47; John 6:67–71, 20:24; Acts 1:26, 6:2, 1 Cor 15:5; Rev 21:14.

to Matthew 19:28 and Luke 22:30, he envisioned them judging the twelve tribes of Israel on twelve thrones.[41] The calling of this specific number of apostles is considered a key piece of evidence for the restoration hypothesis by a number of scholars.[42] It is difficult to deny the probable accuracy of the testimony that Jesus envisioned the Twelve judging the twelve tribes, since Judas Iscariot was included among the Twelve during Jesus's lifetime. As Sanders writes, "It is unlikely that, after the betrayal by Judas, the church would have had Jesus include him as one of those who would sit on a throne judging Israel."[43] The number twelve recalls the number of Israelite tribes, and the image of the Twelve judging the twelve tribes envisions an eschatological judgment scene in which all Israel has been restored and gathered together, including the ten "lost" tribes. The image is highly reminiscent of the gathering, judgment, and covenant renewal scene pictured in Ezekiel 20:33–37. The special role imagined for the inner circle of the Twelve that Jesus gathered in the judgment scene indicates that he saw his group and actions having an integral relationship to this event.

4. The geographical boundaries of Jesus's activities strongly suggests that he envisioned an eschatological restoration. According to the evangelists, Jesus was active not only in Galilee and Judea, but also in the Transjordan (Mark 10:1; Matt 19:1; John 10:40), the region of Tyre and Sidon (Mark 7:24; Matt 15:21), and Samaria (John 4:4). Although these areas were not Jewish-controlled in the first century CE, they were a part of what Freyne has termed "greater Israel," the region allotted to the twelve tribes according to Joshua 13–20 (cf. 2 Sam 24:1–9; 1 Kgs 4:7–19).[44] The sentiment that the ancestral lands, whether or not they were under Jewish control, belonged to "greater Israel" is reflected in this statement attributed by the author of 1 Maccabees to Simon concerning the Jewish seizure of Gentile territory: "We have neither taken

---

41. Cf. also Mark 10:35–45.
42. E.g., John P. Meier, "The Circle of the Twelve: Did It Exist During Jesus' Public Ministry?" *JBL* 116, no. 4 (1997): 635–72 (635); Helen Bond, *The Historical Jesus: A Guide For the Perplexed* (London and New York: T&T Clark, 2012), 96; Allison, *Constructing Jesus*, 71; Fredriksen, *Jesus of Nazareth*, 98; Richard Horsley, *The Prophet Jesus and the Renewal of Israel: Moving Beyond a Diversionary Debate* (Grand Rapids: Eerdmans, 2012), 120–22; Wright, *Jesus and the Victory of God*, 299–300; Meyer, *Aims of Jesus*, 154; Sanders, *Jesus and Judaism*, 98.
43. Sanders, *Jesus and Judaism*, 99.
44. See Freyne, *A Jewish Galilean*, 70–91, cf. Seán Freyne, "The Geography of Restoration: Galilee-Jerusalem Relations in Early Jewish and Christian Experience," *NTS* 47 (2001): 289–311.

foreign land nor seized foreign property, but only the inheritance of our ancestors, which at one time had been unjustly taken by our enemies. Now that we have the opportunity, we are firmly holding the inheritance of our ancestors" (1 Macc 15:33–34). The fact that Jesus was active specifically in the regions of "greater Israel" and not only Judea and Galilee indicates that his intentions involved "Israel" conceived in terms of the traditional idealized national boundaries, rather than Judea and Galilee alone.[45]

5. Two sayings in Matthew refer to the "lost sheep of Israel" as the target of Jesus's mission. The first, Matthew 10:6, comes in Jesus's instructions to the twelve before sending them out to proclaim the "good news of the Kingdom" and heal the sick, raise the dead, and cast out demons. This sending appears to be an extension of the mission that Jesus himself carries out according to Matthew (Matt 4:23–24, 9:35). In the other instance, Jesus states that he was "sent only to the lost sheep of the house of Israel" (Matt 15:24). This statement is made to the "Canaanite" woman in order to deny her request while Jesus is in the region of Tyre and Sidon. The fact that Jesus is said to offer this reply to a Gentile in this geographical setting is striking, since it implies that, even in Gentile territory, Jesus directed his proclamation and healing ministry to other Jews. Nevertheless, we should not exclude the possibility that Jesus's *ultimate* goals were global in scope (cf. Matt 8:11; Luke 13:28–29), since the images of the restored Israel in the Hebrew Bible also envision the blessings of God's restorative rule coming upon the nations as well.[46]

6. In the Lukan and Pauline versions of the Last Supper, Jesus refers to the cup as "the new covenant in my blood" (Luke 22:20; 1 Cor 11:25).[47] There is probably an allusion being made here to Jeremiah 31:31, which envisions a new, restored covenant between God and Israel. The Markan and Matthean versions do

---

45. On restoration of the territory of the Land of Israel in Jesus' thought, see also Joel Willits, "Jesus, the Kingdom and the Promised Land," *JSHJ* 13 (2015): 347–72.

46. See, e.g., Isa 2:2–4; Mic 4:1–8; Zech 8:20–23. Full discussion of this issue is neither possible nor necessary here. For lengthier treatment, see Freyne, *Jesus, A Jewish Galilean*, 109–13; Wright, *Jesus and the Victory of God*, 308–10.

47. Brant Pitre has recently made a forceful and convincing argument in favour of the authenticity of Jesus enacting a new covenant at the Last Supper in Pitre, *Jesus and the Last Supper*, 104–20. Although "historicity" is in itself not among the primary concerns of this study, Pitre's argument is helpful for understanding how to interpret the passage and apply it as evidence for the present project. See also Dunn, *Jesus Remembered*, 816–18; Theissen and Merz, *Historical Jesus*, 422–23; Joachim Gnilka, *Jesus of Nazareth: Message and History*, trans. Siegfried S. Schatzman (Peabody: Hendrickson, 1997), 286.

not mention a "new" covenant. Instead, Jesus calls the wine his "blood of the covenant" (Mark 14:24; Matt 26:28). However, as Seeyoon Kim argues, there is nevertheless an implicit reference to Jeremiah 31:31, since "a covenant established by Jesus' blood can only be a 'new covenant.'"[48] The Mosaic covenant is at the centre of Israel's founding narrative. The action of instituting a "new covenant" is, in effect, equivalent to renewing Israel's constitution. Once again, we are reminded of the image presented in Ezekiel 20:33–37, which envisions God reigning over his people, gathering them in the wilderness, and renewing the covenant (v. 37).[49] The connection between the establishment of "covenant" and "kingdom" is also reflected in some of the Qumran material, specifically 1Q28b V, 18 and 4Q252 V, 1–4. Jesus's "new" covenant fits very well within this tradition, and indicates that he saw his actions as bringing about the restoration of Israel.

The evidence presented here comes together to form a plausible, coherent picture. No single piece of evidence stands alone, as we are able to weave it all together with threads of imagination, interpretation, and inference. The evidence leads me to conclude that Jesus aimed to restore Israel, and that the concept of the "Kingdom of God" in his thought is inextricably tied to that aim.

It is worth noting that, as some scholars have recently argued, the Kingdom is sometimes described in spatial terms, as the heavenly realm.[50] There are also some sayings in the Jesus tradition that may presuppose a spatial conception of the Kingdom.[51] The idea that God's Kingdom exists in the heavenly realms is by no means at odds with the notion that he will exert his reign over the earth. Heaven is where God's reign is already in full effect. When Jesus instructs his disciples to pray, he addresses God as "Our Father in heaven," and then asks that for his Kingdom to *come*, and for his will to be done "on earth as it is in heaven" (Matt 6:9-10; cf. Luke 11:2). The desire expressed here is for the state of the heavenly realms, in which God fully exercises his reign and will, to be extended to the earth. The hope is for the Kingdom to come, not for the faithful to go to it.

There is still much left unanswered. Most importantly, it is not clear

---

48. Seeyoon Kim, *"The 'Son of Man'" as the Son of God* (WUNT 30; Tübingen: Mohr Siebeck, 1983), 62.
49. Cf. Dunn, *Jesus Remembered*, 816–18.
50. Allison, *Constructing Jesus*, 164–203; Pitre, *Jesus and the Last Supper*, 474–76. See 4Q405 23, II, 10–12; Wis 10:10; T. Job 33:1–9.
51. E.g., Luke 13:29, cf. Matt 8:11; Mark 14:25, cf. Matt 26:29, Luke 22:16.

what restoration meant for Jesus, or how he thought it might come about, and what role he would play in bringing it to fruition. To quote Sanders, "We have not yet achieved precision and nuance in understanding just how Jesus thought of restoration and what it would involve."[52] It is worth noting at this point that synagogue research has not yet played a role in helping to clarify Jesus's concept of and plan for restoration, despite the fact that the synagogue was the setting that the Gospels identify as the locus of his proclamation of the Kingdom of God. Why did Jesus proclaim this message of God's redemptive reign in synagogues? What can this setting tell us about how Jesus conceived of his mission?

The interpretive strategy that I will employ in order to address these matters approximates what Runesson has recently dubbed "institution criticism."[53] The basic premise of institution criticism is the use and recognition of institutional realities as explanatory categories.[54] As Runesson writes, "An individual's actions and thoughts evolve and take form as a consequence of a complex dynamic in which socialisation, experience, and innovation are all entangled."[55] Understanding the institutional frameworks which inform these actions and thoughts can thereby be useful for interpretation and contextualization. By setting the Gospel synagogue summary passages alongside the reconstruction of the public synagogue that I have laid out in chapters 2 and 3, we can illuminate the customs, conventions, and sociopolitical mechanics that undergird the actions that these passages describe.

Kingdom and Synagogue

It is important to recognize that Jesus's use of the synagogue as a venue for his proclamation was intentional. There were other options. He did not, for example, operate in a fixed area where the crowds could come to him—as John the Baptist did.[56] This is a striking difference between Jesus and John, especially since at this point, Jesus's message of repentance and eschatology seems to have been in general continuity with that of the Baptist.[57] Alternatively, Jesus could have also stayed

---

52. Sanders, *Jesus and Judaism*, 119. A similar issue is also addressed by Pitre, *Jesus and the Last Supper*, 446–47, who cites this same passage from Sanders.

53. In Anders Runesson, "Placing Paul: Institutional Structures and Theological Strategy in the World of the Early Christ-believer," *Svensk Exegetisk Årsbok* 80 (2015): 43–67.

54. Ibid., 43.

55. Ibid.

56. Mark 1:5, cf. Matt 3:5–6.

57. On continuity with John the Baptist in Jesus's early career, see Robert L. Webb, "Jesus' Baptism by

in Jerusalem and delivered his message in the temple precincts, as his followers would later do (Acts 2:46, 5:42). Travel and synagogue, then, were purposeful elements of Jesus's mission. We are now tasked with getting at the "inside" of the event of his peripatetic synagogue proclamation.

Why did he proclaim *this* message in *this* institution? It is not enough to say that Jesus wanted to find an audience, so he went to synagogues only because he could expect to find one there. While there is perhaps a kernel of truth in this, we must recognize that the synagogue was not the only public space available, and moreover, if we imagine Jesus within synagogue buildings such as the ones discovered at Magdala and Gamla, we are forced to recognize that they could only accommodate a fraction of the town's population.[58] Thus, teaching in a synagogue building could actually limit the size of his audience as opposed to teaching in the open air, as John the Baptist did. More importantly, we must recognize the institutional character of the synagogue. As we have seen in chapters 2 and 3, the public "synagogue" was not just *any* gathering of Jewish people—it was a civic institution with political, societal, legislative, and religious functions. Interacting with synagogues meant interacting not just with people, but with a local-official institution. Any serious answer to our question will need to take into account what a synagogue actually was.

As Ben Meyer has argued, the Hebrew Bible and the literature of the Second Temple period conceived of salvation in terms of "'all Israel' (*kol-yiśrā'ēl*) or 'the people of Israel' (*'am yiśrā'ēl*), the assembly (*qāhāl*), the congregation (*'ēdâ*), and the like; Israel, in short, understood salvation in ecclesial terms."[59] As our discussion above indicates, Jesus appears to have stood firmly in this tradition, as he similarly thought of the redemptive, restorative reign of God as something corporate. The synagogue as Jesus knew it was a corporate entity, and represented the town as a whole. We must recall that the synagogue was a local-official institution in which decisions were made regarding the direction to be taken by the town as a whole.[60] By proclaiming his message of the Kingdom of God in the local synagogues, he was effectively direct-

John: Its Historicity and Significance," in *Key Events in the Life of the Historical Jesus: A Collaborative Exploration of Context and Coherence*, ed. Darrell L. Bock and Robert L. Webb (Tübingen: Mohr Siebeck, 2009), 95–150 (139–41).

58. Cf. the findings of Spigel, *Synagogue Seating Capacities*.

59. Meyer, *Aims of Jesus*, 134, emphasis my own.

60. See also, on this topic, Jordan J. Ryan, "Jesus and Synagogue Disputes: Recovering the Institutional Context of Luke 13:10–17," *CBQ* 79, no. 1 (2017): 41–59.

ing his message not only to the individuals present in the synagogue, but to the town as a corporate, political entity. Jesus was *trying to bring entire locales into the then-outbreaking Kingdom of God, the restored Israel* by announcing its coming within local synagogues and attempting to persuade the assembly to take part in it. So doing would effectively bring towns and villages into the Kingdom of God as Jesus conceived it.

Significant clues are to be found in the summary of Jesus's proclamation in Mark 1:14–15.[61] We must be aware that even within the context of Mark, v. 15 is meant to represent the general voice or spirit of Jesus's pattern of proclamation rather than an actual saying uttered on a specific occasion. Nevertheless, this is significant data. It is clear from v. 15 that the proclamation requires a response. Jesus admonishes his audience to "believe in the good news," that is, the good news that God's reign is at hand. This evidences the fact that Jesus was attempting to persuade his listeners of the truth of what he was proclaiming. In other words, merely delivering the message was not enough—the people needed to accept it, and so, needed to be won over. Belief in the message needed to be accompanied by, as Meyer has put it, a "willed act" of repentance.[62] The town would need to be persuaded, then, not only that the reign of God was at hand, but moreover, that they needed to "repent" and act in a particular way in response. The necessity of the response of repentance is evidenced by the double-tradition saying concerning woes to the Galilean villages of Chorazin, Bethsaida, and Capernaum (Luke 10:13–16; Matt 11:20–24) because they have failed to repent. Luke's version of the saying connects this directly to rejection (10:16), while the Matthean version connects the lack of repentance to liability to judgment (11:24).

There is a precedent for this pattern in the narrative of Jonah, in which a prophet travels to a city, and proclaims a message of impending judgment.[63] A direct reference to the repentance of the Ninevites in the narrative of Jonah can be found within the Jesus tradition, in Luke 11:32/Matthew 12:41. As Carroll writes of the Lukan passage, "the role that Jonah played at Ninevah, Jesus as the Son of Humanity now plays in his own era."[64] In Jonah, as in the Gospels, repentance, much like redemption and judgment, are understood to be corporate, ecclesial things.[65] As the salvation of the Ninevites depended on their being per-

---

61. Cf. Matt 4:17.
62. Meyer *Aims of Jesus*, 137.
63. See esp. Jonah 3:1–10.
64. Carroll, *Luke*, 257.
65. A hard distinction need not be made here between corporate and individual redemption, which is

suaded by Jonah's message (cf. Jonah 3:6–10) and subsequently repenting, so too does Jesus's ultimatum of "repent or perish" (Luke 13:5) imply the same.

A connection between the act of repentance, the Kingdom (*basileia*) of God (v. 1), and a divine act of "gathering" and restoring his people is strongly reflected in Tobit 13:1–6.[66] Verses 5b–6a read as follows:

> He will gather you from all the nations among whom you have been scattered. If you turn to him with all your heart and with all your soul, to do what is true before him, then he will turn to you and will no longer hide his face from you.

The act of gathering the repentant envisioned in this passage is essentially what Jesus appears to be doing in the synoptic Gospels by going throughout the Land, teaching and proclaiming the message of the outbreak of the reign of God in public synagogues.[67] By persuading the assemblies to accept his message and repent, he was gathering them for the coming restoration. This passage indicates the currency of these ideas in the Second Temple period.

That Jesus had the corporate redemption of towns and villages in mind is demonstrated by the aforementioned double-tradition saying pronouncing woes upon Galilean locales in Matthew 11:21–23a/Luke 10:13–15. I cite the Matthean version here in its narrative setting:

> Then he began to reproach the cities in which most of his deeds of power had been done, because they did not repent. "Woe to you, Chorazin! Woe to you, Bethsaida! For if the deeds of power done in you had been done in Tyre and Sidon, they would have repented long ago in sackcloth and ashes. But I tell you, on the day of judgement it will be more tolerable for Tyre and Sidon than for you. And you, Capernaum, will you be exalted to heaven? No, you will be brought down to Hades."[68]

This data indicates several things that are of relevance to our inves-

---

also sometimes present in the tradition (Luke 15:7), since the corporate entity is made up of individuals.

66. Note the parallels here also to Deut 30:1–10.

67. Note the mention of the Father drawing people to Jesus in the Capernaum synagogue discourse in John 6:44. On this, see chapter 8 below.

68. The Lukan version has a different narrative setting. It is set in the context of the sending of the seventy, and it is followed by a saying directed at the seventy: "whoever listens to you listens to me, and whoever rejects you rejects me, and whoever rejects me rejects the one who sent me" (Luke 10:16). The woes against the Galilean cities seem out of place in this narrative context, which is concerned with instructions to the seventy rather than the results of Jesus's own mission. It is probably the case that Luke worked this genuine but contextually displaced saying into this narrative for rhetorical effect.

tigation. First, it is striking that Jesus speaks of the repentance and judgment of *municipalities*. This is indicative of the ecclesial terms of the conception of his mission. I suggest that this saying reflects a failure to persuade the synagogue assemblies of these towns to believe his proclamation and/or to repent in light of it. Second, Jesus made use of "deeds of power" in order to persuade local populations to repent.[69] Third, Jesus was not always successful in his attempts to persuade municipalities to accept his message. These are all significant observations, and each of them will be revisited throughout the rest of the investigation, particularly when we turn to examining individual episodes in the Gospels which are set in synagogues. As we shall see, there is further evidence to support all three. For now, it is sufficient simply to make these observations, and to grasp the relevance of this passage for the matter currently under discussion.

The clearest statement of Jesus's mission on his own lips in the synoptic Gospels is in Mark 1:38 and its parallel in Luke 4:43. In the Markan version, Jesus says, "Let us go on to the neighboring towns, so that I may proclaim the message there also; for that is what I came out to do." This pericope follows the exorcism that was performed in the synagogue at Capernaum and the healing of Peter's mother-in-law. Rather than basing his mission in Capernaum alone, he is, instead, said to consider it his purpose to proclaim the message in other towns (lit. "the next towns") as well. Unlike John the Baptist, Jesus does not wait for the people to come to him.[70] Instead, he travels from town to town to proclaim his message, since this is what he "came out" (Gk. ἐξῆλθον) to do. Jesus's statement of his purpose is then followed by a report that he went throughout Galilee proclaiming the message in synagogues and casting out demons (Mark 1:39, cf. Luke 4:44). Ultimately, the synagogue was where this purpose was carried out, as proclaiming in the synagogue *was* proclaiming to the town.

It is curious that this statement of purpose in Mark 1:38 (and the parallel in Luke 4:43) has not played a more significant role in historical Jesus research.[71] It is possible that this is due to concerns surrounding the "authenticity" of the passage. The Jesus Seminar, for example, considers Mark 1:38 to be a Markan creation, saying that Mark here summarizes "what, for him, was Jesus' purpose (v. 38): to carry his message

---

69. This will be discussed in depth in chapter 7.
70. Cf. Collins, *Mark*, 177.
71. It is particularly surprising that it is passed over by Ben Meyer in *The Aims of Jesus*, since here more than anywhere else in the Gospels do we have a clear statement by Jesus of his purpose.

to neighbouring villages."[72] Let us, for the sake of argument, grant that this saying comes from Mark rather than Jesus. Even if it is a Markan creation, I am not convinced that this saying can be so easily dismissed. Could Mark not have been correct in his summary of Jesus' purpose? What evidence is there to the contrary? Jesus's travels in Galilee and in Judea are integral to the tradition. He did, after all, die in Jerusalem, not Capernaum. If we accept that Jesus was an itinerant, then it is hard to deny that carrying his message to various locales *was* his intent. The mere fact that Mark and Luke consider this to have been Jesus's purpose is significant and relevant for our investigation, especially when we do not consider it in isolation, but alongside the other evidence presented here. By interpreting and treating this data in this way, I am deliberately shifting away from treating the data as mere "testimony" to be either accepted or rejected, toward treating it as *evidence* for the matter at hand.

Jesus's mission to proclaim his message of the coming of the Kingdom of God in the synagogues of Galilee and Judea in order to bring each town into the restored Israel could not be accomplished by him alone. There were simply too many Jewish towns and villages throughout the Land for him to visit.[73] In light of Jesus's aims, the pericopes dealing with the sending out of the twelve and the seventy should be understood as a necessary extension of Jesus's own mission of proclamation.[74]

The double tradition indicates that the twelve were sent out to proclaim the Kingdom of God, as well as to heal and cast out demons (Luke 9:2; Matt 10:7). The sending of the seventy, an event that is unique to Luke, also has Jesus instructing his followers to proclaim the nearness of the Kingdom (Luke 10:9). Mark, however, only mentions that the twelve performed exorcisms and "proclaimed that all should repent" (Mark 6:12–13). In my opinion, Mark (or the Markan memorialization process) has shaped the memory of the event in accordance with his portrait of Jesus's early mission as characterized by exorcisms.[75] At any

---

72. Funk and the Jesus Seminar, *Five Gospels*, 43.
73. The early Roman period in particular saw a dramatic increase in the number of Jewish settlements in Galilee alone. On this, see Uzi Leibner, *Settlement and History in Hellenistic, Roman, and Byzantine Galilee* (TSAJ 127; Tübingen: Mohr Siebeck, 2009), 331–33. Josephus claims that there were 204 Jewish settlements in Galilee (cf. *Life*, 204). It has recently been argued that there is good reason to think that this number is fairly accurate, cf. Chaim ben David, "Were There 204 Settlements in Galilee at the Time of Josephus Flavius?" *JJS* 62, no. 1 (2011): 21–36.
74. Mark 6:6b–13; Matt 10:1–42; Luke 9:1–6; Luke 10:1–12.
75. For a concise comparison of Mark's characteristic portrayal of Jesus as an exorcist with the portraits of Jesus in the other Gospels, see Cees den Heyer, "Historic Jesuses," in *Handbook for the*

rate, the mention of the proclamation of repentance is evidence of the Kingdom proclamation, since the two are inextricably tied together in Mark, as seen earlier in Mark's summary of Jesus's early mission (Mark 1:14–15).

Some scholars have expressed doubt that Jesus ever sent his own followers out on a specific mission during his lifetime, opting instead to see these passages as a retrojection of the early church's missionary activity back into the Jesus movement.[76] The problem with this is that the Gospels describe a mission with a kerygma that is fundamentally different from that of Jesus's post-Easter followers. In the Gospels, Jesus's followers proclaim the Kingdom of God, whereas the post-Easter mission typically proclaims Jesus himself, in terms of his resurrection, lordship, and messiahship.[77] The existence of the post-Easter mission does not preclude there having been a pre-Easter mission, especially when they are apparently quite different in character. It is certainly probable that the memory of Jesus sending his followers out has been colored and impacted to some degree by the situation of the post-Easter mission, but this does not mean that there was no sending at all, or that Jesus's followers did not proclaim the Kingdom in the towns of Judea and Galilee during Jesus's lifetime. To the contrary, the "sending" pericopes constitute crucial data on Jesus's aims, since they indicate that Jesus thought that he required the contributions of others to accomplish his overarching goal, at least at this point in his career. This inference fits quite well into the portrait we have thus far presented.

The idea that is beginning to emerge from the data is that Jesus was travelling throughout the Land of "greater Israel," trying to restore Israel one municipality at a time, bringing each locale into the realized eschatological reign of God by convincing them to believe in his message and to repent in response. This, then, helps to explain *how* Jesus saw the Kingdom of God breaking out in the world, and how he saw his own mission in relation to the realization of that event. The restoration hypothesis, which is now a staple of historical Jesus research, has illuminated Jesus's aims. What we have hit upon now is the method by which Jesus attempted to achieve that end during the early phases of his career, which in turn, impacts our understanding of the way in

---

Study of the Historical Jesus, ed. Tom Holmén and Stanley E. Porter (Leiden and Boston: Brill, 2011), 1079–101 (1086–89).

76. See, e.g., Funk and the Jesus Seminar, *Acts of Jesus*, 86; Francis Wright Beare, "Mission of the Disciples and the Mission Charge: Matthew 10 and Parallels," *JBL* 89, no. 1 (1970): 1–13, esp. 13.

77. Cf. a similar argument made by Graham H. Twelftree, *Jesus the Exorcist: A Contribution to the Study of the Historical Jesus* (WUNT 52; Tübingen: Mohr Siebeck, 1993), 124.

which Jesus conceived of the Kingdom of God and its advent upon the earth.

Understanding Jesus's proclamation of the Kingdom of God in light of the institution of the synagogue also highlights the political dimension of his aims. To be clear, by "political," I do not specifically mean "anti-Roman" or "revolutionary," as the term is too often taken to mean in our discipline. Rather, I use the term much as Alan Storkey does in saying that politics means "all the business of the state – rule, law, nationhood, power, justice, taxation, statehood, international relations, war, and government economic policy."[78] As we will see, the coming of the reign of God proclaimed by Jesus pertains to many of these things.

There is, to be sure, more to Jesus's politics than things having to do with "the state" conceived narrowly in national terms. There is also such a thing as local or municipal politics, which pertains to rule, law, township, power, justice, etc., on the local level. The "political" is, to use Arendtian language, based on human plurality,[79] and so, it is present in different ways and to different degrees wherever that plurality is to be found. We should recognize that the synagogue was a local-official institution, and that there is thus a local political element to Jesus's act of proclamation in synagogues. Nevertheless, the local level cannot be separated entirely from the national level within the aims of Jesus's mission. The national-level aim of restoring Israel had direct ramifications on the local level of the town in which it was proclaimed. The decision to partake in the outbreaking Kingdom of God would entail the acceptance of the proclamation and all that it entails by the synagogue as well as an accompanying response of repentance by the people of that town.

My approach also highlights the importance of persuasion and rhetoric in Jesus's mission. As chapter 3 demonstrated, rhetoric and persuasion of the assembled public was an important aspect of synagogue discourse and proceedings. If the public could not be persuaded, Jesus would accrue shame, his message would go unheeded, and his legal teachings would be rejected within that locale. This is apparently what happened in Bethsaida, Chorazin, and Capernaum, as evidenced by Matthew 11:21–23a/Luke 10:13–15. Further investigation into the methods and means of persuasion that Jesus used in synagogues is warranted, since this will help to further clarify his actions, aims, and mes-

---

78. Alan Storkey, *Jesus and Politics: Confronting the Powers* (Grand Rapids: Baker, 2005), 10.
79. See Hannah Arendt, *The Promise of Politics* (New York: Schocken Books, 2005), 93.

sage. We will look into this further when we examine specific episodes set in synagogues in the following chapters.

Teaching in the Synagogues

All four of the canonical evangelists, either explicitly or implicitly, tell us that Jesus habitually taught in synagogues.[80] Although Mark does not include a general reference to teaching in his summary statement of Jesus's activity in Galilee, there are two specific episodes involving Jesus teaching in a synagogue in Mark.[81] In neither case are we given the content of the teaching. The three other evangelists explicitly describe teaching in synagogues as though it was characteristic of the pattern of his program.[82]

Despite the fact that Matthew, Luke, and John all describe Jesus's teaching in synagogues as though it were frequent and habitual, there are very few preserved instances in the Gospels of Jesus intentionally teaching in synagogue settings.[83] This problem is especially acute for Matthew, who does not specify the content of Jesus's teaching in synagogues, and never sets a specific teaching complex within a synagogue context. In fact, the only sayings that are set within synagogues in Matthew are "prophets are not without honour except in their own country and in their own house" (Matt 13:57), which is not a teaching so much as a response to those who are offended by him, and a saying about healing on the Sabbath in Matthew 12:11–12. Despite this, general reference is made to Jesus's habitual teaching in synagogues not once but *twice* in Matthew (4:23 and 9:35), in addition to a specific reference to Jesus teaching in the synagogue at Nazareth, though the content of that teaching is not given.

A cursory search for the content of Jesus's synagogue teaching in the Gospels produces meagre results. There are two teaching complexes set in synagogues, which convey the content of what was taught. Luke 4:16–30 narrates Jesus's teaching in the synagogue at Nazareth, and John 6:25–59 contains a block of teaching material located in the synagogue at Capernaum. There are also several instances of very short

---

80. Cf. Runesson, "Importance of the Synagogue," 290.

81. Mark 1:21 and 6:2.

82. Matthew 4:23; Luke 4:15; John 18:20. Mark is the only one of the four evangelists who does not directly mention Jesus's teaching as something distinct from proclamation.

83. A similar point is made by Blomberg. He notes that nothing comparable to the teaching in John 6:25–59 is found in the synoptics, "because there we are *never* given in detail the contents of any of Jesus' preaching *in the synagogues*" (emphasis original). See Blomberg, *Historical Reliability of John's Gospel*, 127.

sayings responding to Sabbath controversies that are set in synagogues in Luke 13:15-16, Mark 3:4, and Matthew 12:11-12. However, it is clear that these sayings are occasioned rather than deliberate and are meant to respond to negative reactions to healings or exorcisms performed in synagogues on the Sabbath.

Full discussion of these passages will have to wait for the chapters to follow. For the time being, it is worth noting that these passages share a common element in that they all deal in some way with the interpretation of Jewish scripture.[84] The Sabbath controversies relate, naturally, to the interpretation of the Sabbath laws.[85] John 6:25-59 contains discussion of the story of manna from heaven.[86] Luke 4:16-30 narrates a reading from Isaiah,[87] and makes reference to events from the Elijah and Elisha cycles of 1-2 Kings.[88] The fact that all of these passages involve Jewish scripture in some way fits in well with the general portrait of the synagogue that was presented in chapter 3, since the synagogue was the place where both the Torah and Nevi'im were read and discussed. We can also observe that the acts of "teaching" and "proclaiming" are closely and intricately connected, as the teaching illuminates and clarifies the proclamation.

The paucity of teachings located in synagogues in the Gospels is in tension with the evangelists' unanimous testimony to Jesus's habitual teaching in synagogues. Although this problem has not gone altogether unnoticed,[89] it has not yet been adequately addressed. We are thus left to wrestle with several historical questions. What was Jesus teaching in the synagogues? What purpose did his teaching serve within his broader aims? How did his teaching relate to his proclamation? We are, however, without sufficient evidence in the form of direct testimony by the evangelists to address these questions. This is a case in which the answer cannot be sought through empirical or scissors-and-paste research. If these questions are to be convincingly answered, the answer must be arrived at through inference, interpretation, and imagination. We must rely on reconstruction rather than testimony.

Some answers may lie in the material contained in the Matthean Sermon on the Mount and its parallels in Luke's Sermon on the Plain. A

---

84. Thus, Bovon's comment on Luke 4:15, cf. Mark 1:21, that διδάσκω is understood in the tradition "in terms of the Jewish interpretation of the Scriptures" seems appropriate. Bovon, *Luke*, 1:152.

85. Exod 20:8-11; 23:12, 31:13-17; Deut 5:13-14.

86. Exod 16:1-36; Num 11:1-9.

87. Isa 61:1-2, 58:6.

88. 1 Kgs 17:8-24, 18:1; 2 Kgs 5:1-19.

89. E.g., Raymond E. Brown, *The Gospel According to John* (AB 29A; New Haven: Yale University Press, 2008 [1970]), 826; Joel B. Green, *The Gospel of Luke* (NICNT; Grand Rapids: Eerdmans, 1997), 207.

majority of scholars recognize that the Sermon on the Mount is more likely to be a compilation of Jesus traditions than either an actual "sermon" delivered by Jesus or an original, *ex nihilo* Matthean compositional unity.[90] This view goes at least as far back as John Calvin, who wrote that the Sermon on the Mount was "collected out of his [Jesus'] many and various discourses."[91] Current thought on how Matthew compiled the Sermon on the Mount is summed up by Cees Den Heyer, in saying that "using tradition—the memories of Jesus' statements—he [Matthew] has created *his* Sermon on the Mount."[92] In other words, though the Sermon as a unit was crafted by Matthew, it was woven from earlier memories and traditions about Jesus that he had collected. The artificiality of the narrative setting of the Sermon on the Mount is strongly indicated by the fact that Matthew 5:1 has Jesus leaving the crowds behind and ascending the mountain, where he teaches only his disciples, while the Sermon ends in 7:28–29 with the crowds being astonished at his teachings. Intriguingly, Matthew has lifted this response almost verbatim from Mark 1:22, which describes the reaction of the assembled public to Jesus's teaching in the synagogue at Capernaum. That Luke 6:17–19 sets much of the same material in a "sermon" located at a "level place" amidst a great crowd may serve to indicate that no specific location was attached to these teachings in the earlier oral or written tradition upon which the evangelists drew.

It is my contention that the Sermon on the Mount material represents the sort of things that Jesus taught, and thus, provides a general idea of what his synagogue teaching might have been like. I would also suggest that some, perhaps even many, of the teachings contained in the Sermon on the Mount and the Sermon on the Plain could have

---

90. See, e.g., Ulrich Luz, *Matthew*, rev. ed., 3 vols, (Hermeneia; Minneapolis: Fortress Press, 2007), 1:174; W. D. Davies and D. C. Allison, *Matthew* (ICC; 3 vols.; Edinburgh: T&T Clark, 1988), 1:422; Craig S. Keener, *Matthew: A Socio-Rhetorical Commentary* (Grand Rapids and Cambridge: Eerdmans, 2009), 162–63; John S. Kloppenborg, *Excavating Q* (Minneapolis: Fortress Press, 2000), 90; Christopher M. Tuckett, *Q and the History of Early Christianity: Studies on Q* (Edinburgh: T&T Clark, 1996), 36–37; James A. Brooks, 'The Unity and Structure of the Sermon on the Mount," *Criswell Theological Review* 6, no. 1 (1992): 15–28; Benedict T. Viviano, "The Sermon on the Mount in Recent Study," *Biblical* 78 (1997): 255–65. A comprehensive survey of proponents of this view and the varieties of its instantiations would be so lengthy so as to require its own monograph. This small but broad sample serves our present purpose well. It is worth noting that a small minority have proposed and defended alternative views. This minority includes, most notably, Hans Dieter Betz, *The Sermon on the Mount* (ed. Adela Yarbro Collins; Hermeneia; Minneapolis: Fortress Press, 1995); Jan Lambrecht, *The Sermon on the Mount: Proclamation and Exhortation* (Wilmington: Glazier, 1985), esp. 39–40; and Stanley E. Porter, "The Role of Greek Language Criteria in Historical Jesus Research," in *Handbook for the Study of the Historical Jesus* (ed. Tom Holmén and Stanley E. Porter; Leiden and Boston: Brill, 2011), 1:361–404.

91. John Calvin, *Commentary on Matthew*, 5:1.

92. den Heyer, "Historical Jesuses," 2:1085.

actually been delivered in the synagogues of Galilee. The synagogue summary statements provide a context without content, while in the Sermon on the Mount material, we have content without a historical context. It is thus only matter of making a connection between these two relatively fixed points in order to see how the Sermon material might find a plausible setting in the Galilean synagogues.

Though it is tempting to simply transplant the Sermon material wholesale into Galilean synagogues, the lack of direct evidence necessitates a more cautious and modest approach in most cases. If, however, we treat the Sermon sayings as representative of the kind of thing that Jesus would have been teaching in synagogues in a generic way, we may at least come away with a general picture of what his synagogue teachings were like that can then be further clarified and brought into focus by our examination of episodes explicitly set in synagogues in chapters 8–11.

One particular group of sayings found in the Sermon on the Mount is especially plausible to imagine within a public synagogue setting. Given that the synagogue was the place where the Law was read, interpreted, and discussed, the "antitheses" (Matt 5:21–48) find a natural home within the context of a synagogue gathering. Though I must rely on my historical imagination here, a thread stretched between the datum of the legal content of the antitheses on the one hand and that of the synagogue as place of the Law on the other, it is probable that the antitheses represent actual instances of teaching delivered by Jesus in public synagogue settings. The antitheses also cohere with the teaching complexes mentioned above that *are* explicitly set in synagogues, insofar as they are concerned with the interpretation of Jewish scripture.

The evidence for situating the antitheses in a synagogue context can be summed up in the following manner: i) there is evidence that Jesus taught habitually in synagogues; ii) the synagogues were where the Law was read, interpreted, and discussed; iii) the antitheses concern legal interpretation and practice; and iv) the general nature of the antitheses as interpretation of Jewish scripture coheres with the few instances of Jesus's sayings and teachings unambiguously delivered in synagogue contexts elsewhere in the Gospels. For these reasons, the antitheses make for a good point of departure for this stage of our investigation.

The Antitheses as Synagogue Teaching

The term "antitheses" is a misnomer. It comes from reading Matthew 5:21–48 as constituting a challenge to the Mosaic Law. This interpretation was especially popular with New Questers.[93] Bultmann's views on the topic exemplify this:

> The demands of the Sermon on the Mount have always been regarded as particularly characteristic of the preaching of Jesus. Here we find at the beginning the new set over against the old in strong antitheses, in a peculiar interpretation of the Old Testament which evidently aims to establish its true meaning as against the scribal interpretation, thus completely destroying, as we have before observed, the formal authority of Scripture.[94]

If Bultmann's interpretation is correct, it would be hard to imagine the antitheses being persuasive whatsoever within a synagogue setting. By the very nature of the synagogue institution, scripture and its authority were understood to be central to Jewish civic and religious life. However, other scholars have since pointed out that Jesus here does not actually abrogate the law.[95] Rather, as Sanders puts the matter, the antitheses "affirm the law, but press beyond it," in the sense of making it tighter,[96] since the antitheses generally seem to tighten rather than abrogate the law.[97] This raises the possibility that, with the antitheses, Jesus was actually "building a fence around the Torah,"[98] making stricter laws around the Mosaic Torah in order to prevent trespassing the core instruction. It is certainly easy to imagine such a thing taking place within a synagogue context.

There are a total of six antitheses, five of which deal explicitly with a Mosaic commandment: (1) concerning murder (Matt 5:21–26; on Exod 20:13, cf. Gen 9:5–6), (2) concerning adultery (Matt 5:27–30; on Exod

---

93. E.g., Bultmann, *Jesus and the Word*, 89–90; Käsemann, "Problem of the Historical Jesus," 303; Werner Georg Kümmel, *Theology of the New Testament* (London: SCM, 1974), 52; Georg Strecker, "Die Antithesen der Bergpredigt (Mt 5 21–24 par)," *Zeitschrift für die Neutestamentliche Wissenschaft* 69 (1978): 36–72. Interestingly and perhaps tellingly, Betz, *Sermon on the Mount*, 200–201, finds that Marcion was the first to use the term.

94. Bultmann, *Jesus and the Word*, 89.

95. E.g., Robert H. Gundry, *Matthew: A Commentary on His Literary and Theological Art* (Grand Rapids: Eerdmans, 1982), 82–83; Sanders, *Jesus and Judaism*, 260; Stephen Westerholm, "The Law in the Sermon on the Mount: Matt 5:17–48," *Criswell Theological Review*, 6, no. 1 (1992): 43–56, esp. 53 ("the law is not abolished; it is transcended"); Geza Vermes, *The Religion of Jesus the Jew* (Minneapolis: Fortress Press, 1993), 30–31; Keener, *Matthew*, 181.

96. Sanders, *Jesus and Judaism*, 260.

97. Cf. Keener, *Matthew*, 181; Sanders, *Jesus and Judaism*, 9–10, 156–57.

98. See *m. Avot* 1:1.

20:14), (3) concerning divorce (Matt 5:31–32; on Deut 24:10–4), (4) concerning oaths (Matt 5:33–37; on Deut 23:23), (5) concerning retaliation (Matt 5:38–42; on Exod 21:23–25, cf. Deut 19:21); and (6) concerning love for enemies (Matt 5:43–48; the reference is unclear, though it is generically related to Lev 19:18). Although Luke's Sermon on the Plain does not include the antitheses as a unit, parallels to some of these teachings exist elsewhere in the Jesus tradition. Part of the teaching on murder is paralleled in Luke 12:57–59, the teaching on divorce is widely attested (Matt 19:9; Mark 10:11–12; Luke 16:18; 1 Cor 7:10–11), and parallels to the teachings on retaliation and love for enemies are embedded in Luke 6:27–36.

The fact that there exist different versions of these teachings or portions of these teachings employed in different ways elsewhere in the tradition does not necessarily indicate that the comparisons drawn between Jesus's teaching and the Mosaic Law in the antitheses are artificial Matthean constructions.[99] First, it is probable that the sayings were retold, remembered, and shaped differently within different streams of tradition. Second, if we imagine that Jesus had a relatively extended teaching career, and that he habitually taught in different locales, we must also imagine that he probably repeated aspects of his teaching on different occasions. This actually occurs in the world of the Matthean narrative, as the teaching on divorce is repeated in Matthew 19:9. Third, and most importantly, the teachings in the first five antitheses draw natural comparisons to the Mosaic commandments that they address. Whether or not the antithetical formulation ("you have heard it said"/"but I say to you") is Matthean or dominical is actually beside the point. This is recognized by Dunn, who holds that the antithetical formulation is probably Matthean, but writes nevertheless that "it is equally likely that Jesus was remembered as setting his own teaching on various subjects in some measure over against previous rulings or as giving radical interpretations of particular Scriptures, even if not in such a formulaic manner."[100] The teaching in 5:28 on adultery, for example, needs to be understood in comparison to Exodus 20:14. Thus, even if the antithetical form in which Matthew presents these teachings is a result of memory distortion or Matthean redaction,[101] a point that needs to be proven and not assumed in the

---

99. Cf. Becker, *Jesus of Nazareth*, 288.
100. Dunn, *Jesus Remembered*, 579.
101. E.g., Daniel J. Harrington, *The Gospel of Matthew* (Sacra Pagina 1; Collegeville: Liturgical, 2007 [1991]), 90–91.

first place,[102] an implicit juxtaposition with the Mosaic Law is nevertheless assumed.

The teaching on murder (Matt 5:21–26) is particularly interesting for our purposes, since it deals both with legal interpretation and with ramifications. It is important to note that v. 22, which prescribes legal liability for anger and insults, does not abrogate the Mosaic law referred to in v. 21. Jesus's teaching in v. 22 requires stricter observance, which would actually serve to help prevent transgression of the Mosaic commandment.[103] Indeed, in the narrative of the first murder in Genesis 4:1–16, anger is the root cause of murder (Gen 4:5–7). According to the Cain and Abel narrative, murder entered the world through anger. Thus, the elimination of anger is, in effect, the elimination of the cause for murder, and thereby, of murder itself.

The idea expressed by Jesus in v. 22 is that a person can be held *legally culpable* (ἔνοχος ἔσται τῇ κρίσει) for feelings and displays of anger.[104] There is some question here as to whether this culpability should be understood concretely in terms of human law, or eschatologically in terms of divine judgment.[105] The term κρίσις in vv. 21 and 22a is ambiguous, and could refer to the judgment of either human or divine courts.[106] The reference to liability to Gehenna in v. 22c indicates that there is an eschatological aspect to this culpability,[107] but ἔνοχος ἔσται τῷ συνεδρίῳ (liability to the council) in v. 22b more likely envisions a human court rather than an eschatological judgment.[108]

Derrett argues that only a heavenly court is in mind throughout v. 22.[109] He recognizes that the Greek term ἔνοχος suggests human jurisdictions, but suggests that it translates the Hebrew *ḥayyāv*, which also

---

02. A thorough and convincing argument for attributing the antithetical form to Jesus is offered by Luz, *Matthew*, 1:227–31. In keeping with his major hypothesis, Betz also makes a case for the antitheses being pre-Matthean, though he does not ascribe them to Jesus. See Betz, *Sermon on the Mount*, 212–14.

03. Hence, the suggestion that Jesus is building a "fence" around the Torah. On this concept and the relation of the first antithesis to early rabbinic parallels, see Neudecker Reinhardt, *Moses Interpreted by the Pharisees and Jesus: Matthew's Antitheses in Light of Early Rabbinic Literature* (Subsidia Biblical 44; Rome: Georgian and Biblical Press, 2012), 49–55.

04. Direct association of anger with murder can be found elsewhere in Second Temple Jewish writings. E.g., Sir 22:24; *T. Dan.* 1:7–8; *T. Gad* 4:1–7; *T. Sim.* 2:11; *T. Zeb.* 4:11.

05. Compare, e.g., Keener, *Matthew*, 183–84; J. Duncan M. Derrett, "Ἔνοχος (Mt 5, 21–22) and the Jurisprudence of Heaven," *Filología Neotestamentaria* 19 (2006): 89–97; Joachim Jeremias, *New Testament Theology* (New York: Scribner's, 1971), 149; Luz, *Matthew*, 1:235–36; Davies and Allison, *Matthew*, 1:512.

06. At any rate, Jewish human courts were understood to judge on the basis of divine Law, and thus, represent divine will.

07. Cf., e.g., Keener, *Matthew*, 184.

08. Cf., e.g., Luz, *Matthew*, 1:235; W. D. Davies, *The Setting of the Sermon on the Mount* (Cambridge: Cambridge University Press, 1964), 236–38.

09. Derrett, "Ἔνοχος (Mt 5, 21–22) and the Jurisprudence of Heaven," passim.

has another dimension, that of heavenly jurisprudence. This is an interesting suggestion, especially given the reference to Gehenna in Matthew 5:22. However, even if we grant that the Hebrew *ḥayyāv* does indeed underlie the Greek ἔνοχος, itself an uncertain premise, the fact that *ḥayyāv* can refer to heavenly jurisprudence does not necessarily mean that it does here. Furthermore, ἔνοχος refers in v. 21 to liability for murder, a crime which was tried in human courts,[110] so there is good reason to think that it should not be treated any differently in v. 22.[111] It is difficult to imagine punitive justice for murder being put off entirely until the eschatological judgment, even if Jewish courts did not have the legal ability to execute capital sentences at the time of Jesus.[112] It is clear that capital sentences were carried out by Jews in the first century regardless.[113] It is important to note, moreover, that vv. 23–25 (esp. v. 25) explicitly imagine human relationships and legal systems. Derrett also relies on late rabbinic evidence to make his case. For these reasons, I find this interpretation unconvincing.

If Jesus envisions judgment within the setting of a human court, then this implies that he imagined the legal teaching of v. 22 ideally being put into practice in Jewish communities. The term συνέδριον need not be taken to refer to a national Jewish ruling body in Jerusalem called "the Sanhedrin."[114] The word can refer simply to a gathering or council,[115] and it most likely refers in this case to a local council or a judicial assembly as described in chapter 3.[116] As I have already demonstrated there, the synagogue was the usual place where judgment would have taken place in towns and villages, and where the local council met. We should now also recall that Mark 13:9 connects συνέδρια (note the plural form) with the synagogue judicial system.[117] It thus seems as though Jesus saw the teaching in Matthew 5:22 as some-

---

110. E.g., Josephus, *Ant.* 14.168–77, cf. also 1.102.; *m. Makkot* 1:8–10, 2:1–2, 6, 7–8.
111. Cf. Davies and Allison, *Matthew*, 1: 512: "One in any case cannot solve the problem by thinking of divine judgment, for then the ἔνοχος ἔσται τῇ κρίσει of 5:22 would mean something altogether different from the ἔνοχος ἔσται τῇ κρίσει of 5:21."
112. Contra Keener, *Matthew*, 184.
113. E.g., Josephus, *Ant.* 20.200, *Apion*, 2.206, *Life* 75, 303; Acts 7:58–59.
114. See the description in *m. Sanhedrin*.
115. Cf. Sanders, *Practice and Belief*, 473. See also the entry in LSJ. Sanders has called into question traditional conceptions about "The Sanhedrin" as a supreme legislative assembly.
116. Cf. Davies, *Setting of the Sermon on the Mount*, 238. Like myself, Davies also connects this council to the local synagogue. See also Davies and Allison, *Matthew*, 1:514.
117. Contra scholars who identify the *synedrion* here with the heavenly court, e.g., Derrett, "Jurisprudence," 92; Craig S. Keener, "Matthew 5:22 and the Heavenly Court," *Expository Times* 99 (1987): 46; Kenner, *Matthew*, 184; Samuel Tobias Lachs, *A Rabbinic Commentary on the New Testament; The Gospels of Matthew, Mark, and Luke* (Hoboken: Ktav, 1987), 92–94; R. T. France, *Matthew* (Downers Grove: InterVarsity, 1985), 120.

thing that would be accepted and practiced in the public synagogues *as well as* the eschatological judgment. One would thus be liable for anger to both the human and the divine courts, since anger is the root cause of murder. This makes a good deal of sense if we take Jesus's now-and-not-yet, partially-realized eschatology into account. The outbreak of the Kingdom calls God's people to a radical ethic in the present. Human beings should refrain from acting out of anger, and must recognize that they are liable for their actions to each other in the present time and to God at the eschatological judgment. Human and divine law, much like politics and religion, were inextricable in a public synagogue setting.

Is it possible that Jesus was simply being hyperbolic? Perhaps, but if that is the case, then it is odd that he would invoke an actual law that was tried in Jewish courts in v. 21.[118] Such an interpretation leaves us in the difficult position of understanding that "liability to judgment" in v. 22a means something entirely different than it means in v. 21.[119]

Keener, similar to Derrett, has argued that the συνέδρια in Matthew 5:22 refers to the heavenly court, rather than "the Sanhedrin," that is, the Jerusalem governing body.[120] His argument, too, is mostly based on very late rabbinic evidence, which speaks of a heavenly Sanhedrin. It is also important to note that vv. 23–26 quite clearly depicts a human court. If v. 22 does not, then it is odd that it is surrounded by verses that do envision a human justice system. Moreover, Keener's argument leaves aside altogether the possibility that neither a heavenly court nor the Jewish governing body known as "the Sanhedrin" are in view in this passage, but rather, a local synagogue council.[121] I suggest that this third option is preferable, and best reflects the historical setting of Jesus's rural Galilee, where trials were held in synagogue settings.[122]

How could an earthly court be expected to judge anger? This problem has not gone unnoticed by interpreters.[123] Some scholars have, however, noted some potential parallels in the sectarian documents at Qumran.[124] 1QS 6:24–27, 7:1–5 contains rules and penalties that pertain

18. E.g., Josephus, *Ant.* 14.168–177, cf. also 1.102; *m. Makkot* 1:8–10, 2:1–2, 6, 7–8.

19. In agreement with Davies and Allison, *Matthew*, 1: 512.

20. Craig S. Keener, "Matthew 5:22 and the Heavenly Court," *Expository Times* 99, no. 2 (1987): 46.

21. Examples from the Land include Mark 13:9 (cf. Matt 10:17); *m. Mak.* 1:10; *m. Sanh.* 1:6; *t. Sanh.* 7:1; and perhaps also Josephus, *Life* 68. Similar usage of *synedrion* in the broader Greco-Roman world includes, e.g., Aelius Aristides, *Orations*, 13; Xenophon, *Hellenica*, 1.31; Diodorus Siculus, *Hist. Lib.* 14.82.2, 15.28.4, 17.4.2.

22. See chapter 3, above.

23. E.g., Davies and Allison, *Matthew*, 1:512; Keener, *Matthew*, 182; Becker, *Jesus of Nazareth*, 290–291.

24. Davies, *The Setting of the Sermon on the Mount* 236–38; cf. France, *Matthew*, 120; Gundry, *Matthew*, 85; Keener, *Matthew*, 182. It is also worth noting that *2 Enoch* 44:3 considers anger to be something that will be judged by God, though no mention is made here of a human court.

to outbursts of anger which are to be decided "at a community inquiry" (1QS 6:24). Statements made in anger are also discussed in CD 9:2–6, though a judicial setting is not as clear here as it is in 1QS 6:24–27, 7:1–5.

There are, however, some differences to be aware of. 1QS and CD are both written for sectarian communities. 1QS, which contains the stronger parallels, seems particularly to have been written for a small, specific community. Matthew 5:22a, on the contrary, appears at least on the narrative and dominical levels to envision wider public society and public courts, probably convened in synagogues. Moreover, the parallels in CD and 1QS are both concerned with outward displays of anger. While outward expressions of anger in the form of insults are mentioned in Matthew 5:22, the first part of the teaching seems to be dealing with general anger, that is, the mental state of anger. It is much more difficult to imagine how this could be judged in a court. Perhaps the parallels in the Qumran material can illuminate the matter, by showing how displays of anger could function as evidence of anger, thus providing the court with something to judge.[125] We must nevertheless admit that the situation being depicted here, of a human court judging anger as a criminal action, though hypothetically possible, is intuitively odd and strikingly strict. While it is possible to imagine that a public synagogue court *could* hold someone legally accountable for their anger, it is also hard to imagine such a practice actually being carried out regularly across the Land.

This issue is even more acute with the second antithesis, the teaching on adultery (Matt 5:27–30). Verse 28 equates looking at a woman with lust to committing adultery in one's heart. Although mention of a human court is lacking (compare vv. 22 and 25), adultery was a capital legal offense, punishable by death in Jewish law.[126] Some confirmation of the practice of this law in the first century CE might also be found in Josephus, *Apion* 2.215 and in the *pericope adulterae* (John 7:53–8:11). A straightforward equation of the mental act of lust with adultery would, *ipso facto*, result in a situation in which one could be liable for the act of lust in a human court, and could receive the death penalty for it.[127]

The first two antitheses present a curious problem on the practical level. How are we to imagine these actually being enacted in synagogues across the land? The four other antitheses are somewhat less

---

125. Cf. Davies, *Setting of the Sermon on the Mount*, 236–39.
126. Lev 20:10; Deut 22:22. See also Josephus, *Ap.* 2.215; John 7:53–8:11.
127. However, it is worth stating that I take Matt 5:29–30 to be hyperbolic illustrations of the dangers of lust rather than as literal legal statues. See Keener, *Matthew*, 188; Blomberg, *Matthew*, 109.

problematic as actual laws, insofar as they do not deal with the judgment of mental states as do the first and second antitheses, so this matter pertains mostly to the teachings on murder and adultery. Did Jesus expect these teachings to be accepted and literally practiced as law in the synagogues of the Land?

It is tempting to make the argument that Jesus had a less judicial understanding of the Law, and did not see scripture as statutory law. This position has been extensively argued recently by Thomas Kazen, and has been previously presented by Stephen Westerholm.[128] There is indisputable merit in Westerholm's argument that Jesus understood the Torah as expression of God's loving salvific will. Nevertheless, Matthew 5:21–22 gives me pause. It is worth noting that Kazen does not treat these verses in his recent monograph, and that Westerholm does not discuss them in-depth in *Jesus and Scribal Authority*.[129] The image presented there is that of liability to the divine court as well as human courts, an image made even more concrete in vv. 23–26.[130] This implies that Jesus did have at least some judicial conception of the "Torah."

In my opinion, Jesus did indeed view the Torah as an expression of a loving God's salvific will for his people, but this does not exclude its function as statutory law. We must remember that Jesus was proclaiming the eschatological outbreak of the Kingdom of God, and these teachings must be understood in light of that proclamation.[131] The impracticality of his teachings need not necessarily impact our determination of his expectation that they would be practiced.

What we see in the antitheses is, as Ben Meyer has put it, "Torah for a graced and restored Israel."[132] Herein lies the relevance of the teaching to the proclamation. The restored Israel was to have a restored Law, a new covenant.[133] Jesus's legal teaching was "Torah transformed by reference to the new and public revelation set before Israel in Jesus' proclamation of the reign of God."[134] It is the definitive, fulfilled inter-

---

28. Kazen, *Scripture, Interpretation, or Authority?*, 296–97; Stephen Westerholm, *Jesus and Scribal Authority*, (Coniectanea Biblica New Testament Series 10; Lund: Gleerup, 1978), passim, see esp. 129.

29. See, however, Westerholm, "Sermon on the Mount," 52–53.

30. See also the parallel in Luke 12:58–59. Note that Luke does not attach this saying to a teaching on anger or murder. It is difficult to determine whether Luke or Matthew has redeployed this saying. It is quite possible that Matt 5:25–26 were not originally attached to vv. 21–24 in the Jesus tradition. Nevertheless, vv. 25–26 still indicate that Jesus could think about "law" in terms of a human justice system.

31. Cf. Meyer, *Aims of Jesus*, 137: "all his [Jesus'] words and actions were relative to the reign of God."

32. Meyer, *Aims of Jesus*, 141.

33. Jer 31:31; Luke 22:20; 1 Cor 11:25. See also the use of *diatithēmi* ("to covenant") in connection with the establishment of the Kingdom and the Twelve sitting on twelve thrones. Brant Pitre has recently made a persuasive argument for the reliability of the "new covenant" traditions, in Pitre, *Jesus and the Last Supper*, 108–20.

pretation of the Law, the Torah as it should be practiced during the reign of God. It is in this light that we should read Matthew 5:17. Jesus does not abrogate the Mosaic Torah, but sees himself as bringing it to fulfilment with the proclamation of the reign of God and his commandments for the restored Israel.

The Law taught by Jesus is understood by him to be Torah fulfilled, that is, restored to God's original intent for Israel and for humanity. This thinking is revealed in Matthew 19:3–9, wherein Jesus appeals to the primacy of the marriage ordinance of Genesis 2:24. The logic is that divorce was allowed by Moses because of the hardness of human hearts, "but *from the beginning* it was not so" (Matt 19:8). We must remember that the Torah includes not only the Mosaic cycle of narratives and laws (Exod-Deut), but also Genesis, which deals with pre-Mosaic times. In the teaching of Jesus and the outbreak of reign of God, the Law itself is being renewed and restored to its intended state, the primordial state of *Urzeit*.[135] As with the teaching on divorce, the teaching on anger and murder in Matthew 5:21–22 hearkens back to the primordial *Urzeit*. In the Cain and Abel narrative, murder enters the world as a result of anger. Attacking anger as the root cause of murder would bring the Law back in effect to the primordial state *before* murder had come into the world, since if anger can be avoided, then so too can murder.

Three of the antitheses seem to set aside provisions of the Mosaic Law. These are the teachings on divorce (Matt 5:31–32), oaths (Matt 5:33–77), and *lex talionis* (Matt 5:38–42). We have already dealt with the teaching on divorce above, and have determined that it aims at restoring the Law rather than abrogating it. The teaching on oaths is best understood as an instance of "building a fence around the Torah,"[136] insofar as it aims to prevent the breaking of oaths, which is at the heart of the Mosaic commandment against swearing falsely.[137] It may also aim at preventing the profanation of the divine name (vv. 34–35; cf. Exod 20:7; Deut 5:11). This leaves only the teaching on retaliation (*lex talionis*), which requires explanation. In my opinion, it is an over-

---

134. Meyer, *Aims of Jesus*, 141.
135. Cf. André LaCocque, *Jesus the Central Jew: His Times and His People* (Early Christianity and its Literature 15; Atlanta: Society of Biblical Literature, 2015), 75. By *Urzeit*, Lacocque means the ante-diluvian primordial state of Genesis 1 and 2.
136. Cf. James D. G. Dunn, "Law" in *Dictionary of Jesus and the Gospels, Second Edition*, ed. Joel B. Green, Jeannine K. Brown, and Nicholas Perrin (Downers Grove: IVP Academic, 2013), 505–15 (510); Luz, *Matthew*, 1:263.
137. In basic agreement with Keener, who comments that Jesus "summons his disciples beyond the law's letter to its intention" (*Matthew*, 193).

statement to see this as an abolishment of a Mosaic law. Rather, non-retaliation brings out the divine intent of the Law, summarized in the commandment to love one's neighbor,[138] which Jesus understands to include even enemies (see the sixth antithesis, Matt 5:43–48).

The specific intent behind *lex talionis* is to limit retaliation: only an eye may be taken for an eye, and so forth.[139] Thus, according to Dunn, the teaching on *lex talionis* is "better heard as pressing behind the law to reinforce the social principle behind it."[140] We may conclude, then, that none of the antitheses actually abrogate the Mosaic Law. Rather, they restore it, protect it, and get at the divine intent that undergirds it.

Exegetes have often treated Matthew 5:17 as a Matthean interpretive apology for the antitheses,[141] but as Davies and Allison observe, a pre-Easter *Sitz im Leben* is not impossible, since "Jesus may well have wished to defend his loyalty to Torah against those who made him out to be an antinomian."[142] This interpretation is particularly plausible if we consider the fact that Jesus taught in synagogues, where discussion and debate over the Torah and its interpretation was normative. Given that elsewhere Jesus encounters resistance in synagogue settings to his practice and interpretation of Sabbath law,[143] it is easy to imagine the saying in Matthew 5:17 being offered as a reply, especially if it was accompanied by Jesus's signature Kingdom proclamation.[144]

There are admittedly other possible interpretations in situations such as this one, in which the historian is forced to rely heavily on inference and imagination in addition to the evidence, but that is the nature of history.[145] This is not to say that I do not think that this tradition has been shaped, remembered, and redeployed in the form and place in which it has been preserved in Matthew.[146] Matthew 5:17 is better understood on the historical level as a general response offered

---

138. Mark 12:28–31; Matt 22:34–40; Luke 10:25–28; cf. Rom 13:8–10; Gal 5:14; Jas 2:8.

139. Cf. LaCocque, *Jesus the Central Jew*, 86; Dunn, "Law," 510.

140. Dunn, "Law," 510.

141. A good recent example of this can be found in Schröter, *Jesus of Nazareth*, 153–54. See also the redaction-critical argument in Meier, *A Marginal Jew*, 4:42.

142. Davies and Allison, *Matthew*, 1:482.

143. Mark 3:16 (cf. Luke 6:6–11; Matt 12:9–14); Luke 13:10–17.

144. See also LaCocque, *Jesus the Central Jew*, 76.

145. By envisioning this scenario, I am imagining or inventing no more than those who would see this saying as being composed in response to controversy surrounding the practice of the law in an early community of Christ-believing Jews (e.g., Bultmann, *History of the Synoptic Tradition*, 138, 163).

146. Whether or not 5:17 was accompanied by the elaboration in 5:18–20 on the historical level is a question that is beyond the scope of my present concerns, but it is quite possible the vv. 18–20 represent a collective mnemonic interpretation of v. 17.

by Jesus to criticism of his legal teaching than as an introduction to the antitheses. As such, the meaning of that response is to emphasize that Jesus says nothing that would contradict the original intended meaning of the Mosaic Law. Hence, in the mind of Jesus, the marriage ordinance has primacy over the allowance for divorce (Matt 19:3–9), and the intended sense of the Sabbath Law can be both appealed to and restored (Mark 2:27).

The question still remains as to how Jesus imagined these seemingly idealistic legal sentences actually being practiced. First of all, it is essential to keep Jesus's vision of the eschatological setting of his legal teachings in mind.[147] These were legal teachings for the *restored* Israel under God's reign. The ethics of these legal teachings were, in the words of Ben Meyer, "an ethics of realized eschatology," demands meant for a "community of the transformed."[148] The eschatological transformation of the community of the people of God under God's reign would allow them to meet the challenge of the eschatological Law.

Moreover, we must recognize that the Jesus tradition preserves provisions for reconciliation, forgiveness, and mercy. In this way, it is very much in continuity with early Judaism.[149] Matthew 5:23–24, which illustrates the first antithesis, exhorts a hearer liable for a misdemeanor to seek reconciliation with a brother or sister. Similarly, v. 25 (cf. Luke 12:58–59), which envisions a human justice system, entreats the hearer to come to terms with an accuser (Gk. ἴσθι εὐνοῶν τῷ ἀντιδίκῳ σου) prior to a trial. Elsewhere, in Mark 11:25, Jesus instructs his followers to forgive if they "have anything against anyone" (Gk. ἔχετε κατά τινος). This would naturally apply to the pursuit of justice and civil cases.[150] A Matthean parallel to Mark 11:25 appears in the Sermon on the Mount, in which Jesus tells his followers that if they forgive the trespasses of others, God will also forgive them (Matt 6:14–15). Likewise, in the

---

147. As André LaCocque has argued, the legal teachings of Jesus (particularly the teaching on divorce) reveal his conception that "the new order dawns with his ministry," a return "to *Urzeit*, to Gen 1 and 2," and thus, the Torah accedes "to its transcendental form" (*Jesus the Central Jew*, 75–76).

148. Meyer, *Aims of Jesus*, 142.

149. Cf. Sanders, *Practice and Belief*, 275–78. The topic of early Jewish thought on grace and forgiveness has been much discussed elsewhere, especially in Pauline scholarship. We need not review this topic in depth here. See, e.g., the classic studies of this topic, esp. Claude G. Montefiore, *Judaism and St. Paul* (London: Goschen, 1914), 36–44; Hans Joachim Schoeps, *Paul: The Theology of the Apostle in the Light of Jewish Religious History* (Philadelphia: Westminster, 1961), esp. 196; E. P. Sanders, *Paul and Palestinian Judaism* (Philadelphia: Fortress Press, 1977), passim, esp. 107–82. See also Stephen Westerholm, *Perspectives Old and New on Paul: The "Lutheran" Paul and His Critics* (Grand Rapids: Eerdmans, 2004), 341–51.

150. At least one other exegete connects this passage directly with the pursuit of justice. See Darrell L. Bock, *Mark* (NCBC; New York: Cambridge University Press, 2015), 297.

Lukan Sermon on the Plain, Jesus says "do not judge, and you will not be judged; do not condemn, and you will not be condemned. Forgive, and you will be forgiven" (Luke 6:37).

These passages are evidence of a radical system of reciprocity in forgiveness,[151] grace, reconciliation, and love for enemies. Forgiveness is not to be limited, but continual.[152] We should recognize that civil cases would have been brought against the accused by individual complainants rather than "the state."[153] Faithful citizens living under God's reign are thus expected to avoid the inappropriate excesses such as anger and lust that lie at the root of major infractions of divine law. At the same time, they must be willing to forgive others who commit infractions against them. Only then can they be expected to be forgiven for their own transgressions by their fellow citizens and by God. As the antitheses teach, rather than pursuing recourse, they are to love their enemies and to resist retaliation. Civil suits in the restored Israel would ideally be settled through reconciliation and forgiveness, and would *never even need to appear* in either the human or divine courts. We see this somewhat concretely in the fifth antithesis (Matt 5:38–39). Under the Mosaic Law, the complainant has the right to legal recourse: an eye for an eye and a tooth for a tooth (Lev 24:19–20). However, Jesus exhorts his listeners not to retaliate, but to turn the other cheek. Is this system hopelessly utopian? Perhaps, but what should we expect the literally theocratic Kingdom of God to be, if not utopian?[154]

What happens when we situate these legal teachings within a synagogue setting, their natural *Sitz im Leben*? As has been demonstrated in chapter 3, the synagogue is where the law was both read and interpreted. It was where court cases were settled, and where legal *praxis* was determined. The synagogue was a political arena in which the assembled majority would need to be persuaded of the validity of a given legal interpretation through honor and shame exchanges. Success in such an endeavor would lead to the acceptance of the validity of the interpretation for practice in that locale, and the setting of a legal precedent for the future. From an institution-critical perspective, if we situate the antitheses within a synagogue context, it is likely that they would naturally have been understood by the audience to have practi-

---

51. On reciprocity in early Jewish legal thought, see *m. Sotah* 1:7.
52. Cf. Matt 18:21–22; Luke 17:3–4. Compare *t. Yom.* 4:13.
53. Cf. Alexander, "Jewish Law," 47.
54. In this regard, see Mary Ann Beavis, *Jesus and Utopia: Looking for the Kingdom of God in the Roman World* (Minneapolis: Fortress Press, 2006); cf. Mary Ann Beavis, "Jesus in Utopian Context," in *Jesus in Contiuum*, ed. Tom Holmén (WUNT 289; Tübingen: Mohr Siebeck, 2012), 151–70.

cal legal ramifications if they were accepted, regardless of whether or not this was Jesus's intent.

If Jesus were to present his legal teachings in a public synagogue in a Galilean village, and if the assembly were to be persuaded and to accept his teachings, then that village would be brought under the rule of the "fulfilled" or "restored" Torah for the restored Israel. Matthew has pointed us in the correct direction by portraying Jesus as a new Moses in Matthew 5–7, delivering an eschatologically fulfilled Law for the eschatologically fulfilled people, since this appears to at least reflect the spirit of Jesus's aims despite the mountain setting and the Sermon itself being Matthean elements. The fact that Jesus is portrayed as the new Moses by Matthew is not, contrary to the position of redaction-critical studies and advocates of the criterion of dissimilarity, reason to think that Jesus did not understand himself in this way. To the contrary, the fact that Jesus was remembered this way indicates that he said and did things that led some of his earliest followers to think that he *was* a new Moses.[155]

As we have seen in the discussion above, the proclamation of the Kingdom demands a response, a willed act of repentance, of returning to God. What does this mean, and how is it related to the proclamation? As William Holladay has demonstrated, repentance (שוב) in the Hebrew Bible could have covenantal valences as "conversionary repentance," a return to covenant loyalty.[156] We are reminded here once more of the imagery of the restoration of Israel in Ezekiel 20:33–37, in which the Exodus story is reenacted, and the people are brought under the bond of the covenant. Covenant and Law are inseparable, and so, the response of repentance in light of the outbreak of the Kingdom would entail acceptance of the instruction of the fulfilled Law that Jesus taught.

The connection between repentance, covenant, and restoration is clearly laid out within the Torah itself, in Deuteronomy 30:1–6:

> When all these things have happened to you, the blessings and the curses that I have set before you, if you call them to mind among all the nations where the LORD your God has driven you, and return to the LORD your God, and you and your children obey him with all your heart and with

---

155. See also the arguments for the identification of Jesus as the new Moses in Pitre, *Jesus and the Last Supper*, 108–20.

156. See William L. Holladay, *The Root Subh in the Old Testament* (Leiden: Brill, 1958), esp. 116–57. Cf. also the meaning of the Greek πίστις in BDAG, and its use and translation as "loyalty" in John M. G. Barclay, *Against Apion: Translation and Commentary*, vol. 10 of *Flavius Josephus: Translation and Commentary* (Leiden and Boston: Brill, 2007), 192.

all your soul, just as I am commanding you today, then the LORD your God will restore your fortunes and have compassion on you, gathering you again from all the peoples among whom the LORD your God has scattered you. Even if you are exiled to the ends of the world, from there the LORD your God will gather you, and from there he will bring you back. The LORD your God will bring you into the land that your ancestors possessed, and you will possess it; he will make you more prosperous and numerous than your ancestors. Moreover, the Lord your God will circumcise your heart and the heart of your descendants, so that you will love the Lord your God with all your heart and with all your soul, in order that you may live.

This passage describes what will happen if Israel "returns" (שׁוּב) to the covenant following the calamity that results from covenantal sin. The nation will be gathered and restored, including the territory of the Land. This is what Jesus's call to repentance envisioned as its end goal—the gathering of the people, the renewal of the covenant, and the restoration of the Land. Given that Jesus frequented synagogues and that the Torah was read in the synagogue, it is not unreasonable to think that Jesus could have been familiar with these ideas. Deuteronomy 30:6 also mentions that God will circumcise the hearts of the people, "so that you will love the Lord your God with all your heart and with all your soul," which references the central covenantal statute of the *shema* in Deuteronomy 6:5. Notably, Jesus too references this command, elevating it to the place of the "greatest commandment" in Mark 12:28–31 (cf. Matt 22:36–40; Luke 10:25–28). Keeping this particular central commandment entails the avoidance of covenantal sin, and thus, assures the continuance of the covenant.

The synagogue was not only the physical setting of Jesus's teaching, it also provided the institutional means by which his teachings would come to be practiced throughout the Land. It was the vehicle by which his legal teachings, restored Torah for the restored Israel, could be spread. What good, after all, is a law or a legal teaching if no one practices it? Jesus was not an anti-nomian. His legal teaching played an essential role in his aims and in his program in the synagogues of Galilee. As John P. Meier has put the matter, "the historical Jesus is indeed the halakic Jesus."[157]

We might consider Jesus's legal system to be comparable to covenantal nomism.[158] It requires faithfulness on the part of its adherents to its

---

57. Meier, *A Marginal Jew*, 4:574–75.
58. Cf. Sanders, *Jesus and Judaism*, 335–37; see also Sanders, *Practice and Belief*, 262–75. I would, however, disagree with Sanders' statement that Jesus was not a legal teacher.

commandments of love for enemies, reconciliation, forgiveness, non-retaliation, and resistance of the "root" transgressions of anger or lust in order for it to function. Within it, there is room for grace and forgiveness, but a refusal to adhere to these precepts altogether sets the transgressor outside of the covenantal system, thus denying them access to its benefits. Forgiveness is granted to those who forgive, but is not given to the unmerciful.

This system has some precedent in early Jewish thought, which speaks to its plausibility within Jesus's early Jewish setting. The closest parallel is found in Sirach 28:1–11,[159] which exhort the reader to refrain from anger and to forgive others. Verses 2–3 are particularly instructive: "Forgive your neighbor the wrong he has done, and then your sins will be pardoned when you pray. Does anyone harbor anger against another, and expect healing from the Lord?" Moreover, v. 7 invokes a covenantal framework, and encourages the reader to "remember the covenant of the Most High, and overlook faults." The existence of this sort of approach to forgiveness and anger within a covenantal context in earlier Jewish thought highlights the Jewish nature of Jesus's teaching, and allows us to see Jesus's teaching in the antitheses as part of a trajectory of early Jewish teaching, rather than as a wholly new development.

Jesus's covenantal system of forgiveness and justice is illustrated by the Parable of the Unforgiving Servant in Matthew 18:23–35. The servant in this parable receives mercy in the form of debt forgiveness, but is unwilling to show the same mercy to others by forgiving what they owe him. Because of his lack of mercy for others, the mercy shown to him is reversed, and he is held responsible for what he owes, being handed over to be tortured until he repays the debt. This is explicitly a Kingdom parable (v. 23), meant to demonstrate something about what life under God's reign is like. This parable teaches that, as Klyne Snodgrass writes, "The kingdom comes with limitless grace in the midst of an evil world, but it comes with limitless demand."[160] Here again, we see that participation in the reign of God is not passive. It is active. Its benefits come with demands, and its proclamation requires a response. Thus, the Kingdom requires the persuasion of the people in order for it to be fully realized.

Understanding the synagogue as the setting of Jesus's legal teaching

---

159. Other minor parallels can be found in *T. Zeb.* 5:1–3 and *T. Gad* 6:3.
160. Klyne R. Snodgrass, *Stories With Intent: A Comprehensive Guide to the Parables of Jesus* (Grand Rapids: Eerdmans, 2008), 72.

and proclamation highlights its political nature. As we discussed in chapter 3, discussion of the Law in public synagogue settings was intensely political. It is important to recognize the sort of power dynamics that would have been in play during discourse on the Law in a local-official setting such as the synagogue, where court was held, where councils and town officials met, and where the townspeople gathered. Much was at stake: personal honor and shame, as well as control over the political direction of the town, and precedent for local religio-legal praxis. The synagogue was the arena in which Jesus's political opponents would need to be faced and confronted, and where his teachings would be on trial in front of the assembled public.

The Antitheses in the Web of Historical Imagination

A few words are necessary here on how the antitheses should be treated as evidence for understanding the teaching of the historical Jesus. In previous scholarship, the matter has typically centred upon redaction-critical views of the antitheses.[161] There are three major redaction-critical views: a) the first, second, fourth antitheses are authentic, the others are redactional;[162] b) all of the antitheses go back to Jesus;[163] c) all of the antitheses are redactional and none of them originated with Jesus.[164] However, the wide variety of views, combined with the usual problems associated with the use of redaction criticism to do the work of history, indicate that redaction criticism cannot produce a certain judgment on whether or not the antitheses originated with Jesus. It is better to make a historical argument. The best that we can do is to interpret the data in order to see how it fits within the web of evidence, inference, and imagination.[165]

As with any other data coming from the Gospels, I recognize that

---

61. See the summary of the issues in Luz, *Matthew*, 1:226–27.

62. Bultmann, *History*, 135–36; Martin Albertz, *Die synoptischen Streitgespräche: Ein Beitrag zur Formgeschichte des Urchristentums* (Berlin: Trowitzsch, 1921) 146–51; Robert Guelich, "The Antitheses of Matthew v. 21–28: Tradition and/or Redactional?" *NTS* 22 (1976): 444–57; Davies and Allison, *Matthew*, 1:505; Luz, *Matthew*, 1:228 (though Luz also considers the fourth antithesis to be secondary).

63. Joachim Jeremias, *New Testament Theology I: The Proclamation of Jesus* (trans. John Bowden; New York: Scribner, 1971), 251–53; Hans-Theo Wrege, *Die Überlieferungsgeschichte der Bergpredigt* (WUNT 9; Tübingen: Mohr Siebeck, 1968), 56–57; Alexander Sand, *Das Gesetz und die Propheten: Untersuchungen zur Theologie des Evangeliums nach Matthäus* (BU 11; Regensburg: Pustet, 1974), 48; Keener, *Matthew*, 180–81.

64. M. Jack Suggs, *Wisdom, Christology, and Law in Matthew's Gospel* (Cambridge, MA: Harvard University Press, 1970), 109–14; Ingo Broer, "Die Antithesen und der Evangelist Mattaus," *Biblische Zeitschrift* 19 (1975): 50–63; Sanders, *Jesus and Judaism*, 260–64. The authenticity of the teaching on divorce may be treated as a separate issue by proponents of this hypothesis, since it appears in an alternate form in Matt 19:3–9.

the form in which these sayings have been preserved is the product of interpretation, but this is a normal part of remembering and translation. It is important to keep in mind that we are seeking the *ipsissima vox* rather than the *ipsissima verba*, the general sense of what Jesus taught in the synagogues rather than his precise words.

As the discussion above has endeavoured to demonstrate, the antitheses fit quite plausibly within the context of early public synagogue gatherings. As legal teaching, the antitheses would be quite at home within the synagogues of Galilee. The "fulfilled" Torah evidenced by the antitheses does not at all abrogate the Torah. Instead, it looks more like the "fence around the Torah" spoken of in the early rabbinic/Pharisaic tradition of *m. Avot* 1:1 and 3:13 than it does like the teachings of an antinomian.[166] However, the antitheses do not, as Sanders objects, portray a super-legal Jesus.[167] These teachings need to be understood within the greater context of Jesus's aims. According to Collingwood, the father of modern philosophy of history, the work of historical criticism is done in light of the entire web of the historian's imaginative construction.[168] As the discussion above has endeavoured to demonstrate, the antitheses can only be properly understood on the historical level in light of Jesus's proclamation of the Kingdom of God and the system of grace and restoration that it promises. This is how, rather than extending the law, they bring it to its fulfilment. Once this is grasped, the antitheses can be seen as sitting plausibly not only within the context of early Palestinian Judaism, but perhaps more importantly, within the portrait of Jesus that we are painting on the basis of the evidence at hand.

---

165. An excellent precedent for this kind of historical approach dealing with the same data has been set by Meyer, *Aims of Jesus*, 144–53.
166. Evidence for awareness of the concept of "building a fence around the Torah" in the Second Temple period might be found in the reference to the Pharisees as "builders of the wall" in CD IV, 19–20. See Lawrence H. Schiffman, *Reclaiming the Dead Sea Scrolls: The History of Judaism, the Background of Christianity, the Lost Library of Qumran* (New York: Double Day, 1995), 249; cf. Solomon Schechter, *Fragments of a Zadokite Work* (New York: Ktav 1970 [1910]), xvii (49). It is also worth noting that extra-Torah community laws can be found throughout CD and the Serekh texts.
167. Sanders, *Jesus and Judaism*.
168. Cf. Collingwood, *Idea of History*, 244–45. This is the primary rationale for my preference of Meyer's interpretation of this data over that of Sanders. On this, see appendix A, or alternatively Ryan, "Jesus at the Crossroads of Inference and Imagination," 87.

Conclusion

Jesus aimed to bring about the coming of the Kingdom of God, which is to be understood in terms of the eschatological restoration of the people of God. As the summary statements of his program indicate, this would be accomplished through the acts of proclamation and teaching, which were done primarily in synagogues.

The public synagogue was intrinsic to Jesus's mission. It was the vehicle by which he intended to carry the message of the outbreak of the Kingdom of God to the villages of the Land. Moreover, it was the means by which he would bring the Kingdom about. Because the public synagogue assembly represented the town as a whole, and because the political and legal decisions made in the assembly affected the praxis and direction of the entire locale, it made for the most natural venue for Jesus and his mission.

The synagogue summary statements identify the two primary elements of Jesus program as proclamation and teaching. The two are, of course, intimately connected. The proclamation was of the outbreak of the Kingdom of God, and the national restoration and redemption that it would bring. The exact nature of the teaching is harder to pin down due to a paucity of direct evidence, but our discussion so far has revealed that Jesus's synagogue teaching outlined the Law and practice for a renewed Israel living under the reign of God. Further aspects of Jesus's synagogue teaching will be illuminated in the chapters to follow.

The investigation of the evidence in this chapter has brought to light a hypothesis and a general outline of Jesus's aims and their relation to the synagogue. There is, however, more data to examine. The next three chapters will discuss specific incidents set in synagogues in the Gospels, which will help to more fully flesh out and colour in the broad sketch that has been drawn thus far.

6

The Incident in the Synagogue at Nazareth (Luke 4:16–30; Mark 6:2–6; Matthew 13:54–58)

Introduction

The narrative of Jesus teaching in the synagogue at Nazareth, preserved in various forms in all three synoptic gospels (Luke 4:16–30; Mark 6:2–6; Matt 13:54–58), provides some of the most promising potential evidence for understanding Jesus's use of and interaction with public synagogues. The Lukan version, in particular, provides us with a rare window onto Jesus's specific teachings, rhetoric, and interactions within a synagogue setting.

Luke 4:16–30 presents a greatly expanded telling of the basic events related in Mark 6:2–6 and Matthew 13:54–58. Neither the Markan nor the Matthean versions preserve the content of Jesus's teaching. Luke, however, conveys Jesus's reading from the scroll of Isaiah as well as his subsequent teaching. As a result, Luke's version has the most significance for our purposes by far. Nevertheless, there are some historiographical issues related to this passage to address before we can discuss how to apply the data as evidence for our investigation. A number of scholars have called the reliability of Luke's witness to this event into question, and a reply is warranted. These problems are relevant to the purposes of this project insofar as they have a significant impact on the interpretation of the data and the determination of where and how it fits into the web of historical evidence and imagination that we are constructing.

Historical Plausibility and the Relationship of Luke 4:16–30 to Mark 6:2–6

The issue of the relationship between Luke 4:16–30 and Mark 6:2–6 is a thorny problem. Some scholars have argued that Luke 4:16–30 is, in part, a Lukan composition based upon Mark 6:2–6.[1] If so, the reliability and direct relevance of the passage to the historical level of our investigation would be called into question. Others have suggested that Luke used another source in order to write this scene.[2] In contrast to the former suggestion, this scenario would not exclude the reliability or direct historical relevance of Luke 4:16–30. Both suggestions are theoretically possible. However, I am convinced that the evidence is better explained by regarding this passage as representing genuine memories of the life of Jesus that Luke knew from a source other than Mark than as a Lukan composition.[3]

Luke 4:16–30 describes features of synagogue gatherings that were distinctive to a setting in the public synagogues of the Land rather than the Jewish associations of the diaspora.[4] Luke describes Jesus standing up to read (4:16) and sitting before teaching (v. 20). By contrast, when the same author describes Paul speaking in a diaspora synagogue in Pisidian Antioch, he mentions that Paul stood up to teach.[5] This coheres with Philo's description of Sabbath gatherings in which teach-

---

1. E.g., Bultmann, *History of the Synoptic Tradition*, 31–32; C. F. Evans, *Saint Luke* (Trinity Press International New Testament Commentaries; Philadelphia: Trinity), 266–67; Fitzmyer, *Luke*, 1:526–27; Gerd Lüdemann, *Jesus After 2000 Years: What he really said and did* (London: SCM, 2000), 283. Similarly, see Kelber, *The Oral and the Written Gospel*, 14. See also Steve Moyise, "Jesus and the Scriptures of Israel," in *Handbook for the Study of the Historical Jesus*, ed. Tom Holmén and Stanley E. Porter (Leiden and Boston: Brill, 2011), 1137–67 (1156).
2. John C. Poirier, "Jesus as an Elijianic Figure in Luke 4:16–30," *CBQ* 71, no. 2 (2009): 349–63; Robert C. Tannehill, *The Shape of Luke's Story: Essays on Luke-Acts* (Eugene: Cascade, 2005), 5; John Nolland, *Luke 1–9:20* (WBC 35a; Dallas: Word, 1989), 192; I. Howard Marshall, *The Gospel of Luke: A Commentary on the Greek Text* (NIGTC; Grand Rapids: Eerdmans, 1978), 179.
3. Whether or not that source was oral or written is beyond the purview of the present study, and beyond my ability to determine.
4. Cf. Runesson, *Origins*, 219–20; Runesson, "Importance of the Synagogue," 288–89; Contra Kee, "Transformation," passim.
5. Acts 13:15–16.

ing is done while standing up.[6] This distinction in Luke's portrayal of Jesus's and Paul's postures when teaching in synagogue settings has been noted by both Levine and Runesson.[7] Levine notes the contrast in practice, but makes little of it, suggesting only that there were two alternative practices in use. Runesson, however, takes this as evidence of a distinction between the practices in the Land and the diaspora, citing the passage from Philo mentioned above (*Spec.* 2.62) in support. He does not, however, produce evidence from the Land that mirrors the description of Jesus standing to read and sitting to teach as in Luke 4:16–20.

Which interpretation is to be preferred? Although it is not discussed or cited by Runesson, I have found that there is, in fact, evidence stemming from the Land that supports his conclusion. Perhaps the most important piece of relevant evidence comes from an unattributed tradition preserved in *t. Meg.* 3:12 (cf. also *t. Suk.* 2:11), which concerns the reading of scripture specifically within a synagogue context. According to this passage, the reader "stands and reads and sits down." This practice is assumed and attested in Palestinian traditions found in later rabbinic sources as well.[8] These rabbinic sources find some traction in the first century CE, since Matthew consistently describes Jesus sitting down before teaching.[9] Matthew is typically identified as a Jewish author with knowledge of Palestinian Jewish traditions and culture. Thus, whether these descriptions are based in knowledge of the histor-

---

6. Philo, *Spec.* 2.62.

7. Levine, *Ancient Synagogue*, 158; Runesson, *Origins*, 219, cf. Runesson, "Importance of the Synagogue," 288–89. See also Hugo Grotius, *Annotationes in Novum Testamentum*, 9 vols. (Groningen: W. Zuidema, 1826–34), 3:225.

8. See esp. *b. Meg.* 21a; *y. Meg.* 4:1. On this, see Michael Graves, "The Public Reading of Scripture in Early Judaism," *JETS* 50, no. 3 (2007): 467–87 (485). The tradition preserved in *b. Meg.* 21b concerns the distinction between the Purim reading from Esther, which can be reader either standing or sitting (the Mishnaic rulings around this particular obligatory reading are distinctly more lax than usual) and reading from the Torah, though *t. Meg.* 3:12 probably concerns synagogue scripture readings in general (following the wording at the end of *t. Meg.* 3:11). Nevertheless, the same custom is probably being referred to in *b. Meg.* 21b. Note that, although this tradition is fairly late, it is attributed to a *tanna*, and that, although it comes from the Babylonian Talmud, the only named individual is a Palestinian Rabbi (R. Abbahu). This indicates that this rather late text is probably dealing with an earlier tradition originally stemming from the Land, which may have made its way into the diaspora sometime between the end of the Second Temple period and the compilation of the Babylonian Talmud. The explanation for this tradition, given by R. Abbahu, is both relevant and interesting despite being attested by an *amora*. According to R. Abbahu, one stands while reading from the Torah because Deut 5:31 implies that Adonai was standing while he told Moses the statutes, commandments, and ordinances of the Law, since he tells Moses to "stand here by me." It is, however, most probably the case that this is simply a late explanation given for an early tradition that had become widespread, although the possibility that this practice originated in the Second Temple period because of Deut 5:31 cannot be altogether excluded.

9. Matt 5:1, 13:1–2, 24:3, 26:55. Mention of Jesus sitting before teaching is occasionally found in the other Gospels, in John 8:1; Mark 9:35, 13:3.

ical Jesus that Matthew is conveying, or if they are just details added by the author for the sake of verisimilitude, is of no consequence for the matter at hand.

Once the additional evidence that I have provided here is taken into consideration, we are able to determine that the hypothesis of differing practices in the Land and the diaspora has the most explanatory power. What does this mean for the pericope under discussion? Runesson holds that "it seems as if Luke in fact knew about a custom in Palestine differing from customs in the diaspora and that he intentionally detailed his knowledge of this custom in the paradigmatic text under discussion in order to set the stage for his message as accurately as possible."[10] A friendly amendment to this is in order. It is unlikely that this detail comes from Luke himself. It has been noted by a number of scholars in the past that Luke displays imperfect knowledge of Palestinian geography and that he sometimes removes or replace references in his sources to elements of Palestinian Jewish customs or practices.[11] Given that this is the case, it is rather unlikely that Luke had independent knowledge of synagogue customs and procedures that were unique to the Land, especially to this degree of specificity.[12]

The better explanation in my opinion is that Luke has crafted this scene primarily on the basis of a non-Markan source,[13] and that the detail of this Palestinian Jewish custom comes from that non-Markan source. Whether the form in which Luke received it was written or oral is difficult to determine. Nevertheless, as I will argue, it is possible that the event narrated in Luke 4:16–30 has the memory of an eyewitness from the Land at its core.[14]

---

10. Runesson, *Origins*, 219.

11. E.g., Hans Conzelmann, *Theology of St. Luke* (London: SCM, 1982), 68–73; Fitzmyer, *Luke*, 1:41–42; Mark Allan Powell, *What Are They Saying About Luke?* (New York and Mahwah: Paulist, 1989), 6; Martin Hengel, "Luke the Historian and the Geography of Palestine in Acts of the Apostles," in *Between Jesus and Paul: Studies in Earliest Christianity* (Eugene: Wipf & Stock, 2003 [1983]), 97–128; cf. Martin Hengel, "The Geography of Palestine in Acts," in *The Book of Acts in its Palestinian Setting* (ed. Richard Bauckham; vol. 4 of *The Book of Acts in its First-Century Setting*; Grand Rapids: Eerdmans, 1995), 27–78.

12. As we will see below, there are other aspects of Luke 4:16–30 that reflect the milieu of the Land during the Second Temple period.

13. Cf. A. R. C. Leaney, *A Commentary on the Gospel According to St. Luke* (New York: Harper, 1958), 50–54; Tim Schramm, *Der Markus-Stoff bei Lukas: Eine literarkritische und redaktiongeschichtliche Untersuchung* (SNTS Monograpd Series 14; Cambridge: Cambridge University Press, 1971); Marshall, *Luke*, 179; Nolland, *Luke 1–9:20*, 192; Bovon, *Luke*, 1:150–51; Bock, *Luke*, 1:397; Poirier, "Jesus as an Elijianic Figure," 351–52; Peter W. Flint, "The Qumran Scrolls and the Historical Jesus," in *Jesus Research: New Methodologies and Perceptions* (vol. 2; ed. James H. Charlesworth with Brian Rhea and Petr Pokorný; Grand Rapids: Eerdmans, 2014), 261–82 (281).

14. It bears repeating that all memory is interpreted and that there is no history without interpretation, even in a case such as this, where eyewitness memory is concerned. The eyewitness will have inevitably interpreted the memory in their recollection of it in light of their present cir-

Synagogue scholarship is of further utility for establishing the historical plausibility of this pericope. Catto has argued that the general description of the gathering in Luke 4:16–30 fits well with what is known from Second-Temple-period sources about synagogue services.[15] He also makes an interesting argument about the practice of standing to read and sitting to teach, based on synagogue architecture, that may help to further explain the present matter.[16] He notes, as we have also discussed in chapter 3, that first-century synagogue buildings in the Land exhibit tiered benches with an open area in the middle. Since the focal point of the building is the central area, and as scripture reading was the primary activity of Sabbath synagogue gatherings, Jesus would probably have read while standing in the central floor area. He then went back to his seat. Catto argues that, since Jesus does not seem to be connected to the leadership of the Nazareth synagogue, he probably was not seated in one of the "best seats" (Gk. πρωτοκαθεδρία, cf. Mark 12:39 and parallels) of the synagogue, which Catto identifies with instances of single, untiered benches at the synagogue buildings found at Gamla and Masada. It is more likely that he was seated among the tiered benches. This is convincing, so long as we think that the narrative describes a synagogue building.

If Catto is correct, then it is noteworthy that Jesus would have been seated on one of the tiered benches while teaching, debating and discussing (Luke 4:20–28). This makes a good deal of sense within the context of a public synagogue, and may help to explain the custom of standing to read and sitting to teach or discuss. In chapter 3, we discussed the tiered, quadrilateral seating arrangements in public synagogues. The architectural pattern is reminiscent of civic buildings such as the Hellenistic *bouleutēria* or the modern House of Parliament in the United Kingdom. Returning to your bench, where you could be seated alongside those that you typically agree with and could face and thus easily address your potential opponents seated in other sections, makes practical sense in a setting in which discussion of scripture had religio-political implications and consequences.[17]

---

cumstances. As Chris Keith writes, "If any act of presenting the past necessarily and inextricably requires the frameworks of the present in order to render it intelligible and significant to an individual or group, then no tradition circulates independently of present interpretive frameworks – for those frameworks are the very means by which it circulates." See Chris Keith, "The Narratives of the Gospels and the Historical Jesus: Current Debates, Prior Debates and the Goal of Historical Jesus Research," *JSNT* 38 (2016): 1–30 (17). See also Alan Kirk, "Memory," 169.

15. Catto, *Reconstructing*, 185. Note also the agreement here of McKay, *Sabbath and Synagogue*, 165.

16. Catto, *Reconstructing*, 184–85.

17. Cf. Jordan J. Ryan, "Jesus and Synagogue Disputes," passim.

There is a further feature of the depiction of Jesus's reading from the Isaiah scroll in Luke 4:16–21 that leads me to conclude that it plausibly depicts the specific historical setting of a public synagogue in the Land of Israel. This evidence stems from the content of Jesus's reading from the Isaiah scroll. Perhaps the most curious feature of the reading is that though the reading is primarily from Isaiah 61:1–2, a portion from Isaiah 58:6 (ἀποστεῖλαι τεθραυσμένους ἐν ἀφέσει) is inserted at the end of Luke 4:18, before the reading returns to Isaiah 61:2a in Luke 4:19. A number of exegetes have suggested that this is best explained as an instance of the Jewish hermeneutical method known as gĕzērâ šāwâ.[18] This method fuses together two different passages of scripture, and hinges upon the existence of similar words or phrases in the two passages.[19] In the MT, a connection between Isaiah 61:1–2 and 58:6 is possible through שׁלח, which appears in both of our passages, or through רָצוֹן, which appears in 58:5 and 61:2.[20] Thus, we need not rely on the appearance of ἄφεσις in the LXX of both 61:1 and 58:6 for a connection.[21] In my estimation, the most likely connection is through שׁלח, since this word appears in the portions of both passages that are read by Jesus in Luke 4:18.

While previous scholarship has done well in identifying a Palestinian Jewish hermeneutical method that is likely at work in Luke 4:18–19 in the gĕzērâ šāwâ, whether or not the use of this sort of a method would have been normative or plausible within the context of a *public* scripture reading in a synagogue setting remains to be seen. This has been a missing element in the discussion until now. Evidence derived directly from the late Second Temple period is lacking on this issue, but the Mishnah and the Tosefta contain important data that may shed light on the matter.[22] According to both *m. Meg.* 4:4 and *t. Meg.* 3:19, "they

---

18. E.g., James A. Sanders, "Isaiah in Luke," in *Luke and Scripture: The Function of Sacred Tradition in Luke-Acts*, by Craig A. Evans and James A. Sanders (Minneapolis: Fortress Press, 1993), 14–25 (21); Notley, "Jesus' Jewish Hermeneutical Method," passim; Bock, *Luke*, 1:404–5; Bovon, *Luke*, 1:153.

19. As in *t. Sanh.* 7:11; *Abot R. Nat.* 37. See Herman L. Strack and Günter Stemberger, *Introduction to the Talmud and Midrash*, 2nd ed., trans. Markus Bockmuehl (Minneapolis: Fortress Press, 1996), 18–19. John P. Meier has also made a strong case for the identification of the use of gĕzērâ šāwâ in Jesus's teaching on the love command. See Meier, *A Marginal Jew*, 4:493–94. Although the gĕzērâ šāwâ in Jesus's most clearly defined in early Rabbinic literature, the basic elements of this technique are evidenced at Qumran (see 11QTemple 17:6–8). On this, see Moshe J. Bernstein and Shlomo A. Koyfman, "The Interpretation of Biblical Law in the Dead Sea Scrolls: Forms and Methods," in *Biblical Interpretation at Qumran*, ed. Matthias Henze (Grand Rapids: Eerdmans, 2005), 61–87 (84–86); Moshe J. Bernstein, "Interpretation of Scriptures," *Encyclopedia of the Dead Sea Scrolls*, ed. Lawrence H. Schiffman, 2 vols. (Oxford: Oxford University Press, 2000), 1:376–83 (381).

20. Cf. Bock, *Luke*, 1:405; Sanders, "Isaiah in Luke," 21–25; Notley, "Hermeneutical Method," 53.

21. Indeed, Notley has argued that there is good reason to think that it is more likely that the citations in Luke 4:18–19 rely on a Hebrew text than on the LXX. Notley, "Hermeneutical Method," passim.

22. Readers concerned about relying on early rabbinic traditions here are encouraged to refer to the

[readers] leap [from place to place] in the prophetic lections but not in the Torah lections."[23] The Tosefta passage goes on to specify additional rules: readers should not skip from one prophet to another unless they are reading from the Book of the Twelve, and should not leap from the end of a scroll to the beginning of the same one. This last detail is particularly interesting, since it implies that it is acceptable to skip backward in a scroll, so long as it is done within reasonable limits.

Jesus's reading from the Isaiah scroll in Luke 4:18–19 follows the rules given in these early rabbinic traditions quite well. He leaps around in Isaiah, but does not go outside of it to other prophetic texts. If the material evidence of the Great Isaiah Scroll from Qumran (1Q Isa A) can be taken as an instance of what a typical Isaiah scroll might have looked like in the late Second Temple period, then it is worth noting that it would have been quite easy to skip while reading aloud from Isaiah 61:1 to 58:6, since they are only two columns apart.[24] It is also possible that Jesus simply cited this small portion of 58:6 from memory while reading from 61:1–2.

A few observations can be made at this point. The precise manner in which Jesus presents his reading from Isaiah in Luke 4:18–19 is plausible within the context of a public synagogue scripture reading. Moreover, the method of *gĕzērâ šāwâ* illuminates the purpose behind Jesus's skipping between Isaiah 61:1–2 and 58:6 as a hermeneutical technique. We shall return to this later when we discuss the interpretation of this passage as evidence for our overarching project. These traditions are Palestinian Jewish traditions, rooted in the Land. While it is theoretically possible for Luke to have known about these traditions and to have included them in his composition of the passage for the sake of verisimilitude or local flavour, this seems unlikely and stretches the imagination. Moreover, we will see in the discussion below that, as Steven Notley has argued, the reading could have plausibly been drawn from a Hebrew text, rather than from the LXX.[25] Thus, the potential Hebrew links established between the two Isaianic passages through the technique of *gĕzērâ šāwâ* make the presence of a traditional source

---

important arguments in Geza Vermes, "Improving Methodology," 17–27, esp. 18–21. As Vermes argues, late attestation does not necessarily indicate late origins.

23. Compare *t. Meg.* 3:5, which interestingly mentions that for Passover readers do "skip around" in the Torah readings pertaining to the Passover story.

24. Isa 61:1 is found in column 49 of 1Q Isa A, while the relevant part of 58:6 is in column 47.

25. Cf. Notley, "Hermeneutical Method," 51–54.

possible.[26] If so, it is not necessary to regard this pericope as a free Lukan creation nor is there particular reason to do so on this account.

Another piece of evidence worth raising is the seemingly out of place reference that Jesus makes in Luke 4:23 to an anticipated request to "do here also in your hometown the things that we have heard you did at Capernaum." This saying is found only in Luke, which means that it does not come from Luke's Markan source. However, at this point in Luke's narrative, Jesus has not yet gone to Capernaum.[27] In fact, Luke introduces Capernaum for the first time in Luke 4:31, right after the incident at Nazareth. I am led to conclude that this is indicative of a relocated pre-Lukan tradition rather than a Lukan creation.[28]

Is it possible for the author of Luke to have gained access to an eyewitness account of this event that Mark did not have? It is not particularly difficult to imagine precisely the sort of situation that could have led to Luke gaining access to an eyewitness account of this event based on internal evidence in Luke-Acts. Luke mentions in Acts 1:14 that Mary and Jesus's brothers were present in the Jerusalem church, and knows specifically of the presence of James the Just in the same locale (Acts 12:17, 15:13–21, 21:8–25). Though there are other possibilities, these Nazarene relatives of Jesus are good candidates for the tradent behind this memory.[29]

Intriguingly, the narrative of Acts implies that the author of Luke-Acts had direct contact with one of these Nazarenes. Though the exact nature of the "we" passages in Acts is debated, Paul's trip to Jerusalem in Acts 21:15–18 is narrated in the first-person plural. Verse 18 narrates a meeting with James told in the first-person plural. It is admittedly difficult to know what to make of this, and there is no certainty to be had here. Nevertheless, we should recognize that Luke claims to be aware of accounts of the events of Jesus's life that have been passed on from eyewitnesses and "servants of the word" (Luke 1:2–3), and to have conducted his own investigation. If we were to look for a specific point of direct contact between the author of Luke-Acts and a Nazarene who is likely to have witnessed this event, we may have one here in Acts 21:18. Other interpretations of the data cannot be excluded, but if one accepts that the "we passages" represent the experiences of the author of Luke-Acts, then this is a plausible scenario.[30] My point is not that it

---

26. Bock, *Luke*, 1:405.
27. Note, however, that Luke 4:14–15 depicts Jesus teaching in unspecified Galilean synagogues prior to the incident at Nazareth.
28. Cf. Nolland, *Luke*, 1:192; Bock, *Luke*, 1:389.
29. See Bauckham, *Jesus and the Eyewitnesses*, 297–98.

had to have happened this way, nor does my argument hinge upon this scenario. Of course, it is not actually necessary for Luke to have met the eyewitness behind the tradition, as it could have been passed on orally to him. My point is simply that it is both possible and plausible to think that Luke (or one of his sources) could have acquired knowledge of this tradition from a non-Markan source that stems from an eyewitness account of the event in the Nazareth synagogue.

Our passage is too often dismissed as relevant data on the historical Jesus because it is redactional, and thus, "Lukan."[31] As we have seen, it is far from certain that Luke 4:16–30 is a free "redactional" composition relying upon Mark 6:1–6. At any rate, the question that needs to be asked and explored with regard to Jesus's reading from the Isaiah scroll in the synagogue at Nazareth is not whether or not Luke 4:16–30 is "Lukan." Everything contained with the Gospel of Luke is "Lukan" insofar as it has been interpreted by Luke and employed in the service of the formation of his narrative. There is no uninterpreted memory, and no access to uninterpreted history. We must remember that the past cannot be reobserved, and that all we have access to is evidence of the events, not empirical experience of the past itself.

Saying that a passage is "Lukan" does not mean that it does not correspond to historical reality or that it is not evidence of what happened in the past. Does this passage suit Luke's purposes? Yes, of course it does. However, saying so tells us little about how this passage should serve as evidence in our reconstruction, or even whether or not Jesus read from Isaiah in a public synagogue setting in his hometown. Everything contained within Luke's Gospel suits his purposes in some way. This is true of any narrative work, whether its intent is historical or otherwise. In this, historical criticism has something to learn from the

---

30. Some readers may find this scenario unconvincing on the basis that it relies upon the witness of a famous and named individual in the early church (James the Just). However, as Gerhardsson has argued, it is actually quite likely that, rather than tradition arising from anonymous origins, Jesus's close associates (including James and the Twelve) were authoritative witnesses and bearers of tradition. See Gerhardsson, *Reliability of the Gospel Tradition*, 35–40. Similarly, see Bauckham, *Jesus and the Eyewitnesses*, 290–318. As Gerhardsson rightly complains, "people blithely speak of 'products of the church' (*Gemeindebildungen*) and of traditions which 'circulated in the communities,' instead of asking *who* has formulated, reformulated, or transmitted a certain text" (*Reliability of the Gospel Tradition*, 74). It is also worth pointing out that it is a scenario derived directly from the data, which contains an implicit claim by the Lukan author to have been in contact with James, a Nazarene, and not spun solely out of historical imagination. Moreover, it is worth noting that this is certainly not the only possible or plausible scenario for understanding how Luke could have encountered a Nazarene. Nevertheless, the fact that this particular scenario can be inferred directly from the data makes it a preferable explanation.

31. See, e.g., Becker, *Jesus of Nazareth*, 29–30; Twelftree, "Jesus and the Synagogue," 3126–27; Funk and the Jesus Seminar, *Acts of Jesus*, 274–75; Oakman, *Political Aims of Jesus*, 126.

world of literary criticism. As Jan Fokkelman writes, "every word that the author allows to participate [in a narrative] has a relation to his vision and themes."[32] Likewise, Northrop Frye holds that "one has to assume, as an essential heuristic axiom, that the work *as produced* constitutes the definitive record of the writer's intention."[33] Whether or not a given passage in a Gospel suits its evangelist's purpose is an all-but irrelevant matter altogether for historical inquiry, since the answer will always be "yes." Understanding *how* a passage suits that purpose is useful for exegesis, but may not have much bearing on history. Thus, I would affirm that, within the context of the narrative of Luke-Acts, Luke 4:16–30 functions as a "programmatic introduction" to Jesus's ministry.[34] This is how it has been used by Luke in the creation of his story of Jesus. Nevertheless, this does not mean that it does not evince a historical event, or that it has no correspondence to historical reality.[35]

Redaction-critical questions are, at any rate, the wrong questions to be asking for the purposes of this project.[36] The question that I am more interested in asking is, what does Luke 4:16–21 mean for our study of Jesus and the synagogue?[37] How should it be interpreted? On a more basic level, did Jesus read from Isaiah 61:1–2, perhaps with an interjection from Isaiah 58:6, and apply it to his own career and aims in the context of a public synagogue gathering? If so, what does this mean?

A potential problem arises when we consider the text of Jesus's reading as presented in Luke 4:18–19. As a caveat, we must state the obvious in recognizing that Jesus's reading could not have been identical to what we have in Luke 4:18–19, simply because of the difference in language. Jesus would have been reading in Hebrew, while Luke is writing in Greek. The difference in language is in itself an indication that

---

32. Jan Fokkelman, *Reading Biblical Narrative: A Practical Guide* (Leiden: Deo, 1999), 76.

33. Northrop Frye, *Anatomy of Criticism: Four Essays* (Princeton: Princeton University Press, 1957), 87. Emphasis is my own.

34. Cf., e.g., Freyne, *Jewish Galilee*, 92; Schröter, *Jesus of Nazareth*, 101.

35. The argument that Luke saw Isa 62:1–2, 58:6 as a good summary of Jesus's actions and so used these passages to "programmatically" describe his mission is not convincing. It can be turned on its head, as Jesus himself could just as easily have patterned his activities on what he encountered in those same passages.

36. On asking the right or wrong questions in historical inquiry, see Lonergan, *Method in Theology*, 162–64.

37. Note the specificity of the question. I am not asking only if Luke 4:16–30 is data on the historical Jesus. It surely is, insofar as it indicates at the very least that Jesus was *remembered* as applying Isa 61:1–2 to himself. This fairly nuanced use of Luke 4:16–30 has been employed in the past, by Rodriguez, *Structuring Early Christian Memory*, 139–73; Schröter, *Jesus of Nazareth*, 116; and Freyne, *Jewish Galilee*, 92. However laudable these uses of the passage may be, I am interested in a more specific issue, that of the relationship of Jesus to the synagogue and the role that it played in his aims.

we need to be willing to think *inferentially* about the matter. We cannot ask, "did Jesus read exactly these words?" but we can ask the question, "is it plausible that Jesus read from Isaiah 61:1–2a, perhaps with an interjection from Isa 58:6, and apply it to his own career and aims in the context of a public synagogue gathering?" This is the question that we will consider here. While this means that we are concerned with the *vox* of Jesus as opposed to the *verba*, it is important to keep in mind that the *words* of Jesus as reported by Luke are the evidence from which we can infer the gist of Jesus's *voice*. As a result, we still need to carefully examine the words of Jesus as reported by Luke. This is a fine line, but one that nevertheless must be drawn.

Rodriguez raises an issue worth considering in saying that "Jesus *could not have been* reading words from a page, simply because no such page exists."[38] He raises this in regards to the insertion of Isaiah 58:6 into the reading from 61:1–2a, a problem which I think is sufficiently explained by the tradition of leaping from place to place in readings from the Nevi'im discussed above. Otherwise, Luke 4:18–19 generally follows the text of Isaiah 61:1–2a. One exception to this is the omission of "to heal the brokenhearted" (Gk. ἰάσασθαι τοὺς συντετριμμένους τῇ καρδίᾳ). There are various ways to explain this: it could be due to an intentional omission on Luke's part, an intentional omission by Jesus, an accidental omission by either one of them, or to a corrupt text being used by either Luke or Jesus. There is no way to settle the matter with absolute certainty, but I consider the best explanation to be that the omission originates with Jesus, who skipped ahead in his reading as per the allowance of *m. Meg.* 4:4 (and parallels). The issue is certainly not inexplicable, and we need not leap to the conclusion that the scene depicted is implausible, and thus, must be a Lukan fabrication.

For the most part, both Luke 4:18–19 and the LXX follow the MT fairly closely. In fact, they are so close that, as Notley has pointed out, it is hard to be certain that Luke 4:18–19 is following the LXX rather than MT.[39] In this regard, it is also interesting that the citation of Isa 58:6 uses the infinitive ἀποστεῖλαι in agreement with the MT, while the LXX uses the imperative ἀπόστελλε.[40] However, "recovery of sight to the blind" (τυφλοῖς ἀνάβλεψιν) matches the LXX, but might depart from the MT.[41] The issue here is tricky, because the Hebrew פְּקַח־קוֹחַ refers to

---

38. Rodriguez, *Early Christian Memory*, 162.
39. Notley, "Hermeneutical Method," 50. Alternatively, it could be that Luke knew that Jesus read from Isa 6:1–2, and interjected the small segment from 58:6, but used the LXX in his composition of the scene because he was writing in Greek.
40. See Fitzmyer, *Luke*, 1:533.

"opening," and can have the sense of "to open the eyes wide."[42] Thus, the distance between Luke and the MT here is perhaps not as great as it may initially appear.[43] If we are thinking on the level of the historical Jesus, it is possible, perhaps even probable, that Jesus himself would have taken this as a reference to his healing ministry. What can we thus conclude about the text of the reading from Isaiah featured in Luke 4:18–19 and its relation to the MT? For our purposes, it is sufficient to conclude that they are close enough that if Jesus was reading in Hebrew, the essential voice of his reading would be reflected in the Greek text of Luke 4:18–19 well enough for us to draw historical inferences from it.

The chronology of this event presents a minor problem.[44] Luke positions the incident in synagogue at Nazareth at the beginning of Jesus's career. In Mark, however, it occurs much later, in the middle of Jesus's Galilean period. Matthew's placement of the incident generally follows that of Mark. Whereas the Nazareth incident is the first event taking place in a synagogue to be narrated by Luke, it is the last in both Mark and Matthew.[45]

When did the incident actually take place? It is most likely that it took place sometime after Jesus's public synagogue program had gotten underway. Evidence for this is actually found within the Lukan narrative. Luke does not actually hold that this was Jesus's inaugural teaching event in a synagogue. In fact, Luke 4:14–15 depicts Jesus teaching in Galilean synagogues prior to the Nazareth incident. Moreover, there is the curious reference in Luke 4:23 to the request to "do here also in your hometown the things we have heard you did at Capernaum" discussed above, which presumes that Jesus has already been active there, despite no such event having yet been narrated by Luke at that point. This leads to the conclusion, as mentioned earlier, that this is a relocated tradition.[46] It is important to recognize that the evangelists, though having historical intentions in writing the Gospels,[47] nevertheless purposefully shaped the traditional material into the respec-

---

41. As noted by Rodriguez, "Early Christian Memory," 139.
42. Cf. J. Alex Motyer, *Isaiah* (TOTC 20; Downers Grove: Intervarsity, 1999), 426.
43. It is worth noting that a reading very similar to the LXX variant is attested in Hebrew in 4Q521 2, II, 8, a text which draws upon Isa 61:1. Cf.
44. Cf. David Hill, "The Rejection of Jesus At Nazareth (Luke iv 16–30)," *Novum Testamentum* 13, no. 3 (1971): 162–80 (172–77). However, Hill's discussion is complicated by an outdated conception of synagogue liturgy.
45. Cf. Keith, *Jesus' Literacy*, 144. The similarities between the basic narratives of the accounts make it unlikely that there are two different incidents being narrated, cf. Tannehill, *Shape of Luke's Story*, 4–5.
46. Bock, *Luke*, 1:398.

tive narrative forms of the Gospels as we now have them. This is, of course, what the author of any narrative historical work is tasked with. Luke's chronological placement of the incident at Nazareth comes as a result of the careful crafting of his story.

Luke 4:16–30 and the Problem of Jesus's Literacy

The issue of Jesus's literacy is relevant to the interpretation of Luke 4:16–30. Jesus's literate status is disputed,[48] and a number of scholars have argued that he was illiterate, or at least, not literate enough to read in a public setting. If so, then he could not have read from the Isaiah scroll in the synagogue at Nazareth, and this would impact how we should interpret and use Luke 4:16–30 in our present project.

Before discussing this further, it is necessary to recognize that there is a spectrum of literacy, ranging from general illiteracy to scribal-literacy.[49] There is no need to go over this in detail here, as others have already done so admirably.[50] It is enough for our purposes to simply recognize this fact. We only need to concern ourselves with whether or not Jesus could read *well enough* in order for Luke 4:18–19 to describe a plausible event, not with his ability to write at a scribal level or otherwise.

Arguments based on statistical illiteracy in the Roman world[51] and/or on Jesus's status as a "peasant" or member of the lower class are unconvincing.[52] That most people in Jesus's world were illiterate[53] does not mean that *Jesus* was illiterate. The general problem with this sort

---

47. Cf. David E. Aune, *The New Testament in Its Literary Environment* (ed. Wayne A. Meeks; Library of Early Christianity 8; Philadelphia: Westminster, 1987), 64–65.

48. Examples of scholars arguing for various shades of an illiterate Jesus include Pieter F. Craffert and Pieter J. Botha, "Why Jesus Could Walk on the Sea but He Could Not Read or Write," *Neotestamentica* 39, no. 1 (2005): 5–35; John Dominic Crossan, *The Birth of Christianity: Discovering What Happened in the Years Immediately After the Execution of Jesus* (New York: HarperCollins, 1998), 235; Funk and the Jesus Seminar, *Acts of Jesus*, 274; Keith, *Jesus' Literacy*, 165–88; Keith, *Scribal Elite*, 89–108; Kelber, *Oral and Written Gospel*, 18, cf. 14. Examples of scholars arguing for various shades of a literate Jesus include Craig A. Evans, "Jewish Scripture and the Literacy of Jesus," in *From Biblical Criticism to Biblical Faith: Essays in Honor of Lee Martin McDonald*, ed. William H. Brackney and Craig A. Evans (Macon: Mercer University Press, 2007), 41–54; cf. Evans, *Jesus and His World*, 63–88; Paul Foster, "Educating Jesus: The Search For a Plausible Context," *JSHJ* 4, no. 1 (2006): 7–33 (though Foster comes to no definitive conclusion); Meier, *A Marginal Jew*, 1:268–78.

49. See William V. Harris, *Ancient Literacy* (Cambridge: Harvard University Press, 1989), 5–8.

50. Good extended discussions of this issue can be found in Keith, *Jesus' Literacy*, 89–107; or Meier, *A Marginal Jew*, 1:271–78. Shorter discussions can be found in David E. Aune, "Literacy," in *The Westminster Dictionary of New Testament and Early Christian Literature and Rhetoric* (Louisville: Westminster John Knox, 2003), 275–76; Harry Y. Gamble, "Literacy and Book Culture," in *The Dictionary of New Testament Background*, ed. Craig A. Evans and Stanley E. Porter (Downers Grove: InterVarsity, 2000), 644–48.

51. Cf. the findings of Harris, *Ancient Literacy*, see esp. 22, 272.

52. Examples of this sort of argumentation include Craffert and Botha, "Why Jesus Could Walk on the

of argument is that it does not properly take the existence of exceptions or exceptional people into account.[54] Terminological problems with the term "peasant" aside, we must recognize that Jesus did not lead the life of an ordinary Galilean "peasant," nor did he die the death of one. The root of the problem is that such arguments are founded on inferences about an individual drawn from an analysis of data pertaining to a group to which the individual belongs. This is a form of the "ecological fallacy,"[55] and must be regarded as unconvincing.

Keith takes a nuanced approach to the issue of Jesus's literacy. He describes a "debate" in the synoptic Gospels, in which Jesus is portrayed as scribal-illiterate by Mark and Matthew, but as scribal-literate in Luke.[56] Keith comes to the conclusion that Jesus was not a scribal-literate teacher based on his identification of these competing depictions of Jesus as either scribal-literate or scribal-illiterate in the tradition combined with the statistical unlikelihood of him attaining scribal-literate status as a Galilean craftsman.[57] The two competing portrayals of Jesus's literacy in the synoptic Gospels stem from the fact that there was confusion surrounding Jesus's literate status, which in turn came about because Jesus acted like a scribal-literate teacher though he was, in fact, scribal-illiterate.

I disagree with Keith's conclusion. I question whether Jesus is actually depicted as scribally illiterate in the synoptic tradition. I am also unconvinced that *scribal* literacy is the best term to describe Luke's portrayal of Jesus in 4:16–30. In the first place, I question whether Jesus's literacy should be judged by what is essentially the highest standard on the spectrum of literacy. Scribal literacy is usually associated with writing and a professional literate class.[58] In Jesus's world, a "scribe" (Gk. *grammateus*) was someone with professional writing ability.[59] Luke does not portray Jesus with quite this level of literacy, and

---

Sea," 29; Crossan, *Birth of Christianity*, 235; John Dominic Crossan, *Jesus: A Revolutionary Biography* (New York: HarperCollins, 1994), 25–26; Funk and the Jesus Seminar, *Acts of Jesus*, 274.

53. See, however, the evidence for wider literacy presented in Evans, *Jesus and His World*, 63–88; and the arguments in Foster, "Educating Jesus," passim.

54. Here, I am in agreement with Keith, *Jesus' Literacy*, 168. Keith writes, "the problem with such an approach, regardless of which side of the argument one takes, is that history is littered with exceptions to generalities."

55. See Fischer, *Historians' Fallacies*, 119–20.

56. Keith, *Jesus' Literacy*, 125–146; cf. Keith, *Scribal Elite*, 85–108.

57. Keith, *Jesus' Literacy*, 167–169; cf. Keith, *Scribal Elite*, 89–93.

58. Classically, see Harris, *Ancient Literacy*, 7. Keith recognizes this as well in his description of scribal literacy in first-century Jewish Palestine, in Keith, *Jesus' Literacy*, 110–11. However, he also says that "scribal literacy can also refer to religious authorities who are experts in texts that are determinative for the group's identity" (p. 110). This might be a bit closer to how Jesus is portrayed by Luke.

certainly not as grapho-literate. On the spectrum of literacy, I would say that Luke portrays Jesus as having a level of literacy that lies somewhere between craftsmen's literacy and scribal literacy, though a fair bit closer to scribal literacy than to craftsmen's literacy. It may seem like I am splitting hairs, but this distinction helps to avoid category slippage.

My disagreement with Keith's argument essentially comes down to a difference in interpretation of the evidence. Keith sees evidence of a synoptic portrayal of Jesus as scribally illiterate in Mark 1:22 (cf. Matt 7:28b–29) and Mark 6:3. Mark 1:22 recounts the reaction to Jesus's teaching in the synagogue at Capernaum: "They were astounded at his teaching, for he taught them as one having authority, and not as the scribes." According to Keith,

> In a world where very few received a scribal-literate education, Mark explains the synagogue audience's reaction to Jesus' occupation of a synagogue position typically associated with scribal literacy by contrasting Jesus with those who held scribal literacy. *The crowd's initial astonishment and Mark's own assessment of Jesus' pedagogy both assume, therefore, that Jesus fell outside scribal-literate culture.*[60]

I interpret the passage differently. The reason for the assembly's astonishment is that "he taught them as one having authority, and not as the scribes." The question is, what does this mean? Does it mean that he taught in a way that would clearly mark him as scribally illiterate, or unable to read? It is not clear that it does. In my opinion, it means simply that, in the words of Edwin Broadhead, Jesus's teaching is "distinguished from the scribal tradition by its authority."[61]

What would it mean to teach with authority, as opposed to the way in which the scribes taught? Some scholars have taken this to mean that Jesus did not rely on the opinions of others, as opposed to the scribes, who cited other authorities.[62] I am willing to grant that there may be something to this. However, within the context of the Gospel of

59. See Saldarini, *Pharisees, Scribes, and Sadducees*, 241–42, 273–76.
60. Keith, *Jesus' Literacy*, 129. Emphasis original.
61. Edwin K. Broadhead, *Teaching With Authority: Miracles and Christology in the Gospel of Mark* (JSNTSupp 74; Sheffield: Sheffield Academic, 1992), 59.
62. E.g., France, *Mark*, 102; Vincent Taylor, *The Gospel According to St. Mark* (London: Macmillan, 1963), 172; James A. Brooks, *Mark* (NAC 23; Nashville: Broadman, 1991), 50; Keener, *Matthew*, 256–57; John P. Meier, *Matthew* (New Testament Message 3; Wilmington: Michael Glazier, 1980), 76; Gundry, *Matthew*, 137; Luz, *Matthew*, 1:390. This interpretation is especially common amongst commentators on the Matthean version of the saying, presumably because the interpretation of Mark 1:22 must take Mark 1:27 into account as well, while no such parallel is attached to Matt 7:28b–29.

Mark, it is more likely that this refers to Jesus's authority to work exorcisms and miracles.[63] That, at least, is what Mark meant to say by it.[64] This conclusion is bolstered by Mark 1:27 at the end of the pericope, which follows the account of an exorcism in the synagogue with the following reaction: "They were all amazed, and they kept on asking one another, 'What is this? A new teaching—with authority! He commands even the unclean spirits, and they obey him.'" This response is intuitively odd, since no teaching is actually given, but it is nevertheless clear that the "authority" that Mark is referring to comes from Jesus's command over unclean spirits. Thus, Mark 1:22 tells us not that Jesus's teaching was distinguished from that of the scribes because of his non-literate status, but because he wielded supernatural authority, whereas the scribes did not.

Keith is aware of these more common interpretations of the passage, and replies that "Mark explains the synagogue audience's reaction to Jesus' occupation of a synagogue position typically associated with scribal literacy by contrasting Jesus with those who held scribal literacy."[65] The problem with this interpretation is that it is not actually what the text says, nor is it apparent that this is what Mark is trying to communicate. At issue is not scribal *literacy*, but the difference between the teaching of Jesus and the scribes, which is understood in terms of "authority." Here, we must be attentive to the primacy of the intended sense of the text,[66] and recognize that literacy does not clearly factor into the message that the author is trying to convey.

Mark 6:3 conveys the response of the synagogue assembly at Nazareth to Jesus's wisdom and deeds of power. In the first part of the verse, the crowd asks, "is not this the craftsman?" (Gk. τέκτων). In Matthew, the crowd says, "is this not the craftsman's son?" (Matt 13:55). Luke 4:22 has the crowd say "is this not Joseph's son?" Keith identifies two streams of Jesus-memory here. One, evidenced by Mark 6:3 and Matthew 13:55, remembers Jesus as a craftsman, while the other, evidenced by Luke 4:22, does not.

According to Keith, in Mark 6:3, the offense taken by the assembly at

---

63. Cf. Joshua Starr, "The Meaning of 'Authority' in Mark 1:22," *HTR* 23, no. 4 (1930): 302–5; Richard J. Dillon, "'As One Having Authority' (Mark 1:22) The Controversial Distinction of Jesus' Teaching," *CBQ* 57, no. 1 (1995): 97–112; Robert H. Stein, *Mark* (Baker Exegetical Commentary on the New Testament; Grand Rapids: Baker Academic, 2008), 87.

64. A study of "authority" (ἐξουσία) in Mark is beyond the purview of this project. For a good overview, see James R. Edwards, "The Authority of Jesus in the Gospel of Mark," *JETS* 37, no. 2 (1994): 217–33.

65. Keith, *Jesus' Literacy*, 129.

66. Cf. the argument in Meyer, *Critical Realism*, 17–49.

Jesus's actions stems particularly from his identity as a *tektōn* (craftsman).[67] He rightly notes that the identification of Jesus as a *tektōn* does not automatically indicate that he was an illiterate peasant, since some craftsmen held a functional level of literacy (craftsmen's literacy).[68] However, Keith interprets the "debate" between the synoptic authors in their portrayal of Jesus as a craftsman in terms of the divide between scribal literacy and craftsman's literacy.[69] He summarizes his argument thus: "the accusation of 'craftsman' is simultaneously a denial of scribal literacy; such that if one wishes to affirm scribal literacy, the accusation of craftsman must be removed."[70]

The question, then, is this: is the identification of Jesus as a *tektōn* sufficient warrant to say that Mark portrays him as a teacher lacking a sufficient level of literacy to publically read from a scroll in a synagogue setting? We first need to determine what the Markan crowds mean to say in Mark 6:3. There are no references to scribes in Mark 6:1–6, so any comparison made between Jesus the *tektōn* and scribes must be implicit. Granted, scribes were the usual teachers in synagogues, and Jesus is said to be teaching in a synagogue (v. 2), so it is *possible* that such a contrast is being made. The issue raised by the crowd in vv. 2–3 is that Jesus is speaking wisely and performing "deeds of power," but they take offence at him because they know him. Verse 3 does not only mention that Jesus is a *tektōn*—it also mentions that the crowd knows his family. The issue for the crowds in Mark seems to be Jesus's social status and the crowd's familiarity with him. As Eugene Boring writes, "familiarity, not elitist prejudice against the 'working class,' is a key factor in their rejection."[71] This does not exclude an objection based on Jesus's literate status, but *nor is it necessary* in order to make sense of the narrative.

Could Jesus have been a craftsman who learned to read? I see no compelling reason why this could not be the case. I would argue, as others have in the past, that Jesus was not formally educated as a scribe would have been, but had attained a level of literacy sufficient to read

---

67. Keith, *Jesus' Literacy*, 130.
68. Ibid., 130–31.
69. Ibid., 145.
70. Ibid. The language of "removal" is somewhat problematic, since as I have argued above, it is not clear that Luke is following Mark's account. Nevertheless, we can still say that Luke chose not to include a passage identifying Jesus as a *tektōn* in his Gospel, despite having knowledge of Mark's Gospel, wherein Jesus is identified as a *tektōn*.
71. M. Eugene Boring, *Mark: A Commentary* (NTL; Louisville: Westminster John Knox, 2006), 165. Boring notes that the use of *houtos* with the definite article before *tektōn* "suggests that it is *this* construction worker who is disparaged, not the class as such."

a Hebrew text aloud in a public setting.[72] According to Keith, "the ideas that Jesus (1) was not formally educated but (2) still attained scribal literacy are mutually exclusive at worst and an aberration demanding explanation at best."[73] This is based on Keith's reading of Second Temple evidence concerning education and literacy.[74] A review of this evidence is beyond the purview of the present project, but it is at least worth noting that other scholars have come to different conclusions in their considerations of similar evidence.[75]

My basic objection is that the argument is essentially a more nuanced instantiation of the ecological fallacy. If, as I am willing to do, we grant his reading of the Second Temple evidence, what Keith has demonstrated is that *under usual circumstances*, craftsmen were not scribally literate. He has not demonstrated that *no* craftsman could possibly attain a level of literacy sufficient to read a text aloud in a public setting, though this is what his interpretation of Mark 6:3 requires. Once again, allowance in this sort of discussion needs to be made for the possibility that Jesus was an exceptional individual, and did not adhere to normal statistical patterns, especially given that we have a source depicting Jesus reading in Luke 4:18–19. Another factor worth considering in this regard is the fact that whether or not Jesus was a *tektōn* prior to beginning his ministry, he does not act as a *tektōn* in the Gospel narratives. The actions and stories of Jesus in the Gospels are themselves an aberrance from the typical behavior of a craftsman. This fact, in itself, is an indication that we are dealing with an individual who resists pigeonholing and normative categorization.[76]

How could Jesus, a craftsman, have attained a level of literacy higher than craftsman's literacy?[77] Most likely by participating in synagogue culture. The matter is not beyond explanation. What it would probably take for someone with craftsman's literacy to attain a higher level of literacy, beyond the primary requirement of sufficient time, is access to written texts, and perhaps also access to a literate teacher. As we have seen in chapters 2 and 3, these things could be found in syn-

---

72. Cf. John 7:15. See Meier, *A Marginal Jew*, 1:278; Evans, "Jewish Scripture," 51; Evans, *Jesus and His World*, 80–81.

73. Keith, *Jesus' Literacy*, 115.

74. Ibid., 100–107, 110–12.

75. Foster, "Educating Jesus," passim; Evans, *Jesus and His World*, 63–88.

76. I would not altogether exclude the possibility, combining the testimony of Luke 4:16–30 and Mark 6:3, that the historical Jesus read in the synagogue at Nazareth, and that the crowd reacted to his reading as though it were unusual because of his status as a *tektōn*. Nevertheless, the fact that it would have been unusual, aberrant, or difficult for a *tektōn* to attain the literate status attributed to Jesus in Luke 4:16–30 does not mean that no *tektōn* could do so.

77. In response to Keith, *Jesus' Literacy*, 116.

agogues. While we must admit that it might have been difficult for someone like Jesus to have access to some time, some texts, and a teacher, it is not beyond the realm of what is plausible or possible in the ancient world. From a logical standpoint, to say that it would have been unusual for someone like Jesus to be literate does not mean that it would thereby be impossible or implausible.

Although it is sometimes overstated,[78] contemporary synagogue scholars have often recognized that the Second Temple synagogue had an educational function.[79] Given the work of these other scholars on the matter, a full review of the literature on the educational function of synagogues issue is unnecessary here. There is, however, one relatively new piece of evidence that has not yet received due attention in relation to this issue. I am referring to the secondary room in the recently discovered synagogue at Magdala (see figs. 3.3 and 3.5) containing a limestone "reading stone," discussed in chapter 5 above, at its centre (see figs. 3.5 and 3.6).

As suggested by Runesson, the current best explanation for the function of this piece of furniture is that the grooves were meant to hold scroll rollers, which would facilitate reading.[80] The seating arrangement of the room, with benches surrounding the "reading stone" in a rectangular formation, indicates that the room was likely used for the communal study of texts in a smaller group setting, as one might expect in an educational context.[81] This provides a plausible spatial and institutional setting in which Jesus could have accessed texts and literate people.

The above discussion has endeavoured to demonstrate that the general presentation of the incident in the synagogue at Nazareth in Luke 4:16–30 is historically plausible. Synagogue scholarship has until now been a curiously missing element of the discourse surrounding this passage, its plausibility,[82] and how or whether it should be employed as

---

78. E.g., Alan Millard, *Reading and Writing at the Time of Jesus*, (Sheffield: Sheffield Academic, 2000), 157; Dunn, "Did Jesus Attend the Synagogue?," 221. Compare Levine's more restrained and cautious statement about education in synagogues in Levine, *Ancient Synagogue*, 144–45.

79. Binder, *Into the Temple Courts*, 433–35; Levine, *Ancient Synagogue*, 144–45; Runesson, "Importance of the Synagogue," 292; Twelftree, "Jesus and the Synagogue," 3123–24. To be clear, this does *not* mean that there was an institutional "primary school" education in place in synagogues or that we should imagine that most Jewish children in the Second Temple period could read and write. This is an overstatement and stretches the evidence. It simply means that *some form* of education involving texts took place there.

80. Runesson, "Synagogues Without Rabbis or Christians?"

81. This supports Binder's conjecture that the secondary room at Gamla could have been used for similar purposes. See Binder, *Into the Temple Courts*, 434.

82. On its plausibility, see esp. Catto, *Reconstructing*, 185; Runesson, *Origins*, 217–20; cf. also McKay, *Sabbath and Sacrifice*, 165.

evidence for understanding the historical Jesus. Arguing that the passage serves Luke's purposes does not speak against the historical reality of the event that it recounts, since *everything* in Luke's Gospel serves Luke's purposes simply by virtue of the fact that it was included at all.[83] Luke 4:16–30 is undoubtedly Lukan, and its testimony has been shaped by Luke and by the processes of collective remembering. That is the nature of history, and there does not exist any account of something that happened in the past that is not similarly shaped by the process of remembering. None of this means that it does not recall or evince an event that actually happened. Again, we must remember that history is inferential, and that the evidence is not the past itself, but bears witness to it. A shift in language may help to illustrate this. Rather than saying that this passage "goes back to Jesus," it is better to say that it *tells us about him*. We are, as always, seeking Jesus's voice.

A Historical Interpretation of Jesus's Reading of Isaiah

In this section, I will provide a historical interpretation of Luke 4:16–30. Though we are seeking the *vox* rather than the exact *verba* of Jesus,[84] we will still need to consider the data, the words reported by Luke to have been spoken by Jesus, and interpret it. In so doing, I am treating the words reported by Luke as artifacts or evidence from which to infer the voice of Jesus.

What do Luke 4:16–30 and its shorter synoptic parallels in Mark 6:1–6 and Matt 13:54–58 tell us about Jesus's synagogue ministry and about his aims? Let us begin by considering the import of the basic act of teaching in a synagogue itself (Mark 6:2; Matt 13:54; described but not directly mentioned in Luke's account). As demonstrated in previous chapters, the act of teaching in a synagogue was politically charged due to the local-official nature of the institution.[85] Thus, just by engaging in the act of teaching, Jesus was entering the political arena. It is important to keep this in mind and to let it inform the discussion to follow.

---

83. Contra Binder, *Into the Temple Courts*, 400–402.
84. When it comes to reports of Jesus reading or quoting from a text as in Luke 4:18–19, we may be slightly closer to the *verba* than usual, since the words of the historical Jesus would have been tied to the text. Nevertheless, there are still complicating factors. For example, there is the matter of the translation of the text that was read by Jesus in Hebrew into Greek by the evangelist or the tradents, and the impossibility of objective certainty that an eyewitness remembered exactly where Jesus inserted the segment of Isa 58:6 into the reading of Isa 61:1–2. Moreover, longer discourses such as the one contained in Luke 4:23–27 that follows the reading would naturally have been more difficult to remember with exactitude than short, pithy sayings (cf. Gerhardsson, *Reliability of the Gospel Tradition*, 10).
85. Cf. similar ideas in Runesson, *Origins*, 221–22; Mosser, "Torah Instruction," 540–41.

Standing to read was itself an act of significance. It is unlikely that there was a set lectionary schedule for the Nevi'im in the late Second Temple period.[86] Thus, Jesus would have freely selected the reading. By doing so, he was determining the course of the gathering and shaping it to fit his aims. Most importantly, this means that the specific portions of scripture that he chose to read were themselves significant and selected with purpose and intent.

What did Jesus hope to achieve by reading from Isaiah 61:1–2 and 58:6? What was he trying to communicate? It is clear that Jesus was applying the message of his reading to his own work. This much can be inferred from Luke 4:21, wherein Jesus states that "this scripture has been fulfilled in your hearing." The statement strongly implies that his reading in vv. 18–19 was both meaningful and intentional. The accompanying inference that Jesus understood his reading of the passage to be both meaningful and intentional is thus the logical starting point and initial orientation for our interpretation of the passage.

Luke 4:18a ("the Spirit of the Lord is upon me, because he has anointed me") communicates an understanding of divine agency in Jesus's mission.[87] Jesus is claiming to be acting in accordance with the divine will, insofar as he has been "anointed" by God, in the sense of being commissioned, to carry out his specific task.[88] There is some potential for this data to speak to the problem of Jesus's self-understanding, which may help to illuminate his aims and mission. Some exegetes have noted the connection between the verb *chriō* ("to anoint") and *christos*, the messianic title.[89] However tempting it may be to read further into this, it is important to approach this with caution. It is by no means clear that this particular datum indicates that Jesus

86. Cf. Catto, *Reconstructing*, 181; Runesson, *Origins*, 215; Levine, *Ancient Synagogue*, 154; Bovon, *Luke*, 1:152; Bock, *Luke*, 1:403; Craig S. Keener, *The IVP Bible Background Commentary: New Testament* 2nd ed. (Downers Grove: InterVarsity, 2014), 190; L. Crockett, "Luke iv. 16–30 and the Jewish Lectionary Cycle: A Word of Caution," *JJS* 17, no. 2 (1966): 13–46.

87. On the portrayal of Jesus as a divine agent in the Gospels, see, e.g., Carter, *Matthew and Empire*, 67–70; Gary M. Burge, *The Anointed Community: The Holy Spirit in the Johannine Tradition* (Grand Rapids: Eerdmans, 1987), 200–201. A more specific and "higher" form of "chief" agency is discussed by Paul Owen, "Jesus as God's Agent in Mark's Christology," in *Mark, Manuscripts, and Monotheism* (ed. Chris Keith and Dieter Roth; London and New York: Bloomsbury T&T Clark, 2014), 40–57. On this concept of "chief agency" in early Judaism, see Larry W. Hurtado, *One Lord, One God: Early Christian Devotion and Ancient Jewish Monotheism*, 3rd ed. (London and New York: Bloomsbury T&T Clark, 2015), 17–22.

88. Cf. Carter's comments on Jesus' messianic title in Matthew, *Matthew and Empire*, 67–68.

89. Tannehill, *Luke*, 91; Carroll, *Luke*, 112; David Ravens, *Luke and the Restoration of Israel* (JSNTSupp 119; Sheffield: Sheffield Academic, 1995), 114; R. T. France, *Jesus and the Old Testament: His Application of Old Testament Passages to Himself and His Mission* (Grand Rapids: Baker, 1982), 134; Bock, *Luke*, 1:406–407; Robert H. Stein, *Luke* (NAC 24; Nashville: Broadman, 1992), 156; John Nolland, *Luke* (WBC 35; 3 vols.; Dallas: Word, 1989–1993), 1:196.

had a Davidic messianic self-understanding, nor that a royal messiah is envisioned here at all.[90] Some parallels in Second–Temple-period literature can help to shed light on the breadth of the concept of divine "anointing" at the time of Jesus. In the Damascus Document, prophets are understood to be "anointed" (CD 2:12, 6:1). Similarly, the messenger of Isaiah 52:7 is said to be "anointed with the Spirit" in 11QMelch 2:18.[91] Thus, in my opinion, it is best to understand the anointing in Luke 4:18a in terms of a divine commissioning for the task of proclamation outlined in vv. 18b–19. The notion that the "anointing" is that of divine agent in terms of a prophet or herald is further supported by Jesus's apparent identification of himself as a prophet in v. 24.

It is sometimes suggested that Jesus's use of Isaiah 61:1–2 indicates that he was taking on the role of the Isaianic Servant.[92] However, it is not clear that Isaiah 61:1–2 actually belongs to the Servant song literature.[93] That having been said, the voice of Isaiah 61 describes itself "in the garb of the figure of the servant."[94] Thus, it is plausible and even likely that Jesus would have associated Isaiah 61:1–2 with the Isaianic servant, since the language in Isaiah 61:1–2 reflects that of the Servant material.[95]

Brevard Childs makes the astute point that the fact that Isaiah 61:1–3 was not included among the Servant songs in Isaiah is irrelevant to the New Testament's interpretation of it,[96] and the same could be said for Jesus's understanding of the passage. Ultimately, it is more important for the historical study of Jesus and the Gospels to consider how Isaiah 61 was read in the late Second Temple period than how it was

---

90. Contra Wright, *Jesus and the Victory of God*, 536.

91. Cf. Fitzmyer, *Luke*, 1:530. On this, see John J. Collins, "A Herald of Good Tidings: Isaiah 61:1–3 and Its Actualization in the Dead Sea Scrolls," in *The Quest for Context and Meaning: Studies in Biblical Intertextuality in Honor of James A. Sanders*, ed. Craig A. Evans and Shemaryahu Talmon (Leiden, New York, and Köln: Brill, 1997), 225–40.

92. E.g., Morna D. Hooker, *Jesus and the Servant: The Influence of the Servant Concept of Deutero-Isaiah in the New Testament* (London: SPCK, 1959), 85; France, *Jesus and the Old Testament*, 135; Bock, *Luke*, 1:405–6; Nolland, *Luke*, 1:196; E. Earle Ellis, *The Gospel of Luke* (Eugene: Wipf & Stock: 2003 [1983]), 97–98.

93. Cf. Fitzmyer, *Luke*, 1:529. It has been suggested that Isa 61:1–3 should be identified as a fifth servant song, most notably by W. W. Cannon, "Isaiah 61, 1–3 an Ebed-Jahweh Poem," *ZAW* 47 (1929): 284–88. However, others have argued against this reading, preferring to see the passage as relating to the prophet's self-understanding. See, for example, W. Zimmerli, "Das 'Gnadenjahr des Herrn,'" *Studien zur alttestamentlichen Theologie und Prophetie* (Munich: Kaiser, 1974), 222–34. A good summary of the matter can be found in Brevard S. Childs, *Isaiah: A Commentary* (OTL; Louisville: John Knox, 2001), 502–3.

94. Childs, *Isaiah*, 505. See also Willem A. M. Beuken, "Servant and Herald of Good Tidings: Isaiah 61 as an Interpretation of Isaiah 40–55," in *The Book of Isaiah: Les Oracles et Leurs Relectures Unité et Complexité de L'Ouvrage*, ed. J. Vermeylen (Leuven: Peeters, 1989), 411–42.

95. Cf. Childs, *Isaiah*, 507.

96. Ibid.

composed.[97] 11QMelch casts the anointed prophetic speaker of Isaiah 61:1–2 as an eschatological herald of restoration, and a similar role for the same figure is attested in 4Q521 (2, II, 15). We should note that 11QMelch explicitly draws upon the presentation of the messenger of Isaiah 52:7, a passage which leads into the Servant song of 52:13–53:12. This data indicates that the figure of Isaiah 61:1–2 was recognized in Jewish thought at the time of Jesus as an eschatological herald of restoration, much like the Isaianic Servant is described in the Servant songs, and as Jesus is presented by the synoptic evangelists.

What we can conclude about Jesus's self-understanding from v. 18a is modest, but not insignificant. I find no clear basis in this particular passage on its own for an inference that Jesus understood himself to be the Davidic messiah. It is somewhat more likely that he could have associated the restorative acts that he announces in Luke 4:18–19 with those of the Isaianic servant. Nevertheless, it is clear that Jesus understood his aims, mission, and actions to have divine agency, and to be guided by the Spirit of the Lord.

What did Jesus think that he was commissioned to do? This is precisely what is outlined in vv. 18b–19. Firstly, to "bring good news (Gk. *evangelizō*) to the poor." This requires some unpacking. What is the "good news" and who are "the poor?" In the sayings tradition, "good news" is associated with the proclamation of the outbreak of the Kingdom of God.[98] Similarly, the authors of Matthew and Luke themselves connect "good news" with the concept of the "Kingdom."[99] As discussed in chapter 7, the Kingdom of God is at the heart of Jesus's proclamation. In light of this, it is striking that proclamation of "the good news of the Kingdom" is associated with Jesus's synagogue activities in Luke 4:43–44 and Matthew 4:23 (cf. 9:35). Further light is cast on the matter by Luke 6:20, the first Lukan beatitude, wherein Jesus proclaims that the poor are blessed because the Kingdom belongs to them. Surely this would qualify as "good news" for the poor. Thus, the "good news" to be proclaimed to the poor is that the Kingdom of God, with its trademark reversal of values, is breaking out into the world, and that it belong to, rather than excludes or marginalizes, "the poor."

Who, exactly are "the poor?" The most natural referent of this term (Gk. *ptochoi*) is the economically impoverished.[100] However, some schol-

---

97. On this topic, see Collins, "Isaiah 61:1–3," 229–40.

98. Mark 1:15; Matt 10:7, 24:14; Luke 4:43, 16:16.

99. Matt 4:23, 9:35; Luke 8:1.

100. In other words, those living around or below subsistence level. See the excellent discussion in

ars have pointed out that while the usage of the term in the tradition does include the economically impoverished, it extends beyond this to include the disadvantaged, marginalized, or those of low social status in general.[101] Thus, as Carroll writes, the other disadvantaged members of society mentioned in v. 18 (the captives, the blind, and the oppressed) comprise an illustrative rather than a comprehensive list of the recipients of the good news of the outbreak of the Kingdom.[102] The Lukan form of the beatitudes (6:20–22) are once again helpful for illuminating this matter. The Kingdom belongs to the poor, and blessings and the reversal of fortunes are pronounced upon the outcasts of society: the poor, the hungry, those who mourn, and those who are excluded, reviled and hated.

It is worthwhile to take a moment to consider the implications of proclaiming good news to the poor within the local-official institution that is the public synagogue. The political chord that is struck by this is unmistakable once the institutional context of the venue is understood. The significance of the religiopolitical institutional setting of Jesus's proclamation of good news to the poor within a public synagogue has not been properly appreciated in scholarship, and is missing even from works specifically focused on political exegesis.[103] As discussed above, the proclamation of good news to the poor in the synagogue at Nazareth is related to the macarism of Luke 6:20. The coming of the Kingdom is good news for those on the bottom of the social order, precisely because it envisions a reordering of that order in terms of power and economics. If Luke 4:19 (discussed below) can be taken as an indication, the Kingdom proclamation was bound up with the Jubilee year, which entailed the remission of debt, the redistribution of property, and the freeing of slaves.[104] Yet, as indicated by data elsewhere in the Jesus tradition, there was more to the social reordering that would come about with God's reign. The social order would not just be equalized, it would be reversed, such that the first will be last and the last will be first.[105]

Jesus's mission involves the proclamation of "release to the cap-

---

Ekkehard W. Stegemann and Wolfgang Stegemann, *The Jesus Movement: A Social History of Its First Century* (Minneapolis: Fortress Press, 1999), 70–72, 92–93.

101. Green, *Luke*, 211; Stein, *Luke*, 156.

102. Carroll, *Luke*, 112. See also Schröter, *Jesus of Nazareth*, 116.

103. E.g., John Howard Yoder, *The Politics of Jesus: Vicit Agnus Noster*, 2nd ed. (Grand Rapids: Eerdmans, 1994), 28–32, 60–71; Storkey, *Jesus and Politics*, 163.

104. For political interpretation of the Jubilee year in Jesus's teaching, see Yoder, *Jesus and Politics*, 60–71.

105. Matt 19:30, 20:16; Mark 10:31; Luke 13:30.

tives." What this might have meant in reference to the historical Jesus is difficult to determine with confidence. Various suggestions have been made: Jesus could have been referring to the release of imprisoned debtors,[106] release from demonic bondage,[107] salvific release,[108] or the metaphorical release of the forgiveness of sins.[109] In my view, these are all closely related concepts, and the "release" that Jesus envisioned could well have encompassed all of them. That debt prisoners would be literally released is supported by the proclamation of good news to the impoverished in the same verse, as well as the debt forgiveness that is brought about by the declaration of the Jubilee year in v. 19. The reign of God no doubt involves a radical revision of the social order. We need not, however, limit the sense of release to the literal, economic sense alone. In Jesus's worldview, debt is not the only force that held the people of the Land captive. Demonic forces also bound the people, and elsewhere, we see Jesus releasing a woman "bound" by Satan on the Sabbath in a synagogue setting (Luke 13:10–17). Moreover, in the Hebrew Bible and the Septuagint, "captives" (cf. LXX αἰχμάλωτος) frequently refers to the exiles under the Babylonian and Assyrian empires.[110] The Hebrew Bible conceives of exile as the result of covenantal sin.[111] It thus is quite likely that v. 18 may also envision a release from the captivity of sin.[112]

The outbreak of the Kingdom of God that Jesus proclaims as an agent of God brings about release, not only from present socio-economic and political realities, but also from the spiritual forces of sin and demonic bondage. When dealing with the thought and writings of the world of early Judaism, we must remember not to draw hard lines of separation between the economic, sociopolitical realm and the religious or spiritual realm.[113] The two were inextricably connected, as is illustrated by the example of the concept of exile in the Hebrew Bible: the covenantal sins of the nation are directly connected to the political situation of exile and destruction.[114]

---

106. Fitzmyer, *Luke*, 1:532; Malina and Rohrbaugh, *Social Science Commentary on the Synoptic Gospels*, 243.

107. Green, *Luke*, 212.

108. Beasley-Murray, *Jesus and the Kingdom of God*, 86.

109. Stein, *Luke*, 156.

110. E.g., Tobit 2:2, 7:3; Amos 6:7, 7:11, 17; Nah 3:10; Isa 5:13 52:2, 61:1. Cf. Bock, *Luke*, 409.

111. In relation to its significance for Luke, see Bock, *Luke*, 1:409. The Hebrew Bible evidence he cites comes from Deut 28–32; Ps 79:11, 126:1; Isa 42:7. See also Lam 1, 5, esp. v. 7.

112. Cf. the freeing of prisoners in the Messianic age of salvation envisioned in 4Q521 2 II, 8.

113. Cf. the sociopolitical analyses of exorcism accounts in Amanda Witmer, *Jesus, the Galilean Exorcist: His Exorcisms in Social and Political Context* (LNTS 459; London and New York: T&T Clark, 2012).

114. This is very nicely illustrated by, for example, Lam 1, in which sin is connected to exile directly in vv. 10 and 14.

The "recovery of sight to the blind"[115] most naturally refers to Jesus's healing ministry.[116] Its inclusion alongside the proclamations of release and "good news" for the poor leads to the inference that Jesus understood it to be as much a part of his mission and as much an element of the outbreak of the Kingdom as the other proclamations of Luke 4:18–19. Were this not the case, it could have been omitted, as was done with the mention of the binding of the brokenhearted in Isaiah 61:1.

The recovery of sight to the blind is intrinsically tied to the Kingdom of God insofar as it is about restoration. It is a symbol of realized eschatology, signifying the restoration of the nation.[117] The announcement of the recovery of sight could also have a further symbolic meaning, insofar as it metaphorically represents perception and the transition out of darkness and into light.[118] Furthermore, as will be explored further below in chapter 7, Jesus's healing miracles were not only symbolic, but were also instantiations of the presence of the outbreaking Kingdom of God. They were, in themselves, part of the eschatological blessings of God's restorative reign.

The reply to John's question in Luke 7:22 and Matthew 11:5 reveals that Jesus's healing ministry and his proclamation of good news to the poor were remembered as being intrinsic to his mission and identity. These acts herald the dawn of the eschatological age.[119] This double-tradition saying, along with the similar elements of restoration of sight to the blind and good news proclaimed to the poor in Luke 4:18, is paralleled in 4Q521, a text describing what the Lord will do at the time of judgement.[120] 4Q521 provides us with good comparative data from the thought world of early Judaism, indicating that the sorts of healing actions, and proclamations of release to prisoners and good news to the poor in Isaiah 61:1–2 were understood to have special significance.

---

115. The issue of the problem of the differences between the MT and LXX has already been discussed in this chapter. See above for the argument that Jesus could have understood the act of "opening wide" in the MT to pertain to his healing ministry.

116. Cf. Green, *Luke*, 211; Tannehill, *Luke*, 92; Stein, *Luke*, 156;

117. Cf. Meyer, *Aims of Jesus*, 157. See also Green, *Luke*, 211.

118. Cf. Tannehill, *Luke*, 92.

119. On the eschatological function of Jesus's reading of Isaiah, see Emerson B. Powery, *Jesus Reads Scripture: The Function of Jesus' Use of Scripture in the Synoptic Gospels* (Brill Interpretation Series 63; Leiden and Boston: Brill, 2003), 206. See also Rainer Albertz, "Die 'Atrittspredigt' Jesu im Lukasevangelium auf ihrem alttestamentlichen Hintergrund," *ZNW* 74 (1983): 182–206; Michael Wolter, "Reich Gottes bei Lukas," *NTS* 41 (1995): 541–63, esp. 555. On the relationship between eschatology and Jesus's healing ministry, see Rudolf Bultmann, *Jesus Christ and Mythology* (New York: Scribner, 1958), 12; Meyer, *Aims of Jesus*, 157.

120. 4Q521 2, II. On this, see Craig A. Evans, *Jesus and His Contemporaries: Comparative Studies* (Arbeiten zur Geschichte des antiken Judentums und des Urchristentums 25; Leiden and New York: Brill, 1995), 128–29.

They were elements of the eschatological age, when the God of Israel would judge the earth and make it right again. Jesus's single-sentence interpretation of his reading from Isaiah in Luke 4:22, brief though it is, is particularly meaningful in light of this. The notion that Isaiah 61:1-2 (and 58:6) has been fulfilled *today* meant that the eschatological age, the dawn of the reign of God, was already present and coming to be.

The insertion of "to let the oppressed go free" from Isaiah 58:6 is intriguing, not only because of the fact that is an interpolation from another section of Isaiah, but also because it is identical in essence to "release for the captives."[121] Why go to the trouble of skipping around in the public reading[122] to repeat a point? The answer is probably to be found in the hermeneutical method of *gĕzērâ šāwâ* that Jesus employs here.[123] His reading of Isaiah 61:1-2 is mutually illuminated by his reference to Isaiah 58:6. Isaiah 58 presents an image of the restoration of Jerusalem. Verses 6-7 outlines acts of social justice as the "true fast" that God desires. These deeds of compassion and righteousness include loosening the bonds of injustice, setting the oppressed free (cf. Luke 4:18), feeding the hungry, bringing the homeless poor into one's home, clothing the naked, and not hiding from one's kin. This is followed by vv. 8-9a, which describe the effects of obedience to the demands of the righteous and compassionate actions of the "true fast":

> Then your light shall break forth like the dawn,
> and your healing shall spring up quickly;
> your vindicator shall go before you,
> the glory of the Lord shall be your rear guard.
> Then you shall call, and the Lord will answer;
> you shall cry for help, and he will say, Here I am.

This imagery, of light breaking out of the darkness of night, of healing, of vindication, and of a God who answers cries for help, is the imagery of restoration. The thrust of the passage is, as Brevard Childs has put it, that "it lies at the heart of God's rule to demand mercy and justice for all."[124] This brings to mind the fact that Jesus's proclamation of the Kingdom of God requires a response of repentance. It requires active participation and adherence, not merely passive acceptance.[125] Isaiah

---

21. Cf. Stein's remark about it standing in "synonymous parallelism" with the preceding statements, in Stein, *Luke*, 156.
22. Cf. *m. Meg.* 4:4 and *t. Meg.* 3:19. See the discussion above.
23. Cf. Bock, *Luke*, 1:405; Sanders, "Isaiah in Luke," 21–25; Notley, "Hermeneutical Method," 53. See the discussion above.
24. Childs, *Isaiah*, 478.

58:9b–12 repeats the essence of vv. 6–9a, driving the point home further. The righteous acts of compassion described in vv. 9b–10 result in a description of the literal restoration of Jerusalem:

> Your ancient ruins shall be rebuilt;
> you shall raise up the foundations of many generations;
> you shall be called the repairer of the breach,
> the restorer of streets to live in.

Only once we recognize the intentionality of Jesus's insertion of the line from Isaiah 58 into his reading of Isaiah 61:1–2 and the hermeneutical method that he is employing by doing so is it possible to explain and understand it. By inserting a line from Isaiah 58:6 into his reading, he was pointing toward the promise of restoration and renewal that come as a result of the acts of justice, compassion, and mercy found in Isaiah 58:6–12. It is not difficult to make the connection from this to Jesus's reading of Isaiah 61:1–2, and thus, to his own mission. He heralds the advent of extraordinary deeds of righteousness and compassion (good news to the poor, release to the captives, recovery of sight to the blind, and release for the oppressed), and points to the promise of restoration in Isaiah 58:6–12 that is supposed to come about along with Israel's turn toward obedience to God's desire for justice and mercy. Thus, the insertion of Isaiah 58:6 into Jesus's reading illuminates it by calling to mind the effect of the actions proclaimed in Isaiah 61:1–2.

Jesus's reading culminates in the proclamation of "the year of the Lord's favour" in Luke 4:19. This is commonly identified with the Jubilee year (Lev 25:8–55).[126] The Jubilee year was a year of debt forgiveness and the release of slaves, a year in which "you shall proclaim liberty throughout the land to all its inhabitants" (Lev 25:10). This concept is developed in both Isaiah 58 and 61, which understand the impending redemption from exile, captivity, and oppression "in the eschatological language of jubilary release."[127] This is not to say that the socio-economic dimension of the Jubilee was not also being drawn upon and proclaimed by Jesus. After all, debt forgiveness (Deut 15:1)

---

125. Cf. Lohfink, *Jesus of Nazareth*, 31.
126. E.g., André Trocmé, *Jesus and the Nonviolent Revolution* (Scottdale: Herald, 1973[1961]), passim; Yoder, *The Politics of Jesus*, 30–31; Beasley-Murray, *Jesus and the Kingdom of God*, 86; Sanders, "Isaiah in Luke," 151–52; Bovon, *Luke*, 1:153; Carroll, *Luke*, 12; Robert B. Sloan, *The Favorable Year of the Lord: A Study of Jubilary Theology in the Gospel of Luke* (Austin: Scholar, 1977), passim; Green, *Luke*, 212; Bock, *Luke*, 1:410; Tanehill, *Luke*, 92–93; Charles Perrot, "Luke 4,16–30 et la Lecture Biblique de l'Ancienne Synagogue," *Revue des Sciences Religieuses* 47 (1973): 324–40 (332–33).
127. Green, *Luke*, 212.

and the return of land to its original owner (Lev 25:13) constitute good news for the poor. The equalizing factor of the Jubilee is undoubtedly closely related to the reversal envisioned by Jesus's insistence that the first shall be last and the last shall be first.[128] Nevertheless, it is the specifically eschatological valence of the Jubilee and the liberty it brings that Jesus highlights by reading from these Isaian texts.

The eschatological conception of the Jubilee year of Isaiah 61:1–2 is also present in 11QMelchizedek.[129] This fragmentary text helps to give us an idea of how Isaiah 61:1–2 was read by some other Jews at the time of Jesus and how they conceived of the Jubilee year. 11QMelch explicitly connects the release of prisoners in Isaiah 61:1 to the Jubilee year (II, 1–4). Most importantly, this event is understood eschatologically, "for the last days" (II, 4), and in relation to the time of judgment (II, 9–13). The semi-divine figure of Melchizedek acts in this text as a liberator and judge,[130] freeing those captive under Belial (the typical chief demonic figure in the Qumran sectarian texts) and executing God's vengeance. Notably, the release proclaimed (cf. Isa 61:1) in this text is understood as a freedom from iniquity which will take place at the time of the eschatological Jubilee (11QMelch II, 6–7).

The primary significance of this text for understanding Jesus's reading from Isaiah is that it understands the jubilary release in terms of freedom from sin, and moreover, it sets the release promised by the Jubilee within an eschatological context.[131] Jesus's understanding of Isaiah 61:1–2 differs significantly from 11QMelch insofar as Jesus omits the reference to God's vengeance by ending his reading right before it appears in Isaiah 61:2. Nevertheless, the parallels in 11QMelch demonstrate that an eschatological reading of Isaiah 61:1–2 is undoubtedly plausible within Jesus's early Jewish context. Moreover, the fact that 11QMelch interprets the release of prisoners in terms of the forgiveness of sins is intriguing. Forgiveness of sin, when understood corporately,[132] has covenantal valences, and implies the renewal of God's promises to Israel and the restoration of the nation. If the author of 11QMelch could understand the release of captives in this way, it is certainly plausible to think that Jesus could have as well.

---

28. Matt 19:30, 20:16; Mark 10:31; Luke 13:30.

29. Cf. the observations of Beasley-Murray, *Jesus and the Kingdom of God*, 87; Green, *Luke*, 213.

30. Cf. Peter Flint, *The Dead Sea Scrolls* (Nashville: Abingdon, 2013), 114.

31. Similarly, see Green, *Luke*, 213.

32. It is worth mentioning here that Matthew remembers Jesus as having saved "his people from their sins" (Matt 1:21). This is clearly a corporate, national understanding of sin. The very fact that Matthew remembered Jesus in this way is significant data for the matter at hand.

More intriguing again is the fact that Belial is the one holding the people captive in 11QMelch (II, 13, 25). The divine agent Melchizedek is thus charged with liberating them from demonic bondage. This parallels another incident taking place in a synagogue (discussed below), in which Jesus declares that it is fitting for a woman bound by Satan to be set free on the Sabbath day.[133] It is striking that release from sin and release from diabolic captivity are intertwined in 11QMelch. Given: a) that Jesus sought to bring about restoration, and b) that his work included exorcism and liberation from demonic bondage, it is plausible that Jesus understood jubilary release in a similar way.

Applying the Institution-Critical Lens

It is now time to turn the institution-critical lens onto the passage. How can the institutional context of the public synagogue illuminate our historical interpretation of Jesus's reading at Nazareth?

By reading from the scroll of Isaiah in the synagogue at Nazareth, Jesus intended to announce to the assembly of his hometown that God's reign was breaking out. The time is nigh, the eschatological year of Jubilee is at hand, and restoration is coming. His goal in so doing was not, like Jonah, to simply make the announcement and be done with it without hoping for a response. The inserted reference to Isaiah 58:6 points toward this, indicating that acts of obedience in the form of justice and mercy were requisite for participation in the restored Israel.[134] This is highly reminiscent of the summary of Jesus's Galilean proclamation in Mark 1:15: "the time is fulfilled, and the Kingdom of God is at hand; repent,[135] and believe in the good news." The proclamation of the reign of God needed to be *accepted*.[136] It had to be believed and responded to with repentance. This requirement is what lies at the Collingwoodian "inside of the event."

It is significant that this takes place within a public synagogue setting. As discussed in chapters 2 and 3, the public synagogue was the place where decisions were made for the town as a whole. Further-

---

133. Luke 13:16. The connection between "Sabbath" and "Jubilee" as the Sabbath of Sabbaths is significant here.

134. Cf. the elements of this in Jesus's teaching. E.g., Matt 5:43–45, 9:13, 19:16–21, 25:31–46; Mark 10:17–21; Luke 10:25–37, 14:12–14, 18:18–22.

135. I understand "repentance" in Mark 1:15 much in the same way that Eugene Boring describes it: "in this context, repentance means a reorientation of one's whole life, a turn to the new reality that is dawning, not a return to the past" (Boring, *Mark*, 51).

136. On this, Meyer writes, "the reign of God was a gift; the core of repentance was acceptance of it *as a gift*," and moreover, "there could be no giving without the positive act of receiving" (Meyer, *Aims of Jesus*, 132). See also Boring, *Mark*, 51; Collins, *Mark*, 155.

more, the evidence indicates that the assembled public played a major role in the decision-making process.[137] Persuasion of the public, the conferral of honor, and the recognition of wisdom were required for a proposition to go forward and for a particular interpretation of scripture to be accepted and put into practice. Those with more recognized honor would have been more likely to be successful in convincing the assembly to accept a given interpretation or decision. In the case of Luke 4:16–21, it is not Jesus's act of reading that is on trial. Rather, it is his interpretation of it offered in v. 21, the notion that this scripture has been fulfilled in Jesus's own actions.

The public synagogue assembly represented the town as a whole.[138] As Runesson has observed, one of the primary ideological points of Luke 4:16–30 depends on this, insofar as Jesus's rejection by the synagogue assembly is taken as rejection by his hometown.[139] Similarly, Jesus elsewhere pronounces woes upon other Galilean villages resulting from their failure to repent (Luke 10:13–16; Matt 11:20–24). The idea expressed here is that these locales have failed corporately rather than individually. This likely indicates that Jesus's message was similarly rejected in the public synagogue assemblies of these other villages. As argued in chapter 5, acceptance by the public synagogue assembly of Jesus's proclamation would amount to the village's acceptance of that proclamation. However, Jesus was rejected by the Nazareth synagogue assembly, and thus, by the village as a whole.

The public synagogue was the institutional vehicle through which Jesus would be able to accomplish the fulfilment of what he had read in the synagogue at Nazareth. The proclamation of the coming of the Kingdom and the acceptance of that proclamation were to be accomplished primarily in the synagogue assemblies, as demonstrated in chapter 5. What we see in Luke 4:16–30 is a specific instance of what is described generally in the synagogue summary statements.[140]

Understanding the synagogue setting of this episode highlights its political facets. Although others have commented on the general political nature of the socio-economic elements of Jesus's reading from Isaiah in Luke 4:18–19,[141] the grassroots, municipal, local-level politics of

137. I have argued this at length elsewhere, in Ryan, "Jesus and Synagogue Disputes," passim.
138. See chapter 3 above, esp. the discussions of Josephus, *Vita*, 277–82; Judith 6:16; and *m. Ned.* 5:5. Cf. Ryan, "Tiberias," n.p.; Runesson, *Origins*, 216, 221–22.
139. Runesson, *Origins*, 216.
140. Mark 1:38–39; Matt 4:23, 9:35; Luke 4:15–16, 43–44; John 18:20.
141. E.g., Yoder, *Politics of Jesus*, 28–33; Karl Allen Kuhn, *The Kingdom According to Luke and Acts: A Social, Literary, and Theological Introduction* (Grand Rapids: Baker, 2015), 263; Amanda C. Miller, *Rumors of*

the passage have been missed. In other words, Jesus's reading was not only political in the general sense that anything dealing with poverty, liberation, and oppression is political, or in the way that anything having to do with the Kingdom of God is intrinsically political. It is political in the sense that through this reading Jesus was proclaiming the message of the Kingdom of God, the restoration it would bring, and its socio-economic effects in the local-official assembly. If the assembly had chosen to accept the proclamation, Jesus envisioned it impacting the course of life of the residents of the village. It is important to remember that the setting of the episode depicted in Luke 4:16–30 is rather more like a town hall than a modern place of worship in the West.

It is also worth observing that the synagogue setting afforded Jesus access to the physical text of Isaiah. The rhetorical impact of reading directly from Israel's sacred prophetic scripture and announcing its immediate fulfilment in one's own actions is enormous. The persuasive strength of this action is evident in the assembly's initial reaction in Luke 4:22 (cf. Mark 6:2; Matt 13:54).

The interpreter himself stands trial alongside his interpretation. The importance of personal honor and status in the political arena that was the public synagogue should not be underestimated. Ben Sira's frequent mention of the conferral and recognition of honor or shame in public synagogue settings is illustrative of this.[142] The evergetistic inscriptions found in late antique public synagogues in the Land similarly evidence the important role that honor continued to play in the synagogue in later periods.[143]

Although the assembly recognizes the wisdom of Jesus's words (Mark 6:2; cf. Matt 13:34; Luke 4:22), they nevertheless reject them because they reject *him*, on account of knowing him too well.[144] They know the ordinariness of his family and are familiar with his siblings and parents. They know his "honor status."[145] Jesus is making a claim that goes well beyond the ordinary when he claims to have fulfilled

---

Resistance: Status Reversal and Hidden Transcripts in the Gospel of Luke (Minneapolis: Fortress Press, 2014), 162–65.

142. Sir 1:30, 4:7, 15:5, 21:17, 23:24, 31:11, 38:33, 39:10, 44:15, 41:18.

143. Evergetistic dedicatory inscriptions are ubiquitous in late-antique synagogues. Some well-known examples include those at Beth Alpha, En-Gedi, Capernaum, and Sepphoris. An early precursor can be found in the Theodotus inscription, which comes from an association synagogue. On dedicatory inscriptions in late-antique synagogues, see Hachlili, *Ancient Synagogues*, 517–20, as well as Joseph Naveh, *On Stone and Mosaic: The Aramaic and Hebrew Inscriptions From Ancient Synagogues* (Jerusalem: Israel Exploration Society, 1978), passim.

144. As argued above.

145. Malina and Rohrbaugh, *Social-Science Commentary on the Synoptic Gospels*, 165.

the scripture passages that he has read, and to be anointed by God for the tasks that he describes in vv. 18–19. In modern terms, this would be something like hearing an eloquent high school classmate claim to have fulfilled biblical prophecy and to be on a divinely-appointed mission. Jesus's response that "prophets are not without honor, except in their hometown" (Mark 6:4) is instructive.[146] It underscores the fact that Jesus has not been accorded the honor that his prophetic words deserve, and has been rejected on account of familiarity. The point is that Jesus's proclamation has been rejected because Jesus has been rejected.

The examples from the Elijah and Elisha cycles in Luke 4:25–27 illustrate the point about rejection that Jesus makes in v. 24.[147] Some interpreters take this to refer to Israel's rejection of Jesus and the beginning of the Gentile mission.[148] Such an interpretation may work on the level of the broader narrative of Luke-Acts, but it is hard to square on the historical level with Jesus's statements about being sent to Israel (Matt 10:6, 15:24) and the data locating his mission primarily in synagogues. Moreover, the context of the teaching about Elijah and Elisha, coming right after the saying about a prophet being without acceptance in their hometown in v. 24, leads to the conclusion that it is meant to illustrate the rejection that Jesus meets specifically in his hometown. At any rate, neither Elijah nor Elisha were remembered for giving up on Israel to turn toward the Gentiles.[149] Israel and the Gentiles function metaphorically here, as in a parable. It is, in other words, about being rejected by those closest to you, and not literally about Israel and the Gentiles.

From the perspective of synagogue studies, the sayings contained in Luke 4:23–27 are best understood to be part of the public discussion of the reading and its interpretation rather than as a "sermon" per se.[150]

---

146. On the historical plausibility of this form of the saying, see Collins, *Mark*, 292.

147. Whether the original form of the saying was more like the Markan version (Mark 6:4) or the Lukan version (Luke 4:24) is beyond the point and at any rate unknowable. The intended sense of rejection in one's hometown is conveyed clearly in either form.

148. Robert C. Tannehill, "The Mission of Jesus According to Like iv 16–30," in *Jesus in Nazareth*, ed. Erich Grässer, August Strobel, and Robert C. Tannehill (BZNW 40; Berlin: de Gruyter, 1972), 51–62 (60); Fitzmyer, *Luke*, 1:537; Hill, "Rejection of Jesus," 177; Bock, *Luke*, 1:418; Stein, *Luke*, 160–61. A similar interpretation is held by Bovon, *Luke*, 1:156 who sees it as pointing more toward the fellowship between Jews and Gentiles than to the mission to the Gentiles.

149. Cf. Green, *Luke*, 218; Carroll, *Luke*, 115.

150. Cf. Mosser, "Torah Instruction," 540; Nolland, *Luke*, 1:194–95. The idea that a longer sermon has been omitted from this episode, but that it is preserved in the the Beatitudes and Woes has been proposed by Asher Finkel, "Jesus' Sermon at Nazareth (Luk. 4, 16–30)," in *Abraham unser Vater; Juden und Christen im Gespräch über die Bibel*, ed. Otto Betz, Martin Hengel, and Peter Schmidt (Leiden: Brill, 1963), 106–15. This suggestion is intriguing and imaginative, but ultimately lacks

Jesus's posture indicates that the interpretation of the passage is given in v. 21.[151] What follows from v. 22 onward is debate and discussion. The evangelists all focus on Jesus's words. Thus, we are only given a summary of the crowd's response to Jesus in Luke 4:22, Mark 6:2–3, and Matthew 13:54–56, but we can imagine that there would have been some disputation back and forth between Jesus and his interlocutors.

It is striking that in Mark 6:1–6, when Jesus is not accepted by the public assembly at Nazareth, he is unable to perform deeds of power. Instead, he is only able to cure a few sick people by laying hands upon them. This is indicative of the power held by the assembly of the people in synagogue settings. Public approval carries with it authority. Notably, Jesus's ability to heal is frequently tied to *pistis*, meaning "faith" or "belief."[152] Acceptance entails belief in the proclamation of the Kingdom, and so, participation in the blessings of the restoration that it brings requires that it be accepted. Thus, Jesus is unable to perform the eschatological blessings of restoration to their fullest extent in Nazareth due to the assembly's rejection of him, and by extension, his message.

Conclusion

Luke 4:16–30 presents a historically plausible, detailed account of Jesus's activities in the synagogue at Nazareth. Its account is rooted firmly in the institutional context of the first-century public synagogues of the Land of Israel.

The evidence provided by this passage helps to flesh out the general picture of Jesus's synagogue activities and mission discussed in chapter 5 and presented in the evangelists' synagogue summary statements. By publically reading Isaiah 61:1–2 and Isaiah 58:6 and applying it to himself and his actions, Jesus was claiming to be the divinely appointed prophetic herald of the eschatological restoration envisioned in those passages. His aim was for Nazareth to accept the proclamation, to make the appropriate response of actions that went along with that acceptance, and to thus participate in the Kingdom of God, the restored

---

enough solid evidence to be convincing. As discussed in chapter 5, however, I am nevertheless sympathetic to the notion that Sermon on the Plain or Mount material could be drawn from Jesus's synagogue teaching, though matching the Sermon material to a specific episode or locale is simply not possible.

151. Nolland, *Luke*, 1:194–95; Levine, *Ancient Synagogue*, 157. Mosser, "Torah Instruction," 541 notes a similarity between Jesus's interpretation and the method of interpretation found in the Qumran *pesherim*.

152. Mark 2:5, 5:34–36, 9:23, 10:52; Matt 8:10–13, 9:2, 22, 29, 15:28, Luke 5:20, 7:9, 8:48, 17:19, 18:42.

Israel. Proclamation to the public synagogue was understood to be proclamation to the village, as salvation was conceived in corporate terms, and as the synagogue assembly represented the village as a whole. The public synagogue was thus to be the institutional vehicle by which Jesus could accomplish his mission of proclamation.

The rejection that Jesus experienced in the synagogue at Nazareth hints at a larger pattern of refusal of his proclamation in the Galilean villages. This is evidenced further by the double-tradition woes pronounced on Bethsaida, Chorazin and Capernaum (Luke 10:13; Matt 11:21), by the loss of disciples after Jesus's teaching in the synagogue at Capernaum (John 6:60–6:66), and the anticipation of rejection in the instructions given to his followers prior to sending them out (Mark 6:11; Matt 10:14–15, 16–23; Luke 9:5, 10:10–12).

7

Healings and Exorcisms in Synagogue Settings (Matthew 12:9–14; Mark 3:1–6; Luke 6:6–11 / Mark 1:21–28; Luke 4:31–37)

Introduction

Public synagogues provided the stage for some of Jesus's miracles. Three miracles are explicitly set in synagogues by the evangelists: an exorcism of a man with an unclean spirit in Capernaum,[1] the healing of a man with a withered hand,[2] and the healing of a woman with a bent back.[3] It is also worth noting that the Markan and Matthean synagogue summary statements (Mark 1:39; Matt 4:23, 9:35) closely associate Jesus's miracles (exorcism and healing) with his synagogue activities. Whether or not the healings and exorcisms mentioned in these passages typically took place in the synagogue is difficult to say without more direct evidence. What we can say with certainty is that,

---

1. Mark 1:21–28; cf. Luke 4:31–37.
2. Mark 3:1–6; Matt 12:9–14; Luke 6:6–11. This may have also taken place in Capernaum, as indicated by the *palin* in Mark 3:1.
3. Luke 13:10–17.

according to the synoptic Gospels, healing and exorcism were essential elements of Jesus's program and that some of his miracles took place in synagogues.

This data raises some questions. How did healing and exorcism relate to Jesus's mission of teaching and proclaiming the Kingdom of God in synagogues? Furthermore, what is the significance of the synagogue setting for understanding this data? In other words, what can the institutional setting of the public synagogue contribute to the interpretation of these passages on the historical level?

Before turning to these questions, a few brief words on the historical plausibility of exorcisms and healing miracles are called for, since the issue is somewhat contentious, and with good reason.[4] Modern mainstream scholarship has tended to recognize that there is a historical element to the memories of Jesus as a healer and exorcist.[5] While Christian and Jewish scholars are naturally more inclined to believe in the historical plausibility of miracles, there has also been substantial acknowledgment of the plausibility of Jesus's activities as a healer and exorcist from more skeptical quarters of the guild.[6] This is mostly due to the recognition that these sorts of miracles can be understood as anthropological or psychosomatic phenomena.[7]

We are therefore justified in concluding that the notion that Jesus performed healings and exorcisms is theoretically plausible.[8] More-

---

4. See, for example, Zeba Crook, "On the Treatment of Miracles in New Testament Scholarship," *Studies in Religion* 40, no. 4 (2011): 461–78.

5. E.g., Sanders, *Jesus and Judaism*, 11; E. P. Sanders, *The Historical Figure of Jesus* (London: Penguin, 1995), 132–68; Meier, *A Marginal Jew*, 2:617–31; Eric Eve, *The Healer From Nazareth: Jesus' Miracles in Historical Context* (London: SPCK, 2009), passim; Jan Roskovic, "Jesus as Miracle Worker: Historiography and Credibility," in *Jesus Research: New Methodologies and Perceptions*, vol. 2, ed. James H. Charlesworth with Brian Rhea and Petr Pokorný (Grand Rapids: Eerdmans, 2014), 874–96; Craig S. Keener, *Miracles: The Credibility of the New Testament Accounts*, 2 vols. (Grand Rapids: Baker, 2011), passim; Graham H. Twelftree, *Jesus the Miracle Worker: A Historical and Theological Study* (Downers Grove: IVP Academic, 1999), passim; Evans, *Jesus and His Contemporaries*, 213–27; Becker, *Jesus of Nazareth*, 173; Meyer, *Aims of Jesus*, 99–102; Crossan, *Historical Jesus*, 320–26; Fredriksen, *Jesus of Nazareth*, 114–15; Bond, *Historical Jesus*, 102–8.

6. E.g., Crossan, *Historical Jesus*, 320–26; Funk and the Jesus Seminar, *Acts of Jesus*, 530–32, 566.

7. See, for example, Funk and the Jesus Seminar, *Acts of Jesus*, 531; Bond, *Historical Jesus*, 106–8; Eric Eve, *The Jewish Context of Jesus' Miracles* (JSNTSup 231; Sheffield: Sheffield Academic, 2002), 350–60. On the social-scientific study of exorcism, see M. Ioan Lewis, *Ecstatic Religion: An Anthropological Study of Shamanism and Spirit Possession* (Harmondsworth: Penguin, 1971); Witmer, *Galilean Exorcist*, 22–60; Santiago Guijarro, "The Politics of Exorcism: Jesus' Reaction to Negative Labels in the Beelzebul Controversy," *Biblical Theology Bulletin* 29, no. 3 (1999): 118–29; Esther Miquel, "How to Discredit an Inconvenient Exorcist: Origin and Configuration of the Synoptic Controversies on Jesus' Power as an Exorcist," *Biblical Theology Bulletin* 40, no. 4 (2010): 187–206.

8. It is also worthwhile to recognize that, even if the issue is approached from a theistic perspective, miracles need not be viewed as violations of the created order. As Aquinas writes, "whatever is done by God in created things is not contrary to nature, even though it may seem to be opposed to the proper order of a particular nature" (*Summa Contra Gentiles*, 3.100.2). For the rationale behind

over, belief in the miraculous was common in the ancient Mediterranean world, and Jesus was not the only person in that society who was reputed to have performed healings or exorcisms.[9] It is undeniable that the tradition strongly remembers Jesus as a healer and exorcist. The confluence of this data leads me to infer that it is reasonable to think that Jesus performed acts that were understood by himself and by his contemporaries as healing miracles or exorcisms.

Miracles and Mission

What is the relationship between Jesus's healing miracles and exorcisms and his typical synagogue activities of teaching and proclamation? It is certain that there is one. We have already seen above how Jesus's reading in the synagogue at Nazareth envisioned the incorporation of his healing ministry into the outbreak of the Kingdom of God. Not only are miracles mentioned in the summaries of Jesus's Galilean program in Mark 1:39 and Matthew 9:23-24 (cf. 9:35), but two different episodes (Mark 2:1-12/Matt 9:1-8/Luke 5:17-26; and Mark 3:1-6/Matt 12:9-14/Luke 6:6-11) interweave elements of Jesus's teaching with miracles.[10] Notably, one of these two incidents is set in a synagogue (Mark 3:1-6 and parallels). Furthermore, a direct connection is made between Jesus's exorcisms and the outbreak of the Kingdom of God in Matthew 12:28/Luke 11:20.

Jesus's healings and exorcisms are part and parcel of the realization of the eschatological reign of God.[11] They are signs insofar as they signify the dawn of the Kingdom,[12] but they are also more than signs. They are, in themselves, the outpouring of the renewal and blessings that come with God's reign. The people themselves are physically restored and liberated from demonic domination by the miracles worked at

this, see Aquinas, *Summa Contra Gentiles* 3.100-101; Brian Davies, *The Thought of Thomas Aquinas* (Oxford: Clarendon, 1992), 173-74.

9. Examples from early Jewish tradition besides Jesus include Tob 8:1-3; 4Q560; 11Q5 27.2-4; 11Q11 1,4, 6, 4.4; *Jubilees* 10:1-14; Josephus, *Ant.* 8.45-48; *m. Ber.* 5:5; *b. Ber.* 34b; *m. Sanh.* 10:1. On physicians in the Second Temple period, see Sir 38:1-8. In the Hebrew Bible, Elisha performs healing miracles, in 2 Kings 4:17-37 (perhaps better described as a resuscitation?) and 5:1-14. There are also parallels in the Greco-Roman literature. The most relevant example is that of Apollonius of Tyana. See Philostratus, *Vit. Ap.* 3.39, 4.20.

10. Cf. Twelftree, *Jesus the Exorcist*, 168-69.

11. Variations on this perspective are dominant in mainstream scholarship. E.g., Graham H. Twelftree, "The Miracles of Jesus: Marginal or Mainstream," *JSHJ* 1, no. 1 (2003): 104-24 (121-22); Twelftree, *Jesus the Exorcist*, 170-71; Bond, *Historical Jesus*, 108-9; Allison, *Apocalyptic Prophet*, 197-200; Wright, *Jesus and the Victory of God*, 191-96; Horsley, *Renewal of Israel*, 117-20; Fredriksen, *Jesus of Nazareth*, 110-17; Schröter, *Jesus of Nazareth*, 93-100; Becker, *Jesus of Nazareth*, 170-86.

12. As held by, e.g., Meyer, *Aims of Jesus*, 155-56; Bultmann, *Jesus Christ*, 12-13.

the hands of Jesus and his followers. Hence, the recovery of sight to the blind is proclaimed alongside the promises of liberation and "good news" in Luke 4:18–19, and in the double-tradition version of the Beelzebub controversy (Matt 12:28/Luke 11:20), the Kingdom of God is brought about by the casting out of demons. Thus, the acts of healing and exorcism demonstrate and also realize, at least in part, what Jesus proclaims and teaches.

What is the significance of the public synagogue setting for interpreting the miracles that take place within them? This issue has been underexplored in historical Jesus scholarship. Levine observes that the healings that take place in the Gospels are unique, as miracles in synagogues are not reported in other sources from the Second–Temple period.[13] Rather than taking Jesus's healing activities in synagogues as an anomaly, he instead considers it to be a "facet of synagogue life virtually unknown elsewhere," suggesting that other contemporary sources would have considered it too common to require comment, too embarrassing, or that it was simply ignored.[14]

While it is true that Jesus was by no means the only healer in the late Second Temple period, I disagree with Levine's suggestion. There is not enough corroborative or comparative evidence to interpret the synagogue miracles in the Gospels as witnessing a common synagogue function rather than as something that was particular to and memorable about Jesus's actions within synagogues. An inference to that effect, while hypothetically possible, is not justifiable on the basis of the extant evidence. Moreover, there are indications in the Gospels that healing miracles were rare (though not unique) in Galilean society. This is strongly hinted at by the response to Jesus's healing of the paralytic in Mark 2:12 ("we have never seen anything like this!") and by the amazement with which Jesus's exorcism in the synagogue at Capernaum is met in Mark 1:27. Since Jesus performs many other healing miracles and exorcisms outside of synagogues,[15] it is better to conclude that they are particular to Jesus and his mission rather than to the synagogue setting.

The rhetorical effect of a healing miracle performed within the pub-

---

13. Levine, *Ancient Synagogue*, 47. He does, however, rightly note the healing activity in late antique synagogues reported by John Chrysostom, *Adv. Iud.* 1, 6 in Levine, "Synagogues of Galilee," 141, no. 28. This is fourth-century source is, however, much too late for our purposes, and at any rate speaks to a diaspora context in Antioch.
14. Levine, "Synagogues of Galilee," 140–41.
15. Mark 1:29–34/Matt 8:14–15/Luke 4:38–39; Mark 1:40–45/Matt 8:1–4/Luke 5:12–16; Mark 2:1–12/ Matt 9:1–8/Luke 5:17–26; Mark 5:21–43/Matt 9:18–26/Luke 8:40–56; Mark 7:31–37; Mark 8:22–26; Mark 10:46–52/Matt 20:29–34/Luke 18:35–43; Luke 14:1–6; Luke 17:11–19; John 5:1–18, 9:1–12.

lic synagogue assembly would have been significant. As I have indicated above, I agree with the opinion that miracles were not only signs, nor meant primarily as "proof" or authentication of Jesus's message.[16] However, it is important to recognize the persuasive power that miracles would have had, especially in public settings like a synagogue. This effect is directly witnessed in the acknowledgement of the authority of Jesus's teaching in the synagogue at Capernaum in relation to his ability to command unclean spirits in Mark 1:27. Not only does Jesus proclaim the Kingdom and teach about it, but he visibly brings it into being through performing miracles. The rhetorical impact of such a combination should not be underestimated. Similarly, John 2:23 reports that "many believed in his name because they saw the signs that he was doing." Moreover, Jesus expresses frustration at the lack of repentance of Chorazin, Bethsaida, and Capernaum, despite having seen "deeds of power," which, had they been done in Tyre and Sidon, the inhabitants of those cities "would have repented long ago, sitting in sackcloth and ashes."[17] An indirect witness to the persuasive power of miracles can be found in the various requests that Jesus received for "signs."[18] Thus, the miracles had a sociopolitical function within the discourse of the local-official setting of the public synagogue.

The relationship between "faith" (Gk. *pistis*) and healing in the Jesus tradition is significant in light of the rhetorical effect of the miraculous in public settings.[19] Those who believe are granted the blessings of restoration that come with participation in the outbreaking reign of God.[20] This idea will be explored further below. Performing such acts in synagogues would serve to convince the assembly of the accuracy of Jesus's proclamation and the truth of his divine agency. In the political arena of the synagogue, this would be a powerful method that could be used to win the public over and to convince the assembly to accept his proclamation and teaching. Although only three incidents involving a miracle in a synagogue context are recorded in the Gospels, it is justifiable to imagine that healings often played a role in Jesus's synagogue activities, and that many of these incidents simply were not

---

16. Cf. the discussion of this idea in Twelftree, *Jesus the Exorcist*, 169–70.

17. Luke 10:13–15/Matt 11:20–23.

18. Mark 8:11–12/Matt 12:38–39; Matt 16:1; Luke 11:16, 23:8; John 2:18.

19. Evidence of the connection between faith and healing miracles is found in Mark 2:5, 5:34–36, 9:23, 10:52; Matt 8:10–13, 9:2, 22, 29, 15:28; Luke 5:20, 7:9, 8:48, 17:19, 18:42.

20. Cf. Luke 4:18–19, 7:18–23, 11:20; Matt 11:2–6, 12:28. Note also the connection between the act of salvation (Gk. σῴζω) and healing in Mark 5:34, 6:56, 10:52; Matt 9:22; Luke 6:9, 7:50, 8:36, 48, 50, 17:19, 18:42. On "salvation" as participation in the Kingdom of God, see Mark 10:24–27 (cf. Matt 19:23–26; Luke 18:24–27).

preserved. This inference can reasonably be made by connecting the evidence indicating that the synagogue was Jesus's typical venue (discussed in chapter 5) to the evidence indicating the regularity and frequency of his healing and exorcistic activity with a robust thread of historical imagination.

Exorcism and Synagogues

Exorcism is a very particular sort of miracle, and requires some further discussion. Unlike other healing miracles, it involves not only the healer and the person healed, but also the demon. In exorcisms, making someone well was understood to involve the defeat of an evil or unclean spirit that had power over the individual requiring the exorcism.[21] Within the Jesus tradition, exorcism needs to be understood in light of Jesus's overarching aims and his proclamation of the Kingdom of God.[22] Moreover, it needs to be understood within the wider context of early Jewish demonology and eschatological expectations.

The Gospels present the devil as a chief adversary, and ruler of a kingdom that is in conflict with the Kingdom of God.[23] This is made especially clear in the Beelzebul controversy pericope (Mark 3:22–27; Matt 12:22–30; Luke 11:14–23). The double tradition version of this episode is particularly instructive. Satan is described as the ruler of a kingdom (Gk. *basileia*) (Matt 12:26/Luke 11:18) in opposition to the Kingdom of God, which is brought about by Jesus's exorcistic activity (Matt 12:28/Luke 11:20).[24] Further evidence is found in the double-tradition temptation narrative, wherein the devil tempts Jesus with the kingdoms of the world in return for worship.[25] This indicates that, within the narrative worlds of Luke and Matthew, the kingdoms of the world are the devil's to give.[26] The "historicity" of this narrative aside,

---

21. See Witmer, *Galilean Exorcist*, 22–60.

22. Cf. Twelftree, *Jesus the Exorcist*, 170–71, 217–24; Witmer, *Galilean Exorcist*, 125–29; Craig A. Evans, "Defeating Satan and Liberating Israel: Jesus and Daniel's Visions," *JSHJ* 1, no. 2 (2003): 161–70.

23. The idea of a diabolic 'evil empire' in early Judaism is explored by Elaine Pagels, "The Social History of Satan, the 'Intimate Enemy': a Preliminary Sketch," *Harvard Theological Review* 84:2 (1991) 105–28 (see especially p. 116). See also her further analysis of this idea in the gospels in "The Social History of Satan, Part II: Satan in the New Testament Gospels," *Journal of the American Academy of Religion* 62:1 (1994) 17–58. Some key early Jewish texts involving diabolic rule include 1QS I, 18, 1QM (particularly I, 1; XIII, 11; XIV, 9 XVIII, 1); 4Q390 2, IV; *Jubilees* 1:20, 10:11; *Martyrdom of Isaiah* 2:4.

24. Notably, this episode is fairly widely accepted as "authentic" across a considerable spectrum of perspectives. See, e.g., Twelftree, *Jesus the Exorcist*, 98–113; Funk and the Jesus Seminar, *Five Gospels*, 329–28; Funk and the Jesus Seminar, *Acts of Jesus*, 311–12; Witmer, *Galilean Exorcist*, 109–129; Beasley-Murray, *Kingdom of God*, 95; Meier, *Marginal Jew*, 2:404–23.

25. Matt 4:8–10; Luke 4:5–8.

these episodes reveal that Jesus was remembered as being in conflict with the chief demonic entity, who was understood to rule a kingdom on the earth. There is continuity here, since other New Testament authors also make reference to the devil as "the ruler of this world."[27] We need not draw any far-reaching conclusions from this data beyond the fact that Jesus understood himself to be, and was also remembered as having been, in conflict with a demonic kingdom. This makes good sense when considered in light of the depiction of the establishment of the Kingdom of God in terms of a dualistic struggle between God and demonic forces.[28]

The concept of a diabolic dominion is reflected in early Jewish literature. Some of the most relevant evidence is found in *Jubilees*. In *Jubilees* 1:20, Moses expresses a fear that Israel will be ruled by the spirit of "Beliar"[29] due to covenantal failure predicted in 1:7–14.[30] However, a future time of repentance and restoration is promised in 1:15–18. The connection between covenantal failure and the coming of demonic rule here is clear and noteworthy.[31] *Jubilees* 15:30–34 describes Israel as a nation ruled by God directly under the covenant of circumcision. On the other hand, according to vv. 31–32, "there are many nations and many people, and they all belong to him, but over all of them he caused spirits to rule so that they might lead them astray from following him." There is, then, demonic reign over the Gentile nations, but the covenant allows Israel to be ruled by God. However, future covenantal failure is predicted regarding the ordinance of circumcision in vv. 33–34.

The concept of the reign of "Belial" is similarly reflected in the Qumran sectarian material.[32] Primarily on the basis of 1QS I, 17–18, the reign of Belial has often been understood to refer to the present age of the sectarian texts, which is filled with terrifying trials, and is apparently to come to an end with the eschatological war of God and the Sons of

---

26. Cf., e.g, R.T. France, *The Gospel of Matthew* (NICNT; Grand Rapids: Eerdmans, 2007), 135; Carter, *Matthew and Empire*, 80.

27. John 12:31, 14:40, 16:11; 2 Cor 4:4, Eph 6:11–12; 1 John 5:19, Rev 12:9–17.

28. As discussed in chapter 5 above. See *T. Dan* 5:10–13; 1QM, esp. 6:6; *Assumption of Moses* 10, esp. v. 1; *Sib. Or.* 3.767.

29. On Beliar as the proper name of a chief demonic figure, see Michael Segal, *The Book of Jubilees: Rewritten Bible, Redaction, Ideology and Theology* (JSJSupp, 117; Leiden: Brill, 2007), 255–56. See also S. D. Sperling, "Belial," in *Dictionary of Deities and Demons in the Bible* (Leiden: Brill, 1999), 171. In the New Testament, see 2 Cor 6:15.

30. See James C. VanderKam, *The Book of Jubilees*, 2nd ed., ed. Karel van der Toorn, Bob Becking, Pieter W. van der Horst (Sheffield: Sheffield Academic Press, 2001), 27.

31. Cf. Segal, *Jubilees*, 251.

32. E.g., 1QS I, 16–18; II, 19; IV, 15–26; 1QM XIII, 4; XIV, 8–10; XVIII, 1; 4Q177 III, 8; cf. slightly different formulations in 1QM I, 15; CD IV, 12–13; and XII, 2.

Light against the forces of Belial's dominion in 1QM.[33] Notably, in 1QM I, 2 Belial's army is composed of Gentiles as well as Jews who have not been faithful to the covenant, indicating that covenantal failure results in falling under diabolic dominion.

An eschatological war against Beliar is also mentioned in *T. Dan* 5:10–13, which results in the establishment of the rule of God over Israel "in humility and poverty."[34] Furthermore, in 6:1–2, Dan's children are instructed to be on guard against Satan and his spirits, and to draw near to God and to "the angel who intercedes for you,"[35] who will "stand in opposition to the kingdom of the enemy." In *Martyrdom of Isaiah* 2:4, King Manasseh is said to have turned his father's house so that they serve Beliar, who is identified as "the angel of iniquity who rules this world." This is connected directly to Manasseh's covenantal sins, which are outlined throughout 2:1–6.

There are several inferences about the concept of diabolic dominion in Second Temple period Jewish thought that can be drawn on the basis of this evidence. First, demonic rule is a corporate or national problem, and does not only affect individuals. Second, it is closely related to covenantal sin. Third, God is expected to provide redemption from diabolic dominion. That hope is expressed in terms of an eschatological restoration, sometimes as the result of an eschatological war, and in at least once case (*T. Dan* 5:13), it is directly associated with the reign of God.

These inferences can help to illuminate Jesus's conception of the kingdom of Satan, as similar concepts are reflected in the Jesus tradition. The reign of God is established through the performance of Jesus's exorcisms (Matt 12:28/Luke 11:20). Moreover, in Luke 10:18, Jesus says he "saw Satan fall like lightning" in response to the disciples' report that demons submit to them in his name. As Twelftree notes, in light of the imperfect tense of ἐθεώρεω and its connection to the exorcisms

---

33. E.g., Michael Anthony Knibb, *The Qumran Community* (Cambridge: Cambridge University Press, 1987), 84; Yigael Yadin, *The Scroll of the War of the Sons of Light Against the Sons of Darkness* (London: Oxford University Press, 1962), 232–33; Annette Steudal, "God and Belial," in *The Dead Sea Scrolls: Fifty Years After Their Discovery*, ed. Lawrence H. Schiffman, Emanuel Tov, James C. VanderKam, and Galen Marquis (Jerusalem: Israel Exploration Society, and The Shrine of the Book, Israel Museum, 2000), 332–40 (335); and Loren T. Stuckenbruck, "Protect Them From the Evil One," in *John, Qumran, and the Dead Sea Scrolls*, ed. Mary L. Cole and Tom Thatcher (Atlanta: Society of Biblical Literature, 2011), 139–60 (145–46). On the end of the reign of Belial in 1 QM 1, 5–6, see Brian Schultz, *Conquering the World: The War Scroll Reconsidered* (Leiden and Boston: Brill, 2009), 295–96.

34. On the defeat of Beliar in the *Testaments of the Twelve Patriarchs*, see Graham H. Twelftree, "Exorcism and the Defeat of Beliar in the Testaments of the Twelve Patriarchs," *Vigilae Christianae* 65 (2011): 170–88, esp. 177–79.

35. This is most likely to be identified with Michael, cf. Evans, "Defeating Satan," 165.

reported in v. 17, the fall of Satan seems to be understood as an ongoing process,[36] one that is brought to realization through the exorcisms carried out by Jesus and his followers. The Kingdom of God thus stands over and against Satan's dominion, and its outbreak involves the defeat of Satan and his minions through exorcisms.

The Exorcism of the Demoniac in the Synagogue at Capernaum (Mark 1:21–28/Luke 4:31–37)

With this understanding of exorcisms, their purpose, and their effect in synagogues in mind, we can now turn to Mark 1:21–28/Luke 4:31–37.[37] The scene is set in the synagogue at Capernaum, where Jesus is teaching at a Sabbath gathering (Mark 1:21). We are told that the crowd is impressed with the teaching, since he teaches "with authority" (v. 22). It is significant that the demon's appearance and speech in vv. 23–34 occur while Jesus is teaching, presumably in response. The encounter with the demoniac does not happen immediately upon Jesus's entry into the synagogue,[38] but rises in reaction to what Jesus is teaching and the reception that it receives. The demoniac thus functions in this episode as a type of interlocutor with whom Jesus will need to interact and whom he will need to best in order to be successful and for the recognition of the authority of his teaching to be upheld.

By naming Jesus, the demon is challenging him, as naming an opponent was a means of trying to gain power over them in exorcistic struggles.[39] The verbal challenge indicates that the demon takes a defensive strategy to ward off destruction.[40] It asks, "What have you to do with us, Jesus of Nazareth? Have you come to destroy us? I know who you are, the Holy One of God." The first-person plural used by the demoniac is notable. It does not indicate that the man is possessed by a horde of spirits,[41] but rather, that the demoniac is speaking for demons in gen-

---

36. Twelftree, *Jesus the Exorcist*, 127.

37. Unless otherwise noted, reference will be made primarily to the Markan version of the pericope.

38. According to Twelftree, it is likely that the demoniac did not always show adverse symptoms of his condition (*Jesus the Exorcist*, 60). Comparatively, in Philostratus, *Life of Apollonius*, 4.20, it is not until confronted by Apollonius that the young dandy is aware that he is possessed.

39. As evidenced in *T. Solomon* 3:5–6, 5:2–3; 4Q560 1, 3–5; 11Q11 5, 6. Cf. Witmer, *Galilean Exorcist*, 159–60; Boring, *Mark*, 64; Collins, *Mark*, 168; Darrell L. Bock, *Mark* (NCBC; New York: Cambridge University, 2015), 127.

40. Otto Bauernfeind, *Die Worte der Dämonen im Markusevangelium* (Stuttgart: Kohlhammer, 1927), 6–7; Twelftree, *Jesus the Exorcist*, 64; Witmer, *Galilean Exorcist*, 158–59; Boring, *Mark*, 64; Collins, *Mark*, 169.

41. Cf. Boring, *Mark*, 64. Note the reversion to the use of the first-person singular in saying οἶδά σε τίς εἶ.

eral. In asking "have you come to destroy us?" the demoniac is express-ing fear that the activities of Jesus will destroy not only that particular demon, but demons in general. What is significant here is that *the pos-itive reception of Jesus' teaching in the synagogue at Capernaum entails the destruction of demons*. It is not merely being in the presence of Jesus that occasions this outburst, since it comes not upon Jesus's entrance into the synagogue. The outburst comes in reaction to his teaching and its reception by the crowd, who recognizes its authority.

Although the content of this teaching is not given, it is most rea-sonable to imagine on the basis of the synagogue summary statements that it is an instantiation of Jesus's usual synagogue proclamation of the Kingdom of God and accompanying teaching (see chapter 5). The acceptance of the content of Jesus's program, that is, the outbreak of the Kingdom of God, spells the impending downfall of the diabolic dominion. As synagogues and their locales are brought into the King-dom of God, they are liberated from the effects of diabolic domination. The recognition of authority in Mark 1:27 is not full acceptance,[42] though it is certainly prerequisite for it.

Anthropological studies of negative spirit possession demonstrate that the afflicted person typically comes from a marginal or oppressed sector of society.[43] The ailment functions as an outward expression of that marginalization and oppression, and can act as a discourse that addresses sociopolitical issues.[44] Thus, it is appropriate to understand the notion of the demonic kingdom in the Jesus tradition and the Sec-ond Temple period concept of diabolic dominion as expressions of oppression and marginality from the disadvantaged sector of Galilean society. From a sociopolitical perspective, the societal reordering envi-sioned by Jesus's eschatological proclamation of the Kingdom of God might have been perceived as a threat to the current order.[45] This threat is recognized by the demoniac, and is expressed through the discourse of the challenge by the demoniac and the subsequent exor-cism that Jesus conducts. Moreover, from a sociological perspective,

---

42. Ultimately, it seems that Jesus was not successful in persuading the assembly of Capernaum. See Luke 10:15/Matt 11:23.

43. Lewis, *Ecstatic Religion*, 92–99, 114–19; Witmer, *Galilean Exorcist*, 27; Miquel, "How to Discredit an Inconvenient Exorcist," 193.

44. Michael Lambek, "From Disease to Discourse: Remarks on the Conceptualization of Trance and Spirit Possession," in *Altered States of Consciousness and Mental Health*, ed. Colleen Ward (Newbury Park: Sage, 1989), 36–61 (57); cf. Witmer, *Galilean Exorcist*, 152; Ched Myers, *Binding the Strong Man: A Political Reading of Mark's Story of Jesus* (Maryknoll: Orbis, 2008 [1988]), 146–67 (see also 141–43).

45. On the marginality of the demoniac, see Witmer, *Galilean Exorcist*, 157; Malina and Rohrbaugh, *Social-Science Commentary on the Synoptic Gospels*, 350.

because the synagogue is the local assembly, the public performance of the exorcism would potentially allow the marginalized demoniac to be restored to regular participation in society.

The local-official dimension of the synagogue is important to recall at this point. As discussed in chapter 3, persuasion of the synagogue popular assembly was essential for a presented proposition to go forward.[46] The fact that the demoniac reacts only once the crowd recognizes Jesus's authority is striking.[47] Given that, as we have seen, open discussion was normative in synagogue settings, it is quite likely that this recognition was expressed in the discussion (cf. v. 27), and was perceived by the demoniac, who reacted to it. The demoniac recognizes that acceptance by the synagogue of Jesus's "new teaching" was threatening to the present social order, expressed in terms of diabolic dominion, and thus, engages him in the discourse of an exorcism.

This concept of a covenant community that stands as a bulwark against demonic domination is paralleled in the Qumran sectarian texts. According to 1QS I, 16–18, those entering into the rule of the *yahad* "shall establish a covenant before God in order to carry out all that he commanded and in order not to stray from following him out of any fear, dread, or testing (that might occur) during the dominion of Belial." The implication is that participation in the covenant community will protect the covenanters from the difficulties that will arise during the diabolic dominion. Reference is also made in CD XII, 2 to those over whom the spirits of Belial rule (ימשלו). Those who are unfaithful to the covenant will be given over to destruction at Belial's hand.[48] There are, of course, some very clear differences between the Kingdom of God proclaimed by Jesus and the community concepts of the Qumran sectarians. Nevertheless, a parallel is to be found in the Qumran literature's emphasis on covenantal faithfulness, which must be adhered to during Belial's rule.

It is significant that a public synagogue was the stage for the discourse between Jesus and the demoniac. The rhetorical effect of exorcism performed in the religio-political context of a public synagogue that we have discussed above is evidenced in the pericope at hand. In

---

46. See also Ryan, "Jesus and Synagogue disputes," passim.

47. Both the Markan and Lukan accounts lack a verb indicating that the demoniac "entered" or "came into" the synagogue, instead simply using the imperfect tense of *eimi* (ἦν), which indicates that the demoniac was already amongst the crowd. This is even clearer in the Lukan form of the pericope, as Luke 4:33 drops the Markan εὐθύς in Mark 1:23 (cf. Nolland, *Luke*, 1:206).

48. CD 8.2, 19.14. See John J. Collins, *Apocalypticism in the Dead Sea Scrolls*, repr. ed. (London: Routledge, 1998), 49.

Mark 1:27, the reaction of amazement (θαμβέω) and the recognition of Jesus's authority is directly connected to his ability to command unclean spirits. Likewise, v. 28 indicates the result of the episode, which is that Jesus's fame began to spread throughout Galilee. The performance of a miracle, and especially an exorcism, in the public arena of the synagogue would have served to bolster the persuasive power of Jesus's teaching and proclamation.[49] As indicated by the crowd's response in v. 27, the miracle demonstrated Jesus's authority, and resulted in the spread of his fame throughout the region (v. 28). The exorcistic discourse within the local-official arena of the synagogue has brought Jesus honor and public validation.[50] Although the sociopolitical dimension of exorcism has been explored in prior scholarship,[51] the political context of the synagogue and the rhetorical impact that exorcism would have on synagogue deliberation and discourse has been neglected until now.

There are some factors that are indicative of the plausibility and historical intention of Mark 1:21–28. First of all, the discussion above has rooted our understanding of this incident in the thought world of Second Temple Judaism and its conceptions of demonic dominion, as well as in the anthropological approach to negative spirit possession. Thus, the pericope fits plausibly within the landscape of what is known about the Second Temple period in which it is set, within the realm of the theoretically possible, and within the picture of the past that we are constructing. This is the essential Collingwoodian touchstone of historical criticism.[52] Second, there are elements of the story that go against the grain of Mark's ideal portrayal of Jesus.[53] Several scholars have noted that the defensive show of resistance put up by the demon, especially in its use of Jesus's name as an attempt to gain power over him and its violent exit from the demoniac in v. 26 (Gk. σπαράσσω) are at odds with Mark's tendency to depict Jesus as having full control over

---

49. On the public performance of exorcisms, see Witmer, *Galilean Exorcist*, 27; cf. Arthur Kleinman, *Patients and Healers in the Context of Culture: An Exploration of the Borderland Between Anthropology, Medicine, and Psychiatry* (Berkeley: University of California, 1980), 239, cited here by Witmer.

50. Cf. Malina and Rohrbaugh, *Social-Science Commentary on the Synoptic Gospels*, 150. On the function of honor and shame in public synagogue gatherings, see chapter 3 above, or alternatively, Ryan, "Jesus and Synagogue Disputes," passim.

51. Esp. by Myers, *Binding the Strongman*, 141–43; and Witmer, *Galilean Exorcist*, passim.

52. Collingwood, *Idea of History*, 244.

53. This argument should not be taken as the application of the criterion of dissimilarity or embarrassment. I am not employing them *as* criteria. There are elements of these criteria that are based upon good hermeneutical principles and can serve as indices for inferring the historical intent or plausibility of a given datum. It is these shared principles that may be reflected in this sort of argument. What I am doing here is similar in principle to what is described in Denton, *Historiography and Hermeneutics*, 119; cf. Meyer, *Aims of Jesus*, 86.

negative spirits.[54] In accordance with this, the demoniac's expression of Jesus's identity should be understood in light of the discourse and challenge of exorcisms, rather than as an instantiation of the Markan messianic secret.[55] Thus, we are justified in the direct application and interpretation of this evidence and in the manner of its use within the web of evidence, inference, and imagination that we are constructing here.

Liberating the Woman With the Bent Back (Luke 13:10–17)

The incident taking place in an unidentified synagogue described in Luke 13:10–17 contains a mixture of elements making it of particular interest to the present study. Jesus's teaching within a Sabbath synagogue context is mentioned (v. 10), and a miracle is performed that straddles the line between healing and exorcism (vv. 11–13, cf. v. 16), which occasions a public legal dispute between Jesus and an *archisynagōgos* (vv. 14–17). As we shall see, this pericope describes a fairly high stakes public synagogue debate resulting in an honor and shame exchange.

The description of a legal debate taking place in a public synagogue on the Sabbath in this passage is manifestly plausible, based on the picture of early public synagogues that has been presented on the basis of the evidence in chapters 2 and 3. Moreover, it fits very well into the picture of Jesus that is emerging from the web of evidence, inference, and imagination that we have been constructing. At this point, we should recognize that we must either acknowledge that Jesus engaged in debate in local synagogues, or adopt an extreme skepticism and concede that we can know virtually nothing about his public program at all. This is because, as the evidence has thus far demonstrated: a) the memories of Jesus's public activities are tied to synagogues in the data, and b) public discussion and debate was a typical feature of synagogue gatherings. Thus, *the dispute described in Luke 13:10–17 is precisely the sort of incident that we should expect to have taken place over the course of Jesus' public mission.*[56]

54. Bruce D. Chilton, "An Exorcism of History: Mark 1:21–28," in *Authenticating the Activities of Jesus*, ed. Bruce D. Chilton and Craig A. Evans (New Testament Tools and Studies 28.2; Leiden: Brill, 1998), 215–45, esp. 228–30; Twelftree, *Jesus the Exorcist*, 70–71; Witmer, *Galilean Exorcist*, 162–63. This sort of dissimilarity to the tendencies of the evangelist is not a *criterion* per se, but is an index, a datum indicating historical reference.

55. Contra Wrede, *Messianic Secret*, 33–35; Meier, *Marginal Jew*, 2:649.

56. Contra the findings of Funk and the Jesus Seminar, *Acts of Jesus*, 318–19; Bultmann, *History of the Synoptic Tradition*, 12; cf. also the agnosticism of Meier, *Marginal Jew*, 2:684–85. Sanders expresses

Recently, Nina L. Collins and Twelftree have both independently argued that although Luke 13:10–17 witnesses an event in the life of Jesus, its setting within a synagogue is not original, and comes from Luke's hand.[57] This interpretation is problematic, and is primarily based upon misunderstandings of the institutional context of the synagogue.[58]

Collins maintains that the curing of the woman with the bent back "almost certainly did not take place" within a synagogue.[59] Her argument against locating the incident within a synagogue depends upon her identification of the use of ὄχλος in v. 14 as an inappropriate term to describe the people gathered in the synagogue. Collins observes that "ὄχλος in Greek is used for a 'moving crowd,' a 'throng,' a 'mob,' or a 'multitude.' . . . This term is thus used for a large group of people in an open public space, but most unsuitable for those who have come to a synagogue on the Sabbath, presumably—for the most part—in order to pray."[60] She thereby concludes that the location of the cure within a synagogue is "disproved" by the use of this term.[61] The use of ὄχλος to describe the assembled people belonged to the original story, and was retained by Luke despite resituating the episode within a synagogue.

It is difficult to see how Collins's conception of the synagogue reflects the evidence about early Palestinian synagogues, presented in chapters 2 and 3 of this study. The claim that ὄχλος is an inappropri-

---

a similar agnosticism in *Jewish Law*, 20. He writes, "An assessment of the synoptic conflicts ideally requires us to know things which we cannot know, such as precisely what happened and precisely what the circumstances were." This agnosticism, however, is epistemologically problematic. Sanders is correct that we cannot know these things. However, historical knowledge is, by nature, inferential. The data provides evidence from which we can infer some knowledge of the past. We cannot be concerned with the lack of details that could only be ascertained through empirical means, since seeing is not knowing, and the past cannot, at any rate, be observed. Bultmann's suggestion that this pericope was composed on the basis of Luke 13:15 and modelled on Mark 3:1–6 is problematic. As Twelftree has observed (*Jesus the Miracle Worker*, 296–97), the only point of contact between Luke 13:15 and Luke 13:10–17 is Jesus's defense of his healing on the Sabbath. This is not sufficient warrant to consider the passage to be a Lukan composition. On the unlikelihood of the Lukan wholesale composition of Luke 13:10–17, see Kazen, *Scripture, Interpretation, or Authority?*, 66–71. A number of other scholars have recognized that this pericope memorializes an event in the life of Jesus, e.g., Walter Grundmann, *Das Evangelium nach Lukas* (Theologischer Handkommentar zum Neuen Testament 3; Berlin : Evangelische Verlagsanstalt, 1963), 279; Marshall, *Gospel of Luke*, 556–57; Fitzmyer, *Luke*, 2:1011; Bock, *Luke*, 2:1213. Despite this, Luke 13:10–17 has played a curiously minor role in historical Jesus research.

57. Nina L. Collins, *Jesus, The Sabbath, and The Jewish Debate: Healing on the Sabbath in the 1st and 2nd Centuries CE* (LNTS 474; New York: T&T Clark, 2014), 123–44; Twelftree, "Jesus and the Synagogue," 3127–28.

58. I have argued this at length elsewhere, in Ryan, "Jesus and Synagogue Disputes," passim. The more salient points of the discussion will be touched upon here.

59. Collins, *Jesus, the Sabbath and the Jewish Debate*, 144.

60. Ibid., 126.

61. Ibid., 144.

ate term for a synagogue setting is especially questionable. Luke is not the only first-century author to use the term ὄχλος to refer to people assembled in a synagogue. In *Life* 277, Josephus writes of an assembly that took place in a large synagogue in Tiberias, since it was "able to accommodate a large crowd" (πολὺν ὄχλον ἐπιδέξασθαι δυνάμενον).[62] On another occasion, he also describes the assembled townspeople of the same synagogue as τὸν δημοτικὸν ὄχλον ("the crowd of the populace").[63]

The argument that ὄχλος is the wrong choice of word for people assembled in a synagogue is predicated on a problematic assumption about early synagogue functions. Collins considers the term to be "most unsuitable" for people who have come to a synagogue on the Sabbath to pray.[64] Corporate prayer was simply not the characteristic synagogue function during the Second Temple period. The very existence of communal prayer in Second Temple synagogues has been the subject of much debate over the past few decades.[65] Levine has gone so far as to say that prayer is the "most problematic component" of synagogue worship.[66]

As the discussion in chapters 2 and 3 above has demonstrated, the characteristic function of synagogue assemblies in both the Land and the diaspora was the reading and interpretation of the Jewish scriptures, especially the Torah.[67] Moreover, the interpretation of the Jewish scriptures was a community affair, and could involve heated discussion and debate.[68] Synagogue gatherings would not have been quiet, reflective, and personal, but loud, corporate, and potentially heated or boisterous. Even a "religious" gathering, such as the one described by Josephus in *Life* 290–303, could be animated, politically charged, and

---

62. See *ASSB*, no. 43; cf. the discussion of the synagogue in Tiberias in chapter 3 above.

63. Josephus, *Life*, 284. Cf. Runesson, Binder, and Olsson, *ASSB*, 78.

64. Collins, *Jesus, the Sabbath and the Jewish Debate*, 126.

65. See Levine, *Ancient Synagogue*, 162–69; Catto, *Reconstructing*, 125–42; Solomon Zeitlin, "The Tefillah, the Shemoneh Esreh: An Historical Study of the First Canonization of the Hebrew Liturgy," *JQR* 54 (1964): 208–49; Stefan C. Reif, *Judaism and Hebrew Prayer: New Perspectives on Jewish Liturgical History* (Cambridge: Cambridge University Press, 1993), 44–52; and McKay, *Sabbath and Synagogue*, passim.

66. Levine, *Ancient Synagogue*, 162. Do note, however, the reference to prayer in a synagogue setting in Matt 6:5.

67. As we have already seen, this is widely agreed upon in synagogue scholarship. See, for example, the comments of Hachlili, *Ancient Synagogues*, 47; Catto, *Reconstructing*, 16; and Olsson, "An Evaluation," 134. See also Strange, "Archaeology and Ancient Synagogues," 53–57; Runesson, *Origins*, 193–231; Binder, *Into the Temple Courts*, 399; Levine, *Ancient Synagogue*, 150, 165; Claussen, *Versammlung*, 213; Lawrence H. Schiffman, "The Early History of Public Reading of the Torah," in *Jews, Christians, and Polytheists in the Ancient Synagogue: Cultural Interaction During the Greco-Roman Period*, ed. Steven Fine (New York: Routledge, 2014 [1997]), 44–56, esp. 54.

68. Mosser, "Torah Instruction," 523–51, esp. 550.

even violent.[69] Luke's choice of the term ὄχλος is thus undoubtedly appropriate to describe people assembled in synagogues.

Twelftree has similarly argued that Luke is responsible for the synagogue setting of Luke 13:10–17 for different reasons. His rationale is based on "the fact that the synagogue ruler reprimands the crowd (13:14), not Jesus, and it is 'the Lord' (ὁ κύριος, 13:15), not 'Jesus,' who answers, so that an early church origin of this part of the story seems likely."[70]

That it is "the Lord" rather than "Jesus" who answers the ἀρχισυνάγωγος in v. 15 is irrelevant to the historical level of the passage. This title comes from the narrator, not from a character within the world of the narrative. Luke, in his capacity as the author of his Gospel, is responsible for this nomenclature.[71] What this means is that this feature of the text tells us more about Luke's christology than it does about the historical setting of the passage. Luke, after all, is responsible for the shape of the traditions that he received as they appear in his Gospel. All memory is interpreted, and the memories of Jesus preserved in Luke's Gospel bear his interpretive imprint. Evidence of redaction is not evidence of implausibility or "inauthenticity."

Twelftree is correct to highlight the fact that both Jesus (cf. the plural noun ὑποκριταί in v. 15)[72] and the *archisynagōgos* address the crowd, since it is a curious feature of the text. It appears as though Jesus and the *archisynagōgos* are literally talking past each other.[73] However, the matter can be resolved by properly situating the event within the context of the institutional setting of the synagogue. This is not a detail that speaks to the artificiality of the setting. If anything, it speaks in favor of a synagogue setting rather than against it.

As the evidence examined in chapter 3 has indicated, the public played a major role in decision making and in determining what would go forward in synagogue settings.[74] We have also seen in our discussion of the Gospel evidence thus far that persuasion of the assembly was essential for the conferral of honor and for a given proposition to

---

69. The attempt on Josephus's life at the public fast in the Tiberian synagogue recounted in *Life* 302 and the attempt to stone Jonathan in *Life* 303 can be compared to the rejection of Jesus in the synagogue at Nazareth in Luke 4:28–29.

70. Twelftree, "Jesus and the Synagogue," 3128.

71. The Lukan narrator refers to Jesus as "Lord" (Gk. κύριος) several times in Acts: 9:10–17; 19:5, 13, 15; 28:31.

72. Cf. Bock, *Luke*, 2:1217–18.

73. Both Nolland and Bovon also consider this to be a historically problematic feature of the text. See, e.g., Nolland, *Luke*, 2:722–23; Bovon, *Luke*, 2:281.

74. See also Ryan, "Jesus and Synagogue Disputes," passim.

be accepted and upheld. When the *archisynagōgos* states in v. 14 that "there are six days on which work ought to be done; come on those days and be cured, and not on the Sabbath day,"[75] he is not authoritatively laying down the law. He is, in fact, putting forward a proposition that, as can actually be seen in this very passage, will need to be accepted by the assembly at large.[76] The mechanics of synagogue disputes involved status and the exchange of honor and shame, that is, public reputation, standing in the community and the public recognition of it.[77] It is striking that Jesus's reply to the *archisynagōgos* in vv. 15–16 results in all of his opponents being "put to shame" (κατῃσχύνοντο), since this directly acknowledges that the social mechanics of an honor-and-shame exchange are at play in the narrative.

It is the assembled public that confers and recognizes both honor and shame, just as it is the assembled public that decides the outcome of disputes and legal discourse. Thus, the ἀρχισυνάγωγος directs his complaint to the crowd (ἔλεγεν τῷ ὄχλῳ) rather than to Jesus. His aim in so doing appears to be to persuade the public to adopt his perspective on the law, since it is ultimately the public who will decide the result of this challenge. Moreover, Jesus is not apparently a resident of the town. Future normative Sabbath observation in that locale would thus concern the townspeople, but probably not Jesus. Whereas Twelftree and Nolland have both treated this feature of the text as an indication of the secondary nature of the synagogue setting,[78] I see it as a detail that is best understood *within* a synagogue setting, in which local-official disputes were settled by the opinion of the majority.[79] Although the crowd is being addressed, I agree with Malina and Rohrbaugh that the complaint nevertheless constitutes a challenge to Jesus and his honor,[80] since the charge implies that Jesus's act of healing constitutes work on the Sabbath.

As the discussion of synagogue people and roles in chapter 3 demonstrated, an *archisynagōgos* was a synagogue functionary charged with the oversight of the ceremonial reading and interpretation of the law, and an influential member of the community. Thus, Jesus's opponent

---

75. This presumably refers to the Sabbath commandment in Exod 20:9, cf. Deut 5:13.

76. Refer to the discussion of synagogue people in chapter 3, particularly on the roles of the assembled public and the *archisynagōgos*.

77. Malina and Rohrbaugh, *Social-Science Commentary on the Synoptic Gospels*, 370.

78. Twelftree, "Jesus and the Synagogue," 4:3128.

79. Cf., e.g., Josephus, *Life* 289; Sus 41. For further evidence, see chapter 3. See also Ryan, "Jesus and Synagogue Disputes," passim.

80. Malina and Rohrbaugh, *Social Science Commentary on the Synoptic Gospels*, 282.

would have been recognized as a high status individual with influence in synagogue proceedings.

Meier has noted that the identification of Jesus's adversary in this story as an *archisynagōgos* rather than a Pharisee despite "Luke's great redactional interest in the Pharisees as dialogue partners of Jesus,"[81] may point to pre-Lukan tradition lying behind the passage. I would also add that this speaks to the synagogue context of the incident. An incident involving a Pharisee could be located almost anywhere, but a dispute with an *archisynagōgos* makes the most sense within a synagogue. We should recall at this point that Pharisees had no specific connection or institutional role within Second Temple public synagogues.[82] By contrast, *archisynagōgoi* were intrinsically connected to synagogues, and were influential members of the assemblies which they oversaw. This is a significant detail of the narrative for understanding the passage in its institutional context. Jesus was not being challenged by a member of a rival association, but by a member of the institutional structure of the synagogue itself, who was quite likely also one of its benefactors. This is indicative of the difficulty of the debate that Jesus faced and of the significance of his victory.

The narrative plays out as a synagogue dispute over a legal issue between Jesus and a person of high social status, the outcome of which is decided by persuading the present members of the public. The public recognition of the wisdom of Jesus's reply to the complaint of the *archisynagōgos* results in his gaining honor, the shaming of his opponents, the legal validity of his Sabbath cure, and the setting of a precedent for future practice in that locale.[83]

We have thus far established the plausibility of Luke 13:10–17 and the integrity of its institutional setting. With our new understanding of the dispute between Jesus and the *archisynagōgos* in mind, we may now turn to the interpretation of the rest of the passage.

The episode opens in v. 10 with Jesus teaching on the Sabbath in an unidentified synagogue. Here, we see Jesus carrying out the usual activity of his program,[84] as discussed in chapter 5. The location and chronology of this event is problematic. Within the Lukan narrative, this is the last time that Jesus teaches in a local synagogue.[85] The last

---

81. John P. Meier, *Marginal Jew*, 2:684.
82. Cf. Levine, *Ancient Synagogue*, 40–41.
83. Cf. Runesson, *Origins*, 483 on synagogue disputes and the interpretation of the Law.
84. As noted also by Carroll, *Luke*, 282.
85. Cf. Fitzmyer, *Luke*, 2:1012; Nolland, *Luke*, 2:723; Stein, *Luke*, 373; Bock, *Luke*, 2:1214; Carroll, *Luke*, 282.

identifiable location prior to this pericope is apparently Bethany, given the mention of the home of Mary and Martha in 10:38–42,[86] which probably would set our pericope around that same area, quite near to Jerusalem. However, he is later located far to the north of Bethany, between Samaria and Galilee, in 17:11. This strongly indicates that, as Bock observes, Luke's arrangement of the journey section is "more thematic and topical"[87] than geographical or chronological. Given that this is Luke's intent in the arrangement of the travel narrative, it is likely that the narrative of Luke 13:10–17 has been chronologically and geographically displaced. Moreover, the narrative resembles the earlier period of Jesus's career described in the synoptic synagogue summary statements.[88] This leads to the conclusion that this event likely took place during that earlier phase described by the summary statements, in a synagogue in Galilee or possibly Judea (cf. Luke 4:44). Thus, it is likely that Jesus's teaching pertained to the proclamation of the Kingdom (cf. vv. 18–21) and its accompanying legal praxis.

The woman first appears in v. 11. The presence of women in synagogues in this period would not have been out of the ordinary, as women were participants in synagogue gatherings.[89] The woman is described in v. 11 as "having a spirit of weakness for eighteen years" (Gk. πνεῦμα ἔχουσα ἀσθενείας ἔτη δεκαοκτώ). In Jesus's response to the *archisynagōgos* in v. 16, he says that the woman has been bound by Satan. It is clear that Jesus understands the woman's affliction to be a result of demonic oppression. However, as Twelftree has observed, the miracle is properly a healing and not an exorcism, since Jesus does not address the spirit itself nor Satan, but the woman.[90] Form of the miracle aside, the act of healing is nevertheless seen by Jesus as liberation from Satan (v. 16).

Upon seeing her, Jesus calls the woman over to heal her, apparently interrupting his teaching (v. 12). Joel Green has convincingly argued

86. Although the village in this pericope is unidentified (κώμην τινά), the location of Mary and Martha's home is known from John 12:1–8.

87. Bock, *Luke*, 2:1040.

88. Mark 1:39; Luke 4:15, 43–44; Matt 4:23, 9:35. Cf. Green, *Luke*, 519.

89. This is now generally agreed upon in synagogue scholarship, e.g., Brooten, *Women Leaders*, passim; Frédéric Manns, "La femme et la synagogue à l'époque de Jésus," *Ephemerides Liturgicae* 109, no. 2 (1995): 159–65; Catto, *Reconstructing*, 188–189; McKay, *Sabbath and Synagogue*, 170; Levine, *Ancient Synagogue*, 502–511. For example, refer to Judith 6:16; Acts 16:12–13, 17:1–4, 10–12, 18:26; Josephus, *Ant.*, 14.260. Philo, *Contempl. Life* 66–82; *t. Meg.* 3:11; *b. Sotah* 22a. The archaeological data does not evidence partitions between men and women, as synagogue architecture consists primarily of one large open meeting hall (see chapter 3).

90. Twelftree, *Jesus the Exorcist*, 55; cf. also M. Dennis Hamm, "The Freeing of the Bent Woman and the Restoration of Israel: Luke 13.10–17 as Narrative Theology," *JSNT* 31 (1987): 23–44 (29).

that, on the level of Luke's narrative, this is done "as a consequence and expression of his [Jesus'] mission,"[91] and I am inclined to think that this is the case on the historical level as well. Just as we discussed in light of Jesus's exorcisms above, the act of healing through liberation here is part and parcel of Jesus's synagogue program of the announcement and realization of the Kingdom of God.

Jesus does not pronounce the woman healed, but "set free" (Gk. ἀπολύω).[92] This acknowledges the healing as liberation from a demonic "agent of subjugation" from which she needs to be released.[93] As argued earlier in this chapter and in chapter 6 above, Jesus understood the liberation of captives to be a function of his divine appointment, and victory over the dominion of Satan is bound up with the eschatological outbreak of the Kingdom of God. In other words, *Jesus's work in the synagogue reflected the struggle between the Kingdom of God and Satan's kingdom that he understood to be operative within his mission.*

4Q521 II IV 2, 8 cites Psalm 146:7–8 in the context of the eschatological Messianic age and the establishment of "the eternal Kingdom, describing the acts of God's spirit: "liberating captives, restoring sight to the blind, lifting up the b[ent]."[94] This text has also been raised above in conjunction with Luke 4:18–19. Although it is unlikely that Jesus would have been familiar with this text, it indicates that Psalm 146:7b–8 was read eschatologically by some in the late Second Temple period,[95] and that the act of "lifting up the bent" could have eschatological significance if understood in light of the blessings of the outbreak of the reign of God. Given that v. 10 of that same Psalm refers to the eternal reign of Adonay in the future (Heb. qal imperfect, יִמְלֹ֥ךְ יְהוָ֨ה | לְעוֹלָ֜ם), it is not hard to imagine why this might have been the case.

What is the connection between the legal dispute, Jesus's proclamation of the Kingdom of God, and the healing of the woman with the bent back? The key is found in vv. 15–16. The *archisynagōgos'* charge to the crowd in v. 14 implies that the act of healing constitutes work, and thus, is inappropriate for the Sabbath. As Thomas Kazen has con-

---

91. Joel B. Green, "Jesus and a Daughter of Abraham (Luke 13:10–17): Test Case for a Lucan Perspective on Jesus' Miracles," *CBQ* 51 (1989): 643–54 (652).
92. Compare the usage of "made well" (Gk. ὑγιής) in Mark 5:34 and John 5:6, 14, or "delivered you" (Gk. σῴζω) in Matt 9:22; Mark 5:34, 10:52; Luke 8:48, 17:19.
93. Green, *Luke*, 522.
94. The reconstruction is based on the citation of Psalm 146:7–8, and we can thus be fairly confident of its accuracy. See Émile Puech, "Une apocalypse messianique (4Q521)," *Revue de Qumran* 15 (1992): 475–522 (490); Michael O. Wise and James D. Tabor, "The Messiah at Qumran," *BAR* 16, no. 6 (1992): 60–65 (63); Eric Eve, *Jewish Context*, 190–91.
95. In light of this, it is worth noting the reference in Psalm 146:10 to Adonay's eternal reign.

vincingly shown, there was a tradition of considering non-life-saving acts of healing on the Sabbath, both through medicine and through prayer, to be violations of the Sabbath law in early rabbinic thought.[96] This same unease with the legality of Sabbath healing is expressed in the Gospels (cf. Mark 3:2–4; John 9:14). Jesus's response in vv. 15–16 takes the form of a *qal va-ḥomer* (from lesser to greater) argument.[97] He draws upon the common practice of "loosing" (Gk. λύω) an animal on the Sabbath to allow it to drink,[98] and places it alongside the "loosing" (Gk. λύω) of the woman from her bonds. The latter both parallels and magnifies the former. The idea presented here is not just that it is *acceptable* for a woman to be set free on the Sabbath, but that it is *appropriate*. As the use of δεῖ in v. 16 indicates, it is even *necessary*.[99] As Fitzmyer writes, the use of this verb "alludes to the necessary realization of God's plan of salvation-history, working itself out in Jesus' ministry."[100] The healing, understood in terms of the loosing of Satanic bonds, thus has an eschatological character, as it is bound up with the present realization of the Kingdom of God as it comes to be through Jesus's synagogue program. Here, we see yet another example of the Kingdom of God demonstrably coming into being *within the synagogue*. In this way, the synagogue was to be the birth place of the Kingdom, the restored and renewed Israel.

What made the Sabbath an appropriate and necessary time to effect liberation through healing? As some interpreters have noted, the Deuteronomic Sabbath commandment includes an injunction to remember God's liberation of the Israelites from slavery in Egypt (Deut 5:15).[101] By describing the woman as a "daughter of Abraham," Jesus highlights her status as an Israelite and heir of the Abrahamic covenant.[102] How appropriate, then, that a member of God's people should experience both physical and eschatological liberation on the day appointed to remember God's foundational act of liberation. This certainly speaks to the appropriateness of the Sabbath as an occasion for the woman to be liberated, but I would go beyond this to suggest

---

96. Kazen, *Scripture, Interpretation, or Authority?*, 95–100. See *m. Yoma* 8:6; *m. Shab.* 14:3–4; *t. Shab.* 12:8–14; *t. Shab.* 16:22.

97. Cf. Meier, *Marginal Jew*, 2:684; Bock, *Luke*, 2:1218; Carroll, *Luke*, 284.

98. Jesus apparently takes it for granted that this is common practice, evidenced by his reference to "each of you" (ἕκαστος ὑμῶν), implying that it is typically done. Some reflection of this practice is found in early Rabbinic literature (see *m. Shab.* 5:1–4, 15:1–2; *m. 'Erub.* 2:1–4) and at Qumran (CD 11:5–6; 4Q265 VII, 2–4), cf. Peter W. Flint, "Qumran Scrolls and the Historical Jesus," 274.

99. Fitzmyer, *Luke*, 2:1011; Hamm, "Freeing of the Bent Woman," 33; Tannehill, *Luke*, 220.

100. Fitzmyer, *Luke*, 2:1011.

101. Hamm, "Freeing of the Bent Woman," 27; Carroll, *Luke*, 285.

102. Compare 4 Macc 15:28.

that attention should also be drawn to the Jubilee, the "year of the Lord's favour" which Jesus announces in Luke 4:19 (see above). The Jubilee year is proclaimed in the forty-ninth year (Lev 25:8), the Sabbath of Sabbath years, which, as argued above, takes on eschatological valences in Jesus's teaching. The Jubilee ordinance includes a commandment to "proclaim liberty throughout the land to all its inhabitants" (Lev 25:10). Thus, Jesus's act of setting the woman free from her bondage in this unnamed synagogue instantiates and realizes the eschatological Jubilee and its promise of liberation that Jesus had announced in the synagogue at Nazareth.

Sanders is correct to point out that in this story, Jesus has not actually transgressed the Law by performing work, since no work was performed.[103] However, that does not make the story implausible. It is better to say that he has transgressed a particular *interpretation* of the Law,[104] one that he clearly rejects, rather than the Law itself. To accept the validity of the Sabbath cure is to accept the outbreak of the Kingdom of God that it witnesses and enacts and to set a possible precedent for future acts of healing on the Sabbath in that locale. Thus, by persuading the synagogue of the necessity of the cure, Jesus was causing them to recognize the *availability* of eschatological liberation that it instantiated. It is therefore fitting that in the Lukan narrative, Jesus follows the favourable resolution of the debate with further teachings on the Kingdom in vv. 18–21.

Verse 17 indicates that the assembly resolves the debate in Jesus's favor by highlighting his opponents' accrual of shame. This is the clearest evidence of an occasion upon which Jesus was successful in a public synagogue setting. Mark 1:27–28 also indicates a generally positive reception and the accrual of honor in v. 28. However, the amazement and the recognition of authority expressed there do not ultimately lead to the acceptance of Jesus's proclamation in Capernaum, as indicated by the double-tradition saying of Luke 10:15/Matt 11:23. Ultimately, it would appear as though Jesus failed to convince Capernaum, along with Chorazin and Bethsaida. Thus, Luke 13:10–17 stands alone in the

---

103. Sanders, *Jesus and Judaism*, 266. Cf. also Schröter, *Jesus of Nazareth*, 157.
104. Cf. Sven-Olav Back, "Jesus and the Sabbath," in *Handbook for the Study of the Historical Jesus* (ed. Tom Holmén, and Stanley E. Porter; Leiden and Boston: Brill, 2011, 2597–2633, (2623), who says that Jesus transgressed the Sabbath commandment "as it was understood by teachers of halakha—including Pharisees—in first-century Jewish Palestine." This is quite different from claiming that he transgressed the Sabbath law in itself or that he abrogated it. See also Westerholm, *Scribal Authority*, 95.

Gospels as the sole preserved unambiguous victory in a public synagogue.

Luke 13:18–21 as Synagogue Teaching?

Following the resolution of the dispute between Jesus and the *archisynagōgos* in Luke 13:17, Luke has Jesus deliver two parables in Luke 13:18–21. No change of setting is narrated, which leads to the conclusion that Luke also sets these parables within the public synagogue.[105] Moreover, the use of οὖν in v. 18 indicates that the parables are given in response or connection to what has just occurred in vv. 10–17.[106]

However, the historical setting of these parables is a complicated matter. Nolland rightly notes that, while there is no change of location between vv. 17 and 18, "neither is there any expectation that we should read these paired parables with the crowd or the synagogue ruler of vv. 10–17 as an audience."[107] Moreover, the evangelists disagree about the setting of these teachings. The Parable of the Leaven in vv. 20–21 is extant only in Luke and Matthew (Matt 13:33). This parable belongs to the double tradition, and is usually included in Q by proponents of the Two-Document Hypothesis.[108] Parallels to the Lukan Parable of the Mustard are found in Mark 4:30–32 and Matt 13:31–32.[109] There is substantially less verbal overlap in the Lukan version of this parable and the other versions, though there are some agreements between Matthew and Luke against Mark.[110] Notably, the same pairing of the two parables is found in Matthew. In Matthew, the pair appears in the midst of a large collection of parables (Matt 13:31–33). The Matthean setting for this parabolic discourse is Jesus teaching from a boat to a crowd gathered on a beach (Matt 13:1–2).

It appears as though Matthew's narrative presentation and arrangement of the parables discourse is not intended to be historical. This

---

05. Cf. Fitzmyer, *Luke*, 2:1016; Green, *Luke*, 526.

06. Cf. Fitzmyer, *Luke*, 2:016; Tannehill, *Luke*, 220; Bock, *Luke*, 2:1224–25; Carroll, *Luke*, 286.

07. Nolland, *Luke*, 728.

08. E.g., John S. Kloppenborg, *Q: The Earliest Gospel* (Louisville and London: Westminster John Knox, 2008), 42; Wendy J. Cotter, "The Parables of the Mustard and the Leaven: Their Function in the Earliest Stratum of Q," *Toronto Journal of Theology* 8, no. (1992), 38–51; Zeba Crook, "The Synoptic Parables of the Mustard and the Leaven: A Test-Case for the Two-Document, Two-Gospel, and Farrer-Goulder Hypotheses," *JSNT* 78 (2000): 23–48.

09. See also *Gos. Thom.* 20.

10. There is a tendency amongst Two-Document Hypothesis proponents to think that Luke has followed Q, while Matthew has mostly followed the Markan version, altering it using the wording of Q. See Fitzmyer, *Luke*, 2:1015; Crook, "Synoptic Parables," 26–33; Luz, *Matthew*, 2:257; Adolf Jülicher, *Die Gleichnisreden Jesu*, 2 vols. (Freiburg: J.C.B. Mohr, 1888–89), 2:571; Marshall, *Gospel of Luke*, 559–60.

discourse comes at the turning point of Matthew's narrative, yet also interrupts its flow.[111] Luz's suggestion that Matthew 13's presentation of the parables in narrative form "condenses and anticipates the story of the entire Gospel of Matthew in a concentrated form" adequately and convincingly explains the intent behind Matthew's ingenious arrangement of the parable collection here.[112] Thus, the Lukan setting of the parables is not ruled out on the basis of Matthew's narrative setting of the same parables.[113]

Since Luke 13:10–17 comes from a Lukan special source, it is possible that Luke's knowledge of the connection between vv. 10–17 and the parables in vv. 18–21 comes from that special source. However possible this is, it is also somewhat unlikely due to the close verbal agreement between the Lukan and Matthean versions of the Parable of the Leaven and the agreements against Mark in the Parable of the Mustard. Under the standard source-critical models, Luke would have had to know the parables from both sources, but have chosen to follow Q (cf. 2DH) or Matthew (Farrer-Goulder) despite taking the setting from his special source. This is not impossible, but nor is it particularly convincing. It is more likely that Luke drew these parables as a pair from Q or Matthew, and then used them to illuminate and interpret the story in Luke 13:10–17.

Nevertheless, the fact that Luke situates the parables of vv. 18–21 in a public synagogue is significant, regardless of whether or not they were originally delivered immediately following the event narrated in vv. 10–17. Tradition history aside, *Luke remembers and preserves these parables as synagogue teaching*. This is an important datum in itself. Given that these are explicitly Kingdom parables, this datum further evidences the connection between Jesus's activity in synagogues and his proclamation of the Kingdom of God.

Though it is prudent not to hang too much on Luke's preservation of these parables as synagogue teaching, it is worth considering them as remembered synagogue sayings, since they may give us some idea of the sort of thing that Jesus's teaching and proclamation in the synagogues entailed.[114] Moreover, Luke 13:18–21 is unique in the Jesus tra-

---

111. Luz, *Matthew*, 2:290, 295; Jack Dean Kingsbury, *The Parables of Jesus in Matthew 13* (Richmond: John Knox, 1969), 130.

112. Luz, *Matthew*, 2:295. Space and focus do not permit further discussion of this issue here. For a similar perspective to that of Luz, see the comments of Keener, *Matthew*, 371.

113. Similarly, Bock writes that "it is hard to be certain that a single setting is in view for both Matthew and Luke, though it seems most likely that a single tradition is employed" (*Luke*, 2:1223).

114. For the sake of simplicity, we will deal directly here only with the Lukan form of the parables, since it is Luke alone who memorializes them within a synagogue.

dition in that it presents teachings given in a synagogue setting that are not directly related to Jewish scripture. Thus, what we see here is nonscriptural teaching on the object of Jesus's proclamation, that is, the Kingdom of God. These parables are expressly meant to illustrate something about the Kingdom,[115] and so, we can see here an example of how Jesus used teaching to convey and illuminate his proclamation.

Detailed exegesis of these two parables is not required here, and is beyond the scope of what is necessary for the purposes of this project. Nevertheless, some discussion of the meaning of these parables will serve to show how they might cast some light upon Jesus's synagogue program.

Some interpreters have interpreted these parables in light of perceived negative valences of the image of mustard, and especially leaven.[116] However, it is not clear that mustard or leaven would actually have been seen as negative or contaminating symbols in antiquity.[117] At any rate, placing this at the centre of the interpretation of the parable misses the point, as these negative valences do not seem to be highlighted in any of the extant versions.

A number of interpreters have identified "growth" of something small into something else much larger as the key image in the Parable of the Mustard Seed.[118] Within the context of Jesus's career, the parable would then indicate the coming of the Kingdom in fulfilment of Israel's expectations despite its humble beginnings within Jesus's small band of followers and its slight appearances in Jesus's miracles, such as the one performed in Luke 13:10–13. The Parable of the Leaven could be read in much the same way, as the leaven makes the dough rise, thus evoking the image of growth.[119]

---

115. Explicitly so in v. 18 ("τίνι ὁμοία ἐστὶν ἡ βασιλεία τοῦ θεοῦ, καὶ τίνι ὁμοιώσω αὐτήν;") and v. 20 ("τίνι ὁμοιώσω τὴν βασιλείαν τοῦ θεοῦ;").

116. Funk and the Jesus Seminar, *Five Gospels*, 346–47; Bernard Brandon Scott, *Hear Then the Parable: A Commentary on the Parables of Jesus* (Minneapolis: Fortress Press, 1989), 321–29; 374–77; Douglas E. Oakman, *Jesus and the Economic Questions of His Day* (Studies in the Bible and Early Christianity 8; Lewiston, NY: Edwin Mellen, 1986), 124; Crossan, *Historical Jesus*, 278; Robert W. Funk, "Beyond Criticism in Quest of Literacy: The Parable of the Leaven," *Interpretation* 25 (1971): 149–70 (161).

117. Ryan S. Schellenberg, "Kingdom as Contaminant? The Role of Repertoire in the Parables of the Mustard and the Leaven," *CBQ* 71, no. 3 (2009): 527–43. Cf. also Meier, *Marginal Jew*, 5:194.

118. Dodd, *Parables of the Kingdom*, 142; Arland J. Hultgren, *The Parables of Jesus: A Commentary* (Grand Rapids: Eerdmans, 2000), 396–97; Kümmel, *Promise and Fulfilment*, 128–31; Amy-Jill Levine, *Short Stories by Jesus: The Enigmatic Parables of a Controversial Rabbi* (New York: HarperOne, 2014), 158–59 (though it should be noted that Levine has a somewhat more nuanced interpretation that concentrates on *what* great outcomes arrive from small beginnings rather than *that* this occurs); Joachim Jeremias, *The Parables of Jesus*, 2nd ed., trans. S.H. Hooke (New York: Charles Scribner's Sons, 1963), 149; Nils Dahl, "The Parables of Growth," in *Jesus in the Memory of the Early Church* (Minneapolis: Augsburg Fortress, 1976), 156–66; Bock, *Luke*, 2:1225; Fitzmyer, *Luke*, 2:1016; Cotter, "Parables of the Mustard Seed and the Leaven," 47–48.

The identification of an image of growth in these parables is certainly well made, but there is more to the parable than this.[120] The key issue in both parables is, in my opinion, drawn out by Klyne Snodgrass in saying that "the point is that what one sees with Jesus will lead to what one hopes for in the kingdom."[121] Though it cannot be seen, the tree is already present in the seed, and the promise of fulfilment that will lead to full realization is present in the leaven, despite being "hidden" (Gk. κρύπτω) in the dough.

What, then, does it mean that the Lukan Jesus offers this as a comment on the events of Luke 13:10–17?[122] The Lukan remembered Jesus is saying that the reign of God is already present in what has been done in the synagogue. The batch is already thoroughly leavened, though it has not yet reached full realization. The scene in the synagogue is a seed of what is yet to come, small now, but already present. Although Snodgrass only sees the connection being made between the parables and the act of healing the woman with the bent back,[123] I would expand the connection to include the entirety of the scene in the synagogue, especially the description of Jesus's victory in v. 17, which directly precedes the Ἔλεγεν οὖν ("therefore, he said . . .") of v. 18. It is not just the miracle that indicates the presence of God's reign, *but the positive acceptance of it and Jesus's teaching by the synagogue assembly.*

I do not think that we can be certain in a historical sense about the original setting of these parables. Nevertheless, that they are presented within a synagogue in Luke as a comment on the events of Luke 13:10–17 is a significant historical datum. The fact that these teachings about the Kingdom of God are situated by Luke in a synagogue indicates and confirms that Jesus was strongly remembered in the early tradition as having taught about the Kingdom in synagogues. Moreover, that these parables are offered as a commentary on the event in Luke 13:10–17 and are apparently given as a response to the outcome of that narrative may indicate some memory of a connection between the presence and growth of the Kingdom and the acceptance of Jesus's teaching and miracles in synagogue settings.

---

119. E.g., Fitzmyer, *Luke,* 2:1019; Dahl, "Parables of Growth," passim.

120. Cf. Snodgrass, *Stories With Intent,* 223, 225.

121. Snodgrass, *Stories With Intent,* 225. Compare also Dunn, *Jesus Remembered,* 464. On the element of realized eschatology in these parables, see Dodd, *Parables of the Kingdom,* 142–44.

122. Fitzmyer, *Luke,* 2:016; Tannehill, *Luke,* 220; Bock, *Luke,* 2:1224–25; Carroll, *Luke,* 286; Snodgrass, *Stories With Intent,* 234.

123. Snodgrass, *Stories With Intent,* 234.

Healing the Man with the Withered Hand: Mark 3:1–6/Matthew 12:9–14/Luke 6:6–11

The healing of the man with the withered hand, recounted in Mark 3:1–6 and the parallel accounts in Matthew 12:9–14 and Luke 6:6–11,[124] underscores and exemplifies the religiopolitical dimension of healing miracles in synagogue settings. It is probable that this incident took place in the synagogue at Capernaum, as with the exorcism in Mark 1:21–28/Luke 4:31–37. In Mark 3:1, we are told that Jesus entered the synagogue *again* (Gk. εἰσῆλθεν πάλιν εἰς συναγωγήν), as though he had been there before. This likely refers back to Mark 1:21, the last time that Jesus was in a synagogue in the Markan narrative prior to Mark 3:1.[125] Mark's testimony is all we have to go on for the location of this synagogue. The testimony is plausible and beyond reasonable doubt, so we may at least provisionally infer that the setting of this narrative is the Capernaum synagogue.

The Sabbath setting (Mark 3:2) is integral to the plot of the episode. Twelftree has argued that Mark is responsible for setting this scene in a synagogue,[126] and I have already responded to the redaction-critical dimension of his argument in chapter 4. Nevertheless, it is worth drawing attention to the plausibility of the synagogue setting. If the Sabbath date of the cure is essential to the story, as is the public performance of the cure, then it would seem as though a synagogue would be the natural setting to expect, given that we know that public assemblies took place in synagogue settings on the Sabbath. The assumed public nature of the gathering itself strongly implies a synagogue context. Thus, the synagogue setting is plausible, not only because it is stated in Mark 3:1, but also because it is implied by the circumstances of the story.

The Markan and Matthean versions do not indicate Jesus's purpose in entering the synagogue. Only Luke mentions that Jesus taught in the synagogue on this occasion (Luke 6:6). This may have been an inference on Luke's part, based on his knowledge that Jesus typically taught in synagogues. Nevertheless, it is a reasonable inference, and one with which I am inclined to agree, since it fits with what is known about the general pattern of Jesus's program, as discussed in this chapter and in chapters 5 and 6.

---

124. The treatment of this episode here assumes Markan priority, contra, e.g., C. S. Mann, *Mark: A New Translation with Introduction and Commentary* (AYB; New York: Doubleday, 1986), 24143.

125. France, *Mark*, 148–49; Collins, *Mark*, 206.

126. Twelftree, "Jesus and the Synagogue," 3131.

As with the liberation of the woman with the bent back, it is Jesus who takes the initiative and calls the man with the withered hand forward.[127] He is not sought. Rather, it is he who seeks out the infirm to heal them. This indicates the intentionality of the act. On the one hand, we might consider this to reflect Jesus's charity or mercy, which are undoubtedly virtues in Jewish thought.[128] However, it also reflects the relation of healing to the mission of Jesus, as has been attested throughout this chapter. He seeks to heal the infirm because it falls within his mandate of announcing and bringing about the reign of God.

In terms of the spatial dimension of the synagogue building,[129] it is likely that the healing of the man took place in the open middle floor area, since Jesus asks the man to "get up [from your seat] into the middle" (v. 3; Gk. Ἔγειρε εἰς τὸ μέσον).[130] Since Jesus does not heal by touching in this episode, it is likely that he spoke either from the doorway, as we are not directly told that he took a seat, or from wherever he was seated if we imagine that he took a seat before speaking. Thus, we should imagine that the miracle was on display, so to speak, for all to see. Understanding the spatial element of this event helps us to better understand the expressly public nature of the healing, and illuminates the intent behind Jesus telling the man to rise from his seat and go "into the middle."

The expressly intended public performance of this healing in the middle of the synagogue goes against the grain of the Markan tendency toward secrecy.[131] This is a fairly good indication that pre-Markan tradition lies behind this pericope.[132] Moreover, it speaks to the fully public nature of the historical Jesus's synagogue program, including healings.

Not only does Jesus take the initiative in calling the man forward, he is also the first and only party reported to have spoken in the narrative.[133] In this case, it is Jesus who provokes the Pharisees with the act of healing and the legal question offered in v. 4. The Pharisees do not

---

127. Cf. Boring, *Mark*, 93–94; Collins, *Mark*, 208.
128. E.g., Tob 1:3–8; 4:5–11; Sir 4:1–10.
129. This incident likely takes place in Capernaum, and as discussed in chapter 3, Capernaum had a synagogue building in the first century C.E., as is indicated by the archaeological evidence of the stone basalt pavement beneath the monolithic late antique limestone synagogue. See *ASSB*, no. 8. Thus, it is justified to think of this incident taking place within a synagogue building.
130. Compare the NRSV of Mark 6:3, which reads "come forward." I consider this to be a problematic rendering, since it does not take the spatial context of a synagogue building into account. I am generally in agreement here with Runesson, Binder, and Olsson, *ASSB*, 81.
131. Cf. France, *Mark*, 150.
132. Note that it is an index, not a criterion. See appendix A.
133. Cf. Boring, *Mark*, 93.

offer a reply, as we are told that "they were silent." The negative reception of the act and its accompanying legal teaching in v. 4 is instead expressed in the plot hatched against Jesus outside the synagogue by the Pharisees with the Herodians in v. 6.

The question "is it lawful to do good or to do harm on the Sabbath, to save life or to kill?" that Jesus asks in v. 4 requires some comment. What does this mean? The question frames the necessity of the healing in binary terms of doing good or doing harm, saving a life or killing. This seems intuitively odd, given that the disease in question is a withered hand, and is not life threatening. Allowance is made in early *halakha* for saving a life on the Sabbath,[134] but this would not be directly applicable to the situation in Mark 3:1–6, since no life is in danger.

A convincing interpretation of the intent behind this saying has been proposed by Sven-Olav Back.[135] The Greek word translated as "life" in the NRSV is ψυχή, which can also be translated as "soul." The Hebrew equivalent of ψυχή is נפש. Back notes that, in the Hebrew Bible, disease is construed as a threat to the נפש, which is understood to be in or near "the pit" or *Sheol* because of illness.[136] He proposes that Jesus shared this view of illness, and thus, for Jesus, "even healing a withered hand (as in Mark 3:1–6) is saving a נפש (ψυχή)."[137] Furthermore, Back identifies an eschatological facet of Jesus's saying in Mark 3:4. Just as Jesus understood his healing of the woman with the bent back in Luke 13:10–17 to have an eschatological element insofar as he saw it as releasing her from Satan's bonds, so too does his interpretation of healing a withered hand as "saving a soul" have an eschatological valence. According to Back, within the context of Jesus's healing activity, Mark 3:4 "indicates what happens when a diseased person is confronted with the eschatological and salvific reign of God."[138] A parallel to this idea can be found in 1QHa XI, 19–37, which describes the salvation and renewal of a soul (נפש) from the pit within the eschatological context of the defeat of Belial in the "war of the heroes of heaven" (XI, 36–37). Within Jesus's thought, healing miracles both signify and instantiate the outbreak of God's eschatological reign and the present salvation from the conditions of diabolic domination that it brings.

---

134. E.g., *m. Yoma* 8:6; *t. Shab.* 9:22, 15:11–17; On this, see Kazen, *Scripture, Interpretation, or Authority?*, 84–100; Lutz Doering, *Schabbat: Sabbathalacha und -praxis im antiken Judentum und Urchristentum* (Texts and Studies in Ancient Judaism 78; Tübingen: Mohr Siebeck, 1999), 566–68.

135. Back, "Jesus and the Sabbath," 2625–27.

136. E.g., Job 33:22; Ps 6:5, 30:3–4, 88:4, 107:18.

137. Back, "Jesus and the Sabbath," 2626.

138. Ibid., 2627.

Jesus's saying in Mark 3:4 must be understood as a public challenge, not against the Sabbath law itself, but against any interpretation of the Sabbath law which would consider it forbidden to heal disease and do good on the Sabbath. That the healing also takes place in the central floor area of the synagogue also speaks to the fact that this is a challenge. The silence of Jesus's opponents in v. 4 is curious, especially within a synagogue context wherein discussion and debate over the interpretation of the Law was expected. It is important to recall that more was on the line than just the validity of a given interpretation of the Law. Honor, personal reputation and standing within the community, were also at stake in public synagogue debates.[139] Mark 3:1-6 can be understood as a challenge-riposte scenario in which honor was on the line.[140] In light of this, the rhetorical impact of a miracle in the public setting of a legal dispute should not be underestimated, especially when the miracle is the subject of the dispute. The rhetorical phrasing of Jesus's question would also have made a reply difficult. By equating his act of healing with doing good, the alternative to which is doing evil, and saving a life, the alternative to which is killing, Jesus makes it difficult to raise an objection.[141] The sociopolitical dimension of this pericope is palpable. The event takes place in the very middle of the public assembly. At issue is the interpretation of the Law, and future normative *praxis* along with it.

What was Jesus's motivation for healing the man? Gerd Theissen and Anette Merz suggest that three motivations lie behind Jesus's Sabbath conflicts: an ethical motive, an eschatological motive, and a messianic motive (the demonstration of Jesus' authority).[142] In Mark 3:1-6, there is little evidence to suggest that the demonstration of Jesus's authority or the matter of his messianic identity directly figure into the conflict.[143] However, v. 4 does indicate a concern with ethics, insofar as Jesus asks whether or not it is lawful to "do good" (Gk. ἀγαθοποιῆσαι) on the Sabbath, which is well in line with his teachings elsewhere on the love command and the importance of helping a neighbour in need.[144] A

---

139. See chapter 3 above, cf. Malina and Rohrbaugh, 370.
140. See Malina and Rohrbaugh, 334-35.
141. Cf. Collins, *Mark*, 208-9.
142. Theissen and Merz, *Historical Jesus*, 369.
143. On the Markan level, it is possible to see Mark 3:1-6 as a demonstration of Jesus's lordship over the Sabbath in accordance with the saying that directly precedes it in Mark 2:28. Nevertheless, we are dealing here with the historical level.
144. Mark 12:28-31; Matt 22:37-40; Luke 10:25-37. On Jesus's ethics and this passage, see Luz, *Matthew*, 2:189-90.

concern for eschatology is also reflected, as argued above, by the reference to "saving a soul."

The identification of the dual motivation of ethics and eschatology behind the act of healing helps us to get at the inside of the event. By healing the man, Jesus was not only modelling the sort of ethic that the restored Israel was to practice, but also simultaneously instantiating and demonstrating the coming of the Kingdom. The two are, of course, completely intertwined. The ethic of charity, summed up in Jesus's double love command (Mark 12:28–31 and parallels), is the legal praxis of the Kingdom.

Ched Myers has suggested that the event in question represents "carefully staged political theater."[145] Though I would not call the event "staged," the intentionally public setting of the healing, in the middle of the synagogue floor, suggests that there is some truth to this. It is a political challenge, as well as a demonstration of the coming of the Kingdom and of its ethic. In Jesus's understanding, the Kingdom had come into the midst of the synagogue in Capernaum.

The political character[146] of the healing and challenge that Jesus offered in the synagogue is evident in the plot hatched against Jesus in v. 6 by the Pharisees and the Herodians.[147] Jesus's public actions in the synagogue were viewed as a threat. They imperiled the dominance of the Pharisaic interpretation of the Law in the public synagogues of Galilee, damaged the honor of Jesus's interlocutors (cf. Luke 13:17), and served as a source for the growing recognition of Jesus's claimed divine agency, and thus, authority. Not all politics takes place at the level of nations and empires. As Runesson writes, "a certain town or village could thus be dominated by an influential group striving to control the local-official level ideologically."[148] Thus, the hostile tone toward the Pharisees in the Gospels can be explained by the fact that both Jesus and the movement around him, on the one hand, and the Pharisees on the other tried to exert influence over the public synagogue, and in the end, the Jesus movement was less successful at achieving this end.[149]

---

145. Myers, *Binding the Strong Man*, 162.

146. In general agreement with John P. Meier, "The Historical Jesus and the Historical Herodians," *JBL* 119 (2000): 740–46 (743).

147. Only Mark mentions the collusion of the Pharisees with the Herodians. Luke does not specifically mention the plot (Luke 6:11), instead saying that an unspecified group, presumably the scribes and Pharisees (cf. v. 7) "discussed with one another what they might do to Jesus." Matthew mentions the plot, but omits the Herodians (Matt 12:14). Matthew's omission of the mention of the Herodians can be explained as an attempt to lay blame more squarely upon the Pharisees.

148. Runesson, *Origins*, 221.

149. Ibid., 484.

The hostility of the Pharisees toward Jesus and his particular interpretation of scripture can likewise be understood as an instantiation of a power struggle over control over the local-official level of the towns of Galilee. Moreover, in light of the issue of control, the Pharisees' collusion with the Herodians in Mark 3:6 makes a good deal of sense. Although there has been some dispute over their identity in the past,[150] the Herodians in Mark 3:6 are best understood as supporters, servants, and officials of Herod Antipas.[151] Both the Pharisees and the Herodians would have had a vested interest in exercising control at the local-official level. Moreover, Jesus's prior association with John the Baptist, who was imprisoned and killed by Herod Antipas,[152] may have made him suspect in the eyes of Antipas's supporters. The overt and flagrant public challenge in the synagogue of Capernaum narrated by Mark 3:1–6 would likely have drawn their attention to him.

The historical plausibility of Mark 3:1–6 has sometimes been called in question. As Meier and Sanders both note, Jesus does not actually perform any work in healing the man from a distance by speaking.[153] That may well be, but as I have argued above, Jesus has transgressed a particular *interpretation* of the Sabbath law. As Kazen has noted, if no one thought of healing through speech as problematic in the Second Temple period, then where did the evangelists get the idea that it was? Early rabbinic literature contains a number of prohibitions against healing on the Sabbath using medicine or, more importantly for our purposes, prayer.[154] According to *t. Shab.* 16:22, "they do not pray for a sick person on the Sabbath." The prohibition of prayer for the sick indicates that healing of any sort, whether through manual labor or otherwise, was regarded as unacceptable by some.

As can be ascertained from the above discussion, Mark 3:1–6 also fits in fairly well with what we know of the public synagogue at the time of Jesus. It reflects synagogue architecture, and the synagogue's function as a place where the Law was interpreted and disputed. The silence of Jesus's opponents is curious, but that can be explained in light of the social functions of rhetoric and honor that we have discussed above.

---

150. For a summary of the issues, see Meier, "Historical Herodians," 740–42.
151. Cf. Josephus, *War*, 1.319. I am in agreement on this point with Helen Bond, "Herodian Dynasty," in *Dictionary of Jesus and the Gospels*, 2nd ed., ed. Joel B. Green, Jeannine K. Brown, and Nicholas Perrin (Downers Grove: IVP Academic, 2013), 379–82 (382). On the enmity between Jesus and Herod Antipas in the Gospels, see Jensen, *Herod Antipas in Galilee*, 109–24.
152. Mark 1:14, 6:14–29; Matt 14:1–12; Luke 9:7–9; Josephus, *Ant.*, 18.116–119.
153. Sanders, *Jewish Law*, 21; Meier, *Marginal Jew*, 4:254; Geza Vermes, *Jesus the Jew*, 25.
154. Kazen, *Scripture, Interpretation, or Authority?*, 95–100. See *m. Yoma* 8:6; *m. Shab.* 14:3–4; *t. Shab.* 12:8–14; *t. Shab.* 16:22.

It also fits perfectly into our picture of the past, the web of evidence, inference, and imagination that we have been constructing throughout the present work.

It is hard to regard the whole story as a free composition by Mark.[155] The fact that it goes against the grain of Markan messianic secrecy has already been mentioned above. Moreover, as Twelftree has argued, given the fact that there is no evidence that Sabbath healing was an issue for the early church, the story is best explained as having roots in "the memories of Jesus' audience."[156]

It is, of course, necessary to be aware that the story has been remembered in light of Jesus's eventual crucifixion, just like everything else in the tradition. While it is quite likely that the Pharisees and Herodians discussed how to bring Jesus down,[157] it is important to recall that it was not ultimately they who brought about Jesus's arrest and execution, despite the tradition's tendency to lump the Jewish leadership all together.

Matthew's version of the narrative in Matthew 12:9–14 differs somewhat from his Markan source. The assembly is not silent, but rather, asks Jesus directly whether or not it is lawful to cure on the Sabbath. Jesus replies with a halakhic argument in v. 11: "Suppose one of you has only one sheep and it falls into a pit on the Sabbath; will you not lay hold of it and lift it out? How much more valuable is a human being than a sheep! So it is lawful to do good on the Sabbath."

How should we interpret and apply this data on the historical level? Intriguingly, the Matthean version reflects the context of a public synagogue more clearly than the Lukan or Markan versions. It features back-and-forth discussion and halakhic debate of the "how much more" form. The specific example of an animal that has fallen into a pit on the Sabbath is attested in other early Jewish legal literature, which indicates that it reflects a common stream of argumentation in the Judaism of Jesus' day.[158]

Nevertheless, the priority of Mark's telling of the event should be

---

55. See also Christopher Tuckett, "Jesus and the Sabbath," in *Jesus in Continuum*, ed. Tom Holmén (WUNT 289; Tübingen: Mohr Siebeck, 2012), 411–42 (435–42).

56. Twelftree, *Jesus the Miracle Worker*, 306. Cf. also Arland J. Hultgren, *Jesus and His Adversaries* (Minneapolis: Augsburg Fortress, 1979), 82–84; Rudolf Pesch, *Das Markusevangelium* (Herders theologischer Kommentar zum Neuen Testament; 2 vols.; Frieburg im Breisgau: Herder, 1976), 1:195–96; Davies and Allison, *Matthew*, 2:316.

57. Cf. Twelftree, *Jesus the Miracle Worker*, 305–6.

58. CD XI, 13–14; 4Q265 7, I, 6–7; b. Shab. 128b. Similarly, see t. Shab. 15:11–17. On this, see Meier, *Marginal Jew*, 4:244–245; Luz, *Matthew*, 2:187–88; Keener, *Matthew*, 358; Kazen, *Scripture, Interpretation, or Authority?*, 108–10; Phillip Sigal, *The Halakhah of Jesus of Nazareth According to the Gospel of Matthew* (Studies in Biblical Literature 18; Atlanta: Society of Biblical Literature, 2007), 167–68.

maintained.[159] This does not mean that the Matthean evidence should be dismissed altogether. A similar type of argument involving the rescue of a trapped and fallen animal on the Sabbath is attested elsewhere in the Jesus tradition, in Luke 14:5. Thus, it is clear that Jesus was generally remembered as having made this sort of "how much more" (*qal wahomer*) argument in the context of a dispute over healing on the Sabbath. As Meier writes, Jesus's rhetorical questions about Sabbath observance fit into the *Sitz im Leben* of early-first-century Jewish halakhic debates, and moreover, "fit perfectly into a credible portrait of a truly Jewish Jesus."[160]

How, then, should we interpret the evidence of Matthew 12:9–14? Notably, this is only one of two episodes in all of Matthew that take place in a synagogue, the other being the rejection at Nazareth in Matthew 13:54–58. While Mark apparently sets the episode in the Capernaum synagogue, the geographical location of the incident is not specified in Matthew. In my opinion, Matthew has drawn on traditional remembered material about Jesus in order to formulate a more general summary picture of Jesus's synagogue disputations, including the types of things Jesus would have said and done in synagogues, and most importantly for Matthew, the resulting antagonization of the Pharisees. Thus, we may conclude that the incident represents the *vox Jesu* despite being a Matthean literary construction, and moreover, that this was probably the author's intention.

Conclusion

In this chapter, we have examined how Jesus's healings and exorcisms related to his typical synagogue activities of teaching and proclamation. For Jesus, healings and exorcisms were intrinsic to the realization of the reign of God and were part of the outpouring of eschatological blessings and restoration that came along with it. Rather than seeing healings and exorcisms as a regular part of synagogue activity in the late Second Temple period, I have argued that they were particular to Jesus and related to his mission within the synagogues of the Land. Moreover, from an institution-critical perspective, the rhetorical impact that miracles would have had on public assemblies as a demonstration of Jesus's divine agency and the present realization of the

---

159. Cf. Luz, *Matthew*, 2:186–87; Meier, *Marginal Jew*, 4:259–60; Kazen, *Scripture, Interpretation, or Authority?*, 111.
160. Meier, *Marginal Jew*, 4:267; cf. Theissen and Merz, *Historical Jesus*, 367.

reign of God is significant. The exorcism of the demoniac in the synagogue at Capernaum and the liberation of the woman with the bent back demonstrate the eschatological nature of Jesus's synagogue program as well as the connection between Jesus's proclamation of the Kingdom of God and the overthrow of diabolic dominion. Exorcisms thus appear to have played an important and particular role within Jesus's aims and synagogue program.

The three narratives that we have examined in this chapter have also highlighted the intensely political nature of Jesus's synagogue activities. As with discussion of scripture, the lines between "religion" and "politics" are blurred where Jesus's miracles within synagogue settings are concerned. The healing of the man with the withered hand and the liberation of the woman with the bent back are also both intertwined with conflicts over the interpretation of the Jewish Law, which speaks to Jesus's perspective on the Law and his intention to restore the Law along with the people, as discussed in chapter 5.

This chapter has also highlighted the plausibility of these incidents specifically *within a synagogue context*. The public synagogue setting is integral to the interpretation and understanding of the data examined in this chapter, and should not be bracketed off or considered secondary. Considering these passages in light of their setting within public synagogues rather than in spite of that setting has not only served to help demonstrate the plausibility of these incidents, but also, to more firmly situate Jesus within the historical context of Jewish public society of the late Second Temple period.

8

"I am the Bread of Life":
The Teaching in the Synagogue at
Capernaum (John 6:25–71)

Introduction

Jesus's teaching in the synagogue at Capernaum in John 6:25–71, known as the "Bread of Life" discourse, is the only incident reported to take place in a synagogue in the Fourth Gospel. It is perhaps the most challenging single piece of evidence to interpret that will be considered in this project. However, as we shall see, it is also one of the most potentially revealing about Jesus's aims, self-understanding, and synagogue program.

Much of the interpretive difficulty so far as the historical level of this passage is concerned stems from the nature of the Fourth Gospel. The Gospel of John has only very recently begun to play a more important role in historical Jesus research.[1] In fact, the reticence surrounding the

---

[1] For a summary and evaluation of the history of scholarship on the use of the Fourth Gospel in historical Jesus research, see Dwight Moody Smith, "John: A Source For Jesus Research?" in *Critical Appraisals of Critical Views*, vol. 1 of *John, Jesus, and History*, ed. Paul N. Anderson, Felix Just, and Tom Thatcher (SBL Symposium Series 44; Atlanta: Society of Biblical Literature, 2007), 165–78; cf. Dwight Moody Smith, "Jesus Tradition in the Gospel of John," in *Handbook for the Study of the His-*

use of the Johannine witness in historical Jesus research goes back to the very early years of the First Quest.[2] The details of the developments of recent scholarly conversation around the use of the Fourth Gospel as a historical source in Jesus research need not be recounted in full here. Suffice it to say, recent developments in scholarship have turned toward the recovery of the Johannine voice as a historically valuable source for the study of Jesus.

Applying the Johannine Witness as Historical Evidence

While it is clear that the Gospel of John is an important historical source for the life of Jesus, it must be recognized that it is not historical in quite the same way as the synoptics. The Gospel of John is, in agreement with Paul Anderson's summary of recent scholarship on the relationship of the Fourth Gospel to the historical Jesus, "a deeply theological narration of a story rooted in history."[3] What this means is that the author of the Gospel of John writes history through theological and narrative interpretation.[4] In the words of C. K. Barrett, "John presents in his one book both history and interpretation."[5]

The Johannine mnemonic tradition is undoubtedly theological, and the past is remembered and intentionally interpreted for the reader through its particular theological lens.[6] It is not possible to separate

torical Jesus, ed. Tom Holmén, and Stanley E. Porter (Leiden and Boston: Brill, 2011), 1997–2039; Paul N. Anderson, "The Jesus of History, the Christ of Faith, and the Gospel of John," in The Gospels: History and Christology: The Search of Joseph Ratzinger - Benedict XVI, 2 vols., ed. Bernardo Estrada, Ermenegildo Manicardi, and Armand Puig i Tàrrich (Rome: Libreria Editrice Vaticana, 2013), 2:63–81; See also Blomberg, Historical Reliability of John's Gospel, 17–22; Bond, Historical Jesus, 49–50. It is worth mentioning that there have been some relatively early outliers, e.g., C. H. Dodd, Historical Tradition in the Fourth Gospel (Cambridge: Cambridge University Press, 1963); and relatively more recently, Fredriksen, Jesus of Nazareth, esp. 220–25; Meier, A Marginal Jew, esp. 2:680, 694–98, 798–832, 908–14, 951–56.

2. E.g., David Friedrich Strauss, The Christ of Faith and the Jesus of History: A Critique of Schleiermacher's Life of Christ (Minneapolis: Fortress Press, 1977[1865]), esp. 52–92; Ferdinand Christian Baur, The Church History of the First Three Centuries, 3rd ed., 2 vols., trans. Allan Menzies (London: Williams and Norgate, 1878), esp. 1:25; Albert Schweitzer, The Quest of the Historical Jesus: First Complete Edition, trans. W. Montgomery, J.R. Coates, S. Cupitt, and J. Bowden (Minneapolis: Fortress Press, 2001), 80–83.

3. Paul N. Anderson, "Aspects of Historicity in the Fourth Gospel: Consensus and Convergences," in Critical Appraisals of Critical Views, vol. 1 of John, Jesus, and History, ed. Paul N. Anderson, Felix Just, and Tom Thatcher (SBL Symposium Series 44; Atlanta: Society of Biblical Literature, 2007), 379–86 (380).

4. Cf. Marianne Meye Thompson, "The 'Spiritual Gospel': How John the Theologian Writes History," in Critical Appraisals of Critical Views, vol. 1 of John, Jesus, and History, ed. Paul N. Anderson, Felix Just, and Tom Thatcher (SBL Symposium Series 44; Atlanta: Society of Biblical Literature, 2007), 103–7.

5. C. K. Barrett, The Gospel According to St. John: An Introduction with Commentary and Notes on the Greek Text (London: SPCK, 1960), 118.

6. In terms of the authorial intent of the Gospel of John, it is important to note that the author makes truth claims about the testimony of the Beloved Disciple in 19:35 and 21:24, cf. other gen-

"history" from "theological interpretation," nor is it necessary or appropriate to create a dichotomy between the two,[7] especially given that we are dealing with the work of an author who draws no such line himself. Rather than treating the data in the Fourth Gospel as *either* theological or historical, it is imperative to treat it as *evidence* of the historical events in which it roots its theological narrative and of the intentions of the historical actors who populate it.[8] That is how it will be treated in this project.[9] I am not seeking to convince the reader of one-to-one correlations between the data in John and the events of the past as though seeing is tantamount to knowing.[10] Rather, I aim at the more humble epistemological goal of making inferences about the past by applying the Johannine data as evidence.[11] Thus, the procedure is to infer the essence of what the Johannine Jesus teaches in our passage and, once it has been understood, to then determine how and whether it fits into the picture of the past that we have thus far been constructing.[12] As we will see, the substance, if not the language,[13] of

eral truth claims in 1:14–17. Reference to acts of remembrance of Jesus are found in 1:14, 2:19–22, 14:26, 19:35, 20:30–31, and 21:24–25. We need not separate the author's notion of theological truth entirely from historical truth. For the Johannine author, interpreted theological truth is inextricable from the historical events or memories of them from which it stems. Concerning the import of history for the theology of the Fourth Gospel, see Barrett, *St. John*, 17–118. On John's intention, see Bernier, *Aposynagōgos*, 114–125; for a slightly different approach, on Johannine truth claims and the complex intersection of history and theological narrative in the Fourth Gospel, see Andrew T. Lincoln, "'We Know That His Testimony is True': Johannine Truth Claims and Historicity," in *Critical Appraisals of Critical Views*, vol. 1 of *John, Jesus, and History*, ed. Paul N. Anderson, Felix Just, and Tom Thatcher (SBL Symposium Series 44; Atlanta: Society of Biblical Literature, 2007), 179–97.

7. Cf. Richard Bauckham, *The Testimony of the Beloved Disciple; Narrative, History, and Theology of the Gospel of John* (Grand Rapids: Eerdmans, 2007), 14, 27; Bernier, *Aposynagōgos*, 117. As Bernier writes, the author of the Fourth Gospel is "interested in history not despite but rather *because of* his theology."

8. This point is similar in spirit to that made by Tom Thatcher, *Why John Wrote*, 167.

9. In this, I am generally in line with the thought of Philipp F. Bartholomä, *The Johannine Discourses and the Teaching of Jesus in the Synoptics* (Texte und Arbeiten zum neutestamentlichen Zeitalter 57; Tübingen: Francke, 2012), 81: "the Johannine discourses have to be considered as historically authentic as long as they accurately represent the meaning and substance of what Jesus originally said. In accordance with the historiographical conventions of his own time, the author of the Fourth Gospel does not use direct speech in order to attempt to present a verbatim report of the words of Jesus. Instead he makes use of direct speech in order to communicate to his readers that he is giving them a reliable account of the content of Jesus' teaching. Whether he reached his own standards remains an open question. It will not do, however, to argue that what was reliable for first century readers is simply not reliable enough for us. The fact that John did not use direct speech in our modern way does not preclude him from presenting speeches which we could accept as an accurate or authentic rendition of the general substance of Jesus' teaching."

10. At any rate, this is an epistemologically problematic approach, cf. Lonergan, *Method in Theology*, 186, 238; Collingwood, *Idea of History*, 257–63.

11. This is accomplished by being attentive to the data, interpreting it, making judgments, and evaluating those judgments, cf. Lonergan, *Method in Theology*, 14, 181.

12. In accordance with the discussion concerning method in chapter 1. For further discussion, see appendices A and B.

13. On the difference in language between the synoptic and Johannine Jesus, see Jörg Frey, "From

the Johannine Jesus's teaching in John 6:25–71 reflects that of the synoptic Jesus,[14] and of the portrait of the historical Jesus that we are outlining here.

In my opinion, there is no doubt that Fourth Gospel is an important and valuable source for understanding the historical Jesus. However, in our capacities as historians, the nature of the Fourth Gospel does not permit us to treat it in the same manner that we might treat evidence from the Synoptic Gospels. The Fourth Gospel challenges us to think interpretively and inferentially, to understand its intentions and interpretive tendencies. Here, the need to interpret and understand the data before applying it as evidence is especially pronounced. If we are not willing to think inferentially, if we fall back into the dichotomy of "true" or "false" scissors-and-paste history, then we will be unable to grasp the significance of the vital historical evidence that the Fourth Gospel supplies. In the words of Jörg Frey, "the search for mere historical accuracy may miss the fundamental intention of the Gospel of John."[15] Thus, the aim of this chapter is not to simply demonstrate the "authenticity" or even plausibility of the data, but to understand what it means, and to grasp how John has intentionally presented history and interpretation intertwined. Only once this is done can we understand how and in what ways we can speak of plausibility and begin to think about how to draw inferences about the past from it.

Establishing the Setting

John 6:25–58 is explicitly located within the synagogue at Capernaum by a spatial comment in John 6:59: "he said these things while teaching in the synagogue in Capernaum" (Gk. ταῦτα εἶπεν ἐν συναγωγῇ διδάσκων ἐν Καφαρναούμ). Although some interpreters separate vv. 60–71 from 25–59, there is no explicit change of setting until 7:1. In my opinion, at least vv. 25–66 should be understood to take place in the Capernaum synagogue. This matter will be addressed further below.

---

the 'Kingdom of God' to 'Eternal Life,'" in *Glimpses of Jesus Through the Johannine Lens*, vol. 3 of *John, Jesus, and History*, ed. Paul N. Anderson, Felix Just, and Tom Thatcher (Atlanta: SBL, 2016), 439–58 (441–42).

14. In general agreement with the findings on this passage of Bartholomä, *Johannine Discourses*, 155–90. Bartholomä's review of the Bread of Life discourse concludes that, despite a lack of verbatim agreement with synoptic traditions, "the general picture is one of significant similarities in terms of content between John 6:22–59 and Matthew, Mark, and Luke," (190).

15. Frey, "From the 'Kingdom of God' to 'Eternal Life,'" 458. Further, he writes that "it is more promising to understand and appreciate the process of transformation that has happened not only to the story of Jesus but also (and even more) to the style of his teaching" (458).

The lack of an article attached to συναγωγῇ in v. 59 has led to the suggestion that a general assembly or gathering is in view here, rather than the institutional setting of a public synagogue.[16] However, there are good reasons to locate this passage within the setting of the public synagogue at Capernaum, rather than a general gathering. First, the lack of an article in prepositional phrases is not unusual, and does not preclude the translation of ἐν συναγωγῇ as "in the synagogue."[17] Second, the discourse that is described in John 6:25–71 fits very well within a public synagogue setting. The astute reader will note that the narrative of 6:25–71 coheres with the reconstruction of the synagogue presented in chapters 2 and 3 of this study. Our passage concerns back-and-forth public discussion of a narrative from the Torah, the giving of manna from heaven to the Israelites in Exodus 16 (cf. Num 11:4–9).[18] It is even possible, as some interpreters have suggested, that this discussion was sparked on the historical level by an unnarrated public Torah reading from this Exodus narrative.[19] Third, as Birger Olsson has argued, since the synagogue was the primary gathering place and the location of public scripture reading, "even if we emphasize the gathering more than the place, we are left with the question: where in Capernaum did this crowd of people come together?"[20] The obvious answer, given its attestation in the archaeological record and elsewhere in the Gospels,[21] is the public synagogue of Capernaum.

It is worth pointing out that the above discussion of the setting of the narrative of John 6:25–71 within the context of the public synagogue at Capernaum also speaks to the historical plausibility of the passage in a general sense. By this, I mean that it depicts Jesus engaged in the discussion of scripture, both the Torah (Exodus 16) and Nevi'im (Isa 54:13, cited in v. 45), which would be expected within a synagogue set-

---

16. Leon Morris, *The Gospel According to John* (rev. ed.; NICNT; Grand Rapids: Eerdmans, 1995), 337. This option is raised but rejected by Brown, *John*, 284; Birger Olsson, "'All My Teaching Was Done in Synagogues . . .' (John 18,20)," in *Theology and Christology in the Fourth Gospel: Essays By the Members of the SNTS Johannine Writings Seminar*, ed. Gilbert van Belle, J.G. van der Watt, and P.J. Martin (Leuven: Peeters, 2005), 203–24 (221).

17. Cf. Olsson, "All My Teaching," 221.

18. Olsson, "All My Teaching," 221; Steven A. Graham, "Semitic Language and Syntax Within the Speech of the Johannine Jesus," in *Glimpses of Jesus Through the Johannine Lens* , vol. 3 of *John, Jesus, and History*, ed. Paul N. Anderson, Felix Just, and Tom Thatcher (Atlanta: Society of Biblical Literature), 407–21 (418–19). Although relying on a now-outdated conception of synagogue liturgy, see also Peder Borgen, *Bread from Heaven: An Exegetical Study of the Concept of Manna in the Gospel of John and the Writings of Philo* (NovTSupp 10; Leiden: Brill, 1965), 28–98.

19. Gary M. Burge, *The Gospel of John* (NIV Application Commentary; Grand Rapids: Zondervan, 2000), 197; Andreas J. Köstenberger, *John* (Baker Exegetical Commentary on the New Testament; Grand Rapids: Baker Academic, 2004), 209.

20. Olsson, "All My Teaching," 221.

21. Mark 1:21; Luke 4:31–38, 7:1–5; *ASSB* nos. 4–8.

ting.[22] Moreover, the extended teaching and discourse here provide us with exactly the sort of evidence concerning Jesus's synagogue teaching that we should expect, given the evangelists' unanimous claim concerning the centrality of the synagogue within Jesus's mission (see chapter 5), but which is otherwise lacking, apart from the Lukan version of the incident in the Nazareth synagogue.[23] We will further discuss other aspects of the passage's plausibility or implausibility below, after we have interpreted the data.

Interpreting the Bread of Life Discourse as Historical Evidence

The main body of John 6:25–71 unfolds as an open discussion between Jesus and members of the assembled public. Especially from v. 31 onward, the topic of the discussion is closely tied to the story of the giving of the manna in Exodus 16.[24] Notably, unlike Mark 3:1–6 (and parallels), which is set in the same synagogue, no members of another faction are mentioned, nor does Jesus get into a halakhic legal debate as in Luke 13:10–17. Jesus's conversation partners in vv. 25–58 are referred to either in the third-person plural (vv. 25, 28, 30, 32, 34, 35, 42, 43, 53), referring back to "the crowd" (Gk. ὁ ὄχλος) of v. 22–24, or as οἱ Ἰουδαῖοι ("the Jews"; vv. 41, 52). Here, the term is used generically to refer to residents of the Land (עם הארץ), and does not indicate that they are from Judea in the south, nor is it used to distance the author or Jesus from them.[25] In this case, it denotes the common people of the Capernaum assembly. We should note that they are not hostile to Jesus, nor are they predisposed against his propositions. Thus, what is depicted here is an attempt by Jesus to teach and persuade the public (see chapter 5) to accept what he is teaching rather than a conflict or legal controversy with members of a rival faction.

Within the Johannine narrative, John 6:25–58 functions as an interpretation of the event of the feeding of the five thousand (6:1–15).[26]

---

22. Note that I am not making a specific claim about the plausibility of Jesus's particular reported speech here.
23. Cf. Blomberg, *Historical Reliability of John's Gospel*, 127.
24. That Exod 16 is specifically in view has been convincingly shown by Borgen, *Bread from Heaven*, 59–98; cf. Peder Borgen, "Observations on the Midrashic Character of John 6," *ZNW* 54 (1963): 232–40. See also Jerome H. Neyrey, *The Gospel of John* (NCBC; Cambridge: Cambridge University Press, 2007), 124.
25. Compare the usage in Josephus *Ant.*, passim, or Josephus, *War*, passim. See Gutbrod, *TDNT*, 3:369–91.
26. On the relationship between vv. 1–15 and vv. 25–34, see Maarten J. J. Menken, "Some Remarks on the Course of the Dialogue: John 6:25–34," in *Studies in John's Gospel and Epistles: Collected Essays* (Contributions to Biblical Exegesis & Theology 77; Leuven: Peeters, 2015), 271–83.

The direct interpretive connection between the two is indicated by the first words that Jesus speaks to the crowd in vv. 26–27. We cannot separate memories of the past from the interpretation of the past, and so, whether or not the historical dialogue in the synagogue at Capernaum was offered as a comment on a feeding event is beyond my ability to say with certainty in my capacity as a historian. What is clear, however, is that both the feeding in 6:1–15 and the discourse in vv. 25–58 elicit comparisons between Jesus and Moses. The relationship of Jesus to Moses has come up already in chapter 5, and given its centrality to the discourse in John 6:25–58, we will pay particular attention to this issue in the interpretation to follow.

In v. 28, Jesus is asked what must be done in order to "perform the works of God," to which he replies, "this is the work of God, that you believe in him whom he has sent" (v. 29). Although the phrase "works of God" can refer to mighty things that God has done,[27] in this context, it more likely refers to God's commandments,[28] naturally calling the Torah and covenant to mind.[29]

It is striking that in his response to the question of v. 28, Jesus associates "the work of God," which has a distinct covenantal valence, with belief in him. More specifically, it is "belief" (πιστεύω) in "him whom he [God] has sent," which is Jesus himself. Thus, that belief is bound up with his sending, his mission. Again, if we recognize this as a Johannine interpretation of Jesus, we must nevertheless also recognize it as a dimension of the *remembered* Jesus. Thus, we must ask what this memory of the Johannine Jesus's notion of "belief" or "trust" in himself might have meant for the *historical* Jesus if we are to have any hope of understanding its place in our historical reconstruction. Data cannot be reasonably dismissed apart from understanding, determining what it means for the investigation.[30] This is not historical presumption, it is historical interpretation, a prerequisite for historical judg-

---

27. E.g., consider the usage of this phrase in the Qumran material: 1QS IV, 4; 1QM XIII, 9; 1QH XIII, 36; CD XIII, 7–8. See Köstenberger, *John*, 208; Morris, *John*, 319, no. 80. A synoptic parallel can be found in Matt 5:16 (cf. Bartholomä, *Johannine Discourses*, 165).

28. CD II, 14–15; Bar 2:9–10. Cf. Paul N. Anderson, "John and Qumran: Discovery and Interpretation Over Sixty Years," in *John, Qumran, and the Dead Sea Scrolls: Sixty Years of Discovery and Debate*, ed. Mary L. Coloe and Tom Thatcher (Early Judaism and Its Literature 32; Atlanta: Society of Biblical Literature, 2011), 15–50 (41); Craig S. Keener, *The Gospel of John: A Commentary*, 2 vols. (Peabody: Hendrickson, 2003), 1:678.

29. Cf. "works of the Law" in the NT, e.g., Rom 3:28, 4:2; Gal 2:16, 3:2–12; Jas 2:14–26. See also 4QMMT, cf. Martin Abegg, "Paul, 'Works of the Law,' and MMT," *BAR* 20, no. 6 (1994): 24–36; N. T. Wright, "4QMMT and Paul: Justification, 'Works,' and Eschatology," in *History and Exegesis: New Testament Essays in Honor of Dr. E. Earle Ellis for His 80th Birthday*, ed. Aang-Won Son (New York and London: T&T Clark, 2006), 104–32.

30. Cf. Collingwood, *Idea of History*, 275.

ments. According to Collingwood, the historian's overarching picture of the past, rooted in evidence, serves as the "touchstone" for historical criticism.[31] In accordance with this, we are at this point attempting to determine whether, and if so, how, this data fits into the picture of the past that is emerging from the evidence examined thus far.

On the historical level, belief or trust in Jesus would entail the recognition of Jesus's divine agency, and thus, the truth of his message and proclamation. An exhortation to believe in Jesus's message is associated with his synagogue program in Mark 1:15, and as seen in our study of the incident in the synagogue at Nazareth (Luke 4:16–30 and parallels) above, rejection of the messenger entails rejection of the message. Thus, for the historical Jesus, trust or belief in him was tied up with the recognition and acceptance of his role as prophetic messenger, and thus, also his message.[32] If Jesus was not believed, then his message would not be either. There was, for the historical Jesus, no distinction between belief in the proclaimer and belief in the proclaimed.

There are hints and shades of the historical Jesus's eschatological aim to restore Israel throughout John 6:25–58. This especially comes out in v. 44 (cf. also vv. 37–40), wherein Jesus speaks of those who come to him and are drawn to him by the Father, whom he will raise up "on the last day" (Gk. ἐν τῇ ἐσχάτῃ ἡμέρᾳ). The language of "coming" to Jesus can be found in the synoptic tradition as well in Matthew 11:28. The connection here between eschatology and a group drawn to Jesus brings to mind the eschatological restoration of Israel and the act of gathering the chosen people of God.[33] This stands out all the more in light of the overt Exodus theme that runs throughout our passage, which itself recalls the liberation, gathering, and formation of the nation of Israel. Within the prophetic literature of the Hebrew Bible, there is a tradition of conceiving of the restoration of Israel as a new Exodus.[34] It is my contention that this is the essential background

---

31. Collingwood, *Idea of History*, 242–45. On this, see appendix A.

32. Bartholomä likewise concludes that the content of John 6:29 is generally present in the synoptics: "Both the Johannine and the Synoptic Jesus regard themselves as God's envoy and the importance to believe in Jesus as the one sent by God is expressed in the synoptic teaching tradition as well" (*Johannine Discourses*, 165). On πιστεύω in the Fourth Gospel, see Keener, *John*, 1:25–28. On faith in the NT in general, see Rudolf Bultmann, "πιστεύω" TDNT 6:197–228. Bartholomä identifies a synoptic parallel to v. 29b in Matt 10:40, cf. Luke 10:16 (*Johannine Discourses*, 164–65). Other references to "belief" (πιστεύω) in the synoptic tradition in relation to the aims of Jesus are found in Mark 1:15, 5:36, 9:42 (cf. Matt 18:6).

33. Cf. Horsley and Thatcher, *Renewal of Israel*, 152, though they are speaking about John 12:32. A similar notion of God's *basileia* in relation to a restorative, salvific "gathering" can be found in Tob 13:1–6. On "gathering" and Tob 13:1–6, see chapter 5 above.

34. See Rodrigo J. Morales, *The Spirit and the Restoration of Israel: New Exodus and New Creation motifs in Galatians* (WUNT 2.282; Tübingen: Mohr Siebeck, 2010); John Dennis, "The Presence and Function

for interpreting John 6:25–58 on the historical level. We have already discussed the image of restoration as a reenactment of the Exodus in Ezekiel 20:33–37 in chapter 5. It will serve out purposes to consider just a few more pertinent examples:

> There shall be a highway from Assyria for the remnant that is left of his people, as there was for Israel when they came up from the land of Egypt. (Isa 11:16)

> Therefore, the days are surely coming, says the Lord, when it shall no longer be said, "As the Lord lives who brought the people of Israel up out of the land of Egypt," but "As the Lord lives who brought the people of Israel up out of the land of the north and out of all the lands where he had driven them." For I will bring them back to their own land that I gave to their ancestors. (Jer 16:14–15)

> They shall return to the land of Egypt, and Assyria shall be their king, because they have refused to return to me. . . . They shall come trembling like birds from Egypt, and like doves from the land of Assyria; and I will return them to their homes, says the LORD. (Hos 11:5, 11).

> I will bring them home from the land of Egypt, and gather them from Assyria; I will bring them to the land of Gilead and to Lebanon, until there is no room for them. They shall pass through the sea of distress, and the waves of the sea shall be struck down, and all the depths of the Nile dried up. The pride of Assyria shall be laid low, and the scepter of Egypt shall depart. (Zech 10:10–11)

The currency of this idea in the late Second Temple period is strongly reflected in the actions of Theudas and the enigmatic Egyptian, the Jewish sign prophets:

> Now it came to pass, while Fadus was procurator of Judea, that a certain magician, whose name was Theudas, persuaded a great part of the people to take their effects with them, and follow him to the river Jordan; for he told them he was a prophet, and that he would, by his own command, divide the river, and afford them an easy passage over it; and many were deluded by his words. (Josephus, *Ant.* 20.97–98)

of Second Exodus-Restoration Imagery in John 6," *SNTU* 30 (2005): 105–21 (105–6); Rikki E. Watts, *Isaiah's New Exodus in Mark* (Grand Rapids: Baker, 1997); Richard Bauckham, *The Jewish World Around the New Testament* (Tübingen: Mohr Siebeck, 2008), 339–40; N. T. Wright, "The Lord's Prayer as a Paradigm for Christian Prayer," in *Into God's Presence: Prayer in the New Testament*, ed. Richard N. Longenecker (Grand Rapids: Eerdmans, 2001), 132–54; Brant Pitre, "The Lord's Prayer and the New Exodus," *Letter & Spirit* 2 (2006): 69–96.

There came out of Egypt about this time to Jerusalem, one that said he was a prophet, and advised the multitude of the common people to go along with him to the Mount of Olives, as it was called, which lay over against the city, and at the distance of five furlongs. He said farther, that he would show them from hence, how, at his command, the walls of Jerusalem would fall down; and he promised that he would procure them an entrance into the city through those walls, when they were fallen down. (Josephus, *Ant.* 20.169–170)

Both these figures drew upon the prophetic tradition of a second Exodus.[35] Theudas' attempt to cross the Jordan again was a literal reenactment of the Exodus, reentering the Land where the original Exodus had taken place, and the Egyptian's plan to bring down the walls of Jerusalem, and so, gain entrance to the city mirrors Joshua's conquest of Jericho.[36] A second Exodus, that is, the renewal of Israel and her covenant, is in view here in John 6:25–58 as well.[37] This will become clearer as our discussion progresses below.

Jesus supports his statement in v. 44 with a citation from Isaiah 54:13: "they shall all be taught by God," saying that those who have heard and learned from the Father will come to him. Isaiah 54 is concerned with the gathering (cf. 54:7) and restoration of Israel. Thus, the implication of the citation of this passage by Jesus is that the day of restoration has come, and that God is teaching the people through Jesus.[38] According to John 6:45, those who have "heard and learned," presumably those who have not only heard but have also accepted the teachings, will come to Jesus. As we know from v. 44, only those who come to Jesus will be raised up on the last day. Thus, according to our passage, Jesus understands the regathered Israel who will experience the eschatological blessings to be those who have "come to him" and accepted his teachings. This is very much coherent with the portrait of Jesus that has thus far emerged from the web of evidence, inference, and imagination that we have been constructing. Although there is a distinctly Johannine tenor to the language and presentation of the material, the voice of the historical Jesus known to us also from the synoptics can be heard here if we are only willing to listen.

---

35. Cf. Paul W. Barnett, "The Jewish Signs Prophets – A.D. 40–70 – Their Intentions and Origin," *NTS* 27 (1981): 679–97 (682–83); Evans, *Jesus and His Contemporaries*, 74–76; Pitre, *Jesus and the Last Supper*, 64–65.
36. Cf. Dale Allison, *The New Moses: A Matthean Typology* (Minneapolis: Fortress Press, 1993), 79.
37. Cf. Dennis, "Second Exodus–Restoration Imagery in John 6," 117–18.
38. Dennis, "Second Exodus-Restoration Imagery," 117–18; Alicia D. Myers, *Characterizing Jesus: A Rhetorical Analysis on the Fourth Gospel's Use of Scripture in its Presentation of Jesus* (LNTS 458; London and New York: T&T Clark, 2012), 111.

The concept of "eternal life" is intrinsic to John 6:25–58, and so, some comments on it are necessary since it has not come up in our discussion to this point. In the synoptics, "eternal life" is essentially interchangeable with the "Kingdom of God" (cf. Mark 9:43–47; 10:17–30; Matt 19:23–29; Luke 18:24–30).[39] In John, while the terms "life" and "eternal life" are common, the language of the "Kingdom of God" is rare, and despite its centrality in the synoptics, it only appears twice in the Fourth Gospel. Both appearances of "the Kingdom of God" occur within the narrative of the discussion with Nicodemus (3:3, 5), wherein it is closely related to the concept of "eternal life." The close connection between these two terms in the tradition combined with the rarity of Kingdom terminology in John leads to the conclusion that "eternal life" is essentially the Johannine approximate or substitute for "Kingdom" language.[40] It has also been long recognized in Johannine studies that the concept of "eternal life" has an eschatological valence,[41] which is reflected in our passage in v. 40 wherein "eternal life" is associated with being raised up "on the last day." In fact, the general eschatological flavor of the passage is unmistakable. Beyond the allusions to a second Exodus and the references to "eternal life" and resurrection (Gk. ἀνίστημι), there are also numerous references to "the last day" (vv. 39, 40, 44, 54).[42] All of this, we may note, generally coheres with the portrait of Jesus that we have been constructing thus far.

The story and concept of the giving of manna from Exodus 16 is at the center of our passage. In vv. 30–31, the crowd asks Jesus for a sign so that they may see it and believe, and offer the example of the giving of manna from heaven, citing a form of Ps 78:24: "He gave them bread from heaven to eat."[43] Jesus' response in vv. 32–33, 35 reveals

---

39. See G. R. Osborne, "Life, Eternal Life," in *Dictionary of Jesus and the Gospels* (2nd ed.; ed. Joel B. Green, Jeannine K. Brown, and Nicholas Perrin; Downers Grove, IL: IVP Academic, 2013), 518–22. See also Bartholomä's comments on John 6:40 and its conceptual parallel in Matt 7:21 (*Johnnaine Discourses*, 175).

40. Cf., e.g., Barrett, *St. John*, 179; Leonhard Goppelt, *Theology of the New Testament* (2 vols.; trans. John E. Alsup; ed. Jürgen Roloff; Grand Rapids: Eerdmans, 1981–982); Keener, *John*, 1:328–29; Beth M. Stovell, "Seeing the Kingdom of God, Seeing Eternal Life: Cohesion and Prominence in John 3:1–15 and the Apocryphal Gospels in Terms of Metaphor Use," in *The Language of the New Testament: Context, History, and Development* (Early Christianity in its Hellenistic Context 3; ed. Stanley E. Porter and Andrew W. Pitts; Leiden: Brill, 2013), 439–67; Frey, "From the 'Kingdom of God' to 'Eternal Life," passim.

41. E.g., C. H. Dodd, *The Interpretation of the Fourth Gospel* (repr. ed.; Cambridge: Cambridge University Press, 1968), 144–50, esp. 147; Brown, *John*, 1:cxvii–cxviii; Keener, *John*, 1:328–29.

42. It is worth mentioning the use of the "Son of Man" title in v. 53 may also refer to the tradition of the semi-divine eschatological "Son of Man" in *1 Enoch*. Although the phrase "on the last day" (Gk. τῇ ἐσχάτῃ ἡμέρᾳ) does not appear in the synoptics, Bartholomä observes that the references to the "day of judgment" (e.g., Matt 10:15) or the "day and hour" (e.g., Matt 24:36) point to the same event, and constitute strong conceptual parallels (*Johannine Discourses*, 176).

that the true bread that comes down from heaven and gives life was not given by Moses. Rather, it is Jesus himself who is the "true" bread from heaven, the "bread of life," given by the Father. What this means is that Jesus is himself the sign that the crowd has asked for,[44] the bread given from heaven.

What does it mean for Jesus to have identified himself with the bread from heaven, and moreover, what does it have to do with the gathering of those who are drawn to him? The "bread from heaven" promised by Jesus is fundamentally different from the manna eaten by the Israelites in the desert in Exodus 16. An explicit contrast is made between the original manna and the new "living bread" from heaven in vv. 49–51. Those who ate the original manna died, while those who eat of the new bread from heaven will "live eternally" (Gk. ζήσει εἰς τὸν αἰῶνα).[45] As argued by Dodd, in spite of the miraculous origin of the original manna, it is not like the new bread from heaven, which is "true bread," belonging to the order of existence described as "spirit and truth" in John 4:23.[46] It is understood in salvific and eschatological terms: those who eat of it have eternal life (v. 51), and will be raised on the last day (v. 54).

In post-70 CE Jewish literature, there is attestation of an expectation of the return of the miracle of the manna in the eschatological age.[47] This is noteworthy, but we need not directly identify Jesus's speech in the synagogue at Capernaum with this notion.[48] In fact, it may not be entirely prudent to do so on the historical level, given the typically later date of the attestation of this tradition. It is enough simply to say that Jesus's giving of himself as the new bread from heaven plays upon the eschatological concept of the new Exodus in the Hebrew Bible and

---

43. On the form of the citation, see Borgen, *Bread From Heaven*, 40; Paul N. Anderson, *The Christology of the Fourth Gospel: Its Unity and Disunity in Light of John 6* (WUNT 2.78; Tübingen: Mohr Siebeck, 1996), 202.

44. Cf. Menken, "John 6:25–43," 282–83.

45. Note here the connection to "eternal life" and its connection to eschatology and the concept of the Kingdom of God as discussed above.

46. Dodd, *Interpretation of the Fourth Gospel*, 336.

47. 2 Bar 29:8; Sib. Or. 7:148–49, frag. 3:49; Rev 2:17; *Cant. Rab.* 2.9.3; *Qoh. Rab.* 1.9.1. The only early extant possible reference to eschatological manna that can be dated with confidence to the Second Temple period can be found in 4Q511 X, 9. However, the fragmentary nature of the text makes it very difficult to understand the context or meaning of the reference to manna. On the eschatological manna traditions, see Bruce J. Malina, *The Palestinian Manna Tradition: The Manna Tradition in the Palestinian Targums and Its Relationship to the New Testament Writings* (Leiden: Brill, 1968), passim, esp. 42ff.; Maarten J. J. Menken, *Old Testament Quotations in the Fourth Gospel: Studies in Textual Form* (Contributions to Biblical Exegesis & Theology 15; Kampen: Pharos, 1996), 54–55; Herman N. Ridderbos, *The Gospel According to John: A Theological Commentary*, trans. John Vriend (Grand Rapids: Eerdmans, 1997), 226–27.

48. Contra Pitre, *Jesus and the Last Supper*, 197–201.

Second Temple Judaism, and that the later traditions about the eschatological new manna are drawing from and developing that same concept.

In v. 51, Jesus says, "I am the living bread that came down from heaven. Whoever eats of this bread will live forever; and *the bread that I will give* for the life of the world is my flesh." By identifying himself as the giver of "bread from heaven" in relation to and distinction from the manna of the Exodus, the Johannine Jesus is implicitly but intentionally drawing a parallel between himself and Moses. Deuteronomy 18:15–18 contains expectations of a "prophet like Moses," a Mosaic eschatological figure.[49] Naturally, this figure would factor into the "new Exodus" expectations discussed above,[50] and the hope for a coming Mosaic redeemer is attested in the Second-Temple-period literature.[51] In our passage, John's Jesus is alluding to his self-identification with the new Moses by claiming to give the new bread from heaven.[52]

It has been noted that the servant figure in Isaiah is, in fact, a type of Mosaic figure, insofar as his coming triggers the Isaianic new exodus.[53] Moreover, the new exodus theme is echoed in Isaiah 61, which Jesus applied to himself in the synagogue at Nazareth in Luke 4:18–19, as it speaks of the release of captives (Isa 61:1), and the forging of an eternal covenant (61:8). Thus, the allusion to Jesus's identity as a new Moses coheres fairly well with the connection to the servant figure and new exodus theme that Jesus applies to himself and his actions in the synagogue at Nazareth.[54] It is also worth noting that Jesus explicitly calls himself a "prophet" (Mark 6:4/Matt 13:57/Luke 4:24) in the con-

---

49. On this figure, see, e.g., Allison, *The New Moses*, 73–84; Howard M. Teeple, *The Mosaic Eschatological Prophet* (Philadelphia: Society of Biblical Literature, 1957), passim.

50. Allison, *New Moses*, 73–84; Pitre, *Jesus and the Last Supper*, 58–59.

51. 4Q175 I, 1–8 (which directly references Deut 18:15–18); 1QS IX, 11. Theudas (Josephus, *Ant.*, 20.97–98) and the Egyptian (Josephus, *Ant.*, 20.169–170) are probably imitating Moses and Joshua (in the case of the Egyptian, at least). As Allison writes, "to be like Joshua was to be like Moses" (*New Moses*, 79). Moreover, in agreement with Pitre, *Jesus and the Last Supper*, 65, identifying the Egyptian as a "prophet from Egypt" may be an attempt to identify himself with Moses, who was a prophet from Egypt.

52. Cf. Pitre, *Jesus and the Last Supper*, 228.

53. E.g., Gerhard von Rad, *Old Testament Theology* (2 vols.; trans. D.M.G. Stalker; New York: Harper & Row, 1965), 2:260–61; R. E. Clements, "Isaiah 53 and the Restoration of Israel," in *Jesus and the Suffering Servant: Isaiah 53 and Christian Origins*, ed. William H. Bellinger Jr. and William R. Farmer (Harrisburg: Trinity, 1998), 47–54; Allison, *New Moses*, 68–71; H. P. Hugenberger, "The Servant of the Lord in the 'Servant Song' of Isaiah: A Second Moses Figure," in *The Lord's Anointed*, ed. P.E. Satterthwaite, R.S. Hess, and G.J. Wenham (Grand Rapids: Baker, 1995), 105–40; David Aune, *Prophecy in Early Christianity and the Ancient Mediterranean World* (Eugene: Wipf & Stock, 2003 [1983]), 125; Joachim Jeremias, "Μωϋσῆς," *TDNT*, 4:848–73 (863–64); Pitre, *Jesus and the Last Supper*, 60–62.

54. The coherence between these two synagogue-centered pericopes stemming from very different streams of tradition (Luke 4:16–30 and John 6:25–71) is striking, especially given the limited role that they have both played in historical Jesus research due to concerns over "authenticity."

text of the incident in the Nazareth synagogue, and that it is explicitly a "prophet" promised in Deuteronomy 18:15–18. If we treat John 6:51 and Luke 4:18–19 as memories of Jesus's voice (the *"vox Jesu"*), then these passages offer us some insight into Jesus's understanding of himself and of his mission.[55]

The language of eating the bread of life[56] and eating Jesus's flesh in John 6:51–58 is difficult to interpret. It has frequently been understood to refer to the eucharist.[57] Of course, if it is eucharistic, then vv. 51–58 must be regarded as anachronistic, which would have a major impact on how we treat it as evidence for our present project.[58] However, this interpretation is contentious, as a number of scholars consider this to be a problematic reading.[59] It has been noted that the words of institution themselves are lacking in this passage and that the word used for Jesus's flesh here is σαρξ, rather than σῶμά ("body"), which is used in the eucharistic pericopes in the synoptics (Mark 14:22, Matt 26:26, Luke 22:19) and in 1 Cor 11:24.[60] However, neither of these are conclusive arguments by any means. The Johannine Jesus could be making a general allusion or reference to the eucharist without actually drawing directly on a formalized or standardized tradition or liturgy.

Paul Anderson has argued that the reference to Jesus's "flesh" as bread given for the life of the world is a reference to Jesus's death

---

55. For the sake of preventing misunderstanding about my method, I remind the reader once more that I am *not* claiming that these are the *ipsissima verba* of Jesus, nor even that I am claiming the "authenticity" of these passages in the sense that the previous generation of scholarship conceived of it. Rather, I am treating this data as memories of Jesus' voice, which I am applying as evidence for my investigation, and from which I am making inferences.

56. It is worth noting that the phrase "bread of life" is attested elsewhere in early Judaism, in *Joseph and Aseneth*. See *Jos. Asen.* 8:5, 9–11, 15:5, 6:16, 19:5, 21:21. It is not necessarily alien to Jesus's Second Temple context.

57. Rudolf Bultmann, *The Gospel of John: A Commentary*, trans. G.R. Beasley-Murray, R.W.N. Hoare, J.K. Riches (Philadelphia: Westminster, 1971), 234–37; Maurice Casey, *Is John's Gospel True?* (London and New York: Routledge, 1996), 44–51; Funk and the Jesus Seminar, *The Five Gospels*, 421; Brown, *John*, 1:284–85; Urban C. von Wahlde, *The Gospel and Letters of John*, 2 vols. (Eerdmans Critical Commentary; Grand Rapids: Eerdmans, 2010), 316–25; Lüdemann, *Jesus After 2000 Years*, 473. The related matter of the Bultmannian theory concerning vv. 51–58 as a later interpretation has been demonstrated to be problematic by other scholars, and need not be treated in depth here. See esp. Anderson, *Christology of the Fourth Gospel*, 111; Meredith J. C. Warren, *My Flesh Is Meat Indeed: A Nonsacramental Reading of John 6:51-58* (Minneapolis: Fortress Press, 2015), 34–47; James D. G. Dunn, "John VI – A Eucharistic Discourse?" *NTS* 17, no. 3 (1971): 328–38; Pitre, *Jesus and the Last Supper*, 195–97. Two of the bigger problems pointed out by Pitre are that the language of "eating" holds the unit together, and moreover, vv. 60–64 address *both* the matter of eating and drinking the flesh and blood of Jesus in vv. 51–58 and the teaching on belief in vv. 29 and 35. This strongly suggests that the passage be treated as a unit.

58. Cf. Casey, *Is John's Gospel True?*, 44–45; Brown, *John*, 1:286–287; Funk and the Jesus Seminar, *The Five Gospels*, 421.

59. Warren, *My Flesh Is Meat Indeed*, passim; Pitre, *Jesus and the Last Supper*, 241–42, 249–50; Keener, *John*, 1:689–691; Morris, *John*, 331–33; Köstenberger, *John*, 215; Ridderbos, *John*, 235–37.

60. Cf. Blomberg, *Historical Reliability of John's Gospel*, 126; Köstenberger, *John*, 215.

on the cross rather than to the eucharist per se. In other words, this passage can be read as referring to Jesus's death without taking it to refer specifically to the eucharist. To add to this, Meredith Warren has observed that the late first-century date of the composition of John makes it difficult to speak of a coherent institutionalized eucharist at the time when this text would have been written.[61] Brant Pitre has recently taken up a similar line of argumentation to Anderson, and has applied it to the historical level of the passage. He argues that in this passage, Jesus does not speak about "the eucharist," but rather, about the manna from heaven,[62] which Pitre interprets as referring to Jesus's knowledge of his own impending death that he viewed as redemptive.[63] Thus, John 6:51–58 coheres with Jesus's words and actions at the Last Supper,[64] which Pitre takes to genuinely represent the historical Jesus. This interpretation is certainly not implausible, especially given that some scholars have argued forcefully that Jesus could have anticipated his own death.[65]

Though this is a tempting line of interpretation, I am not entirely convinced that Jesus was teaching about his own death at this early stage in his career, nor that John 6:51–58 can *only* be read as referring to Jesus's death, or that there is no other possible reading on the historical level. Not only did the evangelists remember Jesus in light of his death on the cross, but the crucifixion and death of Jesus also looms large in our *own* society's collective memory of Jesus. In other words, it is difficult not to read the Gospels in light of that collective memory of Jesus as someone who died a sacrificial death, and we may end up reading his death into passages like this one, where it may not have figured in the thought of the historical Jesus.

In my opinion, we need to be willing to allow for multiple layers of meaning in the Johannine traditional material. When dealing with the historical level of the Johannine tradition, it is of the utmost importance to determine the substance of what the words of the Johannine Jesus actually mean to convey in terms of teaching. Once we have determined this, we will be better suited to make decisions about how and whether to apply this data as evidence for our purposes.

---

61. Warren, *My Flesh Is Meat Indeed*, 45–46.
62. Pitre, *Jesus and the Last Supper*, 250.
63. Ibid., 240.
64. Ibid., 241.
65. Scot McKnight, *Jesus and His Death: Historiography, the Historical Jesus, and Atonement Theory* (Waco: Baylor University, 2005), passim; Pitre, *End of Exile*, passim; Wright, *Jesus and the Victory of God*, 563–611; Allison, *Constructing Jesus*, 387–434.

John 6:67–71 is often taken as the Johannine parallel to Peter's confession in the synoptics (Mark 8:27–30; Matt 16:13–20; Luke 9:18–20).[66] In the synoptics, Jesus does not begin to speak of his death until *after* Peter's confession in the synoptic tradition. This would speak against reading John 6:51–58 as a reference to Jesus's death on the historical level. However, some scholars have disagreed with this identification, preferring to see it as a different incident altogether.[67] The rationale against identifying these two pericopes to be remembering the same event is derived from the substantial differences between them, especially in location, circumstances, and wording.[68] However, these differences are not without explanation or reply.

I am not convinced that John 6:67–71 is set in the Capernaum synagogue, nor is it entirely clear that John intended it to be read in that way. It has to be recognized that setting is difficult to follow and somewhat slippery throughout chapter 6 as a whole. Indeed, we are not even told that the discourse beginning in v. 25 takes place in a synagogue until v. 59. Verse 66, as I will argue below, likely refers to something that happened in the synagogue as a result of the discourse between Jesus and the assembly. However, vv. 67–71 seems to refer to another event that occurred as a reaction to the loss of followers, but which did not occur directly after the event of v. 66. We are told in v. 66 that many of Jesus's disciples turned back "and no longer went about with him" (Gk. οὐκέτι μετ᾽ αὐτοῦ περιεπάτουν), which implies that Jesus has been "going around" (περιπατέω) since the events of John 6:25–65, and is no longer in the synagogue.

It is true that the circumstance of Jesus being abandoned by some of his followers is not reflected in the synoptic confession of Peter. However, as Dodd has pointed out, there are hints and traces of that sort of abandonment to be found throughout the synoptic tradition.[69] The double-tradition pericope about Jesus's rejection by Chorazin, Bethsaida, *and especially Capernaum* (Matt 11:20–24, cf. Luke 10:13–15) is worth raising in this regard, and it is worth noting that in Matthew, this saying is given sometime prior to Peter's confession.

The difference in wording between the two confessions is unsurprising, and not particularly problematic. There is very little verbatim agreement between John and the synoptics in general, let alone in this

---

66. Dodd, *Historical Tradition*, 218–22; Köstenberger, *John*, 221; Neyrey, *Gospel of John*, 133–34; Keener, *John*, 1:697.
67. Blomberg, *Historical Reliability of John's Gospel*, 130; Morris, *John*, 343 no. 161.
68. The rationale is summarized and presented well in Morris, *John*, 343 no. 161.
69. Esp. Luke 22:28; cf. also Mark 8:38; Matt 11:6, 13:21, 10:33; Luke 9:62.

passage. This objection does not take the way that John writes history into consideration, nor how collective memory can shape tradition. In the first place, there is little verbatim agreement in the synoptic wording of the confession. Moreover, as discussed above, John writes history through theological interpretation. Thus, we should not expect the Fourth Gospel to attempt or to intend to produce the *ipsissima verba* of Peter, nor even necessarily of prior Semitic tradition without translation (into Greek) and interpretation.

There is, however, a factor that speaks in favor of the identification of John 6:67–71 with the synoptic confession of Peter at Caesarea Philippi. As Dodd has noted, the sequence of the events of John 6 (feeding, voyage, request for a sign, confession) matches that of Mark 8:1–30, which culminates with Peter's confession.[70] This similarity in sequence is an indication that we may be dealing with parallel traditions here. This, combined with the arguments above, points toward a general identification of these two events. This is significant because, according to the synoptic chronology, Jesus does not begin to teach about his death until *after* Peter's confession.[71] All three of the synoptic evangelists maintain the chronological sequence of Peter's confession being followed by Jesus beginning to speak about his death, as Matthew puts it, "from that time on" (Matt 16:21). The teaching in the synagogue at Capernaum in John 6:25–58 *precedes* Peter's confession. Thus, within the context of the historical life of Jesus, if we take the evangelists' chronology into account, it is *less* likely (though admittedly not impossible) that John 6:51–58 would have been a teaching about Jesus's death. Chronology may not be able to settle the matter, but it is relevant data all the same.

Even if we set the chronology issue aside, the key to an alternate reading can be found in v. 35. There, Jesus says: "I am the bread of life. Whoever *comes to* me will never be *hungry*, and whoever *believes in* me will never be *thirsty*." Herein lies the key piece of evidence, the elusive fingerprint, the smoking gun. As Köstenberger has observed, this verse helps to clarify what Jesus means in v. 54 by "eat my flesh" and "drink my blood," as eating is parallel to "coming to" and drinking to "believing in," with Jesus as the object of both actions.[72] If we apply this observation to the level of historical interpretation, then the teachings

---

70. Dodd, *Historical Tradition*, 218–22. This is a remarkable example of Dodd's ability to take an inferential approach to the historical reference of the Fourth Gospel.

71. Mark 8:31; Matt 16:21; Luke 9:21–22.

72. Köstenberger, *John*, 210.

in vv. 51–58 become intelligible within the web of evidence, inference, and imagination that has been emerging throughout the course of this investigation. The language of "eating" and "drinking" Jesus's flesh and blood is symbolic and metaphorical. Verses 53–54 thus indicate that Jesus is saying that those who are gathered to him and who believe in him, those who accept both the proclaimer and the proclamation, will participate in the eschatological blessings of the new Exodus.

A few observations can be made about the form of the discourse of John 6:25–66 from an institution-critical perspective.[73] The discussion described in our passage revolves around the story of the giving of manna, which is drawn from the Torah, and involves back-and-forth dialogue and questioning between Jesus and the assembly as a whole. This can be identified with public synagogue discussion concerning the interpretation of the Torah, as described in chapter 3 above.[74]

In light of the public synagogue discussion setting, the crowd's questions, responses, and reactions (vv. 28, 30–31, 34, 41–42, 52) are significant, as are those of Jesus's followers (vv. 60, 66). The assembly initially reacts positively to Jesus's teachings (v. 34). However, their response turns negative in vv. 41–42. This is in reaction to Jesus's claim to be "the bread that came down from heaven." It is noteworthy that this negative reaction is due to the fact that they know Jesus and his family, similar to the Nazareth synagogue assembly in Mark 6:3 (and parallels). Familiarity with Jesus's origins appears to have been a contributing factor to the rejection of Jesus as proclaimer, which naturally led to the rejection of his proclamation.

The crowd's reaction turns to sharp disputation (μάχομαι) in v. 52 in reaction to the saying in v. 51, wherein Jesus speaks of eating his flesh. This is because the crowd has not grasped the symbolism and metaphor of Jesus's discourse and think that he is speaking of eating the man standing before them.[75] This reaction needs to be understood in light of the negative attitude toward eating human flesh and drinking blood in early Judaism.[76] In light of this, it has sometimes been argued that Jesus's imagery of eating human flesh and drinking blood is implausible, since it is unacceptable to eat human flesh and to drink blood in Judaism.[77] However, we need to be aware that Jesus was speak-

---

73. As discussed above, vv. 67–71 do not belong to a synagogue context.
74. Cf. also the description of such discussions in Mosser, "Torah Instruction," passim.
75. Cf. A. J. B. Higgins, *The Lord's Supper in the New Testament* (Chicago: Alec R. Allenson, 1952), 82.
76. See esp. Deut 28:53–57; cf. Gen 9:3–4; Lev 17:10–12; Deut 12:15–16.
77. E.g., Casey, *Is John's Gospel True?*, 44; cf. Vermes, *Religion of Jesus*, 16; Lüdemann, *Jesus After 2000 Years*, 96–97; Becker, *Jesus of Nazareth*, 341.

ing metaphorically and symbolically—he is not speaking of literally eating his flesh and drinking his blood.[78] No law is broken by the use of this imagery. It is likely, however, that this imagery was provocative and offensive (cf. v. 61) in his Jewish context. In light of this, as Brant Pitre has argued, the reaction of the assembly in v. 52 and of Jesus's followers in v. 60 to this imagery is believable, and is essentially what we should expect.[79] Thus, the description of the crowd's reaction to Jesus's imagery speaks to the plausibility of the narrative rather than to its implausibility.

The negative reaction of the crowd is mirrored by some of Jesus's disciples in v. 60, who speak of the difficulty of the teachings given in the synagogue. The end result of the discourse is described in v. 66, in which we are told that "many of his disciples turned back and no longer went about with him." To summarize, despite initial positive reactions, Jesus is rejected by the assembly of Capernaum due to unwillingness to accept the special identity that he claims for himself (vv. 41–42) resulting from the crowd's familiarity with Jesus and his family, and due to the difficult and offensive nature of his teaching about the bread of life (v. 52). This rejection at the synagogue in Capernaum is echoed by some of those who were already committed to following Jesus, as witnessed by vv. 60, 66. The significance of this data is that *it provides evidence of an event that is strongly implied and even expected in the synoptic Gospels,*[80] but never actually narrated: Jesus's rejection by the assembly at Capernaum, including some of those who had previously followed him.

In light of this, the synoptic evangelists' agreement that Jesus did not begin to teach about his own death until after Peter's confession may be a significant datum. What we see in John 6:25–66 is further evidence that Jesus was not very successful in his synagogue program, and was rejected not only by Nazareth, but also by Capernaum, which was the center and staging ground of Jesus's peripatetic mission. The double tradition also witnesses rejection at Bethsaida and Chorazin. Was the rejection at Capernaum the final straw that led to Jesus changing his approach to carrying out his mission? A hypothesis is beginning to emerge from the evidence: Jesus's synagogue program was not as successful as he had hoped, and his rejection in various Galilean syn-

---

78. Cf. Jonathan Klawans, *Purity, Sacrifice, and the Temple: Symbolism and Supersessionism in the Study of Ancient Judaism* (Oxford: Oxford University Press, 2006), 216; Pitre, *Jesus and the Last Supper*, 430.

79. Pitre, *Jesus and the Last Supper*, 231.

80. Luke 10:15; Matt 11:23–24.

agogues led to the formulation and expression of another means of achieving his aims through his own death as Israel's suffering servant (cf. Isa 53:4–12), and the new Moses.[81] The comment on Caiaphas's speech offered by the Johannine narrator in John 11:51–52 may speak to this, since there the act of "gathering" the children of God is directly associated with Jesus's death on behalf of the nation. This narrative comment may reflect a genuine memory of Jesus's aims that the author adapted to the context of his narrative.

Once it has been interpreted and understood, the data in John 6:25–71 is historically plausible as evidence concerning the historical Jesus from which to draw inferences about the past. As has been argued above, it fits perfectly within the setting of the first-century synagogue, within the thought of Jesus, and within the context of early Judaism. Most importantly, it fits very well into the picture of Jesus and especially his aims that is being constructed here on the basis of evidence, inference, and imagination. This data has played a surprisingly minimal role in previous research on the historical Jesus, despite filling some gaps in our knowledge and cohering remarkably well with what can be known about Jesus's thought, teaching, and aims from the synoptic Gospels. Once we truly and consciously strive to shift our concentration to the *ipsissima vox*, and recognize the nature of John's approach to history and the importance of interpretation and inference in historical investigation, it becomes clear that John 6:25–71 has a role to play within the study of the historical Jesus and his aims.

Conclusion

This chapter has sought to determine the relevance of John 6:25–71 to the study of the historical Jesus and his mission as it was carried out within public synagogues. Like Luke 4:16–30, this passage has played a minimal role in previous scholarship on the historical Jesus due to concerns surrounding its "authenticity." The discussion above has attempted to apply the data of John 6:25–71 as evidence within our historical reconstruction by interpreting it in light of current scholarship on John's relationship to history, the aims of the historical Jesus, and early synagogues. In this passage, we are presented with a remembered, interpreted artifact of Jesus's teaching in the synagogue at Capernaum. I have endeavored to treat it *as* an artifact, evidence for

---

81. Note that Moses dies on behalf of Israel's sin (Deut 4:21–22).

the thing being remembered and interpreted, rather than treating it simply as the literal *verba*.[82]

Our examination of John 6:25–71 has determined that once it is properly understood and interpreted as a distinctively Johannine artifact of the remembered Jesus, the data that is provided fits very well within current understandings of the aims of the historical Jesus and within contemporary scholarship on synagogues. In fact, it has proven to be fairly significant evidence, providing insight into Jesus's self-understanding and eschatology.

Moreover, it sheds light on Jesus's failure to persuade the assembly of Capernaum, which is hinted at but never narrated in the synoptic Gospels, and the potential relationship of that failure to the turning point in Jesus's mission, the final trip to Jerusalem, and his eventual death. Thus, the evidence provided by John 6:25–71 illuminates not only Jesus's thought, but also the shape of his career.

82. It is worth mentioning that other scholars have recently taken comparable approaches to the Johannine data. A number of notable essays on interpretive historical approaches to the words of Jesus contained in the Fourth Gospel have recently been published in Paul N. Anderson, Felix Just, and Tom Thatcher, eds., *Glimpses of Jesus Through the Johannine Lens*, vol. 3 of *John, Jesus and History* (Atlanta: SBL, 2016). Three essays in this volume that deserve particular mention in this regard are R. Alan Culpepper, "Jesus Sayings in the Johannine Discourses: A Proposal," 353–82; Michael Theobald, "Johannine Dominical Sayings As Metatexts of Synoptic Sayings of Jesus: Reflections On a New Category Within Reception History," 383–405; and Jörg Frey, "From the 'Kingdom of God' to 'Eternal Life': The Transformation of Theological Language in the Fourth Gospel," 439–58.

9

To Jerusalem: The *Aposynagōgos* Passages and the Relationship between the Temple and Synagogue

Introduction

The goal of this chapter is to determine the relevance of the *aposynagōgos* passages (John 9:22, 12:42, 16:2) and John 18:20 to the present project. While the other major passages that we have examined pertain primarily to Jesus's activity in Galilee and to the towns and villages of the Land of Israel, the data that we will discuss in this chapter is set in Jerusalem. As we will see, this data also pertains in some sense to the Jerusalem temple. Because of this, it will be necessary to investigate the relationship between the synagogue and temple and the relevance of this connection for our present project.

This chapter aims at being brief and exploratory rather than comprehensive. The limits of space and scope do not allow for in-depth interaction with the rich history of scholarship surrounding the *aposynagōgos* passages nor with Jesus's perspective on the Jerusalem temple. Instead, I will focus my efforts here on the two related issues of: i) interpreting the *aposynagōgos* passages as evidence pertaining to events that took place during Jesus's lifetime within the context of the concerns of the present project, and ii) the relationship between the synagogue and temple in the aims of Jesus.

The Temple, Festivals, and National Assembly in the Aims of Jesus

In John 18:20, Jesus says, "I have spoken openly to the world; I have always taught in synagogues and in the temple, where all the Jews come together."[1] As discussed in chapter 5, "synagogues" (συναγωγή) here most likely refers to the public assemblies that Jesus taught in outside of Judea. It is remarkable that there are no narrated instances of Jesus teaching in a "synagogue" in Jerusalem. This is most likely because, as discussed in chapter 2, the temple was the local gathering place and also the locus of "synagogue" activities for Jerusalem.[2] Although there were undoubtedly association synagogues in Jerusalem,[3] the evidence discussed in chapters 5–8 shows that Jesus was primarily active in public synagogues, whereas there are no narratives in the Gospels that clearly take place in association settings. The most likely explanation is that, as we have seen throughout the discussion in the preceding chapters, Jesus's mission and aims more directly concerned public assemblies than associations. It would thus appear to be the case that John 18:20 implies that the temple replaced local public synagogues as the primary venue for Jesus's mission and program while he was in Jerusalem.

Jerusalem and its temple were of central importance in early Jewish thought and society.[4] The preeminence of Jerusalem was due in large

---

1. Whether or not John 18:20 reports an actual saying that was literally spoken by Jesus is irrelevant. For example, the Jesus Seminar assigned John 18:20 a "black" rating, indicating that they do not think that Jesus said this (Funk, Hoover, and the Jesus Seminar, *The Five Gospels*, 461). The rationale behind this decision is that it does not qualify as an aphorism or parable, and there is nothing about it that would have prompted those present to remember it. The saying probably communicates an aspect of historical reality regardless of any assessment of its "authenticity." This is because all four gospels contain manifold evidence that Jesus taught in synagogues and the temple (on the temple, see Mark 11:11, 15, 27, 12:35, 14:49; Matt 21:12, 14–15, 23, 26:55; Luke 2:46, 19:45, 47, 20:1, 21:37, 22:53; John 2:14, 5:14, 7:14, 28, [8:2], 8:20, 10:23, 11:56). The unanimity of the sources on this matter, combined with the apparent centrality of these institutions within the evangelists' narratives of Jesus's career and mission make it difficult to deny the essential accuracy of the statement in John 18:20 short of adopting an extreme historical skepticism.
2. See also Binder, *Into the Temple Courts*, passim (e.g., 31–39).
3. See Acts 6:9–10, 24:12; *CIJ* 2.1404 (*ASSB* nos. 18, 19, and 26).
4. Lengthy discussion of the evidence pertaining to Jerusalem's central importance is beyond the scope of this project, and has been sufficiently covered by other scholars. For more in-depth treatments of this topic, see Lawrence H. Schiffman, "The Importance of the Temple for Ancient Jews," in *Jesus and Temple: Textual and Archaeological Explorations*, ed. James H. Charlesworth: Minneapo-

part to the temple, described by Josephus as the "one temple for the one God."[5] According to the author of *Jubilees*, Zion was "the centre of the navel of the universe" (*Jub* 8:13). As the only legitimate place of sacrifice in mainstream Judaism of the Land and the seat of the High Priest, the temple was understandably the cultic centre of the Jewish world. Pilgrimage and the temple tax also gave the temple a pivotal economic importance.[6] The chief political significance of the temple is tied to its role as the place of public assembly (see chapter 4), and to its role as the seat of the High Priesthood, which was tied to royal governance throughout the Hasmonean period.[7]

The Jerusalem temple's eminence and influence extended to Galilee.[8] This is demonstrated especially through the references to Galileans who made pilgrimages to Jerusalem in the late Second Temple period.[9] The importance of Jerusalem for Galilee is also reflected in the archaeological record. The recent discovery of the "Magdala stone," discussed in chapter 5 above, is important evidence of the centrality of the Jerusalem temple in Galilean society, as well as the connection between synagogues and the temple.[10] Bronze coins from the First Jewish Revolt bearing the inscription "for the redemption of holy Jerusalem" have also been found at Gamla, indicating the importance of Jerusalem and its temple for the rebels in Galilee.[11] Of less certain relevance, incense shovels, which might be connected to priestly culture and the temple cult in Jerusalem,[12] have also been found in Galilean locales.[13]

Zion, which signifies Jerusalem and its temple, also had a special

lis: Fortress Press, 2014), 75–93; Timothy Wardle, *The Jerusalem Temple and Early Christian Identity* (WUNT 2.291; Tübingen: Mohr Siebeck, 2010), 13–30; Freyne, *A Jewish Galilean*, 92–109.

5. Josephus, *Ag. Ap.*, 2.193.

6. See Wardle, *Jerusalem Temple*, 23–27.

7. Refer to Josephus, *Ant.* 13.301, cf. *War*, 1.70; 1 Macc 14. On the royal priesthood, see C. Fletcher-Louis, "Priests and Priesthood," in *Dictionary of Jesus and the Gospels*, 2nd ed., ed. Joel B. Green, Jeannine K. Brown, and Nicholas Perrin (Downers Grove: IVP Academic, 2013), 699–700.

8. Cf. Mordechai Aviam, "Reverence for Jerusalem and the Temple in Galilean Society," in *Jesus and Temple: Textual and Archaeological Explorations*, ed. James H. Charlesworth (Minneapolis: Fortress Press, 2014), 123–44; Mark A. Chancey, *The Myth of a Gentile Galilee* (SNTS Monograph Series 118; Cambridge: Cambridge University Press, 2002), 54–55.

9. Josephus, *War*, 2.232; Luke 2:22, 41, 13:1. Cf. Sean Freyne, "Behind the Names: Galileans, Samaritans, *Ioudaioi*," in *Galilee through the Centuries: Confluence of Cultures*, ed. Eric M. Meyers (Winona Lake: Eisenbrauns, 1999), 39–56 (54–55).

0. Cf. Aviam, "Reverence for Jerusalem," 132–42.

1. See Aviam, "Reverence for Jerusalem," 142–43. Concerning the inscription, refer to Danny Syon, *Gamla III: The Shmarya Gutman Excavations 1976–1989: Finds and Studies Part 1* (IAA Reports 56; Jerusalem, 2014), 120–22; Danny Syon, "Yet Again on the Bronze Coins Minted at Gamla," *Israel Numismatic Research* 2 (2007): 117–22.

2. Cf., e.g., Leonard Victor Rutgers, "Incense Shovels at Sepphoris?," in *Galilee Through the Centuries: Confluence of Cultures*, ed. Eric M. Meyers (Winona Lake: Eisenbrauns, 1999), 177–98.

3. Eric M. Meyers, Ehud Netzer, and Carol L. Meyers, *Sepphoris* (Winona Lake: Eisenbrauns, 1999), 25; Israel Antiquities Authority, "Special Bronze Implements were Discovered in Archaeological Exca-

importance within early Jewish eschatology. In the Book of Isaiah, Zion plays a key role in the visions of future restoration.[14] The hopes for the restoration of Zion are also reflected in literature from the Second Temple period.[15] The centrality of Zion in early Jewish tradition about the coming restoration is noteworthy, given the role that the temple played in Jesus's program while in Jerusalem. This is especially the case with the healing miracles that he conducted within its precincts, since as we have seen in chapters 6 and 7, these healings had eschatological significance and were closely tied to Jesus's conception and goal of the restoration of Israel.

In chapter 2, we briefly discussed how the temple was the place of public assembly in Jerusalem,[16] and how "synagogue" activities, including Torah reading and judgment took place there.[17] The temple was, in other words, where Jerusalemite local-official assemblies gathered.[18] Moreover, the temple was, like the synagogue, public space. There is, however, a notable difference between Jesus's activities in the temple and in the local synagogues, insofar as there are no indications that Jesus's actions in the temple took place in the context of such official gatherings at the temple. The fact that local-official assemblies took place at the temple does not mean that Jesus took part in them or was present at them.

The synoptic Gospels only record one journey made to Jerusalem during Jesus's adulthood. That trip was also his last. The timing of

vations at Magdala – a 2,000 Year Old Jewish Settlement on the Sea of Galilee," http://www.antiq-uities.org.il/Article_eng.aspx?sec_id=25&subj_id=240&id=4190.
14. Cf. Freyne, *A Jewish Galilean*, 97–109. See, e.g., Isa 1:28, 2:2–4, 24:23, 35:10, 46:13, 51:3, 11, 52:2, 59:20, 62:10–12.
15. Tob 13:9–17; Sir 36:13–19; *Pss. Sol.* 11:1–3; 11Q5 XXII, 1–15. Cf. Freyne, *A Jewish Galilean*, 109.
16. *War* 1.122, 2.1–5, 2.294–295, 2.320–324; *Ant.* 17.200–201. See also Binder, *Intro the Temple Courts*, passim.
17. An objection to the existence of a synagogue on the temple mount has been raised by Sidney B. Hoenig, "The Supposititious Temple-Synagogue," in *The Synagogue: Studies in Origins, Archaeology and Architecture* (ed. Joseph Gutmann; Library of Biblical Studies; New York: Ktav, 1975), 55–71. However, the objection is based upon a narrow and problematic definition of a "synagogue" as an architectural space. As Runesson has written, "his [Hoenig's] definition of 'synagogue' is too narrow. 'Synagogue' defined as a public assembly may indeed use different types of public space, including the temple courts: it need not be an architecturally confined area having walls and ceilings" (Runesson, *Origins*, 365; cf. also Bernier, *Aposynagōgos*, 67–68). At any rate, as Leen Ritmeyer's work on the spatial dimension of the Jerusalem temple has shown, there was an abundance of public space that could have been used for assemblies or civic functions, both indoors and open air, within the temple precincts. See Leen Ritmeyer, *The Quest: Revealing the Temple Mount in Jerusalem* (Jerusalem: Carta, 2006); Ritmeyer, "Imagining the Temple," passim. One of the most notable pieces of archaeological evidence pertaining to official assembly on the temple mount is the existence of Herodian period rock-cut chambers just west of the Triple Gate, which Ritmeyer suggests may have belonged to one of the council-houses mentioned in *m. Sanh.* 11:2 (Ritmeyer, "Imagining the Temple," 43).
18. Cf., e.g., *m. Sanh.* 11:2; *War* 1.122, 2.1–5, 2.294–295, 2.320–324; *Ant.* 17.200–201.

the final journey to Jerusalem is significant, since it occurred around Passover.[19] Due to pilgrimage, Passover was a time of *national assembly*, when Jews travelled from around the Land and even the diaspora to gather at Jerusalem and its temple.[20] Presence at the three pilgrimage festivals (Passover, Weeks, and Booths) was technically required by the Torah (Exod 23:17, 34:23; Deut 16:16), though it is unlikely that every Jew living in the Land was able to comply with this. Sanders reasonably estimates that the average Palestinian Jew made one pilgrimage per year, with Passover being the most popular of the three festivals.[21] Josephus provides attendance estimates for two different Passovers in the mid-60s CE, one at 2,700,000 attendees and the other at 3,000,000.[22] While these numbers are undoubtedly exaggerations, the very fact that they are so exaggerated reflects the sense of the immense size of the Passover festival and the incredible number of Jews who travelled from afar to attend it. Sanders provides the much more reasonable estimate of 300,000–500,000 attendees.[23] This would have been a very significant percentage of the Jewish population of the Land, which was probably under one million.[24]

By shifting his target venue from public synagogues to the Jerusalem temple at Passover, Jesus was moving his mission from the local to the national stage. No longer was he speaking to a local village assembly, but rather, to the *qāhāl* (LXX *ekklēsia* or *synagōgē*, both of which are synagogue terms) of Israel,[25] the assembly of the Jewish nation.[26] This undoubtedly raised the stakes for him and his mission, and set the stage for his arrest and execution. Moreover, Passover was directly concerned with the commemoration of the Exodus event. If there was ever a time to bring his message of restoration and a new Exodus to

---

19. Mark 14:1; Matt 26:2; Luke 22:1; John 12:1.
20. See Josephus, *Ant.*, 17.213–14.
21. Sanders, *Judaism: Practice and Belief*, 127.
22. Josephus, *War*, 26.420–27 and 2.280 respectively.
23. Sanders, *Judaism: Practice and Belief*, 128. Sanders estimates the total Jewish population of Palestine at under one million (p. 127).
24. Cf., e.g., Magen Broshi, "The Population of Western Palestine in the Roman–Byzantine Period," *BASOR* 236 (1979): 1–10; Sanders, *Judaism: Practice and Belief*, 127; David M. Fouts, "The Demographics of Ancient Israel," *Bulletin of Biblical Research* 7, no. 2 (2007): 1–10; Jack Pastor, *Land and Economy in Ancient Palestine* (London: Routledge, 2012[1997]), 6–8.
25. See Korner, "*Ekklēsia* as a Jewish Synagogue Term," 53–78. On *ekklēsia* as a term for the popular assembly, see Korner, "Before Church," 29–51. See also Kyriakoula Papademetriou, "The Dynamic Semantic Role of Etymology in the Meaning of Greek Biblical Words. The Case of the Word ἐκκλησία," in *Biblical Lexicology: Hebrew and Greek: Semantics - Exegesis - Translation*, ed. Eberhard Bons, Jan Joosten, and Regine Hunziker–Rodewald (Beihefte zur Zeitschrift für die alttestamentliche Wissenschaft 443; Berlin and Boston: De Gruyter, 2015), 261–80.
26. Cf. H. J. Fabry, קָהָל, in *TDOT*, eds. G. Johannes Botterweck and Helmer Ringen (Grand Rapids: Eerdmans, 1974-), 12:561.

the national stage, it was at Passover.[27] In light of this, we should note the significance of John 18:20. Jesus always taught in the synagogue and temple, places "where all the Jews come together." It thus seems as though *Jesus specifically sought out the primary places of Jewish assembly* as the stage and arena to carry out his aims. This makes a good deal of sense in light of our discussion of Jesus's aims up to this point, which involved the "gathering" or restoration of Israel. The significance of the temple in Jewish restoration eschatology and its central significance for Jews of the Land of Israel during the Second Temple period help to further illuminate the role that it played in Jesus's aims.

Throughout the course of John's narrative, Jesus travels to Jerusalem several times. Notably, these trips are always made during festivals.[28] If we take this Johannine evidence into account alongside the synoptics, it shows that Jesus was remembered as having travelled to Jerusalem specifically for times of national assembly. Special emphasis, of course, should be placed on Jesus's final trip for Passover, which was the largest festival. What I infer from this data is that Jesus's aims in relation to the temple as a venue for his proclamation, teaching, and actions were more likely tied to its role as the setting of gathering of the nation, rather than to its role as the place where the local-official assembly of Jerusalem gathered.

There is a marked parallelism between Jesus's actions in the temple and in the synagogues. The synoptic Gospels only narrate Jesus's final trip to Jerusalem during his adult lifetime. During this final period of his life, the synoptic evangelists tell us that Jesus was habitually teaching in the temple.[29] Matthew also reports that Jesus was carrying out healing miracles in the temple (Matt 21:14),[30] which was similarly a

---

27. Cf., on this point, Fredriksen, *Jesus of Nazareth*, 257.

28. John 2:13, 5:1, 7:14, 37, 10:22–23, 12:12. On Jesus's pilgrimages in recent scholarship, see Michael Allen Daise, "Jesus and the Jewish Festivals: Methodological Reflections," in *Jesus Research: New Methodologies and Perceptions*, vol. 2, ed. James H. Charlesworth with Brian Rhea and Petr Pokorný (Grand Rapids: Eerdmans, 2014), 283–304.

29. On habitual teaching, see Luke 19:47, 21:37–38; Mark 14:49 (cf. Matt 26:55; Luke 22:52).

30. The historical accuracy of Matt 21:14 has sometimes been called into question. The rationale for this is that the parallel account in Mark lacks mention of these healings, thus leading some scholars to conclude that it is a Matthean addition to Mark's account (e.g., Meyer, *Marginal Jew*, 2:746; Funk and the Jesus Seminar, *Acts of Jesus*, 231). According to Funk and the Jesus Seminar, "Matthew has supplied out of his imagination the additional material found in vv. 14–16" (*Acts of Jesus*, 231). However, this is a contentious conclusion, as it excludes the very real possibility that Matthew could have had additional information that Mark either did not have access to, or omitted. A historical argument is preferable to one based solely on redaction criticism. As discussed in chapter 7, it is clear that Jesus was remembered as a healer, and if he was active in the temple precincts, it is quite likely that he would have performed healings and have been sought out for his ability do so. In fact, the evidence of the strong memory of Jesus as a healer, combined with the memory of Jesus being active in the Jerusalem temple, themselves provide two fixed points of evidence,

part of his synagogue program (see chapter 7 above). Moreover, Jesus is said to have discussed the interpretation of Torah in the temple precincts, as indicated by the "Greatest Commandment" pericope (Mark 12:28–34; cf. Matt 22:34–40) and by the discussion about the resurrection that precedes it (Mark 12:18–27; cf. Matt 22:23–33; Luke 20:27–40), in which Jesus references and interprets Exodus 3:6.

The evangelists report that Jesus enjoyed popular success in the temple on his final journey to Jerusalem. Mark directly connects the popular success of Jesus's program in the temple with the advent of the plot to kill Jesus by the temple-based authorities.[31] According to Mark 11:18, following Jesus's demonstration in the temple, the chief priests and scribes "kept looking for a way to kill him; for they were afraid of him, *because the whole crowd was spellbound by his teaching.*" While Jesus's mission may have been faltering on the local level in some of the synagogues of Galilee (see chapters 6 and 8), it had begun to gain momentum on the national stage in the Jerusalem temple during Passover, and thus, in the *qāhāl* (Gk. *ekklēsia*) of Israel. The switch from the local to the national level was initially a success.

The Gathering of Israel and *Aposynagōgos*

Why would the priestly authorities be afraid on account of the popularity of Jesus's teaching? The Passover setting is important to take into account. Not only was Passover a time of national assembly, it was also a time when the Exodus was remembered, and as such, it commemorated the liberation of the Hebrew people and the establishment of Israel as an independent nation.

The Johannine evidence is worth bringing into the conversation on this point. John 11:47–53 indicates a connection between the plot to kill Jesus initiated by the temple authorities and the threat of Roman intervention:

So the chief priests and the Pharisees called a meeting of the council, and said, "What are we to do? This man is performing many signs. If we let

---

and once they connected with a thread of historical imagination, the most reasonable inference to draw would be that Jesus performed healings in the temple. Thus, Matt 21:14 provides a witness to what we would have already been able to determine by means of inference from evidence and imagination in true Collingwoodian fashion.

31. On this point on the historical level, see Adele Reinhartz, "The Temple Cleansing and the Death of Jesus," in *Purity, Holiness, and Identity in Judaism and Christianity: Essays in Memory of Susan Haber* (ed. Carl S. Ehrlich, Anders Runesson, and Eileen M. Schuller; WUNT 305; Tübingen: Mohr Siebeck, 2013), 100–111.

him go on like this, everyone will believe in him, and the Romans will come and destroy both our holy place and our nation." But one of them, Caiaphas, who was high priest that year, said to them, "You know nothing at all! You do not understand that it is better for you to have one man die for the people than to have the whole nation destroyed." He did not say this on his own, but being high priest that year he prophesied that Jesus was about to die for the nation, and not for the nation only, but to gather into one the dispersed children of God. So from that day on they planned to put him to death.

There are three inferences that I would like to draw attention to from this data. First, according to John, some of the Jerusalem elites expressed concern that Jesus's movement was gaining momentum, and that if he were allowed to continue, the Romans would consider it to be a threat. Whether or not the direct speech in John 11:47–48 reflects the actual *verba* of the Jerusalem elites is beside the point. What vv. 47–48 communicate is a memory[32] that around the time of his final Passover, Jesus's movement was picking up steam, and this was perceived as a threat to the Jerusalem temple and to the people of Israel because of the possibility of Roman intervention.[33] The likelihood of this scenario is strongly suggested by the accounts of Jewish populist movements centered around charismatic leaders from the late Second Temple period known to us from Josephus that were ended by Roman intervention.[34] Given this evidence and the fact that Jerusalem and the temple were indeed laid to waste in 70 CE, we can be certain that this was a reasonable fear, and that what John presents here is a likely scenario. The second inference, closely related to the first, is that according to John, the plot of the elites against Jesus took shape as a result of the popularity of Jesus's movement in Jerusalem (cf. vv. 49–50).

The third and final inference is that John remembered and understood Jesus's intentions surrounding this final trip to Jerusalem in terms of "assembling" or "gathering" (Gk. συνάγω) the dispersed children of God. Moreover, the Johannine author sets this event just prior to Passover. The combination of "assembling" the children of God and

---

32. It goes almost without saying that this memory, like all memory, has been interpreted in light of later events. This is indicated by the explicit interpretation offered by the narrator in vv. 51–52.

33. Cf. Horsley and Thatcher, *John, Jesus & the Renewal of Israel*, 173. On the unlikelihood that this was an *ex nihilo* composition from the Johannine imagination alone, see Dodd, *Historical Tradition*, 24–25.

34. These include Theudas (*Ant.* 20.97–99; cf. Acts 5:36), the "Egyptian" (*Ant.* 20.169–172; *War* 2.261–263; cf. Acts 21:38), Athronges (*Ant.* 17.278–284; *War* 2.60–65), an unnamed Samaritan (*Ant.* 18.85–87), Simon of Perea (*Ant.* 17.273–277; *War* 2.57–59), and Menachem (*War* 2.433–450). Cf. the argument in Bernier, *Aposynagōgos*, 102–3. On these messianic claimants and their relevance for historical Jesus research, see Evans, *Jesus and His Contemporaries*, 53–81.

Passover brings to mind Jesus's aim of restoration, specifically in terms of a new Exodus. This memory, though it comes from John and not from the lips of Jesus, is nevertheless a mnemonic historical artifact and should be considered as evidence in its own right.

In chapter 4, we discussed the merits of Jonathan Bernier's post-Martynian hypothesis on the *aposynagōgos* passages.[35] Bernier has made a convincing case that, on the basis of current synagogue research, the *aposynagōgos* passages can be taken to plausibly refer to events that took place during the life of Jesus. According to Bernier, a fear developed over the course of Jesus's career that the popularity of the movement that formed around him might lead to Roman intervention. Thus,

> To counter these threats, a coalition of Jerusalem–based elite persons entered into a probably informal agreement to pressure those who were sympathetic to Jesus to abandon those sympathies. One of the ways in which they did this was to exert their informal influence such as to exclude those who appeared sympathetic to Jesus from Jerusalem's public assembly.[36]

Bernier argues that being made *aposynagōgos* would have meant exclusion from participation in the public assembly (or "synagogue") of Jerusalem, and thus from participation in civic and religious affairs. Given that John 12:42 describes a fear of being made *aposynagōgos* within the context of the Passover festival, it seems likely that some of those who were sympathetic to Jesus feared being unable to participate in the festal assembly at the temple. Thus, I would go beyond Bernier and suggest that being made *aposynagōgos* would have been exclusion not just from Jerusalem's local assembly, but also from participation in national assemblies.

The threat of making Jesus's followers *aposynagōgoi* would have severely limited his ability to persuade members of the Jewish public and to find sympathizers in Jerusalem.[37] It would also have been an effective political move by the elites against Jesus and his movement.

---

35. As presented in Bernier, *Aposynagōgos*, passim.

36. Ibid., 138.

37. Bernier argues that there was no formal mechanism for making someone *aposynagōgos*. Rather, on the basis of John 16:2, he notes that the Johannine Jesus associates being made *aposynagōgos* with physical, even lethal, violence, and thus suggests that a person would have been excluded from participation in the public assembly under threat of violence, perhaps even mob or police violence (Ibid., 73–74). Violence is, of course, an effective threat in itself. Whether or not this suggestion is correct, the threat of exclusion from the public and national assembly would in itself have been a significant deterrent for would-be sympathizers with Jesus or potential members of his movement.

After all, how could Jesus bring about the restoration of Israel if those who were sympathetic to his movement were excluded from participation in the *qāhāl* (Gk. *ekklēsia* or *synagōgē*) of Israel? The success of this strategy is attested by John 12:42, which states that "many, even of the authorities, believed in him. But because of the Pharisees they did not confess it, for fear that they would be put out of the synagogue."

That these Jerusalem elites chose to employ this tactic indicates the importance of the public assembly both within Second Temple period Jewish society and within the aims of Jesus. This reading of the *aposynagōgos* passages fits into the picture of the synagogue that we have formed from the evidence examined in chapters 2 and 3, and into the picture of the career, actions, and aims of Jesus that has emerged over the course of chapters 5–8. Thus, if Bernier's hypothesis is accepted, then the *aposynagōgos* passages serve as evidence and confirmation of what I have been constructing and arguing up to this point.

Conclusion

This chapter has explored some aspects of Jesus's use of the temple as his primary venue in Jerusalem while he was there. By moving from local public synagogues to the temple at Passover, Jesus had shifted his program from the local level to the national level of public assembly. Given that Jesus had been met with rejection in some of the Galilean locales, the switch from the local to the national stage was a shift in strategy, though his aim, the restoration of Israel, appears to have remained constant (cf. John 11:52).

The Passover setting and the significance of the temple in early Jewish traditions concerning restoration eschatology suggest that Jesus's use of the temple as a venue was not only a matter of convenience, but also closely intertwined with his aims. By bringing his message to the temple at Passover, when the nation assembled there, Jesus was engaging the *qāhāl* of Israel with his mission. There could be no better opportunity to "gather" the children of God (cf. John 11:52) for a new Exodus than at the festival that commemorated the original Exodus event, when the people of Israel were assembled at Zion.

The evidence examined above indicates that Jesus was initially successful at the temple during Passover, and that he was rapidly gaining supporters and sympathizers. However, out of a rational fear of Roman intervention, some of the Jerusalem elite saw Jesus's movement as a threat. Thus, they threatened to exclude his sympathizers from the assembly and plotted to kill Jesus before he attracted unwanted military attention from Rome. Ultimately, the national assembly was at the center of the events in Jerusalem. For Jesus, it was a matter of gathering the *qāhāl* of Israel in preparation for the outbreak of the Kingdom of God. For a certain faction of the Jerusalem elites, however, it was a matter of keeping order in order to prevent a catastrophe. Thus, the mission that began in the synagogues of Galilee would come to its end upon a Roman cross outside the walls of Jerusalem.

Conclusion

The overarching intent of this project has been to bring the study of the historical Jesus into conversation with current research on early synagogues. Our discussion began by noting the centrality and importance of the synagogue in Jewish societal, political, and religious life in the Land during the late Second Temple period, and by similarly observing its prominence within the narratives of the life and career of Jesus of Nazareth in the canonical Gospels. Nevertheless, as my review of the history of scholarship in Chapter 4 has shown, synagogue scholarship has been a missing element in historical Jesus research. Throughout this study, we have seen how reconstructions and understandings of "the synagogue" in the study of Jesus and the Gospels have often been driven by assumptions and by analogies made to modern synagogues, while interaction with current scholarship on ancient synagogues has been minimal. I have attempted to make some headway into bringing the findings of recent research on the synagogue into the study of the historical Jesus. In so doing, I hope to help to recover yet another piece of Jesus's Jewish context that has been frequently misunderstood or neglected.

One of the findings of my research has been that understanding the public synagogue in light of the extant material and literary evidence speaks greatly to the historical plausibility of narratives involving synagogues in the Gospels. Furthermore, such an understanding helps to produce better informed interpretations and judgments about those narratives. It is interesting that interpretations of and judgments about the plausibility or "authenticity" of the passages treated in this project have been made so frequently in previous scholarship, apart from an adequate understanding of early synagogues.

There are three distinct areas of the discipline of historical Jesus research to which I hope this study can make contributions. First, I have argued that we should look to philosophy of history and historiography for a way forward out of the morass of current debates over method. The work on philosophy of history, hermeneutics, and historiography in the Appendices can help advance the current discussions around method in historical Jesus research.

Second, the reconstruction of the synagogue—specifically *as Jesus knew it*—can help to better focus future research on Jesus and the Gospels, wherever synagogues are concerned. As we have seen, historical portraits of "the synagogue" in New Testament scholarship are often complicated by anachronism, anatopism, anatypism, or some combination of the three. Moreover, most synagogue scholarship is (of course) not focused specifically on Jesus, so nonspecialist readers with an interest in Jesus or the Gospels are often left to discern for themselves what is pertinent to that interest, which can result in confusion. By prioritizing data pertaining to public synagogues stemming from the Land in the late Second Temple period in chapter 3, I have attempted to provide a current and working understanding of the synagogue as it was known to Jesus, which should be of use and interest to future researchers on Jesus and the Gospels. What both the archaeological and textual evidence has shown is that, in agreement with mainstream synagogue scholarship, the synagogues that Jesus interacted with were local-official public institutions that are best described as religiopolitical town halls.

Third, and most importantly, the historical investigation of the role of the synagogue in the aims of Jesus helps to clarify our understanding of Jesus's mission and also helps us to better understand the data involving synagogues in the Gospels. We have found that the public synagogue played a key role in Jesus's mission and that it was intrinsic, rather than incidental, to his aim of restoring or regathering Israel and its people. Jesus made use of and interacted with the institutional structure of the synagogue as a platform for advancing his proclamation, his teaching, and his cause.

This is the basic scenario that I have presented on the basis of the evidence: Jesus aimed to persuade public synagogues, which were local-official assemblies, of his proclamation of the present and impending outbreak of the Kingdom of God, which can be understood in terms of the eschatological restoration of Israel under the reign of God. By persuading them to accept his proclamation, which required a willed act of repentance, Jesus understood himself as bringing that locale into the regathered and restored Israel. By accepting Jesus's proclamation, a given synagogue assembly would participate in the eschatological blessings of the outbreak of the Kingdom of God. Thus, Jesus was *bringing the Kingdom of God as he conceived of it into existence by persuading local pubic synagogue assemblies to participate in it.*

However, Jesus met rejection and resistance in several Galilean synagogues. According to the evidence that we have examined, the difficulty of the content of Jesus's teaching, disagreement over his interpretation of the Law, and familiarity with Jesus and his family were contributing factors to the rejection that Jesus faced in synagogues. At best, the extant evidence indicates that the results of Jesus's mission in the synagogues were mixed. There is at least one clear instance preserved in the Gospels of a victory within a synagogue setting in Luke 13:10–17. However, Jesus and his message were rejected in the synagogues of Nazareth and Capernaum, and probably also in the synagogues of Chorazin and Bethsaida. It is likely that there were more victories and rejections than those that have been preserved. Nevertheless, the extant data gives us some idea as to how Jesus and his proclamation were received in the public synagogues. It is clear that the synagogue mission was not a complete success.

The mixed results that Jesus received in the synagogues appear to have led to a change in his tactic and approach to achieving his aims. It is worth noting that, with only one exception, Jesus does not appear in a *local* public synagogue after beginning to speak of the necessity of his death in any of the four Gospels. The exception is Luke 13:10–17, which I have argued is chronologically displaced and belongs to an earlier phase of Jesus's career. In the Gospel narratives, from the incident at Caesarea Philippi on, Jesus seems to have focused his efforts more on the *national* assembly of the Jerusalem temple at Passover and other festivals than on the local public synagogue assemblies. In this, the Johannine evidence helps to flesh out the broader picture of Jesus's activity in Jerusalem and its temple during festivals, which were times of national public assembly.

Our study has also highlighted the importance of "institution criticism" for understanding the rhetorical and political dimensions of Gospel narratives set in synagogues. Grasping the institutional context of the synagogue as a setting impacts the interpretation of these narratives and helps to shed light on politics at the local level in the Jesus tradition. Moreover, by understanding the synagogue and interpreting these narratives in light of that understanding, we are able to recover just a little bit more of Jesus's Jewish context. These elements have, until now, been missing in historical Jesus research.

In line with modern synagogue scholarship and archaeological discoveries, this project has painted a picture of the synagogue as a vital and integral part of Jewish life in the Land of Israel during the late Second Temple period. *So too was it a vital and integral part of the life and mission of Jesus of Nazareth.* If nothing else, I hope that the reader will be persuaded by this point, and that the synagogue narratives in the Gospels will play a more substantial role in future historical Jesus scholarship rather than being discarded as "redactional" or "inauthentic." The fact that the synagogue narratives have had such a minimal role in previous historical studies of historical Jesus speaks to the failure of the methods used throughout the Third Quest and beyond to truly recover a Jesus who is at home and engaged in the Jewish society of his day.

The present work has presented a picture of the historical Jesus and the role of the synagogue in his aims that is located at the crossroads of evidence, inference, and imagination. It is at that crossroads that historians encounter the past. Since there is no objectivity without subjectivity, this has been an interpretive endeavor, and I have no doubt that others may interpret the same evidence differently. Nevertheless, what I have aimed to present here is a plausible scenario built from inferences and imagination rooted in evidence. Insofar as I am a historian, I can do no more and no less, for that is the nature of history.

Appendix A:
Outlining the Practice of History:
A Historiographical Approach to Jesus

Introduction

The primary aim of this essay is to outline the philosophy and method that are employed in this work. The method proposed below is primarily inspired by the thought of R. G. Collingwood and Bernard Lonergan. Collingwood provides a historiographical foundation, while Lonergan contributes a hermeneutic and grounded epistemology, both of which are necessary for historical investigation. Collingwood's seminal thought on the nature and practice of history, primarily contained in his posthumously published work, *The Idea of History*,[1] has the potential to form the basis of a sound procedure for historical Jesus research.

Unlike many other notable theoretical works of the twenty and twenty-first centuries, Collingwood's work is concerned not only with the nature of history, but also with the infrastructure of history,[2] the "nuts and bolts" of method and procedure. The emphasis of his historiographical thought on evidence, interpretation, imagination, and questioning provides some initial orientation for navigating through the darkness of history.[3]

---

1. Collingwood, *The Idea of History*.
2. On the "superstructure" and "infrastructure" of history, see Leon J. Goldstein, *Historical Knowing* (Austin: University of Texas, 1976), 141. On Collingwood and the infrastructure of history, see Jan van der Dussen, *History as a Science: The Philosophy of R. G. Collingwood* (Dordrecht and Heidelberg: Springer, 2012), ix.
3. This point is further addressed in appendix B, in relation to the postmodern turn to the subject.

Appendix B will introduce certain aspects of Lonergan's work that can further build upon Collingwood's insights, and which may function as a corrective to certain elements of his understanding of history that I consider problematic. The end result will be a procedure that is distilled from Collingwood's philosophy of history resituated within a Lonerganian critical-realist epistemological framework. Ben Meyer once remarked that Collingwood himself never did provide a satisfactory theory of knowledge, and thus, Lonergan offers "the most trenchant contemporary follow-up on Collingwood."[4] In other words, Lonergan's cognitional theory offers an epistemological corrective and update of Collingwood's insights into the nature and practice of history.

Although Collingwood is among the most influential figures in the philosophy of history and historiography, the effects of his contributions, methodological foundations, and insights into the nature of history itself have not yet been properly incorporated into historical Jesus research. This is not to say that Collingwood has never been cited or utilized in our field.[5] However, as Ben Meyer has put it, "Many cite Collingwood but few follow him in the effort to free history from irrelevant baggage."[6]

Due to early misapprehension and misrepresentation of his thought in combination with the emergence of the criteria of authenticity as a methodological standard in the mid-twentieth century, crucial dimensions of Collingwood's contributions to historical method have been passed over by the historical Jesus enterprise. Incorporating Collingwood's thought at this juncture may serve to fill the need for a robust historical procedure, and will also serve as a corrective for some of the problems that have arisen in the discipline. Simply put, a Collingwoodian historiography is incompatible with the quest for the "authentic" Jesus. The methodological insights presented in *The Idea of History* can only properly be applied in a post-scissors-and-paste historiographical landscape.[7] Given that this is where our discipline appears to be

---

4. Meyer, *Critical Realism*, 150.
5. There are indeed occasional references to Collingwood in scholarship on the historical Jesus. Some recent examples of works that cite Collingwood in various capacities include Robert L. Webb, "The Historical Enterprise and Historical Jesus Research," in *Key Events in the Life of the Historical Jesus*, ed. Darrell L. Bock and Robert L. Webb (WUNT 247; Tübingen: Mohr Siebeck, 2009), 9–93; Bernier, *Aposynagōgos*; Jens Schröter, "The Criteria of Authenticity in Jesus Research and Historiographical Method," in *Jesus, Criteria, and the Demise of Authenticity*, ed. Christ Keith and Anthony Le Donne (London and New York: T&T Clark, 2012), 49–70; Le Donne, *Historiographical Jesus*.
6. Meyer, *Critical Realism and the New Testament*, 148.
7. As we will see in section 2.4 below, Collingwood is harshly critical of a "scissors-and-paste"

headed, the methodological dimensions of *The Idea of History* now have much to offer the discipline. It is only once we have broken out of the scissors-and-paste paradigm that Collingwood's vision of the historian's task can be truly appreciated.

Rather than being superseded by postmodernism, Collingwood anticipates the postmodern turn toward the subject,[8] and offers the historiographical and theoretical resources to incorporate the insights of postmodernism and move on from it.[9] In other words, Collingwood offers a way to span the gap between subject and object in history. For this reason, Collingwood's work has a place in the aftermath of the postmodern turn to the subject. Both Collingwoodian idealism and Lonerganian critical realism have the awareness and resources necessary to help bridge the gap between subjectivity and objectivity. This is a great strength of both traditions, and leaves both Collingwood and Lonergan largely unphased by the postmodern turn toward the subject in history without a need to retreat into empiricism.[10] We will discuss these issues further in appendix B. For now, it is sufficient to note that the advent of postmodernism has not rendered these thinkers obsolete.

On the contrary, *The Idea of History* has continued to generate conversation and secondary scholarship throughout the mid- to late twentieth century up to today, as a cursory glance through the bibliography of the recently published Collingwood research companion will confirm.[11] In fact, according to Marnie Hughes-Warrington, "Present-day Collingwood scholars are only just beginning to chart and understand this extraordinarily wide vision of history."[12]

---

approach to history, which is history constructed by excerpting and combining the testimonies of different authorities.

8. Cf. van der Dussen, *History as a Science*, ix. See also Hayden White's favourable treatment of Collingwood in Hayden White, *Tropics of Discourse: Essays in Cultural Criticism* (Baltimore: Johns Hopkins, 1978), 59–62.

9. For a summary of the postmodern critique of history, see F.R. Ankersmit, "Historiography and Postmodernism," *History and Theory* 28, no. 2 (1989): 137–53. For reactions to the postmodern critique in New Testament studies see, e.g., Pieter F. Craffert, "Multiple Realities and Historiography: Rethinking Historical Jesus Research," in *The New Testament Interpreted: Essays in Honor of Bernard C. Lategan*, ed. Cilliers Breytenbach, Johan C. Thom, and Jeremy Punt (Leiden and Boston: Brill, 2007), 87–116; Beth M. Sheppard, *The Craft of History and the Study of the New Testament* (Atlanta: Society of Biblical Literature, 2012), 164–69.

10. Compare, for example, E. H. Carr, *What is History?*, 2nd ed., ed. R. W. Davies (Harmondsworth and New York: Penguin, 1987 [1961]); Geoffrey R. Elton, *The Practice of History*, 2nd ed. (Oxford: Blackwell, 2001 [1967]); and more recently, perhaps also Richard J. Evans, *In Defense of History*, new ed. (London: Granta, 2001 [1997]).

11. James Connelly, Peter Johnson and Stephen Leach, *R. G. Collingwood: A Research Companion* (London: Bloomsbury, 2014).

12. Marnie Hughes-Warrington, *Fifty Key Thinkers on History*, 2nd ed. (Oxon: Routledge, 2008), 43.

Where We Stand: The Criteria of Authenticity and Social Memory Theory in Current Research

Since the turn of the millennium, the study of the historical Jesus has seen significant advancements and developments. Some of the most notable of these advancements include the recovery and understanding of the Fourth Gospel as a source for the historical Jesus,[13] as well as the increasing role played by archaeological evidence.[14] These same years have also seen the rise of the use of social memory theory in historical Jesus research as well as the decline of the traditional criteria-based approach. While there had been a number of objections to the criteria approach in earlier decades,[15] dissatisfaction with the criteria and recognition of their limitations has come to a head, and there is a pressing need for more robust foundations.[16]

13. The proceedings and findings of the "John, Jesus, and History" section of the Society of Biblical Literature have been both influential and exemplary in this regard. This section has thus far produced three publications: Paul N. Anderson, Felix Just, and Tom Thatcher, eds., *Critical Appraisals of Critical Views*, vol. 1 of *John, Jesus, and History* (SBL Symposium Series 44; Atlanta: Society of Biblical Literature, 2007); Paul N. Anderson, Felix Just, and Tom Thatcher, eds., *Aspects of Historicity in the Fourth Gospel*, vol. 2 of *John, Jesus, and History* (Atlanta: Society of Biblical Literature, 2009); and Paul N. Anderson, Felix Just, and Tom Thatcher, eds., *Glimpses of Jesus Through the Johannine Lens*, vol. 3 of *John Jesus and History* (Atlanta: Society of Biblical Literature, 2016). Some examples of other important publications concerning the use, applicability, and recovery of the Fourth Gospel as a source for the historical Jesus include Craig L. Blomberg, *The Historical Reliability of John's Gospel: Issues and Commentary* (Downers Grove: InterVarsity, 2001); Paul N. Anderson, *The Fourth Gospel and the Quest for Jesus: Modern Foundations Reconsidered* (London and New York: Continuum, 2007); Tom Thatcher, *Why John Wrote a Gospel: Jesus - Memory - History* (Louisville: John Knox, 2006); Bernier, *Aposynagōgos*; Dwight Moody Smith, "Redaction Criticism, Genre, Narrative Criticism, and the Historical Jesus in the Gospel of John," in *Jesus Research: New Methodologies and Perceptions*, vol. 2 of *Jesus Research*, ed. James H. Charlesworth, with Brian Rhea and Petr Pokorný (Grand Rapids: Eerdmans, 2014), 624–33; Horsley and Thatcher, *John Jesus, & the Renewal of Israel*.
14. For examples, see James H. Charlesworth, ed., *Jesus and Archaeology* (Grand Rapids: Eerdmans, 2006); Jonathan L. Reed, *Archaeology and the Galilean Jesus: A Re-Examination of the Evidence* (Harrisburg: Trinity International Press, 2000); Craig A. Evans, *Jesus and His World: The Archaeological Evidence* (Louisville: Westminster John Knox, 2012); James H. Charlesworth, ed., *Jesus and Temple: Textual and Archaeological Explorations* (Minneapolis: Fortress Press, 2014); Seán Freyne, *The Jesus Movement and Its Expansion: Meaing and Mission* (Grand Rapids: Eerdmans, 2014); Roland Deines, "Galilee and the Historical Jesus in Recent Research," in *Galilee in the Late Second Temple and Mishnaic Periods: Life, Culture, and Society*, vol. 1, ed. David A. Fiensy and James Riley Strange (Minneapolis: Fortress Press, 2014), 11–48; as well as the methodological essays in "Section 2: Archaeology and Topography: Perceiving Jesus in His World," in James H. Charlesworth, ed., with Brian Rhea and Petr Pokorný, *Jesus Research: New Methodologies and Perceptions*, vol. 2, Grand Rapids: Eerdmans, 2014), 103–97.
15. As mentioned above in chapter 1. For an overview of early objections or proposed modifications to the criteria approach, see Donald L. Denton, *Historiography and Hermeneutics in Jesus Studies: An Examination of the Work of John Dominic Crossan and Ben F. Meyer* (JSNTSup 262; London and New York: T&T Clark, 2004), 195–208.
16. Some recent examples include Stanley E. Porter, "How Do We Know What We Think We Know? Methodological Reflections on Jesus Research," in *Jesus Research: New Methodologies and Perceptions*, vol. 2 ed. James H. Charlesworth, with Brian Rhea and Petr Pokorný (Grand Rapids: Eerdmans, 2014), 82–99; Freyne, *The Jesus Movement*; Freyne, *Jesus, A Jewish Galilean: A New Reading of the Jesus*

The publication of the essays collected in *Jesus, Criteria, and the Demise of Authenticity* has been a key indication that the tide has been turning against the criteria approach.[17] The rationale for such a claim lies in the concerted challenge to the criteria and to the search for authenticity that the contributors represent, which is indicative of a growing state of dissatisfaction with the criteria approach in the discipline as a whole. While the contributors differ in opinion as to whether the criteria should be abandoned or reformed, all of them express general discontent with the criteria approach in one way or another.[18] The critiques of the criteria approach present real and crucial issues, all of which raise questions about its methodological viability. As will be seen below, I have some additional reservations about the criteria approach of my own.

The contributions to *Demise of Authenticity* provide a good starting point for understanding the problems that the criteria approach faces. However, while it does a good job of identifying problems, it does little in the way of providing solutions. Nevertheless, in the conclusion, Chris Keith briefly details an approach to the historical Jesus, based upon the findings of social memory theory.[19] This "memory approach" is described in more detail elsewhere in his work.[20] With the memory approach, Keith has identified an emerging trend in historical Jesus research, which he considers to have the potential to provide a way forward in a post-criteria landscape.

The core principle of the "memory approach" is the application of social memory theory to the gospel data,[21] and especially, the recognition of the character of Jesus traditions as collective memory.[22] Con-

Story; Bernier, *Aposynagōgos*; Horsley and Thatcher, *John, Jesus & the Renewal of Israel*. The work of Annette Merz and Gerd Theissen concerning dissimilarity and plausibility also merits mention here, e.g., in Theissen and Merz, *The Historical Jesus*, cf. also Dagmar Winter, "Saving the Quest for Authenticity from the Criterion of Dissimilarity: History and Plausibility," in *Jesus, Criteria, and the Demise of Authenticity*, ed. Chris Keith and Anthony Le Donne (London and New York: T&T Clark, 2012), 115–31.

17. Keith and Le Donne, eds., *Demise of Authenticity*.

18. For example, compare the opinion of Chris Keith, "The Indebtedness of the Criteria Approach to Form Criticism and Recent Attempts to Rehabilitate the Search for an Authentic Jesus," in *Jesus, Criteria, and the Demise of Authenticity*, ed. Chris Keith and Anthony Le Donne (London and New York: T&T Clark, 2012), 25–48, with that of Winter, "Saving the Quest."

19. Chris Keith, "Concluding Remarks," in *Jesus, Criteria, and the Demise of Authenticity*, ed. Chris Keith and Anthony Le Donne (London and New York: T&T Clark, 2012), 200–205.

20. See esp. Keith, *Jesus' Literacy*, 27–70; and Keith, *Against the Scribal Elite*, 67–84.

21. For a good introduction to social memory theory and to the Jesus tradition as social memory, see Alan Kirk, "Social and Cultural Memory," in *Memory, Tradition, and Text: Uses of the Past in Early Christianity*, ed. Alan Kirk and Tom Thatcher (Semeia 52; Atlanta: Society of Biblical Literature, 2005), 1–24, and Alan Kirk and Tom Thatcher, "Jesus Tradition as Social Memory," in *Memory, Tradition, and Text: Uses of the Past in Early Christianity*, ed. Alan Kirk and Tom Thatcher (Semeia 52; Atlanta: Society of Biblical Literature, 2005), 25–42.

trary to appearances, remembering is not done in isolation. All memory is social. As Maurice Halbwachs, the progenitor of social memory theory, has maintained, "the mind reconstructs its memories under the pressures of society."[23] Individual memory is a part or aspect of group memory, "since each impression and each fact, even if it apparently concerns a particular person exclusively, leaves a lasting memory only to the extent that one has thought it over – to the extent that it is connected with the thoughts that come to us from the social milieu."[24] Understanding the processes of human remembering, how the social milieu impacts individual remembering, and how communities commemorate,[25] is of interest to history. This is because it helps historians to understand the nature of the surviving traces of the past that are used as evidence in the historical endeavour.[26]

A central tenet of the memory approach is the notion that the past is remembered and thus interpreted in light of the present in commemorative activities.[27] The result is that, as Keith writes, "there is no memory, no preserved past, and no access to it, without interpretation."[28] While the criteria approach attempts to separate authentic traditions from the interpretations around them, the "memory approach" recognizes that this cannot be done, since there are no uninterpreted traditions to separate.[29] This is not to say that the past is inaccessible, or eclipsed by the present.[30] Although the past is anchored in the present, the present is nevertheless "constituted by the past."[31] The

---

22. The now classic work of Maurice Halbwachs has been influential in this endeavour. See, e.g., Maurice Halbwachs, *On Collective Memory*, trans. Lewis A. Coser (Chicago: University of Chicago Press, 1992), esp. 35–189.

23. Ibid., 51.

24. Ibid., 53.

25. Cf. Le Donne, *Historiographical Jesus*, 60.

26. Social memory theory has been utilized in various forms for historiographical purposes by a number of historians. A few notable examples include Pierre Nora, "Between Memory and History: Les Lieux de Mémoire," *Representations* 26 (1989): 7–24; Pierre Nora, *Realms of Memory: Rethinking the French Past*, trans. Arthur Goldhammer (New York: Columbia University Press, 1996); Yael Zerubavel, *Recovered Roots: Collective Memory and the Making of Israeli National Tradition* (Chicago: University of Chicago Press, 1995); Barry Schwartz, *Abraham Lincoln and the Forge of National Memory* (Chicago: University of Chicago Press, 2000); Barry Schwartz., *Abraham Lincoln in the Post-Heroic Era: History and Memory in Late Twentieth-Century America* (Chicago: University of Chicago Press, 2008); Jan Assman, *Religion and Cultural Memory*, trans. Rodney Livingstone (Stanford: Stanford University Press, 2006).

27. Cf., e.g., Keith, *Jesus' Literacy*, 54ff.; Kirk, "Social and Cultural Memory," 20ff.; Le Donne, *Historiographical Jesus*, 42; Dale C. Allison, *Constructing Jesus: Memory, Imagination, and History* (Grand Rapids: Baker Academic, 2010), 4.

28. Keith, *Jesus' Literacy*, 61.

29. Cf. Ibid.

30. This is essentially the position described as "continuitism." A good summary and defence of this position can be found in Anthony Le Donne, "The Problem of Selectivity in Memory Research: A Response to Zeba Crook," *JSHJ* 11 (2013): 77–97.

past is indeed remembered, though not without interpretation. However, scholars should not simply discard the interpretations, since it is through the interpretations of the past that connections to the actual past are preserved.[32] Thus, Le Donne posits that "matters of emphasis, perspective, and interpretation are *the very basis* for memory's existence."[33] According to the "memory approach," the historian's task is to explain the existence of the memories of Jesus in the Gospels, by accounting for the interpretations in the Gospels rather than by dismissing them.[34] This task runs contrary to traditional methods for studying the historical Jesus, which make use of the criteria and redaction criticism in order to free authentic traditions from the redactional frameworks in which they are embedded.[35]

There are now a considerable number of scholars who are incorporating the insights of social memory theory into their work on Jesus and the Gospels.[36] Of course, not all of these scholars employ social memory theory in the same manner, nor do they necessarily all agree about how much of the "present" is represented in the traditions preserved in the Gospels. Nevertheless, Keith's "memory approach" identifies and highlights some of the common threads and underlying foundations of this trend in current research. It is important, however, to distinguish the proponents of the "memory approach" from those scholars who utilize social memory theory to establish the historical reliability of the Gospel traditions, since these are two distinct approaches.[37]

31. Schwartz, *Forge of National Memory*, 302.
32. Keith, *Jesus' Literacy*, 65; Alan Kirk, "Memory," in *Jesus in Memory: Traditions in Oral and Scribal Perspectives*, ed. Werner H. Kelber and Samuel Byrskog (Waco: Baylor University Press, 2009), 155–72 (169).
33. Le Donne, *Historiographical Jesus*, 51.
34. Keith, *Jesus' Literacy*, 66.
35. For a classic description of this traditional method, see Perrin, *What Is Redaction Criticism?*, 68–74.
36. Some examples include Allison, *Constructing Jesus*; Samuel Byrskog, "A New Quest for the *Sitz im Leben*: Social Memory, the Jesus Tradition, and the Gospel of Matthew," *NTS* 52 (2006): 319–336; Dennis C. Duling, "Social Memory and Biblical Studies: Theory, Method, and Application," *BTB* 36, no. (2006): 2–3; Zeba Crook, "Collective Memory Distortion and the Quest for the Historical Jesus," *JSHJ* 11, no. 1 (2013): 53–76; Werner H. Kelber, "The Generative Force of Memory: Early Christian Traditions as Processes of Remembering," *BTB* 36, no. (2006): 15–22; Werner H. Kelber and Samuel Byrskog, eds., *Traditions in Oral and Scribal Perspectives* (Waco: Baylor University Press, 2009); Kirk, "Social and Cultural Memory"; Kirk, "Memory"; Kirk and Thatcher, "Jesus Tradition as Social Memory"; Le Donne, *The Historiographical Jesus*; Rafael Rodríguez, *Structuring Early Christian Memory: Jesus in Tradition, Performance, and Text* (LNTS 407; London and New York: T&T Clark, 2010); Jens Schröter, *From Jesus to the New Testament: Early Christian Theology and the Origin of the New Testament Canon*, trans. Wayne Coppins (Waco: Baylor University Press, 2013); Jens Schröter, "The Criteria of Authenticity in Jesus Research and Historiographical Method"; Thatcher, *Why John Wrote a Gospel*.
37. Especially Richard Bauckham, *Jesus and the Eyewitnesses: The Gospels as Eyewitness Testimony* (Grand Rapids: Eerdmans, 2006); and Robert K. McIver, *Memory, Jesus, and the Synoptic Gospels* (RBS 59; Lei-

Social memory theory has brought some valuable insights to the study of the historical Jesus. Nevertheless, the "memory approach" is not a method, nor does it provide the historian with a clear path for moulding the raw data into history. The historian's craft does not consist solely of recognizing and understanding elements of the present in the past. Keith has rightly avoided calling this procedure a "method," preferring the more modest term "approach." In his own words, "no formal method has replaced the criteria approach. Recent post-criteria Jesus research has, however, exhibited a shared set of assumptions that I and others have referred to as the 'Jesus-memory approach' or simply 'memory approach' in light of the prominent role of social memory theory."[38] This caution is judicious. The "memory approach" may provide some initial orientation as a way to understand the data and in what way it might be used as evidence for the historian's investigation.

A well-defined historiographical procedure or philosophy of history is still lacking. Although memory research has provided a useful tool for historical investigation, historical reconstruction is not achieved solely through the recognition of the interpretive imprint of the present on memories of the past (called "distortion"), *but by asking historical questions of the data provided by those memories and other sources, whether literary or material, interpreting the data, applying that data as evidence, inferring historical knowledge from it, and connecting the evidence by means of the historical imagination.*

Addressing Some Problems and Misconceptions: The Doctrine of ReEnactment, Idealism, and the Role of Testimony in History

Collingwood is notoriously difficult to understand, and is prone to being misconstrued.[39] Further complicating the matter is the fact that

---

den and Boston: Brill, 2012). This approach has attracted criticisms, e.g., Judith C.S. Redman, "How Accurate are Eyewitnesses? Bauckham and the Eyewitnesses in Light of Psychological Research," *JBL* 129 (2010): 177–97; Paul Foster, "Memory, Orality, and the Fourth Gospel: Three Dead-Ends in Historical Jesus Research," *JSHJ* 10, no. 3, 2012: 191–227; Crook, "Collective Memory Distortion"; John S. Kloppenborg, "Memory, Performance, and the Sayings of Jesus," *JSHJ* 10 (2012): 97–132. See also the response to Crook by Anthony Le Donne, "The Problem of Selectivity", and Crook's reply, Zeba A. Crook, "Gratitude and Comments to Anthony Le Donne," *JSHJ* 1 (2013): 98–105. A response to Foster can be found in Stanley E. Porter and Hughson T. Ong, "Memory, Orality, and the Fourth Gospel: A Response to Paul Foster with Further Comments for Future Discussion," *JSHJ* 12 (2014): 143–64, replied to in Paul Foster, "Memory, Orality, and the Fourth Gospel: An Ongoing Conversation with Stan Porter and Hughson T. Ong," *JSHJ* 12 (2014): 165–83.

38. Chris Keith, *Scribal Elite*, 81.

39. Awareness of this issue is frequently reflected in the secondary literature. See, e.g., Peter Johnson, *Collingwood's The Idea of History*, xiii; van der Dussen, *History as a Science*, 283; William H. Dray, *History as Re-Enactment: R. G. Collingwood's Idea of History* (Oxford: Clarendon, 1995), 5; Louis O. Mink,

his seminal work in the philosophy of history, *The Idea of History*, was compiled and published posthumously, with the definitive revised and expanded edition being published almost half a century later in 1993.[40] A great deal of the misunderstanding is related to the controversial doctrine of reenactment. It is best to address this matter straightaway in order to alleviate confusion.

One of Collingwood's more important contributions to the theory of history and to the practice of history is his distinction between the inside and the outside of historical events.[41] By the "outside" of the event, Collingwood essentially means the physical dimension of the event, including bodies, the movement of bodies, geography, etc. The "inside" of the event is that which "can only be described in terms of thought," that is, the thought of the historical actors.[42] The two are sides of the same coin, and Collingwood rightly maintains that history is concerned with *both* the outside and the inside of event.[43]

Although this is, in itself, not particularly controversial, Collingwood also states that the historian discerns the thoughts that are the object of historical inquiry only by "re-thinking them in his own mind."[44] Thus, he maintains that the historian "must re-enact the past in his own mind."[45] This might be considered reasonable so far as the outside of an event is concerned, but the re-thinking of the thought of historical actors is an intuitively eccentric proposition.

Even if we grant that the thoughts of a historical actor exist to be rethought by a historian in the present, one of the most serious problems with the doctrine of reenactment remains. It is questionable to suppose that one can actually rethink the thoughts of another without having access to the direct experience of their historical context, including all of the specific individual experiences that shaped their thoughts. This is at the core of David Hackett Fischer's objection that

Mind, History, and Dialectic: The Philosophy of R. G. Collingwood (Middletown: Wesleyan University Press, 1969), 158–60. I have dealt with some of the misunderstandings of Collingwood's thought by New Testament scholars in further depth elsewhere, in Jordan J. Ryan, "Jesus at the Crossroads of Inference and Imagination: The Relevance of R. G. Collingwood's Philosophy of History for Current Methodological Discussions in Historical Jesus Research," *JSHJ* 13, no. 1 (2015): 66–89.

40. R. G. Collingwood, *The Idea of History*, 1st ed., ed. T.M. Knox (Oxford: Clarendon, 1946); R. G. Collingwood, *The Idea of History*, ed. Jan van der Dussen, rev. and enl. ed. (Oxford: Clarendon, 1993). Unless otherwise stated, all further references will be made to the revised and enlarged edition.

41. Collingwood, *Idea of History*, 213. This concept will be further discussed in appendix B.

42. Ibid., 213.

43. Ibid., 214.

44. Ibid., 215.

45. Ibid., 282.

reenactment requires the historian to actually *be* the person whose thoughts they are reenacting—which is impossible.[46]

Despite the peculiarity of this particular idea, there is no need to reject or disregard Collingwood entirely on this basis alone. There are two reasons for this. First, it must be recognized that reenactment is not actually a methodological matter or tool, but an epistemological doctrine pertaining to Collingwood's understanding of history itself. Second, Collingwood's genuinely methodological insights, which will be discussed below, can be applied independently of this doctrine and still hold their validity if reenactment is removed. A cursory survey of the secondary literature reveals a serious concern among Collingwood's later interpreters to clarify that the doctrine of reenactment is *not* methodological and that it is a critical mistake to treat it as such.[47] The doctrine of reenactment in Collingwood's thought is best understood not as a "method" but as a "condition" for history,[48] or more simply, as a description of what historical knowledge entails.

Collingwood was essentially a philosophical idealist, and he developed his philosophy of history in opposition to the prevailing realism of his day. This sort of realism is basically identical to what Lonergan calls "naïve" realism,[49] which is to be distinguished from his own "critical" realism. The doctrine of reenactment is essential to the antirealist aspect of Collingwood's understanding of the nature of history. Johnson calls it a "load-bearing doctrine," and once it is removed, "you are left with history as realism understands it."[50] It thereby comes as

---

46. Although he mistakenly conceives of it as a method, Fischer otherwise presents a reasonable objection to the reenactment of past thought in David Hackett Fischer, *Historians' Fallacies: Toward a Logic of History* (New York: Harper & Row, 1970), 196–97. He writes, "To require a historian to rethink Brutus' thought before he killed Caesar is to require him to become Brutus. And this he cannot do, any more than Disko Troop (of Rudyard Kipling's *Captains Courageous*) could convert himself into a twenty-pound cod. For Brutus did not merely think different things than Collingwood thought – he thought them differently . . . some thought which interests historians cannot be separated from feeling, or from thinking structures which exist within limits of space and time."

47. For example, Johnson, *Collingwood's The Idea of History*, 54; van der Dussen, *History as a Science*, 263; Alan Donagan, "The Verification of Historical Theses," *Philosophical Quarterly* 6 (1956): 193–208 (207). The exhaustive review and evaluation of the history of interpretation of the doctrine of reenactment in van der Dussen, *History as a Science*, 85–96 is highly recommended. Although some early interpreters tended to view reenactment as a method, the view that it is a doctrine or condition for history has stood the test of time and won out.

48. Cf. Johnson, *Collingwood's The Idea of History*, 54; William H. Dray, "R. G. Collingwood and the Acquaintance Theory of Knowledge," *Revue Internationale de Philosophie* 11 (1957): 420–32 (432); Dray, *History as Re-Enactment*, 59; Donagan, "Verification of Historical Theses," 206–7; Robert G. Shoemaker, "Inference and Intuition in Collingwood's Philosophy of History," *The Monist* 53 (1969): 100–115 (112–13). Similarly, van der Dussen, *History as a Science*, 292–94, though van der Dussen notes the doctrine's relevance for method, despite not being a method in itself.

49. E.g., Bernard Lonergan, *Method in Theology* (Toronto: University of Toronto Press, 2007), 263–64.

50. Johnson, *Collingwood's The Idea of History*, 54.

no surprise that Lonergan omits it from his own account of history in *Method in Theology*, which is heavily influenced by Collingwood.[51] In speaking of Collingwood's "Copernican revolution" in historical inquiry, Lonergan says, "unfortunately it is contained in an idealist context. But by introducing a satisfactory theory of objectivity and of judgment, *the idealism can be removed* without dropping the substance of what Collingwood taught about the historical imagination, historical evidence, and the logic of question and answer."[52]

Lonergan, and Ben Meyer after him,[53] were thus able to apply certain aspects of Collingwood's methodological insights within a critical realist framework. As both Lonergan and Meyer demonstrate, Collingwood's methodological insights do not depend on these other aspects of his thought and require serious consideration by the historian whether in light or in spite of them. Although I recognize its purpose and place within Collingwood's thought, the doctrine of reenactment need not be retained, since it overcomplicates matters and entails the acceptance of an essentially idealist epistemology.[54] Following Lonergan, I propose that the substance of Collingwood's methodological approach to history, once it has been distilled from the framework in which it appears in *The Idea of History*, can be resituated within a Lonerganian "critical-realist" epistemology, which leaves no need for the reenactment of past thought.

Rudolf Bultmann made use of some particular aspects of Collingwood's thought in the influential Gifford Lectures (1955), later published as *History and Eschatology*.[55] Bultmann's reading of Collingwood would subsequently come to have a substantial impact on the New Quest for the historical Jesus.[56] However, as several scholars have since pointed out, Bultmann egregiously misunderstood Collingwood.[57] As a result, Collingwood was put into the service of a historical project and procedure that was antithetical and contrary to the foundations of his

---

1. Bernard Lonergan, *Method in Theology*, 175–234.

2. Ibid., 206, emphasis my own.

3. E.g., Meyer, *Critical Realism and the New Testament*, 147ff.

4. Cf. Jasper Hopkins, "Bultmann on Collingwood's Philosophy of History," *Harvard Theological Review* 58, no. 2 (1965): 227–33 (231). According to Hopkins, Collingwood's methodological statements concerning evidence "can be held fast, even though his bizarre metaphysical theory about what it means to recapture a past thought be rejected."

5. Rudolf Bultmann, *History and Eschatology: The Presence of Eternity* (New York: Harper, 1957), 122–47.

6. For a summary and critique of the manner in which Collingwood was applied by proponents of the New Quest, see Paul Merkley, "New Quests for Old: One Historian's Observations on a Bad Bargain," *Canadian Journal of Theology* 16, no. 3 (1970): 203–18.

7. Hopkins, "Bultmann on Collingwood's Philosophy of History," 227–33; Merkley, "New Quests for Old"; Meyer, *Critical Realism and the New Testament*, 148–150; van der Dussen, *History as a Science*, 82–83.

philosophy and historiography. Thus, Ben Meyer writes that "for years Bultmann and his followers indulged in the habit of citing Collingwood on history. This is ironic, for virtually nothing of Collingwood's drive to free history of alien inhibitions and prohibitions passed into their practice."[58]

Curiously, Bultmann concentrated on the problematically idealist aspects of Collingwood's philosophy of history, and endorsed Collingwood's theory of historical reenactment as a method.[59] Jasper Hopkins considers Bultmann's interpretation of Collingwood to be at least partially responsibility for the neglect of Collingwood by theologians.[60] Given Bultmann's towering presence in historical Jesus research, it is even more likely that this is the case in our specific subfield.

Now that the ground-clearing work has been done, we may turn to the methodological insights that will form the basis for the procedure of the present historical investigation. Throughout this undertaking, it must be kept in mind that *The Idea of History* is a posthumous composite work whose concern is to present a philosophy of history rather than a comprehensive method. As such, it does not systematically lay out a clear historiographical procedure, nor is that its purpose. Thus, a historical method must be distilled from its insights. This is the task now set before us.

The Shortfalls of Scissors-and-Paste

Collingwood's concept of scissors-and-paste is particularly relevant to the current discussions in historical Jesus research concerning the criteria of authenticity. Scissors-and-paste is history constructed by excerpting and combining the testimonies of different authorities.[61] Historical criticism, in Collingwood's estimation, is nothing more than an advanced instance of scissors-and-paste. The primary question it is concerned with asking is: "shall we incorporate this statement in our own narrative or not?" The methods developed to this end are intended to answer either affirmatively or negatively.[62] Authentic statements are included in the history, while the inauthentic statements are discarded. The historian is then left to consider the impli-

---

58. Meyer, *Critical Realism and the New Testament*, 150.
59. Bultmann, *History and Eschatology*, 130–31.
60. Hopkins, "Bultmann on Collingwood's Philosophy of History," e.g., 227.
61. Collingwood, *Idea of History*, 257.
62. Ibid., 259.

cations of the statements that have been included, disregarding that which has been cast aside as inauthentic.

Scissors-and-paste history is problematic because it creates an inflexible dichotomy between authentic and inauthentic traditions.[63] We should note here that Collingwood's insight in this regard finds confirmation in the challenges presented to the distinction between authentic/inauthentic by social memory theory. Scissors-and-paste is primarily interested in asking one particular question of the data, namely, "is this statement true or false?"[64] For Collingwood, the better question is "what does this mean?"[65] More specifically, this entails asking and answering the questions "what did the author mean by it?" and subsequently "what does this mean for my investigation?"

In a murder case, a detective might discover that the statement of an individual who claims to have committed the crime but was incapable of so doing for one reason or another is false.[66] This false statement, however, should not simply be discarded—it raises further questions, requires explanation, and despite being false, may yet be evidence for the matter at hand. Why might the witness lie about committing the crime? Perhaps to protect someone else. This knowledge can then be used by the detective to advance the investigation. So it is also with the historian's task. Even "inauthentic" data requires explanation, and by understanding the statement and what light it may shed, one transforms the statements of one's sources or authorities into evidence for the question at hand. It is for this reason that extreme skepticism or minimalism, in which "inauthentic" traditions are simply discounted from the investigation altogether, must be rejected.[67]

This does not mean that it is not at all worth knowing whether a statement corresponds to historical reality.[68] Collingwood readily acknowledges that some statements may need to be rejected.[69] However, a judgment on the correspondence of a statement to historical

---

63. The scissors-and-paste character of certain approaches in historical Jesus research has also been noted by Pieter F. Craffert, *The Life of a Galilean Shaman: Jesus in Anthropological-Historical Perspective* (Eugene: Wipf and Stock, 2008), 6, 33, 254.

64. Collingwood, *Idea of History*, 261.

65. Ibid., 275.

66. Cf. Collingwood's detective story, written to illustrate historical method, in Collingwood, *Idea of History*, 266–82. The analogy between the task of the detective, who puts together a picture of the past on the basis of traces of the past in the present in the form of testimony and material evidence, and the historian is celebrated and further examined in the collection of essays edited by Robin W. Winks, *The Historian as Detective: Essays on Evidence* (New York: Harper Torchbooks, 1970).

67. Hence, Collingwood's biting dismissal of skepticism, and the hard distinction he makes between the critic and the skeptic in *Idea of History*, 252. This point has also been applied by Chris Keith. See Keith, *Jesus' Literacy*, 63–64.

68. Historical judgments of truth and falsehood will be discussed in appendix B.

reality can really only be made with confidence once a statement is understood, and even if the judgment is negative, the statement may still be of use in some way other than in its literal sense. Here, we are again reminded of the example of a murder case in which a witness is lying, wherein knowledge of the fact that they are lying and the precise content of the lie may itself be helpful evidence for reconstructing the past. Moreover, the validity of any judgment will ultimately stand or fall in one way or another on the basis of its relationship to evidence. This could be, for instance, evidence indicating a problem with the statement (for example, historical implausibility or anachronism), or evidence that favors an alternative construction or a dissenting witness.

It is striking how well Collingwood's critique of scissors-and-paste complements recent work in historical Jesus research utilizing social memory theory. Since there is no memory without interpretation,[70] Keith has remarked that even if a tradition about Jesus is considered false, the proper approach to that tradition is not to ask *whether* or not Jesus was misremembered, and to discard it if he was, but rather, to ask *how* Jesus was misremembered and "proceed to explain what socio-historical conditions led to the production of that memory."[71] This basic notion that data, even traditions that are suspected to be false, should be explained and understood rather than discarded is both similar to and confirmatory of Collingwood's critique of scissors-and-paste.

The key to escaping the trap of scissors-and-paste is the ability to treat data as evidence for a question or investigation, rather than as testimony. I suggest that the discipline of historical Jesus research needs to reconsider its obsession with "historicity" or "authenticity." This does not mean that historical truth should be abandoned. I must stress once more that this does not mean that we will never need to determine whether something did or did not happen, or whether a witness is telling the truth. However, as anyone who has ever read a good detective novel will know, the truth or falsity of a statement is not always as interesting for the purposes of reconstructing the past as the very fact that it is made to begin with. Evidence comes in many forms, so the historian's task is not to simply sift traditions in order to separate "authentic" from "inauthentic," but to understand the data, know

---

69. As is the case with his comparison of the accounts of Suetonius and Tacitus on Nero's policy and the evacuation of Britain, in Collingwood, *Idea of History*, 244–45.
70. Keith, *Jesus' Literacy*, 61.
71. Ibid., 64.

what is relevant, and how to apply it as evidence to the investigation and questions at hand.

Data and Evidence

History is constructed in relation to evidence. This is the most fundamental aspect of the historian's task. Knowledge of the past is not direct, as it is in the empirical sciences, but inferred, mediated through evidence. Evidence forms the framework upon which the historical reconstruction hangs, and the truth of a reconstruction is justified by an appeal to evidence.[72] However, relevant data cannot simply be gathered and arranged, because data requires interpretation. Thus, at its most basic level, history is a discipline concerned with *interpretation*.[73] E. H. Carr puts the matter well in saying that it is untrue that "the facts" speak for themselves, since "the facts speak only when the historian calls on them."[74]

What exactly counts as evidence? According to Collingwood, there is a correlation between a historical question and evidence, and thus, "Anything is evidence which enables you to answer your question – the question you are asking now."[75] In other words, evidence is not something that comes readymade. All data is potentially evidence for something. Data becomes actualized as evidence once it is applied to a historical inquiry, and so, what is to be used as evidence becomes clear as the inquiry progresses.[76] Evidence exists within the context of an investigation. In other words, something can only be evidence when it is contemplated historically.[77] Thus, Collingwood remarks that "you can't collect your evidence before you begin your thinking."[78] The key notion here is that the historical enterprise is not simply about gathering information independent of an investigation or question. Rather, history involves the *application* of data as evidence in an investigation.

Collingwood's understanding of evidence purposefully encourages the historian to consider the potential contribution that can be made

---

72. Cf. Collingwood, *Idea of History*, 246.
73. Cf. Sheppard, *Craft of History*, 15–16. On interpretation as the formal task of history, see Collingwood, *Idea of History*, 368–70. The importance of interpretation for history is also recognized and discussed by Johann Gustav Droysen, *Outline of the Principles of History*, trans. E. Benjamin Andrews (Boston: Ginn & Company, 1897), 26ff.
74. Carr, *What is History?*, 11. Carr's understanding and use of the term "facts" is problematic, but this can be corrected by replacing what he considers to be "fact" with "evidence."
75. Collingwood, *Idea of History*, 281.
76. Cf. Johnson, *Collingwood's The Idea of History*, 71.
77. Cf. Collingwood, *Idea of History*, 247.
78. Ibid., 281.

not only by literary sources, but also by nonliterary sources. This includes, for example, archaeological sources and material data, which can be contributed through such things as numismatics, ceramics, and architecture,[79] as well as topography and geography. Collingwood was no armchair philosopher of history, but was himself both an accomplished historian *and* archaeologist of Roman Britain,[80] and is well known for his emphasis upon the interpretation of archaeological data within historical reconstruction.[81] By contrast, archaeology has only relatively recently come to play a significant role in historical Jesus research.[82]

Material evidence can be used to establish a historical context beyond what literary sources provide, operating outside of what is remembered. For example, archaeology, including numismatics, ceramics, and architecture, has played a major part in recent efforts to reconstruct the economy of Galilee,[83] which has, in turn, been used in Jesus research to interpret and contextualize Jesus and the movement around him.[84] Archaeological evidence breaks down the scissors-and-paste paradigm, in which data is primarily considered in terms of its "authenticity" or "inauthenticity," since it is typically nonsensical to consider provenanced archaeological data (from excavations properly conducted) in terms of "authenticity." Provenanced archaeological data requires interpretation, not verification. Moreover, grounding a reconstruction in material evidence alongside literary evidence prevents the historian from falling into the trap of confusing literary analysis with historical reconstruction,[85] and from slavery to the

---

79. On this, see Collingwood, *Idea of History*, 386. Concerning the use of numismatics in historical Jesus research, see David Hendin, "Jesus and Numismatics: The Importance of Coins in Reconstructing Jesus and His World," in *Jesus Research: New Methodologies and Perceptions*, ed. James H. Charlesworth, with Brian Rhea and Petr Pokorný, 2 vols. (Grand Rapids: Eerdmans, 2014), 2:190–97.

80. See especially R. G. Collingwood, *Roman Britain* (rev. ed.; Barnes and Noble, 1994); and R. G. Collingwood, *The Archaeology of Roman Britain*, rev. ed., ed. I.A. Richmond (repr.; London: Bracken Books, 1996).

81. See van der Dussen, *History as a Science*, 268–71.

82. On this, refer to James H. Charlesworth, "Jesus Research and Archaeology: A New Perspective," in *Jesus and Archaeology*, ed. James H. Charlesworth (Grand Rapids and Cambridge: Eerdmans, 2006), 11–63.

83. E.g., Morten Hørning Jensen, *Herod Antipas in Galilee: The Literary and Archaeological Sources on the Reign of Herod Antipas and its Socio-Economic Impact on Galilee* (WUNT 215; Tübingen: Mohr Siebeck, 2010); David A. Fiensy and Ralph K. Hawkins, eds., *The Galilean Economy in the Time of Jesus* (Early Christianity and its Literature 11; Atlanta: Society of Biblical Literature, 2013); and the chapters on economy in David A. Fiensy and James Riley Strange, eds., *Galilee in the Late Second Temple and Mishnaic Periods: Life, Culture, and Society* (Minneapolis: Fortress Press, 2014), esp. 263–387.

84. See esp. Freyne, *The Jesus Movement*, 90–132; and Oakman, *Political Aims of Jesus*. Jensen also makes judicious use of similar data in his reconstruction of the reign of Herod Antipas in Jensen, *Herod Antipas in Galilee*.

authority of witnesses. As soon as material evidence is cast alongside literary sources, the historian is required to use the historical imagination and reconstruction in order to connect the two.

Evidence thus plays a dual role in history. First, it is one of the primary building materials, the robust skeletal framework, of history. Second, evidence is the standard of plausibility for historical constructions, the solid bedrock in which a construction is grounded. A reconstruction that is unable to explain relevant evidence, or that is lacking in evidence must be considered problematic.[86] This does not mean that sources should be simply reproduced. Evidence requires interpretation, since data can only be reasonably applied as evidence if it is understood. A historian may even disagree with a statement in a source, but by interpreting it, may find that it is applicable to the investigation in some other way apart from the literal sense of the statement.[87]

Inference

Historical knowledge is inferential knowledge. It is not like empirical knowledge. According to Collingwood, the business of history is "to study events not accessible to our observation, and to study these events inferentially, *arguing to them from something else which is accessible to our observation*, and which the historian calls 'evidence' for the events in which he is interested."[88] This principle is self-evidently true, since historical events belong to the past and cannot be observed in the present, although they can be argued to from their traces in the present.[89] We see here how essential the historian is to the practice of history, since inference requires not only evidence, but a historian to infer historical knowledge from the evidence. Nevertheless, history is not subjective belief, but a type of knowledge, an inferential knowledge. Historical knowledge is grounded in evidence, from which it is inferred, but with which it is not identical. This concept is fundamental to the practice of history, and yet its applicability within historical investigation is far too easily underestimated.

85. Cf. the now famous critique of Hooker, "On Using the Wrong Tool," passim.
86. A concrete example of such a problematic reconstruction can be found in H.C. Kee's denial of the existence of pre-70 CE synagogue buildings, which is treated in chapter 4 of this study. See Kee, "Transformation of the Synagogue," passim.
87. Cf. Marc Bloch, *The Historian's Craft*, trans. Peter Putnam (New York: Alfred A. Knopf, 1953), 64.
88. Collingwood, *Idea of History*, 251–52.
89. Cf., e.g., Sheppard, *The Craft of History*, 70–71; Denton, *Historiography and Hermeneutics*, 106–7; Lonergan, *Method in Theology*, 206; Johnson, *Collingwood's The Idea of History*, 77.

The methodological upshot of understanding history to be inferential is that a clear distinction must be made between history itself and the evidence used to construct it. The historian is not interested in the evidence in itself, but in the inferences that may be drawn from the evidence.[90] In other words, history is something that is inferred by the historian from the evidence, not derived from it directly. So far as literary evidence is concerned, the historian is not enslaved to the testimony of witnesses, nor to historical authorities, because the historian's picture is his or her own to create on the basis of what can be inferred from the witnesses or authorities. Consequently, it is not enough to simply establish the "reliability" or "authenticity" of a source or a piece of evidence. There are questions to be asked and data to interpret beyond what the witnesses can provide.

We must remember at this point that history can enlighten us when memory fails, when something was not recorded, or not observed.[91] Memory provides some of the raw data necessary for the historian's task, but history is not reducible to memory.[92] The presence of memory distortion, misremembering, redaction, or minor errors in a source does not mean that the past cannot be reconstructed from it, since knowledge of the past is inferred, and thus does not need to be tied to the exact content of a statement. As the discussion of the problem of scissors-and-paste indicated above, historical knowledge can even be inferred from an untruthful witness, since it does not stand or fall on the "authenticity" of statements.

The fact that historical knowledge is inferential knowledge rather than direct empirical knowledge is not a cause for concern. Inference is a regular element of human cognition. As Robin Winks has put it, "we all make inferences daily, and we all collect, sift, evaluate, and then act upon evidence. Our alarm clocks, the toothpaste tube without a cap, warm milk at the breakfast table, and the bus that is ten minutes late provide us with evidence from which we infer certain unseen actions."[93] Despite being inferential, history is not made-up, invented, or pulled out of thin air. Evidence, traces of the past in the present which can be observed by the historian,[94] grounds inference. There is

---

90. Cf. Johnson, *Collingwood's The Idea of History*, 45.

91. Ibid.

92. Collingwood, *Idea of History*, 366–67; cf. 252–53; 486–88.

93. Robin W. Winks, introduction to *The Historian as Detective: Essays on Evidence*, ed. Robin W. Winks (New York: Harper & Row, 1970), xiii–xxiv (xvi).

94. See Collingwood, *Idea of History*, 251.

no history without evidence, since there is nothing to make inferences from.

The Historical Imagination

The concept of inference dovetails into imagination. Collingwood insists that historians must go beyond their sources in two ways.[95] One of these is through criticism of the evidence, the processes of deciding how the sources will be used and in what measure,[96] with which historical Jesus research is intimately familiar. The other is through *construction*. Throughout the history of the quest for the historical Jesus, the critical aspect of history has had a tendency to eclipse the constructive element.[97] However, history is both critical and constructive. Construction allows historians to arrive at knowledge that may have been unknown to the authors of the sources, or that was forgotten, withheld, or omitted. It can also allow for the rediscovery and use of something that went unmentioned because it was assumed and went without saying within the author's temporal and cultural milieu, as is the case with much contextual and background information.

The historical imagination is the constructive element in history.[98] The historian's task requires the interpolation of information between the data,[99] making connections and filling in gaps. According to Collingwood, knowledge inferred in this way is "essentially something imagined."[100] This does not mean that what the historian reconstructs is not "real," in the sense of being fictional or untrue. As Collingwood says, "If we look out over the sea and perceive a ship, and five minutes later look again and perceive it in a different place, we find ourselves obliged to imagine it as having occupied intermediate positions when we were not looking."[101] This is precisely how the constructive act of writing history should operate. Perception of the two positions of the

95. Ibid., 240.
96. Cf. Lonergan, *Method in Theology*, 206.
97. The traditional methods used in historical Jesus research are designed to facilitate criticism. This is clearly the case with the criteria of authenticity. As the names indicate, the same goes for form, redaction, and source criticism. Indeed, the ever-increasing multiplication of methodologies in Biblical studies labelled with the word "criticism" is indicative of an obsession with criticism in our discipline.
98. One of the best in-depth treatments of this aspect of Collingwood's thought can be found in Marnie Hughes-Warrington, *How Good an Historian Shall I Be? R. G. Collingwood, The Historical Imagination, and Education* (British Idealist Studies Series 2: Collingwood 2; Exeter: Imprint Academic, 2004).
99. Collingwood, *Idea of History*, 240.
100. Ibid., 241.
101. Ibid.

ship provides points of data to work with. The imagination fills the gap between them. Thus, the narrative that emerges of the ship travelling between points A and B is firmly rooted in evidence—it is not arbitrary.

The historian's construction consists of a web, composed of threads of imagination stretched between nodes of evidence, which provide relatively fixed points for the imaginative threads.[102] In order for a construction to be truly historical, it must be firmly embedded in evidence.[103] The points are *relatively* fixed, because the historian is responsible for the interpretation, use, and application of evidence in a construction.[104] These points of evidence are responsible for the strength and viability of a construction. More and stronger evidence will result in more robust connections and imaginative threads between those points of evidence. The plausibility of a web of historical construction is derived from the strength of its evidence and the interweaving and connectivity of the threads between the nodes.[105] This is one of the most important distinctions separating history from historical fiction.[106] Both history and historical fiction must be consistent and localized in time and space. However, as Collingwood writes, "the historian's picture stands in a peculiar relation to something called evidence," since the truth of a historical statement can be justified by an appeal to the evidence.[107] A construction consisting of too much imagination and not enough evidence will cease to be history, and will instead fall into the realm of historical fiction.[108]

This does not, however, mean that something is untrue simply because it is not stated directly in the sources. Scholars must be careful when they claim that "there is no evidence" to support a given hypothesis when what is really meant is that there is no direct statement in the sources or authorities of the content of the hypothesis. To do so is to relinquish one's autonomy as a historian and to fall into the problematic practice that Collingwood calls "scissors-and-paste."[109] Instead, the historian must be able to ask the right questions and apply the

---

102. Ibid., 242–43. Cf. also Lonergan, *Method in Theology*, 189.
103. Cf. Johnson, *Collingwood's The Idea of History*, 48.
104. Collingwood, *Idea of History*, 242–43. For further discussion of this, see Dray, *History as Re-enactment*, 197–98. This premise fits quite well with Meyer's notion of "data control," in Meyer, *Aims of Jesus*, 81–87.
105. In agreement with Dray, *History as Re-enactment*, 197.
106. Collingwood, *Idea of History*, 246.
107. Ibid.
108. An excellent unpacking of the distinction between history and fiction can be found in Hughes-Warrington, *How Good an Historian Shall I Be?*, 136–38.
109. Cf., e.g., Collingwood, *Idea of History*, 256; R. G. Collingwood, *Principles of History*, ed. William H. Dray and Jan van der Dussen (Oxford: Oxford University Press, 1999), 150.

right evidence to those questions. Because anything is evidence which enables the historian to answer the question that he or she is asking,[110] evidence goes well beyond the realm of direct statements by the sources or authorities. On the contrary, because history can only be inferred from evidence, reconstructions that are imaginative but not rooted in the evidence are suspect and tantamount to fiction.

Let us consider an example in order to illustrate this. The recent archaeological discoveries at Magdala have produced very interesting finds and results for our understanding of first-century Galilee. However, there are no clear, direct statements in the Gospels that locate Jesus in Magdala proper. Did Jesus ever visit Magdala? The location of the site places it within the range of the Galilean peripatetic ministry of Jesus, which is described in the gospels as taking place along the Sea of Galilee (Matt 4:18, 15:29, Mark 1:16, 3:7–8, 7:31, John 6:1). The pattern of Jesus' ministry involved the synagogues of Galilee (Matt 4:23, 9:35, Mark 1:39, Luke 4:15, John 18:20), and a synagogue has indeed been discovered at Magdala. Magdala's location between Nazareth and Capernaum places it on the route by which Jesus would have travelled between the two, a journey which is depicted occurring twice in the synoptic gospels (Matt 4:15, Luke 4:16, 31). A journey from Cana to Capernaum is also depicted in the Gospel of John, which could also have taken Jesus through Magdala (John 2:1, 12). Moreover, the name of one of his followers, Mary Magdalene, probably indicates that she hailed from Magdala. All of this data constitutes evidence for our question. Although no authority tells us directly that Jesus visited Magdala, if we connect the fixed points of evidence by means of historical imagination, we are able to go beyond the statements of the sources and infer that Jesus probably visited or passed through Magdala at some point in time, and that he *may* have been active there for short periods of time.

The application of the historical imagination to the study of the historical Jesus is immediately apparent. There are innumerable gaps and lacunae in the Gospel narrative. For example, in the Gospel of John, Jesus will be located in Galilee in one episode, and then in Judea in the next, or vice versa (e.g., John 2:12, 13; John 5:1, 6:1). As in the example of the ship cited above, travel and intervening time must be imagined between the two episodes. A more pertinent example for the present project concerns Jesus's teaching in the synagogues. In several places

---

0. Collingwood, *Idea of History*, 282.

in the synoptics, we are told that Jesus preached and taught in the synagogues, but we are not told the content of that teaching beyond the fact that, in some instances, he was "proclaiming the Kingdom" (Matt 4:23, 9:35; Mark 1:21, 6:2; Luke 4:44, 6:6, 13:10). It is not possible to reconstruct the precise words or content of Jesus's teaching on these occasions, but it may be possible to employ the historical imagination to reconstruct the basic premises and tenets of his teaching in the synagogues in a general way on the basis of data pertaining to Jesus's teaching while in Galilee, data pertaining to synagogue teaching and practices, and clues within the Gospel synagogue episodes themselves.

Another application of the concept of the historical imagination that has been passed over in historical Jesus research involves a recognition of the reciprocity between the imaginative web and the points of evidence between which it is stretched. Just as the web of imagination depends on the evidence that grounds it, so too is the evidence itself supported by the web. As Collingwood writes, "It is thus the historian's picture of the past, the product of his own *a priori* imagination, that has to justify the sources used in its construction."[111] The interpretive web is not dependent on the independently established historicity of data. On the contrary, it serves as the "touchstone" by which the truth of alleged facts are determined.[112] The validity of the "facts" cannot be determined apart from a picture of the past. It is ultimately the historian's picture of the past *as a whole* rather than individual traditions or facts that matters and does the work of historical criticism. After all, if the picture as a whole is coherent, this supports the truth of the facts used to ground it. Thus, according to Collingwood, historical criticism of the sources is done "by considering whether the picture of the past to which the evidence leads him is a coherent and continuous picture, one that makes sense."[113] This cannot be accomplished within any historiographical paradigm which proceeds by establishing the truth of traditions prior to engaging in the work of interpretation and construction.[114]

---

111. Collingwood, *Idea of History*, 245.
112. Ibid., 244.
113. Ibid., 245.
114. It is worth noting that Denton observes that this is a major aspect of Collingwood's thought which has been passed over by Meyer. See Denton, *Historiography and Hermeneutics*, 122.

The Role of Question and Answer

As our discussion has demonstrated thus far, evidence plays an essential role in historical investigation, but it is not the object or end goal of history. The historian's task is not only to gather and sift evidence, but to infer historical knowledge from it by understanding it and putting it to the question.[115] As Marc Bloch has said, "Even those texts of archaeological documents which seem the clearest and the most accommodating will speak only when they are properly questioned."[116]

Historical method proceeds by asking questions of the data and answering them by making recourse to evidence.[117] As Collingwood has famously said, "Knowing involves asking questions and answering them."[118] The form of the questions, which we might also call "problems," is irrelevant, since what matters are their content and the answers that they will lead to. Questions may be either implicit or explicit, specific or general, but whatever the case may be, questions are the driving force of an investigation,[119] giving it direction and shape. In Lonerganian terms, questions are crucial for the development of understanding. Thus, Lonergan writes, "The understanding that has been achieved on a determinate point can be complemented, corrected, revised, only if further discoveries on that very point can be made. Such discoveries can be made *only if further relevant questions arise*."[120] Hence, if there are no further relevant questions, then a certain judgment can be considered to be true.[121]

There is a correlation between questions and evidence.[122] They are intimately related. Evidence, as discussed above, is anything that enables the historian to answer the question being asked. Conversely, there is a very real sense in which historical problems (or questions) themselves arise only when the historian possesses potential evidence bearing on that problem in the first place. Thus, Collingwood says "The historian does not first think of a problem and then search for evidence

5. Cf. Collingwood, *Idea of History*, 278ff.; Lonergan, *Method in Theology*, 187; Johnson, *Collingwood's The Idea of History*, 82ff.
6. Bloch, *Historian's Craft*, 64.
7. Cf. also Fischer, *Historian's Fallacies*, 3–4, in which Collingwood is cited favourably. Fischer eloquently writes that, "Without questions of some sort, a historian is condemned to wander aimlessly through dark corridors of learning."
8. R. G. Collingwood, *The New Leviathan*, (rev. ed. David Boucher; Oxford: Clarendon, 2000), 74.
9. In Collingwood's words, "The question is the charge of gas, exploded in the cylinder-head, which is the motive force of every piston-stroke." Collingwood, *Idea of History*, 273.
0. Lonergan, *Method in Theology*, 191. Emphasis is my own.
1. Ibid., 191.
2. Collingwood, *Idea of History*, 281.

bearing on it; it is his possession of evidence bearing on a problem that alone makes the problem a real one."[123] This may seem circular, since something can only be evidence in relation to a question, but there is undoubtedly a certain truth to it. It is more of a spiral than a circle. As Collingwood points out, when legitimate historical questions are asked, questions that are possible to answer,[124] historians already have some tentative idea of the data that might serve as evidence to address them.[125] When scholars investigate whether Jesus travelled to Jerusalem for one Passover or for multiple Passovers, they are only able to do so because they are aware that there is evidence that speaks to the problem in the first place.

The procedure of question and answer raises some critical questions for the traditional methods and procedures in historical Jesus research. The criteria of authenticity are not objectively pan-applicable questions, because the most relevant questions will differ from case to case. Many investigations will not depend on asking whether or not a certain pericope is multiply attested, doubly dissimilar, coherent with other sayings attributed to the historical Jesus, or embarrassing for the early church. The criteria may indeed sometimes pose questions worth asking, but even in these cases, they should be treated as indices rather than criteria.[126] Failure to satisfy the requirements of any given criterion is not warrant in itself to disregard a saying or to omit it from one's history. Asking the questions that the criteria provide may sometimes be helpful for interpreting the data, but history cannot functionally proceed by recourse to the questions that they ask alone.[127] History is an autonomous discipline, and the historian must operate autonomously, finding and asking for themself the most relevant and crucial questions as they arise over the course of an investigation.

In reality, the criteria can only offer a limited set of questions, and the most important or relevant questions for a given historical study will probably exist outside of their boundaries. There are instances in

---

123. R. G. Collingwood, "The Limits of Historical Knowledge," *Philosophy* 3, no. 10 (1928): 213–22 (222).
124. By this, I mean that historical questions are really only worth asking if there is some evidence that will allow them to be answered in one way or another. For example, it is pointless, if not somewhat absurd, to ask what Peter's favourite colour was, because there is no evidence (at least that I am aware of) that will enable us to answer that question. However, it is possible, historically speaking, to ask where Peter died, or whether he was behind the composition of 1 Peter, since there is evidence available to investigate these matters. Even if the investigation of that evidence results in *aporia* or a tentative answer, the question is still valid, due to the existence of evidence that speaks to it.
125. Collingwood, *Idea of History*, 281.
126. Cf. Meyer, *The Aims of Jesus*, 86.
127. Cf. Denton, *Historiography and Hermeneutics*, 120–21.

which the very nature of the question or data itself may go beyond what the criteria were designed to deal with. This problem is related to the fact that the criteria only deal with what is conveyed directly by the sources. They are really only designed to ask *whether* Jesus did or said something. They are incapable of asking, for example, *why* or *to what end*.[128] For Collingwood, the key question that the historian asks of a given datum is not "is this true or false?" but "what does this mean?"[129]

I readily admit that there are some good historiographical impulses underlying the criteria. Those impulses may be relevant as indices of the potential plausibility of a tradition. The principles underlying the criteria, that the fact that a given tradition is, e.g., multiply attested, or doubly dissimilar, or embarrassing may be an indication of its direct reference to historical reality, have some value as stock arguments in favor of the plausibility of a tradition. Nevertheless, their negative application as literal criteria that are used to strain out "inauthentic" traditions, is problematic and reflects the limited scope of history conceived by earlier iterations of the Quest.

In Collingwood's eyes, even critical history, such as that employed by John Dominic Crossan in *The Historical Jesus: The Life of a Mediterranean Jewish Peasant*,[130] in which some material is considered to be earlier and authentic, while other material is regarded as late and thus discarded, essentially handles data as testimony.[131] Even when those materials which are considered to be "late" or "inauthentic" are discarded, one is left with the "early" or "authentic" material, which is then incorporated into one's history and accepted as historically referential testimony.[132]

The procedure of question and answer is probably best understood as a hermeneutics.[133] In light of this, the question "what does this mean?" is of particular importance to the practice of history. This is

---

8. This finds traction in Meyer's concepts of historical interpretation and explanation, in *Aims of Jesus*, 76–78.

9. Collingwood, *Idea of History*, 275.

0. Referring to the methods employed in Crossan, *Historical Jesus*.

1. In this regard, see especially Collingwood, *Idea of History*, 258–59.

2. In general, one might apply this sort of critique to most works which are primarily concerned with "authenticity" or proceed by the sifting and separating out of material that belongs to Jesus as opposed to the evangelists or the early church. An obvious example of this sort of procedure is the publication of the results of the Jesus Seminar, Funk, Hoover, and The Jesus Seminar, *The Five Gospels* and those works by fellows of the Seminar which are based upon these results, such as Stephen J. Patterson, *The God of Jesus: The Historical Jesus and the Search for Meaning* (Harrisburg: Trinity Press International, 1998). Even more sophisticated variants of this sort of historiographical procedure, such as Meier, *A Marginal Jew*, are vulnerable to this critique.

3. Cf. Mink, *Mind, History, and Dialect*, 131ff.; van der Dussen, *History as a Science*, 274–75. Although

the implicit question being asked every time data is interpreted. It is the most basic question to be asked, whether implicitly or explicitly, of data relevant to the historical problem at hand. This is because interpretation, not authenticity, is at the heart of the historian's task. Beth Sheppard has done an excellent job of emphasizing this in her introduction to history and historiography for students of the New Testament, *The Craft of History*.[134] It is only a mild hyperbole to state, as she does, that "the historian's primary task can be boiled down to one word: 'interpretation.'"[135] Seeking understanding, knowing what something means, whether it be a statement in a literary source, a coin hoard found during an archaeological excavation, a particular palaeographic form of a letter in a papyrus manuscript, the architecture of an ancient building, or the plan of a town revealed by ground-piercing radar, is the core of the historical enterprise. In the words of E. H. Carr, "the belief in a hard core of historical facts existing objectively and independently of the interpretation of the historian is a preposterous fallacy, but one which it is very hard to eradicate."[136] This does not mean that there are no "facts," or worse, that history is whatever any given historian wants it to be. Again, we recall that the historian's picture of the past *must* be rooted in evidence—its truth depends on it. Conversely, data does not speak for itself, and requires interpretation in order to function as evidence for an investigation. There can be no history without evidence, but there is also no evidence without interpretation.

When addressing questions or problems, one may be faced with several possible explanations that provide varying answers, as a situation may arise in which strong direct evidence supporting any one particular hypothesis is lacking.[137] When this is the case, it is appropriate to make what is termed an "inference to the best explanation." As defined by C. Behan McCullagh, inference to the best explanation "proceeds by judging which of the plausible hypotheses provides the best explanation of what is known about the creation of the evidence in question."[138] In other words, the hypothesis that best explains the most evidence is to be preferred. As a consequence, even suspect statements

Collingwood calls it a "logic," Mink rightly observes here that it is not actually a theory of logic so much as it is a hermeneutics, which supplements but does not replace formal logic.

134. Sheppard, *The Craft of History*.
135. Ibid., 15.
136. Carr, *What is History?*, 12.
137. C. Behan McCullagh, *The Logic of History: Putting Postmodernism in Perspective* (London: Routledge, 2004), 49.
138. McCullagh, *Logic of History*, 49.

should be explained rather than discarded, since through explanation, they may yet speak to the matter at hand.

Conclusion

The primary aim of this essay has been to lay the groundwork for a historical method that is rooted in the philosophy of history and historiographical theory. As my discussion has endeavored to show, the historian's task involves asking historical questions, interpreting data and applying it as evidence for the questions being asked, inferring historical knowledge from the evidence, and connecting the evidence together with robust threads of historical imagination. Thus far, the foundation of the method that I have proposed has been distilled primarily from and in relation to Collingwood's seminal philosophy of history, especially his insights into the nature of history. A healthy amount of input from the thought and work of his later interpreters and from other historians and philosophers, such as Carr, van der Dussen, Fischer, Johnson, McCullagh, and Meyer, has helped to further temper and hone the raw ideas that I have drawn from Collingwood.

The fact that Collingwood and the philosophy of history in general have thus far played a relatively minor role in historical Jesus research is striking, and may be an indication of the degree to which New Testament studies have developed in relative isolation from other disciplines.[139] We should note that when Käsemann advanced the criterion of dissimilarity in his 1953 Marburg lecture, Collingwood's severe critique of scissors-and-paste had already been published and was available for some time in the first edition of *The Idea of History* (1946). Even now, as New Testament scholarship is introduced through social memory theory to the notion that interpreted or distorted traditions should be understood rather than discarded altogether, it is important to recognize that this insight had already been brought to bear in *The Idea of History* many decades prior.

Although much has been gained in our discussion thus far in terms of fundamentals and basic method, there is still more ground to cover. In particular, the discussion in this essay has highlighted the impor-

---

139. It is worth noting that this may be changing. Shortly after I published an article in *JSHJ* in 2015, suggesting the relevance of Collingwood's thought for the historical Jesus, Donald Denton also published an article later that same year in the same journal that briefly, but pointedly discusses the relevance of Collingwood's thought for the study of the historical Jesus. See Donald L. Denton, "Being Interpreted by the Parables: Critical Realism as Hermeneutical Epistemology," *JSHJ* 13, no. 2–3 (2015): 232–54. Note also that Denton combines elements of Collingwood's thought with Lonergan's epistemology.

tance of interpretation in history. As a result, some further discussion of hermeneutics in appendix B will serve to help round out the methodological discussion here. I have also indicated some discomfort on my part with the idealist epistemological trappings of Collingwood's methodological insights, especially with the doctrine of reenactment. It will therefore be necessary to propose an alternative epistemological and hermeneutical theoretical framework, in order to determine how to approach the sources, the data, and the evidence that is set before us. This includes the task of making judgments in history, a key aspect of historical investigation and method. In other words, we have now laid the foundations for a historiographical method, but we have yet to determine how to approach the sources and evidence themselves.

Appendix B:
Approaching the Sources:
Hermeneutics, Truth, and Knowledge in the Practice of History

Introduction

In appendix A, we laid the foundations for the practice and principles of history. The discussion thus far has underscored the importance of interpretation in history. As Collingwood has demonstrated in his critique of scissors-and-paste, the pivotal question for historical investigation is not "is this statement true or false," but "what does this mean?"[1] Interpretation, understanding the meaning of relevant data and evidence is thus the beating heart of history.

There is a need for a firm epistemological grounding for our historical investigation and procedure. History, after all, is concerned with a certain type of knowledge, knowledge of the past. The burden of the present essay is to elaborate on these two matters—epistemology and interpretation—in order to lay out a basic hermeneutical framework that will be useful for our historical project. Bernard Lonergan's cognitional theory and "transcendental method" provides a suitable basis for this,[2] and will be introduced in this essay in order to fill the need

---

1. Collingwood, *The Idea of History*, 275.
2. This theory is initially outlined in depth in Bernard Lonergan, *Insight: A Study of Human Understanding* (Collected Works of Bernard Lonergan 3; ed. Frederick E. Crowe and Robert M. Doran; 5th ed.; Toronto: University of Toronto Press, 1992). It appears in a concise and summarized, though more developed form in Lonergan, *Method in Theology*, esp. 3–25.

both for an epistemological and a hermeneutical foundation for our historiography.[3] Lonergan's cognitional theory provides us with a clear picture of what we are doing when we are knowing, and attention paid to the process can sharpen our ability to acquire knowledge of the past.

As we have seen in the previous essay, both Lonergan and Meyer were heavily influenced by Collingwood and have a tendency to cite him favorably in their work on the philosophy of history and historical method, although they reject the more idealist dimensions of his thought.[4] As a result, their thoughts on history are very much compatible with the elements of Collingwood's understanding of history and the historian's craft that we have retained and presented here. Intention and the determination of the "aims" of historical actors plays an important role in the thought of both Meyer and Collingwood, and as such, we will discuss the role of intention and the "inside of the event" in historical investigation in this essay. Because the determination of the role of the synagogue in the aims of Jesus is the central question addressed by this project, this particular topic has specific and special relevance for our historical investigation.

As we shall see in this essay, judgment is an essential aspect of Lonergan's hermeneutics and of the cognitional process. It is also an essential element of the historian's task. Historians frequently need to make judgments throughout the course of historical investigations. How can historians judge truth from falsehood about past events when the past is not directly observable? How can we be confident about the veracity of our reconstructions and of the testimony employed in them? Due to its relevance to past and present concerns in historical Jesus research, the issue of judgment and truth in history will be taken up toward the end of this essay.

Whose "Critical Realism?"

The Lonerganian cognitional theory is sometimes referred to as "critical realism," the term by which Meyer consistently refers to it in *Critical Realism and the New Testament*.[5] This term has been popularized in biblical studies by N. T. Wright, who uses it to refer to his own

---

3. A treatment of the relevance of Lonergan's cognitional theory and hermeneutics in light of current developments in historical Jesus research can be found in Jonathan Bernier, *The Quest for the Historical Jesus After the Demise of Authenticity: Toward a Critical Realist Philosophy of History in Jesus Studies* (LNTS 540; London and New York: T&T Clark, 2016).

4. On this, see also Denton, "Being Interpreted by the Parables," 241–43.

5. Meyer, *Critical Realism*.

hermeneutics and historiographical theory.[6] However, Wright's presentation of "critical realism" differs in a number of significant respects from that of Lonergan. This has caused some confusion around "critical realism" and Lonergan in New Testament studies. This problem is further compounded by the existence of other philosophical traditions that employ the name "critical realism," especially that of Roy Bhaskar.[7] As a result, there is a tendency in New Testament scholarship to confuse and conflate the thought of Lonergan and Meyer with that of Wright and Bhaskar.

The issue of the varieties of "critical realism" has already been treated by Denton,[8] and does need to be discussed in depth here. However, despite Denton's work in this regard, instances of insufficient distinction between the various traditions called by this name have continued to persist.[9] A few words about Wright's brand of "critical realism" are necessary, since he is perhaps the figure most associated with this nomenclature in New Testament studies. According to Wright, critical realism is

. . . a way of describing the process of 'knowing' that acknowledges the *reality of the thing known, as something other than the knower* (hence 'realism'), while also fully acknowledging that the only access we have to this reality lies along the spiralling path of *appropriate dialogue or conversation between the knower and the thing known* (hence 'critical').[10]

It must be noted that this basic definition of Wright's "critical realism" differs in form and substance from Lonergan's cognitional theory, which will be discussed below. There is also some considerable distance here between what is "real" in Wright's "critical realism" and what is "real" in that of Meyer and Lonergan. As seen above, what is "real" for Wright is the reality of the object of knowledge as something other than the knower. However, according to Meyer, "Critical realism locates the issue of real/unreal at the level of sense only insofar as

---

6. See esp. N. T. Wright, *The New Testament and the People of God* (Christian Origins and the Question of God 1; Minneapolis: Fortress Press, 1992), 32–46.
7. E.g., Roy Bhaskar, *A Realist Theory of Science* (London: Verso, 2008 [1975]).
8. Denton, *Historiography and Hermeneutics*, 210–25.
9. Some more recent examples of insufficient distinction or even conflation of philosophical theories termed "critical realism" without sufficient qualification of the differences between them include Robert B. Stewart, *The Quest of the Hermeneutical Jesus: The Impact of Hermeneutics on the Jesus Research of John Dominic Crossan and N.T. Wright* (Lanham: University Press of America, 2008), 77–88, 112–13, 113nn4–5; Andrew Wright, *Christianity and Critical Realism: Ambiguity, Truth and Theological Literacy* (London: Routledge, 2013), 51; Webb, "Historical Enterprise," 28n55.
10. Wright, *People of God*, 35. Emphasis is original.

sense knowledge provides data for higher level operations that terminate in judgment. It is perfectly true that what is sensed is, but this is ascertained not by the senses alone but by understanding and judgment taking account of sense data."[11] In other words, the "real" is that which is not only sensed, but is also known by means of the cognitive process. Therefore, it is the object *known* by the critical process of experience, understanding, and judgment that is real. All of these facts lead to the conclusion that, although they are not unrelated, Wright's critical realism is distinct from Lonergan's cognitional theory.

Lonergan's Cognitional Theory: "Transcendental Method"

According to Lonergan, cognitional theory is the primary field that lies behind hermeneutics.[12] His cognitional theory simultaneously provides both a robust epistemology and a hermeneutical framework, and so, it will be presented here as an alternative to and corrective for Collingwood's idealist trappings and as a useful procedure in itself for historical investigation.[13] What Lonergan provides in his cognitional theory is not so much an account of what knowledge is, so much as it is an account of what human beings are doing when we are knowing.

The central premise of Lonergan's cognitional theory is that seeing is not knowing.[14] As Collingwood has already shown us in the previous essay, this is self-evidently the case so far as knowledge of the past is concerned, since the past is not observable, but must be inferred, argued to "from something else accessible to our observation."[15] Lonergan posits a cognitive process made up of operations taking place on four levels of consciousness and intentionality. These levels are the empirical level, the intellectual level, the rational level, and the responsible level.[16] The empirical level is concerned with sensory perception, the intellectual level with inquiry and understanding, the rational level with reflection and judgment, while the responsible level

---

11. Meyer, *Critical Realism*, xi.
12. Bernard Lonergan, *Early Works on Theological Method* (Collected Works of Bernard Lonergan 22; 3 vols.; ed. Robert M. Doran and Robert C. Croken; Toronto: University of Toronto Press, 2010), 1:209.
13. Cf. Ben F. Meyer, *Critical Realism and the New Testament*, ix–x. According to Meyer, he learned from Lonergan that "there was a realism that made room with the idealists for every ambition of intelligence but that, correcting the concessions and oversights in idealist critique, went decisively beyond idealism as well."
14. Cf. Lonergan, *Insight*, 437.
15. Collingwood, *Idea of History*, 251–52.
16. Lonergan, *Method in Theology*, 9. See also Lonergan, *Insight*, 298.

is the level on which human beings are concerned with their own operations and goals, carrying out decisions on possible courses of action.[17]

Cognitive operations are carried out on these levels, each one building on the last. In order, these operations are experiencing, understanding, judging, and deciding, each of which is a conscious and intentional act.[18] Each of these operations also function in order in each of the four operations at all four levels. Experience itself involves experiencing, understanding, judging, and deciding, as does understanding, and so on.[19]

So far as historiography is concerned, knowing the past involves experiencing, understanding, judging, and evaluating it.[20] Corresponding to this are four "functional specialties" or disciplines, which Thomas McPartland rightly identifies as "differentiations of cognitive activities appropriate to the different cognitive levels of encountering the past and being oriented to the future."[21] The disciplines are research (experiencing the data), interpretation (understanding what the data means), history (applying the data as evidence, marshalling, weighing, and judging the evidence in relation to a question), and dialectic (evaluating trends, discerning horizons, and aiming at a comprehensive viewpoint).[22]

Reducing one's account of knowledge to sense experience short-circuits the cognitional process, ignoring the importance of the operations carried out at the intellectual, rational, and responsible levels. History is not reducible to gathering and experiencing the data, to research, alone. Sensory experience nevertheless plays a crucial role in the cognitive process, since the senses provide the data for knowledge.[23] In this, Lonergan is close to his Thomist roots, since Aquinas reckoned that "whatever is in our intellect must have previously been in the senses."[24] The cognitive operation of experience requires the knower to *be attentive*, to attend to the data taken in by the senses. For

17. Lonergan, *Method in Theology*, 9.
18. Ibid., 14.
19. Ibid., 14–15.
20. Cf. Thomas McPartland, *Lonergan and Historiography: The Epistemological Philosophy of History* (Columbia and London: University of Missouri Press, 2010), 35.
21. McPartland, *Lonergan and Historiography*, 35.
22. Lonergan, *Method in Theology*, 127–30; cf. McPartland, *Lonergan and Historiography*, 35, specifically relating the functional specialties to historiography. Note that there are a total of eight functional specialties in *Method in Theology*, but we need only concern ourselves with the first four for our present purposes.
23. Cf. Denton, *Historiography and Hermeneutics*, 83.
24. Thomas Aquinas, *Quaestiones Disputatae de Veritate*, q2 a3.

history, this means that attention must be paid to the traces of the past in the present.

Knowledge does not stop at sense perception. Once the senses have made the data available, the knower then inquires upon the data, asking questions of it, in order to understand it.[25] This requires the knower to *be intelligent* in the sense of being inquiring and insightful, to ask the right questions of the data, and to be able to answer them in order to understand it and to derive insight from it. After some datum becomes present to the senses, one wonders about it, then formulates that wonder as a question, comes to an answer to the question, and then weighs the validity of the answer.[26] As this process occurs, questions may arise naturally and spontaneously, but they are shaped and sharpened, ordered and made exact, and an answer is sought, culminating in understanding. Data, and hence experience, are central to this process. Here, one is reminded of Collingwood's "logic" of question and answer, and the role of evidence in investigation.[27]

In the practice of history, interpretation is understanding what something means, whether it be a written text, material evidence, or anything else.[28] As such, and as per our discussion in the previous essay, the primary question around which understanding revolves is "what does this mean?" Answering this question will require the historian to be attentive, to be intelligent, and to be reasonable—to experience the data, to inquire of it seeking understanding, and to judge the correctness of one's interpretation. Only once this is done can he or she state the meaning of the text. How can the historian or exegete be confident in his or her interpretation, and thus judge it to be correct? In short, this requires the historian to have answered the question "what does this mean?" and all other relevant questions,[29] which entails grasping sufficient evidence or the necessary conditions to be met for the proposition to stand.[30] In order to do this, one must be able to transcend one's own horizon, coming into a fuller horizon overlapping with that of the author, enabling the historian to reconstruct the context of the author's thought and speech.[31]

---

25. See Lonergan, *Insight*, 297–98. On asking questions leading to the possibility of making a judgment, see *Method in Theology*, 162–63.

26. Cf. Ben F. Meyer, *Reality and Illusion in New Testament Scholarship: A Primer in Critical Realist Hermeneutics* (Collegeville: Liturgical, 1994), 5.

27. This point of contact between Lonergan and Meyer is noted by Denton, *Historiography and Hermeneutics*, 114–16.

28. Cf. Lonergan, *Method in Theology*, 127.

29. Ibid., 162–63.

30. Meyer, *Reality and Illusion*, 27.

Understanding leads to judgment. Judgment requires the knower to *be reasonable*. This entails reflection, marshalling the evidence, passing judgment on the accuracy of a statement.[32] As Meyer writes, "insight is made complete in judgment,"[33] as in this stage in the cognitive process, one makes a pronouncement on the understanding produced by one's inquiry, deeming it to be "true," "false," "certain," or "probable."[34] This is done *on the basis of evidence*,[35] which up to this point must be sufficiently grasped in order for a judgment to be accurate. Here, we see yet another clear point of contact with the Collingwoodian practice of history, wherein the truth of a statement about the past is related to and can be justified by an appeal to the evidence.[36]

The final operation is evaluation, which requires the knower to *be responsible*.[37] Everyone is bound to their own horizons, which are the products of one's own experiences, the limits of what one knows and cares about.[38] History, almost by definition, involves the study of people, actors, and authors, whose horizons differ from our own. The historian's task, however, is not to dismantle one's own horizon in order to come into that of the past, but to *transcend* one's own horizon, expanding it to include that of the past.[39] This means *being responsible*.

The basic pattern of operations described above are what Lonergan calls "transcendental method."[40] It is "transcendental" in the sense that "the results envisaged are not confined categorically to some particular field or subject,"[41] and it is thus applicable as a hermeneutic to any act of knowing.[42] It may be summed up simply in the following

---

31. Lonergan, *Method in Theology*, 163.

32. Ibid., 9. Cf. also Meyer, *Reality and Illusion*, 24.

33. Ibid.

34. Ibid.

35. Ibid., 27.

36. Collingwood, *Idea of History*, 246.

37. This is probably the most difficult of Lonergan's cognitional operations. Notably, it seems to be absent from his original formulation of the cognitional theory in *Insight* (see Lonergan, *Insight*, 296–303). There is no need to discuss it in depth here, and so I will focus on those elements of its correlative functional specialty, dialectic, which are most pertinent to historiography. For a more full treatment of this cognitive operation and its place in historiography, see McPartland, *Lonergan and Historiography*, 38–43; or Meyer, *Reality and Illusion*, 40–58.

38. Meyer, *Reality and Illusion*. Cf. Lonergan, *Method in Theology*, 236.

39. Cf. McPartland, *Lonergan and Historiography*, 38.

40. Lonergan, *Method in Theology*, 13.

41. Ibid., 14.

42. It is worth mentioning that the use of Lonerganian "critical realism" in New Testament studies has recently been critiqued by Stanley E. Porter and Andrew W. Pitts, "Critical Realism in Context: N.T. Wright's Historical Method and Analytic Epistemology," *JSHJ* 13, no. 2–3 (2015): 276–306. The essential thrust of their argument is that critical realism has been made irrelevant by developments in epistemology set in motion by Edmund Gettier in his article "Is Justified True Belief Knowledge?" *Analysis* 23 (1963): 121–23. They attempt to fit Lonerganian critical realism into the "internalism" vs. "externalism" debate, arguing that Lonerganian critical realism is thoroughly

instructions: "be attentive, be intelligent, be reasonable, be responsible."[43]

internalist, and untenable due to Gettier's critique of internalism. I find this to be a puzzling argument. It is problematic to identify Lonergan as an internalist, and any attempt to identify him as one is likely to result from a gross misapprehension of Lonergan's project in *Insight* and *Method in Theology*. From a Lonerganian perspective, the whole debate between externalism and internalism should be regarded as wrongheaded, predicated on problematic understandings of objectivity, and what is internal or external. A Lonerganian account of knowledge can hardly be defined as "justified true belief" as it is for internalism. As Andrew Beards writes, "The definition of knowledge given by some analytical philosophers as 'justified true belief' is not one adopted by Lonergan. Rather he prefers to follow Aristotle and Aquinas in saying that out knowing processes aim at the intentional identity between knower and known." See Andrew Beards, *Method in Metaphysics: Lonergan and the Future of Analytic Philosophy* (Toronto: University of Toronto Press, 2008), 345–46. The extent of the distance between Lonergan and the definition of knowledge as "justified true belief" can be seen with clarity in his critique of the epistemology of Gilson and Kant by appealing to the concept of horizon, in Bernard Lonergan, "Metaphysics as Horizon," *Cross Currents* 16, no. 4 (1966): 481–94. The problem that Lonergan identifies in that article is the notion that objectivity is a matter of perception, and thus that knowing is perceiving. The Gettier-style problems raised by Porter and Pitts are designed to counter a type of epistemology that holds to precisely this sort of "seeing is knowing" account of knowledge, wherein knowing occurs when data produces justification for belief. The account of critical realism that Porter and Pitts present ignores the final, crucial step of the cognitive process, dialectic, and with it, the important concepts of horizon and transcendence. These concepts do not appear in their critique of critical realism, which is unfortunate precisely because they problematize the notion of objectivity and the dichotomy of "internal" and "external" as presented by Gettier-style problems. Beyond this matter, Beards further addresses Gettier-style problems from a critical realist perspective, writing that "most of our judgments about reality are probable. We can say that we are *justified* in holding that belief *x* is probably true of reality, with a high degree of probability, and that belief *y* is probably true of reality, but with a lower degree of probability. When therefore some data, some evidence, could possibly interpreted in some other way (as an illusion perhaps) we are *not justified* in saying more than that proposition *x* is probably true of reality. This is what we should say, strictly speaking, or what we are justified in believing in cases in which the belief is *de facto* true while the evidence of itself does not give certainty" (*Method in Metaphysics*, 346, emphasis original). Note here the importance of authentic subjectivity. This why Lonergan, in his account of judgment in historical investigation, considers it essential to ensure that all possible relevant questions have been answered in order to consider a judgment to be true (*Method in Theology*, 191). From a critical realist perspective, a major problem with an internalist account of knowledge is that the knower needs to perceive through sensory data, but the knower cannot be certain that the information that they have matches up with reality. For the critical realist, internalism amounts to a sophisticated version of "seeing is knowing," and so, should be rejected as wrongheaded. Jonathan Bernier has offered a response to Porter and Pitts, in Jonathan Bernier, "A Response to Porter and Pitts' 'Wright's Critical Realism in Context,'" *JSHJ* 14, no. 2 (2016): 186–93, to which Porter and Pitts gave a reply in Stanley E. Porter and Andrew W. Pitts, "Has Jonathan Bernier Rescued Critical Realism?" *JSHJ* 14, no. 3 (2016): 1–7. Bernier argues that Porter and Pitts have misidentified Lonergan as an internalist, an issue that is not sufficiently answered or addressed in Porter and Pitts reply, which continues to evince a problematic account of Lonerganian critical realism. To conclude, it is difficult to see how Gettier-style problems apply to a Lonerganian critical realist account of knowing, or how they are relevant to Lonergan at all. It seems as though Porter and Pitts have grossly misunderstood Lonergan, and thus, their critique is not a serious challenge to critical realism. A more potent critique comes from the postmodernists, which will be treated below. For more on the problems of knowledge as justified true belief from a critical realist perspective, see Andrew Beards, "Knowledge and Our Limits: Lonergan and Williamson," *The Lonergan Review* 5, no. 1 (2014): 77–108.

43. Cf. Lonergan, *Method in Theology*, 20.

Subjectivity, Objectivity, and Bridging the Postmodern Gap

The problem of subjectivity and objectivity in history is central to the postmodern challenge to traditional history.[44] A critical aspect of the postmodern critique of history is that history has failed to deliver on its promise of objectivity. Frank Ankersmit, for example, has claimed that "we no longer have any texts, any past, but just interpretations of them."[45] Similarly, in light of Hayden White's thought on history, Keith Jenkins says that "to write a history is to construct one kind of narrative rather than another, not to represent the past 'plain.'"[46] Does postmodernism render thinkers such as Lonergan and Collingwood obsolete? The short answer to this is "no."

I must confess that I consider the nomenclature "postmodern" to be unfortunate, since it implies supersession, as though earlier thought has simply been replaced.[47] Postmodernism has made valuable contributions, and has greatly expanded the discussion of subjectivity in historiography beyond the purview of the debate, mostly between E. H. Carr and G. R. Elton, of the mid-twentieth century.[48] Nevertheless, Collingwood and Lonergan are hardly superseded by postmodernism.[49] If anything, their philosophies provide helpful ways to navigate the postmodern critique of history.

As we have seen in Appendix A, Collingwood is, in some ways, a forerunner of postmodern historiography.[50] His emphasis on the historian and the interpretation of evidence in history spelt the downfall of naïve realism and introduced a thinking subject into historiographical theory.[51] Nevertheless, as I have mentioned already, unlike that of the postmoderns, Collingwoodian history also concerns the "infastructure" of history,[52] the evidence and the processes of interpreting the

---

44. A good summary of the basic challenge presented by postmodernism to traditional, especially empiricist history, can be found in Callum G. Brown, *Postmodernism for Historians* (London and New York: Routledge, 2013), 26–30. For summaries of the issue and its pertinence to historical Jesus studies, see Pieter F. Craffert, "Multiple Realities and Historiography," 87–116.

45. Ankersmit, "Historiography and Postmodernism," 137.

46. Keith Jenkins, *Why History? Ethics and Postmodernity* (London and New York: Routledge, 1999), 86. See further, Hayden White, *Metahistory: The Historical Imagination in Nineteenth-Century Europe* (Baltimore and London: Johns Hopkins, 1975), e.g. 433–34.

47. Note, of course, that Lonergan and Meyer were both active after the advent of postmodernism.

48. See Carr, *What is History?*, passim; Elton, *The Practice of History*, passim.

49. An excellent Lonerganian response to postmodernism can be found in James L. Marsh, "Postmodernism: A Lonerganian Retrieval and Critique," in *Postmodernism and Christian Philosophy*, ed. Roman T. Ciapalo (Washington, DC: Catholic University of America Press, 1997), 149–67.

50. Cf. van der Dussen, *History as a Science*, ix. Note, in this regard, Hayden White's favorable treatment of Collingwood in White, *Tropics of Discourse*, 59–62. Collingwood has not really been in the crosshairs of postmodernism to the extent that the empiricists have been.

51. Hence Carr's reaction to Collingwood in Carr, *What is History?*, esp. 26–29.

evidence that go into the historian's construction of the past. Attentiveness to evidence grounds subjectivity, a fact too often neglected by postmodern theorists. Ankersmit has argued that evidence does not point to the past, but only to other interpretations of it.[53] This is true to some extent, insofar as evidence requires interpretation, but evidence also necessarily tempers the historian's subjective imagination and points toward conclusions, favoring certain hypotheses over others.

Lonergan's functional specialty of dialectic (corresponding to responsibility) and his framing of the relationship between subject and object are helpful for bridging the postmodern problem of subjectivity in history.[54] Dialectic involves the transcendence of one's own horizons without abandoning one's own perspective. There are, of course, innumerable horizons, many of which are opposed to others. Responsibility entails a willingness to understand and incorporate the perspectives of others who "differ radically from oneself,"[55] which provides the opportunity for reflection and self-scrutiny. Carried to its ultimate conclusion, this means striving toward a universal viewpoint. This objectivity, which is so often coveted and appealed to in the practice of history, is not achieved by abandoning one's own subjectivity. Objectivity is to be found in authentic subjectivity. As Meyer eloquently writes, "Truth, in fine, ripens on the tree of the subject, and objectivity is the fruit of subjectivity at its most intense and persistent."[56]

History requires a historian, an attentive, intelligent, reasonable thinker, without whom there is no history, but only scattered data. The historian must be comfortable with their own subjectivity. Objectivity as authentic subjectivity will entail the transcendence and expansion of one's horizons, but not the abandonment of oneself, of one's own perspective or experience, since all of this will be included in the expanded horizon.

E. H. Carr was concerned that Collingwood had gone too far toward total subjectivity by emphasizing the role of the historian in history, leading him to the complaint that in Collingwood's view, "the facts of history are nothing, interpretation is everything."[57] Carr's own work

---

52. van der Dussen, *History as a Science*, ix.
53. Ankersmit, "Historiography and Postmodernism," 145.
54. See the Lonerganian responses to postmodernism, in McPartland, *Lonergan and Historiography*, 153ff.; and Robert Doran, *Theology and the Dialectics of History* (Toronto: University of Toronto Press, 1990), 153–58.
55. Lonergan, *Method in Theology*, 253.
56. Meyer, *Critical Realism*, 140. See also Lonergan, *Method in Theology*, 292. Lonergan considers the subject to be "the rock" upon which the knower builds, in Lonergan, *Method in Theology*, 21–22.

thus represents an attempt to find a middle ground between "the Scylla of an untenable theory of history as an objective compilation of facts, of the unqualified primacy of fact over interpretation, and the Charybdis of an equally untenable theory of history as the subjective product of the mind of the historian."[58] Here is an example of a historian who is uncomfortable with his own subjectivity, and yet has an acute awareness of its import.

Carr is certainly correct that there is room for both objectivity and subjectivity in history. Nevertheless, it is a gross exaggeration to say that the "facts of history" are inconsequential for Collingwoodian history, since in Collingwood's view, history must be rooted in evidence or it is no history at all. It is true that there can be multiple interpretations of the same data, and that evidence can be understood in different ways, resulting in different conclusions. This does not completely relativize history altogether. We must recall that the cognitive process does not end at understanding, but proceeds from understanding to judgment. Historical knowledge requires adjudication between possible conclusions, which means *being reasonable*. In cases where multiple reconstructions are possible, the reconstruction with the most explanatory power and scope, the one able to explain the most evidence in the simplest way, is to be preferred.[59] The fact that multiple interpretations are possible does not mean that some are not better than others. There may be no recipe for history, but there is reason and logic to it.

A fear of subjectivity in the practice of history is akin to fear of one's own shadow. The only way to be free of it is to retreat into darkness. The postmodern turn to the subject does contain important insights and raises crucial questions, but these can be incorporated into a Lonerganian perspective.[60] The Lonerganian notion of responsibility, through commitment to authentic subjectivity, allows the historian to escape the battle between objectivity and subjectivity altogether by rejecting a dichotomy between the two and recognizing that they are intimately related.

57. Carr, *What is History?*, 27.
58. Ibid., 29.
59. Cf. C. Behan McCullagh, *The Logic of History*, 49–52.
60. Cf. Marsh, "Lonerganian Retrieval," 166.

Understanding the Data

If data is to be applied as evidence in an investigation, it must be understood.[61] Comprehending what an author means to convey, or grasping the intention behind statements in the gospels is important for understanding the data that the author provides, and thus helps to determine *whether* something might potentially provide data concerning a specific question, and moreover, *how* it might be applied as evidence.[62] However, understanding an author is not the end goal of historical interpretation. In the words of Meyer, "To understand Caesar it is not enough to understand what Suetonius meant to say about him."[63] In order to understand Jesus, it is not enough to understand what the evangelists meant to say about him. One must also understand what Jesus meant by what he said, and why he did the things that he did.

Meyer considered it necessary to control the data used in a historical investigation, by which he meant that it must be understood, and that it must be established as potential data on Jesus, meaning that its historical authenticity needs to be determined.[64] I agree that data must be understood, but the establishment of authenticity, whether it be on the basis of criteria or indices,[65] slips back into the practice of scissors-and-paste. Properly speaking, the judgment of the "truth" or "falsehood" of a statement is relative to the knowledge that is inferred from it. In other words, judgments of "truth" or "falsehood" cannot be made apart from interpretation and understanding. In fact, so doing short-circuits the cognitive process, cutting out the intellectual level.

So far as statements in the gospels are concerned, understanding means apprehending what the evangelist meant by a given statement, and what it means for Jesus.[66] Of course, the two are interrelated, since the evangelist is obviously impacted by the Jesus tradition, and because Jesus's words are conveyed to us only through the evangelists in the

---

61. On understanding and data control, see Meyer, *Aims of Jesus*, 80–87.
62. Meyer correctly argues that authorial intention is not only contained in the writer, and thus, extrinsic to the text. It is also contained within the text, being its main intrinsic determinant. In agreement with Meyer, *Critical Realism and the New Testament*, 20, cf. also the longer discussion of the relationship between the reader and the author on pp. 36–41. It is not possible to engage in extended discussion of authorial intention and interpretation, but readers are encouraged to refer to the above passages on this matter, as well as the work of Seán Burke, *The Death and Return of the Author: Criticism and Subjectivity in Barthes, Foucault and Derrida*, 3rd ed. (Edinburgh: Edinburgh University Press, 2008).
63. Meyer, *Aims of Jesus*, 77.
64. Ibid., 81.
65. Ibid., 85–87.
66. Ibid., 80–81.

first place. At any rate, as Meyer acknowledges, this cannot be done at the outset of an investigation, since data are not entirely understood in the holistic sense in their role as evidence until the inquiry is complete,[67] and their place in the web of evidence and imagination is clear. The process, then, is a spiral, moving back and forth from evidence to reconstruction.

Intention and "The Inside of the Event"

Collingwood makes a clear distinction between "the inside of the event," which can be described in terms of the thoughts of historical actors, and the "outside of the event," which is the physical element in historical events.[68] He quite rightly asserts that the historian is never interested in one to the exclusion of the other.[69] Collingwood thus emphasizes the importance of understanding the thoughts of historical agents, since the "outside of the event" is ultimately intertwined with and explained by the "inside of the event." Even the effect of natural phenomena on human history involves the interaction and interface of those phenomena with human thoughts, acts, and intentions. This is one of the ways in which history differs from empirical science, since thought is not something that can be observed empirically.[70] This emphasis on thought led Collingwood to the conclusion that the historian can rediscover the thoughts of historical actors by reenacting them in one's own mind, that is, to the doctrine of reenactment.

Although we have critiqued this aspect of Collingwood's thought above, we should not throw out the baby with the bathwater. The core concept that an action is "the unity of the outside and the inside of an event,"[71] thus highlighting the importance of the thought behind physical action and events in history, is itself a keen insight into the object and nature of history, and need not be tied to the rethinking of past thoughts. Human action does not proceed without some thought, some motivation, some intention, to move it forward. It is not enough, then, for the historian to say that Jesus went about the countryside of Galilee, teaching and proclaiming his message in the synagogues without some understanding of the motivation behind it. This is akin to what a detective does when uncovering the motive in a criminal investigation. Just

67. Ibid., 81.
68. Collingwood, *Idea of History*, 213.
69. Ibid.
70. Ibid., 214.
71. Ibid., 213.

as a detective can uncover and understand the motive behind a criminal act by inferring it from available evidence, so too can the historian infer the inside of the event, the intention that impels physical action, from evidence. There is no need to consider this to be a literal rethinking of past thoughts. Rather, it is the act of coming to as much of an understanding of the human intention behind an event as possible on the basis of what can be critically observed and examined, which we call evidence.

The fact that thought cannot be seen does not mean that it cannot be grasped or understood. Meyer, picking up on Collingwood's distinction between the inside and outside of the event, makes the astute observation that the outside of the Jesus event, that which can be described in terms of time and place, constitutes data for understanding the inside of the event.[72] Even without a direct statement of intention,[73] the historian does not simply pull the inside of historical events out of thin air, but rather, infers it from what is available for examination.

Meyer made a concerted attempt to understand the inside of the Jesus event in *The Aims of Jesus*. According to Meyer, historical interpretation proper consists of "the discovery of what historical agents really intended and the effective mediation of this discovery to a given audience."[74] Thus, his project in *Aims of Jesus* endeavored to uncover the intentions of Jesus. However, this dimension of his historiography has sometimes been dismissed as dealing with matters that are inaccessible or beyond the purviews of historical fact.[75] The role of the discovery of the inside of the event in historical interpretation should not be confused with groundless psychologizing,[76] nor with the search for exis-

---

72. Meyer, *Critical Realism and the New Testament*, 166–67.
73. Direct statements of intention can also come with their own sets of interpretive problems. The author of Luke conveys the intention behind the writing of his gospel in Luke 1:1–4. Since he is conveying his own intention, unless the historian has reason to think he is not being truthful, this statement may convey knowledge that can accepted on the historian's authority at face value. However, not every direct statement of the intentions of historical actors can or should be taken at face value. When, for instance, the same author (Luke) communicates Jesus' intentions behind telling the parable of the ten minas (Luke 19:11, compare the Matthean version in Matt 25:14–30, which is without a statement of Jesus's intent), we must be aware that Luke is, on *his* own authority as the author of his gospel, inferring Jesus' intention from the content of the parable. The statement conveys Luke's interpretation of the parable, and is, in turn, motivated by Luke's thought and intention. This is not to say that it is necessarily incorrect. Whether Luke's inference is correct or not is up to the exegete or historian to decide for oneself on the basis of the evidence.
74. Meyer, *Aims of Jesus*, 77. See also Denton, *Historiography and Hermeneutics*, 107–8.
75. E.g., Seán Freyne, *Galilee, Jesus and the Gospels* (Philadelphia: Fortress Press, 1988), 25; Gerd Theissen and Dagmar Winter, *Die Kriterienfrage in der Jesusforschung: vom Differenzkriterium zum Plausibilitätskriterium* (Novum Testamentum et Orbis Antiquus 34; Göttingen: Vandenhoeck & Ruprecht, 1997), 155. On the reception, both positive and negative, of Meyer's concept of intention in historical Jesus research, see Denton, *Historiography and Hermeneutics*, 109–10.
76. Cf. Meyer, *Reality and Illusion*, 104.

tential selfhood, as seen in the work of James Robinson.[77] The intentions of historical actors are conveyed through their actions, which provide data for the apprehension of the inside of historical events. To deny the accessibility of the inside of the event is to deny the ability to apprehend meaning in physical and communicative events (such as speaking or writing), and to fall back into scissors-and-paste, in which all one has access to is the brute fact of what did or did not happen, with no ability to explain why or what any given datum means.

In saying that the discovery of the inside of the event is essential to the historian's task, I am not denying a role to the outside of the event, nor am I diminishing its import. To the contrary, they are two sides of the same coin and cannot be separated. It has sometimes been objected that not all past events can be explained in terms of human thought and intention.[78] Other factors, such as natural events, or the existence of natural resources in a particular location, might determine the course of the past apart from human intent.

The existence of elements in the past that cannot be described in terms of thought does not mean that human intention is irrelevant to history or to the events impacted by such elements. Louis Mink has rightly pointed out that "these natural facts are relevant to history *only* to the extent that they enter the consciousness of men."[79] The study of weather is properly meteorology, and the study of natural features of the earth is properly geography. Natural events and other extraneous factors are significant to the historian insofar as they are a part of the outside of the event. The historian might be interested in how extreme weather, for example, affects human aims and endeavors, and how humans react to such extreme weather events.

Insofar as I am a historian, I am not interested in the storm that shipwrecked Paul off the coast of Malta *in itself*, but I might be interested in how it impacted Paul's experiences and aims, and what he did and said as a result of the shipwreck. The storm belongs to that which is described in terms of time and place, that is, the outside of the event. There are indeed events in the past that are not the product of human thought, but the historian's interest in them only extends as far as they

---

77. James M. Robinson, *A New Quest of the Historical Jesus* (London: SCM, 1959), esp. 39. On how the notion of intention as existential selfhood egregiously misapprehends the Collingwoodian distinction between the inside and outside of events, see Merkley, "New Quests for Old," esp. 205–7.

78. E.g., Alan Donagan, *The Later Philosophy of R.G. Collingwood* (Oxford: Clarendon, 1962), 203; Norman Wilson, *History in Crisis? Recent Directions in Historiography* (Upper Saddle River: Prentice Hall, 1999), 43. See also the discussion of and reply to this sort of objection in Mink, *Mind, History, and Dialectic* 170–73; and Denton, *Historiography and Hermeneutics*, 111–13.

79. Mink, *Mind, History, and Dialectic*, 171.

affect human action. This is not to say that natural phenomena are of no interest whatsoever, since they frequently affect human beings, and can even shape their actions, thoughts, outcomes, and intentions. In this way, they may be of relevance to a historical investigation, though understanding them is not the ultimate goal of history in itself.

Truth, Judgment, and Evidence in History

Thinking historically means thinking critically. Not all testimony corresponds directly to historical reality—eyewitnesses lie, people forget, memory is distorted, documents are forged, and artifacts are counterfeited. Because of this, historians need to be able to make judgments in order to discern between truth and falsehood. As we have learned from Lonergan's transcendental method, making historical judgments means marshaling and weighing *evidence*, not collecting authentic testimony.

Historical Jesus scholarship has had an unhealthy obsession with authentic testimony. The remedy to this affliction is to treat the data as evidence for a premise rather than testimony to be accepted or rejected. We have already been alerted to this by Collingwood's problematization of scissors-and-paste history. However, the historian must also be cognizant of the truth and falsehood of testimony, and must be able to make historical judgments.[80] How, then, should the statements of the evangelists be used in historical investigation? How can the historian be certain that what he or she has employed is "true," and that the investigation has not been led astray by false testimony?

Since the time of Käsemann until now, mainstream historical Jesus scholars have typically used the criteria of authenticity to ensure that the testimony that they have included in their reconstructions is "authentic" by filtering out the "inauthentic" testimony. The use of criteria gives the historical Jesus enterprise the illusion of objectivity by establishing firm ground rules and by appearing to eliminate the historian and his or her biases from the equation. I say that this is only an illusory objectivity because true historical objectivity does not con-

---

80. Collingwood was cognizant of this issue, and wrote a detective story titled "Who Killed John Doe?" in which all of the witnesses are lying in order to illustrate how a historian proceeds on the basis of evidence and asking questions in such situations, in Collingwood, *Idea of History*, 266–82. For examples of other major twentieth-century historical theorists dealing with the problem of testimony, see Bloch, *Historian's Craft*, 79–137; Jacques Barzun and Henry F. Gradd, "A Medley of Mysteries: A Number of Dog That Didn't Bark," in *The Historian as Detective: Essays on Evidence*, ed. Robin W. Winks (New York: Harper Torchbooks, 1970), 213–31; Michael Oakeshott, *Experience and Its Modes*, repr. ed. (Cambridge: Cambridge University Press, 1994[1933]), 114–17.

sist of the establishment of criteria meant to mitigate the historian's own perspective, especially not when the criteria themselves reflect the biases of those who formulated them. As we have seen, in Lonergian terms, true objectivity means authentic subjectivity.[81] What this means for history is being attentive to the data and how it fits into the investigation as evidence. It simply means being able to say, "I want X to be true, but the evidence indicates Y."

When I say that Jesus taught and proclaimed the message of the Kingdom in the synagogues of Galilee, citing relevant Gospel passages, I am not merely presuming the "authenticity" of the passages in the Gospels that state that Jesus did these things (i.e., Mark 1:39; Matt 4:23; Luke 4:15; John 18:20). What I am doing is *citing these passages as evidence* in favor of the premise that Jesus taught and proclaimed the message of the Kingdom in the synagogues of Galilee. This is an important distinction. What I am doing is placing my premise on trial, and the sources in the witness box. I am able to say that Jesus did these things because I have gone through a cognitive process of marshalling and weighing the evidence culminating in a reasonable judgment that this is the case. The nature of our craft is that the fact that a source states that Jesus did or said something is, in itself, the initial and typically strongest evidence that he did. I am not credulously presuming that Jesus taught and proclaimed in the Galilean synagogues, I am inferring it from the evidence at hand.

In some cases, the historian may have reason to think that there is a problem with a witness' testimony. This may arise in the course of interpreting the passage, or when bringing the passage into dialogue with other evidence. It may be that the historian has some piece of testimony that does not fit into his or her web of evidence and imagination since it comes into conflict with other evidence. If this happens, then the historian cannot simply discard the testimony, but must first understand it, since it may yet prove to be relevant to the investigation. Whatever the case may be, any such judgment, if it is to be a reasonable judgment, requires the marshalling and weighing of evidence, since the validity of a judgment ultimately stands or falls on evidence. In the words of Michael Oakeshott, "what really happened" must be replaced by "what the evidence obliges us to believe" as the goal of history, since "all that history has is 'the evidence;' outside this lies nothing at all."[82]

---

81. Lonergan, *Method in Theology*, 292.

82. Michael Oakeshott, *Experience and Its Modes*, 107–8. We must be reminded here that imagination

Direct verification of testimony is frequently impossible in history, since the past, by its very nature, is unobservable. In historical Jesus research, it is quite often the case that the Gospels provide the only evidence that Jesus said or did some particular thing, and there is insufficient external evidence to clearly confirm or deny an inference made on the basis of the Gospel traditions. This may cause some anxiety, since it leaves us with the sense that history is imprecise and unscientific, unlike the empirical sciences which require direct verification through observation. However, history is not like the empirical sciences. If anything, it is more than a science, since it is an inferential discipline whose object of study is unobservable, and thus, requires much more than empirical data.[83]

Marc Bloch wrote that criticism of testimony is a subtle art, and that "there is no recipe for it."[84] Nevertheless, Bloch points out that criticism typically involves comparison.[85] For example, two sources may agree against a third, or the validity of a statement by one witness may not permit the truth of another. In cases such as these, the hypothesis that best explains the evidence is to be preferred. Critical thinking in history is not merely a matter of verification of data, of establishing the authenticity of everything that the historian uses. It is a matter of attending to the evidence, interpreting the evidence, and making judgments based on the evidence in a responsible manner. If testimony, which appears on the surface to be relevant to the investigation, is to be considered suspect, a reason to do so must first arise, and the decision to do so must be supported by evidence. I am not suggesting that we should revert to historical credulity in favour of the sources, nor that the "burden of proof" should be ignored altogether. What needs to be proven are the historian's premises, which are inferred from the data. These premises are supported by applying the data as evidence. The traditions preserved in the Gospels, *are themselves* the initial evidence, the proof for the historian's inferences. Other evidence may arise which calls the literal validity of the traditions into question. If so, the historian must adjust his or her inferences accordingly on the basis of a reasonable judgment.

Let us consider an example of how this might work in the context of an investigation. Assume, for the sake of this exercise, that we are

plays a role in history, but that imagination must itself be rooted in evidence. Oakeshott may be overstating his point here, but the basic sentiment is accurate.

83. Cf. Collingwood, *Idea of History*, 249–52.
84. Bloch, *Historian's Craft*, 110.
85. Ibid., 110–11.

investigating Jesus's attitudes toward Gentiles. The Abgar tradition preserved by Eusebius in *Hist. eccl.* 1.13 contains written correspondence between Jesus and Abgar V of Edessa (1.13.6–10). Included in this passage is a Greek translation of a letter written by Jesus (either by his own hand or through an *amanuensis*, Ananias the courier) to Abgar V, under a heading reading "ΤΑ ΑΝΤΙΓΡΑΦΕΝΤΑ ΥΠΟ ΙΗΣΟΥ ΔΙΑ ΑΝΑΝΙΟΥ ΤΑΧΥΔΡΟΜΟΥ ΤΟΠΑΡΧΗΙ ΑΒΓΑΡΩΙ." The testimony of this tradition is potentially tempting to accept as directly correlative to historical reality for a number of reasons, not the least of which is that it would provide an example of something composed by Jesus himself, addressed to a Gentile ruler. Attentiveness to potential data uncovers this tradition, from which we might formulate (for example) the premise that Jesus composed a letter during his own lifetime to a Gentile ruler. The testimony of the tradition itself might function as evidence for this premise, but first requires interpretation.

Jesus's letter appears to refer to a saying in John 20:29: "Blessed art thou who didst believe in me not having seen me, for it is written concerning me that those who have seen me will not believe on me, and that those who have not seen me will believe and live."[86] This is problematic because, even if we grant that the things that Jesus claims are written concerning him are loosely derived from Hebrew Bible texts (e.g., Isa 6:9–10), itself an uncertain premise, the opening of the letter still appears to refer to John 20:29, the events of which would not have occurred by the time the letter was written. The letter also states that Jesus will send one of his disciples to Abgar after he has been "taken up." Although traditions preserved in the Gospels depict Jesus speaking about his death and resurrection, nowhere else is there evidence that Jesus spoke of his ascension prior to his death. It is admittedly possible to conceive of a world in which Jesus *could* have thought that he would be "taken up" after completing his mission on earth and in which the opening of the letter is independent of John 20:29. However, the more parsimonious explanation, the hypothesis that best explains the evidence with the least resistance, is that the letter was composed after Jesus's lifetime, by someone with knowledge of both John and Acts, perhaps to legitimate the Edessene church in the eyes of the authorities.

Thus, after interpreting the evidence, we are able to make a judgment, which is that the tradition is not apparently relevant in a direct

---

86. Cited in Eusebius, *Hist. eccl.* 1.13.10.

sense to the investigation of Jesus's attitude to Gentiles. Nevertheless, it may be useful in other ways or for other investigations, since everything is evidence for something. For example, the Abgar tradition depicts a mission to a Gentile ruler that is legitimized by Jesus, but which is not undertaken by him, and which does not commence until after his lifetime. This indicates an awareness that Jesus did not himself missionize Gentiles, and that the mission to the Gentiles began during the apostolic age. Thus, the tradition may be of use to the investigation after all, even though its testimony is not literally "authentic."

Conclusion

There is a certain compatibility between Collingwood's "idea of history" and Lonergan's cognitional theory, insofar as both deny that knowledge of the past can be attained by empirically attending to the data. Both require a knower, a historian, to understand the data and to make reasonable judgments on the basis of the evidence grasped by inquiring into the meaning of the data. The result of this combination is a more robust and defensible philosophy of history, resulting in a clearer historiographical approach. Lonergan's cognitional theory, or "transcendental method," provides both a hermeneutic and a satisfactory epistemological basis upon which to build my historical reconstruction. Knowledge of the past, like any other type of knowledge, is attained by experiencing, understanding, judging, and deciding, in that order. This means being attentive, being intelligent, being reasonable, and being responsible.

Appendix C: Additional Notes on Secondary Rooms in Synagogue Buildings

Some synagogues had additional rooms aside from the main hall. These rooms provide some additional insight into synagogue functions and roles. The Gamla synagogue (figs. 5.1–2), for example, features a number of small additional rooms both near the building's entrance and at the back of the hall.[1] The largest and most significant of these rooms is what the excavators refer to as a "study room," a rectangular room seating about 25 people at the back of the synagogue with benches lining at least three of the four walls.[2] This "study room" was not entered directly through the main hall, but through another room off of the main assembly area, though it did have a window opening onto the main hall. Zvi Yavor has quite reasonably noted that the small size and arrangement of the room suggests that the room was used for study in smaller groups, though he also notes that other communal functions could have taken place there.[3]

My opinion, and without further evidence it can be nothing more than opinion, is that while the room was probably used for study, it may have also been used to hold meetings of smaller subgroups or councils, such as the *prōtoi* or *presbytēroi*, away from the main congregation. The window on to the main hall may have been used for communication between the assembly and the council.

The synagogue at Magdala (figs. 5.4a and 5.4b) has two rooms in

---

1. See Yavor, "Architecture and Stratigraphy," 55–58.
2. Ibid., 56. The bench on the western side may have been too narrow to serve as seating.
3. Ibid., 55–56. Previously, it was also suggested that the room might have been a place for impure people or others not allowed into the main assembly hall, in Syon and Yavor, "Gamla – Old and New," 10.

addition to the main assembly hall. The smaller of these two rooms is located in a short hallway off of the main room. It features a mosaic floor, and may have been used for storage, perhaps for Torah scrolls.[4] The larger of the auxiliary rooms at Magdala is referred to by the excavators as "the vestibule," so-called because the synagogue's entrance has been reconstructed on the western side of the room.[5] Like the main hall, this room also features benched seating (fig 5.5). A limestone block with two semi-cylindrical grooves along either end of its upward face stands in the centre of the room (fig 5.6), in the middle of a small basalt frame on the floor. The excavators have suggested that this block may have been the base for a chair or table,[6] but I think it is more likely that this served as a small table for reading scrolls. Scroll rollers could be placed in the two grooves, allowing the reader to easily scroll back and forth between various sections of the text.

I find the identification of this room as a vestibule to be somewhat problematic. First, the architectural elements of the synagogue's entryway were discovered out of context, and were not reconstructed in their current location until 2013–2014 (fig 5.7).[7] Second, the reconstructed entrance is made awkward by the presence of the limestone block and its frame, which sits in the path of anyone who would have entered the room by such a doorway. The stone frame and the block's location at the room's central focal point strongly indicates that it was a key element of the room's design, so it is curious to have the entrance located in a place which would appear to disrupt this. Third, the synagogue is located on the Western limit of the town. If the entrance was on the west side of the building, congregants would first need to exit the town by the road located to the south of the building in order to come around to the doorway, which seems odd. I suggest that the entrance may have been located either on the east side of the main hall, where there was a clear gap in the wall before the building's reconstruction, or on the south side. There is a small hallway that abuts the road on the south side of the building, which seems to be the most natural place for the entrance to have been located.

---

4. Cf. Bauckham and De Luca, "Magdala As We Now Know It," 106–7.
5. See Avshalom-Gorni and Najar, "Migdal."
6. Ibid.
7. I first came to this site as a participant in the 2012 excavation season, and at that time, the elements of the doorway were not yet incorporated into the reconstruction of this room. Note, however, that according to the publication of Avshalom-Gorni and Najar, "Magdala," the remains of the entrance were not discovered. It is possible that they mean that the remains of the entrance were not discovered *in situ*, since in personal conversation, Arfan Najar indicated that he believed that the architectural elements of the entryway depicted in fig. 5.7 belonged to the synagogue.

As it stands, the best clues to the function of this secondary room are the limestone block and the seating arrangement. I infer from this evidence that, much like the secondary "study room" in the synagogue at Gamla, this secondary room was probably used for teaching and studying involving texts in smaller groups,[8] and perhaps also for meetings of smaller councils and subgroups. It is worth mentioning that a secondary room with benches lining at least three of its walls was also discovered at the late-first-century synagogue at Khirbet Qana.[9] This room is quite comparable in form to the "study room" at Gamla, and so, we should imagine that it had similar functions to the Gamla synagogue's "study room."

The synagogue at Masada features a small additional room. It was under the floor of this room that the portions of scrolls of Deuteronomy and Ezekiel, mentioned above, were found buried.[10] This led Yadin to suggest that this was a sort of *genizah*, though it is unclear as to whether the texts were buried while the rebels were living at Masada or whether the texts were buried before they took their own lives.[11] It is, however, somewhat natural to imagine that the texts may have been kept in this room while they were in use. At any rate, this is indicative of the presence or storage of sacred texts in the synagogue buildings of the Land and sacred texts, not only the Torah, but also the Nevi'im, just as in Luke's depiction of Jesus's reading from Isaiah in Luke 4:16–21.

The presence of an oven on its floor and the discovery of an *ostracon* bearing an inscription "Priest's Tithe" just outside this room led Yadin to propose that it served as living quarters for a priest who was responsible for maintaining the building.[12] This data dovetails nicely with the evidence from the Theodotos inscription, coming from what was probably an association synagogue in Jerusalem, which mentions guest rooms.[13] It is thus clear that synagogues could provide housing, and that we should be careful not to exclude such nonreligious or liturgical functions from our historical imaginations.

---

8. As suggested also by Mordechai Aviam, "Zwischen Meer und See – Geschichte und Kultur Galiläas von Simon Makkabäus bis zu Flavius Josephus," in *Bauern, Fischer und Propheten - Galiläa zur Zeit Jesu*, ed. Jürgen K. Zangenberg and Jens Schröter (Darmstadt: Verlag Philipp von Zabern), 13–38 (35); Bauckham and De Luca, "Magdala As We Now Know It," 106. Note also that according to Avshalom Gorni and Najar, "Magdala," "the vestibule might also have been a kind of small seminary used for studying."

9. See Richardson, *Building Jewish*, 66; *ASSB* no. 3.

10. See Yadin, "Masada," 21–22 for an account of this discovery.

11. Ibid., 21.

12. Yadin, "Excavation of Masada," 78.

13. *ASSB* no. 26; *CIJ* 2.1404.

Works Cited

Abegg, Martin. "Paul, 'Works of the Law,' and MMT." *BAR* 20, no. 6 (1994): 24–36.

Abrahams, Israel. "The Freedom of the Synagogue." In *Studies in Pharisaism and the Gospels*. 2 vols., 1:1–17. Cambridge: Cambridge University Press, 1917.

Albertz, Martin. *Die synoptischen Streitgespräche: Ein Beitrag zur Formgeschichte des Urchristentums*. Berlin: Trowitzsch, 1921.

Albertz, Rainer. "Die 'Atrittspredigt' Jesu im Lukasevangelium auf ihrem alttestamentlichen Hintergrund." *ZNW* 74 (1983): 182–206.

Alexander, Philip S. "Jewish Law in the Time of Jesus: Towards a Clarification of the Problem." In *Law and Religion: Essays on the Place of the Law in Israel and Early Christianity*, 44–58. Edited by Barnabas Lindars. Cambridge: J. Clarke, 1988.

Allison, Dale C. *The New Moses: A Matthean Typology*. Minneapolis: Fortress Press, 1993.

_____. *Constructing Jesus: Memory, Imagination, and History*. Grand Rapids: Baker Academic, 2010.

Anderson, Paul N. "Aspects of Historicity in the Fourth Gospel: Consensus and Convergences." In *Critical Appraisals of Critical Views*, vol. 1 of *John, Jesus, and History*, 379–86. Edited by Paul N. Anderson, Felix Just, and Tom Thatcher. SBL Symposium Series 44. Atlanta: Society of Biblical Literature, 2007.

_____. *The Christology of the Fourth Gospel: Its Unity and Disunity in Light of John 6*. WUNT 2.78. Tübingen: Mohr Siebeck, 1996.

_____. *The Fourth Gospel and the Quest for Jesus: Modern Foundations Reconsidered*. London and New York: Continuum, 2007.

_____. "The Jesus of History, the Christ of Faith, and the Gospel of John." In *The Gospels: History and Christology: The Search of Joseph Ratzinger - Benedict XVI*, 2:63–81. 2 vols. Edited by Bernardo Estrada, Ermenegildo Manicardi, and Armand Puig i Tàrrich. Rome: Libreria Editrice Vaticana, 2013.

_____. "John and Qumran: Discovery and Interpretation Over Sixty Years." In *John, Qumran, and the Dead Sea Scrolls: Sixty Years of Discovery and Debate*, 15–50. Edited by Mary L. Coloe and Tom Thatcher. Early Judaism and Its Literature 32. Atlanta: Society of Biblical Literature, 2011.

Anderson, Paul N., Felix Just, and Tom Thatcher, eds. *Aspects of Historicity in the Fourth Gospel*. Vol. 2 of *John, Jesus, and History*. Atlanta: Society of Biblical Literature, 2009.

_____, eds. *Critical Appraisals of Critical Views*. Vol. 1 of *John, Jesus, and History*. SBL Symposium Series 44. Atlanta: Society of Biblical Literature, 2007.

_____, eds. *Glimpses of Jesus Through the Johannine Lens*. Vol. 3 of *John Jesus and History*. Atlanta: Society of Biblical Literature, 2016.

Ankersmit, F. R. "Historiography and Postmodernism." *History and Theory* 28, no. 2 (1989): 137–53.

Arendt, Hannah. *The Promise of Politics*. New York: Schoken Books, 2005.

Ascough, Richard S. "Paul, Synagogues, and Associations: Reframing the Question of Models for Pauline Christ Groups." *JJMJS* 2 (2015): 27–52.

Ascough, Richard S., Philip A. Harland, and John S. Kloppenborg. *Associations in the Greco-Roman World: A Sourcebook*. Waco: Baylor University Press, 2012.

Assman, Jan. *Religion and Cultural Memory*. Translated by Rodney Livingstone. Stanford: Stanford University Press, 2006.

Atkinson, Kenneth. "On Further Defining the First-Century Synagogue: Fact or Fiction? A Rejoinder to H.C. Kee." *NTS* 43 (1997): 491–502.

Aune, David E. "Literacy." In *The Westminster Dictionary of New Testament and Early Christian Literature and Rhetoric*, 275–76. Louisville: Westminster John Knox, 2003.

_____. *The New Testament in Its Literary Environment*. Edited by Wayne A. Meeks. Library of Early Christianity 8. Philadelphia: Westminster, 1987.

_____. *Prophecy in Early Christianity and the Ancient Mediterranean World*. Grand Rapids: Eerdmans, 1983. Repr., Eugene: Wipf & Stock, 2003.

Avery-Peck, Alan J., and Jacob Neusner, eds. *The Special Problem of the Ancient Synagogue*. Vol. 4 of *Judaism in Late Antiquity*, Part 3: *Where We Stand: Issues and Debates in Ancient Judaism*. Leiden: Brill, 2001.

Avi-Yonah, Michael. "Some Comments on the Capernaum Excavations." In *Ancient Synagogues Revealed*, 60–62. Edited by Lee I. Levine. Jerusalem: Israel Exploration Society, 1981.

Aviam, Mordechai. "The Decorated Stone at Migdal: A Holistic Interpretation and a Glimpse into the Life of Galilean Jews at the Time of Jesus." *Novum Testamentum* 55 (2013): 205–20.

_____. "Reverence for Jerusalem and the Temple in Galilean Society." In *Jesus and Temple: Textual and Archaeological Explorations*, 123–44. Edited by James H. Charlesworth. Minneapolis: Fortress Press, 2014.

_____. "Zwischen Meer und See – Geschichte und Kultur Galiläas von Simon Makkabäus bis zu Flavius Josephus." In *Bauern, Fischer und Propheten - Galiläa zur Zeit Jesu*, 13–38. Edited by Jürgen K. Zangenberg and Jens Schröter. Darmstadt: Verlag Philipp von Zabern, 2012.

Aviam, Mordechai, and William Scott Green. "The Ancient Synagogue: Public Space in Ancient Judaism." In *Judaism From Moses to Muhammad: An Interpretation*, 83–200. Edited by Jacob Neusner, William Scott Green, and Alan J. Avery-Peck. Leiden and Boston: Brill, 2005.

Avshalom-Gorni, Dina, and Arfan Najar. "Migdal: Preliminary Report." *Hadashot* 125 (2013), http://www.hadashot-esi.org.il/report_detail_eng.aspx?id=2304&mag_id=120.

Back, Sven-Olav. "Jesus and the Sabbath." In *Handbook for the Study of the Historical Jesus*, 2597–633. Edited by Tom Holmén and Stanley E. Porter. Leiden and Boston: Brill, 2011.

Bahat, Dan. "The Second Temple in Jerusalem." In *Jesus and Temple: Textual and Archaeological Explorations*, 59–74. Edited by James H. Charlesworth. Minneapolis: Fortress Press, 2014.

Barclay, John M. G. *Against Apion: Translation and Commentary*. Flavius Josephus: Translation and Commentary 10. Leiden and Boston: Brill, 2007.

_____. *Jews in the Mediterranean Diaspora: From Alexander to Trajan (323 BCE - 117 CE)*. Berkeley and Los Angeles: University of California Press, 1996.

Barnett, Paul W. "The Jewish Signs Prophets – A.D. 40–70 – Their Intentions and Origin." *NTS* 27 (1981): 679–97.

Barrett, C. K. *The Gospel According to St. John: An Introduction With Commentary and Notes on the Greek Text*. London: SPCK, 1960.

Barth, Karl. *Church Dogmatics, vol. 1:2: The Doctrine of the Word of God*. London: T&T Clark, 1956.

Bartholomä, Philipp F. *The Johannine Discourses and the Teaching of Jesus in the Synoptics*. Texte und Arbeiten zum neutestamentlichen Zeitalter 57. Tübingen: Francke, 2012.

Barton, John. *Holy Writings, Sacred Texts: The Canon in Early Christianity*. Louisville: Westminster John Knox, 1997.

Barzun, Jacques, and Henry F. Gradd. "A Medley of Mysteries: A Number of Dog That Didn't Bark." In *The Historian as Detective: Essays on Evidence*, 213–31. Edited by Robin W. Winks. New York: Harper Torchbooks, 1970.

Bauckham, Richard. "Further Thoughts on the Migdal Synagogue Stone." *Novum Testamentum* 57 (2015): 113–35.

_____. *Jesus and the Eyewitnesses: The Gospels as Eyewitness Testimony.* Grand Rapids: Eerdmans, 2006.

_____. *The Jewish World Around the New Testament.* Tübingen: Mohr Siebeck, 2008.

_____. *The Testimony of the Beloved Disciple: Narrative, History, and Theology in the Gospel of John.* Grand Rapids: Eerdmans, 2007.

Bauckham, Richard, and Stefano De Luca. "Magdala As We Now Know It." *Early Christianity* 6 (2015): 91–118.

Bauer, Georg Lorenz. *Beschreibung der gottesdienstlichen Verfassung der alten Hebräer.* 2 vols. Leipzig: Weygand, 1805–6.

Bauernfeind, Otto. *Die Worte der Dämonen im Markusevangelium.* Stuttgart: Kohlhammer, 1927.

Baur, Ferdinand Christian. *The Church History of the First Three Centuries.* 3rd ed. 2 vols. Translated by Allan Menzies. London: Williams and Norgate, 1878.

Beards, Andrew. "Knowledge and Our Limits: Lonergan and Williamson." *The Lonergan Review* 5, no. 1 (2014): 77–108.

_____. *Method in Metaphysics: Lonergan and the Future of Analytical Philosophy.* Toronto: University of Toronto Press, 2008.

Beare, Francis Wright. "Mission of the Disciples and the Mission Charge: Matthew 10 and Parallels." *JBL* 89, no. 1 (1970): 1–13.

Beasley-Murray, G. R. *Jesus and the Kingdom of God.* Grand Rapids: Eerdmans, 1986.

_____. "Jesus and the Kingdom of God," *Baptist Quarterly* 32 (1987): 141–47.

Beavis, Mary Ann. *Jesus and Utopia: Looking for the Kingdom of God in the Roman World.* Minneapolis: Fortress Press, 2006.

_____. "Jesus in Utopian Context." In *Jesus in Contiuum*, 151–70. Edited by Tom Holmén. WUNT 289. Tübingen: Mohr Siebeck, 2012.

Becker, Jürgen. *Jesus of Nazareth.* Translated by James E. Crouch. New York and Berlin: Walter de Gruyter, 1998.

Bernier, Jonathan. *Aposynagōgos and the Historical Jesus in John: Rethinking the Historicity of the Johannine Expulsion Passages.* Biblical Interpretation 122. Leiden and Boston: Brill, 2013.

_____. *The Quest for the Historical Jesus After the Demise of Authenticity: Toward a Critical Realist Philosophy of History in Jesus Studies.* LNTS 540. London and New York: T&T Clark, 2016.

_____. Review of Stephen K. Catto, *Reconstructing the First-Century Synagogue: A Critical Analysis of Current Research.* RBL. November 16, 2008.

_____. "A Response to Porter and Pitts' 'Wright's Critical Realism in Context.'" *JSHJ* 14, no. 2 (2016): 186–93.

Bernstein, Moshe J. "Interpretation of Scriptures." In *Encyclopedia of the Dead Sea Scrolls* 1:376–83. Edited by Lawrence H. Schiffman. 2 vols. Oxford: Oxford University Press, 2000.

Bernstein, Moshe J., and Shlomo A. Koyfman. "The Interpretation of Biblical Law in the Dead Sea Scrolls: Forms and Methods." In *Biblical Interpretation at Qumran*, 61–87. Edited by Matthias Henze. Grand Rapids: Eerdmans, 2005.

Betz, Hans Dieter. *The Sermon on the Mount*. Edited by Adela Yarbro Collins. Hermeneia. Minneapolis: Fortress Press, 1995.

Beuken, Willem A. M. "Servant and Herald of Good Tidings: Isaiah 61 as an Interpretation of Isaiah 40–55." In *The Book of Isaiah: Les Oracles et Leurs Relectures Unité et Complexité de L'Ouvrage*, 411–42. Edited by J. Vermeylen. Leuven: Peeters, 1989.

Bhaskar, Roy. *A Realist Theory of Science*. London: Verso, 2008.

Binder, Donald D. *Into the Temple Courts: The Place of the Synagogues in the Second Temple Period*. SBL Dissertation Series 169. Atlanta: Society of Biblical Literature, 1999.

———. "The Mystery of the Magdala Stone." In *A City Set on a Hill: Essays in Honor of James F. Strange*, 17–48. Edited by Daniel A. Warner and Donald D. Binder. Fayetteville: Borderstone Press, 2014.

Black, C. Clifton. "Redaction Criticism." In *Encyclopedia of the Historical Jesus*, 491–94. Edited by Craig A. Evans. New York and London: Routledge, 2007.

Bloch, Marc. *The Historian's Craft*. Translated by Peter Putnam. New York: Alfred A. Knopf, 1953.

Blomberg, Craig L. *The Historical Reliability of John's Gospel: Issues and Commentary*. Downers Grove: InterVarsity Press, 2001.

———. *The Historical Reliability of the Gospels*. 2nd ed. Downers Grove: IVP Academic, 2007.

Bock, Darrell L. *Luke*. 2 vols. BECNT. Grand Rapids: Baker, 1994.

———. *Mark*. NCBC. New York: Cambridge University Press, 2015.

Bockmuehl, Markus. *This Jesus: Martyr, Lord, Messiah*. Downers Grove: InterVarsity Press, 1994.

Bond, Helen. "Herodian Dynasty." In *Dictionary of Jesus and the Gospels*, 379–83. 2nd ed. Edited by Joel B. Green, Jeannine K. Brown, and Nicholas Perrin. Downers Grove: IVP Academic, 2013.

———. *The Historical Jesus: A Guide For the Perplexed*. London and New York: T&T Clark, 2012.

Boring, M. Eugene. *Mark: A Commentary*. New Testament Library. Louisville: Westminster John Knox, 2006.

Borgen, Peder. *Bread from Heaven: An Exegetical Study of the Concept of Manna in the Gospel of John and the Writings of Philo*. NovTSupp 10. Leiden: Brill, 1965.

_____. "Observations on the Midrashic Character of John 6." *ZNW* 54 (1963): 232–40.

Botterweck, G. J., and Helmer Ringgren, eds. *Theological Dictionary of the Old Testament*. Translated by John T. Willis et al. 8 vols. Grand Rapids: Eerdmans, 1974–2006.

Bovon, François. *A Commentary on the Gospel of Luke*. 3 vols. Hermeneia. Minneapolis: Fortress Press, 2002.

Bowman, Alan K. *The Town Councils of Roman Egypt*. Toronto: A. M. Hakkert, 1971.

Brandon, S. G. F. *Jesus and the Zealots*. New York: Charles Scribner's Sons, 1967.

Broadhead, Edwin K. *Teaching With Authority: Miracles and Christology in the Gospel of Mark*. JSNTSupp 74. Sheffield: Sheffield Academic, 1992.

Broer, Ingo. "Die Antithesen und der Evangelist Mattaus." *Biblische Zeitschrift* 19 (1975): 50–63.

Brooks, James A. *Mark*. NAC 23. Nashville: Broadman, 1991.

_____. "The Unity and Structure of the Sermon on the Mount," *Criswell Theological Review* 6, no. 1 (1992): 15–28.

Brooten, Bernadette J. "Female Leadership in the Ancient Synagogue." In *From Dura to Sepphoris: Studies in Jewish Art and Society in Late Antiquity*, 25–223. Edited by Lee I. Levine and Zeev Weiss. Portsmouth: Journal of Roman Archaeology, 2000.

_____. *Women Leaders in the Ancient Synagogue*. Brown Judaic Studies 36. Chico: Scholar's Press, 1982.

Broshi, Magen. "The Population of Western Palestine in the Roman-Byzantine Period." *BASOR* 236 (1979): 1–10.

Brown, Callum G. *Postmodernism for Historians*. London and New York: Routledge, 2013.

Brown, Raymond E. *Community of the Beloved Disciple: The Life, Loves, and Hates of an Individual Church in New Testament Times*. New York: Paulist, 1979.

_____. *The Gospel According to John*. AYB 29. 2 vols. New York: Doubleday, 1970. Repr., New Haven: Yale, 2008.

_____. *An Introduction to the Gospel of John*. Edited by Francis J. Maloney. New York: Doubleday, 2003.

Bryan, Steven M. "Jesus and Israel's Eschatological Constitution." In *Handbook for the Study of the Historical Jesus*, 2835–853. Edited by Tom Holmén and Stanley E. Porter. Leiden and Boston: Brill, 2011.

Bultmann, Rudolf. *The Gospel of John: A Commentary*. Translated by G. R. Beasley-Murray, R. W. N. Hoare, and J. K. Riches. Philadelphia: Westminster, 1971.

_____. *History and Eschatology: The Presence of Eternity*. New York: Harper, 1957.

_____. *History of the Synoptic Tradition*. Translated by John Marsh. Peabody: Hendrickson, 1963. Translation of *Geschichte der Synoptischen Tradition*. Göttingen: Vandenhoeck & Ruprecht, 1931.

_____. *Jesus and the Word*. Translated by Louise Pettibone Smith and Erminie Huntress Lantero. London: Collins, 1958. Translation of *Jesus*. Berlin: Deutsche Bibliotek, 1926.

_____. *Jesus Christ and Mythology*. New York: Scribner, 1958.

_____. "Liberal Theology and the Latest Theological Movement." In Gregory W. Dawes, *The Historical Jesus Quest: Landmarks in the Search for the Jesus of History*, 242–68. Louisville: Westminster John Knox, 2000. Repr. from Rudolf Bultmann, *Faith and Understanding*. New York: Harper & Row, 1969. Translation of *Glauben und verstehen*. Tübingen: Mohr Siebeck, 1933.

_____. *The Theology of the New Testament (1948-1953)*. Translated by Kendrick Grobel with an introduction by Robert Morgan. Waco: Baylor University Press, 2007.

Burge, Gary M. *The Anointed Community: The Holy Spirit in the Johannine Tradition*. Grand Rapids: Eerdmans, 1987.

_____. *The Gospel of John*. NIV Application Commentary. Grand Rapids: Zondervan, 2000.

Burke, Seán. *The Death and Return of the Author: Criticism and Subjectivity in Barthes, Foucault and Derrida*. 3rd ed. Edinburgh: Edinburgh University Press, 2008).

Byrskog, Samuel. "A New Quest for the *Sitz im Leben*: Social Memory, the Jesus Tradition, and the Gospel of Matthew." *NTS* 52 (2006): 319–36.

Calvert, D. G. A. "An Examination of the Criteria for Distinguishing the Authentic Words of Jesus." *New Testament Studies* 18 (1972): 209–18.

Cannon, W. W. "Isaiah 61, 1–3 an *Ebed-Jahweh* Poem," *ZAW* 47 (1929): 284–88.

Carr, E. H. *What is History?* 2nd ed. Edited by R. W. Davies. Harmondsworth and New York: Penguin, 1987.

Carroll, John T. *Luke: A Commentary*. New Testament Library. Louisville: Westminster John Knox, 2012.

Carson, D. A. "Redaction Criticism: On the Legitimacy and Illegitimacy of a Literary Tool." In *Scripture and Truth*, 119–42. Edited by D. A. Carson and John D. Woodbridge. Grand Rapids: Baker Book House, 1992.

Carter, Warren. *John and Empire: Initial Explorations*. New York: T&T Clark, 2008.

_____. *Matthew and Empire: Initial Explorations*. Harrisburg: Trinity Press, 2001.

Casey, Maurice. *Is John's Gospel True?* London and New York: Routledge, 1996.

Catto, Stephen K. *Reconstructing the First-Century Synagogue: A Critical Analysis of Current Research*. LNTS 363. London and New York: T&T Clark, 2007.

Chancey, Mark A. *The Myth of a Gentile Galilee*. SNTS Monograph Series 118. Cambridge: Cambridge University Press, 2002.

Charlesworth, James H., ed. *Jesus and Archaeology*. Grand Rapids: Eerdmans, 2006.

_____. "Jesus Research and Archaeology: A New Perspective." In *Jesus and Archaeology*, 11–63. Edited by James H. Charlesworth. Grand Rapids and Cambridge: Eerdmans, 2006.

_____, ed. *Jesus and Temple: Textual and Archaeological Explorations*. Minneapolis: Fortress Press, 2014.

Charlesworth, James H., with Brian Rhea and Petr Pokorný, eds. *Jesus Research: New Methodologies and Perceptions*. Grand Rapids: Eerdmans, 2014.

Childs, Brevard S. *Isaiah: A Commentary*. Old Testament Library. Louisville: John Knox, 2001.

Chilton, Bruce D. "An Exorcism of History: Mark 1:21–28." In *Authenticating the Activities of Jesus*, 215–45. Edited by Bruce D. Chilton and Craig A. Evans. New Testament Tools and Studies 28.2. Leiden: Brill, 1998.

Choi, Junghwa. *Jewish Leadership in Palestine from 70 CE to 1135 CE*. AJEC 83. Leiden and Boston: Brill, 2013.

Claussen, Carsten. "Meeting, Community, Synagogue – Different Frameworks of Ancient Jewish Congregations in the Diaspora." In *The Ancient Synagogue From its Origins until 200 C.E.*, 144–67. Edited by Birger Olsson and Magnus Zetterholm. Stockholm: Almqvist & Wiksell, 2003.

_____. *Versammlung, Gemeinde, Synagoge: die hellenistisch-jüdische Umfeld der frühchristlichen Gemeinden*. Studien zur Umwelt des Neuen Testaments 27. Göttingen: Vandenhoeck & Ruprecht, 2002.

Clements, R. E. "Isaiah 53 and the Restoration of Israel." In *Jesus and the Suffering Servant: Isaiah 53 and Christian Origins*, 47–54. Edited by William H. Bellinger Jr. and William R. Farmer. Harrisburg: Trinity, 1998.

Cohen, Shaye J. D. "Were Pharisees and Rabbis the Leaders of Communal Prayer and Torah Study in Antiquity?" In *Evolution of the Synagogue: Problems and Progress*, 89–105. Edited by Howard Clark Kee and Lynn H. Cohick. Harrisburg: Trinity Press International, 1999.

Collingwood, R. G. *The Archaeology of Roman Britain*. Rev. ed. Edited by I. A. Richmond. London: Bracken Books, 1996.

_____. *The Idea of History*. 1st ed. Edited by T. M. Knox. Oxford: Clarendon, 1946.

_____. *The Idea of History*. Rev. and enl. ed. Edited by Jan van der Dussen. Oxford: Clarendon, 1993.

_____. "The Limits of Historical Knowledge." *Philosophy* 3, no. 10 (1928): 213–22.

_____. *The New Leviathan*. Rev. ed. Edited by David Boucher. Oxford: Clarendon, 2000.

_____. *Principles of History*. Edited by William H. Dray and Jan van der Dussen. Oxford: Oxford University Press, 1999.

_____. *Roman Britain*. Rev. ed. Barnes and Noble, 1994.

Collins, John J. *Apocalypticism in the Dead Sea Scrolls*. London: Routledge, 1998.

_____. "A Herald of Good Tidings: Isaiah 61:1–3 and Its Actualization in the Dead Sea Scrolls." In *The Quest for Context and Meaning: Studies in Biblical Intertextuality in Honor of James A. Sanders*, 225–40. Edited by Craig A. Evans and Shemaryahu Talmon. Leiden, New York, and Köln: Brill, 1997.

Collins, Nina L. *Jesus, The Sabbath, and The Jewish Debate: Healing on the Sabbath in the 1st and 2nd Centuries CE*. LNTS 474. New York: T&T Clark, 2014.

Connelly, James, Peter Johnson, and Stephen Leach. *R. G. Collingwood: A Research Companion*. London: Bloomsbury, 2014.

Conzelmann, Hans. *Acts of the Apostles*. Hermeneia. Philadelphia: Fortress Press, 1987.

_____. *Theology of St. Luke*. London: SCM, 1982.

Corbo, Virgilio. "La Citta romana di Magdala." In *Studia Hierosolymitana in onore del P. Bellarmino Bagatti*, 365–68. Edited by I. Mancini and M. Piccirillo. Jerusalem: Franciscan Printing Press, 1976.

_____. "Resti della sinagoga del primo secolo a Cafarnao." In *Studia Hierosolymitana*, 3:313–57. 3 vols. 3rd ed. Edited by G. C. Biottini. Jerusalem: Franciscan Printing, 1982.

_____. "Scavi Archaelogici a Magdala." *Liber Annuus* 24 (1974): 5–37.

Cotter, Wendy J. "The Parables of the Mustard and the Leaven: Their Function in the Earliest Stratum of Q." *Toronto Journal of Theology* 8, no. (1992): 38–51.

Craffert, Pieter F. *The Life of a Galilean Shaman: Jesus in Anthropological-Historical Perspective*. Eugene: Wipf & Stock, 2008.

_____. "Multiple Realities and Historiography: Rethinking Historical Jesus Research." In *The New Testament Interpreted: Essays in Honor of Bernard C. Lategan*, 87–116. Edited by Cilliers Breytenbach, Johan C. Thom, and Jeremy Punt. Leiden and Boston: Brill, 2007.

Craffert, Pieter F., and Pieter J. J. Botha. "Why Jesus Could Walk on the Sea but He Could Not Read or Write." *Neotestamentica* 39, no. 1 (2005): 5–35.

Crockett, L. "Luke iv. 16–30 and the Jewish Lectionary Cycle: A Word of Caution." *JJS* 17, no. 2 (1966): 13–46.

Crook, Zeba. "Collective Memory Distortion and the Quest for the Historical Jesus." *JSHJ* 11, no. 1 (2013): 53–76.

_____. "Gratitude and Comments to Anthony Le Donne." *JSHJ* 1 (2013): 98–105.

_____. "On the Treatment of Miracles in New Testament Scholarship." *Studies in Religion* 40, no. 4 (2011): 461–78.

_____. "The Synoptic Parables of the Mustard and the Leaven: A Test-Case for the Two-Document, Two-Gospel, and Farrer-Goulder Hypotheses." *JSNT* 78 (2000): 23–48.

Crossan, John Dominic. *The Birth of Christianity: Discovering What Happened in the Years Immediately After the Execution of Jesus.* New York: HarperCollins, 1998.

_____. *God and Empire: Jesus Against Rome, Then and Now.* New York: HarperCollins, 2007.

_____. *The Historical Jesus: The Life of a Mediterranean Jewish Peasant.* San Francisco: HarperCollins, 1991.

_____. *Jesus: A Revolutionary Biography.* New York: HarperCollins, 1994.

Cullmann, Oscar. *Jesus and the Revolutionaries.* New York: Harper Collins, 1970.

Culpepper, R. Alan. "Jesus Sayings in the Johannine Discourses: A Proposal." In *Glimpses of Jesus Through the Johannine Lens,* vol. 3 of *John, Jesus and History,* 353–82. Edited by Paul N. Anderson, Felix Just, and Tom Thatcher. Atlanta: SBL, 2016.

Dahl, Nils. "The Parables of Growth." In *Jesus in the Memory of the Early Church,* 156–66. Minneapolis: Augsburg, 1976.

Daise, Michael Allen. "Jesus and the Jewish Festivals: Methodological Reflections." In *Jesus Research: New Methodologies and Perceptions,* 283–304. Edited by James H. Charlesworth with Brian Rhea and Petr Pokorný. Grand Rapids: Eerdmans, 2014.

David, Chaim ben. "Were There 204 Settlements in Galilee at the Time of Josephus Flavius?" *JJS* 62, no. 1 (2011): 21–36.

Davies, W. D. *The Setting of the Sermon on the Mount.* Cambridge: Cambridge University Press, 1964.

Davies, W. D., and D. C. Allison. *Matthew.* ICC. 3 vols. Edinburgh: T&T Clark, 1988.

Davies, Brian. *The Thought of Thomas Aquinas.* Oxford: Clarendon, 1992.

Dawes, Gregory W., ed. *The Historical Jesus Quest: Landmarks in the Search for the Jesus of History.* Louisville: Westminster John Knox, 2000.

Deines, Roland. "Galilee and the Historical Jesus in Recent Research." In *Galilee in the Late Second Temple and Mishnaic Periods: Life, Culture, and Society.* Vol. 1 of *Galilee in the Late Second Temple and Mishnaic Periods,* 11–48. Edited by David A. Fiensy and James Riley Strange. Minneapolis: Fortress Press, 2014.

Deissmann, Gustav Adolf. *Light from the Ancient East: the New Testament Illustrated by Recently Discovered Texts of the Graeco-Roman World.* 4th ed. New York: George H. Doran, 1927.

Dennis, John. "The Presence and Function of Second Exodus-Restoration Imagery in John 6." *SNTU* 30 (2005): 105–21.

Denton, Donald L. *Historiography and Hermeneutics in Jesus Studies: An Examination of the Work of John Dominic Crossan and Ben F. Meyer.* JSNTSupp 262. London and New York: T&T Clark, 2004.

Derrett, J. Duncan M. "'Ενοχος (Mt 5, 21–22) and the Jurisprudence of Heaven." *Filología Neotestamentaria* 19 (2006): 89–97.

deSilva, David. "The Wisdom of Ben Sira: Honour, Shame, and the Maintenance of the Values of a Minority Culture." *CBQ* 58 (1996): 433–55.

Dibelius, Martin. *Die Formgeschichte des Evangeliums.* 3rd ed. Edited by Günther Bornkamm. Tübingen: Mohr Siebeck, 1971.

Dillon, Richard J. "'As One Having Authority' (Mark 1:22) The Controversial Distinction of Jesus' Teaching." *CBQ* 57, no. 1 (1995): 97–112.

Dodd, C. H. *Historical Tradition in the Fourth Gospel.* Cambridge: Cambridge University Press, 1963.

_____. *The Interpretation of the Fourth Gospel.* Cambridge: Cambridge University Press, 1968.

_____. *The Parables of the Kingdom.* London: James Nisbet & Co., 1935.

Doering, Lutz. *Schabbat: Sabbathalacha und -praxis im antiken Judentum und Urchristentum.* Texts and Studies in Ancient Judaism 78. Tübingen: Mohr Siebeck, 1999.

Domeris, W. R. "Shame and Honor in Proverbs: Wise Women and Foolish Men." *Old Testament Essays* 8, no. 1 (1995): 86–102.

Donagan, Alan. *The Later Philosophy of R. G. Collingwood.* Oxford: Clarendon, 1962.

_____. "The Verification of Historical Theses." *Philosophical Quarterly* 6 (1956): 193–208.

Doran, Robert. *Theology and the Dialectics of History.* Toronto: University of Toronto Press, 1990.

Dray, William H. *History as Re-Enactment: R. G. Collingwood's Idea of History.* Oxford: Clarendon, 1995.

_____. "R. G. Collingwood and the Acquaintance Theory of Knowledge." *Revue Internationale de Philosophie* 11 (1957): 420–32.

Droysen, Johann Gustav. *Outline of the Principles of History.* Translated by E. Benjamin Andrews. Boston: Ginn & Company, 1897.

Duling, Dennis C. "Social Memory and Biblical Studies: Theory, Method, and Application." *BTB* 36, no. (2006): 2–3.

Dunn, James D. G. "Did Jesus Attend the Synagogue?" Pages 206–22 in *Jesus and Archaeology.* Grand Rapids: Eerdmans, 2006.

_____. *Jesus Remembered.* Christianity in the Making 1. Grand Rapids: Eerdmans, 2003.

_____. "John VI – A Eucharistic Discourse?" *NTS* 17, no. 3 (1971): 328–38.

_____. "Law." In *Dictionary of Jesus and the Gospels,* 505–15. Edited by Joel B.

Green, Jeannine K. Brown, and Nicholas Perrin. 2nd ed. Downers Grove: IVP Academic, 2013.

Dussen, Jan van der. *History as a Science: The Philosophy of R. G. Collingwood*. Dordrecht and Heidelberg: Springer, 2012.

Edwards, James R. "The Authority of Jesus in the Gospel of Mark." *JETS* 37, no. 2 (1994): 217–33.

Eisenberg, Azriel. *The Synagogue Through the Ages*. New York: Bloch Publishing Company, 1974.

Eisler, Robert. *Iēsous Basileus ou Basileusas*. 2 vols. Heidelberg: Carl Winters Universitäitsbuchhandlung, 1929–1930.

Elbogen, Ismar. *Jewish Liturgy: A Comprehensive History*. Translated by Raymond P. Scheindlin. Philadelphia: The Jewish Publication Society, 1993. Translation of *Der jüdische Gottesdienst in seiner geschichtlichen Entwicklung*. Leipzig: Fock, 1913.

Ellis, E. Earle. *The Gospel of Luke*. Eugene: Wipf & Stock: 2003.

Elton, Geoffrey R. *The Practice of History*. 2nd ed. Oxford: Blackwell, 2001.

Evans, C. F. *Saint Luke*. Trinity Press International New Testament Commentaries. Philadelphia: Trinity.

Evans, Craig A. "Authenticity Criteria in Life of Jesus Research." *Christian Scholar's Review* 19, no. 1 (1989): 6–31.

_____. "Defeating Satan and Liberating Israel: Jesus and Daniel's Visions." *JSHJ* 1, no. 2 (2003): 161–70.

_____. *Jesus and His Contemporaries: Comparative Studies*. Arbeiten zur Geshichte des antiken Judentums und des Urchristentums 25. Leiden and New York: Brill, 1995.

_____. *Jesus and His World: The Archaeological Evidence*. Louisville: Westminster John Knox, 2012.

_____. "Jewish Scripture and the Literacy of Jesus." In *From Biblical Criticism to Biblical Faith: Essays in Honor of Lee Martin McDonald*, 41–54. Edited by William H. Brackney and Craig A. Evans. Macon: Mercer University Press, 2007.

Evans, Richard J. *In Defense of History*. New ed. London: Granta, 2001.

Eve, Eric. *The Healer From Nazareth: Jesus' Miracles in Historical Context*. London: SPCK, 2009.

_____. *The Jewish Context of Jesus' Miracles*. JSNTSupp 231. Sheffield: Sheffield Academic, 2002.

Fiensy David A., and Ralph K. Hawkins, eds. *The Galilean Economy in the Time of Jesus*. Early Christianity and its Literature 11. Atlanta: Society of Biblical Literature, 2013.

Fiensy, David A., and James Riley Strange, eds. *Galilee in the Late Second Temple* and *Mishnaic Periods: Life, Culture, and Society*. Minneapolis: Fortress Press, 2014.

Fine, Steven. *Art and Judaism in the Greco-Roman World: Toward A New Jewish Archaeology*. 2nd ed. Cambridge: Cambridge University Press, 2010.

_____. "From Meeting House to Sacred Realm." In *Sacred Realm: The Emergence of the Synagogue in the Ancient World*, 21–47. Edited by Steven Fine. New York and Oxford: Oxford University Press, 1996.

_____, ed. *Jews, Christians, and Polytheists in the Ancient Synagogue: Cultural Interaction during the Greco-Roman Period*. Baltimore Studies in the History of Judaism. London: Routledge, 1999.

_____. *This Holy Place: On the Sanctity of the Synagogue During the Greco-Roman Period*. Christianity and Judaism in Antiquity 11. Notre Dame: University of Notre Dame Press, 1997.

Finkel, Asher. "Jesus' Sermon at Nazareth (Luke 4, 16–30)." In *Abraham unser Vater: Juden und Christen im Gespräch über die Bibel*, 106–15. Edited by Otto Betz, Martin Hengel, and Peter Schmidt. Leiden: Brill, 1963.

Finkelstein, Louis. "The Origin of the Synagogue." In *Proceedings of the American Academy for Jewish Research 1928-1930*, 49–59.

_____. "The Origin of the Synagogue." In *The Synagogue: Studies in Origins, Archaeology, and Architecture*, 3–13. Edited by Joseph Gutman. New York: Ktav, 1975.

Fischer, David Hackett. *Historians' Fallacies: Toward a Logic of History*. New York: Harper & Row, 1970.

Fitzmyer, Joseph A. *The Gospel According to Luke*. 3 vols. AYB 28. New York: Doubleday, 1981.

Flesher, Paul V. M. "Palestinian Synagogues Before 70 C.E.: A Review of the Evidence." In *Historical Analysis and Archaeological Discovery*. Vol. 2 of *Ancient Synagogues*, 1:27–39. Edited by Dan Urman and Paul V. M. Flesher. Leiden: Brill, 1995.

Fletcher-Louis, C. "Priests and Priesthood." In *Dictionary of Jesus and the Gospels*, 699–700. Edited by Joel B. Green, Jeannine K. Brown, and Nicholas Perrin. 2nd ed. Downers Grove: IVP Academic, 2013.

Flint, Peter W. "The Qumran Scrolls and the Historical Jesus." In *Jesus Research: New Methodologies and Perceptions*, 261–82. Edited by James H. Charlesworth with Brian Rhea and Petr Pokorný. Grand Rapids: Eerdmans, 2014.

Foerster, Gideon. "Notes on Recent Excavations at Capernaum." In *Ancient Synagogues Revealed*, 57–59. Edited by Lee I. Levine. Jerusalem: Israel Exploration Society, 1981.

Fokkelman, Jan. *Reading Biblical Narrative: A Practical Guide*. Leiden: Deo, 1999.

Foster, Paul. "Educating Jesus: The Search For a Plausible Context." *JSHJ* 4, no. 1 (2006): 7–33.

_____. "Memory, Orality, and the Fourth Gospel: Three Dead-Ends in Historical Jesus Research." *JSHJ* 10, no. 3, (2012): 191–227.

_____. "Memory, Orality, and the Fourth Gospel: An Ongoing Conversation with Stan Porter and Hughson T. Ong." *JSHJ* 12 (2014): 165–83.

Fouts, David M. "The Demographics of Ancient Israel." *Bulletin of Biblical Research* 7, 10.2 (2007): 1–10.

France, R. T. *Jesus and the Old Testament: His Application of Old Testament Passages to Himself and His Mission.* Grand Rapids: Baker, 1982.

_____. *Matthew.* Downer's Grove: InterVarsity Press, 1985.

Fredriksen, Paula. *Jesus of Nazareth, King of the Jews: A Jewish Life and the Emergence of Christianity.* London: Macmillan, 1999.

Frey, Jean-Baptiste, ed. *Corpus Inscriptionum Judaicarum.* 2 vols. Rome: Pontifical Biblical Institute, 1936–1952.

Frey, Jörg. "From the 'Kingdom of God' to 'Eternal Life.'" In *Glimpses of Jesus Through the Johannine Lens,* vol. 3 of *John, Jesus, and History,* 439–58. Edited by Paul N. Anderson, Felix Just, and Tom Thatcher. Atlanta: SBL, 2016.

Freyne, Seán. "Behind the Names: Galileans, Samaritans, *Ioudaioi.*" In *Galilee Through the Centuries: Confluence of Cultures,* 39–56. Edited by Eric M. Meyers. Winona Lake: Eisenbrauns, 1999.

_____. *Galilee, Jesus and the Gospels.* Philadelphia: Fortress Press, 1988.

_____. "The Geography of Restoration: Galilee-Jerusalem Relations in Early Jewish and Christian Experience." *NTS* 47 (2001): 289–311.

_____. *Jesus, A Jewish Galilean.* London and New York: T&T Clark, 2004.

_____. *The Jesus Movement and Its Expansion: Meaing and Mission.* Grand Rapids: Eerdmans, 2014.

Friedländer, M. *Synagoge und Kirche in ihren Anfängen.* Berlin: Georg Reimer, 1908.

Frye, Northrop. *Anatomy of Criticism: Four Essays.* Princeton: Princeton University Press, 1957.

Funk, Robert W. "Beyond Criticism in Quest of Literacy: The Parable of the Leaven," *Interpretation* 25 (1971): 149–70.

_____. *Honest to Jesus: Jesus for a New Millennium.* San Francisco: HarperSanFrancisco, 1993.

Funk, Robert W., Roy W. Hoover, and the Jesus Seminar. *The Five Gospels: What Did Jesus Really Say?* New York: HarperCollins, 1997.

Funk, Robert W., and the Jesus Seminar. *The Acts of Jesus: The Search for the Authentic Deeds of Jesus.* New York: Polebridge Press, 1998.

Gamble, Harry Y. "Literacy and Book Culture." In *The Dictionary of New Testament Background*, 644–48. Edited by Craig A. Evans and Stanley E. Porter. Downers Grove: InterVarsity Press, 2000.

Gerhardsson, Birger. *Memory and Manuscript: Oral Tradition and Written Transmission in Rabbinic Judaism and Early Christianity*. Acta Seminarii Neotestamentici Upsaliensis 22. Lund: C.W.K. Gleerup, 1961.

_____. *The Reliability of the Gospel Tradition*. Grand Rapids: Baker Academic, 2001.

Gnilka, Joachim. *Jesus of Nazareth: Message and History*. Translated by Siegfried S. Schatzman. Peabody: Hendrickson, 1997.

Goldstein, Leon J. *Historical Knowing*. Austin: University of Texas, 1976.

Goodacre, Mark. "Criticizing the Criterion of Multiple Attestation: The Historical Jesus and the Question of Source." In *Jesus, Criteria, and the Demise of Authenticity*, 152–69. Edited by Chris Keith and Anthony Le Donne. London and New York: T&T Clark: 2012.

Goodman, Martin. "Sacred Scriptures and 'Defiling the Hands.'" *JTS* 41 (1990): 99–107.

Goppelt, Leonhard. *Theology of the New Testament*. 2 vols. Translated by John E. Alsup. Edited by Jürgen Roloff. Grand Rapids: Eerdmans, 1981–1982.

Grabbe, Lester L. "Synagogue and Sanhedrin in the Frist Century." In *Handbook for the Study of the Historical Jesus*, 1723–44. Edited by Tom Holmén and Stanley E. Porter. Leiden: Brill, 2011.

Graham, Steven A. "Semitic Language and Syntax Within the Speech of the Johannine Jesus." In *Glimpses of Jesus Through the Johannine Lens*. Vol. 3 of *John, Jesus, and History*, 407–21. Edited by Paul N. Anderson, Felix Just, and Tom Thatcher. Atlanta: Society of Biblical Literature.

Grant, Robert M. *Historical Introduction to the New Testament*. New York: Harper & Row, 1963.

Graves, Michael. "The Public Reading of Scripture in Early Judaism." *JETS* 50, no. 3 (2007): 467–87.

Green, Joel B. *The Gospel of Luke*. NICNT. Grand Rapids: Eerdmans, 1997.

_____. "Jesus and a Daughter of Abraham (Luke 13:10–17): Test Case for a Lucan Perspective on Jesus' Miracles." *CBQ* 51 (1989): 643–54.

Griffiths, J. Gwyn. "Egypt and the Rise of the Synagogue." In *Ancient Synagogues: Historical Analysis and Archaeological Discovery*, 3–16. Edited by D. Urman et al. Studia Post-Biblica 1. Leiden: Brill, 1995.

Grotius, Hugo. *Annotationes in Novum Testamentum*. 9 vols. Groningen: W. Zuidema, 1826–34.

Grundmann, Walter. *Das Evangelium nach Lukas*. Theologischer Handkommentar zum Neuen Testament 3. Berlin: Evangelische Verlagsanstalt, 1963.

Guelich, Robert. "The Antitheses of Matthew v. 21–28: Tradition and/or Redactional?" *NTS* 22 (1976): 444–57.

Guijarro, Santiago. "The Politics of Exorcism: Jesus' Reaction to Negative Labels in the Beelzebul Controversy." *BTB* 29, no. 3 (1999): 118–29.

Gundry, Robert H. *Matthew: A Commentary on His Literary and Theological Art.* Grand Rapids: Eerdmans, 1982.

Gutmann, Joseph. "Synagogue Origins: Theories and Facts." In *Ancient Synagogues: The State of Research*, 1–6. Edited by Joseph Gutmann. Brown Judaic Studies. Chico: Scholars Press, 1981.

Haber, Susan. "Common Judaism, Common Synagogue? Purity, Holiness, and Sacred Space at the Turn of the Common Era." In *"They Shall Purify Themselves": Essays on Purity in Early Judaism*, 161–79. Edited by Adele Reinhartz. Atlanta: Society of Biblical Literature, 2008.

Hachlili, Rachel. *Ancient Jewish Art and Archaeology in the Land of Israel.* HdO. Leiden and New York: Brill, 1988.

_____. *Ancient Synagogues – Archaeology and Art: New Discoveries and Current Research.* HdO 105. Leiden and Boston: Brill, 2013.

_____. "The Origin of the Synagogue: A Re-Assessment." *JSJ* 28 (1997): 34–47.

_____. "Synagogues: Before and After the Roman Destruction of the Temple." *BAR* 41, no. 3 (2015), n.p.

Hakola, Raimo. *Identity Matters: John, the Jews, and Jewishness.* Leiden: Brill, 2005.

Hakola, Raimo, and Adele Reinhartz. "John's Pharisees." In *In Quest of the Historical Pharisees*, 131–47. Edited by Jacob Neusner and Bruce D. Chilton. Waco: Baylor University Press, 2007.

Halbwachs, Maurice. *On Collective Memory.* Translated by Lewis A. Coser. Chicago: University of Chicago Press, 1992.

Hamm, M. Dennis. "The Freeing of the Bent Woman and the Restoration of Israel: Luke 13.10–17 as Narrative Theology." *JSNT* 31 (1987): 23–44.

Har–Even, Binyamin. "Khirbet Tawani. A settlement from the Second Temple, Roman– Byzantine and early Muslim periods." *The Frontier and Desert in the Land of Israel* 7 (2012): 15–29.

Har–Even, Binyamin. "A Second Temple Synagogue at Horvat Diab in Western Benjamin." *Qadmoniot* 151 (2016): 49–53.

Harland, Philip A. *Associations, Synagogues and Congregations: Claiming a Place in Ancient Mediterranean Society.* Minneapolis: Fortress Press, 2003.

Harrington, Daniel J. *The Gospel of Matthew.* Sacra Pagina 1. Collegeville: Liturgical Press, 1994.

_____. *Jesus Ben Sira of Jerusalem: A Biblical Guide to Living Wisely.* Interfaces. Collegeville: Liturgical Press, 2005.

Harris, William V. *Ancient Literacy.* Cambridge: Harvard University Press, 1989.

Hasson, Nir. "Roman-era Structure Thought to Be Synagogue Found in Golan Heights." *Haaretz*, December 26, 2014.

_____. "Archaeologists in Israel Find Ancient Synagogue Predating Second Temple Ruin," *Haaretz*, August 16, 2016, http://www.haaretz.com/israel-news/1.736752.

Heemstra, Marius. *The Fiscus Judaicus and the Parting of the Ways.* Tübingen: Mohr Siebeck, 2010.

Hendin, David. "Jesus and Numismatics: The Importance of Coins in Reconstructing Jesus and His World." In *Jesus Research: New Methodologies and Perceptions*, 190–97. Edited by James H. Charlesworth, with Brian Rhea and Petr Pokorný. 2 vols. Grand Rapids: Eerdmans, 2014.

Hengel, Martin. "Luke the Historian and the Geography of Palestine in Acts of the Apostles." In *Between Jesus and Paul: Studies in Earliest Christianity*, 97–128. Philadelphia: Fortress Press, 1983. Repr., Eugene: Wipf & Stock, 2003.

Hengel, Martin. "The Geography of Palestine in Acts." In *The Book of Acts in its Palestinian Setting*. Vol. 4 of *The Book of Acts in its First-Century Setting*, 27–78. Edited by Richard Bauckham. Grand Rapids: Eerdmans, 1995.

_____. *The Pre-Christian Paul.* London: SCM, 1991.

_____. "Proseuche und Synagoge: Jüdische Gemeinde, Gotteshaus und Gottesdienst in der Diaspora und in Palästina." In *The Synagogue: Studies in Origins, Archaeology and Architecture*, 27–54. The Library of Biblical Studies. Edited by J. Gutmann. New York: Ktav, 1975.

Hengel, Martin, and Roland Deines. "E. P. Sanders' 'Common Judaism.'" *JTS* 46, no. 1 (1995): 1–70.

Herford, R. Travers. *The Pharisees.* London: G. Allen, 1924.

Heyer, Cees den. "Historic Jesuses." In *Handbook for the Study of the Historical Jesus*, 1079–101. Edited by Tom Holmén and Stanley E. Porter. Leiden and Boston: Brill, 2011.

Higgins, A. J. B. *The Lord's Supper in the New Testament.* Chicago: Alec R. Allenson, 1952.

Hill, David. "The Rejection of Jesus At Nazareth (Luke iv 16–30)." *Novum Testamentum* 13, no. 3 (1971): 162–80.

Hoenig, Sidney B. "The Ancient City-Square: The Forerunner of the Synagogue." In *Judentum:Allemeines, palestinisches Judentu*, 448–76. Edited by W. Haase. ANRW 2:19:1. Berlin: de Gruyter, 1979.

_____. "The Suppositious Temple-Synagogue." In *The Synagogue: Studies in Origins, Archaeology and Architecture*, 55–71. Edited by Joseph Gutmann. Library of Biblical Studies. New York: Ktav, 1975.

Holladay, William L. *The Root Subh in the Old Testament.* Leiden: Brill, 1958.

Holmén, Tom. "Authenticity Criteria." In *Encyclopedia of the Historical Jesus*, 43–54. Edited by Craig A. Evans. New York and London: Routledge, 2007.

Hooker, Morna D. *Jesus and the Servant: The Influence of the Servant Concept of Deutero-Isaiah in the New Testament*. London: SPCK, 1959.

_____. "On Using the Wrong Tool." *Theology* 75 (1972): 570–81.

Hopkins, Jasper. "Bultmann on Collingwood's Philosophy of History." *Harvard Theological Review* 58, no. 2 (1965): 227–33.

Hoppe, Leslie J. *The Synagogues and Churches of Ancient Palestine*. Collegeville: Liturgical Press, 1994.

Horsley, Richard A. *Archaeology, History, and Society in Galilee: The Social Context of Jesus and the Rabbis*. Valley Forge: Trinity Press International, 1996.

_____. *Galilee: History, Politics, People*. Valley Forge: Trinity Press International, 1995.

_____. *Jesus: Power, People, and Performance*. Minneapolis: Fortress Press, 2008.

_____. *Jesus and Empire*. Minneapolis: Fortress Press, 2003.

_____. *The Prophet Jesus and the Renewal of Israel: Moving Beyond a Diversionary Debate*. Grand Rapids: Eerdmans, 2012.

_____. "Synagogues in Galilee and the Gospels." In *Evolution of the Synagogue: Problems and Progress*, 46–96. Edited by Howard Clark Kee and Lynn H. Cohick. Harrisburg: Trinity Press International, 1999.

Horsley Richard A., and Tom Thatcher, *John, Jesus, and the Renewal of Israel*. Grand Rapids: Eerdmans, 2013.

Horst, P. W. van der. "Was the Synagogue a Place of Sabbath Worship Before 70 C.E.?" In *Jews, Christians, and Polytheists: Cultural Interaction during the Greco-Roman Period*, 18–43. Edited by Steven Fine. London: Routledge, 1999.

Hughes-Warrington, Marnie. *Fifty Key Thinkers on History*. 2nd ed. Oxon: Routledge, 2008.

_____. *How Good an Historian Shall I Be? R. G. Collingwood, The Historical Imagination, and Education*. British Idealist Studies Series 2: Collingwood 2. Exeter: Imprint Academic, 2004.

Hultgren, Arland J. *Jesus and His Adversaries*. Minneapolis: Augsburg, 1979.

_____. *The Parables of Jesus: A Commentary*. Grand Rapids: Eerdmans, 2000.

Hurtado, Larry W. *One Lord, One God: Early Christian Devotion and Ancient Jewish Monotheism*. 3rd ed. London and New York: Bloomsbury T&T Clark, 2015.

Instone-Brewer, David. "1 Corinthians 7 in the Light of the Jewish Greek and Aramaic Marriage and Divorce Papyri." *Tyndale Bulletin* 52, no. 2 (2001): 225–43.

Jenkins, Keith. *Why History? Ethics and Postmodernity*. London and New York: Routledge, 1999.

Hørning Jensen, Morten. *Herod Antipas in Galilee: The Literary and Archaeological Sources on the Reign of Herod Antipas and its Socio-Economic Impact on Galilee.* WUNT 215. Tübingen: Mohr Siebeck, 2010.

Hugenberger, H. P. "The Servant of the Lord in the 'Servant Song' of Isaiah: A Second Moses Figure." In *The Lord's Annointed*, 105–40. Edited by P. E. Satterthwaite, R. S. Hess, and G.J. Wenham. Grand Rapids: Baker, 1995.

Israel Antiquities Authority. "Special Bronze Implements were Discovered in Archaeological Excavations at Magdala – a 2,000 Year Old Jewish Settlement on the Sea of Galilee," http://www.antiquities.org.il/Article_eng.aspx?sec_id=25&subj_id=240&id=4190 N.p.

Jeremias, Joachim. *New Testament Theology I: The Proclamation of Jesus.* Translated by John Bowden. New York: Scribner, 1971.

_____. *The Parables of Jesus.* Translated by S. H. Hooke. 2nd ed. New York: Charles Scribner's Sons, 1963.

Jost, Isaak M. *Geschichte der Israeliten seit der Zeit der Maccabäer bis auf unsre Tage.* Berlin: Schlesingerschen Buch und Musikhandlung, 1822.

Jülicher, Adolf. *Die Gleichnisreden Jesu.* 2 vols. Freiburg: J. C. B. Mohr, 1888–1889.

Juster, Jean. *Les Juifs dans l'Empire Romain: leur condition juridique, économique et sociale.* Paris: Paul Geuthner, 1914.

Kähler, Martin. *The So-Called Historical Jesus and the Historic Biblical Christ.* Translated by Carl E. Braaten. Philadelphia: Fortress Press, 1964.

Käsemann, Ernst. "The Problem of the Historical Jesus." In *Essays on New Testament Themes*, 15–47. Translated by J. W. Montague. London: SCM, 1964.

Kazen, Thomas. *Scripture, Interpretation, or Authority?: Motives and Arguments in Jesus' Halakic Conflicts.* WUNT 320. Tübingen: Mohr Siebeck, 2013.

Kee, Howard Clark. "The Changing Meaning of Synagogue: A Response to Richard Oster," *NTS* 40 (1994): 281–83.

_____. "Defining the First-Century Synagogue: Problems and Progress." *NTS* 41 (1995): 481–500.

_____. "The Transformation of the Synagogue After 70 C.E.: Its Import for Early Christianity." *NTS* 36 (1990): 1–24.

Kee, Howard Clark, and Lynn H. Cohick, eds. *Evolution of the Synagogue: Problems and Progress.* Harrisburg: Trinity Press International, 1999.

Keener, Craig S. *Acts: An Exegetical Commentary.* 4 vols. Grand Rapids: Baker Academic, 2012.

_____. *The Gospel of John: A Commentary.* 2 vols. Peabody: Hendrickson, 2003.

_____. *Matthew: A Socio-Rhetorical Commentary.* Grand Rapids and Cambridge: Eerdmans, 2009.

_____. "Matthew 5:22 and the Heavenly Court." *Expository Times* 99, no. 2 (1987): 46.

_____. *Miracles: The Credibility of the New Testament Accounts.* 2 vols. Grand Rapids: Baker, 2011.

_____. *The IVP Bible Background Commentary: New Testament.* 2nd ed. Downers Grove: InterVarsity Press, 2014.

Keith, Chris. "Concluding Remarks." In *Jesus, Criteria, and the Demise of Authenticity,* 200–205. Edited by Chris Keith and Anthony Le Donne. London and New York: T&T Clark, 2012.

_____. "The Indebtedness of the Criteria Approach to Form Criticism and Recent Attempts to Rehabilitate the Search for an Authentic Jesus." In *Jesus, Criteria, and the Demise of Authenticity,* 25–48. Edited by Chris Keith and Anthony Le Donne. London and New York: T&T Clark, 2012.

_____. *Jesus Against the Scribal Elite: The Origins of the Conflict.* Grand Rapids: Baker Academic, 2014.

_____. *Jesus' Literacy: Scribal Culture and the Teacher from Galilee.* LNTS 413. London: T&T Clark, 2011.

_____. "The Narratives of the Gospels and the Historical Jesus: Current Debates, Prior Debates and the Goal of Historical Jesus Research." *JSNT* 38 (2016): 1–30.

Keith, Chris, and Anthony Le Donne, eds. *Jesus, Criteria, and the Demise of Authenticity.* London and New York: T&T Clark, 2012.

Kelber, Werner H. "The Generative Force of Memory: Early Christian Traditions as Processes of Remembering." *BTB* 36, no. 1 (2006): 15–22.

_____. *The Oral and the Written Gospel: The Hermeneutics of Speaking and Writing in the Synoptic Tradition, Mark, Paul, and Q.* Bloomington: Indiana University Press, 1983.

Kelber, Werner H., and Samuel Byrskog, eds. *Traditions in Oral and Scribal Perspectives.* Waco: Baylor University Press, 2009.

Killebrew, Ann E. "Village and Countryside." In *The Oxford Handbook of Jewish Daily Life in Roman Palestine,* 189–209. Edited by Catherine Hezser. Oxford and New York: Oxford University Press, 2010.

Kim, Seeyoon. *"The 'Son of Man'" as the Son of God.* WUNT 30. Tübingen: Mohr Siebeck, 1983.

Kingsbury, Jack Dean. *The Parables of Jesus in Matthew 13.* Richmond: John Knox, 1969.

Kirk, Alan. "Social and Cultural Memory." In *Memory, Tradition, and Text: Uses of the Past in Early Christianity,* 1–24. Semeia 52. Edited by Alan Kirk and Tom Thatcher. Atlanta: Society of Biblical Literature, 2005.

_____. "Memory." In *Jesus in Memory: Traditions in Oral and Scribal Perspectives,*

155–72. Edited by Werner H. Kelber and Samuel Byrskog. Waco: Baylor University Press, 2009.

_____. "Memory." In *Handbook for the Study of the Historical Jesus*, 809–42. Edited by Tom Holmén and Stanley E. Porter. Leiden and Boston: Brill, 2011.

Kirk, Alan, and Tom Thatcher, eds. "Jesus Tradition as Social Memory." In *Memory, Tradition, and Text: Uses of the Past in Early Christianity*, 25–42. Semeia 52. Edited by Alan Kirk and Tom Thatcher. Atlanta: Society of Biblical Literature, 2005.

_____. *Memory, Tradition, and Text: Uses of the Past in Early Christianity*. Semeia 52. Atlanta: Society of Biblical Literature, 2005.

Kittel, Gerhard, and Gerhard Friedrich, eds. *Theological Dictionary of the New Testament*. Translated by Geoffrey W. Bromiley. 10 vols. Grand Rapids: Eerdmans, 1964–1976.

Klawans, Jonathan. *Purity, Sacrifice, and the Temple: Symbolism and Supersessionism in the Study of Ancient Judaism*. Oxford: Oxford University Press, 2006.

Kleinman, Arthur. *Patients and Healers in the Context of Culture: An Exploration of the Borderland Between Anthropology, Medicine, and Psychiatry*. Berkeley: University of California, 1980.

Kloppenborg, John S. "*Collegia* and *Thiasoi*: Issues in Function, Taxonomy and Membership." In *Voluntary Associations in the Ancient World*, 16–30. Edited by John S. Kloppenborg and Stephen G. Wilson. London: Routledge, 1996.

_____. "Dating Theodotos (*CIJ* II 1404)." *JJS* 51, no. 2 (2000): 243–80.

_____. "Disaffiliation in Associations and the ἀποσυναγωγός of John." *HTS Teologeise Studies* 61, no 1, article 962 (2011). N.p.

_____. *Excavating Q*. Minneapolis: Fortress Press, 2000.

_____. "Memory, Performance, and the Sayings of Jesus." *JSHJ* 10 (2012): 97–132.

_____. *Q: The Earliest Gospel*. Louisville and London: Westminster John Knox, 2008.

_____. "The Theodotos Synagogue Inscription and the Problem of First-Century Synagogue Buildings." In *Jesus and Archaeology*, 236–82. Edited by James H. Charlesworth. Grand Rapids: Eerdmans, 2006.

Knibb, Michael Anthony. *The Qumran Community*. Cambridge: Cambridge University Press, 1987.

Kohl, Heinrich and Carl Watzinger. *Antike Synagogen in Galiläa*. Leipzig: Henrichs, 1916.

Korner, Ralph J. "Before Church: Political, Ethno-Religious, and Theological Implications of the Collective Designation of Pauline Christ-Followers as *Ekklēsiai*." PhD diss., McMaster University, 2014.

_____. "*Ekklēsia* as a Jewish Synagogue Term: Some Implications for Paul's Socio-Religious Location" *JJMJS* 2 (2015): 53–78.

Köstenberger, Andreas J. *John*. Baker Exegetical Commentary on the New Testament. Grand Rapids: Baker Academic, 2004.

Krause, Andrew R. "Rhetoric, Spatiality, and the First-Century Synagogue: The Description and Narrative Use of Jewish Institutions in the Works of Flavius Josephus." PhD diss., McMaster University, 2015.

Krauss, Samuel. *Synagogale Altertümer*. Berlin: Hildesheim, 1922.

Kuhn, Karl Allen. *The Kingdom According to Luke and Acts: A Social, Literary, and Theological Introduction*. Grand Rapids: Baker, 2015.

Kümmel, Werner Georg. *Promise and Fulfilment: The Eschatological Message of Jesus*. Translated by Dorothea M. Barton. SBT 23. Naperville: Allenson, 1957.

_____. *Theology of the New Testament*. New Testament Library. Translated by John E. Steely. London: SCM, 1974.

Lachs, Samuel Tobias. *A Rabbinic Commentary on the New Testament: The Gospels of Matthew, Mark, and Luke*. Hoboken: Ktav, 1987.

LaCocque, André. *Jesus the Central Jew: His Times and His People*. Early Christianity and its Literature 15. Atlanta: Society of Biblical Literature, 2015.

Lambek, Michael. "From Disease to Discourse: Remarks on the Conceptualization of Trance and Spirit Possession." In *Altered States of Consciousness and Mental Health*, 36–61. Edited by Colleen Ward. Newbury Park: Sage, 1989.

Lambrecht, Jan. *The Sermon on the Mount: Proclamation and Exhortation*. Wilmington: Glazier, 1985.

Le Donne, Anthony. *The Historiographical Jesus: Memory, Typology, and the Son of David*. Waco: Baylor University Press, 2005.

_____. "The Problem of Selectivity in Memory Research: A Response to Zeba Crook." *JSHJ* 11 (2013): 77–97.

Leaney, A. R. C. *A Commentary on the Gospel According to St. Luke*. New York: Harper, 1958.

LeFebvre, Michael. *Collections, Codes, and Torah: The Re-Characterization of Israel's Written Law*. OTS 451. London and New York: T&T Clark, 2006.

Leibner, Uzi. *Settlement and History in Hellenistic, Roman, and Byzantine Galilee*. TSAJ 127. Tübingen: Mohr Siebeck, 2009.

Leon, Harry J., and Carolyn Osiek. *The Jews of Ancient Rome*. Updated ed. Peabody: Hendrickson, 1995.

Lessing, G. E., ed. *Fragments from Reimarus: Consisting of Brief Critical Remarks on the Object of Jesus and His Disciples as Seen in the New Testament*. Translated by Charles Voysey. London: Williams and Norgate, 1879.

Levine, Amy-Jill. *Short Stories by Jesus: The Enigmatic Parables of a Controversial Rabbi*. New York: HarperOne, 2014.

Levine, Lee I. *The Ancient Synagogue: The First Thousand Years.* 1st ed. New Haven and London: Yale University Press, 2000.

———. *The Ancient Synagogue: The First Thousand Years.* 2nd ed. New Haven and London: 2005.

———. "The First-Century Synagogue: Critical Reassessments and Assessments of the Critical." In *Religion and Society in Roman Palestine: Old Questions, New Approaches,* 70–102. Edited by Douglas R. Edwards. New York: Routledge, 2004.

———. "The Synagogues of Galilee." In *Galilee in the Late Second Temple and Mishnaic Periods: Life, Culture, and Society,* 129–50. Edited by David A. Fiensy and James Riley Strange. Vol. 1 of *Galilee in the Late Second Temple and Mishnaic Periods.* Minneapolis: Fortress Press, 2014.

———. *Visual Judaism in Late Antiquity: Historical Contexts of Jewish Art.* New Haven: Yale University Press, 2012.

Lewis, M. Ioan. *Ecstatic Religion: An Anthropological Study of Shamanism and Spirit Possession.* Harmondsworth: Penguin, 1971.

Lincoln, Andrew T. "'We Know That His Testimony is True': Johannine Truth Claims and Historicity." In *Critical Appraisals of Critical Views,* vol. 1 of *John, Jesus, and History,* 179–97. Edited by Paul N. Anderson, Felix Just, and Tom Thatcher. SBL Symposium Series 44. Atlanta: Society of Biblical Literature, 2007.

Liddell, Henry George, Robert Scott, Henry Stuart Jones, and Roderick McKenzie. *A Greek-English Lexicon.* Rev. and updated ed. Oxford and New York: Clarendon, 1996.

Loffreda, Stanislao. "Ceramica Ellenistico-Romana nel Sottosuolo della Sinagoga di Cafarnao." In *Studia Hierosolymitana,* 3:273–313. 3rd ed. Edited by G. C. Biottini. 3 vols. Jerusalem: Franciscan Printing, 1982.

———. "The Late Chronology of the Synagogue of Capernaum." In *Ancient Synagogues Revealed,* 52–56. Edited by Lee I. Levine. Jerusalem: Israel Exploration Society, 1981.

———. *Recovering Capharnaum.* Jerusalem: Franscican Printing, 1993.

Lohfink, Gerhard. *Jesus of Nazareth: What He Wanted, Who He Was.* Translated by Linda M. Maloney. Collegeville: Liturgical Press, 2012.

Lonergan, Bernard. *Early Works on Theological Method.* Collected Works of Bernard Lonergan 22. 3 vols. Edited by Robert M. Doran and Robert C. Croken. Toronto: University of Toronto Press, 2010.

———. *Insight: A Study of Human Understanding.* Collected Works of Bernard Lonergan 3. Edited by Frederick E. Crowe and Robert M. Doran. 5th ed. Toronto: University of Toronto Press, 1992.

_____. *Method in Theology*. Toronto: University of Toronto Press, 2007.

Löw, Leopold. "Der synagogale Rituus." *Monatschrift für Geschichte und Wissenshaft des Judenthums* 33 (1884).

Lüdemann, Gerd. *Jesus After 2000 Years: What He Really Said and Did*. London: SCM, 2000.

Luz, Ulrich. *Matthew*. Hermeneia. 3 vols. Rev. ed. Minneapolis: Fortress Press, 2007.

Ma'oz, Zvi. "The Synagogue of Gamla and the Typology of Second-Temple Synagogues." In *Ancient Synagogues Revealed*, 35–41. Edited by Lee I. Levine. Jerusalem: Israel Exploration Society, 1981.

_____. "When Were the Galilean Synagogues First Constructed?" *Eretz Israel* 25 (1996): 416–26.

Mack, Burton. *A Myth of Innocence: Mark and Christian Origins*. Philadelphia: Fortress Press, 1988.

Magen, Yitzhak, Yoav Tzionit, and Orna Sirkis. "Khirbet Badd 'Isa – Qiryat Sefer." In *The Land of Benjamin*, 179–241. Edited by Noga Haimovich-Carmin. JSP 3. Jerusalem: Israel Antiquities Authority, 2004.

Magness, Jodi. "A Response to Eric M. Meyers and James F. Strange." In *The Special Problem of the Ancient Synagogue*. Vol. 4 of *Judaism in Late Antiquity*. Part 3: *Where We Stand: Issues and Debates in Ancient Judaism*, 79–91. Edited by Alan J. Avery-Peck and Jacob Neusner. Leiden: Brill, 2001.

Malina, Bruce J. *The Palestinian Manna Tradition: The Manna Tradition in the Palestinian Targums and Its Relationship to the New Testament Writings*. Leiden: Brill, 1968.

Malina, Bruce J., and Richard L. Rohrbaugh. *Social-Science Commentary on the Synoptic Gospels*. 2nd ed. Minneapolis: Fortress Press, 2003.

Mann, C. S. *Mark: A New Translation With Introduction and Commentary*. AYB. New York: Doubleday, 1986.

Manns, Frédéric. "La femme et la synagogue à l'époque de Jésus." *Ephemerides Liturgicae* 109, no. 2 (1995): 159–65.

Manson, T. W. *The Teaching of Jesus: Studies of its Form and Content*. Cambridge: Cambridge University Press, 1931.

Marcus, Joel. "*Birkat ha-Minim* Revisited." *NTS* 55 (2009): 523–51.

Marsh, James L. "Postmodernism: A Lonerganian Retrieval and Critique." In *Postmodernism and Christian Philosophy*, 149–67. Edited by Roman T. Ciapalo. Washington, DC: Catholic University of America Press, 1997.

Marshall, I. Howard. *The Gospel of Luke: A Commentary on the Greek Text*. NIGTC. Grand Rapids: Eerdmans, 1978.

Martyn, J. Louis. *History and Theology in the Fourth Gospel*. New York: Harper and Row, 1968.

_____. *History and Theology in the Fourth Gospel.* Rev. and enl. ed. Nashville: Abingdon, 1979.

_____. *History and Theology in the Fourth Gospel.* New Testament Library. 3rd ed. Louisville and London: Westminster John Knox, 2003.

McCollough, C. Thomas. "Final Report on the Archaeological Excavations at Khirbet Qana: Field II, the Synagogue." *ASOR Blog,* November 19, 2013, http://asorblog.org/2013/11/19/final-report-on-the-archaeological-excavations-at-khirbet-qana-field-ii-the-synagogue.

_____. "Khirbet Qana." In *The Archaeological Record From Cities, Towns, and Villages.* Vol. 2 of *Galilee in the Late Second Temple and Mishnaic Periods,* 127–45. Edited by David A. Fiensy and James Riley Strange. Minneapolis: Fortress Press, 2015.

McCullagh, C. Behan. *The Logic of History: Putting Postmodernism in Perspective.* London: Routledge, 2004.

McIver, Robert K. *Memory, Jesus, and the Synoptic Gospels.* RBS 59. Leiden and Boston: Brill, 2012.

McKay, Heather A. "Ancient Synagogues: The Continuing Dialectic between Two Major Views." *Currents in Research: Biblical Studies* 6: (1998) 103–42.

_____. *Sabbath and Synagogue: The Question of Sabbath Worship in Ancient Judaism.* Religions in the Greco Roman World 122. Leiden, New York, and Köln: Brill, 1994.

McKnight, Scot. *Jesus and His Death: Historiography, the Historical Jesus, and Atonement Theory.* Waco: Baylor Universite, 2005.

McPartland, Thomas. *Lonergan and Historiography: The Epistemological Philosophy of History.* Columbia and London: University of Missouri Press, 2010.

Meier, John P. "The Circle of the Twelve: Did It Exist During Jesus' Public Ministry?" *JBL* 116, no. 4 (1997): 635–72.

_____. "The Historical Jesus and the Historical Herodians." *JBL* 119 (2000): 740–46.

_____. *A Marginal Jew: Rethinking the Historical Jesus.* 5 vols. New York: Doubleday, 1991–2016.

_____. *Matthew.* New Testament Message 3. Wilmington: Michael Glazier, 1980.

Menes, A. "Tempel und Synagoge," *ZAW* 9 (1932): 268–76.

Menken, Maarten J. J. *Old Testament Quotations in the Fourth Gospel: Studies in Textual Form.* Contributions to Biblical Exegesis & Theology 15. Kampen: Pharos, 1996.

_____. "Some Remarks on the Course of the Dialogue: John 6:25–34." In *Studies in John's Gospel and Epistles: Collected Essays,* 271–83. Contributions to Biblical Exegesis & Theology 77. Leuven: Peeters, 2015.

Merkley, Paul. "New Quests for Old: One Historian's Observations on a Bad Bargain." *Canadian Journal of Theology* 16, no. 3 (1970): 203–18.

Meyer, Ben F. *Aims of Jesus*. PTMS 48. Eugene: Pickwick, 2002.

_____. *Critical Realism & the New Testament*. PTMS 17. Eugene: Pickwick, 1989.

_____. *Reality and Illusion in New Testament Scholarship: A Primer in Critical Realist Hermeneutics*. Collegeville: Liturgical Press, 1994.

Meyers, Eric M., and Mark A. Chancey. *Alexander to Constantine*. Archaeology of the Land of the Bible 3. New Haven: Yale University Press, 2012.

Meyers, Eric M., Ehud Netzer, and Carol L. Meyers. *Sepphoris*. Winona Lake: Eisenbrauns, 1999.

Meyers Eric M., and Carol L. Meyers. *Excavations at Ancient Nabratein: Synagogue and Environs*. Meiron Excavation Project 6. Winona Lake: Eisenbrauns, 2009.

_____. "Nabratein: Synagogue and Environs." In *The Archaeological Record From Cities, Towns, and Villages*. Vol. 2 of *Galilee in the Late Second Temple and Mishnaic Periods*, 404–13. Edited by David A. Fiensy and James Riley Strange. Minneapolis: Fortress Press, 2015.

Millard, Alan. *Reading and Writing at the Time of Jesus*. Sheffield: Sheffield Academic, 2000.

Miller, Amanda C. *Rumors of Resistance: Status Reversal and Hidden Transcripts in the Gospel of Luke*. Minneapolis: Fortress Press, 2014.

Minissale, Antonino. "The metaphor of 'falling': hermeneutic key to the Book of Sirach." In *The Wisdom of Ben Sira: Studies on Tradition, Redaction, and Theology*, 253–75. Edited by Angelo Passaro and Giuseppe Bellia. Deuterocanonical and Cognate Literature Studies 1. Berlin and New York: Walter de Gruyter, 2008.

Mink, Louis O. *Mind, History, and Dialectic: The Philosophy of R. G. Collingwood*. Middletown: Wesleyan University Press, 1969.

Mitchell, Edwin Knox. "The Jewish Synagogue and the Relation of Jesus to It." *The Biblical World* 16, no.1 (1900): 10–17.

Miquel, Esther. "How to Discredit an Inconvenient Exorcist: Origin and Configuration of the Synoptic Controversies on Jesus' Power as an Exorcist." *Biblical Theology Bulletin* 40, no. 4 (2010): 187–206.

Modrzejewski, Joseph Mélèze. "What is Hellenistic Law? The Documents of the Judaean Desert in the Light of the Papyri from Egypt." In *Law in the Documents of the Judaean Desert*, 7–21. Edited by R. Katzoff and D. Schaps. JSJSup 96. Leiden and Boston: Brill, 2005.

Montefiore, Claude G. *Judaism and St. Paul*. London: Goschen, 1914.

Moore, Carey A. *Daniel, Esther, and Jeremiah: The Additions*. AB 44. New York: Doubleday, 1977.

Morales, Rodrigo J. *The Spirit and the Restoration of Israel: New Exodus and New Creation motifs in Galatians*. WUNT 2.282. Tübingen: Mohr Siebeck, 2010.

Morgenstern, J. "The Origin of the Synagogue." *Studi Orientalistici* 2 (1956): 192–201.

Morris, Leon. *The Gospel According to John*. Rev. ed. NICNT. Grand Rapids: Eerdmans, 1995.

Morton, Russell. "Quest of the Historical Jesus." In *Encyclopedia of the Historical Jesus*, 472–79. Edited by Craig A. Evans. New York and London: Routledge, 2007.

Mosser, Carl. "Torah Instruction, Discussion, and Prophecy in First-Century Synagogues." In *Christian Origins and Hellenistic Judaism: Social and Literary Contexts for the New Testament*, 523–51. Texts and Editions for New Testament Study 10. Edited by Stanley E. Porter and Andrew W. Pitts. Leiden and Boston: Brill, 2013.

Motyer, J. Alex. *Isaiah*. TOTC 20. Downers Grove: Intervarsity, 1999.

Moxnes, Halvor. "Honor and Shame." *Biblical Theology Bulletin* 23, no. 4 (1993): 167–76.

Moyise, Steve. "Jesus and the Scriptures of Israel." In *Handbook for the Study of the Historical Jesus*, 1137–67. Edited by Tom Holmén and Stanley E. Porter. Leiden and Boston: Brill, 2011.

Myers, Alicia D. *Characterizing Jesus: A Rhetorical Analysis on the Fourth Gospel's Use of Scripture in its Presentation of Jesus*. LNTS 458. London and New York: T&T Clark, 2012.

Myers, Ched. *Binding the Strong Man: A Political Reading of Mark's Story of Jesus* Maryknoll: Orbis, 2008.

Naveh, Joseph. *On Stone and Mosaic: The Aramaic and Hebrew Inscriptions From Ancient Synagogues*. Jerusalem: Israel Exploration Society, 1978.

Netzer, Ehud. "Did the Magdala Springhouse Serve as a Synagogue?" In *Synagogues in Antiquity*, 165–72. Edited by A. Kasher, A. Oppenheimer, and U. Rappaport. Jerusalem: Yad Izhak Ben Zvi, 1987.

_____. *Masada III: The Buildings*. Jerusalem: Israel Exploration Society, 1991.

_____. "A Synagogue from the Hasmonean Period Recently Exposed in the Western Plain of Jericho." *Israel Exploration Journal* 49 (1999): 203–21.

Neusner, Jacob. *The Tosefta: Translated from the Hebrew with a New Introduction*. 2 vols. Peabody: Hendrickson, 2002.

Neyrey, Jerome H. *The Gospel of John*. NCBC. Cambridge: Cambridge University Press, 2007.

Nicholson, Ernest W. *Preaching to the Exiles: A Study of the Prose Tradition in the Book of Jeremiah*. Oxford: Basil Blackwell, 1970.

Nickelsburg, George W. E. *Jewish Literature Between the Bible and the Mishnah*. 2nd ed. Minneapolis: Fortress Press, 2005.

Nodet, Étienne. *The Historical Jesus?: Necessity and Limits of an Inquiry*. Jewish and Christian Texts in Contexts and Related Studies. Translated by J. Edward Crowley. London and New York: T&T Clark, 2008.

Nolland, John. *Luke*. WBC 35. 3 vols. Dallas: Word, 1989–1993.

Nora, Pierre. "Between Memory and History: Les Lieux de Mémoire." *Representations* 26 (1989): 7–24.

_____. *Realms of Memory: Rethinking the French Past*. Translated by Arthur Goldhammer. New York: Columbia University Press, 1996.

Notley, R. Steven. "Jesus' Jewish Hermeneutical Method in the Nazareth Synagogue." In *Exegetical Studies*. Vol. 2 of *Early Christian Literature and Intertextuality*, 46–59. Edited by Craig A. Evans and H. D. Zacharias. London: T&T Clark, 2009.

Oakeshott, Michael. *Experience and Its Modes*. Repr. ed. Cambridge: Cambridge University Press, 1994.

Oakman, Douglas E. *Jesus and the Economic Questions of His Day*. Studies in the Bible and Early Christianity 8. Lewiston: Edwin Mellen, 1986.

_____. *The Political Aims of Jesus*. Minneapolis: Fortress Press, 2012.

Olsson, Birger. "'All My Teaching Was Done in Synagogues . . .' (John 18,20)." In *Theology and Christology in the Fourth Gospel: Essays By the Members of the SNTS Johannine Writings Seminar*, 203–24. Edited by Gilbert van Belle, J.G. van der Watt, and P.J. Martin. Leuven: Peeters, 2005.

_____. "The Origins of the Synagogue: An Evaluation." In *The Ancient Synagogue From Its Origins Until 200 C.E.: Papers Presented at an International Conference at Lund University, October 14-17, 2001*, 132–38. Edited by Birger Olsson, and Magnus Zetterholm. CBNTS 39. Stockholm: Almqvist & Wiksell, 2003.

_____. Review of Stephen K. Catto, *Reconstructing the First-Century Synagogue: A Critical Analysis of Current Research*. RBL, November 16, 2008.

Olsson, Birger, and Magnus Zetterholm, eds. *The Ancient Synagogue From its Origins until 200 C.E.* CBNTS 39. Stockholm: Almqvist & Wiksell, 2003.

Onn, Alexander and Y. Rafyunu. "Jerusalem: Khirbeth a-ras." *Hadashot Arkheologiyot*, 100 (1993).

Osborne, G. R. "Life, Eternal Life." In *Dictionary of Jesus and the Gospels*, 518–22. 2nd ed. Edited by Joel B. Green, Jeannine K. Brown, and Nicholas Perrin. Downers Grove: IVP Academic, 2013.

Oster, Richard E. "Supposed Anachronism in Luke-Acts' Use of ΣΥΝΑΓΩΓΗ." NTS 39 (1993): 178–208.

Otzen, Benedikt. *Tobit and Judith*. Sheffield: Sheffield Academic Press, 2002.

Owen, Paul. "Jesus as God's Agent in Mark's Christology." In *Mark, Manuscripts, and Monotheism*, 40–57. Edited by Chris Keith and Dieter Roth. London and New York: Bloomsbury T&T Clark, 2014.

Pagels, Elaine. "The Social History of Satan, the'Intimate Enemy': a Preliminary Sketch." *Harvard Theological Review* 84, no. 2 (1991): 105–28.

_____. "The Social History of Satan, Part II: Satan in the New Testament Gospels." *Journal of the American Academy of Religion* 62, no. 1 (1994): 17–58.

Papademetriou, Kyriakoula. "The Dynamic Semantic Role of Etymology in the Meaning of Greek Biblical Words. The Case of the Word ἐκκλησία." In *Biblical Lexicology: Hebrew and Greek: Semantics - Exegesis - Translation*, 261–80. Edited by Eberhard Bons, Jan Joosten, and Regine Hunziker-Rodewald. Beihefte zur Zeitschrift für die alttestamentliche Wissenschaft 443. Berlin and Boston: De Gruyter, 2015.

Pastor, Jack. *Land and Economy in Ancient Palestine*. London: Routledge, 2012.

Patterson, Stephen J. *The God of Jesus: The Historical Jesus and the Search for Meaning*. Harrisburg: Trinity Press International, 1998.

Perrin, Norman. *Rediscovering the Teaching of Jesus*. London: SCM, 1967.

_____. *What Is Redaction Criticism?* Guides to Biblical Scholarship. Minneapolis: Fortress Press, 1969.

Perrot, Charles. "Luke 4,16–30 et la Lecture Biblique de l'Ancienne Synagogue." *Revue des Sciences Religieuses* 47 (1973): 324–40.

_____. "La synagogue dans le Nouveau Testament." *Le Monde De la Bible* 57 (1989): 36–39.

Pesch, Rudolf. *Das Markusevangelium*. Herders theologischer Kommentar zum Neuen Testament. 2 vols. Frieburg im Breisgau: Herder, 1976.

Pitre, Brant. *Jesus and the Last Supper*. Grand Rapids: Eerdmans, 2015.

_____. "The Lord's Prayer and the New Exodus." *Letter & Spirit* 2 (2006): 69–96.

Poirier, John C. "Jesus as an Elijianic Figure in Luke 4:16–30." *CBQ* 71, no. 2 (2009): 349–63.

Porter, Stanley E. *Criteria for Authenticity in Historical Jesus Research*. Sheffield: Sheffield Academic Press, 2000.

_____. "A Dead End or a New Beginning? Examining the Criteria for Authenticity in Light of Albert Schweitzer." In *Jesus Research: An International Perspective*, 16–35. Edited by James H. Charlesworth and Petr Pokorný. Grand Rapids: Eerdmans, 2009.

_____. "How Do We Know What We Think We Know? Methodological Reflections on Jesus Research." In *Jesus Research: New Methodologies and Perceptions*, 82–99. Edited by James H. Charlesworth, with Brian Rhea and Petr Pokorný. Grand Rapids: Eerdmans, 2014.

_____. "The Role of Greek Language Criteria in Historical Jesus Research." In

Handbook for the Study of the Historical Jesus, 361–404. Edited by Tom Holmén and Stanley E. Porter. Leiden and Boston: Brill, 2011.

Porter, Stanley E., and Hughson T. Ong. "Memory, Orality, and the Fourth Gospel: A Response to Paul Foster with Further Comments for Future Discussion." *JSHJ* 12 (2014): 143–64.

Porter, Stanley E., and Andrew W. Pitts. "Critical Realism in Context: N.T. Wright's Historical Method and Analytic Epistemology." *JSHJ* 13, no. 2–3 (2015): 276–306.

_____. "Has Jonathan Bernier Rescued Critical Realism?" *JSHJ* 14, no. 3 (2016): 1–7.

Powell, Mark Allan. *What Are They Saying About Luke?* New York and Mahwah: Paulist, 1989.

Powery, Emerson B. *Jesus Reads Scripture: The Function of Jesus' Use of Scripture in the Synoptic Gospels*. Brill Interpretation Series 63. Leiden and Boston: Brill, 2003.

Puech, Émile. "Une apocalypse messianique (4Q521)." *Revue de Qumran* 15 (1992): 475–522.

Rad, Gerhard von. *Old Testament Theology*. 2 vols. Translated by D. M. G. Stalker. New York: Harper & Row, 1965.

Rajak, Tessa, and David Noy. "Archisynagogoi: Office, Title, and Social Status in the Greco-Jewish Synagogue." *The Journal of Roman Studies* 83 (1993): 75–93.

Ravens, David. *Luke and the Restoration of Israel*. JSNTSupp 119. Sheffield: Sheffield Academic, 1995.

Redman, Judith C. S. "How Accurate are Eyewitnesses? Bauckham and the Eyewitnesses in Light of Psychological Research." *JBL* 129 (2010): 177–97.

Reed, Jonathan L. *Archaeology and the Galilean Jesus: A Re-Examination of the Evidence*. Harrisburg: Trinity International Press, 2000.

Reich, Ronny. "The Synagogue and the *Miqweh* in Eretz-Israel in the Second Temple, Mishnaic and Talmudic Periods." In *Ancient Synagogues: Historical Analysis and Archaeological Discovery*, 289–97. Edited by Dan Urman and Paul Virgil McCracken Flesher. Leiden and Boston: Brill, 1998.

Reich, Ronny, and Marcela Zapata Meza. "A Preliminary Report on the *Miqwa'ot* of Migdal." *IEJ* 64, no. 1 (2014): 63–71.

Reif, Stefan C. *Judaism and Hebrew Prayer: New Perspectives on Jewish Liturgical History*. Cambridge: Cambridge University Press, 1993.

Reinhardt, Neudecker. *Moses Interpreted by the Pharisees and Jesus: Matthew's Antitheses in Light of Early Rabbinic Literature*. Subsidia Biblical 44. Rome: Georgian and Biblical Press, 2012.

Reinhartz, Adele. "Reading History in the Fourth Gospel." In *What We Have

Heard from the Beginning: The Past, Present, and Future of Johannine Studies, 190–94. Edited by Tom Thatcher. Waco: Baylor University Press, 2007.

———. "The Temple Cleansing and the Death of Jesus." In *Purity, Holiness, and Identity in Judaism and Christianity: Essays in Memory of Susan Haber,* 100–111. Edited by Carl S. Ehrlich, Anders Runesson, and Eileen M. Schuller. WUNT 305. Tübingen: Mohr Siebeck, 2013.

Reiser, Marius. *Jesus and Judgment: The Eschatological Proclamation in Its Jewish Context.* Minneapolis: Fortress Press, 1997.

Renan, Ernest. *Life of Jesus.* Translated by William G. Hutchinson. London: Walter Scott, 1893.

Rensberger, David. *Johannine Faith and Liberating Community.* Philadelphia: Westminster, 1988.

Reynolds, Joyce. "Cities." In *The Administration of the Roman Empire,* 15–52. Edited by David Braund. Exeter: University of Exeter, 1988.

Richey, Lance Byron. *Roman Imperial Ideology and the Gospel of John.* Washington, DC: The Catholic Biblical Association of America, 2007.

Ridderbos, Herman N. *The Gospel According to John: A Theological Commentary.* Translated by John Vriend. Grand Rapids: Eerdmans, 1997.

Riesner, Rainer. "Synagogues in Jerusalem." In *The Book of Acts in its Palestinian Setting,* 179–210. Edited by Richard Bauckham. Grand Rapids: Eerdmans, 1995.

Ritmeyer, Leen. "Imagining the Temple Known to Jesus and to Early Jews." In *Jesus and Temple: Textual and Archaeological Explorations,* 19–57. Edited by James H. Charlesworth. Minneapolis: Fortress Press, 2014.

———. *The Quest: Revealing the Temple Mount in Jerusalem.* Jerusalem: Carta, 2006.

Richardson, Peter. "An Architectural Case for Synagogues as Associations." In *The Ancient Synagogue From Its Origins Until 200 C.E.: Papers Presented at an International Conference at Lund University, October 14–17, 2001,* 90–117. Edited by Birger Olsson, and Magnus Zetterholm. CBNTS 39. Stockholm: Almqvist & Wiksell, 2003.

———. *Building Jewish in the Roman East.* Waco: Baylor University Press, 2004.

———. "Early Synagogues as Collegia in the Diaspora and in Palestine." In *Voluntary Associations in the Graeco-Roman World,* 90–109. Edited by John S. Kloppenborg and Stephen G. Wilson. London: Routledge, 1996.

Riddle, Donald Wayne. "Jesus in Modern Research." *The Journal of Religion* 17, no. 2 (1937): 170–82.

Ritschl, Albrecht. "Instruction in the Christian Religion." In *Three Essays,* 219–92. Translated by Philip Hefner. Eugene: Wipf & Stock Publishers, 2005.

Rivkin, Ellis. "Ben Sira and the Non-Existence of the Synagogue: A Study in Historical Method." In *In the Time of the Harvest: Essays in honor of Abba Hillel Sil-*

ver on the Occasion of his 70th Birthday, 320–54. Edited by D. J. Silver. New York: Macmillan, 1963.

_____. *A Hidden Revolution*. Nashville: Abingdon, 1978.

Robinson, James M. *A New Quest of the Historical Jesus*. London: SCM, 1959.

Rocca, Samuel. *Herod's Judea: A Mediterranean State in the Classic World*. Eugene: Wipf & Stock, 2008.

Rodríguez, Rafael. "The Embarrassing Truth About Jesus: The Criterion of Embarrassment and the Failure of Historical Authenticity." In *Jesus, Criteria, and the Demise of Authenticity*, 132–51. Edited by Chris Keith and Anthony Le Donne. London and New York: T&T Clark, 2012.

_____. *Structuring Early Christian Memory: Jesus in Tradition, Performance, and Text*. LNTS 407. London and New York: T&T Clark, 2010.

Roskovic, Jan. "Jesus as Miracle Worker: Historiography and Credibility." In *Jesus Research: New Methodologies and Perceptions*, 874–96. Vol. 2. Edited by James H. Charlesworth with Brian Rhea and Petr Pokorný. Grand Rapids: Eerdmans, 2014.

Rowley, H. H. *Worship in Ancient Israel: Its Forms and Meaning*. London: SPCK, 1967.

Runesson, Anders. "Architecture, Conflict, and Identity Formation: Jews and Christians in Capernaum From the 1st to the 6th Century." In *The Ancient Galilee in Interaction: Religion, Ethnicity, and Identity*, 231–57. Edited by Harold W. Attridge, Dale Martin, and Jürgen Zangenberg. Tübingen: Mohr Siebeck, 2007.

_____. "Entering a Synagogue With Paul: First-Century Torah Observance." In *Torah Ethics and Early Christian Identity*, 11–26. Edited by Susan J. Wendel and David M. Miller. Grand Rapids: Eerdmans, 2016.

_____. "The Historical Jesus, the Gospels, and First-Century Jewish Society: The Importance of the Synagogue for Understanding the New Testament." In *A City Set on a Hill: Festschrift in Honour of James F. Strange*, 265–97. Edited by Daniel Warner. Fayetteville: Borderstone Press, 2014.

_____. "The Nature and Origins of the First-Century Synagogue." *Bible and Interpretation*, July 2004. http://www.bibleinterp.com/articles/Runesson-1st-Century_Synagogue_1.shtml.

_____. "Placing Paul: Institutional Structures and Theological Strategy in the World of the Early Christ-believer." *Svensk Exegetisk Årsbok* 80 (2015): 43–67.

_____. *The Origins of the Synagogue: A Socio-Historical Study*. CBNTS 37. Stockholm: Almqvist & Wiksell, 2001.

_____. "Saving the Lost Sheep of the House of Israel: Purity, Forgiveness, and Synagogues in the Gospel of Matthew." *Melilah* 11 (2014): 8–24.

_____. "Synagogues Without Rabbis or Christians? Ancient Institutions Beyond

Normative Discourses." Paper presented at the "Erasure History: Approaching the Missing Sources of Antiquity" conference, Toronto, ON, November 11, 2011.

Rutgers, Leonard Victor. "Incense Shovels at Sepphoris?" In *Galilee Through the Centuries: Confluence of Cultures*, 177–98. Edited by Eric M. Meyers. Winona Lake: Eisenbrauns, 1999.

Ryan, Jordan J. "Jesus at the Crossroads of Inference and Imagination: The Relevance of R. G. Collingwood's Philosophy of History for Current Methodological Discussions in Historical Jesus Research." *JSHJ* 13, no. 1 (2015): 66–89.

_____. "Jesus and Synagogue Disputes: The Institutional Context of Luke 13:10–17." *CBQ* 79, no. 1 (2017): 41–59.

_____. "Tiberias." N.p. in *Lexham Bible Dictionary*. Edited by John D. Barry and Lazarus Wentz. Bellingham: Lexham Press, 2012.

Safrai, Shmuel. "Oral Tora." In *The Literature of the Sages Part One: Oral Tora, Halakha, Tosefta, Talmud, Externa Tractates*, 35–119. Edited by Shmuel Safrai and Peter J. Tomson. Vol. 1 of *Literature of the Sages*. Philadelphia: Fortress Press, 1987.

Safrai, Ze'ev. *The Economy of Roman Palestine*. London: Routledge, 1994.

Sanders, E. P. *The Historical Figure of Jesus*. London: Penguin, 1995.

_____. *Jesus and Judaism*. Philadelphia: Fortress Press, 1985.

_____. *Jewish Law From Jesus to the Mishnah: Five Studies*. London: SCM, 1990.

_____. *Paul and Palestinian Judaism*. Philadelphia: Fortress Press, 1977.

Sanders, James A. "Isaiah in Luke." In *Luke and Scripture: The Function of Sacred Tradition in Luke-Acts*, 14–25. Edited by Craig A. Evans and James A. Sanders. Minneapolis: Fortress Press, 1993.

Saldarini, Anthony J. *Pharisees, Scribes and Sadducees in Palestinian Society: A Sociological Approach*. Biblical Resource Series. Grand Rapids: Eerdmans, 2001.

Sand, Alexander. *Das Gesetz und die Propheten: Untersuchungen zur Theologie des Evangeliums nach Matthäus*. Biblische Untersuchungen 11. Regensburg: Pustet, 1974.

Schams, Christine. *Jewish Scribes in the Second-Temple Period*. JSOTSupp 291. Sheffield: Sheffield Academic Press, 1998.

Schechter, Solomon. *Fragments of a Zadokite Work*. New York: Ktav, 1970.

Schellenberg, Ryan S. "Kingdom as Contaminant? The Role of Repertoire in the Parables of the Mustard and the Leaven." *CBQ* 71, no. 3 (2009): 527–43.

Schiffman, Lawrence H. "The Early History of Public Reading of the Torah." In *Jews, Christians, and Polytheists in the Ancient Synagogue: Cultural Interaction During the Greco-Roman Period*, 38–49. Edited by Steven Fine. New York: Routledge, 2014.

_____. "The Importance of the Temple For Ancient Jews." In *Jesus and Temple:*

Textual and Archaeological Explorations, 75–93. Edited by James H. Charlesworth. Minneapolis: Fortress Press, 2014.

_____. *Reclaiming the Dead Sea Scrolls: The History of Judaism, the Background of Christianity, the Lost Library of Qumran.* New York: Double Day, 1995.

Schlatter, Adolf. *Der Glaube im Neuen Testament.* 2nd ed. Stuttgart: Calwer Verlag, 1896.

_____. *Die Theologie des Neuen Testaments. Zweiter Teil: Die Lehre der Apostel.* Calw & Stuttgart: Verlag der Vereinsbuchhandlung, 1910.

Schnabel, Eckhard J. *Law and Wisdom from Ben Sira to Paul.* WUNT 16. Tübingen: Mohr Siebeck, 1985.

Schoeps, Hans Joachim. *Paul: The Theology of the Apostle in the Light of Jewish Religious History.* Philadelphia: Westminster, 1961.

Schramm, Tim. *Der Markus-Stoff bei Lukas: Eine literarkritische und redaktiongeschichtliche Untersuchung.* SNTS Monograpd Series 14. Cambridge: Cambridge University Press, 1971.

Schröter, Jens. "The Criteria of Authenticity in Jesus Research and Historiographical Method." In *Jesus, Criteria, and the Demise of Authenticity*, 49–70. Edited by Chris Keith and Anthony Le Donne. London and New York: T&T Clark, 2012.

_____. *From Jesus to the New Testament: Early Christian Theology and the Origin of the New Testament Canon.* Translated by Wayne Coppins. Waco: Baylor University Press, 2013.

Schultz, Brian. *Conquering the World: The War Scroll Reconsidered.* Leiden: Brill, 2009.

Schürer, Emil. *Die Gemeindeverfassung der Juden in Rom in der Kaiserzeit nach den Inschriften dargestellt.* Leipzig: J. C. Hinrichs, 1879.

_____. *A History of the Jewish People in the Time of Jesus.* Edited by Geza Vermes, Fergus Millar, and Matthew Black. 2 vols. Rev. ed. Edinburgh: T&T Clark, 1973–1986.

Schwartz, Barry. *Abraham Lincoln and the Forge of National Memory.* Chicago: University of Chicago Press, 2000.

_____. *Abraham Lincoln in the Post-Heroic Era: History and Memory in Late Twentieth-Century America.* Chicago: University of Chicago Press, 2008.

Schweitzer, Albert. *Das Abendmahl: im Zusammenhang mit dem Leben Jesu und der Geschichte des Urchristentums.* Tübingen and Leipzig: Mohr Siebeck, 1901.

Schweitzer, Albert. *The Mystery of the Kingdom of God: The Secret of Jesus' Messiahship and Passion.* Translated by Walter Lowrie. New York: Dodd, Mead and Company, 1914.

_____. *The Quest of the Historical Jesus: A Critical Study of its Progress from Reimarus to Wrede.* Translated by W. Montgomery. New York: Macmillan, 1968. Translation of *Von Reimarus zu Wrede: eine Geschichte der Leben-Jesu-Forschung*. Tübingen: Mohr Siebeck, 1906.

_____. *The Quest of the Historical Jesus: First Complete Edition*. Translation W. Montgomery, J. R. Coates, S. Cupitt, and J. Bowden. 1906. Minneapolis: Fortress Press, 2001.

Scott, Bernard Brandon. *Hear Then the Parable: A Commentary on the Parables of Jesus*. Minneapolis: Fortress Press, 1989.

Segal, Michael. *The Book of Jubilees: Rewritten Bible, Redaction, Ideology and Theology*. JSJSupp, 117. Leiden: Brill, 2007.

Shanks, Hershel. *Judaism in Stone: The Archaeology of Ancient Synagogues*. New York: Harper & Row, 1979.

Sheppard, Beth M. *The Craft of History and the Study of the New Testament*. RBS 60. Atlanta: Society of Biblical Literature, 2012.

Shoemaker, Robert G. "Inference and Intuition in Collingwood's Philosophy of History." *The Monist* 53 (1969): 100–115.

Sigal, Phillip, *The Halakhah of Jesus of Nazareth According to the Gospel of Matthew*. Studies in Biblical Literature 18. Atlanta: Society of Biblical Literature, 2007.

Sigonius, Carolus. *De republica Hebraeorum libri VII*. Coloniae: 1583.

Silber, Mendel. *The Origin of the Synagogue*. New Orleans: Steeg, 1915.

Smith, Dwight Moody. "The Contribution of J. Louis Martyn for Understanding the Gospel of John." Introduction to *History and Theology in the Fourth Gospel*, by J. Louis Martyn. 3rd ed. New Testament Library. Louisville: Westminster John Knox, 2003.

_____. "Jesus Tradition in the Gospel of John." In *Handbook for the Study of the Historical Jesus*, 1997–2039. Edited by Tom Holmén and Stanley E. Porter. Leiden and Boston: Brill, 2011.

_____. "John: A Source For Jesus Research?" In *Critical Appraisals of Critical Views*. Vol. 1 of *John, Jesus, and History*, 165–78. Edited by Paul N. Anderson, Felix Just, and Tom Thatcher. SBL Symposium Series 44. Atlanta: Society of Biblical Literature, 2007.

_____. "Redaction Criticism, Genre, Narrative Criticism, and the Historical Jesus in the Gospel of John." In *Jesus Research: New Methodologies and Perceptions*, 624–33. Edited by James H. Charlesworth, with Brian Rhea and Petr Pokorný. Grand Rapids: Eerdmans, 2014.

Smith, Stephen. "The Changing Face of Redaction Criticism." *Churchman* 107 (1993): 130–45.

Skeehan, Patrick W., and Alexander A. Di Lella. *The Wisdom of Ben Sira: A New Translation and Commentary*. AYB 39. New Haven: Yale, 2007.

Sloan, Robert B. *The Favorable Year of the Lord: A Study of Jubilary Theology in the Gospel of Luke*. Austin: Scholar, 1977.

Snodgrass, Klyne R. *Stories With Intent: A Comprehensive Guide to the Parables of Jesus*. Grand Rapids: Eerdmans, 2008.

Sperling, S. D. "Belial." Page 171 in *Dictionary of Deities and Demons in the Bible* Leiden: Brill, 1999.

Spigel, Chad. *Ancient Synagogue Seating Capacities: Methodology, Analysis, and Limits*. Texte und Studien zum antiken Judentum 149. Tübingen: Mohr Siebeck, 2012.

_____. "First Century Synagogues." *Bible Odyssey*. http://www.bibleodyssey. org/places/related-articles/first-century-synagogues.

Stacy, David. "Was there a synagogue in Hasmonean Jericho?" *Bible and Interpretation*, 2004. http://www.bibleinterp.com/articles/Hasmonean_Jericho. shtml.

Starr, Joshua. "The Meaning of 'Authority' in Mark 1:22." *Harvard Theological Review* 23, no. 4 (1930): 302–5.

Stegemann, Ekkehard W., and Wolfgang Stegemann. *The Jesus Movement: A Social History of Its First Century*. Minneapolis: Fortress Press, 1999.

Stein, Robert H. *Luke*. NAC 24. Nashville: Broadman, 1992.

_____. *Mark*. BECNT. Grand Rapids: Baker Academic, 2008.

Steudal, Annette. "God and Belial." In *The Dead Sea Scrolls: Fifty Years After Their Discovery*, 332–40. Edited by Lawrence H. Schiffman, Emanuel Tov, James C. VanderKam, and Galen Marquis. Jerusalem: Israel Exploration Society, and The Shrine of the Book, Israel Museum, 2000.

Stewart, Eric C. *Gathered Around Jesus: An Alternative Spatial Practice in the Gospel of Mark*. Matrix: The Bible in Mediterranean Context 6. Eugene: Wipf & Stock, 2009.

Stewart, Robert B. *The Quest of the Hermeneutical Jesus: The Impact of Hermeneutics on the Jesus Research of John Dominic Crossan and N.T. Wright*. Lanham: University Press of America, 2008.

Storkey, Alan. *Jesus and Politics: Confronting the Powers*. Grand Rapids: Baker, 2005.

Stovell, Beth M. "Seeing the Kingdom of God, Seeing Eternal Life: Cohesion and Prominence in John 3:1-15 and the Apocryphal Gospels in Terms of Metaphor Use." In *The Language of the New Testament: Context, History, and Development*. Early Christianity in its Hellenistic Context 3, 439–67. Edited by Stanley E. Porter and Andrew W. Pitts. Leiden: Brill, 2013.

Strack, Herman L., and Günter Stemberger. *Introduction to the Talmud and Midrash*. Translated by Markus Bockmuehl. 2nd ed. Minneapolis: Fortress Press, 1996.

Strange, James F. "Ancient Texts, Archaeology as Text, and the Problem of the First Century Synagogue." In *Evolution of the Synagogue*, 27–45. Edited by

Howard C. Kee and Lynn H. Cohick. Harrisburg: Trinity Press International, 1999.

_____. "Archaeology and Ancient Synagogues up to about 200 C.E." Pages 37–62 in *The Ancient Synagogue From Its Origins Until 200 C.E.: Papers Presented at an International Conference at Lund University, October 14-17, 2001*. Edited by Birger Olsson, and Magnus Zetterholm. CBNTS 39. Stockholm: Almqvist & Wiksell, 2003.

_____. "First Century Galilee from Archaeology and from the Texts." Pages 39–48 in *Archaeology and the Galilee: Texts and Contexts in Graeco-Roman and Byzantine Periods*. Edited by Douglas R. Edwards and C. Thomas McCollough. Atlanta: Scholars Press, 1997.

Strauss, David Friedrich. *The Christ of Faith and the Jesus of History: A Critique of Schleiermacher's Life of Christ*. Translated by Leander E. Keck. Philadelphia: Fortress Press, 1977.

Strecker, Georg. "Die Antitheses der Bergpredigt (Mt 5 21–24 par)." *Zeitschrift für die Neutestamentliche Wissenschaft* 69 (1978): 36–72.

Stuckenbruck, Loren T. "Protect Them From the Evil One." In *John, Qumran, and the Dead Sea Scrolls*, 139–60. Edited Mary L. Cole and Tom Thatcher. Atlanta: Society of Biblical Literature, 2011.

Suggs, M. Jack. *Wisdom, Christology, and Law in Matthew's Gospel*. Cambridge, MA: Harvard University Press, 1970.

Sukenik, Eleazar Lipa. *Ancient Synagogues in Palestine and Greece*. London: Oxford University Press, 1934.

Syon, Danny. *Gamla III: The Shmarya Gutman Excavations 1976-1989: Finds and Studies Part 1*. IAA Reports 56. Jerusalem, 2014.

_____. "Yet Again on the Bronze Coins Minted at Gamla." *Israel Numismatic Research* 2 (2007): 117–22.

Syon, Danny, and Zvi Yavor. "Gamla – Old and New." *Qadmoniot* 121 (2001): 2–33. Hermann Samuel Reimarus. *Reimarus: Fragments*. Edited by Charles H. Talbert. Translated by Ralph S. Fraser. Eugene: Wipf & Stock, 2009.

Talmon, Shemaryahu. "Hebrew Fragments From Masada." In *Masada VI: Yigael Yadin Excavations From 1963-1965: Final Reports*. Jerusalem: Israel Exploration Society, 1999.

Tannehill, Robert C. *Luke*. Abingdon New Testament Commentary. Nashville: Abingdon, 1996.

_____. "The Mission of Jesus According to Luke IV 16–30." In *Jesus in Nazareth*, 51–62. Edited by Erich Grässer, August Strobel, and Robert C. Tannehill. BZNW 40. Berlin: de Gruyter, 1972.

_____. *The Shape of Luke's Story: Essays on Luke-Acts*. Eugene: Cascade, 2005.

Taylor, Vincent. *The Gospel According to St. Mark*. London: Macmillan, 1963.

Tcherikover, Victor. *Hellenistic Civilization and the Jews.* Repr. ed. Grand Rapids: Baker Academic, 2011.

Teeple, Howard M. *The Mosaic Eschatological Prophet.* Philadelphia: Society of Biblical Literature, 1957.

Thatcher, Tom. *Why John Wrote a Gospel: Jesus - Memory - History.* Louisville: Westminster John Knox, 2006.

Theissen, Gerd, and Annette Merz. *The Historical Jesus: A Comprehensive Guide.* Translated by John Bowden. Minneapolis: Fortress Press, 1998.

Theissen, Gerd, and Dagmar Winter. *Die Kriterienfrage in der Jesusforschung: vom Differenzkriterium zum Plausibilitätskriterium.* Novum Testamentum et Orbis Atiquus 34. Göttingen: Vandenhoeck & Ruprecht, 1997.

_____. *The Quest for the Plausible Jesus: The Question of Criteria.* Translated by M. Eugene Boring. Louisville: Westminster John Knox, 2002.

Theobald, Michael. "Johannine Dominical Sayings As Metatexts of Synoptic Sayings of Jesus: Reflections On a New Category Within Reception History." In *Glimpses of Jesus Through the Johannine Lens*, vol. 3 of *John, Jesus and History*, 383–405. Edited by Paul N. Anderson, Felix Just, and Tom Thatcher. Atlanta: SBL, 2016.

Thompson, Marianne Meye. "The 'Spiritual Gospel': How John the Theologian Writes History." In *Critical Appraisals of Critical Views.* Vol. 1 of *John, Jesus, and History*, 103–7. Edited by Paul N. Anderson, Felix Just, and Tom Thatcher. SBL Symposium Series 44. Atlanta: Society of Biblical Literature, 2007.

Tiede, David L. "The Exaltation of Jesus and the Restoration of Israel in Acts 1." *Harvard Theological Review* 79:1–3 (1986): 278–86.

Tiller, Patrick. "The Sociological Settings of the Components of 1 Enoch." In *The Early Enoch Literature*, 237–55. Edited by Gabriele Boccaccini and John J. Collins. JSJSupp 121. Leiden and Boston: Brill 2007.

Trebilco, Paul R. *Jewish Communities in Asia Minor.* SNTS 69. Cambridge and New York: Cambridge University Press, 1991.

Trocmé, André. *Jesus and the Nonviolent Revolution.* Scottdale: Herald, 1973.

Trümper, Monika. "The Oldest Synagogue Building in the Diaspora: The Delos Synagogue Reconsidered." *Hesperia* 74, no. 4 (2004): 513–98.

Tuckett, Christopher M. *Q and the History of Early Christianity: Studies on Q.* Edinburgh: T&T Clark, 1996.

Tuckett, Christopher M. "Form Criticism." In *Jesus and Memory: Traditions in Oral and Scribal Perspectives*, 21–38. Edited by Werner Kelber and Samuel Byrskog. Waco: Baylor University Press, 2009.

_____. "Jesus and the Sabbath." In *Jesus in Continuum*, 411-42. Edited by Tom Holmén. WUNT 289. Tübingen: Mohr Siebeck, 2012.

Twelftree, Graham H. "Exorcism and the Defeat of Beliar in the Testaments of the Twelve Patriarchs." *Vigilae Christianae* 65 (2011): 170–88.

———. "Jesus and the Synagogue." In *Handbook for the Study of the Historical Jesus*, 3105–34. Edited by Tom Holmén and Stanley E. Porter. Leiden: Brill, 2011.

———. *Jesus the Exorcist: A Contribution to the Study of the Historical Jesus*. WUNT 52. Tübingen: Mohr Siebeck, 1993.

———. *Jesus the Miracle Worker: A Historical and Theological Study*. Downers Grove: IVP Academic, 1999.

———. "The Miracles of Jesus: Marginal or Mainstream." *JSHJ* 1, no. 1 (2003): 104–24.

VanderKam, James C. *The Book of Jubilees*. Edited by Karel van der Toorn, Bob Becking, and Pieter W. van der Horst. 2nd ed. Sheffield: Sheffield Academic Press, 2001.

Vermes, Geza. *Jesus the Jew: A Historian's Reading of the Gospels*. Philadelphia: Fortress Press, 1973.

———. *The Real Jesus: Then and Now*. Minneapolis: Fortress Press, 2010.

———. "Reflections on Improving Methodology in Jesus Research." In *Jesus Research: New Methodologies and Perceptions, The Second Princeton-Prague Symposium on Jesus Research*, 17–27. Edited by James H. Charlesworth, with Brian Rhea and Petr Pokorný. Grand Rapids: Eerdmans, 2014.

———. *The Religion of Jesus the Jew*. Minneapolis: Fortress Press, 1993.

Viviano, Benedict T. "The Sermon on the Mount in Recent Study," *Biblical* 78 (1997): 255–65.

Wahlde, Urban C. von. *The Gospel and Letters of John*. 2 vols. Eerdmans Critical Commentary. Grand Rapids: Eerdmans, 2010.

Waldow, H. E. von. "The Origin of the Synagogue Reconsidered." In *From Faith to Faith: Essays in Honour of Donald G. Miller on his Seventieth Birthday*, 269–86. Edited by D. Y. Hadidian. Pittsburgh: Pickwick Press, 1979.

Wardle, Timothy. *The Jerusalem Temple and Early Christian Identity*. WUNT 2.291. Tübingen: Mohr Siebeck, 2010.

Warren, Meredith. *My Flesh Is Meat Indeed: A Nonsacramental Reading of John 6:51-58*. Minneapolis: Fortress Press, 2015.

Watts, James W., ed. *Persia and Torah: The Theory of Imperial Authorization of the Pentateuch*. Atlanta: Society of Biblical Literature, 2001.

———. "The Political and Legal Uses of Scripture." In *From the Beginnings to 600*. Vol. 1 of *The New Cambridge History of the Bible*, 345–64. Edited by James Carleton Paget and Joachim Schaper. Cambridge: Cambridge University Press, 2013.

Watts, Rikki E. *Isaiah's New Exodus in Mark*. Grand Rapids: Baker, 1997.

Webb, Robert L. "The Historical Enterprise and Historical Jesus Research." In *Key Events in the Life of the Historical Jesus*, 9–93. Edited by Darrell L. Bock and Robert L. Webb. WUNT 247. Tübingen: Mohr Siebeck, 2009.

———. "Jesus' Baptism by John: Its Historicity and Significance." In *Key Events in the Life of the Historical Jesus: A Collaborative Exploration of Context and Coherence*, 95–150. Edited by Darrell L. Bock and Robert L. Webb. Tübingen: Mohr Siebeck, 2009.

Weinfeld, Moshe. *Deuteronomy 1-11: A New Translation with Introduction and Commentary*. AB 5. New York: Doubleday, 1991.

———. *Deuteronomy and the Deuteronomic School*. Oxford: Oxford University Press, 1972.

Weingreen, Jacob. "Origin of the Synagogue." *Hermathena* 98 (1964): 68–84.

Weiss, Johannes. *Jesus' Proclamation of the Kingdom of God*. Translated by Richard Hyde Hiers and David Larrimore Holland. Philadelphia: Fortress Press, 1971.

Westerholm, Stephen. *Jesus and Scribal Authority*. CBNTS 10. Lund: Gleerup, 1978.

———. "The Law in the Sermon on the Mount: Matt 5:17–48." *Criswell Theological Review*, 6, no. 1 (1992): 43–56.

———. *Perspectives Old and New on Paul: The "Lutheran" Paul and His Critics*. Grand Rapids: Eerdmans, 2004.

White, Hayden. *Metahistory: The Historical Imagination in Nineteenth-Century Europe*. Baltimore and London: Johns Hopkins, 1975.

———. *Tropics of Discourse: Essays in Cultural Criticism*. Baltimore: Johns Hopkins, 1978.

White, L. Michael. *Building God's House in the Roman World: Architectural Adaptation Among Pagans, Jews, and Christians*. Vol. 1 of *The Social Origins of Christian Architecture*. Harvard Theological Studies 42. Valley Forge: Trinity Press International, 1996.

———. "Reading the Ostia Synagogue: A Reply to A. Runesson." *Harvard Theological Review* 92 (1992): 222–37.

———. *The Social Origins of Christian Architecture*. 2 vols. Valley Forge: Trinity Press International, 1996–1997.

———. "Synagogue and Society in Imperial Ostia: Archaeology and Epigraphic Evidence." *Harvard Theological Review* 92 (1999): 409–33.

Willits, Joel. "Jesus, the Kingdom and the Promised Land." *JSHJ* 13 (2015): 347–72.

Wilson, Norman. *History in Crisis? Recent Directions in Historiography*. Upper Saddle River: Prentice Hall, 1999.

Winks, Robin W. *The Historian as Detective: Essays on Evidence*. New York: Harper Torchbooks, 1970.

_____. Introduction to *The Historian as Detective: Essays on Evidence*. Edited by Robin W. Winks. New York: Harper & Row, 1970.

Winter, Dagmar. "Saving the Quest for Authenticity from the Criterion of Dissimilarity: History and Plausibility." Pages 115–31 in *Jesus, Criteria, and the Demise of Authenticity*. Edited by Chris Keith and Anthony Le Donne. London and New York: T&T Clark, 2012.

Wise, Michael O., and James D. Tabor. "The Messiah at Qumran." *BAR* 16, no. 6 (1992): 60–65.

Witmer, Amanda. *Jesus, the Galilean Exorcist: His Exorcisms in Social and Political Context*. LNTS 459. London and New York: T&T Clark, 2012.

Wolter, Michael. "Reich Gottes bei Lukas." *NTS* 41 (1995): 541–63.

Wrede, William. *The Messianic Secret*. Translated by J. C. G. Greig. 1901. London: James Clarke & Co., 1971.

Wrege, Hans-Theo. *Die Überlieferungsgeschichte der Bergpredigt*. WUNT 9. Tübingen: Mohr Siebeck, 1968.

Wright, Andrew. *Christianity and Critical Realism: Ambiguity, Truth and Theological Literacy*. London: Routledge, 2013.

Wright, N. T. "4QMMT and Paul: Justification, 'Works,' and Eschatology." in *History and Exegesis: New Testament Essays in Honor of Dr. E. Earle Ellis for His 80th Birthday*. Edited by Aang-Won Son. New York and London: T&T Clark 2006.

_____. "Doing Justice to Jesus: A Response to J.D. Crossan." *Scottish Journal of Theology* 50, no. 3 (1997): 359–79.

_____. *Jesus and the Victory of God*. Christian Origins and the Question of God vol. 2. Minneapolis: Fortress Press, 1996.

_____. "The Lord's Prayer as a Paradigm for Christian Prayer." In *Into God's Presence: Prayer in the New Testament*, 132–54. Edited by Richard N. Longenecker. Grand Rapids: Eerdmans, 2001.

_____. *The New Testament and the People of God*. Christian Origins and the Question of God 1. Minneapolis: Fortress Press, 1992.

Yadin, Yigael. "The Excavation of Masada 1963/1964: Preliminary Report." *Israel Exploration Journal* 15 (1965): 1–120.

_____. *The Scroll of the War of the Sons of Light Against the Sons of Darkness*. London: Oxford University Press, 1962.

_____. "The Synagogue at Masada." In *Ancient Synagogues Revealed*, 19–23. Edited by Lee I. Levine. Jerusalem: Israel Exploration Society, 1981.

Yoder, John Howard. *The Politics of Jesus: Vicit Agnus Noster*. 2nd ed. Grand Rapids: Eerdmans, 1994.

Zangenberg, Jürgen K. "Archaeological News From the Galilee: Tiberias, Magdala and Rural Galilee." *Early Christianity* 1 (2010): 471–84.

Zeitlin, Solomon. "The Political *Synedrion* and the Religious Sanhedrin." *Jewish Quarterly Review* 36, no. 2 (1945): 109–40.

_____. "The Tefillah, the Shemoneh Esreh: An Historical Study of the First Canonization of the Hebrew Liturgy." *JQR* 54 (1964): 208–49.

Zerubavel, Yael. *Recovered Roots: Collective Memory and the Making of Israeli National Tradition.* Chicago: University of Chicago Press, 1995.

Zimmerli, W. "Das 'Gnadenjahr des Herrn.'" In *Studien zur alttestamentlichen Theologie und Prophetie*, 222–34. Munich: Kaiser, 1974.

Zissu, Boaz, and Amir Ganor. "Horvat 'Ethri – A Jewish Village From the Second Temple Period and the Bar Kokhba Revolt in the Judean Foothills." *JJS* 60, no. 1 (2009): 90–136.

Zunz, L. *Die gottesdienstlichen Voträge der Juden.* Berlin: A. Asher, 1832.

Index of Names

Index of Texts